Fodor's 5th Edition

W9-AWY-635

Portugal

Fodor's Travel Publications • New York, Toronto, London, Sydney, Auckland
www.fodors.com

CONTENTS

Destination Portugal 5
Great Itineraries 24
Fodor's Choice 28

1 LISBON 33
Exploring Lisbon 37
CLOSE-UP *Prince Henry the Navigator* 56
Dining 58
Lodging 67
Nightlife and the Arts 74
Outdoor Activities and Sports 78
Shopping 80
Lisbon A to Z 83

2 LISBON'S ENVIRONS 90
The Estoril Coast 95
Sintra, Sintra Environs, and Queluz 102
The Setúbal Peninsula 109
Lisbon's Environs A to Z 114

3 ESTREMADURA AND THE RIBATEJO 118
Estremadura 123
The Ribatejo 133
CLOSE-UP *Bullfighting* 134
Estremadura and the Ribatejo A to Z 143

4 ÉVORA AND THE ALENTEJO 146
Évora and Environs 152
The Upper Alentejo 160
CLOSE UP: *Azulejos* 163
The Lower Alentejo 170
Évora and the Alentejo A to Z 176

5 THE ALGARVE 179
Faro and Environs 186

The Eastern Algarve 191
The Central Algarve 193
Lagos and the Western Algarve 204
The Algarve A to Z 210

6 COIMBRA AND THE BEIRAS
214
Coimbra and Environs 219
CLOSE-UP Fado 228
The Western Beiras 231
The Eastern Beiras 246
Coimbra and the Beiras A to Z 256

7 OPORTO AND THE NORTH
260
Oporto 266
Oporto's Environs: The Coast and
the Douro 277
The Minho and the Costa Verde 282
Trás-os-Montes 294
Oporto and the North A to Z 299

8 MADEIRA 304
Funchal 311
Side Trips from Funchal 321
Western Madeira 322
Central Peaks and the Village
of Santana 325
Porto Santo 327
Madeira A to Z 329

9 BACKGROUND AND
ESSENTIALS 332
Portraits of Portugal 333
Smart Travel Tips A to Z 342
Portuguese Vocabulary 371

INDEX 376

ABOUT OUR WRITERS 384

MAPS

LISBON

Exploring Lisbon (Lisboa) 40
Exploring Belém 54
Lisbon Dining 59
Lisbon Lodging 68

LISBON'S ENVIRONS

The Estoril Coast, Sintra,
and Queluz 94
The Setúbal Peninsula 95

ESTREMADURA AND THE
RIBETEJO 122

ÉVORA AND THE ALENTEJO

The Upper Alentejo 150
The Lower Alentejo 151
Évora 154

THE ALGARVE 185

Faro 187
Lagos 205

COIMBRA AND THE BEIRAS

The Beiras 220–221
Coimbra 224

OPORTO AND THE NORTH

The North: Douro, Minho,
and Trás-os-Montes 265
Oporto (Porto) 268

MADEIRA 310

Funchal 312

EUROPE 368–369

PORTUGAL 370

Circled letters in text correspond to letters on the photo-
graphs. For more information on the sights pictured, turn to
the indicated page number Ⓐ on each photograph.

DESTINATION PORTUGAL

If you find that Portugal is a little more given to flourishes than the rest of Europe, you've gotten the point. The essence of the country is that despite its compact size, its architecture, people, and terrain defy expectations with any number of dramatic contrasts. Although the weather along the coast is almost perpetually mild, bracing Atlantic waters temper the warmth of the beaches. And the coastal towns crowded with sun seekers differ markedly from the verdant valleys and rugged mountains where visitors are few and centuries-old traditions are cherished. Even within Lisbon, Portugal's exotic differences are apparent—from the Alfama's twisting streets, a remnant of the Moorish occupation, to the austere Romanesque cathedral. The challenge of planning a trip to Portugal is deciding which of its enchanting aspects to explore.

LISBON

Ⓑ▷ 55

You won't be in Lisbon for long before you begin to sense that this city is different from other European capitals—a little more traditional and old world, a place that's immediately likeable. No small part of this appeal is the way that Lisbon, in its churches, monuments, and public spaces, bears the mark of its remarkable heritage with comfortable pride. You'll notice this as soon as you step into the Ⓕ**Rossio**, the square at the heart of the city, where locals are at ease pulling up café chairs and perusing newspapers against a backdrop of splashing fountains. Many grand buildings in the city's old quarters reflect the riches that poured in from Asia, South America, and Africa during the Age of Discovery. The 16th-century Ⓔ**Casa dos Bicos**, the appropriately named House of Pointed Stones, is typical of the town houses built for wealthy merchants and bankers. The Ⓐ**Convento do Carmo**, now in partial ruin but once the largest convent in Lisbon, testifies that the church got its

Ⓒ▷ 55

share of the pie, too. To see the grandest monuments, though, you must travel out to Belém at the southern edge of the city. Here, the unique Portuguese late-Gothic architecture known as Manueline came to full flower in the ©**Mosteiro dos Jerónimos,** a famous monastery, and the crenelated Ⓓ**Torre de Belém**, with its commanding view of the Tagus River. Even the modern Ⓑ**Monumento dos Descobrimentos** makes a bow to the past, honoring Vasco da Gama and the other great navigators—and proving that in Lisbon tradition remains close to the heart.

Ⓔ 41

Ⓕ 44

LISBON

The best way to explore this compact city is on foot, perhaps with an occasional jaunt on a funicular railway such as the Ⓚ**Elevador da Bica** or another of the charming old public conveyances that prove to be especially handy as you navigate yet another of the seven hills on which Lisbon is built. At just about every turn, you are likely to come upon a sweeping view of city and river. What passes here as ordinary decoration often astounds visitors; residents may take the playful artistry of Lisbon's buildings and monuments for granted, but you will likely be captivated. In the Ⓗ**Alfama**, the centuries-old section of town with the strongest signs of the Moorish presence, narrow, twisting streets and flights of steps lead uphill past

such monuments as the Sé (cathedral) and Azurara Palace to the lofty Castelo de São Jorge, where well-preserved Moorish walls encircle the remnants of a royal residence. One of the best experiences is to stumble onto a thrilling vista, like the one of the Alfama from the sun-drenched ⓘ**Miradouro Santa Luzia,** where you can linger at café tables. Eventually you come to the ⓙ**Mercado Avenida 24 de Julho**, or another crowded venue where the vendors unwittingly provide the entertainment. At each of these colorful markets, vibrant produce and fresh seafood spill from the stalls, and it becomes clear that this city takes its food seriously. When you catch the scent of roasting coffee, follow your nose. Inevitably you will be led to the ⓖ**Café a Brasileira** or a similarly decorative old haunt where you can join locals in one of their favorite rituals, sitting back with a decadent pastry and savoring the considerable delights of this lovely city.

⟨J⟩ 81

⟨K⟩ 86

Ⓐ 108

Palaces, gardens, fishing ports, long stretches of sparkling sea—all of these pleasures are within easy reach of Lisbon. Estoril, with its gardens and glitzy casino, is the first stop along the coast that stretches west from the capital. If you want a place that's a little more quaint and colorful, push on to the fishing village–cum–resort of Ⓒ**Cascais**. Nearby, nature displays its force at Ⓔ**Cabo da Roca**, where violent surf crashes into the granite cliffs that mark the westernmost point of continental Europe.

AROUND LISBON

Ⓑ 108

Ⓒ 98

ⒹⱭ102

ⒺⱭ107

The rolling inland hills were once a retreat of rulers and royal families, whose residences rise above wooded valleys. The whimsical chimneys and domes of the Ⓓ**Palácio Nacional de Sintra** fill the horizon in a flourish of 14th-century Moorish fancy, while the rococo Ⓑ**Palácio Nacional de Queluz** is more sedate but every bit as romantic. A stroll along the gravel paths of the famous gardens is likely to take you back to the 18th century—especially if the local children of Ⓐ**Queluz** are donning traditional dress for a festival. South of Lisbon, beach resorts are the allure of the Costa da Caparica, but a stroll through the old working port of Ⓕ**Setúbal** proves that the sea continues to provide more than a playground.

ⒻⱭ110

ESTREMADURA AND THE RIBATEJO

Water shapes the character of both these provinces. The sea is never far from sight in coast-hugging Estremadura, though seafaring days are but a distant memory in Ⓐ**Óbidos**, where the harbor that once lapped against the village walls has long since silted up. Ⓒ**Nazaré**, meanwhile, still makes its living from the sea—from fishing, as well as from sun seekers. The same is true of the old town of Ⓕ**Ericeira**, where sunbathers and surfers alike can indulge in their favorite pastimes. Coastal valleys once witnessed many a bloody fight between rival groups, including the Moors.

Ⓐ 127

Ⓑ 138

Ⓒ 129

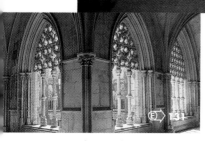

®⟩ 140

E⟩ 131

These battles nonetheless left at least one positive legacy—extraordinary monasteries, such as the one at Ⓔ**Batalha**, built to celebrate a Portuguese victory over the Spanish. The Tagus River flows through the Ribatejo, where vast plains spread out from the river's banks. Although strategic fortifications line the river, the most famous monument is at Ⓑ**Fátima**, where the Virgin Mary allegedly appeared to three young shepherds; millions of pilgrims still flock here every year to pay homage. In Tomar, the impressive Ⓓ**Convento de Cristo**, an amalgam of 12th- to 16th-century styles that was once the headquarters of the order of the Knights Templar, is a reminder of the religious struggles that have defined the region.

Ⓕ⟩ 124

ÉVORA AND THE ALENTEJO

In this vast, nearly empty, and deeply rural region that sprawls across southern Portugal, you'll come across many gently rolling hills topped with cork trees. In fact, cork production—not for those looking for a fast turnaround, since the trees can be stripped only once every nine years—is typical of the slower, more traditional, largely agricultural way of life here. Shepherds still don the *pelico*—a sheepskin vest—around the town of Ⓓ**Beja**, and villages produce local crafts, like the handwoven blankets

Ⓑ 160

and rugs, from sleepy ⑧**Reguengos de Monsaraz**. Beaches on the rugged west coast are uncrowded and peaceful, too, but times have not always been so easy. ©**Monsaraz**, one of many heavily fortified towns and villages, bears testimony to bloody skirmishes that have erupted in the region for the past two millennia. Évora, the ancient, still flourishing capital, has witnessed the passing of Roman legions, Moors, medieval dynasties, and Renaissance geniuses. The city displays this heritage proudly in its impressive architecture—including the Ⓔtemplo Romano, Iberia's finest Roman temple, and the bustling central square, Ⓐ**Praça do Giraldo,** with a church and a handsome fountain.

©▷ 160

Ⓓ▷ 170

Ⓔ▷ 155

THE
ALGARVE

Ⓐ 200

Appealing, yes—perhaps even a bit too appealing for its own good—Portugal's southernmost coastal region is deservedly popular with millions of annual vacationers who throng here for sun, sandy beaches, superb golf, and all the other trappings of the seaside resorts. Join the crowds in such haunts as the umbrella-filled strand at Ⓓ**Praia de Dona Ana** near Lagos and in Albufeira, the busiest resort of them all. Sooner or later, though, you must leave your beach chair and explore

the Algarve's untrammeled corners. Your wanderings should take you past the extraordinary rocky outcroppings that spill into the sea all along the coastline, such as those near ©**Lagos**, as well as down the quiet back streets that crisscross the old town of ®**Faro**, the prosperous provincial capital. Enchanting Tavira blends the salty tang of a traditional fishing port with the charm of no less than 37 churches, most from the 17th and 18th centuries. Inland, you'll discover quiet, intriguing towns like Moorish Silves, and at the southwestern edge of Europe you'll come to Cabo São Vincente, the so-called "end of the world" where Henry the Navigator launched his far-flung expeditions. Take time, also, to indulge in small pleasures that seem never

to change—a plate of grilled sardines or other fish in the still-flourishing fishing port of Ⓐ**Portimão**, perhaps, or the spectacle of the setting sun viewed from the battlements of the Ⓔ**Fortaleza de Sagres**.

Ⓔ▷ 208

COIMBRA AND THE BEIRAS

This expanse of central Portugal, sweeping from the Atlantic beaches to the mountainous border with Spain, is the country's heartland, deeply rooted in national traditions. In fact, the region's treasures, both man made and natural, often qualify as the best or most authentically Portuguese in the country. In the monasteries and cathedrals, for example, built with wealth garnered during 16th-century seafaring expeditions, you'll often come upon stunning examples of the Manueline style, that distinctly Portuguese form of architecture. Also found only in Portugal are the brightly painted *moliceiros*—kelp boats—that glide gracefully along shallow stretches of the ©**Ria de Aveiro** as their owners harvest seaweed. The Mondego River, immortalized in poetry as the most Portuguese of rivers, meanders from one end of the region to the other. On its banks rises Coimbra, a city that has been settled since prehistoric times and has played a crucial role in the country's development. Its importance as a Roman way

235

station comes to life in the ⒺⒻ**Museu Machado de Castro**, where vaulted passageways in the basement are relics from the Roman era; the upstairs galleries hold an impressive collection of sculpture and paintings. Coimbra is best known, though, for its university, with one of the world's finest libraries, the baroque Ⓑ**Biblioteca Joanina**. Attractive little Ⓓ**Luso** draws health seekers from all corners of the globe to the country's most famous thermal waters. The road east ends with a climb along the highest road in the country into the Ⓐ**Parque Nacional da Serra da Estrela**, a domain of alpine peaks, dense forests, and Portugal's only ski slopes.

Ⓔ 224

Ⓕ 224

OPORTO AND THE NORTH

Cosmopolitan Oporto is Portugal's economic center, but it's not business that's likely to bring you north. Rather, it's the chance to explore the tranquil terrain beyond the city's churches and museums. On the Costa Verde, you might be able to find your own solitary stretch of beach. On a visit to the pilgrimage center of Ⓐ**Bom Jesus do Monte**, however, you're apt to meet picnicking Portuguese families. In the province of Ⓑ**Minho**, where a fanciful shawl is still everyday garb, the attraction is seeing centuries-old traditions, such as the making of ceramics in Ⓒ**Barcelos**. All these pleasures are enhanced by a glass of *vinho verde* (green wine), made from grapes cultivated in the rich Ⓓ**Douro** and Minho regions.

Ⓑ 282

Ⓒ 288

Ⓓ 277

Wine connoisseurs around the world, from George Washington to Napoléon Bonaparte, have long savored Madeira's eponymous export, but a sip of this heady elixir provides only a taste of the island's many delights. Foremost among these is the balmy year-round temperature, ensured by warm Atlantic currents. The promise of clear skies, a brisk midwinter dip in the sea, and excellent weather for fishing or for hiking along an extensive network of footpaths keeps northern Europeans arriving

MADEIRA

Ⓑ ▷ 367

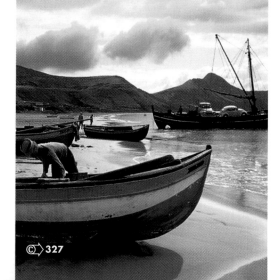

Ⓒ ▷ 327

year-round. The subtropical climate keeps the ⓓ**Jardim Botânico** in bloom in all seasons, and the deep mountain ravines around villages such as ⓕ**Curral das Freiras** are perennially verdant. Almost as colorful is the island's distinctive thatch-roofed architecture, most likely encountered these days in remote outposts such as ⓔ**Santana.** In the busy waterfront capital of ⓐⓑ**Funchal** you'll discover plenty of local color, too, especially when costumed dancers whirl through the streets during yet another festival. And just when you think you've exhausted all the pleasures this small island has to offer, you can sail off to ⓒ**Porto Santo**, a nearby islet blessed with the one commodity Madeira doesn't have—long expanses of sandy beaches.

GREAT ITINERARIES

Leiria

Alcobaça

Óbidos

ESTREMADURA

Sintra

Lisbon

Setúba

Highlights of Portugal
13 to 15 days

From the Algarve, Portugal's southernmost region of gorgeous beaches, vibrant resorts, and secluded hill villages, the route strikes north through the country's major towns. Landscapes along the way include the picturesque coast and arid plains of the south; vibrant Lisbon and its lush environs; and the rivers, valleys, forests, and mountains of the north. Begin with two days in Faro, the Algarve's historic capital, visiting its Old Town and making side trips to towns such as riverside Tavira.

ÉVORA
2 days. Évora's Roman, Moorish, and Renaissance heritage provides a compelling architectural feast. Study the temple ruins, graceful squares, royal palaces, and striking churches—then stay overnight in the Pousada dos Lóios, a converted monastery, or another historic lodging. ☞ *Évora and Environs in Chapter 4.*

LISBON
3 days. Don your walking shoes and range across the seven hills of the Portuguese capital. Explore the intricate alleyways of the Moorish Alfama; the checkerboard grid of the Baixa (Lower Town); the cobbled contours of the Bairro Alto (Upper Town); and the superb architectural details of Belém. Don't miss Portugal's finest museum collections—the Museu Calouste Gulbenkian and the Museu de Arte Antiga (Museum of Ancient Art). ☞ *Chapter 1.*

ÓBIDOS TO LEIRIA
1 or 2 days. A slow drive from Lisbon through the fertile Estremadura region rewards

you with a glimpse of the celebrated monumental architecture that dominates Óbidos, Alcobaça, and Batalha. At journey's end, the medieval castle at the former royal residence of Leiria is one of Portugal's unsung gems. ☞ *Estremadura in Chapter 3.*

COIMBRA
1 or 2 days. The country's most prestigious university town is home to timeworn buildings, romantic squares and gardens, and colorful traditions—including the singing of the mournful fado, that most characteristic Portuguese folk music. ☞ *Coimbra and Environs in Chapter 6.*

OPORTO
2 days. Gateway to the north and center of the country's port wine industry, Oporto repays careful investigation. Look beyond the solid commercial nature of Portugal's second-largest city and you'll uncover staunch Gothic mansions, an impressive cathedral, and a vibrant riverside pier, the Cais da Ribeira, where you can tuck into fresh fish at an authentic *tasca* (tavern). ☞ *Oporto in Chapter 7.*

BRAGA
1 day. Its Romanesque cathedral, Museu de Arte Sacra (Museum of Religious Art), and Paço dos Arcebispos (Archbishops' Palace) announce Braga's credentials as Portugal's religious nerve center. The Easter processions are justly famous, while year-round pilgrims climb the steep steps of the sanctuary-church of nearby Bom Jesus do Monte. ☞ *The Minho and the Costa Verde in Chapter 7.*

VIANA DO CASTELO
1 day. A low-key Portuguese resort, Viana makes a refreshing change from the international Algarve beach towns. Chug across the Lima River by ferry to the local beach,

stroll the well-kept streets of the late-medieval center, visit the bustling Friday market, or enjoy the views from the Santa Luzia basilica. ☞ *The Minho and the Costa Verde in Chapter 7.*

By Public Transportation
Trains and buses serve all the towns on this itinerary, but connections in the deep south and far north can be time-consuming. The Algarve railway line between Lagos and Vila Real is a useful means of nipping along the south coast—the entire route takes 3 to 4 hrs. From Faro, it is less than 3 hrs to Évora or around 4 hrs to Lisbon by car or express bus. Fast, frequent

13 Tomar

Marvão

Portalegre

N18

98 km

Estremoz

150 km N4 N4 N255

N4
164 km N114

Vila
Viçosa

Évora

N18

245 km

Beja

N18

N2

Castro Verde

N123

N264

bufeira

N125

Tavira

29 km N125

Faro Olhão

VILA VIÇOSA
1 day. Heartland of the royal Bragança family since the 15th century, Vila Viçosa once held sway over much of Portugal. Time (and the eventual declaration of the Republic) reduced the town's influence, but the marble Ducal Palace still has the capacity to thrill. Its rich interior apartments, armory, and treasury detail the golden lives of Portugal's last royal family. ☞ *The Upper Alentejo in Chapter 4.*

SETÚBAL
1 day. If the 15th-century Igreja de Jesus—a church that is the country's earliest example of Manueline architecture—wasn't enough reason to visit, you'll find all the excuses you need in the mighty shape of the Castelo de São Filipe, which lords over the town. The dramatically situated castle is now a luxury *pousada* (inn), where you can indulge yourself in style. ☞ *The Setúbal Peninsula in Chapter 2.*

SINTRA
2 or 3 days. To fully appreciate aristocratic Sintra—retreat of the royals—you need to stay a night or two. Visits to the Palácio Nacional de Sintra, the extraordinarily decorated Paláio Nacional de Pena, and the Castelo dos Mouros (Moorish Castle) are mandatory. Less exalted attractions round out the experience: crafts shopping, a visit to edge-of-the-world Cabo da Roca, and tours of the gardens of Monserrate. ☞ *Sintra, Sintra Environs, and Queluz in Chapter 2.*

ESTREMADURA
2 days. In the region of Estremadura, whose lands were bitterly contested by the Moors and the Spanish, stand three of the country's most alluring sights. Start in

Monumental Portugal
10 or 11 days

Portugal has the eye-catching monuments befitting a land of conquest, discovery, and glory. A stunning range of castles, palaces, monasteries, churches, and ancient ruins lies scattered across the heart of the country, beginning near the border with Spain.

MARVÃO
1 day. The nation was forged—and defended—in its fortified border towns, of which Marvão is a classic example. A strategic site since Roman times, the clifftop castle has panoramic views worth every tiring step of the walk up through town. ☞ *The Upper Alentejo in Chapter 4.*

trains and buses run from Lisbon to Leiria (1 hr), Coimbra (2 hrs), and Oporto (3 to 4 hrs). The journey by car, train, or bus from Oporto to either Braga or Viana do Castelo is around an hour.

Óbidos, part of whose medieval castle is a lovingly adapted pousada. Nearby, the spectacular church and monastery of Alcobaça was built following a 12th-century victory over the Moors. More than 200 years later, the church and monastery at Batalha was erected, a majestic commemoration of the Portuguese victory at the Battle of Aljubarrota. ☞ *Estremadura in Chapter 3.*

TOMAR

1 day. The medieval Knights Templar made their headquarters in the graceful town of Tomar. Investigate the gardens, cloisters, and church of their Convento de Cristo before turning your attention to the preserved Jewish Quarter, whose synagogue is the oldest in Portugal. ☞ *The Ribatejo in Chapter 3.*

CONÍMBRIGA

1 day. No Roman ruins in Portugal are more impressive than those of Conímbriga, once a flourishing town on the route between Lisbon and Braga. Step back in time as you view the mosaic floors, original Roman road (still rutted by cart wheels), and aqueduct. ☞ *Coimbra and Environs in Chapter 6.*

VISEU

1 day. Holding a commanding position in the western Beiras region, the provincial capital of Viseu has a trio of visually rich Old Town squares. The prosperous mix of imposing public buildings, spacious boulevards, and shady parks is a real treat. ☞ *The Western Beiras in Chapter 6.*

By Public Transportation
You'll need a car to make the most of this tour or you'll spend much of your time waiting for connections. That said, if you base yourself in Lisbon you can easily see Setúbal (45 min), Sintra (40 min), and the Estremadura sights (1 to 2 hrs) by public transport from there. Coimbra gives you direct access to Conímbriga (25 min) and Viseu (2 hrs). Only Marvão and Vila Viçosa remain resistant to day-trip sightseeing—you'll need a car for these.

Byways and Backwaters
9 to 11 days

The mellow pleasures of Portugal are often found away from the bustling towns and high-profile attractions. This meandering tour of the northern rivers, valleys, and mountains steers clear of the crowds and highlights local life and culture.

MONÇÃO

1 or 2 days. Now a peaceful border town on a serene stretch of the Minho River, Monção is home to a castle that is the only reminder of more hectic times. The local wine—the sprightly *vinho verde* (green wine)—encourages long lunches, or follow the river downstream as far as Caminha, with its fortified town hall. ☞ *The Minho and the Costa Verde in Chapter 7.*

PONTE DE LIMA

1 or 2 days. A charming Roman bridge is the "ponte" in question, spanning the Lima River, known as the River of Oblivion to the Romans, who were sorely taken with its ethereal beauty. Riverside promenades, mansions, elegant manor-house accommodations, and a traditional twice-monthly market are the town's gentle attractions. ☞ *The Minho and the Costa Verde in Chapter 7.*

BARCELOS

1 day. Plan your trip so your arrival here coincides with the Thursday market, one of Portugal's greatest participatory experiences. Organized by locals for locals—that's the key here—the market is chockablock with ceramics, baskets, toys, foodstuffs, agricultural supplies, clothes,

shoes, and household equipment. ☞ *The Minho and the Costa Verde in Chapter 7.*

AMARANTE

1 day. If you're looking for love, touching the saintly effigy in the Convento de São Gonçalo is recommended by the locals. The rest of the day, stroll across the pretty bridge, wander along the riverbanks, or rent a rowboat. These are the kind of lazy activities that might turn out to provide your best memories of Portugal. ☞ *Oporto's Environs: The Coast and the Douro in Chapter 7.*

CHAVES

1 day. Just a few miles from the Spanish border, Chaves once bore the brunt of any attack. Its sturdy fortress is its most prominent feature, but the engaging late-medieval streets, tiled churches, a local museum, and thermal springs provide more pacific pastimes. ☞ *Trás-os-Montes in Chapter 7.*

BRAGANÇA

1 day. Within the walls of the Cidadela lies a superbly preserved medieval village. Soak it up, then descend to the modern town where the people of Bragança go about their business in the shops and sidewalk cafés of a typical country town. ☞ *Trás-os-Montes in Chapter 7.*

Monção
N101
N13 · 45 km
Caminha
N13 · 56 km
N201
na do Castelo
IN201 · 32 km
Ponte de Lima
N13 · 57 km
Barcelos
N103
N103 · 85 km
Braga
N101
A3 · 53 km
Oporto
A1 · 106 km

SPAIN

Minho
Lima

N103
Bragança
Chaves · 100 km
N2 · 111 km
Vila Real
N15
Amarante

Douro

Douro

159 km

Castelo Rodrigo
36 km
Trancoso · Pinhel
Almeido
26 km
100 km

IP3
Viseu
IP3 · 79 km
A1
IP3
Coimbra

Sortelha

A1 · 67 km
Conímbriga
A1 · 80 km
ia
N1 · 56 km
Batalha
N113 · Tomar

Tejo

Marvão
Portalegre
N18 · 98 km
Estremoz
N4 · N4 N255
N4 · 150 km
Vila Viçosa
N10
N4 · 164 km · N114
túbal
Évora

THE EASTERN BEIRAS

2 days. The rocky highlands of the Eastern Beiras region are for anyone with an interest in rugged, off-the-beaten-track adventure. In out-of-the-way towns like Trancoso, Pinhel, Castelo Rodrigo, and Almeida—each deeply affected through the years by emigration—every castle wall tells a story, while every abandoned house or tower harbors a ghost or two.
☞ *The Eastern Beiras in Chapter 6.*

SORTELHA

1 day. It's not quite the land that time forgot, but Sortelha comes as close as anywhere in Portugal. Ancient walls, crumbling houses, cobbled streets, and simple back-to-basics accommodations all contribute to the age-old atmosphere.
☞ *The Eastern Beiras in Chapter 6.*

By Public Transportation
A car is essential to follow the route outlined above, but be prepared for some tortuous cross-country rides in the mountainous Trás-os-Montes and Eastern Beiras.

FODOR'S
CHOICE

A

B

C

D

E

F

G

H

I

Even with so many special places in Portugal, Fodor's writers and editors have their favorites. Here are a few that stand out.

MEMORABLE MUSEUMS

Museu Calouste Gulbenkian, Lisbon. This relatively small museum stands out for the quality of its pieces: Egyptian artifacts, Greek and Roman coins and statuary, Chinese porcelain, Japanese prints, 16th- and 17th-century Persian tapestries. The European art section represents all major schools from the 15th through the 20th centuries. ☞ p. 50

Museu de Arte Antiga, Lisbon. A 17th-century palace is home to beautifully displayed Portuguese art (mainly from the 15th through 19th centuries), Flemish paintings, French silver, Portuguese furniture and tapestries, and Asian ceramics. ☞ p. 57

Ⓓ **Museu Machado, Coimbra.** This wonderful 12th-century palace contains one of Portugal's finest sculpture collections. ☞ p. 224

Ruins and Museum, Conímbriga. In a bucolic setting southwest of Coimbra, these ruins and an adjacent museum constitute one of the Iberian Peninsula's most important archaeological sites. ☞ p. 230

SPIRITUAL STRUCTURES

Igreja de São Roque, Lisbon. Don't be fooled by the plain facade: inside, the side chapels of this Renaissance church are superbly decorated with rare stones and mosaics that resemble oil paintings. ☞ p. 46

Ⓗ **Mosteiro, Alcobaça.** Grateful for a decisive battle won, a king built this impressive church and monastery in the 12th century. ☞ p. 130

Ⓘ **Mosteiro dos Jerónimos, Lisbon.** Belém's famous monastery is a supreme example of the Manueline style, with elaborate sculptural details. ☞ p. 55

Mosteiro Palácio Nacional, Mafra. An enormous 18th-century complex containing a

monastery, a basilica, and a grand palace, this was built to celebrate a royal birth. ☞ p. 123

Sé Velha, Coimbra. Constructed in the 12th century, the Old Cathedral, made of massive granite blocks crowned by battlements, looks more like a fortress than a house of worship. ☞ p. 223

Templo Romano, Évora. This temple is one of the finest Roman ruins on the Iberian Peninsula. ☞ p. 155

SPOTS FOR A STROLL

Ⓖ **Parque Nacional da Peneda-Gerês.** Nearly 173,000 acres were set aside in 1970 to protect this region of wild mountain, lakes, woods, and remote hilltop villages. ☞ p. 293

Praça de Dom Duarte, Viseu. The rough stone pavement, splendid old houses, wrought-iron balconies, and views of an ancient cathedral have a magical effect. ☞ p. 240

Praça do Giraldo, Évora. This arcade square was once a Roman forum. ☞ p. 153

Ⓕ **Rossío, Lisbon.** The city's main square since the Middle Ages is a grand space with ornate fountains and renowned cafés. ☞ p. 44

TOWNS THAT WILL CHARM YOU

Batalha. The church of Santa Maria da Vitoria, built to commemorate a Portuguese victory over Spain, is here. It contains the tomb of Henry the Navigator. ☞ p. 131

Câmara de Lobos. Date palms climb the hillsides, and pastel cottages dot the landscape of this tranquil coastal village that Sir Winston Churchill, a frequent visitor to Madeira, painted several times. ☞ p. 322

Ⓒ **Cascais.** This former fishing village still feels like a small town. Visit the harbor, with its fishing boats and yachts, and the old squares full of lace shops, cafés, and restaurants. ☞ p. 98

Ⓔ **Coimbra.** An attractive town on the River Mondego, the first capital of Portugal is

best known for its ancient university. ☞ p. 223

Ⓐ **Évora.** The flourishing hub of the rich agricultural Alentejo region, Évora is also a university center and one of the world's great architectural treasures. ☞ p. 153

Guimarães. As you wander narrow, cobbled streets—past small bars that open onto sidewalks and pastel houses where flowers bloom on windowsills—you can feel centuries slip away. ☞ p. 286

Oporto. Clinging to a hill above the Douro River, Portugal's second-largest city is a curious mix of late-20th-century industrial capitalism, fin-de-siècle grandeur, and run-down, medieval-feeling neighborhoods. ☞ p. 266

Santana. Thatch-roof A-frame cottages line the cobblestone streets in this storybook town inland from the northeast coast of Madeira. ☞ p. 326

Ⓑ **Silves.** The Algarve's intriguing former Moorish capital has many charms, from its lively market to its mighty fortress. ☞ p. 199

Sintra. Horse-drawn carriages and elegant old, hotels lend a 19th-century air to Sintra; gardens, wooded paths, and scenic vistas make it even more agreeable. ☞ p. 102

Viana do Castelo. Northern Portugal's folkloric heart beats in this lovely city on an estuary of the Lima River. Be prepared to yield the road to oxcarts calmly plodding alongside men with weather-beaten faces or women carrying baskets on their heads piled with turnip greens. ☞ p. 289

Vila do Conde. This Costa Verde town, with beaches and a sardine fleet, celebrates its lace makers during June's Feast of St. John. The handiwork of these artistic women is sold in local shops and at roadside stands. ☞ p. 278

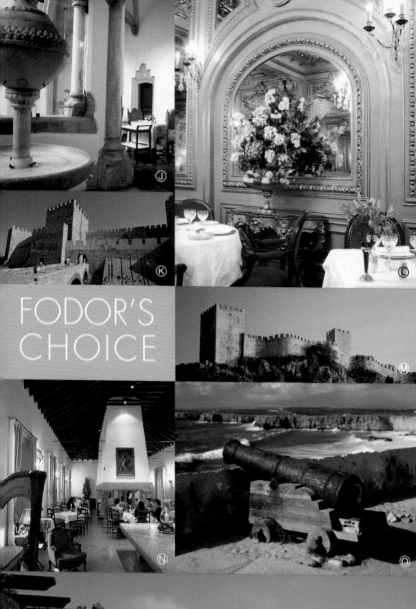

FODOR'S
CHOICE

CASTLES AND FORTS

Ⓚ **Castelo de São Jorge, Lisbon.** Imposing St. George's Castle, set on one of the highest hills in the city's Moorish Alfama District, is a grand place to get your bearings with its supreme views. ☞ p. 41

Cidadela, Bragança. This grand castle and walled village in the remote Trás-os-Montes region shows you how good it must have been to be king. ☞ p. 296

Ⓞ **Fortaleza de Sagres, Sagres.** Enormous walls high above the sea encircle the buildings here, among them a captivating chapel. ☞ p. 208

Ⓜ **Óbidos.** With its narrow streets, massive castle, and impressive walls and battlements, Óbidos is a bit of medieval Portugal transported to the 21st century. ☞ p. 126

Palácio Nacional, Queluz. Inspired in part by Versailles, this salmon-pink rococo edifice took 40 years to complete. The formal grounds are complete with ponds, a canal, fountains, and statues. ☞ p. 108

DINING

Ⓛ **Tavares Rico, Lisbon.** Superb French-inspired food, an excellent wine list, and a splendid Edwardian dining room have brought fame to this restaurant—founded as a café in the 18th century. $$$$ ☞ p. 61

Ⓝ **Restaurante de Cozinha Velha, Queluz.** Formerly the kitchen of the Queluz Palace, this restaurant—part of the Pousada de Dona Maria I—takes advantage of its heritage: certain dishes are based on 18th-century recipes. $$$–$$$$ ☞ p. 108

Palace Hotel Buçaco, Buçaco. This extravagant restaurant has a carved-wood ceiling, massive Manueline windows, and cuisine worthy of the decor. $$$ ☞ p. 245

O Celeiro, Funchal. Traditional Portuguese cooking—including Algarve-style seafood stews served in copper-lidded pots—attracts locals and tourists alike. $$–$$$ ☞ p. 315

A Ruína, Albufeira. For charcoal-grilled seafood—especially sardines and tuna steak—you'll find few places that top this rustic beachside restaurant. $$–$$$ ☞ p. 197

Bonjardim, Lisbon. Nicknamed "Rei dos Frangos" ("King of Chickens"), Bonjardim specializes in superbly spit-roasted chicken; the frenzied waiters are great entertainment. $–$$$ ☞ p. 63

Pedro dos Leitões, Curia. Between Coimbra and Oporto several restaurants specialize in suckling pig. A meal at one such establishment—the ever-popular "Suckling Pig Pete"—is a must. $$ ☞ p. 242

Redondel, Vila Franca de Xira. Feast on hearty regional fare inside the walls of a famous bullring. $$ ☞ p. 135

LODGING

Four Seasons Hotel The Ritz, Lisbon. Tapestries and fine paintings decorate the public areas, and guest rooms have luxurious bathrooms, private terraces, and elegant furnishings. $$$$ ☞ p. 67

Reids, Funchal. Wonderfully old-fashioned and long popular with aristocrats and British tycoons, Reids is one of the world's most gracious hotels. $$$$ ☞ p. 316

Hotel Palácio, Estoril. During World War II, exiled European courts lived in this 1930s hotel. The attractive and elegant rooms can be your home away from home, too—that is, when you're not teeing off on the championship golf course or dining poolside. $$$–$$$$ ☞ p. 97

Pousada de Santa Marinha, Guimarães. Vast stretches of tiled walls depicting 18th-century Portuguese life decorate this mountaintop structure that began life as a monastery in the 12th century. Nowadays you can spend a very comfortable night in what used to be a monk's cell. $$$ ☞ p. 287

Pousada de São Felipe, Setúbal. The location in a

16th-century hilltop castle, the views from the rooms and ramparts, and the interior awash in azulejo tiles are no less than splended. $$$ ☞ p. 111

Ⓙ **Pousada dos Lóios, Évora.** In the 15th-century monastery opposite the Roman Temple of Diana, this pousada is among Portugal's most opulent. $$$ ☞ p. 158

Ⓟ **Quinta das Sequóias, Sintra.** This former 19th-century manor house, on 40 wooded acres, is a lovely small hotel; the half-dozen rooms have charming furniture and period touches. $$$ ☞ p. 104

Albergaria Senhora do Monte, Lisbon. Views from this small, unpretentious hotel in the oldest part of town are some of the best in Lisbon. $$ ☞ p. 72

Grande Hotel do Porto, Oporto. This turn-of-the-century beauty has wonderfully ornate public rooms and cheerful guest quarters that combine chandeliers with satellite TV. $$ ☞ p. 275

Pousada do Arieiro, Madeira. At this cozy hotel above the tree line, mountain views and traditional island cuisine are the attractions. $$ ☞ p. 326

Dona Inês, Coimbra. This modern glass-and-marble hotel on the banks of the Mondego is just a few minutes' walk from Coimbra's commercial district. $ ☞ p. 230

Grão Vasco, Viseu. The location in a wooded park a few steps from the main square offers city conveniences and rural tranquility. $ ☞ p. 240

Pousada de São Pedro, Castelo de Bode. Built in 1946 to house engineers constructing the dam on the River Zêzere, this pousada sits on a hill above the lake they created. $ ☞ p. 141

1 LISBON

Start with the tongue, then move to the back of the throat to say Lisbon's name, "Lisboa" in Portuguese. Slightly strange at first, the sound soon seems zesty and sensuous, like the charismatic city itself. No longer the sleepy outpost that the country's haunting fado music celebrates, Lisbon is now a beguiling 21st-century European capital. Its people have accepted the dual challenge of the new millennium: preserving their proud history while moving forward with new confidence. They are true descendants of their *descobrador* (discoverer) ancestors.

L YING NORTH OF THE RIO TEJO (Tagus River) estuary and spread over a string of seven hills, Lisbon offers an intriguing variety of faces to anyone with the energy to negotiate its switchback streets. In the city's oldest parts, tiny, stepped alleys are lined with pastel-color houses and crossed by laundry hung out to dry; here and there you come across a *miradouro*, a natural vantage point with spectacular city and river views. In the grand 18th-century center, wide boulevards are bordered by black-and-white mosaic cobblestone sidewalks. Clanking *elétricos* (trams) still maneuver through the streets; there's a legacy of fine art nouveau buildings, too, and everywhere—on church walls, around fountains, and in restaurants and bars—you'll see the striking blue-and-white *azulejos* (painted and glazed ceramic tiles) for which the country is famous.

By Jules Brown

Updated by
Alys Bohn

The city was probably founded by the Phoenicians, who traded from its port. It was not until 205 BC, however, when the Romans linked it by road to the great Spanish cities of the Iberian Peninsula, that Lisbon prospered. The Visigoths followed in the 5th century and built the earliest fortifications on the site of the Castelo de São Jorge, but it was with the arrival of the Moors in the 8th century that Lisbon came into its own. The city flourished as a trading center during the 300 years of Moorish rule, and the Alfama—the oldest district of Lisbon—retains its intricate Arab-influenced layout. In 1147 the Christian army led by Dom Afonso Henriques took the city after a ruthless siege that lasted 17 weeks. To give thanks for the end of Moorish rule, Dom Afonso planned a great cathedral, and the building was dedicated three years later. A little more than a century after that, the rise of Lisbon was complete when the royal seat of power was transferred here from Coimbra, and Lisbon was declared capital of Portugal.

The next great period—that of *os descobrimentos* (the discoveries)—began with the 15th-century voyages led by the great Portuguese navigators to India, Africa, and Brazil. The wealth realized by these expeditions was phenomenal: gold, jewels, ivory, porcelain, and spices helped finance grand buildings and impressive commercial activity. Late-Portuguese Gothic architecture—called Manueline (after the king Dom Manuel I)—assumed a rich, individualistic style, characterized by elaborate sculptural details, often with a maritime motif. Torre de Belém and the Mosteiro dos Jerónimos (Belém's tower and monastery) are supreme examples of this period.

With independence from Spain in 1640 and assumption of the throne by successive dukes of the house of Bragança, Lisbon became ever more prosperous, only to suffer calamity on November 1, 1755, when the city was hit by the last of a series of earthquakes. Two-thirds of Lisbon was destroyed, and tremors were felt as far north as Scotland; 40,000 people in Lisbon died, and entire sections of the city were swept away by a tidal wave.

Under the direction of the prime minister, the Marquês de Pombal, Lisbon was rebuilt quickly and ruthlessly. The medieval quarters were leveled and replaced with broad boulevards; the commercial center, the Baixa, was laid out in a grid; and the great Praça do Comércio, the riverfront square, was planned. Essentially this is how downtown Lisbon appears today—an elegant 18th-century layout that remains as pleasing in modern times as it was intended to be 250 years ago.

Of course, there are parts of Lisbon—particularly several dreary suburbs beyond the city center—that lack charm. Even some of the handsome downtown areas have lost their classic Portuguese appearance as the city and its residents have become more cosmopolitan: shiny new office blocks have replaced some 19th- and 20th-century art nouveau buildings and sit alongside others. And the aging trams that tourists so love now share the streets with a growing fleet of new "fast trams" as well as belching buses and predictably proliferating automobiles.

However, much of the modernization—particularly the infrastructure upgrades—has improved the city. Moreover, Lisbon moved into the international limelight after hosting the 1998 World Exposition (Expo), which took "The Oceans" as its theme—an appropriate choice for a nation that first conquered the seas in the 16th century. Expo left favorable impressions on the millions who visited Lisbon at that time; and even those Lisboetas who claim to have opposed it now applaud its legacy, which includes the transformation of Expo's site into an expansive riverfront area, Parque das Nações.

The planners who conceived and developed the plans for Expo during a 10-year period had far more in mind, though, than simply creating a site for Expo events. The riverside has been revitalized, public buildings spruced up, the metro (subway) system overhauled and extended, and an impressive new bridge across the Tagus River completed. The capital has become number one among European-Atlantic ports of call for cruise ships, whose passengers now disembark directly onto a lively, reincarnated waterfront.

But, as the city has palpably changed in recent years, its intrinsic lovable, slightly disorganized, one-of-a-kind charm has not vanished in the contemporary mix. Despite all the growth and progress, you're never far from a hidden courtyard, a quiet garden, or a sweeping viewpoint.

Pleasures and Pastimes

Dining

Lisbon is only now beginning to see signs of the celebrity chefs of other European capitals, but it still rejects the snobbery and slavery to style that can affect dining elsewhere. And there's no doubt that the city takes its food seriously; many businesses have recently *cut* their lunch break to an hour and a half. The smell of coffee is the first thing to hit you each morning, issuing from a thousand pastry-filled cafés. By lunchtime even the humblest backstreet restaurant has chalked up its dishes of the day, depending on what was available at the market that morning—thick vegetable soup, grilled fresh fish, clams sprinkled with seasonal herbs, and chicken barbecued right in the window. And where you eat is half the experience: closeted in the dining room of an old mansion, looking out over the river from a designer warehouse-restaurant, or soaking up the downtown street scenes at an outdoor table.

With the exception of some very expensive restaurants with French-influenced menus, most places serve home-style Portuguese cuisine—grilled sardines and squid, simple steaks and cutlets drenched in olive oil and garlic, fresh seafood (always ask the price before ordering), spit-roast chicken, lamb chops, and casseroles. Local specialties include *açorda* (a thick bread-and-shellfish stew sprinkled with cilantro), *ameijoas á bulhão pato* (clams in garlic sauce), and different varieties of *bacalhau* (dried salt cod) or *bife* (steak). *Caldeirada* is a simple fish stew that varies from restaurant to restaurant, and once a week any local place worth its salt dishes up a *cozido*—a boiled meat stew that's an acquired taste.

In addition, the capital serves the best of the country's regional foods, including *porco á alentejana* (pork and clams) from the Alentejo, lampreys from the Minho, game, and many seasonal items. If you want still more variety, try restaurants that specialize in colonial Portuguese food—principally Brazilian, but also Mozambican and Goan (Indian) cuisine. Vegetarians can enjoy wonderful Portuguese breads, and most chefs are adept at choosing delectable vegetables at the market and then cooking them pleasingly al dente.

Wine is good and reasonably priced, with the *vinho da casa* (house wine) usually more than drinkable and increasingly offered by the glass. It's a custom to finish your meal with a glass of port. If you stop by the renowned Instituto do Vinho do Porto (☞ Exploring Lisbon, *below*) during your visit, you can taste different varieties and pick your favorite. Locals set more store by a glass of Moscatel de Setúbal, a rich dessert wine from across the river that's available everywhere.

Almost all Lisbon restaurants permit smoking throughout. If you're smoke-averse, choose a large, high-ceilinged room such as those along Lisbon's trendy riverfront, avoiding the upper-level sections; take advantage of one of the many outdoor dining rooms; or try dining at some of the top restaurants, including some at the best hotels, which often have powerful filtration systems. You can also try dining early, when the number of nonsmokers tends to be greater.

Lodging

In Lisbon you're spoiled for choice when it comes to finding a room for the night—classy accommodations overlooking the park, modern business hotels on central avenues or in historic houses with gardens, or family-run guest houses in the Old Town. The only snag is that accommodations are not the bargain restaurants are, although top-rated hotel prices are a tad lower than in some other European capitals.

You can still find reasonably priced rooms among the city's dozens of modest *pensões* (guest houses), most of which cost less than 8,000$00 a night. Be warned, however, that the decor may leave something to be desired, the toilet may be down the hall, and you may have to share a shower with other guests. The quality varies greatly from one guest house to another, but the best are spotless and friendly, and many are concentrated downtown, around the Rossío and the Praça dos Restauradores, as well as in the Bairro Alto. In summer it's often difficult to find a pensão with vacancies, so you may have to go door to door looking for a suitable place. The tourist office (☞ Visitor Information *in* Lisbon A to Z, *below*) can provide an up-to-date list of reliable places.

Even in the city's hotels, you still may want to ask to see a room before you agree to take it: street noise can be a problem and, conversely, quieter rooms at the back don't always have great views (or, indeed, any views). Also, some hotels charge the same rate for each of their rooms, so by checking out a couple you might be able to get a better room for the same price. This is especially true of the older hotels and inns, where no two rooms are exactly alike. And, if rooms for nonsmokers are unavailable, stale smoke can permeate one room, yet be totally absent in its clone down the hall.

Lisbon hosts trade fairs and conventions and is busy year-round, so it's best to secure a room in advance of your trip. Peak periods are Easter–June and September–November; budget pensões are particularly busy in summer. Despite the high year-round occupancy, substantial discounts—sometimes 30%–40%—abound from November through February. Even pensões drop their prices by a couple of thousand escudos at this time, so it's always worth asking.

Museums

Lisbon has some splendid museums, and all of them are reasonably priced. Standouts include the Museu Calouste Gulbenkian and the Museu de Arte Antiga, which have the finest collections of art and artifacts in the country. The singular Museu do Azulejo concentrates on the art of the country's famous ceramic tiles.

EXPLORING LISBON

The center city is small enough to cover on foot, but because of Lisbon's hills, you should be careful not to underestimate the distances or the time it takes to cover them. Places may appear close to one another on a map when they actually are on different levels, and the walk can be fearsomely steep. Public transportation is excellent, entertaining, and a bargain to boot. Marvelous old trams, buses, the metro, and turn-of-the-century funicular railways and elevators can transport you up the hills. If time is short or energy lags, taxis are a genuine bargain and can be summoned with a phone call. And, wherever you are, the river is never far away: chances are either you'll be looking over it or walking alongside it.

The center of Lisbon stretches north from the spacious Praça do Comércio—one of the largest riverside squares in Europe—to the Rossío, a smaller square lined with shops and cafés. The district in between is known as the Baixa (Lower Town), an attractive grid of parallel streets built after the 1755 earthquake and tidal wave destroyed much of the city.

The Alfama, the old Moorish quarter that survived the earthquake, lies east of the Baixa. In this part of town are the Sé (the city's cathedral) and, on the hill above, the Castelo de São Jorge (St. George's Castle). West of the Baixa, sprawled across another of Lisbon's hills, is the Bairro Alto (Upper Town), an area of intricate 17th-century streets, peeling houses, and churches. Five kilometers (3 miles) farther west is Belém, site of the famous Jerónimos Monastery, as well as several royal palaces and museums. A similar distance to the northeast, Lisbon's Parque das Nações pivots around the spectacular Oceanário de Lisboa (Lisbon Oceanarium).

The modern city begins at Praça dos Restauradores, adjacent to the Rossío. From here the main Avenida da Liberdade stretches northwest to the landmark Praça Marquês de Pombal, bordered by the green expanse of the Parque Eduardo VII beyond.

Numbers in the text correspond to numbers in the margin and on the Exploring Lisbon and Exploring Belém maps.

Great Itineraries

You could easily spend a week in Lisbon, exploring its neighborhoods, parks, and "hidden" squares and streets; visiting its museums; and passing time in its agreeable café-bars. But it's easy to get a feel for the city in even a couple of days. By using taxis and public transportation, you can combine multiple neighborhoods in a single day of sightseeing— the Alfama and the Baixa fit together particularly well, and the Chiado and the Bairro Alto make a good unit. Four days, then, is a reasonable compromise, allowing you time to see the major sights and quite a few of the minor ones, too.

IF YOU HAVE 2 DAYS

To view all of Lisbon's major attractions in two days, you'll have to get up early. Starting in the **Rossío,** the main downtown square, stroll through the Baixa, pausing to window-shop or take a coffee in a café.

You can then wander into the Alfama quarter by way of the cathedral, the **Sé**, following the winding streets past lookout points and churches as far as the **Castelo de São Jorge,** atop a hill. From here the views are magnificent, and there are plenty of cafés and restaurants nearby when it's time for lunch. A tram ride takes you back down to the Baixa, where in the riverside **Praça do Comércio** you pick up another tram for the rattling ride west through the suburbs to Belém to see the magnificent **Mosteiro dos Jerónimos,** as well as the acclaimed **Torre de Belém** and the **Monumento dos Descobrimentos.** On the way back to the city center, you can stop off at the **Museu de Arte Antiga.**

Your second day can be less hectic. Start with a walk through the Chiado shopping area, followed by a ride up to the Bairro Alto on the **Elevador de Santa Justa.** In the Bairro Alto you can easily fill up the morning browsing in the galleries and stores, visiting the **Igreja de São Roque** and its small museum, and popping into the **Instituto do Vinho do Porto** for a glass of port. Lunch is best taken at one of the small taverns or smarter restaurants. In the afternoon, you can return to the Baixa by the second of the elevators—the **Elevador da Glória**—and then take the metro uptown to the Fundação Calouste Gulbenkian. Here, you can spend three or four hours viewing the collections in the **Museu Calouste Gulbenkian** (at press time scheduled to reopen after renovations in January 2001) and the adjacent **Centro de Arte Moderna.** Alternatively, depending on your interests, take the metro to Parque das Nações to visit the excellent **Oceanário de Lisboa.**

IF YOU HAVE 4 DAYS

On the first day, spend the morning in the Baixa, where the shops and cafés are most inviting. At the riverside Praça do Comércio, you can even take a ferry across the river and back for fine views of the city. Have lunch in the suburb of Cacilhas, where the ferry docks, or return to **Praça dos Restauradores,** just north of the Rossío, where a side street just off the square—Rua das Portas de Santo Antão—is lined with well-known fish restaurants. Spend the afternoon in the Alfama, taking in the Sé, the Castelo de São Jorge, and the **Museu de Artes Decorativas.**

On your second day, catch a tram out toward Belém. Spend half the day exploring the monastery and monuments; you'll also have time for at least one of the specialty museums—**Museu da Marinha, Museu Nacional de Coches,** or **Museu de Arte Popular.** On your way to or from Belém, stop for a morning or afternoon at the Museu de Arte Antiga.

Your two remaining days can be split between old and modern Lisbon. One full day should involve seeing the Chiado shopping area and exploring the Bairro Alto. Devoting a full day, rather than half as above, to these areas means that you can pop into the **Convento do Carmo** archaeological museum and make a side trip to the **Jardim da Estrêla,** or you can make more time for a trip out to the Oceanarium.

On the final day, walk the length of the boulevard-like Avenida da Liberdade to the city's main park, **Parque Eduardo VII,** where the greenhouses are a treat. From here, it's a simple metro ride to the Museu Calouste Gulbenkian and the adjacent Centro de Arte Moderna. Some people spend a full day just in these two galleries, or you could take the metro farther north toward the **Jardim Zoológico** and the **Palácio dos Marqueses da Fronteira.**

When to Tour Lisbon

It's best not to visit at the height of summer, when the city positively steams and lodgings are expensive and crowded. Winters are generally mild and usually accompanied by bright blue skies, but for optimum Lisbon weather, visit on either side of summer, in May or late

September through October. The city's major festivals are in June, the so-called *santos populares* (popular saints), comprising days of riotous celebration dedicated to saints Anthony, John, and Peter.

The Alfama

The Moors, who imposed their rule on most of the southern Iberian Peninsula during the 8th century, left their mark on much of Lisbon but nowhere so evidently as in the Alfama district. Here narrow, twisting streets and soaring flights of steps wind up to an imposing castle on one of the city's highest hills. This is a grand place to get your bearings and take in supreme views. Because its foundation is dense bedrock, the district—a jumble of whitewashed houses with flower-laden balconies and red-tile roofs—has survived the wear and tear of the ages, including the great 1755 earthquake. The timeless alleys and little squares have a notoriously confusing layout, but the Alfama is relatively compact, and you'll keep circling back to the same buildings and streets. In the Moorish period this was a thriving area, and in the 15th century—as evidenced by the probable site of an ancient synagogue on Beco das Barrelas—it was an important Jewish quarter. Although now a somewhat run-down neighborhood, it has a down-to-earth charm—particularly during the June festivals of the santos populares—and smart bars and restaurants are slowly moving in.

A Good Walk

The Alfama's streets and alleys are very steep, and its levels are connected by flights of stone steps, which means it's easier to tour the area from the top down. Take a taxi up to the castle or approach it by Tram 28 from Rua Conceição in the Baixa or Bus 37 from Praça da Figueira.

From the Moorish **Castelo de São Jorge** ①, follow the castle walls around, and you'll emerge close to the **Museu da Marioneta** ②, with its unique collection of Portuguese and foreign puppets. From here, it's a 10-minute walk down Rua de Santa Marinha and Rua São Vicente to the **Mosteiro de São Vicente** ③, where you can examine the tombs of the Bragança dynasty and climb to the roof-terrace for amazing city views. From outside the church, a short ride on Tram 28 (or a 10-minute walk) takes you to the Alfama's prettiest square, **Largo das Portas do Sol,** whose terrace offers more glorious views of the streets below, dotted with drying laundry draped across the stepped alleys. Just off the square you'll find the **Museu de Artes Decorativas** ④, with its splendid decorative arts collections; down the hill about 300 ft is the view-laden **Miradouro Santa Luzia** ⑤. Head southwest from the miradouro along Rua do Limoeiro, which eventually becomes Rua Augusto Rosa. This route takes you past the **Sé** ⑥—Lisbon's cathedral—and to complete your tour of this district, you can then walk around and below the cathedral to the **Casa dos Bicos** ⑦, a mansion that survived the 1755 earthquake. From here it's an easy walk to the adjacent Baixa district, or retrace your steps to the cathedral, outside which Tram 28 stops before heading to the Baixa. Finally, buses from the main, waterfront Avenida Infante D. Henrique run from the Baixa up toward Santa Apolónia station if you want to take a look at the Alfama's most distant museum, the **Museu Militar** ⑧.

TIMING

Allow two to three hours to walk the route, perhaps more on a hot day, when you'll want to rest on the castle grounds or stop for drinks in a café. A visit to the Museu de Artes Decorativas will occupy at least an hour, although other museums and churches require much less attention. Note that museums are closed on Monday, and that churches generally close for a couple of hours in the middle of the day.

Exploring Lisbon (Lisboa)

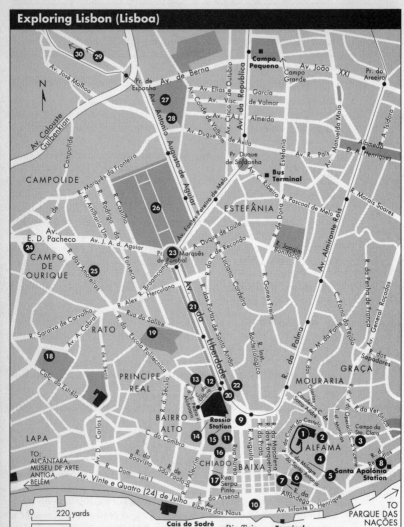

Amoreiras **24**

Aqueducto das
Aguas Livres **25**

Avenida da
Liberdade **21**

Casa dos Bicos **7**

Castelo de São
Jorge **1**

Centro de Arte
Moderna **28**

Convento do
Carmo **15**

Elevador da
Glória **12**

Elevador de
Santa Justa **11**

Igreja de São
Roque **14**

Instituto do
Vinho do Porto **13**

Jardim Botânico . . .**19**

Jardim da
Estrêla **18**

Jardim
Zoológico **30**

Miradouro
Santa Luzia **5**

Mosteiro de São
Vicente **3**

Museu da
Marioneta **2**

Museu de Artes
Decorativas **4**

Museu do
Chiado **17**

Museu Calouste
Gulbenkian **27**

Museu Militar **8**

Palácio dos
Marqueses da
Fronteira **29**

Parque
Eduardo VII **26**

Praça do
Comércio **10**

Praça dos
Restauradores **20**

Praça Marquês de
Pombal **23**

Rossío **9**

Rua das Portas de
Sto. Antão **21**

Rua Garrett **16**

Sé **6**

Sights to See

❼ Casa dos Bicos (House of Pointed Stones). For a view of a Lisbon town house that survived the 1755 earthquake, take a look at this 1523 Italianate dwelling. Built for the wealthy Albuquerque family, the building has a striking facade studded with pointed white stones in diamond shapes. The interior is similarly impressive, although it's not usually open to the public except when it hosts occasional special exhibitions—check with the tourist office for upcoming events. ✉ *Rua dos Bacalhoeiros,* ☎ *no phone.*

★ ❶ Castelo de São Jorge (St. George's Castle). Although this castle was constructed by the Moors, the site on which it stands dates from the 5th century, when the Visigoths first raised a fort here. At the castle's main entrance is a **statue of Dom Afonso Henriques,** who in 1147 besieged the castle and ultimately drove the Moors from Lisbon. Within the preserved Moorish walls and the castle's ramparts and towers (restored in 1938) are the scant remnants of a palace that was the residence of the kings of Portugal until the 16th century. The well-kept grounds are home to swans, turkeys, ducks, ravens, and other birds, and the outer walls encompass the (restored) medieval church of Santa Cruz, a few simple houses, and more restaurants and souvenir shops. Panoramic views of Lisbon can be seen from the walls; watch the uneven footing. ✉ *Entrances at Largo do Chão da Feira and Largo do Menino de Deus,* ☎ *no phone.* 🎟 *Free.* ☉ *Apr.–Sept., daily 9–9; Oct.–Mar., daily 9–7.*

❺ Miradouro Santa Luzia. Hop off Tram 28 at the Miradouro Santa Luzia, a terrace-garden viewpoint that takes in the Alfama and the river. It catches the sun all day, and a nearby café provides outdoor seats and welcome drinks. The adjacent **Igreja de Santa Luzia** (Church of Santa Luzia) is a sorry sight these days. Its exterior was once adorned with fine azulejos depicting the siege of the castle. They're gone, but heartfelt graffiti—AQUI HAVIA HISTORIA-CULTURA. AGORA—0 ("Here there once existed history and culture. Now—nothing")—makes its point. ✉ *Largo da Santa Luzia.*

❸ Mosteiro de São Vicente (St. Vincent's Monastery). The bright Italianate facade of the twin-towered monastery heralds an airy church with a barrel-vault ceiling, the work of accomplished Italian architect Filippo Terzi (1520–97). Finally completed in 1704, the church has a superbly tiled cloister depicting the fall of Lisbon to the Moors. The former refectory is the pantheon of the Bragança dynasty, who were the first rulers of an independent Portugal. Here, among the great, solid tombs and weighty inscriptions, lies Catherine of Bragança, who married Charles II of England in 1661. There's little to see—save a medieval cistern and a richly decorated entrance hall—but it is worth the entrance fee to climb up to the towers and terrace, which offer sweeping views over the Alfama, city, and river. From here you can see the huge white dome of **Santa Engrácia**—the church immediately behind and below São Vicente in Campo de Santa Clara—which doubles as the country's **Panteão Nacional** (National Pantheon), housing the tombs of Portugal's former presidents as well as cenotaphs dedicated to its most famous explorers and writers. The pantheon is open Tuesday through Sunday 10 to 5, and admission is 250$00. ✉ *Largo de São Vicente,* ☎ 21/888–5652. 🎟 *Church free; monastery 400$00.* ☉ *Church Tues.–Sat. 9–12:30 and 3–6, Sun. 9–12:30 and 2–5; monastery Tues.–Sun. 10–6.*

☖ ❷ Museu da Marioneta (Puppet Museum). The intricate workmanship that went into the creation of the puppets on display is remarkable, and it's not just kids' stuff either: during the Salazar regime, puppet shows were used to mock the pretensions and corruption of the reigning politicians. The collection encompasses both Portuguese and foreign puppets. Occasionally the museum staff performs a traditional puppet show; inquire at the museum or tourist office about upcoming events. ⊠ *Largo Rodrigues de Freitas 19,* ☎ *21/886–5794.* ⊠ *500$00.* ☉ *Tues.–Sun. 10–1 and 2–6.*

❹ Museu de Artes Decorativas (Museum of Decorative Arts). The museum is housed in the beautifully restored 17th-century Azurara Palace. Its furnishings, dating from the 15th through 19th centuries, have been lovingly restored and maintained and include *arraiolos* (traditional, hand-embroidered Portuguese carpets) that are brightly colored and based on imported Arabic designs. Other exhibits range from silver work and ceramics to paintings and jewelry. With so many rich items to preserve, the museum has developed into a major center for restoration: specialized crafts such as bookbinding, carving, and cabinetmaking are all undertaken here by highly trained staff, and you can view the restoration work by appointment. ⊠ *Largo das Portas do Sol 2,* ☎ *21/886–2183.* ⊠ *800$00.* ☉ *Tues.–Sun. 10–5.*

NEED A
BREAK?

At **Largo das Portas do Sol,** you'll find a number of small café-bars with outside seats from which you can watch ships on the Tagus River. **Cerca Moura** (⊠ Largo das Portas do Sol 4, ☎ 21/887–4859)—named after the Moorish walls that surround the district—is one of the best.

---

❽ Museu Militar (Military Museum). Military museums rarely rise above the run-of-the-mill, but Lisbon's gets a high score, not so much for its exhibits as for its location. Sited inside the huge Corinthian-style barracks and arsenal complex, opposite Santa Apolónia station, the museum has a spirit of derring-do. As you clatter through endless, echoing rooms of weapons, uniforms, and armor you may be lucky enough to be followed at a respectful distance by a guide who, without speaking a word of English, can convey exactly how that bayonet was jabbed or that gruesome flail swung. The museum is on the eastern edge of the Alfama, at the foot of the hill; the metro or any bus to Santa Apolónia station will take you there. *Largo de Santa Apolónia,* ☎ *21/888–2131.* ⊠ *400$00.* ☉ *Tues.–Sun. 10–5.*

❻ Sé. Lisbon's cathedral was founded in 1150 to commemorate the defeat of the Moors; to rub salt in the wound, the conquerors built the sanctuary on the site where Moorish Lisbon's main mosque once stood. Aside from the austere Romanesque interior and a fine rose window, there's little to detain you. You might, however, want to visit the splendid 13th-century **cloister** and the treasure-filled **sacristy,** which, among other things, contains the relics of the martyr St. Vincent. According to legend, the relics were carried from the Algarve to Lisbon in a ship piloted by ravens. ⊠ *Largo da Sé,* ☎ *21/886–6752.* ⊠ *Cathedral free, cloister 100$00, sacristy 300$00.* ☉ *Cathedral daily 9–noon and 2–6; sacristy daily 10–1 and 2–6.*

OFF THE
BEATEN PATH

MUSEU DO AZULEJO (Azulejo Museum) – To fully understand the craftsmanship that goes into making the ubiquitous azulejos, visit this magnificent museum at the 16th-century Madre de Deus convent and cloister. Some of the ceramics exhibited here date from the 1700s. Displays range from individual glazed tiles to superbly detailed decorative and pictorial panels. The 118-ft *Panorama of Lisbon* (1730) is a beautifully detailed study of the city and waterfront and is reputedly the country's longest azulejo piece. The richly furnished convent church contains some sights of its own: of note are the gilt baroque decoration and lively azulejo works depicting the life of St. Anthony. There's also a little café-bar and a gift shop that sells tile reproductions. ⊠ *Rua Madre de Deus 4 (Bus 59 from Praça da Figueira or Bus 105 from Praça Martim Moniz to the northeastern suburb of Xabegras),* ☎ *21/814–7747.* ⊠ *350$00.* ⊘ *Tues. 2–6, Wed.–Sun. 10–6.*

The Baixa

The earthquake of 1755, a massive tidal wave, and subsequent fires killed thousands of people and reduced proud 18th-century Lisbon to rubble. But within 10 years, frantic rebuilding under the direction of the king's minister, the Marquês de Pombal, had given the city a new look: a neoclassical grid design. You can still see this perfectly today in the impressive Baixa, the main shopping and banking district that stretches from the riverfront to the square known as the Rossío. Pombal intended the various streets to house workshops for certain trades and crafts, something that's still reflected in street names such as Rua dos Sapateiros (Cobblers' Street) and Rua da Prata (Silversmiths' Street). Near the impressive neoclassical arch at the bottom of Rua Augusta, street stalls selling jewelry and ethnic items sometimes appear on weekends. You may have seen the arch before in the movie *Gulliver's Travels,* in which the Lilliputians wheeled Ted Danson, as Gulliver, through it.

A Good Walk

Begin your exploration at Lisbon's main meeting place and crossroads, the Praça Dom Pedro IV. Its popular name, **Rossío** ⑨, matches the names of the metro station opening onto it and the train station just to the north. Note Dom Pedro's statue here; astride his horse, he sits on a pedestal flanked by fountains and wave-patterned paving stones. King for a year, he gave the people a popular charter, then abdicated in favor of his daughter Maria.

Take a moment to admire Rossío's national theater, the Teatro Nacional de Dona Maria II, named for Dom Pedro's daughter-successor (at night the 1846 neoclassical facade is dramatically illuminated). Its left side fronts the square Largo de São Domingos, with the Palácio da Independência (where restoration leaders met before overthrowing Portugal's Spanish occupiers in 1640) on your right. Straight across the Largo de São Domingos, notice (or step inside) the church of the same name; Inquisition sentences were once determined on its site. Just steps south toward Rua dos Correeiros, the Largo turns into the Praça da Figueira, with its statue of Prince Henry the Navigator's father, King João I. Take time to explore the shops and cafés that surround the pigeon-filled square.

Now you are in the heart of Baixa, the Marquês de Pombal's 18th-century gift to the directionally challenged. It's almost impossible to get lost in its compact core, where the streets are laid out on a grid. Rua Augusta is straight ahead; use it as your point of reference, explore the surrounding streets, which run parallel or at right angles and in many cases are for pedestrians only. Take half an hour or half a day; you're never far from a café in which to revive and regroup. Besides offering opportunities for shopping and people-watching, Rua Augusta also has Roman tunnels underneath No. 62–74, open on some summer Thursday afternoons.

When you're done wandering the gridded streets of Baixa, head down Rua Augusta toward the river and go through the neoclassical arch, Arco da Vitória, into the former 16th-century marketplace, **Praça do Comércio** ⑩, now lined with 18th-century buildings, at the street's end.

The route described above allows you to enjoy a generally downhill trajectory. But if you're determined to see as many sights as possible, consider reversing the itinerary. Once you reach the Rossío, a short walk down Rua Aurea will take you to the **Elevador de Santa Justa** ⑪, which will carry you up the Bairro Alto for an afternoon's exploration (☞ The Bairro Alto and Chiado, *below*).

TIMING

You could hike the Baixa from top to bottom in half an hour, but quadruple that for exploring the sights and poking into shops. Now add an hour or more for people-watching or lingering in a classic café, enjoying the charm of Rossío's somehow-satisfying chaos.

Sights to See

★ ⑪ **Elevador de Santa Justa.** The Santa Justa street elevator, built in 1902 by Raul Mésnier, is one of Lisbon's more extraordinary structures. Sitting inside its own Gothic-style tower, it whisks you from the Baixa up to Largo do Carmo in the Bairro Alto in less than a minute, saving you a very steep walk. ⊠ *Rua Aurea and Rua de Santa Justa,* ☎ *21/363–2044.* ⌑ *150$00; free with tourist pass.* ⊙ *Daily 7 AM–midnight.*

⑩ **Praça do Comércio.** When the Marquês de Pombal completed his neoclassical plan for Lisbon, he offset the gridded streets with the enormous riverfront Praça do Comércio. Known also as the Terreiro do Paço, after the royal palace (the Paço) that once stood here, it's lined with serene, arcaded 18th-century buildings, now given a fresh lick of yellow paint, while steps—once used by occupants of the royal barges that docked here—lead up from the water onto the square. The equestrian statue is of Dom José I, king at the time of the earthquake and subsequent rebuilding. In 1908, amid unrest that was later to lead to the declaration of a republic, King Carlos and his eldest son, Luís Filipe, were assassinated as they drove through the square in a carriage. Later, during the 1974 revolution, the Praça do Comércio and its surrounding government buildings were among the first places to be occupied by rebel troops. The square itself is a hub for public transportation (trams to Belém leave from here, and ferries cross the Tagus at this point), and it's also worth coming here on Sunday morning, when a market of old coins and banknotes takes place under the arches of the arcade.

NEED A BREAK?

One of the original buildings on Praça do Comércio houses the **Café Martinho da Arcada** (⊠ Praça do Comércio 3, ☎ 21/887–9259), a literary haunt since 1782. The main rooms now contain an expensive restaurant full of old-style atmosphere; adjacent to it is a more modest café-bar.

★ ⑨ **Rossío.** Lisbon's main square since the Middle Ages is popularly known as the Rossío, although its official name is Praça Dom Pedro IV (whom the central statue commemorates). It's a grand space—although rather overwhelmed by circling traffic these days—with ornate French fountains and, on its northern edge, the mid-19th-century **Teatro Nacional** (National Theater), built on the site of the earlier Palace of the Inquisition. Public executions were once carried out in the Rossío; slightly less dramatic performances these days are on show in the theater (productions are in Portuguese). However, you'll probably do what the locals do when they come to the Rossío: pick up a newspaper at a newsstand and sit at one of the cafés that lines the east and west sides of the square. These are good places to have your shoes shined by one of the roaming shoe shiners who ply their trade in the square—just make sure you establish the price first.

The Bairro Alto and Chiado

Lisbon's most chic shopping district lies west of the Baixa grid. Chiado's narrow, often-cobbled streets lead uphill to Lisbon's Bairro Alto. The streets follow the contours of the hills, which can make getting around a bit confusing. Although a calamitous 1988 fire destroyed much of Chiado, including many of the older shops in the vicinity of Rua Garrett, an ambitious rebuilding program has restored some of the fin-de-siècle facades. And a fashionable new retail complex, hotel, and metro station on the site of the old Armazéns do Chiado—once Lisbon's largest department store—has given the district a modern focus. Above all, the area remains a fashionable place to shop. Scattered along Rua Garrett and Rua do Carmo you'll find some of the best shoe stores in Europe, glittering jewelry shops, hip boutiques, and a host of cafés and delis selling drinks, snacks, and pastries.

Although the settlement of the Bairro Alto dates from the 17th century, most of the buildings are from the 18th and 19th centuries and are an appealing mixture of small churches, warehouses, antiques and art galleries, artisans' shops, and town houses with wrought-iron balconies.

The best way to tour this area is on foot. The backstreets are filled with the sounds of daily life: children scuffle amid the drying laundry, women carry huge bundles from shop to shop, and old men clog the doorways of barrooms. Historically, the Bairro Alto has always had a reputation as being rather rough-and-ready, and there's still a thriving red-light district and back alleys where it would be unwise to venture after dark. On the whole, however, it's safe to walk around; indeed, the Bairro Alto has more bars, restaurants, fado (traditional Portuguese music) clubs, and discos than anywhere else in the city, and the arrival of smart boutiques and trendy eateries has signaled the start of gentrification.

A Good Walk

As the Bairro Alto is spread across steep hills, the least taxing way to explore is from the top down. From Praça dos Restauradores, you can catch the **Elevador da Glória** ⑫, a creaking funicular railway that deposits you immediately across the street from the wonderful **Instituto do Vinho do Porto** ⑬. After sampling from the institute's collection of port wines, turn right and walk down Rua São Pedro de Alcântara. At Largo Trindade Coelho, on your left, is the **Igreja de São Roque** ⑭, with its associated museum. From the southeast corner of the church's square, follow Rua Nova da Trindade downhill and take a left at the second corner, Rua da Trindade. This small street leads toward Largo do Carmo, a pretty square on which stands the **Convento do Carmo** ⑮, a charming ruin housing an interesting archaeological museum.

If you want to browse among the shops of the Chiado before exploring the Bairro Alto, then you can follow the above tour in reverse. You might want to start with the sophisticated new Chiado Shopping Center, with its collection of midsize shops and smart boutiques ensconced behind the elegantly restored historic facade. Also make time for a diversion down Rua Serpa Pinto, off **Rua Garrett** ⑯, the Chiado's main street, to see what's on display at the **Museu do Chiado** ⑰, the district's major art gallery. Then for a comfortable ascent to the Bairro Alto, take Rua do Carmo north from the eastern end of Rua Garrett over to the lower terminus of the Elevador de Santa Justa (☞ The Baixa, *above*). The upper station of the elevator is down a narrow alley behind the Convento do Carmo, from which you can proceed in backwards order to São Roque Church and the Port Wine Institute. Or hike up the steep hill from Rua Garrett to Largo do Carmo; Calçada do

Sacramento will take you straight there, or head up Rua Serpa Pinto and jog east on Travessa do Carmo.

The Bairro Alto is also the best starting point for side trips to two of the city's hidden gardens. From the Elevador de Santa Justa, you can make the lengthy trip across the quarter (by tram if you prefer) to the **Jardim da Estrêla** ⑱ on the western edge of the district. From the Elevador da Glória, it's a 20-minute walk north to the **Jardim Botânico** ⑲, which is also the site of the **Museu de História Natural.**

TIMING

The Bairro Alto is remarkably compact, and it takes very little time to walk from one end to the other; an hour would cover it. But once you start diving off into the side streets and lingering in the shops, galleries, and bars, you'll find you can happily spend a morning or afternoon here. Neither the Igreja de São Roque nor the Convento do Carmo will occupy you for more than half an hour. If you don't like crowds, avoid the Bairro Alto late at night, especially on weekends, when seemingly the whole of Lisbon comes here to eat, drink, and party.

Sights to See

⑮ **Convento do Carmo** (Carmo Convent). The partially ruined Convento do Carmo—once Lisbon's largest convent—was severely damaged in the 1755 earthquake, but open-air summer orchestral concerts are held beneath its majestic archways. Its sacristy houses the **Museu Arqueológico do Carmo** (Archaeological Museum), a small but worthy collection of ceramic tiles, medieval tombs, ancient coins, and other city finds. It's unlikely to delay you long, but the lovely square outside is one of the nicer places in the city to pull up a café seat. ⊠ *Largo do Carmo,* ☎ *21/346–0473.* ☞ *500$00.* ☉ *Apr.–Sept., daily 10–6; Oct.–Mar., daily 10–1 and 2–5.*

⑫ **Elevador da Glória.** One of the finest approaches to the Bairro Alto is via the Elevador da Glória, a funicular railway on the western side of Avenida da Liberdade, near Praça dos Restauradores. The elevator runs up the steep hill and takes only about a minute to reach the São Pedro de Alcântara Miradouro, a viewing point that looks out over the castle and the Alfama. ⊠ *Calçada da Glória,* ☎ *21/363–2044.* ☞ *150$00; free with tourist pass.* ☉ *Daily 7 AM–midnight.*

★ ⑭ **Igreja de São Roque** (Church of St. Roque). Filippo Terzi, the architect who designed São Vicente on the outskirts of the Alfama, was also responsible for completing this Renaissance church. Curb your impatience with its plain facade and venture inside. Its eight side chapels are superbly decorated, several with statuary and art dating from the early 17th century. But if one stands out, it's the last chapel on the left before the altar, the extraordinary 18th-century **Capela de São João Baptista** (Chapel of St. John the Baptist): designed and built in Rome, with rare stones and mosaics that resemble oil paintings, the chapel was taken apart, shipped to Lisbon, and reassembled here in 1747. You may find a guide who will escort you around the church and switch on the appropriate lights so the beauty of the chapels is revealed. Adjoining the church, the **Museu de Arte Sacra** (Museum of Sacred Art) displays a surprisingly engaging collection of clerical vestments and liturgical objects, the capes and drapes delicately embroidered in gold, while the jewel-encrusted crosses and goblets glitter in their cases. ⊠ *Largo Trindade Coelho,* ☎ *21/346–0361.* ☞ *Church free; museum 150$00, free Sun.* ☉ *Church daily 8:30–5; museum Tues.–Sun. 10–1 and 2–5.*

★ ⑬ **Instituto do Vinho do Porto** (Port Wine Institute). In the cozy, clublike lounge, you can taste some of the institute's more than 300 types and vintages of port—from extra-dry white varieties to red vintages. Service can be slow, but eventually someone will bring you a wine list, and you can order by the glass or bottle. ⊠ *Rua de São Pedro de Alcântara 45,* ☎ *21/347–5707.* 🖃 *Free; prices of tastings vary, starting at 200$00.* ⊙ *Mon.–Sat. 10–10.*

⑲ Jardim Botânico. Lisbon's main botanical gardens, the hillside Jardim Botânico, were first laid out in 1874. Hidden between backstreets about 2 km (1 mi) north of the Bairro Alto, they make a restful stop, with 10 acres of paths, benches, and nearly 15,000 species of subtropical plants; there's also a 19th-century meteorological observatory. The gardens form part of the **Museu de História Natural** (Natural History Museum), whose buildings contain mineral and geological displays and zoological and anthropological exhibits. ⊠ *Rua da Escola Politécnica 58; weekday entrance also at Rua do Alegria, near Av. da Liberdade,* ☎ *21/396–1521.* 🖃 *Gardens 200$00, museum free.* ⊙ *Gardens May–Oct., weekdays 9–8, weekends 10–8; Nov.–Apr., weekdays 9–6, weekends 10–6; guided tours (reservations required) year-round Sat. at 11. Museum weekdays 10–5.*

⑱ Jardim da Estrêla. (Estrêla Gardens). Inside the attractively laid out gardens, old men sit at tables playing card games. Watch them a while, stroll the shaded paths, and then pull up a chair in the outdoor café for a drink or a snack. Towering over the southwestern side is the 18th-century **Basilica da Estrêla,** which is open 7:30–1 and 3–7. This spacious baroque basilica has an unusually restrained interior and offers views of the city from its *zimborio* (dome). The gardens lie on the western edge of the Bairro Alto. You can walk here, although it's more pleasant to catch Tram 28, which runs from Rua do Loreto, near Praça Luís de Camões, just west of Largo do Carmo.

⑰ Museu do Chiado. Open again after extensive renovations, the Chiado's prime art gallery—built on the site of a former monastery—specializes in 19th- and 20th-century contemporary art. The museum also hosts temporary exhibitions of international film, paintings and sculpture; keep an eye out for details in the local papers or check with the tourist board. ⊠ *Rua Serpa Pinto 6,* ☎ *21/343–2148.* 🖃 *400$00, free Sun. until 2 PM.* ⊙ *Tues. 2–6, Wed.–Sun. 10–6.*

⑯ Rua Garrett. The Chiado's principal street is lined with old department stores and a series of comfortable, turn-of-the-century, wood-paneled coffee shops that attract locals and tourists alike. The most famous of these cafés is **A Brasileira** (⊠ Rua Garrett 120, ☎ 21/346–9541), which features a life-size statue of Portugal's national poet, Fernando Pessoa, seated at an outside table.

The Modern City

The attractions of 19th- to 20th-century Lisbon are so diverse (and so far-flung) that, even excluding the 21st-century developments in the making along the waterfront, they defy attempts to see the area as a whole. Near the large square Praça dos Restauradores, north of Rossío, the southern reaches of the modern city do echo some of the Baixa. And many visitors are enchanted with the impressive Avenida da Liberdade. With its 10 parallel rows of trees, it's a favorite place in which to linger and an easy-to-find reference point if you get lost in the surrounding backstreets. North of the city's main park, Parque Eduardo VII, the modern city stretches into residential suburbs, with only the occasional attraction to tempt the tourist. What particular attractions there are—namely Portugal's finest museum and a clutch of other diversions—can all be reached by public transportation, or taxi if time is short.

A Good Tour

Since modern Lisbon's attractions are widely dispersed, you may need to return another day to see everything. But to begin your exploration of modern Lisbon, start where half the city's neighborhoods do: at the plaza where downtown meets uptown, **Praça dos Restauradores** ⑳, a.k.a. Restoration Square. Arriving at the Restauradores metro station, note its enamel-on-ceramic painting and decorative tiles. A good first stop on the plaza is Palácio Foz, which houses Portugal's main tourist office (☞ Visitor Information *in* Lisbon A to Z, *below*), where you can pick up information on the entire country. Glance at some of its walls and ceilings painted by early 20th-century artists. Before leaving the Praça dos Restauradores, peer in at the palatial lobby of the Avenida Palace Hotel, built by long-lived architect José Monteiro (1849–1942). And at the square's center, note the patterned paving around the obelisk dedicated to the end of Spanish occupation and restoration of Portuguese rule in 1640.

At the top of the square, start up the gently sloping **Avenida da Liberdade** ㉑ where, on a mild morning, you can stop for a late breakfast at almost any sidewalk café. (Along the way you might want to detour to **Rua das Portas de Santo Antão** ㉒, a pedestrian-only street full of seafood restaurants that runs parallel to Avenida da Liberdade one block to the east.) Despite its lack of famous landmarks, the Avenida da Liberdade's leafy mile is a favorite for stress-free strolls evocative of a traditional, lazier Lisbon. When you leave at its northern end, you pass through the **Praça Marquês de Pombal** ㉓.

If shopping is your bag you could head left down Avenida J.A. d. Aguiar to the **Amoreiras** ㉔ shopping center. Or, if you've called ahead for a group tour, you can turn left on Rua das Amoreiras from Avenida J.A. d. Aguiar to see the impressively engineered inner reservoir of Lisbon's **Aqueduto das Aguas Livres** ㉕. But to continue your exploration of the city's sights, walk around the Praça Marquês de Pombal to the right (**Parque Eduardo VII** ㉖ will be on your left); veer right one block on Avenida Fontes; and turn left up Avenida António Augusto de Aguiar, to the **Museu Calouste Gulbenkian** ㉗. Better, avoid this relatively boring half-hour walk by riding two stops on the metro from Rotunda (at Praça Marquês de Pombal) to São Sebastião or three to Palhavã. This is Portugal's most important museum and home to European, Egyptian, Greek, Roman, and Asian art. Adjoining the museum is the **Centro de Arte Moderna** ㉘, with many sculptures and a fine collection of mostly Portuguese art. Be sure to roam the pretty gardens on the two museums' grounds. Now is the time to hail a taxi or ask the reception desk of the museum to call one. (You can also catch the metro at Palhavã to Sete Rios, then walk 10 to 20 minutes west along Rua São Domingos de Benfica.) The next stop is the **Palácio dos Marqueses da Fronteira** ㉙, which yields pure pleasure. This 17th-century home of the modern Marquises de Fronteira, near the **Jardim Zoológico** ㉚ and on the border of Parque Florestal de Monsanto, is exquisite. Allow time to enjoy the delightful gardens if weather permits.

TIMING

In expansive modern Lisbon, choosing sights according to your mood and the weather is not out of line, and you'll have to make some choices about the places you see to complete your visit in a day. It could take three hours to do justice to the Gulbenkian alone—especially if you have lunch on the premises. The palace and its gardens justify another hour easily; add another for walking (or two if you eschew any taxis or metro), and perhaps another hour for shopping and a coffee on the Avenida da Liberdade.

Sights to See

㉔ Amoreiras. Before the Parque das Nações site was developed, Lisbon could count its postmodern architectural triumphs on one finger—namely the gigantic pink-and-blue Amoreiras, a striking commercial-and-residential complex west of Parque Eduardo VII. Designed by Tomás Taveira in 1985 and visible from just about everywhere in town, the gleaming complex still turns heads; inside, there's a huge shopping center, a 10-screen movie theater, a food court—there's even a chapel. On weekends it seems all of Lisbon turns out to roam the corridors. ⊠ *Av. Eng. Duarte Pacheco,* ☏ *21/381–0200.* ⊙ *Shops and restaurants daily 9 AM–11 PM. Metro: Rotunda.*

㉕ Aqueduto das Aguas Livres. Lisbon was formerly provided with clean drinking water by means of the Aqueduct of Free Waters (1729–48), built by Manuel da Maia and stretching for more than 18 km (11 mi) from the water source on the outskirts of the modern city. Astoundingly, it survived the 1755 earthquake, and today its most graceful section consists of 14 arches that soar 200 ft over the pretty neighborhood square of Largo das Amoreiras. The aqueduct itself is off-limits unless you book a group tour, but the square is also the site of the associated **Mãe d'Agua,** an internal reservoir capable of holding more than a million gallons of water. This extraordinary structure is used for art exhibitions and other cultural displays, giving you the chance to view the vast holding tank, the lavish internal waterfall, and the associated machinery. ⊠ *Largo das Amoreiras,* ☏ *21/813–5522 (for tours of aqueduct). Metro: Rotunda.*

㉑ Avenida da Liberdade. The city's main downtown spine—Avenida da Liberdade—was laid out in 1879, but what started life as an elegant rival to the Champs Élysées has lost some of its allure in recent decades. Many turn-of-the-century mansions and art deco buildings that once graced the avenue have been demolished, whereas others have been turned into soulless office blocks, and both sides of the avenue hum with the constant roar of traffic. However, certain historic facades have been retained, and halfway up on the western side the few theaters that make up Lisbon's surviving downtown theater district congregate in **Parque Mayer.** It's worth a leisurely stroll up the 1½-km (1-mi) length of the avenue at least once, from Praça dos Restauradores to the Parque Eduardo VII, if only to cool off with a drink in one of the city's surviving *esplanadas* (garden cafés)—there are two, set among the plane trees, in the middle of the avenue.

OFF THE
BEATEN PATH
CAMPO PEQUENO – Nothing grabs your attention quite so suddenly as the city's circular, redbrick, Moorish-style bullring, an over-the-top confection built in 1892 with small cupolas atop its four main towers. The ring holds about 9,000 people who crowd in to watch weekly bullfights, held every Thursday at 10 PM from June through September; at other times it's used as the venue for circuses and similar events. ⊠ *Praça de Touros do Campo Pequeno, Av. da República,* ☏ *21/793–2093. Metro: Campo Pequeno.*

㉘ Centro de Arte Moderna (Modern Art Center). In the gardens outside the Fundação Calouste Gulbenkian (Calouste Gulbenkian Foundation), sculptures hide in every recess. You may want to spend a little time here before following signs through the garden to the foundation's modern art museum, where modern and contemporary Portuguese and foreign art are displayed on two floors. There's also a special section set aside for drawings and prints. Although the range of exhibits here is more limited than that of the **Museu Calouste Gulbenkian** (☞ *below*) itself, modern art fans will appreciate this venue for the finest collection of its sort in Portugal. Naturally, Portuguese artists are best represented: look for pieces by Amadeo de Sousa Cardoso, whose painting style varied greatly in his short life; abstract works by Viera da Silva; and the childhood themes explored in the paintings of Paula Rego. ⊠ *Rua Dr. N. Bettencourt,* ☎ *21/795–0241.* 💷 *500$00, free Sun.* ⊙ *Tues.– Sun. 10–5. Metro: Palhavã.*

☟ ㉚ **Jardim Zoológico** (Zoological Gardens). With a menagerie of 2,000 animals from more than 370 species, the city zoo is always a popular spot. Admission is pricey, but in addition to the usual habitats and enclosures there's a children's zoo, with miniature houses and small animals; dolphin shows at 11 and 3; a new, inhabitant-friendly reptile house; and even a cemetery for dogs. Future plans include a new gorilla house, the establishment of an Amazonian ecosystem, and new "free range"– style areas for the larger animals. There are snack bars and restaurants on site, or you can pack a lunch for a picnic. ⊠ *Estrada de Benfica 158,* ☎ *21/726–8217.* 💷 *1,800$00.* ⊙ *Daily 10–8. Metro: Sete Rios.*

★ ㉗ **Museu Calouste Gulbenkian.** At press time the museum was closed for fairly extensive renovation but scheduled to reopen in January 2001. Set on its own lush grounds, the museum of the celebrated Calouste Gulbenkian Foundation, a cultural trust, houses treasures collected by Armenian oil magnate Calouste Gulbenkian (1869–1955) and donated to the people of Portugal in return for tax concessions. The Calouste Gulbenkian Museum is the main part of the foundation's buildings and is easily Portugal's finest museum. The collection it houses is split in two: one part is devoted to Egyptian, Greek, Roman, Islamic, and Asian art and the other to European acquisitions. Both holdings are relatively small, but the quality of the pieces on display is magnificent, and you should aim to spend at least two hours here or even the better part of a day. English-language notes are available throughout the museum.

You might first visit the astounding Egyptian Room, highlighted by a haunting gold mummy mask. Greek and Roman coins and statuary, Chinese porcelain, Japanese prints, and a set of rich 16th- and 17th-century Persian tapestries follow. The European art section has pieces from all the major schools from the 15th through the 20th centuries. A room of vivid 18th-century Venetian scenes by Francesco Guardi and paintings by Rembrandt, Peter Paul Rubens, Claude Monet, and Pierre-Auguste Renoir stimulate the senses, as do the Italian and Spanish ceramics, gleaming French furniture, textiles, and art nouveau jewelry.

If it's all too much to take in at one time, break up your visit with a stop in the pleasant café-restaurant in the basement. There's an exhibition room here, too, featuring temporary displays of art. As you leave the museum, you can buy superb (and inexpensive) posters and postcards at the main desk. The foundation also houses two concert halls, where music and ballet festivals are held in winter and spring—modestly priced tickets are available at the box office. ⊠ *Av. de Berna 45,* ☎ *21/795–0236.* 💷 *500$00, free Sun.* ⊙ *Tues.–Sun. 10–5. Metro: Palhavã.*

㉙ **Palácio dos Marqueses da Fronteira.** Built in the late 17th century, the Palace of the Marquises, often called the Palácio Fronteira, remains one of the most beautiful houses in the capital, containing splendid reception rooms with 17th- and 18th-century decorative tiles, contemporary furniture, and paintings. The stunning grounds harbor a terraced walk, a topiary garden, and statuary and fountains. Some of the city's finest azulejos adorn the fountains and terraces and depict hunting scenes, battles, and religious themes. The palace is northwest of the city, in the suburb of São Domingo de Benfica. ⊠ *Largo de São Domingo de*

Benfica 1, ☎ 21/778–4599 or 21/778–2030. ▨ Weekdays, gardens 300$00, palace and gardens 1,000$00; Sat., gardens 500$00, palace and gardens 1,500$00. ☉ June–Sept., Mon.–Sat. for guided tours 4 times daily; arrive between 10:30 and noon. Oct.–May, Mon.–Sat., 2 tours daily, at 11 AM and noon. Metro: Sete Rios.

㉖ Parque Eduardo VII. Established at the beginning of the 20th century, the city's main park was named to honor the British monarch's 1903 visit here during his brief reign. The sloping, formal gardens are used by surprisingly few of Lisbon's residents.The park attracts visitors, however, with the magnificent views from the avenue at the top of the park— where modernistic towers topped by concrete wheat sheaves stand like sentinels—and Lisbon's best-kept horticultural secret, its two **estufas**: the *estufa fria* (cold greenhouse) and *estufa quente* (hot greenhouse), which contain rare flowers, trees, and shrubs from tropical and subtropical climes. These are gorgeous grottoes in which to stroll, and the estufa fria is also one of the city's most bizarre concert and exhibition venues, used by orchestras, soloists, and artists. ⊠ ☎ 21/388–2278 *for information on greenhouses. ▨ Greenhouses 95$00. ☉ Park daily dawn–dusk, greenhouses Apr.–Sept., daily 9–6; Oct.–Mar., daily 9–5. Metro: Rotunda.*

⑳ Praça dos Restauradores. This square, which is adjacent to Rossío train station, marks the beginning of modern Lisbon. Here the broad, tree-lined Avenida da Liberdade starts its northwesterly ascent, and there's also a useful metro station. The name commemorates the uprising in 1640 against Spanish rule, which ushered in the era of Portuguese independence; an obelisk (raised in 1886) commemorates the event. There's little else of interest in the square itself, save the elegant 18th-century **Palácio Foz**, on the west side, which houses the main tourist office (and, until the outbreak of World War I, contained a casino). The only building to rival the palace is the superbly restored **Eden** building, just to the south, an art deco masterpiece of Portuguese architect Cassiano Branco, now revamped to house the Orion Eden apartment-hotel and a Virgin Megastore.

㉓ Praça Marquês de Pombal. As a pointed reminder of who was responsible for the layout of the city before you, dominating the Praça Marquês de Pombal is a central statue of the Marquês himself, designer of the new Lisbon that emerged from the ruins of the 1755 earthquake. A close look at the base of the statue reveals representations of both the earthquake and tidal wave that engulfed the city, while a female figure with outstretched arms signifies the joy at the emergence of the re-fashioned city. After years of construction work, the statue and landscaped square now look terrific, and there are impressive new entrances into the metro station (indeed, the plaza is also known as the Rotunda, which is the name of the metro station here). The square is effectively a large roundabout—and a useful orientation point, since it stands at the northern end of Avenida da Liberdade with Parque Eduardo VII just behind. New buildings with classic facades are rising along its rim. Still, after you see the statue of the Marquis—looking steadily south toward his major creation, the Baixa—that's pretty much it.

㉒ Rua das Portas de Santo Antão. If you want to eat seafood in the center of Lisbon, you come to Rua das Portas de Santo Antão, a pedestrian-only street of fish restaurants, with waiters lurking at every door. There's a varied range of eating places—cafés to high-class restaurants—but most display great tanks of lobsters and fish on ice slabs; choose your meal and then sit outside on the cobblestones to enjoy it. If you're daring, you can later pop into one of the street's few surviving stand-up *ginginha* bars—cubbyholes where unshaven gents and local characters throw down shots of the eyewateringly strong cherry brandy. The street is on the eastern side of Praça dos Restauradores, a block east from the square and running parallel to it.

Parque das Nações

As Belém (☞ *below*), at Lisbon's western edge, celebrates the explorers who set out to sea centuries ago, the Parque das Nações, which lies an equal distance 5 km (3 mi) northeast of the city center, has risen to revitalize Lisbon's waterfront. Expo '98 was conceived not just to attract tourism but also—even primarily—to spur the development of Lisbon's riverfront and create new directions for the city's expansion. Before, empty warehouses and refuse filled the site, once a landing area for seaplanes. The Expo location—in its new incarnation, the Parque das Nações—has been pivotal in putting a revitalized Tagus River back at the heart of the city.

In addition to the popular Oceanário de Lisboa, apartments, hotels, restaurants, stores, a marina, and acres of landscaped parkland are adding to the area's growing popularity. The vast trade fair and exhibition center, Feira Internacional Lisboa (FIL), has relocated here, hosting frequent conventions and trade shows (some open to the public), plus diverse Sunday markets (which in summer are held outdoors by the river from 10 to 7).

The Atlântico Pavilion holds major cultural and sports events, and at press time had just completed a 200-meter track for the World Indoor Athletics Championship in March 2001. Public- and private-sector planners are working on continued development, with more businesses expected to relocate to this and surrounding areas. Expect the changes here to continue, and enjoy the marked contrasts between this new development and the 13th- to 20th-century Lisbon just minutes away.

A Good Walk

To start this walk take the metro or a train to the Estação do Oriente. Distinguished by its handsome vaulted ceilings, white metal columns, and inner atriums, the station was designed by architect Santiago Calatrava of Spain. From the station, cross Avenida D. João II toward the river and meander east along one of two parallel esplanades toward the **Torre Vasco da Gama** at the end of the park. Or take the steps-saving cable car—open 11–7 weekdays and 10–8 Sunday—to the tower. The cost for the cable car is 500$00 one-way. Forget walking and take the elevator up the Torre Vasco da Gama for an unparalleled view of the Vasco da Gama Bridge. Back at ground level, walk back along the esplanades in the direction you came from, past families at play, mime artists, musicians, and souvenir shops. As you walk, look over the fleet of restaurants, cafés, and bars. Their fare zooms from Uruguayan to regional Portuguese, ice cream to beer. And on weekend nights anywhere along Lisbon's riverfront, just as you think you're the last to leave a nightspot, a new wave of patrons—ready to party until shortly before dawn—will let you know how uncool you are. Off the esplanades, the **Oceanário de Lisboa,** Europe's largest aquarium, was planned to outlast Expo, and it is doing so brilliantly.

If cooling off sounds good, turn left as you leave the Oceanarium, heading west and a bit inland, to the park's Water Gardens—a series of small gardens focusing in turn on glaciers, streams, waterfalls, and waves. Stepping stones over pools allow you to pass between the waterfalls. If you're ready for some serious shopping, find it at the Vasco da Gama Shopping Center, just across Avenida D. João II and two minutes' walk along it. This is where Portuguese suburbanites and families come to play, bowl, stock up on groceries, eat, watch films at a 10-screen cinema, and, oh yes, shop. The center's shops are open 10 AM to 11 PM, midnight on Saturday. Some of the public transportation back to Lisbon ends at midnight, too, but then taxis are waiting at the station until all hours.

TIMING

You can spend anything from a couple of hours to most of the day or night here, especially if you spend the usual two hours or so at the Oceanarium and stay to party or shop long after dark. Sundays, allot some time for the markets at the north end of the park.

Sights to See

★ **Oceanário de Lisboa** (Lisbon Oceanarium). The centerpiece of Expo, renamed after the event, is a stunning glass-and-stone complex that rises from the river and is reached by footbridge. It's the largest aquarium in Europe (containing 25,000 fish, seabirds, and mammals) and the first ever to incorporate selected world ocean habitats (North Atlantic, Pacific, Antarctic, and Indian) within a single environment. You view the connected tanks and display areas from above and then from underwater; clever use of acrylic walls means that tropical fish and penguins look as if they inhabit the same space. Exhibitions tell you more about the environments you're experiencing, and at the end you can sink onto a bench in one of the "contemplation" areas and just watch the fish swim by. A 30-minute behind-the-scenes tour is offered on Wednesdays, Fridays, and weekends. ⊠ *Esplanada D. Carlos I (Doca dos Olivais)*, ☎ *21/891–7002, 21/891–7006, 21/891–7007, or 21/891–7008.* ☞ *1,700$00.* ☼ *Daily 10–7.*

NEED A BREAK?

For pure nectar on a hot day, find one of the many stands or cafés displaying huge bowls of oranges. They have juice machines on which, for about $2, they'll squeeze what seems like a dozen of them for you.

Torre Vasco da Gama (Vasco da Gama Tower). At the park's easternmost edge and rising 480 ft above it, this graceful white tower is Portugal's tallest structure. Its 345-ft Crow's Nest observation deck (reached by three spectacular panoramic glass elevators) seems to put you eye-to-eye with the 18-km (11-mi) Vasco da Gama Bridge as well as lets you see across Lisbon to the Atlantic Ocean. You could lunch up here in the panoramic restaurant, but it suits expense account budgets better than those of most tourists. ⊠ ☎ *21/896–9867.* ☞ *500$00.* ☼ *Daily 10–8 (until 10 PM June–Aug., Fri.–Sat.).*

Belém, Alcântara, and the Museu de Arte Antiga

To see the best examples of the uniquely Portuguese late-Gothic architecture known as Manueline, head for Belém, at the far southwestern edge of Lisbon. If you are traveling in a group of three or four, taxis are the cheapest means of transportation. Otherwise, for a more scenic—if bumpier—20- to 30-minute journey, take Tram 15 from Praça do Comércio, which stops outside the Jerónimos Monastery; Tram 18 runs from Praça do Comércio directly to the Palácio de Ajuda. It's worth noting that almost all the sights in Belém, including the Museu de Arte Antiga, are closed Monday; conversely, Sunday sees free or reduced admission at many attractions.

The tram passes through the wealthy district of Lapa, with its Museu de Arte Antiga (Ancient Art Museum), and a little farther on (at about the halfway point to Belém) you'll pass under the magnificent 25 of April Bridge, spanning the Tagus River, one of the city's great landmarks. This is in the Alcântara district of Lisbon, whose dockside—

Alcântara . . .31

Centro
Cultural de
Belém 37

Jardim
Botânico da
Ajuda 42

Monumento
dos Descobri-
mentos 35

Mosteiro dos
Jerónimos . . .41

Museu da
Marinha . . .39

Museu de
Arte
Antiga 33

Museu de
Arte
Popular 36

Museu
Nacional de
Coches 34

Palácio da
Ajuda 43

Planetário
Calouste
Gulbenkian . . .40

Ponte 25 de
Abril 32

Torre de
Belém 38

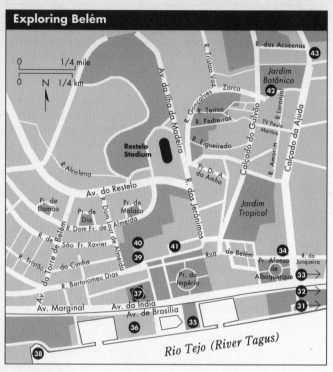

Exploring Belém

particularly the Doca de Santo Amaro—has seen major recent redevelopment as a nightlife destination.

Sights to See

31 Alcântara. The docks are alive with music in Alcântara, where late-night bars attract Lisbon's in-crowd. Here in the lee of the huge 25 of April Bridge the old wharves have been given a makeover, and you can now walk along the landscaped riverfront all the way from Belém (a 30-minute stroll). At **Doca de Santo Amaro,** under the bridge on its east side, a line of fashionable bars, restaurants, and clubs has emerged from the shells of former warehouses, and on the terrace in front of the marina, the party goes on until late into the night. During the day, the easiest way to get here is by train from Cais do Sodré station or on Tram 15; at night, take a taxi.

37 Centro Cultural de Belém (Belém Cultural Center). Built of pink granite and marble, this modernist building won few friends when it was built in 1991, although all of Lisbon now appreciates the cultural activities it offers. The center contains exhibition space, a restaurant, and a concert hall, and it has fine views of the monastery and the river from its roof gardens and terrace bar. Stop by reception to pick up an events brochure. ⊠ *Praça do Império,* ☎ *21/361–2400.* ⊙ *Exhibition hall and café daily 11–8, terrace bar weekdays 3–9.*

42 Jardim Botânico da Ajuda (Ajuda Botanical Gardens). The oldest botanical garden in Portugal was laid out in 1768 by the Italian botanist Vandelli. It has been thoroughly restored in recent years and is an enjoyable place to spend an hour or so, especially on a summer's afternoon. You can stroll up here from the river at Belém, or take Tram 18 from downtown, which terminates near here. The many species of flora, labeled in Latin, are in several greenhouses covering 10 acres; if you call in advance you can arrange a guided tour. ✉ *Calçada da Ajuda,* ☎ *21/362–2503.* ✍ *250$00.* ⊙ *June–Sept., Tues.–Sun. 10–7; Oct.– May, Tues.–Sun. 10–6.*

㉟ Monumento dos Descobrimentos (Monument of the Discoveries). Built in 1960, the monolithic white slab was designed as a modern tribute to the country's seafaring explorers. Fittingly, it was erected to commemorate the 500th anniversary of the death of mariner-king Prince Henry the Navigator and was built on what was the departure point for many voyages of discovery, including those of Vasco da Gama for India and—during Spain's occupation of Portugal—of the Spanish Armada for England in 1588. Henry is at the prow of the monument, facing the water; lined up behind him are the Portuguese explorers of Brazil and Asia, as well as other national heroes, including Luís de Camões the poet, who can be recognized by the book in his hand. On the ground adjacent to the monument, an inlaid map shows the extent of the explorations undertaken by the 15th- and 16th-century Portuguese sailors. Walk inside and take the elevator to the top for river views. ✉ *Av. de Brasília,* ☎ *no phone.* ✍ *320$00.* ⊙ *Tues.–Sun. 9:30–7.*

★ **㊶ Mosteiro dos Jerónimos** (Jerónimos Monastery). Conceived and commissioned by Dom Manuel I, the enormous bulk of Belém's famous monastery was financed largely by treasures brought back from the *descobrimentos* (discoveries) of Africa, Asia, and South America. Construction began in 1502 under the supervision of Diogo de Boitaca (architect of the pioneering Igreja de Jesus at Setúbal) and his successor, João de Castilho, a Spaniard.

It's a supreme example of the Manueline style of building (named after king Dom Manuel I), which represented a marked departure from the prevailing Gothic. Much of the design is characterized by elaborate sculptural details, often with a maritime motif. João de Castilho was responsible for the superb southern portal, which forms the main entrance to the church: the figure on the central pillar is Henry the Navigator, and the canopy shows a hierarchy of statues contained within niches. Inside, the remarkably spacious interior contrasts with the riot of decorative detail on the six nave columns, which disappear into a complex latticework ceiling.

Don't leave the monastery without visiting the Gothic- and Renaissance-style **double cloister**, the lower level of which was also designed to stunning effect by Castilho. The arches and pillars are heavily sculpted with marine motifs. ✉ *Praça do Império,* ☎ *21/362–0034.* ✍ *Cloister 500$00, free Sun.* ⊙ *June–Sept., Tues.–Sun. 10–6:30; Oct.–May, Tues.– Sun. 10–1 and 2:30–5.*

NEED A BREAK? For a real taste of Lisbon, stop at the impressive **Fabrica dos Pasteis de Belém** (✉ Rua de Belém 86–88, ☎ 21/363–7423), a bake shop–café that serves delicious, hot custard pastries sprinkled with cinnamon and powdered sugar. Although you can buy these treats throughout Lisbon, those made here are the best.

㊳ Museu da Marinha (Maritime Museum). There are two museums in the complex of buildings adjoining the Jerónimos Monastery, but the large, well-laid-out Maritime Museum is the most inviting. Here you get a real grasp of the importance of the seafaring tradition in Portugal through maps and maritime codes, navigational equipment, full-size and model ships, uniforms, and weapons. ✉ *Praça do Império,* ☎ *21/362–0210.* ✍ *500$00, free Sun. 10–1.* ⊙ *Tues.–Sun. 10–6.*

PRINCE HENRY THE NAVIGATOR

THE LINKAGE OF ENGLAND and Portugal and the beginning of Portugal's Age of Discovery can be traced back to the 14th century, when England's John of Gaunt gave his daughter, Philippa of Lancaster, in marriage to King João I. The couple's third son, Infante Dom Henrique, is known widely today as Prince Henry the Navigator. By the end of his lifetime (1394–1460), this multidimensional soldier-scientist had conceptualized, funded, and inspired discoveries beyond the borders of the world that Europe knew. Scholars today, however they assess later misuses of exploration and conquest, generally agree that the prince paved the way for explorers such as Vasco da Gama and Ferdinand Magellan.

Strangely for a royal family in those (or any) times, João and Philippa raised six intelligent, apparently happy children. Alternately contemplative and restlessly athletic, Henry persuaded his father to let the four boys earn their knighthoods in an invasion of Morocco and the capture of its fortress at Ceuta. If the prince had not led his 70 soldier-filled ships to a victory worthy of Spielberg replay, Portugal's Age of Discovery might have been very different. As it is, visitors to Lisbon can stop at breezy Belém on the Tagus River, where, at the prow of the ship-shaped *Monumento dos Descobrimentos* (Monument to the Discoveries), Prince Henry stands, leading other Portuguese explorers and even King Afonso V.

At least three achievements secured Henry this place in the vanguard of explorers. In the Algarve, where he was governor, he founded a nearly legendary marine navigation school, which applied scientific principles to what was previously a haphazard endeavor. He also sent ships where none had gone before—especially around Cape Bojador, the "impassable wall" jutting out from West Africa at the end of the European-known ocean. And he required that expeditions chart the seas as they sailed. Charts that these expeditions made of Cape Bojador later led Vasco da Gama to sail around it, then past the Cape of Good Hope and on to India.

Seen through the prism of history, Prince Henry seems a royal contradiction. He earned his knighthood defeating infidels and was eventually named Grand Master of the Order of Christ, the successor to the Knights Templar. But since he lived before the Inquisition began, he may have met some of the Latin-, Greek-, and Hebrew-speaking scholars who came to the royal court. Second, his ships engaged in Africa's lucrative slave trade, but he himself lived simply and, having given away his profits to fund further expeditions, died broke. The navigator-prince was not technically a navigator, and he rarely boarded a ship, but he pointed the way for generations of future explorers.

★ ㉝ **Museu de Arte Antiga** (Ancient Art Museum). The only museum in Lisbon to approach the status of the Gulbenkian is this one. Housed in a 17th-century palace, it has a beautifully displayed collection of Portuguese art—mainly from the 15th through 19th centuries—that superbly complements the Gulbenkian's general collection. Indeed, Gulbenkian himself donated several pieces to this museum, which opened in 1883.

Of all the holdings, the religious works of the Portuguese school of artists (characterized by fine portraiture with a distinct Flemish influence) stand out, especially the acknowledged masterpiece of Nuno Gonçalves, the *St. Vincent Altarpiece*. Painted between 1467 and 1470 for St. Vincent Chapel in Lisbon's cathedral, the altarpiece has six panels showing the patron saint of Lisbon receiving the homage of king, court, and citizens. Sixty figures can be identified, including Henry the Navigator, the archbishop of Lisbon, and sundry dukes, monks, fishermen, knights, and religious figures. In the top left corner of the two central panels is a figure purported to be that of Gonçalves himself.

Besides the Portuguese works, there are pieces by early Flemish painters who influenced the Portuguese. Other European artists are well represented, too, and although few of the works are really first-rate, there are interesting examples by artists as diverse as Hieronymous Bosch, Hans Holbein, Brueghel the Younger, and painter to the Spanish court Diego Velázquez. There are also extensive collections of French silver, Portuguese furniture and tapestries, Asian ceramics, and other works—such as Japanese folding screens and pieces fashioned from Goan ivory—from former Portuguese colonies.

Tram 15 from Praça do Comércio drops you at the foot of a steep flight of steps below the museum. Otherwise, Buses 27 or 49 from Rotunda run straight to Rua das Janelas Verdes. Coming from Belém, Buses 27 and 49 run from Rua de Belém across from the monastery and stop near the museum on their way back to downtown Lisbon. ⊠ *Rua das Janelas Verdes,* ☎ *21/367–6021 or 21/396–4151.* ☞ *500$00.* ☉ *Tues. 2–6, Wed.–Sun. 10–6.*

㊱ **Museu de Arte Popular** (Popular Art Museum). Housed in this squat building are examples of the country's folk art, principally a fascinating collection of ceramics, costumes, furniture, domestic and farm implements, and other ethnographic pieces. Displays are organized according to the province from which the objects came. ⊠ *Av. de Brasília,* ☎ *21/321–1675.* ☞ *400$00.* ☉ *Tues.–Sun. 10–12:30 and 2–5.*

㉞ **Museu Nacional de Coches** (National Coach Museum). This museum houses one of the largest collections of these vehicles in the world in buildings that once accommodated a riding school. The oldest coach on display was made for Phillip II of Spain in the late 16th century, and among the most stunning exhibits are three gold conveyances created in Rome for King John V in 1716. This collection of gloriously painted, gilded baroque vehicles is dazzling, and it's one of the most popular collections in Lisbon. ⊠ *Praça Afonso de Albuquerque,* ☎ *21/ 361–0850.* ☞ *450$00, free Sun. 10–1.* ☉ *June–Sept., Tues.–Sun. 10– 1 and 2:30–6:30; Oct.–May, Tues.–Sun. 10–1 and 2:30–5:30.*

㊸ **Palácio da Ajuda** (Ajuda Palace). In 1802 construction began on this palace, which was intended as a royal residence; its last regal occupant (Queen Maria) died here in 1911. Today the overblown, fussily designed building is home to a museum of 18th- and 19th-century paintings, furniture, and tapestries—hardly unique in Lisbon and, frankly, hardly an essential sight, although temporary exhibitions keep things interesting. It's a 20-minute walk north along Calçada da Ajuda from the coach museum, but Bus 14 and Tram 18 run this way, too. ⊠ *Largo da Ajuda*, ☎ *21/363–7095.* 🖾 *500$00, free Sun. 10–2.* ☉ *Thurs.–Tues. 10–5. Guided tours arranged on request.*

🖰 ⓰ **Planetário Calouste Gulbenkian** (Calouste Gulbenkian Planetarium). In Belém, behind the Maritime Museum, the planetarium presents interesting astronomical shows and displays several times a week. A bulletin posted in the window announces the current program, or you can get updates from the tourist office in Palácio Foz (☞ Visitor Information *in* Lisbon A to Z, *below*). ⊠ *Praça do Império*, ☎ *21/362–0002.* 🖾 *400$00.* ☉ *Schedules vary; check in advance.*

⓷ **Ponte 25 de Abril** (25 of April Bridge). Completed in 1966 and originally dedicated to Dr. Antonio de Oliveira Salazar, Lisbon's first suspension bridge across the Tagus River earned a name change after the 1974 revolution, which lurched into action on April 25 of that year. Standing 230 ft above the water and stretching almost 2½ km (1½ mi), it's a spectacular sight from any direction, although most gasps are reserved for the view from the top downward. Crossing by car, bus, or train is a thrill every time. It's the most heavily trafficked route in Lisbon, however; avoid driving during peak hours.

★ ⓷ **Torre de Belém** (Belém Tower). The openwork balconies and domed turrets of the fanciful Belém—the Portuguese word for Bethlehem— Tower make it perhaps the purest Manueline structure in the country. Although it was built in the early 16th century on an island in the middle of the Tagus River, today the chalk-white tower stands near what has become the north bank—evidence of the river's changing course. Built to defend the port entrance, the tower served as a prison from the late 16th through the 19th centuries; its inmates were incarcerated in the dungeons. Cross the wood gangway and walk inside, not necessarily to see the rather plain interior but to clamber up the steep stone steps to the very top. From this vantage point you'll have a bird's-eye view of the Tagus and central Lisbon. ⊠ *Av. da India*, ☎ *21/321–6892.* 🖾 *400$00.* ☉ *June–Sept., Tues.–Sun. 10–6:30; Oct.–May, Tues.–Sun. 10–1 and 2:30–5.*

DINING

Almost all restaurants offer an *ementa turistica* (tourist menu), a setprice meal, most often served at lunchtime. Meals vary in quality and can be limited in scope, but generally include three courses, a drink, and coffee, all for about 3,000$00. At all restaurants, be wary of eating anything brought as an appetizer that you haven't specifically ordered—typically bread and butter, olives, and such. You'll be charged extra—typically a few dollars—for these *couvert* items even if you eat just one olive; prices always appear on the menu. It's also best to avoid items that shouldn't sit out of the refrigerator too long. Lisbon's restaurants usually serve lunch from noon or 12:30 until 3 and dinner from 7:30 until 11; many establishments are closed on Sunday or Monday.

Inexpensive restaurants typically don't accept reservations. In the traditional *cervejarias* (beer hall–restaurants), which frequently have huge dining rooms, you'll probably have to wait for a table, but usually not more than 15 or 20 minutes. In the Bairro Alto, many of the reasonably priced *tascas* (taverns) are on the small side: if you can't reserve a table, either wait in line or move on to the next place. Throughout Lisbon, dress for meals is usually casual, but exceptions are noted below. For price categories, *see* the chart under Dining *in* Smart Travel Tips A to Z.

Lisbon Dining

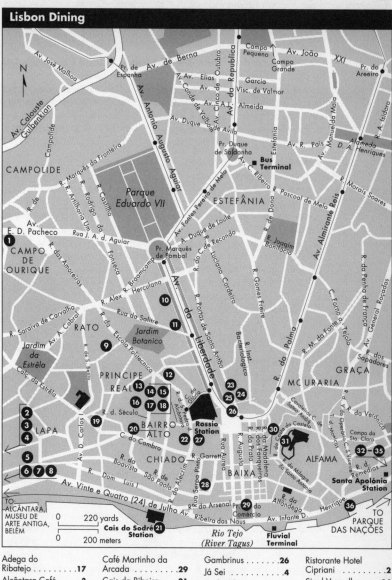

Adega do
Ribatejo **17**

Alcântara Café **3**

Os Alentejanos **34**

Algures na
Mouraria **30**

Andorra **23**

As Barrigas **13**

Bonjardim **25**

Bota Alta **18**

Brasuca **20**

Café Martinho da
Arcada **29**

Cais da Ribeira . . .**21**

Cantinho da Paz . .**19**

Casa Faz Frio **12**

Casa do Leão **31**

Cervejaria
Trindade **27**

Comida de Santo . .**9**

Doca Peixe **8**

Espaço Lisboa **6**

Gambrinus **26**

Já Sei **4**

Jardim do
Marisco **36**

O Madeirense **1**

Pap' Açorda **16**

República da
Cerveja **33**

Restaurante
Panorâmico Torre
Vasco da Gama . . .**32**

Ribadouro **11**

Ristorante Hotel
Cipriani **2**

Sinal Vermelho **14**

Solmar **24**

Sua Excêlencia **5**

Tagide **28**

Tavares Rico **22**

O Terraço **10**

Tertúlia do Tejo . . .**7**

Uruguay **35**

Vá e Volte **15**

Restaurants

African

$–$$ ✕ **Algures na Mouraria.** For a taste of Portugal's colonial past take a trip into the narrow alleys of the Mouraria district, on the west side of the castle, where this simple restaurant serves up dishes from Angola. Chicken cooked with ginger, or stewed in palm nut oil, and spicy beef all make regular appearances on the menu. Beer's probably your best bet, but there's a short Portuguese wine list, too. If you want dinner, come early; this place closes at 9:30 PM. ⊠ *Rua das Farinhas 1, Mouraria,* ☎ *21/887–2470. No credit cards. Closed Sun.*

Brazilian

$$ ✕ **Comida de Santo.** Excellent Brazilian food served in a funky, brightly painted dining room and accompanied by lively Brazilian music keeps this place packed until closing time, at 1 AM. Come early and enjoy classic dishes, such as *feijoada* (meat-and-bean stew) or *vatapá* (a spicy shrimp dish). Order a *caipirinha* (cocktail made with *cachaça,* a rum-like Brazilian liquor) while you're waiting—they're lethal. The restaurant is down a side street off Rua Escola Politécnica, near the botanical gardens—easy to miss if you're not on the ball. You have to ring the bell for entrance. ⊠ *Calçada Engenheiro Miguel Pais 39, Rato,* ☎ *21/396–3339. Reservations essential. AE, DC, MC, V.*

$–$$ ✕ **Brasuca.** In a converted mansion on the edge of the Bairro Alto, the food is Brazilian, and the welcome is warm. With its open fire, its alcove, and its intimate dining rooms, eating here is very much like dining in someone's home. Brazilian dishes such as *picadinho á mineira* (minced beef with onions, peppers, and bananas) or *moqueca* (fish or shrimp in coconut) are always reliable, although there are mainstream Portuguese dishes for the less adventurous. The beer is Brazilian, too, or you may prefer to sip a caipirinha. The restaurant is off Rua do Século—not the easiest place to find, but worth it once you do. ⊠ *Rua João Pereira da Rosa 7, Bairro Alto,* ☎ *21/342–8542. AE, DC, MC, V. Closed Mon.*

Contemporary

$$$$ ✕ **Restaurante Panorâmico Torre Vasco da Gama.** There's always a view from atop the towering Expo landmark. On one side it's the city and the hills beyond; on the other it's the lacy span of the Vasco da Gama Bridge floating above the Tagus River—at its most romantic when its lights bisect the inky night. One starter of carpaccio of salmon with lime juice and virgin olive oil reflects the cuisine's international face, whereas the chef's fish soup with cheese takes a Portuguese approach. A grouper fillet with oyster sauce on spinach with leeks is highly recommended, while vegetarians and vegans welcome a char-grilled vegetable plate. If you resist the dessert trolley temptations such as fluffy cheesecake, coffee comes with a small, dark chocolate. ⊠ *Torre Vasco da Gama, end of esplanade, Parque das Nações,* ☎ *21/893–9550. Reservations essential. AE, MC, V. Closed Mon.*

Eclectic

$$$–$$$$ ✕ **O Terraço.** With views over the city from the top floor of the Tivoli Lisboa (☞ Lodging, *below*) hotel, O Terraço could put its feet up and not worry too much about the food. All praise, then, that the restaurant's grill turns out such high-quality dishes as prime rib, lamb cutlets, the freshest fish, and shrimp with spicy oil. Here traditional salt cod is baked with potatoes and baby onions; for something different, try the mixed-fish curry. The restrained elegance here makes this one of the few hotel-restaurants worth the splurge; in summer there's no nicer place to sit than out on the terrace. ⊠ *Av. da Liberdade 185, Baixa,* ☎ *21/353–2181. Reservations essential. AE, DC, MC, V.*

\$\$–\$\$\$\$ ✕ **Casa do Leão.** The location—on the grounds of St. George's Castle—couldn't be better. In summer, terrace-garden seating grants spectacular views of the center of Lisbon. As for the food, it's a high-quality mix of Portuguese and international dishes. Squid comes on a skewer with shrimp, bacon, and peppers; the lamb chops are a standout entrée. You may want to finish with a dish of Portuguese cheeses. ⊠ *Castelo de São Jorge, Alfama,* ☎ *21/887–5962. AE, MC, V.*

\$\$ ✕ **República da Cerveja.** This large, lively eating and drinking—or maybe drinking and eating—spot, pulses with energy. It's not easy to categorize, but with its German chef and Portuguese manager who arrived via Missouri, it's attractive even if you're not tempted by the wide array of draft and bottled beers. A changing blackboard menu posts German and Portuguese specialties. Steak is always there—perhaps flavored with oysters or cooked with laurel, wine, and smoked ham and topped with pickles. Pizzas and burgers dominate the late-night menu (served until 1 AM, until 4 AM Thursday through Saturday nights) that comes with live music or a show on Thursday, Friday, and Saturday. ⊠ *On river at Parque des Nações,* ☎ *21/460–0934. AE, V.*

French

\$\$\$\$ ✕ **Tavares Rico.** Superb food, an excellent wine list, and a handsome
★ Edwardian dining room have made this one of Lisbon's most famous and formal restaurants. Established as a café in the 18th century, Tavares Rico pleases its customers with the splendor of its furnishings, the quality of its service, and its consistently good French-inspired menu. Caviar pushes the price of a meal right up, but there's nothing wrong with lowering your sights—the sole cooked in champagne sauce is a classic, and there are game birds available in season, served roasted in a rich wine sauce. Portuguese tastes can be assuaged by the bacalhau or the *sopa* (soup) alentejana, a garlic, bread, and egg concoction. ⊠ *Rua Misericórdia 35–37, Chiado,* ☎ *21/342–1112. Reservations essential. Jacket and tie. AE, DC, MC, V. Closed Sat. No lunch Sun.*

Indian

\$–\$\$\$ ✕ **Cantinho da Paz.** The trick is finding this place (take a taxi), but once you're through the unassuming entrance you'll be glad you made the effort. It's a joyful mom-and-pop establishment that specializes in the cuisine of Goa—so spicy curries abound. The shrimp curry is rich in coconut and cream. The English-speaking owner is happy to guide you through the menu. ⊠ *Rua da Paz 4, off Rua dos Poiais de São Bento, Bairro Alto,* ☎ *21/396–9698. Reservations essential. V. Closed Mon.*

Italian

\$\$\$\$ ✕ **Ristorante Hotel Cipriani.** Why choose northern Italian cuisine in Portugal when you have *ristorantes* and pizzerias on every corner back home? Cipriani's ambience and cuisine are reason enough for prosperous Lisboetas as well as tourists and guests of the Lapa Palace, where it's located. The service is as five-star for a solo traveler scanning a book as for the designer-clad quartet celebrating a major milestone, and music, played nightly (except Monday) on a 12-string Portuguese guitar, approaches concert quality. Try cannelloni stuffed with ricotta and zucchini as a starter, or maybe a shrimp and spinach-stuffed puff pastry with oyster sauce. Sauteed monkfish on a bed of ratatouille or citrus-glazed duck might follow (with waiters whipping off domed silver covers in perfect sync), then perhaps a spice-flavored souffle with Grand Marnier sauce. Wines range from monumental to relatively modest. ⊠ *Rua Pau de Bandeira 2, Lapa,* ☎ *21/394–9434. Reservations essential. AE, MC, V.*

Portuguese

\$\$\$\$ ✕ **Tagide.** In a fine old house that looks out over the Baixa and the Tagus River (reserve a table by the window), you can have one of Lisbon's great dining experiences. Careful restoration has created an elegant dining room lined with 17th-century tiles—a lovely backdrop for sampling the impressive list of Portuguese regional dishes, including the famous *presunto* (smoked ham) from Chaves, stuffed squid from the Algarve, or the classic *porco á alentejana* (Alentejo-style pork). There's also a smaller selection of French-influenced dishes available, but this is one place where you really should indulge in the Portuguese fare. ⊠ *Largo Academia das Belas Artes 18–20, at bottom of Rua Ivens, Chiado,* ☎ *21/346–0570. Reservations essential. AE, DC, MC, V. Closed weekends.*

$$$–$$$$ ✕ **Sua Excêlencia.** In this cozy little town house restaurant, put your-
  ★ self in the hands of the English-speaking owner, Mr. Queiroz, who will personally talk you through the outstanding Portuguese dishes on the menu. Specialties include smoked swordfish (an Algarve favorite), baked bacalhau, and Angolan-style chicken. This is a handy place for those staying at York House or at As Janelas Verdes (☞ Lodging, *below*), and it provides an intimate dining experience after a hectic day's sightseeing. ⊠ *Rua do Conde 34, Lapa,* ☎ *21/390–3614. MC, V. Closed Wed. and Sept. No lunch weekends.*

$$–$$$$ ✕ **Alcântara Café.** Locals bring visitors to the Alcântara Café when they want to impress them, and it rarely fails. Its glorious design impressively combines wood, leather, velvet, and steel to re-create something of the 1920s in Lisbon. Old Portuguese specialties highlight the menu, and fish is always a good choice—try the prawns in lemon sauce. There's a large wine list, too, and a splendid bar if you want to sip an aperitif before dinner or stay on afterward—drinks are served until 2 AM. The restaurant is outside the city center, near the 25 of April Bridge (close to the nightlife of the Doca de Santa Amaro), and the kitchen stays open until 1 AM. ⊠ *Rua Maria Luísa Holstein 15, Alcântara,* ☎ *21/363–7176. AE, DC, MC, V. No lunch.*

$$–$$$$ ✕ **Café Martinho da Arcada.** This famous café-restaurant, founded in 1782 beneath the arcades of Praça do Comércio, was once frequented by the Portuguese poet Fernando Pessoa and other literary stars. These days the lunchtime crowd in its wood-paneled dining room is mainly businesspeople from the surrounding shops and offices. The menu offers regional Portuguese cuisine; sometimes there's a colonial splash with the occasional Brazilian dish. Try a *cataplana* (clam stew) from the Algarve, especially if you won't be heading south on this trip. ⊠ *Praça do Comércio 3, Baixa,* ☎ *21/887–9259. MC, V. Closed Sun.*

$$–$$$$ ✕ **Já Sei.** Set beside the river in Belém, this is a fine lunchtime stop, especially in summer, when you can sit on the attractive outdoor terrace. Smooth service and impressive meals—the *arroz de marisco* (seafood rice) for two is particularly memorable. ⊠ *Av. de Brasília 202, Belém,* ☎ *21/321–5969. Reservations essential. AE, DC, MC, V. Closed Mon. No dinner Sun.*

$$–$$$$ ✕ **Pap' Açorda.** A former bakery in the heart of the Bairro Alto now
  ★ holds one of the district's most happening restaurants. Art and media types scramble for the closely packed tables in the minimalist interior. The menu lists cutting-edge versions of Portuguese classics—grilled sea bass; breaded veal cutlets; and, of course, açorda itself, that bread-based stew, rich in seafood and flavored with cilantro. There's a good wine list (all Portuguese) and a long bar by the door where those unwise enough not to have made a reservation wait for a table. ⊠ *Rua da Atalaia 57, Bairro Alto,* ☎ *21/346–4811. Reservations essential. AE, DC, MC, V.*

$$$ ✕ **Espaço Lisboa.** If you can't get a table with a view of the 25 of April Bridge just outside, not to worry: there's space to spare in the interior of this multilevel former warehouse. While waiting for a table, toss some escudos into a murmuring fountain, sink into a leather armchair in a small, candelabra-lighted bar, or inspect the burlap sacks of nuts in the vintage grocer's shop. And whether you're seated in the small mezza-

nine or on the spacious ground level under lofty rafters, find an excuse (like a trip to the loo) to check out the kiosk with old newspapers, a café museum, and more. Menu choices may include chicken sausage invented—it's said—to help supposedly converted Jews avoid eating pork during the Inquisition; *leitão assado* (suckling pig roasted in a wood-burning oven); and *encharcada do ovos,* Portugal's delicious concoction of eggs and sugar. ⊠ *Rua da Cozinha Econômica 16, Doca de Santo Amaro, Alcantâra* ☎ *21/361–0201. AE, MC, V. Closed Tues.*

$$$ ✕ **Os Alentejanos.** Like the cuisine, the decor charmingly evokes the Alentejo region just south of the capital: fans reach down from the ceiling, cooling diners at picnic-style or red-, white-, and green-checkered tables, and tables wines come in earthenware jugs that decorate a small bar. To capture the frugal, flavorful Alentejana heritage, start with a fragrant soup made mainly from herbs and bread, then move on to pork sauteed with fresh clams or a traditional lamb stew. Vegetarians can ask for the region's typical chickpeas or green beans. Reservations are advised at dinner and for peak-season lunches. ⊠ *Facing the Oceanarium, Parque das Nações,* ☎ *21/895–6116. AE, MC, V.*

$$–$$$ ✕ **Cais da Ribeira.** Converted from an old fisherman's warehouse, this small restaurant, perched on the waterfront behind Cais do Sodré station, specializes in fish grilled over charcoal, as well as a filling caldeirada. The pretty, split-level wooden interior makes good use of the old warehouse space. Whatever you order, the views over the river will complement your meal nicely. ⊠ *Cais do Sodré,* ☎ *21/342–3611. AE, DC, MC, V. Closed Sun. and Mon. No lunch Sat. and Tues.*

$$–$$$ ✕ **O Madeirense.** Although it's in the Amoreiras shopping center, Lisbon's only Madeiran restaurant makes you feel as if you're on the island itself: rural scenes adorn the walls, the waitstaff wear traditional costumes, and the place is filled with wood, rattan, and rubber plants. But this is no mere theme restaurant; the cooking is assured, and the consistent quality of the food and service appeals to the mainly business clientele. Start with a glass of Madeira wine while you ponder the menu: the traditional *espetada*—a skewer of steak fillet, rubbed with salt and spices—is hung above the table from a stand so you can serve yourself. Tuna and swordfish make an appearance on the menu, too, and you might try the fried corn-cube appetizer. ⊠ *Loja 3027, Amoreiras shopping center, Av. Eng. Duarte Pacheco,* ☎ *21/381–3147. Reservations essential. AE, DC, MC, V.*

$–$$$ ✕ **Bonjardim.** Set in an alley between Praça dos Restauradores and Rua
★ Portas de Santo Antão and known locally as "Rei dos Frangos" ("King of Chickens"), Bonjardim specializes in superbly cooked spit-roasted chicken, best eaten with fries and a salad. The restaurant is crowded at peak times (8 PM–10 PM), but you shouldn't have to wait long, and watching the frenzied waiters is entertainment in itself. An overflow dining room on the opposite side of the alley serves the same menu and offers the same good deals. ⊠ *Travessa de S. Antão 11, Baixa,* ☎ *21/342–4389. AE, DC, MC, V.*

$–$$$ ✕ **Bota Alta.** This wood-paneled tavern is one of the Bairro Alto's oldest and most favored eateries. There's little space between the tables, but this only enhances the buzz: lines form outside by 8 PM. Once you've secured a table, choose from a menu strong on traditional Portuguese dishes—perhaps bacalhau cooked in cream, homemade sausages, steaks in wine sauce, or grilled fish. The house wine comes in ceramic jugs and is very good. ⊠ *Travessa da Queimada 37, Bairro Alto,* ☎ *21/342–7959. AE, DC, MC, V. Closed Sun. No lunch Sat.*

$$ ✕ **Tertúlia do Tejo.** Nothing is pretentious at this dockside restaurant, where plank floors establish the ambience downstairs, while upstairs there's an agreeable madhouse of long tables and camaraderie. Large red umbrellas shade many of the esplanade tables. The *pratos do dia* (daily specials) are somewhat predictable, but if you try melon with smoked ham or *caldho verde* (green soup) as a starter, and then follow it with something grilled, you can't go wrong. Although reservations are advised at dinner, it looks as if you could just drop in on even the busiest nights and sit down. ⊠ *Doca de Santo Amaro, Alcantâra* ☎ 21/395–5552. AE, DC, MC, V.

$–$$ ✕ **Adega do Ribatejo.** There are fado clubs aplenty in the Bairro Alto, but none so accessible as this thoroughly enjoyable, tiled *adega* (tavern). Primarily it's a restaurant, and the food is reasonably good. Dishes such as steaks, bacalhau, veal, and fried fish are often on the changing menu. At the nightly singing sessions, professional musicians serenade you with ear-splitting renditions of traditional songs. The manager works the tables and sings himself on occasion; even the cooks sometimes get in on the act. Note that there's a minimum charge of 2,000$00, and you'll probably have to wait in line unless you arrive before 8 PM. ⊠ *Rua Diário de Noticias 23, Bairro Alto,* ☎ 21/346–8343. MC, V. *Closed Sun.*

$–$$ ✕ **Andorra.** On the renowned Baixa street of fish restaurants, the Andorra is a perfect place for a simple lunch; from the terrace you can watch the lively street scenes and smell the charcoal-grilled sardines. The friendly staff serves plates of well-cooked Portuguese favorites, and you can choose from a short wine list that caters to most tastes. ⊠ *Rua Portas de S. Antão 82, Baixa,* ☎ 21/342–6047. MC, V. *Closed Sun.*

$–$$ ✕ **As Barrigas.** The clientele are a well-traveled lot judging by the postcards that line the walls of this cozy, wood-paneled adega, but the cooking stays firmly in Portugal. House specialty is a rich arroz *de polvo* (with octopus), and there are steaks, a fish of the day, and other tavern standards. And the restaurant's name? It means "the stomachs," which you'll appreciate once you've waded through their large portions. ⊠ *Travessa da Queimada 31, Bairro Alto,* ☎ 21/347–1220. V.

$–$$ ✕ **Casa Faz Frio.** This traditional wine cellar—complete with wood beams, stone floors, paneled booths, blue tiling, and bunches of garlic suspended from the ceiling—is of a type that's fast disappearing. The list of Portuguese dishes changes daily, and although there's not a large choice, you'll usually find steak, rice dishes, bacalhau, grilled pork, and quail. Surroundings are simple but convivial, and you'd be hard pressed to spend more than 3,000$00, including drinks and coffee. ⊠ *Rua de Dom Pedro V 96–98, Bairro Alto,* ☎ 21/346–1860. *No credit cards.*

$–$$ ✕ **Cervejaria Trindade.** The Trindade is a classic 19th-century Bairro ★ Alto beer hall–restaurant with colorful tiles, vaulted ceilings, and frenetic service. It's a lively spot, and, like at all cervejarias, you can pop in for a beer and a snack or eat a full meal. On the whole, the food is relatively inexpensive and hearty, with such dishes as açorda and steaks forming the mainstay, although if you opt for the grilled seafood you can expect the tab to rocket. The garden is an enjoyable spot for dining in summer. ⊠ *Rua Nova da Trindade 20, Bairro Alto,* ☎ 21/342–3506. AE, DC, MC, V.

$–$$ ✕ **Sinal Vermelho.** At this update of a traditional adega, the split-level ★ dining room is traditionally tiled, and the food is thoroughly Portuguese, but the prints on the wall are modern, the clientele firmly professional (and in-the-know tourist), and the wine list wide-ranging (if completely Portuguese). Start, perhaps, with a plate of clams drenched in oil and garlic and follow with a fresh seafood dish; the meat dishes are less inspiring, although if you feel daring, you might try the tripe or the kidneys. ⊠ *Rua das Gáveas 89, Bairro Alto,* ☎ 21/346–1252. *Reservations essential.* AE, MC, V. *Closed Sun.*

$–$$ ✕ **Vá e Volte.** For one-plate budget Bairro Alto fare, look no farther. In a restaurant that's little more than a bar with a couple of small dining rooms, the owner, his wife, the cook, and a small staff keep the meals coming with speed and good humor. Fried or grilled fish or meat dishes are served with enough salad, potatoes, and vegetables to keep the wolf from the door, and the *arroz doce* (rice pudding) is homemade. The house wine is fine, but even if you choose a regional specialty, the price won't break the bank. ⊠ *Rua do Diário de Notícias 100, Bairro Alto,* ☎ *21/342–7888. AE, MC, V. Closed Mon.*

Seafood

$$$–$$$$ ✕ **Gambrinus.** On a busy street that's full of fish restaurants, Gambrinus stands alone, with more than 70 years of experience in serving the finest fish and shellfish. In a series of somber, dark-paneled dining rooms, you're led through the intricacies of the day's seafood specials by waiters who know their stuff. Prawns, lobster, and crab are always available; seasonal choices such as sea bream, sole, and sea bass are offered grilled or garnished with clam sauce. There are meat dishes, too, but they're rather beside the point here. ⊠ *Rua Portas de S. Antão 23–25, Baixa,* ☎ *21/346–8974 or 21/342–1466. AE, DC, MC, V.*

$$–$$$$ ✕ **Solmar.** This restaurant is renowned for its seafood, and the decor drives the point home: a central fountain is the focus, and a huge mosaic of an underwater scene continues the oceanic theme. Some have complained that Solmar is resting on its laurels, but the cooking remains more hit than miss. In winter the restaurant entices diners with wild boar or venison. There are also cheaper snacks available in the adjacent café, where locals pop in throughout the day for coffee and cakes. ⊠ *Rua Portas de S. Antão 108, Baixa,* ☎ *21/342–3371. AE, DC, MC, V.*

$$$ ✕ **Doca Peixe.** If the name of the restaurant—which means "fish dock"—didn't clue you in to the type of cuisine served here, a display of the day's catch on ice at the entrance plus a small aquarium within would do so. Choose esplanade tables under yellow umbrellas almost under the 25 of April Bridge; the cool, tile-floored ground floor within; or upstairs, where there are slightly better river views. In the center of the restaurant a busy staffer slices well-aged ham, weighs the fish customers choose from the icy display, and turns out juicy fresh fruit salad. You might start with an asparagus or tomato and mozzarella salad, or with oysters on the half shell. Sea bass or bream cooked in traditional garlic, tomato, and onion and cod with turnip leaves are recommended main course choices. *Bifinhas com molho de madeira*—small steaks in Madeira wine—is a meaty alternative. ⊠ *Esplanada at Doca de Santo Amaro, Armazém 14,* ☎ *21/397–3565. AE, MC, V. Closed Tues.* ✧

$$$ ✕ **Jardim do Marisco.** "Seafood Garden" occupies an attractive section of a flourishing converted warehouse. A white ceiling tops metal rafters high above the cool grays and warm woods of a dining area overlooking a riverfront esplanade near Lisbon's major cruise ship area. For a starter, consider traditional vegetable *sopa* (soup) or Portuguese oysters on ice, perhaps followed by a lavish portion of bean-based stew with meat or seafood or *espetadas de gambas piri pire* (spicy shrimp brochette). ⊠ *Doca Jardim do Tabaco, Pavilion A/B, Av. D. Henrique 21,* ☎ *21/882–4242. AE, MC, V.* ✧

$–$$ ✕ **Ribadouro.** One of the oldest beer halls in Lisbon—a bustling basement restaurant on the main avenue—Ribadouro has been brightened up. Sensibly, however, there has been no monkeying around with the tried-and-tested menu. First and foremost it's a seafood joint, with a counter full of fresh shellfish priced by weight—go easy, since this can be a costly way to eat. If you stick to the regular fish and meat dishes, you can't go wrong. When crowds spill out of the nearby theaters, you may have to wait for a table; try to arrive before 8 PM on weekends. ⊠ *Av. da Liberdade 155, Rato* ☎ *21/354–9411. AE, DC, MC, V.*

Uruguayan

$$$ ✕ **Uruguay.** The sound of soft music welcomes you into Uruguay's compact, glass-walled interior, where the rafters are draped with white canvas panels. The sight and aroma of meats on the large grill means this is no place for vegetarians. Portions are generous, but if you want a starter, a good choice is warm salad with goat's milk cheese accompanied by home-baked raisin bread. Few diners resist the grilled brochettes, but you could opt instead for roast chicken. If a country fruit tart or brownie sounds tempting, consider sharing. ⊠ *Parque das Nações, Cais dos Argonautas F3, by the Water Gardens,* ☎ *21/895–5445. AE, V.*

Café-Bars and Pastelarias

Lisbon has some glorious old cafés, and you should make an effort to visit a couple. Most are wonderfully decorated and have rich interiors of burnished and carved wood, mirrors, and tiles. Also, many cafés have outdoor seating, so you can order a coffee, beer, or snack and watch the city pass by. *Pastelarias* (pastry shops) are perhaps the city's greatest contribution to the gastronomic arts: be sure to sample some pastries and cakes at one of the places listed below, all of which serve drinks, too.

✕ **Café a Brasileira.** Less exclusive than it once was, this coffeehouse in the heart of the shopping district is still the most famous of Lisbon's old haunts. A bronze statue of Portugal's poet-writer Fernando Pessoa sits just outside. For a feel of bygone days and enjoyment of the literary and art memorabilia on the walls, it's best to come before dark: at night every table is taken over by beer-drinking young people. ⊠ *Rua Garrett 120, Chiado. Closed Sun.*

✕ **Café Martinho da Arcada.** A stand-up café under the arches, next to the famous restaurant of the same name (☞ *above*), this is a welcome stop for a coffee and specialty *pastéis de nata* (cream cake) before catching your tram to Belém. Tradition oozes from the tiled walls, and the waiters rush to and fro, while the hard-working bakers prepare scrumptious pastries behind the bar. ⊠ *Praça do Comércio 3, Baixa. Closed Sun.*

✕ **Café Nicola.** With its grand interior and suitably aloof waiters, this traditional café is one of the priciest spots for sitting down and taking in downtown. ⊠ *Praça Dom Pedro IV 24, Rossío, west side of Baixa.*

✕ **Casa Chineza.** Join the locals for a midmorning stand-up snack and coffee at this Baixa pastelaria. Enjoy the pastry, admire the fine decor, and then on with the shopping! ⊠ *Rua Aurea 274–278, Baixa.*

✕ **Confeiteria Cister.** All who—perhaps en route to the Livraria Britanica or British Consulate—wander into this small neighborhood café feel they have discovered it. Choose an enticing cake or two (or a more-ordinary sandwich), then find a spot at one of the polished wood tables, where patrons, young and old, are lingering with a friend, a newspaper, or perhaps just a large cup of coffee. ⊠ *Rua da Escola Politécnica 107.*

✕ **Galeto.** There's not much that this café doesn't serve, from cakes and sandwiches to full meals, from early to late every day. Pull up a stool at one of the long wooden counters, and take a break from the modern city outside. ⊠ *Av. da República 14. Metro: Saldanha.*

✕ **Leiteria a Camponeza.** This is an old-fashioned *leiteria* (specializing in milk products and pastries), whose blue-tiled walls display bucolic scenes. The coffee, cakes, and sandwiches are all good. ⊠ *Rua dos Sapateiros 155–157, Baixa. Closed Sun.*

✕ **Pastelaria Suiça.** This huge café-pastelaria stretches all the way back to the adjacent Praça da Figueira. Outdoor tables are at a premium, especially on nice days. But the relaxed ambience (even a single beer or coffee can hold your table for an hour) makes them worth the wait and slightly higher prices. ⊠ *Rossío 96, east side, Baixa.*

✕ **Versailles.** In the modern part of the city, the Versailles (founded in 1929) has retained its grand furnishings. Behind its bar massive mahogany display cases groan with chocolates, port wines, and liqueurs. Homemade cakes and hot chocolate are house specialties. ⊠ *Av. de República 15. Metro: Saldanha.*

LODGING

If you've arrived without accommodations, stop by the airport tourist information desk or at the downtown tourist office (☞ Visitor Information *in* Lisbon A to Z, *below*). The staff at either location can provide you with a list of hotels and pensões. It's not a complete list, by any means, but it will get you started in the search for a room.

All lodgings listed below include private bathrooms unless otherwise noted; in budget places, this often means a cubicle shower and a sink in the room, with toilet down the hall. Breakfast is usually included, but not always at hotels in the $ and $$ categories (and not always in the $$$$ category either, which seems a bit mean-spirited). For price categories, *see* the chart under Lodging *in* Smart Travel Tips A to Z.

$$$$ 🏨 **Four Seasons Hotel The Ritz Lisbon.** You know you're in good hands
★ from the minute you step into the spacious marble reception area and discover a lounge-bar with a terrace overlooking the park. The Ritz is second to none for its excellent service and comfortable surroundings. Public rooms have tapestries, antique reproductions, and fine paintings. There's more space in the corridors than in most hotels' guest rooms, and the accommodations live up to expectations: large, light, and airy, they have luxurious bathrooms, private terraces, and elegant furnishings. Rooms in the back with views of the park are the best choice; on a clear day you can see the castle and the river from the upper floors. A superb buffet breakfast, as well as lunch and dinner, is served at the Varanda restaurant, which, like the bar and lounge, has a wonderful terrace. ⊠ *Rua Rodrigo da Fonseca 88, 1099-039,* ☎ *21/383–2020,* ℻ *21/383–1783. 264 rooms, 20 suites. Restaurant, bar, snack bar, no-smoking floor, room service, exercise room, shops, baby-sitting, laundry service. AE, DC, MC, V. Metro: Rotunda.* 🐾

$$$$ 🏨 **Hotel Dom Pedro Lisboa.** The richly furnished, slightly exotic lobby here hums with comings, goings, and clusters of conversation. Set in the Amoreiras Business Center and facing the shopping center, the 263-room hotel has its own gallery of luxury boutiques as well. Rooms and suites come with rich fabrics and polished wood furniture, including executive desks and other amenities for the prosperous business travelers who favor the hotel. The ultra-secure Presidential Suite was picked for President Clinton's 2000 visit. Vacationers who love to shop enjoy the Amoreiras location and weekend rate reductions. ⊠ *Av. Eng. Duarte Pacheco 24, 1070-109,* ☎ *21/389–6600,* ℻ *21/389–6601. 254 rooms, 9 suites. 2 restaurants, 3 bars, no-smoking floors, room service, in-room safes, laundry service. AE, DC, MC, V.* 🐾

$$$$ 🏨 **Lapa Palace.** This 19th-century former town house in Lisbon's leafy Lapa section is one of the more elegant hotels in Portugal and, arguably, Europe—a pricey place that's worth every escudo. Despite its antique furnishings and lavish use of marble, the effect is warm and welcoming. Fresh flowers are as ubiquitous as perfect taste. Diverse accommodations will have luxurious amenities that could include a stereo with a CD collection; glass-door showers that evoke a waterfall; or a Jacuzzi tub. From your room you might see terraced lawns, a step-under waterfall, the heated garden pool, or perhaps the city and river. What-

Lisbon Lodging

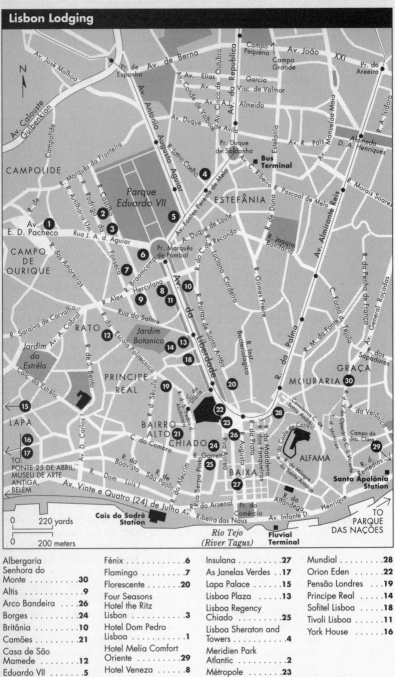

Albergaria
Senhora do
Monte **30**
Altis **9**
Arco Bandeira **26**
Borges **24**
Britânia **10**
Camões **21**
Casa de São
Mamede **12**
Eduardo VII **5**

Fénix **6**
Flamingo **7**
Florescente **20**
Four Seasons
Hotel the Ritz
Lisbon **3**
Hotel Dom Pedro
Lisboa **1**
Hotel Melia Comfort
Oriente **29**
Hotel Veneza **8**

Insulana **27**
As Janelas Verdes . .**17**
Lapa Palace **15**
Lisboa Plaza **13**
Lisboa Regency
Chiado **25**
Lisboa Sheraton and
Towers **4**
Meridien Park
Atlantic **2**
Métropole **23**

Mundial **28**
Orion Eden **22**
Pensão Londres **19**
Principe Real **14**
Sofitel Lisboa **18**
Tivoli Lisboa **11**
York House **16**

ever the vista from your room, you can enjoy a 180-degree city view from the terrace of the Rio Tejo Bar, where comfortable chairs and sofas invite guests to savor their drinks or tea with the view. In sum, there's nothing not to like here; this is what five-star luxury is all about. ⊠ *Rua Pau de Bandeira 4, 1249-021,* ☎ *21/395–0005,* 𝔽𝔸𝕏 *21/395–7164. 101 rooms, 7 suites. 3 restaurants, bar, room service, in-room safes, 1 outdoor pool, 1 indoor lap pool, health club, shops, baby-sitting, laundry service, business services. AE, DC, MC, V.* 🐾

$$$–$$$$ 🏨 **Altis.** This large, boxy modern lodging has a broad range of facilities, including an art gallery and a heated indoor lap pool. Its virtue is reliability, which is why it hosts a lot of business travelers. The mezzanine bar-lounge above the lobby is a relaxing spot, and rooms are comfortable, if unexceptional; those on higher floors have some fine views of Parque Eduardo VII, as does the top-floor restaurant. ⊠ *Rua Castilho 11, 1269-072,* ☎ *21/314–2496,* 𝔽𝔸𝕏 *21/354–8696. 290 rooms, 13 suites. 2 restaurants, 3 bars, room service, pool, sauna, exercise room, shops, laundry service. AE, DC, MC, V. Metro: Rotunda.*

$$$–$$$$ 🏨 **Lisboa Sheraton & Towers.** Even Americans who usually avoid staying in chain hotels appreciate this Sheraton overlooking modern Lisbon. Its many advantages include a huge reception area with a comfortable bar, a staff that speaks especially fluent English, an agreeable restaurant, and attractive, modestly sized guest rooms with many amenities. Refurbished tower rooms have parquet floors, coffeemakers, a 24-hour club lounge, and private "butler" check-in and -out. Ask about their executive-style "smart rooms" with extra desk space and computer and fax-modem outlets. The top-floor Panoramic Bar is the perfect place for an aperitif. The hotel is near Parque Eduardo VII and the Gulbenkian Museum's gardens, but otherwise your days will start and end with a bus or taxi ride. ⊠ *Rua Latino Coelho 1, 1069-025,* ☎ *21/357–5757,* 𝔽𝔸𝕏 *21/354–7164. 377 rooms, 7 suites. Restaurant, 2 bars, grill, in-room safes, room service, heated outdoor pool, massage, sauna, health club, shops, laundry service, business services. AE, DC, MC, V. Metro: Picoas.* 🐾

$$$–$$$$ 🏨 **Meridien Park Atlantic.** Business travelers like the distinctive Park Atlantic for its location—right by Parque Eduardo VII—and facilities, but there's plenty for vacationers to admire, too, including the split-level atrium with its cozy brasserie and separate conservatory-style bar. All the sleek, recently decorated rooms have smart bathrooms and soundproofing; more to the point, they all have fantastic views over the city and park. ⊠ *Rua Castilho 149, 1099-034,* ☎ *21/383–0400.* 𝔽𝔸𝕏 *21/ 383–3231. 313 rooms, 17 suites. Restaurant, bar, no-smoking floors, beauty salon, sauna, shops, baby-sitting, laundry service, business services. AE, DC, MC, V. Metro: Rotunda.* 🐾

$$$–$$$$ 🏨 **Tivoli Lisboa.** On Lisbon's main avenue, this well-run property has
★ a large public area and bar furnished with inviting armchairs and sofas. There's enough marble in the public areas to make you fear for the future supply of the stone, but grandness gives way to comfort in the rooms, where there's fresh decor, well-equipped bathrooms, and a moderate amount of space. In warmer months the outdoor pool and garden offer respite from the bustling city; the grill on the top floor presents wonderful views of the city and the Tagus. There's also a restaurant off the lobby where a filling morning buffet is served. ⊠ *Av. da Liberdade 185, 1269-050,* ☎ *21/353–2181,* 𝔽𝔸𝕏 *21/357–9461. 327 rooms, 15 suites. Restaurant, 2 bars, coffee shop, grill, room service, pool, 2 tennis courts, shops, baby-sitting, laundry service. AE, DC, MC, V. Metro: Avenida.*

$$$ 🏨 **Britânia.** This fine restored town house hotel occupies one of the few buildings from the 1940s near the Avenida da Liberdade to have survived unscathed. It's the work of accomplished architect Cassiano

Branco and originally housed studio apartments, hence the larger than usual rooms and bathrooms. But it's the art deco touches throughout that really impress—from the original marble panels in the bathrooms to the period furniture, "porthole" windows in the facade, columns and candelabra in the lobby, and murals in the bar. Staff members are really friendly, and although only a modest buffet breakfast is served, good restaurants are within walking distance. ✉ *Rua Rodrigues Sampaio 17, 1150-278,* ☎ *21/315–5216,* FAX *21/315–5021. 30 rooms. Dining room, bar. AE, DC, MC, V. Metro: Rotunda.*

$$$ 🖼 **Fénix.** Anyone who remembers the Fénix from days gone by is in for a pleasant surprise. As the Praça Marquês de Pombal has emerged a better, brighter place, so has this hotel. The views from the front rooms, overlooking the square, are exceptional; rooms on the other side overlook the park. All rooms are spacious, harmoniously decorated in shades of pastel pink, and have plenty of closet space, comfortable armchairs, gleaming bathrooms, TVs, and phones. The basement restaurant, O Bodegon, serves good Spanish and Portuguese food in rustic surroundings. ✉ *Praça Marquês de Pombal 8, 1269-133,* ☎ *21/386–2121,* FAX *21/386–2131. 119 rooms, 4 suites. Restaurant, 2 bars, room service, laundry service. AE, DC, MC, V. Metro: Rotunda.*

$$$ 🖼 **Hotel Melia Comfort Oriente.** If you'd like a room overlooking the Parque das Nações's riverfront, restaurants, and Oceanarium and to have the Vasco da Gama Shopping Center just down the street, this is the place. Comfortable if somewhat bland, the hotel is often filled when a major convention or fair is taking place at the park's exhibition center. Otherwise, you might find a river- and bridge-view room when they're scarce in mid-city. Excellent train and metro transportation puts you downtown in about 15 minutes. Rooms are functional and not unattractive. Junior suites add tiny kitchenettes and a sofa bed. ✉ *Av. D. Joáo II, Parque das Nações, 1990-083,* ☎ *21/386–2191,* FAX *21/386–1216. 90 rooms, 26 suites. Restaurant, bar, in-room safes, no-smoking rooms, laundry service. AE, MC, V.* 🍽

$$$ 🖼 **As Janelas Verdes.** On the same street as the Ancient Art Museum,
★   this late-18th-century mansion hotel was once the home of Portuguese novelist Eça de Queirós. Its 17 guest rooms have been marvelously restored and are individually furnished to a high standard—bathrooms are particularly pleasing, and some rooms have direct access to the garden by an exterior staircase. Fittings, furnishings, paintings, and tilework throughout are in keeping with the building's historic character; in the ivy-covered patio garden you can eat breakfast and imagine yourself in a different age. The hotel isn't central, although it's halfway to Belém (the tram stops nearby) and close to the Sua Excêlencia restaurant. Reservations are vital here, and rates in winter are slightly reduced. ✉ *Rua das Janelas Verdes 47, 1200-690,* ☎ *21/396–8143,* FAX *21/396–8144. 17 rooms. Dining room, bar. AE, DC, MC, V.*

$$$ 🖼 **Lisboa Plaza.** This comfortable, welcoming, family-owned hotel
★   behind Avenida da Liberdade has been in business for more than 40 years, and the experience shines through every aspect of its operation. Service is friendly and helpful, and ongoing renovations have smartened up the guest rooms and public areas without detracting from their character. Pastel colors, prints on the walls, attractive ornaments, dried-flower arrangements, and well-stocked marble bathrooms all add to the charm. The best rooms are at the back, looking up to the botanical gardens; those at the front are closer to the main road and don't have the views, but double glazing keeps everything nice and quiet. An excellent buffet breakfast is included in the room rate. ✉ *Travessa do Salitre 7, 1269-066,* ☎ *21/346–3922,* FAX *21/347–1630. 94 rooms, 12 suites. Restaurant, bar, no-smoking rooms, room service, laundry service, business services. AE, DC, MC, V. Metro: Avenida.*

$$$ ⊞ **Lisboa Regency Chiado.** Arriving at the tiny ground-floor entrance to this hotel you'll assume the taxi (or Jaguar limo, on request) has dropped you at some office building near Lisbon's Avenida da Liberdade. Never assume. The new boutique hotel is a small showcase of style, occupying the 6th to 8th floors of Lisbon's recently reconstructed Armazéns do Chiado building (Chiado Shopping Center). From the hotel's spacious public rooms and terrace, you look through a three-story window at Lisbon's tile rooftops and famed Eiffel-designed elevator tower, cathedral, and St. George's Castle beyond. Designer Pedro Espirito Santo blended elements of 16th-century Portugal, Macao, and other former colonies with dramatic results. Guest rooms mix antiques with 21st-century amenities like data ports and fax and printer facilities. ⊠ *Rua Nova de Almada 114, 1200-129,* ☎ *21/325–6100 or 21/325–6200,* ℻ *21/325–6161. 40 rooms, 1 suite. Breakfast room, lounge, bar, in-room safes, room service, laundry service. AE, DC, MC, V.* ✎

$$$ ⊞ **Orion Eden.** Take one of downtown's most exciting art deco buildings—the former Eden theater and movie house—and combine it with the French apartment-hotel chain Orion and you've got a winning combination. The understated lobby gives little hint, but upstairs, studio and one-bedroom apartments (for two and four people, respectively) look out through a garden and beyond to the city below. Each has a compact, well-equipped kitchenette, as well as a tiled bathroom, modern furniture, and satellite TV. But the biggest thrill is on the top floor, where a breakfast bar opens out onto a terrace with rooftop views of the castle; a small outdoor pool here gets the sun all day. Room rates are discounted for longer stays; breakfast is not included. ⊠ *Praça dos Restauradores, 1250-187,* ☎ *21/321–6600,* ℻ *21/321–6666. 75 studios, 59 1-bedroom apartments. Bar, breakfast room, kitchenettes, refrigerators, pool. AE, MC, V. Metro: Restauradores.*

$$$ ⊞ **Principe Real.** This small hotel close to the botanical gardens has a large repeat clientele, which enjoys the friendly atmosphere. There's a real old-fashioned warmth and charm, from the rattling elevator to the lovely antiques in the rooms, which all follow harmonious color schemes in blue and green. If there's a grumble it's that the compact bathrooms need to be upgraded, but this fails to spoil the overwhelmingly positive impression. Each day starts with glorious views accompanying the complimentary buffet breakfast in the top-floor restaurant, where terrace dining is encouraged in fine weather. ⊠ *Rua da Alegria 53, 1250,* ☎ *21/346–2116,* ℻ *21/342–2104. 23 rooms. Restaurant, bar. AE, DC, MC, V. Metro: Avenida.*

$$$ ⊞ **Sofitel Lisboa.** Set right in the middle of the Avenida da Liberdade, the Sofitel is a handsome, modern hotel with a high-tech edge to its design. Rooms are pleasingly contemporary in style, decorated in attractive colors, and comfortably appointed. The intimate piano bar makes a good stop after a day's touring, and you can sit by a window in the Cais da Avenida restaurant for sidewalk views of the attractive central artery. ⊠ *Av. da Liberdade 123–125, 1269-038,* ☎ *21/342–9202,* ℻ *21/342–9222. 166 rooms, 4 suites. Restaurant, bar, room service, laundry service, business services. AE, DC, MC, V. Metro: Avenida.*

$$$ ⊞ **York House.** A convent in the 17th century, this attractive inn is near
★ the Museum of Ancient Art and has a shady courtyard garden, where drinks and meals are served. Despite its somewhat inconvenient location west of the center, York House is on tram and bus routes from downtown and has a loyal following (especially among English visitors); you'll need to book well in advance. The charm of the place is apparent in the vine-covered staircase that climbs to the garden from the street and in the individually decorated guest rooms with original details, good reproduction furniture (including four-poster beds), and

lovely rugs; corridors, too, are tiled and spread with rugs—surely an improvement on the austerity of convent days here. Winter rates here are a good deal. ✉ *Rua das Janelas Verdes 32, 1200-692,* ☎ *21/396–2435,* FAX *21/397–2793. 34 rooms. Restaurant, bar. AE, DC, MC, V.*

$$ ☎ **Albergaria Senhora do Monte.** This small, unpretentious hotel in
★ the oldest part of town, near St. George's Castle, offers fine views of Lisbon, especially at night, when the castle is softly illuminated. The four junior suites have terraces, allowing you to make the most of the hotel's location, but these cost an extra 10,000$00 a night. Other rooms have all been recently modernized and given a pastel-colored makeover. The top-floor grill has a picture window (making breakfast a real pleasure), the neighborhood is quiet, and parking is available. It's a steep walk every time you return to the Albergaria, but Tram 28 runs nearby. ✉ *Calçada do Monte 39, 1100-250,* ☎ *21/886–6002,* FAX *21/ 887–7783. 24 rooms, 4 suites. Bar, grill. AE, DC, MC, V.*

$$ ☎ **Eduardo VII.** This reasonably priced hotel is well situated near the park of the same name, although you'll have to rely on public transportation to see the rest of the city. Its anonymous 1930s exterior opens up to reveal 10 floors of shipshape rooms that are short on space, but smart and comfortable. The hotel's singular attraction is the superb view of the Lisbon skyline from the top-floor Varanda restaurant and Lanterna bar—a fine treat. ✉ *Av. Fontes Pereira de Melo 5, 1060-114,* ☎ *21/353–2141,* FAX *21/353–3879. 136 rooms, 4 suites. Restaurant, bar. AE, DC, MC, V. Metro: Rotunda.*

$$ ☎ **Flamingo.** It may have seen better days, but this old-fashioned, city center hotel is reliable and offers good-value lodgings. The staff is friendly, and the small, simply furnished guest rooms are pleasant enough for the price (note that those in front tend to be noisy). There's a spartan dining room where breakfast is served, and a rather more agreeable bar (festooned with images of flamingos), which is the epitome of high 1970s' fashion. There's also a pay parking lot next door (guests receive a 20% discount), a bonus in this busy area. ✉ *Rua Castilho 41, 1250,* ☎ *21/386–2191,* FAX *21/386–1216. 39 rooms. Restaurant, bar. AE, DC, MC, V. Metro: Rotunda.*

$$ ☎ **Hotel Veneza.** Although you might be somewhat startled by its unusual decor highlighted by an elaborate 19th-century staircase contrasting with modern murals, you'll enjoy this 1886 hotel's superb central location, welcoming service, and intimate size. Amenities like satellite TV are unusual for the price. There's no restaurant, but there are plenty of cafés nearby. ✉ *Av. da Liberdade 189, 1250-141,* ☎ *21/352–2618,* FAX *21/352–6678. 38 rooms. Minibars. AE, DC, MC, V.*

$$ ☎ **Métropole.** The mere existence of a turn-of-the-century hotel right on the glorious Rossío plaza has been known to bring a Cheshire Cat grin to the faces of some regular Lisbon visitors. It's a gem, from its balconied facade to its '20s-style bar and lounge. Elegant, light-filled guest rooms have antique furnishings and an inviting atmosphere. Those in front overlook the square—with its flower sellers and cascading fountain—the Alfama, and St. George's Castle; other quarters provide constantly changing tableaux of life in the Baixa. A substantial breakfast buffet is included in the room price. ✉ *Rossío 30, 1100-200,* ☎ *21/346–9164,* FAX *21/346–9166. 36 rooms. Bar, breakfast room, meeting room. AE, DC, MC, V. Metro: Rossío.*

$$ ☎ **Mundial.** A few steps from both the Rossío and Restauradores squares, this large, bustling property has been expanded recently, although its essential charms have been retained. A new wing overlooks the landscaping and fountains of Praça Martim Moniz. Rooms here have elegant light-wood furniture, firm mattresses, and well-equipped bathrooms; expect the rooms in the original building to be upgraded in similar fashion over the next couple of years. Breakfast (included in

the rate) is served in the rooftop restaurant, Varanda de Lisboa, which has panoramic views of the Baixa on one side, Alfama on the other— no wonder the hotel dubs it "Lisbon's eighth hill." ⊠ *Rua Dom Duarte 4, 1100-198, ☎ 21/884–2000, FAX 21/887–9129. 245 rooms, 10 suites. Restaurant, bar, coffee shop, room service. AE, DC, MC, V. Metro: Rossío.*

$ 🏨 **Arco Bandeira.** The forbidding staircase from the street does this
★   place no favors, but keep going to the top. The family owners have scattered their best furniture and treasured souvenirs with a liberal hand, and the simple rooms in this friendly fourth-floor pensão are reason-ably quiet, given its location at the bottom of the Rossío. Common areas, including the shared bathrooms, are spotless if a little old-fashioned; some rooms have excellent views of Praça da Figueira. The staff is very friendly and used to tourists (although they don't speak much English). You'll pay less than 6,000$00 a night most of the year, making this pensão a great bargain. ⊠ *Rua dos Sapateiros 226, 1100, ☎ 21/342–3478. 8 rooms. No credit cards. Metro: Rossío.*

$ 🏨 **Borges.** In the heart of the Chiado, the Borges is as old-fashioned as the glove shops, department stores, and shoe-shine stands that can still be found in this district. It's much favored by European tour groups and is convenient for those who plan to shop until they drop. Rooms really need to be spruced up; if the furniture and rather tatty decor was ever stylish, it would be difficult to remember when. But the bathrooms are better than those of many hotels in this price range, and you'll have no trouble finding a staff member who can speak En-glish. Although the hotel offers a breakfast plan, having coffee and a pastry at the famous Café Brasileira (just steps away) is a better bet. ⊠ *Rua Garrett 108–110, 1200-503, ☎ 21/346–1951, FAX 21/342–6617. 99 rooms. Bar, breakfast room. MC, V. Metro: Baixa/Chiado.*

$ 🏨 **Camões.** Typical of Bairro Alto guest houses, the Camões spreads its simple rooms across a couple of floors of an apartment building and is overseen by a bustling matron. At these prices, don't expect great comfort; do expect clean, bright rooms with beds that don't sag. Rooms facing the street have little balconies—which make for noisy nights but give you a window onto traditional Bairro Alto life. There's a small breakfast room, or you can step out into the neighborhood for coffee and pastries. ⊠ *Travessa do Poço da Cidade 38, 1250, ☎ 21/346–7510. 13 rooms, 7 with bath. Breakfast room. No credit cards. Metro: Baixa/Chiado.*

$ 🏨 **Casa de São Mamede.** The Casa de São Mamede—in the middle of the Rato district—is a real survivor. One of the first private houses to be built in Lisbon after the 18th-century earthquake, it has been hand-somely restored and transformed into a relaxed guest house. A fresh paint job and new carpets have brightened the rooms, each endowed with antique, country-style furniture. There are charming details in the public areas: tiles in the dining room, a grand staircase, stained-glass windows. Only breakfast is served, but you're just a 10-minute walk from the Bairro Alto (or a long, steep hike from the metro). ⊠ *Rua da Escola Politécnica 159, 1250-100, ☎ 21/396–3166, FAX 21/395–1896. 28 rooms. Dining room. MC, V. Metro: Avenida.*

$ 🏨 **Florescente.** One block from Praça dos Restauradores, on a street well known for its many seafood restaurants, this inn has a prime po-sition. Rooms are spread across four floors (there's no elevator) and vary in quality; ask if you can see a selection and pick your own quar-ters rather than having them assigned to you. The best rooms are airy and freshly painted, with their own small bathrooms and TVs; you may not be too impressed by the cheaper choices on the upper floors, where you share bathrooms. Although not even breakfast is served, you couldn't be better placed for downtown cafés and restaurants. ⊠ *Rua*

Portas de Santo Antão 99, 1150-266, ☎ *21/342–6609,* FAX *21/342–7733. 72 rooms, 50 with bath. AE, MC, V. Metro: Restauradores.*

$ 🏨 **Insulana.** One of a series of long-standing, modest hotels in the Baixa shopping streets, the Insulana has the edge over most and generally has space even when others are full—possibly due to it being a little hidden away, up two flights of stairs through a clothes shop. Decor is a bit dark and dated, but it's a clean and hospitable place to rest your head; ask for a room at the rear to minimize disturbance from street noise. A light breakfast is included. ✉ *Rua da Assunção 52, 1100-044,* ☎ *21/342–3131. 32 rooms. Bar, breakfast room. No credit cards. Metro: Baixa/Chiado.*

$ 🏨 **Pensão Londres.** This modest bed-and-breakfast is a surprisingly agreeable choice in the "you-get-what-you-pay-for" category. Expect a modest but indisputably clean room, with or without bath, starting on the third floor of a former residence in the Bairro Alto section. Higher floors have good rooftop views. ✉ *Rua Dom Pedro III 53, 1250,* ☎ *21/346–2203,* FAX *21/346–5682. 40 rooms, 13 with bath. Breakfast room. DC, MC, V.*

NIGHTLIFE AND THE ARTS

Lisbon has an extensive arts-and-nightlife scene, and you'll find listings of music, theater, film, and other entertainment in the monthly *Agenda Cultural* booklet, available from the tourist office. Also, the Friday editions of both the *Diário de Notícias* and *O Independente* newspapers have separate magazines with entertainment listings. Although written in Portuguese, listings are fairly easy to decipher.

It's best to buy tickets to musical and theatrical performances at the box offices, but you can also get them at special booths around the city: there's one in Praça dos Restauradores, near the main post office, called **ABEP** (☎ 21/347–5824 or 21/342–5360).

Nightlife

Lisbon has an extremely active nightlife, revolving mostly around bars and discos, which open late (10 PM). On weekends the mobs are shoulder to shoulder in the street, as each passing hour heralds a move to the next trendy spot. For a less boisterous evening out, visit an *adega típica* (traditional wine cellar) to hear fado. Still other venues host a variety of live events, from rock and roll to African music.

Bars

For late-night partying, there are two main areas as well as an up-and-coming strip along the Tagus. The **Bairro Alto,** long the center of Lisbon's nightlife, is still best if you don't want to walk too far between drinks. Most bars here are fairly small and idiosyncratic, and stay open until 3 AM or so. Larger, designer bars started opening a few years ago along and around **Avenida 24 de Julho,** where—because this isn't a residential area (as the Bairro Alto still is)—bars can stay open until 5 or 6 AM. The latest hot spot is farther along the riverbank, next to the bridge at **Alcântara,** where the Doca do Santo Amaro and Doca de Alcântara both have fashionable terrace-bars and restaurants, some converted from old warehouses. Whichever district you choose, note that not all bars have signs outside, so to find the latest places you may have to follow the crowds or try a half-open door. Don't expect to have a quiet drink: the company is generally young and excitable.

Apollo XIII (✉ Travessa da Cara 8, Bairro Alto, ☎ 21/342–4952) draws students into its tiny drinking den. **Bar Artis** (✉ Rua Diário de Notícias 95, Bairro Alto, ☎ 21/342–4795) is a laid-back meeting place for jazz buffs. The most refined place to start off your evening is the relaxed **Instituto do Vinho do Porto** (✉ Rua de São Pedro de Alcântara 45, Bairro Alto, ☎ 21/347–5707; closed Sun.), a formidable old building where you can sink into an armchair and sample port. For a more bizarre experience, visit the **Pavilhão Chinês** (✉ Rua Dom Pedro V 89, Bairro Alto, ☎ 21/342–4729), a comfortable bar that's decorated with extraordinary bric-a-brac from around the world—statues, tankards, ceramics, baubles, and toys. At **Portas Largas** (✉ Rua da Atalaia 105, Bairro Alto, ☎ 21/846–1379)—a tiled tavern with barn doors—a mostly (but not exclusively) gay crowd spills out into the street; sangria is the house drink. **A Tasca** (✉ Travessa de Queimada 13–15, Bairro Alto, ☎ 21/342–4910) is a bright bar with tequila as its specialty drink.

Heading down toward Avenida 24 de Julho, the late-night crew stops off at **O'Gillin's** (✉ Rua das Remolares 8–10, Cais do Sodré, ☎ 21/342–1899), a popular Irish bar across the road from the train station, with regular live music nights. At **Trifásica** (✉ Av. 24 de Julho 66, ☎ 21/395–7576) the music—loud though it is—takes second place to the snooker tables. **Rock City** (✉ Rua Cintura do Porto de Lisboa, Armazém 255, Santos, ☎ 21/342–8636) is terrific in summer—a riverside bar-restaurant with tropical garden, live bands, and lots of atmosphere. At Alcântara you can take your pick of party places at the Doca do Santo Amaro. **Doca de Santo** (✉ Doca do Santo Amaro, Alcântara, ☎ 21/396–3522) has a great palm-lined esplanade. If you prefer a quieter drink in an older part of town, seek out **Cerca Moura** (✉ Largo das Portas do Sol 4, ☎ 21/887–4859), in the Alfama, which has outdoor seating and river views.

Discos and Clubs

Again, discos and clubs are split between two areas: the Bairro Alto and the Avenida 24 de Julho, with a smattering of cool, upscale places in the suburbs of Santos and Alcântara (note that new discos open and close frequently in Lisbon). Most charge a cover of about 2,000$00–3,000$00 (more on weekends), which usually includes one drink. Some clubs have strict door policies, and bouncers may scrutinize you and your clothes—it's best to ask around first about the age of the patrons. Clubs are open from about 11 PM until 4 or 5 AM; few get going until well after midnight.

Fragil (✉ Rua da Atalaia 126, Bairro Alto, ☎ 21/346–9578; closed Sun.–Mon.) is a long-standing favorite that attracts a partly gay crowd. For a mixture of funk, pop, and soul, **Três Pastorinhos** (✉ Rua da Barroca 111–113, Bairro Alto, ☎ 21/346–4321) is a very groovy joint. **Keops** (✉ Rua da Rosa 157–159, Bairro Alto, ☎ 21/342–8773) raises eyebrows with its funky Egyptian decor. **Kapital** (✉ Av. 24 de Julho 68, ☎ 21/395–5963) is typical of the high-fashion, high-price venues down on the *avenida*; its terrace is its nicest feature. **Kremlin** (✉ Escadinhas da Praia 5, ☎ 21/390–8768; closed Sun.–Mon. and Wed.) continues to attract the trendiest Lisboetas, although no one turns up much before 2 AM (it stays open until 7 AM). The hottest club is **Lux** (✉ Av. Infante D. Henrique, near Sta. Apolónia, ☎ 21/882–0890). It's rumored that John Malkovich is one of the owners. A 1,000$00 minimum drink-cum-cover is charged at the door.

Clubs in Alcântara tend to be more exclusive than most in the city; it's also a ways out, and you'll need to come back by taxi. The ritzy **Alcântara Mar** (✉ Rua da Cozinha Econômica 11, ☎ 21/363–6432; closed Mon.–Tues.) is one of the most enjoyable of the discos, with over-the-top decor and a well-heeled clientele.

Fado

One of Lisbon's most famous nighttime diversions is going to an adega típica to hear fado, a haunting music rooted in African slave songs.

During colonial times fado was exported to Portugal; later, Lisbon's Alfama was recognized as the birthplace of the style, and today most performances occur in the Bairro Alto. In the adegas típicas food and wine are served, and fado plays late into the night: the singing starts at 10 or 11, and the adegas often stay open until 3 AM. Unfortunately, it's becoming increasingly difficult to find an authentic adega, since tourism has encouraged proprietors to charge high prices for sometimes very average food and dilute real fado with other, more "accessible" forms of music. It's always best to ask around for a recommendation.

Senhor Vinho (✉ Rua do Meio à Lapa 18, Bairro Alto, ☎ 21/397–7456; closed Sun.) is an institution and attracts some of Portugal's most accomplished fado singers. **Lisboa a Noite** (✉ Rua das Gaveas 69, Bairro Alto, ☎ 21/346–2603; closed Sun.) is more touristy (and more expensive) than most, but visitors always enjoy the flamboyant shows. One of the oldest fado clubs is **Adega do Machado** (✉ Rua do Norte 91, Bairro Alto, ☎ 21/342–8713; closed Mon.), a typical, bustling place. For fado at budget prices, consider a meal in the **Adega do Ribatejo** (✉ Rua Diário de Noticias 23, Bairro Alto, ☎ 21/346–8343), a popular local haunt, where there's live entertainment nightly. The best place in the Alfama is **Parreirinha d'Alfama** (✉ Beco do Espírito Santo 1, ☎ 21/886–8209), a little club with highly rated singers. **João de Praça** (✉ Rua S. João de Praça 92–94, Alfama, ☎ 21/888–2694) is popular with locals who come to hear the guitar playing of owner Mário Pacheco. **Timpanas** (✉ Rua Gilberto Rola 24, Alcântara, ☎ 21/397–2431; closed Mon.) is farther from the center of town than all the others but is one of the most authentic.

Gay and Lesbian Clubs

Lisbon has a well-established gay and lesbian scene, concentrated primarily in and around the Bairro Alto. **Trumps** (✉ Rua Imprensa Nacional 104b, Rato, ☎ 21/397–1059; closed Mon.) is the city's biggest gay disco. **Memorial** (✉ Rua Gustavo de Matos Sequeira 42, Rato, ☎ 21/396–8891; closed Mon.) is popular with both gay and lesbian visitors and can get packed on the weekends. **Finalmente** (✉ Rua da Palmeira 38, Bairro Alto, ☎ 21/347–2652; closed Sun.) has one of the best sound systems in town and attracts a high-camp crowd. **Fragil** (☞ Discos and Club, *above*), although not exclusively gay, does attract a good, mixed crowd of people.

Live Music

For a change from fado, there are plenty of places offering live rock, pop, and jazz. Big-name American and British bands, as well as the superstar Brazilian singers so beloved in Portugal, often play in Lisbon's large concert halls and stadiums. Local newspapers have details of upcoming performances; keep an eye out for advertising posters around the city. Advance tickets may be bought at the venue or at the ticket booth in Praça dos Restauradores.

The best jazz joint is the **Hot Clube de Portugal** (✉ Praça da Alegria 39, Rato, ☎ 21/346–7369; closed Sun. and Mon.), which puts on a wide variety of gigs most nights, starting at about 10 PM. The main downtown venue for rock concerts is the **Coliseu dos Recreios** (✉ Rua Portas de Santo Antão 96, ☎ 21/343–1677), an old restored theater in the Baixa.

African music is immensely popular in Lisbon, with touring groups from Cabo Verde and Angola playing regularly alongside homegrown talent. The **Ritz** (✉ Rua da Glória 55, ☎ 21/342–5140; closed Sun. and Mon.) is Lisbon's biggest African club. It's on the edge of the Bairro Alto, in a rather seedy area, but is renowned as a friendly place where you can dance to live music. **Pê Sujo** (✉ Largo de São Martinho 6, Alfama, ☎ 21/886–5269; closed Mon.) specializes in live Brazilian music, which goes down smoothly with superb *caipirinhas* (a cocktail of limes and a rum-like liquor).

The Arts

The prime mover behind Lisbon's artistic and cultural scenes is the **Fundação Calouste Gulbenkian** (✉ Av. de Berna 45, ☎ 21/793–5131), which not only presents exhibitions and concerts in its buildings but also sponsors events throughout the city. The foundation publishes a frequently updated schedule of activities, which you can pick up at the reception desk. The tourist-information office can also assist with inquiries about upcoming events.

The **Centro Cultural de Belém** (✉ Praça do Império, Belém, ☎ 21/361–2400) puts on a full range of reasonably priced concerts and exhibitions, featuring national and international artists and musicians. Its monthly program of events is available at the reception desk inside the center. There's also a major concert and exhibition program mounted at **Culturgest** (Caixa Geral de Depósitos, Rua Arco do Cego, ☎ 21/795–3000; Saldanha), an auditorium and exhibition center sponsored by a Portuguese bank.

Art Galleries

The Centro Cultural de Belém (☞ *above*) has an ever-changing program of art exhibitions, and Lisbon's major art museums and commercial buildings often put on temporary exhibitions alongside their permanent collections; you'll find details in the local press. In addition, the city's gallery count has passed 100 and is growing. If you're staying at the Meridien Park Atlantic, Altis, or Hotel Dom Pedro Lisboa, you needn't even step outside to peruse their galleries. Most galleries are closed Sunday and daily 1–3, and will insure and ship whatever you buy.

At the Centro Cultural de Belém (☞ *above*), **Galeria Arte Periférica** is a good source of contemporary art, particularly by younger artists. **Galeria Barata** (✉ Av. de Roma 11A) is a mainly modern art gallery that doubles as a bookshop—or vice versa. You might spot works of London-based Paula Rego at **Galeria 111** (✉ Campo Grande 113-A, ☎ 21/797–7418), arguably Portugal's best known gallery. In Lisbon's historic cathedral area, **Loja da Calçada** (✉ Calçada de S. Vicente 96, ☎ 21/886–2780) is a small shop that concentrates on individual discoveries.

Other galleries of interest include **Galeria de Arte Cervejaria Trindade** (✉ Rua Nova da Trindade 20, Bairro Alto, ☎ 21/342–3506), **Galeria de São Bento** (✉ Rua do Machadinho 1, Bairro Alto, ☎ 21/397–4325), **Galeria Novo Século** (✉ Rua do Século 23A, Bairro Alto, ☎ 21/342–7712), and **Movimento Arte Contemporânea** (✉ Rua do Sol ao Rato 9, Rato, ☎ 21/385–0789).

Concerts

Classical music concerts are staged from about October through June by the Fundação Calouste Gulbenkian, which has three concert halls. Of particular interest is the **Early Music and Baroque Festival,** held in churches and museums around Lisbon every spring. You may also be in town during a performance of the **Nova Filarmonica,** a national orchestra that gives concerts around the country throughout the year. The **Orquestra Metropolitana de Lisboa** (☎ 21/362–3830) performs a regular program at various city venues. Consult local newspapers for details.

Other venues where regular concerts take place include the **Centro Cultural de Belém** (☞ *above*), **Culturgest** (☞ *above*), the **Teatro Nacional** de São Carlos (☞ Theater, *below*), the **Sé** (☞ The Alfama, *above*), the **Igreja do Carmo** (⊠ Largo do Carmo, for summer outdoor concerts), and the **Basílica da Estrêla** (☞ Jardim da Estrêla *in* The Bairro Alto and Chiado, *above*).

Film

All films shown in Lisbon appear in their original language accompanied by Portuguese subtitles, and you can usually find the latest Hollywood releases playing around town. Ticket prices are low (around 800$00) and even cheaper on Monday; it's best to get to the movie theater early on any day to be assured a seat. Some theaters are in preserved art deco buildings and are attractions in their own right.

There are dozens of movie houses throughout the city, including a couple on Avenida da Liberdade. A modern cinema complex in the **Amoreiras shopping center** (⊠ Av. Eng. Duarte Pacheco, ☎ 21/383–1275) has 10 screens. There's also a multiscreen cinema at the **Colombo Shopping Center** (⊠ Av. Col. Militar, Benfica, ☎ 21/711–3200). Portugal's national film theater, the **Instituto da Cinemateca Portuguesa** (⊠ Rua Barata Salgueiro 39, ☎ 21/354–6279), has regular daily screenings: this is the place to catch contemporary Portuguese films and art-house reruns.

Theater

Plays are performed in Portuguese at the **Teatro Nacional de Dona Maria II** (⊠ Praça Dom Pedro V, Baixa, ☎ 21/347–2246), Lisbon's principal theater. Performances are given August–June, and there's the occasional foreign-language production, too. The **Teatro Nacional de São Carlos** (⊠ Rua Serpa Pinto 9, Baixa, ☎ 21/346–5914) hosts an opera season September–June.

OUTDOOR ACTIVITIES AND SPORTS

Participant Sports

There are few sports facilities in Lisbon; for most activities—fishing, horseback riding, water sports—you'll have to go outside the city (☞ Outdoor Activities and Sports *in* Chapter 2).

Boating

Clube Naval (⊠ Cais do Gás, Letra H, Cais do Sodré, ☎ 21/346–9354; Metro: Cais do Sodré), which offers opportunities for sailing and canoeing, is directly on the river. The office is open weekdays 10–1 and 3–7.

Bowling

Bowling International de Lisboa (⊠ Alameda dos Oceanos, near Oriente Station, ☎ 21/891–9193) is worth the ride to Parque das Nações. It's large, noisy, and popular, with 30 lanes in high demand on weekends.

Golf

There are a half dozen golf courses in Lisbon's environs, most of which are concentrated along the Estoril Coast. Indeed, if you're planning to play golf and plan no city-style dining, fado, or nightlife, consider staying at one of the hotels outside Lisbon that offer special golf packages (☞ Chapter 2).

The 18-hole, par 69 golf course at **Lisboa Sport Club** (⊠ Casal da Carregueira, near Belas, ☎ 21/431–0077) is about 20 minutes by car from the city at Queluz.

Swimming

If your hotel doesn't have a pool, you can visit one of the city's municipal pools, including the indoor **Piscina Municipal do Areeiro** (⊠ Av. de Roma, ☎ 21/848–6794) and the **Piscina dos Olivais** (⊠ Av. Dr. Francisco Luís Gomes, 5 km [3 mi] northeast of town, ☎ 21/851–4630). The **Lisboa Sport Club** (☞ *above*) also has a swimming pool. Another option is the **Aquaparque de Lisboa** (⊠ Av. das Descobertas, ☎ 21/321–5217), a complex of pools, slides, waterfalls, cafés, and restaurants open daily 9:30–8 in Restelo Park, near Belém.

The **Piscina do Ateneu** (⊠ Rua Portas de Santo Antão 102, ☎ 21/342–2365; Metro: Restauradores or Rossío) is perfectly positioned in the center of Baixa for easy access. It's closed on Sunday and public holidays. The **Hotel Altis** (⊠ Rua Barata Salgueiro 52, ☎ 21/355–4110 or 21/314–2496) offers an hour's use of its indoor lap pool to nonguests for about $15.

Tennis

For information about reserving a court at any of the facilities below, ask the tourist office (☞ Visitor Information *in* Lisbon A to Z, below), or ask the concierge or reception desk at your hotel to phone ahead. The **Centro de Tennis de Monsanto** (⊠ Parque Florestal de Monsanto, Estrada do Alvita, ☎ 21/363–8073) is in Lisbon's large, lovely public park. The two public tennis courts making up **Campos de Tennis do Campo Grande** (⊠ Jardim do Campo Grande; Metro: Entrecampos) are within the gardens. The **Lisbon Racquet Center** (⊠ Rua Alferes Malheiro), a club adjoining the woods in Alvalade, has nine courts.

Spectator Sports

Bullfighting

Although some might not call bullfighting a sport, it's a spectacle that's popular with locals and many visitors. The events are held on Thursday (and some Sundays) between Easter and September in the ornate Praça de Touros (bullring) at **Campo Pequeno** (☞ *also* The Modern City *in* Exploring Lisbon, *above*). Some people defend the Portuguese bullfight as entertainment because the bull is not killed in the ring but rather is wrestled to the ground by a group of *forçados* (a team of eight men who fight the bull) dressed in traditional red-and-green costumes. Nonetheless, any bull injured during the contest is later killed. The first-class riding skills displayed by the *cavaleiro* (horseback fighter) during the event are undeniable. After the cavaleiro performs, the forçados goad the bull into charging them, and one man throws himself across the horns (which have been padded) while the other men pull the bull down by grabbing hold of whatever bits they can, including the tail. ⊠ *Praça de Touros do Campo Pequeno, Av. da República,* ☎ *21/793–2093.* ⊡ *3,000$00–9,000$00, depending on seats.* ☉ *Performances start at 10* PM. *Metro: Campo Pequeno.*

Soccer

If you so much as leave your hotel room while visiting Lisbon, you'll be reminded that the city will be host to the Euro 2004 Football Championship. Both major stadiums are undergoing renovations. Soccer is Portugal's most popular sport, and Lisbon has three teams, which play at least weekly during the September–May season. The most famous team is **Benfica.** Matches are held in the northwest part of the city, at the huge Estádio da Luz (⊠ Av. Gen. Norton Matos, ☎ 21/726–0321; Metro: Col. Militar–Luz), one of Europe's biggest stadiums. A great rival of Benfica, the **Sporting Clube de Portugal** plays at the Estádio José Alvalade (☎ 21/759–9459; Metro: Campo Grande), near Campo Grande in the north of the city.

You can buy tickets on the day of a game at the stadiums, but for most big matches, you should purchase tickets in advance from the booth in Praça dos Restauradores. Plan to arrive at the stadium early, because there's usually a full program of entertainment first, including children's soccer, marching bands, and fireworks. (Note: always be wary of pickpockets in the crowd.)

SHOPPING

Shopping in Lisbon ranges from the merely pleasant to off the charts, largely because there are still many independent boutiques and few large stores, and the salespeople are courteous almost everywhere. Handmade goods, such as leather handbags, shoes, gloves, embroidery, ceramics, and basketwork, are sold throughout the city. And, apart from top designer fashions and high-end antiques and porcelain, prices are moderate. Most shops are open weekdays 9–1 and 3–7 and Saturday 9–1; shopping malls and supermarkets often remain open until at least 10, sometimes until midnight. Some are also open on Sunday. Credit cards—and Visa in particular—are widely accepted.

Districts

In 1988 a fire destroyed much of the Baixa's **Chiado,** Lisbon's smartest shopping district. Now the area, and especially the new complex housed behind the restored facade of the historic **Grandes Armazéns do Chiado** building, is being compared to a phoenix. The 11-year project, under the supervision of Portugal's acclaimed architect, Álvaro Siza Vieira, is now a stylish, multilevel shopping center. And its surroundings include plenty of small, choice stores on and around the Rua Garrett. The rest of the district, made up of the grid of streets from the Rossío to the Tagus River, remains a fine place to shop, with small stores given over mainly to fashion, jewelry, shoes, and delicatessen foods. Excellent shops continue to open in the residential districts in the north of the city, at **Praça de Londres** and **Avenida de Roma.**

Of the shopping centers, a central one is **Amoreiras** (⊠ Av. Eng. Duarte Pacheco; Metro: Rotunda), west of Praça Marquês de Pombal, which contains a multitude of shops selling clothes, shoes, food, crystal, ceramics, and jewelry. It also has a hairdresser, restaurants, and 10 movie screens, and is open daily 9 AM–11 PM. It's now been eclipsed as a shopping experience, however, by **Colombo** (⊠ Av. Col. Militar, Benfica; Metro: Col. Militar–Luz), the largest shopping center in the Iberian peninsula, with 19 department stores, more than 400 shops and restaurants, a leisure center, and a multiscreen cinema open daily 9 AM–11 PM; the metro station has an exit right inside the mall. The newer **Vasco Da Gama Shopping Center** (⊠ Av. D. João II; Metro: Oriente) teams well with a trip to Lisbon's new Parque das Nações neighborhood. And for charisma and cachet, a favorite is the resurrected **Chiado** area in Baixa, steps from the Avenida da Liberdade.

Markets

Lisbon has several markets and, although you are unlikely to find authentic antiques, you may find something traditional to take home. The best-known market is the **Feira da Ladra** (⊠ Campo de Santa Clara, Alfama), a flea market held on Tuesday morning (8 AM–1 PM) and all day Saturday. There's a market that sells mostly clothes at **Praça de Espanha;** it's open Monday–Saturday 9–5 and near the Palhavã metro stop. The best place for food, kitchenware, and general household items is the covered market at **Praça do Chile,** open Monday–Saturday 9–5, at the Arroios metro station. There's also a general market, including produce, near the Picoas metro stop at the **Mercado 31 de Janeiro** (⌂ Rua E. V. da Silva, near Sheraton Hotel); it's open Monday–Saturday 8–2. Locals in the Alfama shop at the **Mercado do Chão do Loureiro** (⌂ Calçada do Marq. do Tancos, off Costa do Castelo), open Monday–Saturday 8–2. Most atmospheric of all is probably the **Mercado Avenida 24 de Julho,** opposite Cais do Sodré station, open Monday–Saturday 6–2, where the traders are entertainment in themselves.

Specialty Stores

Antiques

Most of Lisbon's antiques shops are in the district of Rato and in the Bairro Alto along one long street, which changes its name four times as it runs southward from Largo do Rato: Rua Escola Politécnica, Rua Dom Pedro V, Rua da Misericórdia, and Rua do Alecrim. Look on the nearby Rua de São Bento for more stores. One of the best-known antiques shops is **Solar** (⌂ Rua Dom Pedro V 68–70, Bairro Alto).

A cluster of shops on Rua Augusto Rosa, between the Baixa and Alfama, concentrates on antiques—furnishings, silver, china, and more. **Cunha Rosa E. Fernandes** (⌂ Rua Augusto 18) is crowded with furniture, ceramics, and art. **Francoise Baudry** (⌂ Rua Augusto Rosa 4) has framed landscapes and other paintings among its collection. **Ricardo Hogan** (⌂ Rua Augusto Rosa 9) has an eclectic collection that lends itself to unpredictable discovery. The helpful, bilingual owners of **Ferroelo Antiquidades** (⌂ Rua Nova de S. Mamede 6, Rato) will guide you through their collection, which includes some silver and fine furnishings.

Ceramics

Viuva Lamego (⌂ Largo do Intendente, Graça; Metro: Intendente; and ⌂ Calçada do Sacramento, Chiado) offers the largest selection of tiles and pottery in Lisbon—and at competitive prices. **Vista Alegre** (⌂ Largo do Chiado 18, Chiado; ⌂ Loja 2080, Amoreiras shopping center; ⌂ Rua Ivens 52, Chiado) founded its porcelain factory in 1824, and you can buy perfect reproductions of their original table services and ornaments. The **Fábrica Sant'Ana** (⌂ Rua do Alecrim 95, Chiado), founded in the 1700s, sells wonderful hand-painted ceramics and tiles based on antique patterns; the pieces sold here may be the finest in the city. Also try **Aresta Viva** (⌂ Rua Antero de Quental 22; Metro: Intendente), producers of handmade and hand-painted tiles, some based on 16th-century designs seen at the Museu do Azulejo. For handcrafted modern pottery, **Casa Ribeiro da Silva** (⌂ Travessa Fiéus de Deus 69, Bairro Alto) is worth a visit.

Clothing

Although Lisbon isn't on the cutting edge of fashion and design, the city is increasingly fashion-aware and according celebrity status to a rising tide of designers. ModaLisboa has become an annual fashion event showing and promoting the creations of Portuguese designers, who include Ana Salazar, Maria Gambina, Miguel Viera, and at least a dozen more. Their creations are featured alongside the more established fashion names in a variety of stores. Praça de Londres and Avenida de Roma—both in the modern city—form one long run of haute-couture stores and fashion outlets.

Augustus (⌂ Centro Comercial Roma, Loja 36, Av. de Roma) for women and **David and Monteiro** (⌂ Av. de Roma 49) for men are representative of what's on offer. For big international names under one roof, **Colombo** or **Amoreiras** shopping centers (☞ Shopping Districts, *above*) can't be beat. Designer-clothes stores are starting to creep into the Bairro Alto: **Manuel Alves** and **José Manuel Gonçalves** have stores on Rua da Rosa at No. 39 (menswear) and at No. 85 (women's). **Outra Face da Lua** (⊠ Rua do Norte 86; Metro: Baixa/Chiado) is about as unconventional as Lisbon shopping gets. Is it named "the other side of the moon" because it doesn't open until late in the evening—or perhaps because it dispenses an eclectic mix of clothes and music, tea and tattoos?

For women's designer clothes, visit **Ana Salazar** (⊠ Rua do Carmo 87, Chiado). **José Antonio Tenente** (⊠ Travessa do Carmo 8, Chiado) also has some great collections of women's clothing. **Eldorado** (⊠ Rua do Norte 23–25, Bairro Alto) sells antique clothing. And if there isn't a little girl in your life, some of the dresses in saucy prints at **Maison Louvre** (⊠ Rossío 106) will make you want to go out and adopt one.

Food and Wine

There are some excellent delicatessens in the Baixa that sell fine foods, including delicious regional cheeses, and a wide selection of wines, especially varieties of port—one of Portugal's major exports. Supermarkets also sell local wines, and so do—oddly enough—shops that purvey dried cod, which you'll see stacked outside on the sidewalk or hanging in the window. Rua do Arsenal has several such stores. **Manuel Tavares** (⊠ Rua da Betesga 1a, Baixa), just off the Rossío, has a particularly good selection of vintage ports and wines and also sells cheese and chocolate. At **Napoleão** (⊠ Rua dos Fanqueiros 70, Baixa) the helpful staff speaks English and can recommend vintages. The **Instituto do Vinho do Porto** (⊠ Rua de São Pedro de Alcântara 45, Bairro Alto) offers more than 100 varieties to sample and bottles to buy; it also has a very handy and well stocked duty-free store at the airport.

Other popular gourmet items are fresh chocolates, marzipan, dried and crystallized fruits, and pastries, on sale in most of the city's pastelarias. Try the **Pastelaria Suiça** (⊠ Rossío 96), which has a particularly large selection of sweets.

Handicrafts

A showroom for traditional carpets is **Almoravida** (⊠ Rua da Senhora da Glória 130, Graça). **Arameiro** (⊠ Praça dos Restauradores 62) is a place for lace, especially the spidery *rendas de bilros* variety made in Portugal's north. Near the Castelo de São Jorge, you'll find **A Bilha** (⊠ Rua do Milagre de Santo António 10, Alfama), which sells embroidery, lace, copper, gold, and silver. For embroidered goods and baskets from the Azores, stop by **Casa Regional da Ilha Verde** (⊠ Rua Paiva de Andrade 4, Baixa). **Pessoa de Carvalho** (⊠ Costa do Castelo 4) is an old Alfama house that sells candles, glassware, jewelry, and other unique handicrafts. For paper or art supplies or to find a small engraving or watercolor as a souvenir, **Au Petit Peintre** (⊠ Rua de S. Nicolau 104, Chiado) has been around since 1909. **Tricana** (⊠ Av. Praia da Vitória 48, Saldanha), near the Lisboa Sheraton & Towers, specializes in rugs, including classic hand-woven Arriolas rugs and some lovely modern variations thereof.

The Bairro Alto is full of little crafts shops with stylish, contemporary ceramics, wooden sculpture, linen, and clothing. **Pais Em Lisboa** (Rua do Teixeira 25, Bairro Alto) updates traditional handicrafts. At **Francesinha** (Rua da Barroca 96–98, Bairro Alto), hand-painted ceramics sit alongside fabrics, wrought ironwork, and simple jewelry.

Jewelry

The Baixa is a good place to look for jewelry: Rua Aurea (formerly and often still called Rua do Ouro) was named for the goldsmiths' shops installed here under Pombal's 18th-century city plan—the trade has flourished here ever since. **Sarmento** (⊠ Rua Aurea 251, Baixa) has characteristic Portuguese gold- and silver-filigree work. For antique silver and jewelry visit **António da Silva** (⊠ Praça Luís de Camões 40, Chiado).

Leather Goods

Shoe shops can be found all over the city, but they may have limited selections of large sizes because the Portuguese tend to have small feet. The better shops, however, can make shoes to order. Gloves are sold or custom-made in specialty shops in the Rua do Carmo and Rua Aurea.

You'll find fine leather handbags and luggage at **Casa da Siberia** (⊠ Rua Augusta 254, Baixa). **Coelho** (⊠ Rua da Conceição 85, Baixa) is excellent for leather belts and can also make leather-back fabric belts from your own material. Visit **Ulisses** (⊠ Rua do Carmo 87, Chiado) for a good selection of leather gloves. A reliable shoe store, with a good range of sizes and brand names, is **Sapateria Bandarra** (⊠ Rua da Santa Justa 78, Baixa).

Music

If you want to take home some soulful fado music, the best place to check out Portuguese CDs is in a branch of **Valentim de Carvalho** (⊠ Rossío 59, Baixa). Chart hits and other purchases are best made from the huge **Virgin Megastore** (⊠ Praça dos Restauradores, Baixa) inside the beautifully renovated art deco Eden building.

LISBON A TO Z

Arriving and Departing

By Airplane

International and domestic flights land at Lisbon's small, modern Portela Airport, north of the city. There's a tourist office here as well as a currency exchange bureau. **TAP** (☎ 21/841–6990 or 21/386–4080), the Portuguese national airline, flies to Lisbon from New York, Newark, and Boston; it also links Lisbon with other European capitals. **Continental** (☎ 21/383–4000) has a daily service between Newark and Lisbon. **Air France** (☎ 21/790–0020), **British Airways** (☎ 21/342–3118), and **Alitalia** (☎ 21/353–6147) also have service to Lisbon.

BETWEEN THE AIRPORT AND CENTER CITY

There are no trains or subways between the airport and the city, but getting downtown by bus or taxi is simple and inexpensive.

By Bus. A special bus, Aerobus 91, runs every 20 minutes, 7 AM–9 PM, from outside the airport into the city center; tickets, bought from the driver, cost 430$00 or 1,000$00 and allow one or three days of travel, respectively, on all Lisbon's buses and trams; TAP passengers can claim a free ride—check with the airline at the airport. The journey takes 30 minutes, and the bus stops at several useful points, including Praça Marquês de Pombal, Avenida da Liberdade, the Rossío, Praça do Comércio, and the Cais do Sodré train station.

City Buses 44 and 45 cost only 150$00 one-way and depart every 15–30 minutes 5 AM–1:40 AM from the main road in front of the terminal building. They pass through Praça dos Restauradores en route to the Cais do Sodré train station (from there you can continue by rail to Estoril and Cascais).

By Car. Car-rental firms and the tourist-information office at the airport provide free maps of Lisbon and its environs. The drive to the city center takes 20–30 minutes, depending on traffic conditions.

By Taxi. Taxis in Lisbon are so cheap, and the airport is so close to the city center, that many visitors make a beeline straight for a cab (lines form at the terminal). Expect to pay 1,500$00–2,000$00 to most destinations in the city center and around 6,000$00 if you're headed for Estoril or Sintra. If you put luggage in the trunk, add on another 300$00.

By Bus

Plans are underway to reorganize Lisbon's bus terminal system, bringing the main services together in one terminal at the Estação Oriente railway and Metro station. Until that happens, however, perhaps in 2001, the system remains confusing. The best solution by far is to have a travel agency take care of your booking. Most travel agents can sell you a bus ticket in advance; if you buy from the company ticket office at the main terminal, give yourself plenty of time to purchase before you depart. In summer it's wise to reserve a ticket at least a day in advance for destinations in the Algarve. There are four daily departures from Lisbon for the Algarve and Oporto; towns closer to the capital have more frequent service. Most international buses and domestic express buses, including those to and from the Algarve, operate from within the **main bus terminal** (⊠ Av. Casal Ribeiro 18, ☎ 21/354–5439), which is very near Praça Duque de Saldanha. The Saldanha and Picoas metro stations are just a few minutes' walk away.

Terminals at **Praça de Espanha** (Pavalhã metro) and **Campo Pequeno** (Campo Pequeno metro) serve Setúbal-Sesimbra and the northwest coast of Portugal, respectively; the terminal at **Campo das Cebolas,** at the end of Rua dos Bacalheiros, east of Praça do Comércio, is for destinations in the Minho and Algarve; buses to and from Mafra operate from Largo Martim Moniz, northeast of Praça da Figueira.

By Car

Lisbon sees some of the most reckless driving in all of Portugal. Add to this the notoriously difficult parking situation in the city center and in the cramped older quarters, and there's much to be said for not using a car in the capital. Nevertheless, most of the country's highways originate in Lisbon, including the fast roads west to Estoril (A5/IC15), south to Setúbal (A2/IP1, via the 25 of April Bridge), and north to Oporto (A1/IP1). The second trans-Tagus crossing via the spectacular Vasco da Gama Bridge, north of the city center, is an alternative route to Setúbal and provides easier access for the main highway routes east to Spain.

By Train

International trains from France and Spain and long-distance domestic service from Oporto and the north arrive at and depart from the **Santa Apolónia station** (⊠ Av. Infante D. Henrique), on the riverfront to the east of Lisbon's center. One daily train runs to and from Paris; two daily trains to and from Madrid; and frequent daily trains to and from Oporto from 7 AM to midnight. To reach the Rossío or Avenida da Liberdade from the station, take a taxi or Bus 9, 39, 46, or 90 from outside the station. A new metro station here connects you with the subway system (*see* Getting Around, *below*). Some long-distance and suburban trains stop at the **Oriente** station at the Parque das Nações, which is also connected to the metro system.

Local trains to Sintra and all destinations in Estremadura use the central **Rossío station,** an unmistakably neo-Manueline building that stands between Praça dos Restauradores and the Rossío itself. Trains to Sintra run daily every 15 minutes from 6 AM to 2:40 AM; three trains daily run to towns in Estremadura. For information, tickets, and platforms take the escalators through the station building to the top floor.

Trains along the coast to Estoril and Cascais arrive at and depart from the waterfront **Cais do Sodré station,** a 10-minute walk west of the Praça do Comércio. Departures both ways are regular—every 15–30 minutes, 5:30 AM–2:30 AM. Buses 44, 45, and 91 run between Cais do Sodré and the central Lisbon squares; a new metro station provides easy access, and there's a taxi stand outside the station.

Traveling by train to the Algarve and the south of the country is somewhat more complicated than train travel to other destinations. The **Barreiro station** is on the opposite side of the Tagus River but is linked to Lisbon by a ferry that docks at the Terminal Fluvial (also known as Sul e Sueste), adjacent to Praça do Comércio. The fare is included in the train-ticket price. There are seven daily trains to the Algarve, the first of which leaves at 6:40 AM and the last one—an overnight service—at about midnight.

For **information about train service** from any station in Lisbon (or the rest of the country), call ☎ 21/888–4025 daily 8 AM–11 PM.

Getting Around

The best way to see central Lisbon is on foot. It's a small city by any standard, and most of the points of interest are contained within the well-defined older quarters. Just remember that the city is hilly and has cobblestone sidewalks that can make walking tiring (especially in the hot summer), even when you wear comfortable shoes. At some point you'll probably want to use the public-transportation system, if only to sample the old trams and funicular railways and elevators that link sections of the city.

If you're staying in Lisbon for more than a few days, consider reducing transportation costs by buying one of the various transport passes. A **tourist pass** for unlimited rides on a tram or bus costs 430$00 for one day's travel, 1,000$00 for three days; four-day passes (1,600$00) and seven-day passes (2,300$00) are also valid on the metro and the elevator. You can buy tourist passes at the Cais do Sodré station, Restauradores metro station, and other terminals. Otherwise, you pay a flat fee of 150$00 to the driver every time you ride a bus, tram, or the elevator; it's cheaper to buy your ticket in advance from a kiosk (found at major squares and bus terminals), where your 150$00 gets you a ticket valid for two journeys. All buses, trams, and elevators are operated by **Carris,** the city's public transportation company, which has an information line (☎ 21/363–9343). The metro has a different ticketing system (☞ *below*).

The other option is to buy a **Lisboa Card** (24 hours, 2,100$00; 48 hours, 3,500$00; 72 hours, 4,500$00), a special pass that allows free travel on all public transportation and free entry into 26 museums and galleries—including all the major city attractions. It's on sale at the **Lisboa Card central office** (✉ Rua Jardim do Regedor 50, Baixa, ☎ 21/343–3672), off the east side of Praça dos Restauradores, as well as at major sights and attractions throughout the city.

A note of warning: avoid traveling on public transportation during rush hours, especially on the metro, which gets jammed. Also, be aware that pickpockets ply their trade on crowded trains, buses, and trams. Keep an eye on your possessions, and carry wallets in inside pockets and bags and backpacks with the fastening facing your body. If your hotel lacks a convenient safe, consider stashing some documents and cash in a fashion-defying money belt.

By Bus

Buses are generally quicker than trams. Each stop is posted with full details of routes, so you can easily figure out which bus to take. City buses operate 6:30 AM to midnight, and useful buses are detailed in the text where relevant. For a spectacular journey across the 25 of April Bridge over the Tagus River take a bus from Praça de Espanha to Costa da Caparica or Setúbal. When you board, insert your ticket in the ticket-punch machine behind the driver and wait for the pinging noise. For **information on bus routes,** call ☎ 21/363–2044.

By Ferry

Ferries still cross the Tagus, although there are fewer now that Lisbon has two great bridges rather than one. For details of Lisbon-area destinations accessible by ferry, *see* Lisbon's Environs A to Z *in* Chapter 2.

By Funicular and Elevador

Small funicular-railway systems and an ingenious vertical elevator (both are called "elevador") link some of the high and low parts of Lisbon. The Elevador de Santa Justa whisks you from Rua de Santa Justa in the Baixa up to Largo do Carmo in the Bairro Alto. Of the funicular railways, the most useful are the Elevador da Glória, which runs from Calçada da Glória, just behind Praça dos Restauradores, to Rua de São Pedro de Alcântara in the Bairro Alto, and the Elevador da Bica, which runs from Rua do Loreto down to Rua Boavista, northwest of Cais do Sodré. Departures on all three services are every few minutes from 7 AM to 11 PM.

By Metro

The Metropolitano is modern and efficient, and it's considerably more useful now that it has been extended to serve some of the city's newer areas. The new Oriente station connects the recently developed Parque das Nações to the rest of the city, and you'll also find the metro useful for transport to and from the Gulbenkian Foundation and to Praça de Espanha for the bus across the 25 of April Bridge to Setúbal; there are stops en route along Avenida da Liberdade and at the Parque Eduardo VII. The metro operates 6:30 AM to 1 AM; individual tickets cost 70$00 and a 10-ticket strip, a *caderneta,* costs 550$00. There's also a one-day (200$00) or seven-day (620$00) Passe Metropolitano (Metro Pass), available at stations, for use just on the metro system. Insert your ticket in the ticket-punch machine at the barrier. For **metro information,** call ☎ 21/355–8547.

By Taxi

Taxis are plentiful and cheap, and if two to four people are traveling together, a cab is often the cheapest option. Drivers use meters but can take out-of-towners for a ride, literally, by not taking the most direct route. If you book a cab from a hotel or restaurant, it's a good idea to have someone speak to the driver so there are no "misunderstandings" about your destination. Rates start at 300$00, and most city journeys will run 600$00 and up in Lisbon's increasingly dense traffic. Of course small tips—10% or so—for reliable drivers are appreciated. Supplementary charges are added at night, on weekends, for luggage, and for journeys outside the city limits. You may hail cruising vehicles, but it's sometimes difficult to get drivers' attention; there are taxi stands at most main squares. Remember that when the green light is on, it means the cab is already occupied. To phone a cab (which will add 150$00 to the fare), try **Radio Taxis** (☎ 21/815–5061), **Autocoope** (☎ 21/793–2756), or **Teletaxi** (☎ 21/815–2076).

By Tram

Lisbon's elétrico system—built by British engineers at the end of the last century—is one of the most amusing and enjoyable ways to get around, especially if you can board one of the clunky old wooden ones (and remember to secure your bag and wallet against pickpockets). Sadly, though, the system has shrunk over the years as increased auto traffic has taken its toll; meanwhile many of the older carriages have been replaced by sleek new supertrams, emblazoned with ads. Still, for a taste of the old days, catch Tram 28 for an inexpensive tour of the city from the Alfama; Tram 15 will take you to Belém, and Tram 18 to the Palácio de Ajuda, also in Belém. Stops are indicated by PARAGEM (stop) signs on the sidewalks, and every stop has a route map for each tram that passes that way. The system operates 6:30 AM to midnight; insert your ticket in the ticket-punch machine by the driver.

Contacts and Resources

Banks and Currency Exchange

Most major banks have offices in the **Baixa,** and there are currency-exchange facilities at the **airport** (open 24 hours) and at **Santa Apolónia train station** (daily 8:30–8:30). Large hotels and some travel agencies also offer exchange facilities, but the rates are usually poor. Few savvy travelers use them anyway; ATMs are ubiquitous and offer better rates. They will spit out crisp escudos until December 31, 2001, colorful euros thereafter.

Car Rental

It's often much cheaper to arrange car rental in conjunction with your airline ticket or by contacting a car company directly or via a travel agent. But if you've left it until you arrive in Portugal, all the major car-rental companies have offices at the airport and at Santa Apolónia station. In central Lisbon you'll find **Avis** (⊠ Av. Praia da Vitória 12c, ☎ 21/356–11760; 21/849–9947 airport; 0800/221002; Metro: Saldanha), **Budget** (⊠ Av. Visconde Valmor 36B, ☎ 21/797–1377; 21/847–8803 airport; Metro: Saldanha), **Europcar** (⊠ Av. António Augusto de Aguiar 24, ☎ 21/353–5115; 21/847–3181 airport; 21/886–1573 Santa Apolónia station; Metro: Saldanha), and **Hertz** (⊠ Rua do Castilho 72, Rato, ☎ 21/381–2430; 21/849–2722 airport; 0800/221231). Smaller local car-rental companies are also represented in Lisbon; the tourist office has full details.

Embassies

Canada (⊠ Av. da Liberdade 144, Baixa, ☎ 21/347–4892). **United Kingdom** (⊠ Rua São Bernardo 33, Rato, ☎ 21/392–4000). **United States** (⊠ Av. das Forças Armadas, Entre Campos, ☎ 21/727–3300).

Emergencies

Ambulance: ☎ 21/321–7777. **Doctors and Hospitals:** Many doctors who have trained abroad speak English. Ask the staff at your hotel or at the embassy to recommend a reliable local doctor. One clinic with English-speaking doctors or other staff is **Clínica Médica Internationale de Lisboa** (⊠ Rua António Augusto Aguiar 40, ☎ 21/351–3310). Also, you can contact the **British Hospital** (⊠ Rua Saraiva de Carvalho 49, ☎ 21/395–5067 or 21/397–6329), which has English-speaking doctors and nurses. Other hospitals include **Hospital São José** (⊠ Rua José A. Serrano, ☎ 21/886–2131), **Hospital de São Francisco Xavier** (⊠ Est. Forte A. Duque, ☎ 21/321–7351), and **Hospital Santa Maria** (⊠ Av. Prof. Egas Moniz, ☎ 21/797–5171; 21/793–2762 emergency). **Fire:** ☎ 21/342–2222 or 21/606060. **General:** ☎ 112.

Police: (☏ 21/346–6141). For **general** problems or in case of theft, the **Tourism Police** (✉ Rua Capelo 13, near Teatro de São Carlos, ☏ 21/346–6141) has an office open 24 hours. If you need to make a claim against your travel insurance, you must file a report here. **Pharmacies:** Hours of operation and listings of druggists that stay open late are posted on most pharmacy doors. Local newspapers also carry a current list of pharmacies that have extended hours. In town, useful pharmacy addresses include **Farmácia Azevedo Filhos** (✉ Rossío 31, Baixa, ☏ 21/342–7478), **Farmácia Barral** (✉ Rua Augusta 225, Baixa, ☏ 21/346–1534), and **Farmácia Durão** (✉ Rua Garrett 92, Baixa, ☏ 21/324–4166).

English-Language Bookstores

Many bookstores downtown carry at least a few English-language novels and guidebooks. **Livraria Bertrand** (✉ Rua Garrett 73, Chiado) and **Livraria Portugal** (✉ Rua do Carmo 72, Chiado) have a broader selection than most. The English-language selection at **Livraria Buchholz** (✉ Rua Duque de Palmela 4, ☏ 21/317–0580) far exceeds most vacation needs. CDs are downstairs, books up, and classical music plays throughout. **Livraria Britanica** (✉ Rua de S. Marçal 63, ☏ 21/342–8472), across from the British consulate, specializes in English-language books. For American and European newspapers, go to one of the several small newsstands at the bottom of Praça dos Restauradores or on the Rossío, but expect periodicals to be a day or two out of date.

Guided Tours

Beware of unauthorized guides who approach you outside popular monuments and attractions: they are usually more concerned with "guiding" you to a particular shop or restaurant. This is not to suggest that persons offering you a tour of the interior of a church or museum should be ignored—knowledgeable people associated with the particular institution often volunteer their services for a tip of 200$00 or so.

ORIENTATION TOURS

Many companies organize half-day tours of Lisbon and its environs and full-day trips to more distant places of interest. Reservations can be made through any travel agency or hotel; some tours will pick you up at your door. A half-day tour of Lisbon will cost about 6,000$00. A full-day trip north to Obidos, Nazaré, and Fatima will run about 15,000$00 (including lunch), as will a full day east on the "Roman Route" to Évora and Monsaraz. Contact any of the following companies: **Citirama** (✉ Av. Praia da Vitória 12-B, ☏ 21/355–8567; Metro: Saldanha), **Gray Line Tours** (✉ Av. Praia da Vitória 12-B, ☏ 21/352–2594; Metro: Saldanha), or **Top Tours** (✉ Av. Duque de Loulé 108, ☏ 21/315–5877; Metro: Rotunda).

PERSONAL GUIDES

For names of personal guides, contact Lisbon's main tourist office (☞ Visitor Information, *below*) or the **Syndicate of Guide Interpreters** (✉ Rua do Telhal 4, ☏ 21/346–7170; Metro: Avenida), open weekdays 9–1 and 2–5:30. It can provide an English-speaking guide for half-day (11,000$00) or full-day (19,000$00) tours; the price remains the same for up to 20 people.

Telephones and Mail

The area code for Lisbon and its surrounding area (including Cascais, Estoril, and Sintra) is 21. To access Lisbon from abroad, dial 351 (Portugal's country code), then 21 plus the number. From within Portugal, you need just 21 plus the number. Pay phones are abundant and either take coins only or coins and phone cards (825$00 or 2,100$00; available at post offices). For information, dial 118; operators often speak English or will find a colleague who does.

If you have an AT&T, MCI, or Sprint calling card, you can enter the appropriate access number from your hotel phone (and some public phones) to be connected with an English-speaking operator to make an international call. Be aware that you cannot get this service from all phones in the city. The phone office at the post office in Praça dos Restauradores (☞ *below*) is the best place to make long-distance calls, but expect to take a numbered ticket and wait your turn in line. There's another office on the northwestern corner of the Rossío, at No. 65, that's open daily 8 AM–10 PM. At both locations you can use your Visa card. You can also make direct-dialed long-distance calls from most phone booths on the street, although it's easiest if you use a phone card.

The **main post office** (⊠ Praça do Comércio) receives *poste restante* (general delivery) mail and is open Monday–Saturday 8:30–6. You'll need your passport to collect your mail. The **post office** on the eastern side of Praça dos Restauradores, at No. 58, is open Monday–Saturday 8 AM–10 PM, Sunday 9–6.

Travel Agencies
You can save yourself a lot of time by buying train or bus tickets from travel agencies. Main branches generally have an employee who speaks English. Major agencies include **Abreu** (⊠ Av. da Liberdade 158–160, Baixa, ☎ 21/347–6441), **American Express** (⊠ c/o Top Tours, Av. Duque de Loulé 108, ☎ FAX 21/315–5877; Metro: Rotunda), and **Marcus & Harting** (⊠ Rossío 45–50, Baixa, ☎ 21/346–9271).

Visitor Information
Portugal's main tourist office in Lisbon, **Investimentos, Comércio e Turismo de Portugal** (ICEP), is in the **Palácio Foz** (⊠ Praça dos Restauradores, ☎ 21/346–3643), at the Baixa end of Avenida da Liberdade, open Monday–Saturday 9–8, Sunday 10–6. The staff speaks English, and there are plenty of free brochures and maps. The **airport tourist office** (☎ 21/849–3689) is open daily 6 AM–2 AM. Both offices are closed December 25 and January 1. The **Linha Verde Turista** (tourist information help line) is at ☎ 0800/296296.

2 LISBON'S ENVIRONS

Lisbon's backyard is rich in possibilities: drive coastal roads that thread their way along breathtaking seaside cliffs, or laze about on a sandy beach or leafy mountainside, sipping a glass of the delicious local wine. At night, enjoy the active nightlife of the region's resort towns or retire to a room in a converted palace, castle, or country mansion.

By Jules Brown

Updated by
Alys Bohn

S UCH FAMOUS DESTINATIONS as the Estoril Coast, Sintra, the palace at Queluz, even the city of Setúbal and its Manueline church, are all within an hour of Lisbon. You can see the greater part of Lisbon's environs by using the capital as a base. Within a 50-km (31-mi) stretch north and south of the Rio Tejo (Tagus River) you'll find a succession of attractive coastal resorts and important towns. These are no mere dormitory suburbs of the city but are instead endowed with unique traditions and characteristics.

Much of the region is the most southerly part of the historic province of Estremadura (☞ Chapter 3), which reaches as far north as Alcobaça and borders on the province of Ribetejo to the east. This was the first land taken back from the Moors in the 12th century under the Christian Reconquest, which had originated farther north in the region of the Douro River: Estremadura means "farthest from the Douro River," an indication of the early extent of the Christian advance against the Moors. Although the region encompasses glistening coastline, broad river estuaries, wooded valleys, and green mountains, its proximity to Lisbon means it tends to be heavily populated and geared toward the capital's needs: beaches, restaurants, and rural hotels are filled with people escaping from the city, and coastal roads are often congested with slow-moving traffic.

Lisbon and Lisbon's environs are complementary; they have served each other through history. Even the country's earliest rulers appreciated the importance of one to the other. It was the Moors who first built a castle northwest of the capital at Sintra as a defense against Christian forces under Dom Afonso Henriques, which moved steadily southward after the victory at Ourique in 1139. The castle at Sintra fell to the Christians in 1147, a few days after they defeated the Moors in Lisbon.

Once the Christian Reconquest had been consolidated in Estremadura, there was a less pressing need for defensive measures. The early Christian kings instead adopted the lush hills and valleys of Sintra as a summer retreat and designed estates and glorious palaces that survive today. Similarly, Lisbon's 18th- and 19th-century nobility desired a more leisurely life outside the city and so developed small resorts along the Estoril Coast; the amenities and ocean views are still greatly sought after (although the ocean itself is not as clean as it could be). For swimming, modern Lisboetas look a little farther afield—across the Tagus to the beaches and resorts of the Costa da Caparica and the southern Setúbal Peninsula. In whichever direction you travel and whatever your interests, you will be delighted with all that Lisbon's environs have to offer.

Pleasures and Pastimes

Dining

City dwellers make a point of crossing the Tagus to the suburb of Cacilhas to eat platefuls of *arroz de marisco* (rice with shellfish); *linguado* (sole) is especially popular, as are the mounds of shellfish displayed in restaurant windows. One of Caparica's summer delights is the smell of grilled sardines wafting from restaurants and beachside stalls. Seafood, naturally, is also the specialty along the Estoril Coast—even the inland villages here and on the Setúbal Peninsula are close enough to the sea to be assured a steady supply of quality fish.

In Sintra *queijadas* (sweet cheese tarts) are a local specialty, whereas in the Azeitão region of the Setúbal Peninsula, locals swear by the *queijo fresco,* a delicious white sheep's-milk cheese. Lisbon's environs also produce good wines, many of which are offered in local restaurants. From

Colares comes a light, smooth red, a fine accompaniment to a hearty lunch; Palmela, the demarcated wine-growing district of Setúbal, produces distinctive amber-color wines of recognized quality; in the Setúbal Peninsula, the Fonseca winery produces a splendid dessert wine called Moscatel de Setúbal. For price categories, *see* the chart under Dining *in* Smart Travel Tips A to Z.

Golf

The superb golf courses near Lisbon attract players from far and wide. Most are the creations of renowned golf-course designers, and the climate means that you can play year-round. Many hotels offer golf privileges to guests; some places even have their own courses.

Lodging

Outside Lisbon, you can stay in *pousadas,* inns that are members of the Turismo de Habitição organization. Pousadas often are in converted historic buildings, and they generally have superior facilities and restaurants. The three in this region are at Queluz, Setúbal, and Palmela. Under the Turismo de Habitação system, old manor houses and country estates offer rooms and sometimes meals. All lodgings listed with this association are in rural areas and provide comfortable accommodations. Since they typically have few rooms, availability is limited. Regardless of where you stay, in summer it's essential that you book in advance. Out of season, many places discount their prices substantially; particularly good deals are noted. For price categories, *see* the chart under Lodging *in* Smart Travel Tips A to Z.

Sailing

There are sailing clubs at Cascais, Sesimbra, and Setúbal, among others. It's often possible to arrange a weeklong sail with some of the clubs in the coastal towns. Check with your local sailing organization to see if it has reciprocity with any Portuguese marinas.

Shopping

Lisbon's environs have shopping opportunities galore, from clothes sold in smart Cascais and Estoril boutiques to the ceramics and woven and leather goods featured at roadside stalls and at weekly village markets. The area is also the site of several traditional country fairs and markets offering a variety of local handicrafts and foods. Quality and prices vary greatly, so you'd do well to shop around before buying. Prices are fixed almost everywhere, although with a firm command of the Portuguese language you may be able to negotiate a small discount at some of the local markets and roadside stalls.

Exploring Lisbon's Environs

To the west of Lisbon, the Estoril Coast consists of a series of small beaches and rocky coves, at its most delightful around the towns of Estoril and Cascais; farther north, the Atlantic makes itself felt in the windswept beaches and capes beyond Guincho. Yet just a few miles inland, the Sintra hills are as charming a rural retreat as you could wish for, crisscrossed by minor roads and dotted with old monastic buildings, estates, gardens, and market villages.

To the south, across the Tagus River, the contrast couldn't be more pronounced. The beaches of the Costa da Caparica combine to form a 20-km (12½-mi) sweep of sand, backed for the most part by the flat, wine-producing country of the Setúbal Peninsula. The landscape changes only in the south, where the peaks of the Serra da Arrábida rise above a rugged coastline that shelters small fishing villages and resorts. The only city of any size in the region, Setúbal, is just to the east of here, an obvious stop en route to Évora or the Algarve.

Great Itineraries

With a car you can cover the main sights north and south of the Tagus in two days, although this gives you little time to linger. A week's touring wouldn't be too long to spend, particularly if you plan to soak up the sun at a resort or take an in-depth look at Sintra, whose beautiful surroundings alone can occupy two or three days of exploring.

All the main towns and most of the sights in the area are accessible by train or bus from Lisbon. Consequently, you can see the entire region in a series of day trips from the capital. This is really the best way to see the seaside resorts of the Estoril Coast, west of Lisbon, and the beaches of the Costa da Caparica, south across the Tagus: parking space and accommodations in both destinations are extremely limited in summer. The palace at Queluz also makes a good day trip: it's only 20 minutes northwest of Lisbon by train, and many visitors take this in on the way to or from Sintra. Using Lisbon as your base, a realistic time frame for visiting the major sights is four days: one each for the Estoril Coast, Queluz and Sintra, Caparica, and Setúbal.

Numbers in the text correspond to numbers in the margin and on the Estoril Coast, Sintra, and Queluz map and the Setúbal Peninsula map.

IF YOU HAVE 2 DAYS

Start in Lisbon and drive to **Estoril** ①, where you can soak up the atmosphere in the gardens and on the seafront promenade. From here, it's only a short distance to 🔟 **Cascais** ②, where you can have a leisurely alfresco lunch. For the rest of the day, you can explore the lovely little cove beaches, and the **Boca do Inferno** ③ is just a short walk way. The next day, it's less than an hour's ride north to **Sintra** ⑤, where before lunch you'll have time to see the Sintra Palace and perhaps climb to the **Castelo dos Mouros** ⑦. After lunch, head back to Lisbon, stopping in **Queluz** ⑪ to see the Palácio Nacional de Queluz on the way. For dinner, you might cross the Tagus from Lisbon to **Cacilhas** ⑫ for seafood.

You could, of course, reverse this itinerary and spend the night in Sintra instead of Cascais. There are frequent trains to Estoril and Cascais, buses from there to Sintra, and train service back to Lisbon, via Queluz.

IF YOU HAVE 4 DAYS

From Lisbon, head for **Queluz** ⑪ and its Palácio Nacional and have lunch in the old kitchen-restaurant. In the afternoon, make the short drive to 🔟 **Sintra** ⑤, where you can spend the rest of the day seeing the sights in and around the town. Consider having dinner in the adjacent village of **São Pedro de Sintra** ⑥, where there are several recommended restaurants. The next day, head first to the extraordinary **Palácio Nacional de Pena** ⑧ before driving west to the headland of **Cabo da Roca** ⑩—the westernmost point of mainland Europe—and then wind south to the wonderful beach at **Guincho** ④ in time for a late lunch. In the afternoon, stick to the coastal road as it heads east toward 🔟 **Cascais** ②, where you can spend the night.

On the third day, drive back into Lisbon via **Estoril** ① and cross the Tagus River by the mighty Ponte 25 de Abril, and then detour for lunch at either **Cacilhas** ⑫ or **Costa da Caparica** ⑬. It's then only an hour's drive to the region's two attractive pousadas, one at 🔟 **Palmela** ⑭, the other 10 km (6 mi) down the road in 🔟 **Setúbal** ⑮. At either, you're perfectly poised to continue farther east or south into Portugal; if you're heading back to Lisbon, however, drive through the **Serra da Arrábida** ⑱ on your fourth morning and make time for lunch at an esplanade restaurant in **Sesimbra** ⑲. From there, you can return to Lisbon in around 90 minutes.

The Estoril Coast, Sintra, and Queluz

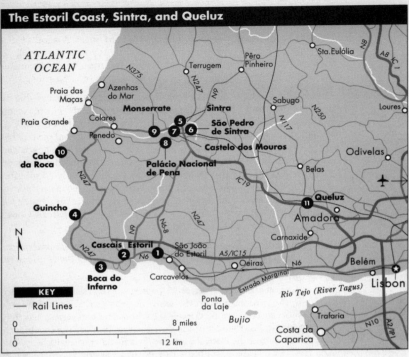

Seven days exploring this region will allow the luxury of two nights in 🏨 **Sintra** ⑤, providing time to see all the surrounding sights with ease. On the third day, you can then drive straight to **Cabo da Roca** ⑩ and then south to **Guincho** ④, if you fancy a half day at the beach before following the coast around to 🏨 **Cascais** ②. Two nights spent here allow you really want to get to know the town and give sufficient time for a walk or train ride along the coast to **Estoril** ① and back.

When it's time to leave, drive back into Lisbon and aim for lunch at either **Cacilhas** ⑫ or **Costa da Caparica** ⑬, across the Tagus River. Your night might be spent at one of two pousadas, in 🏨 **Palmela** ⑭ or 🏨 **Setúbal** ⑮, leaving you with a stop for lunch in the region around **Vila Nogueira de Azeitão** ⑰ and a short, pleasant drive through the **Serra da Arrábida** ⑱ to occupy your final full day. If you spend the night in the attractive fishing port and resort town of 🏨 **Sesimbra** ⑲, you'll have time to visit the region's second windswept cape, **Cabo Espichel** ⑳, before driving back to Lisbon.

When to Tour Lisbon's Environs

If you're in the area in summer, particularly July and August, you *must* reserve a hotel room in advance. If you can, travel to the coastal areas in spring or early fall: the crowds are much thinner, and it could be warm enough for a brisk swim in April and October.

That said, most of the region's festivals are held during summer, and you may want to be there during one of them. In São Pedro de Sintra, the annual *Festa de São Pedro* (St. Peter's Day) celebration is on June 29; there are summer music and arts festivals in Sintra, Cascais, and Queluz; September in Palmela sees the *Festa das Vindimas* (Grape Harvest Festival); while the Feira de Santiago takes place in Setúbal at the end of July. Year-round markets include the famous country fair

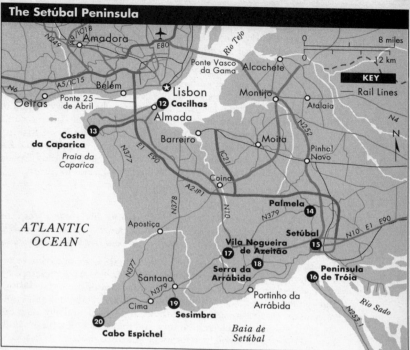

The Setúbal Peninsula

in São Pedro de Sintra (second and fourth Sunday of every month) and a similar affair in Vila Nogueira de Azeitão (first Sunday of every month). Finally, note that most museums and palaces in the region close for one day a week. If it's vital that you see a particular sight, always check the opening hours before you go.

THE ESTORIL COAST

The Estoril Coast extends for 32 km (20 mi) west of Lisbon, taking in the major towns of Estoril and Cascais plus some smaller settlements that are part suburb, part beach town. It's a favored residential area, thanks to its proximity to the capital, and the charms of the rocky coastline and the good climate—the coast has milder winters than Lisbon—make it one of the country's most popular resort areas. Some, rather fancifully, know it as the Portuguese Riviera, and certainly the casino at Estoril and the rich villas and hotels along the coast lend the region a cachet, bolstered by the patronage over the years of wealthy expatriates and even exiled royalty.

Rich visitors aside, the Estoril Coast is where much of Lisbon comes to the beach, and you can count on sharing a visit in summer with great throngs of day-trippers and tourists. Not only are the towns and beaches crowded, but the ocean—sparkling from a distance—suffers from a long-standing pollution problem. The quality of the water varies greatly from beach to beach, and although ongoing works are slowly rectifying the situation, you are strongly advised to avoid swimming in an area unless the water has been declared safe. Look for a blue Council of Europe flag, which signals clean water and beach; consult local tourist offices (☞ Visitor Information *in* Lisbon's Environs A to Z, *below*) if you're unsure.

None of this should suggest that you avoid the Estoril Coast. Many of the beaches are fine, the waterfront towns are attractive, and the train ride along the shore offers striking views. Sailboarding and surfing are popular sports, and many local beaches have rental outfits.

Unless you intend to tour the wider region, taking the train from Lisbon is a better option than driving (☞ Getting Around *in* Lisbon's Environs A to Z, *below*). This section has been arranged accordingly, with coverage of Estoril first, followed by Cascais, which marks the end of the train line; from there, it's a short walk to the Boca do Inferno and a brief bus ride to the magnificent beach at Guincho. If you choose to drive, leave Lisbon via the Estrada Marginal (follow signs for Cascais and Estoril) and take the scenic coastal route (the N6), or the faster Auto-Estrada da Oeste Highway (A5/IC15), which runs from Lisbon to Estoril.

Estoril

❶ *26 km (16 mi) west of Lisbon. (The train runs directly to Estoril, or get off at the previous station, São João do Estoril, and walk 2 km [1¼ mi] along the seafront promenade path, a fine route with excellent views.)*

Estoril perhaps makes too much of its reputation as an exclusive resort. In the 19th century, its gardens and mansions were preferred by the European aristocracy, who wintered here in comfort and seclusion. But reminders of those days are now few: new residential and commercial developments stretch on either side of town, and although Estoril still has plush hotels, restaurants, and sports facilities, there's little beyond these to keep you here for long. The town presents its best face right in the center, where today's jet set descends on the casino, set at the top of the formal gardens of the **Parque do Estoril.** This overlooks the sea and is lined on both sides by several pleasant cafés; down on the beachfront **Tamariz esplanade,** there are more alfresco restaurants, some summer nightlife, and an open-air seawater swimming pool. The best and longest local beach is at **Monte Estoril,** which adjoins Estoril's beach; here you'll find rest rooms and beach chairs for rent, as well as plenty of shops and snack bars.

Those interested in Portugal's mid-20th-century history might check out the **Museu Exílio,** a collection of memorabilia, mostly black-and-white photos with captions in Portuguese, focusing on Estoril's community of exiles, most notably King Carol of Romania. The collection is kept above the post office. ⌧ *Av. Aida,* ☎ *21/468–4493.* ⌧ *Free.* ⊙ *Weekdays 9:30–6:30, Sat. 10–12:30.*

The **Estoril Casino** opened in the center of town in 1968, and besides the gambling salons, there are a nightclub, several bars, and a couple of restaurants. Tour groups often make an evening of it, with dinner and a floor show (☞ Guided Tours *in* Lisbon's Environs A to Z, *below*), but it's a pricey night out. But most visitors are content to feed one of the 1,000 slot machines in the main complex and then check out the other entertainment options: art exhibitions, a movie theater, free nightly cabaret performances and, every summer, musical concerts and ballets. Note that to enter the gaming rooms (but not to use the slots), you must pay 500$00 and show your passport to prove that you're 21. ⌧ *Parque do Estoril,* ☎ *21/466–7700.* ⌧ *Gaming rooms 500$00, dinner with show from 8,500$00.* ⊙ *Casino, bars, and restaurants 3 PM–3 AM, floor show nightly at 11. Reservations essential for restaurant and show. AE, DC, MC, V.*

Dining and Lodging

$$$–$$$$ ✕ **A Choupana.** Just east of town, this restaurant has views of Cascais Bay from its picture windows. It's a reliable establishment, where you

can ask the English-speaking staff about the daily specials. Fresh seafood is the mainstay—try the *cataplana,* a tangy, typically Portuguese dish of clams and chicken. Live music usually accompanies dinner, and in summer there's dancing nightly until 2. ⊠ *Estrada Marginal, São João do Estoril,* ☎ *21/468–3099. AE, DC, MC, V.*

$$$–$$$$ ✕ **The English Bar.** Well it's not English, and it's not a bar. But get beyond the initial confusion, and you're in for a good meal. Surroundings are baronial, with plenty of burnished wood, heavy drapes, and oak beams. The menu is an international hybrid: choose from game in season, fresh fish, chicken curry, even Indonesian *saté* (skewered, charcoal-broiled meats served with a peanut sauce); shellfish soup makes a fine starter. It's near Monte Estoril's Estoril Eden hotel (☞ *below*) and the pedestrian underpass to the beach. ⊠ *Av. Sabóia, off Av. Marginal,* ☎ *21/468–0413. AE, DC, MC, V. Closed Sun.*

$$$–$$$$ ✕⊞ **Hotel Palácio.** During World War II, exiled European courts
★ waited out the war in this luxurious 1930s hotel facing the town's central park. Rooms are splendidly appointed, furnished in Regency style, and those on the first, third, and fifth floors have balconies. The public areas make a grand statement, too, adorned with monumental columns, tile floors, and chandeliers. A comfortable bar and lounge have views over the outdoor pool to the park beyond. A fine buffet breakfast is included, and there's no more-elegant spot in town to dine than the Four Seasons Grill ($$–$$$$), which serves buffets around the garden pool in summer and adjusts its menus seasonally (reservations essential; jacket and tie). Golfers who stay here can tee up on the 18-hole championship course at the Clube de Golfe do Estoril. ⊠ *Rua do Parque, Parque do Estoril, 2769-504,* ☎ *21/468–0400,* 𝖥𝖠𝖷 *21/ 468–4867. 132 rooms, 30 suites. Restaurant, 2 bars, room service, pool, massage, sauna, golf privileges, 4 tennis courts, exercise room, horseback riding, baby-sitting. AE, DC, MC, V.*

$$–$$$ ⊞ **Estoril Eden.** Looking for a good base with the kids? The comfortable studios and suites in this modern apartment hotel are reasonably sized and equipped with satellite TV, fold-out beds, and a basic kitchenette. Ask for one of the front rooms, which have superb views of the coast. Children might enjoy the free summer-entertainment program and the good sports and leisure facilities; parents can keep an eye on things from the poolside café. The ocean is just a few minutes' walk away via an underpass that starts behind the Monte Estoril train station. ⊠ *Av. Sabóia, 2769-502,* ☎ *21/467–0573,* 𝖥𝖠𝖷 *21/467–0848. www.mausturismo.pt/phguide/hotels/estede.htm 162 units. Restaurant, bar, café, kitchenettes, indoor pool, pool, massage, sauna, golf privileges, exercise room, nightclub, baby-sitting, children's programs. AE, DC, MC, V.*

$$ ⊞ **Hotel Lido.** Set on a quiet street overlooking the lush green hillside above Estoril, the Lido is a modest hotel whose amenities compensate for any lack of real style. The simple rooms all look the same—strong colors, clean lines, identical furniture—but they have balconies with fine views and there's a pool, a garden, and a lounge bar. Off-season discounts are substantial; prices can fall well into the $ category in winter. The hotel is signposted for drivers from the casino; otherwise, it's a steep 15-minute walk from the center of Estoril. ⊠ *Rua do Alentejo 12, 2765-188,* ☎ *21/468–4098,* 𝖥𝖠𝖷 *21/468–3665. 56 rooms, 6 suites. Restaurant, bar, pool, billiards, baby-sitting. AE, DC, MC, V.*

Nightlife

Other than **Estoril Casino** (☞ *above*), nightlife in Estoril is based around several well-known bars and clubs, most of which are open 10 PM–3 AM. The young and the restless head out to **Forte Velho** (⊠ Av. Marginal, São João do Estoril, ☎ 21/468–1337), a medieval fort on the edge of town that has been converted into a lively dance club. **Frolic** (✉ Parque do Estoril, ☎ 21/468–1219), in front of the casino next to the café-restaurant of the same name, is a mainstream disco that attracts a sophisticated clientele. In summer, try the **Absurdo Bar** (✉ Tamariz esplanade, ☎ 21/467–5418) for dancing to Brazilian music.

Outdoor Activities and Sports

AUTO RACING

The **Autódromo do Estoril** (Estoril Autodrome), on the Estoril–Sintra road, 5 km (3 mi) north of Estoril, hosts Formula 1 car racing on its newly rebuilt track, and can accommodate 40,000 spectators. Ask for details at the Estoril tourist office (☞ Visitor Information *in* Lisbon's Environs A to Z, *below*).

GOLF

Clube de Golfe do Estoril (✉ Av. da República, ☎ 21/468–0176) is the oldest in the region and has an immaculate 18-hole championship course, with special rates and privileges for guests staying at the Hotel Palácio. On the Estoril–Sintra road, 7 km (4 mi) north of Estoril, the **Estoril Sol** (✉ Linhó, ☎ 21/923–2461) has a scenic nine-hole course on the fringes of the Serra de Sintra. **Penha Longa** (✉ Lagoa Azul, ☎ 21/924–9022), 9 km (5 mi) north of Estoril, features superb views, an 18-hole course, golf clinics, and putting greens.

TENNIS

Many of the larger hotels in Estoril have tennis courts, or contact the **Clube de Tenis do Estoril** (✉ Av. Amaral, ☎ 21/468–1675 or 21/466–2770).

Shopping

Each July and August Estoril holds the **Feira do Artesanato,** an open-air crafts fair, near the casino. Every evening from 5 until midnight stalls sell local arts and crafts and Portuguese foods. The town of **Carcavelos,** 7 km (4 mi) southeast of Estoril, has a busy Thursday market that sells food, clothes, and crafts; you can reach it by local train.

Cascais

★ ❷   *3 km (2 mi) west of Estoril; the train runs directly here, or you can walk along the seafront promenade.*

Once a mere fishing village, the town of Cascais—with three small, sandy bays—is now a heavily developed resort packed with shops, restaurants, and hotels. Despite the masses of people, Cascais (unlike neighboring Estoril) has retained some of its small-town character—most visible around the harbor, with its fishing boats and yachts, and in the old streets and squares off Largo 5 de Outubro, behind the Hotel Baia, where you'll find lace shops, cafés, and restaurants. The beaches are very attractive, too, although bear in mind the pollution problems here: unless signs indicate otherwise, stay out of the sea.

The **Igreja de Nossa Senhora da Assunção** (Church of Our Lady of the Assumption), with its plain white facade, is the most graceful church in Cascais. Inside is an elegant golden altar and fine paintings by 17th-century Portuguese artist Josefa de Óbidos—a rare instance of a female artist of that day gaining an international reputation. ✉ *Largo da Assunção,* ☎ *no phone.* 💰 *Free.* ⏲ *Daily 9–1 and 5–8.*

For an understanding of the rapid development in Cascais since the last century, visit the modern single-story building that houses the **Museu do Mar** (Museum of the Sea). Here, the town's former role as a fishing village is traced through model boats and fishing gear, period clothing, analysis of local fish, and some splendid old photographs and paintings. The museum is opposite the Pavilhão de Cascais (Cascais Pavilion), just a short walk west of the center. ⊠ *Av. da República,* ☎ *21/486–1377.* ⊠ *250$00, free Sun.* ⊙ *Tues.–Sun. 10–5.*

The most relaxing spot in Cascais, apart from the beach, is the municipal **Parque do Marechal Carmona,** open daily 9–6, where there's a shallow lake, a café, a small zoo, and tables and chairs set out under the trees for picnickers.

One of Cascais's elegant 19th-century town houses now serves as the **Museu Conde de Castro Guimarães,** a charming museum that displays 18th- and 19th-century paintings, ceramics, furniture, and some archaeological artifacts excavated nearby. It's set in the grounds of the Parque do Marechal Carmona. ⊠ *Estrada da Boca do Inferno,* ☎ *no phone.* ⊠ *250$00, free Sun.* ⊙ *Tues.–Sun. 11–12:30 and 2–5.*

Dining and Lodging

$$–$$$$ ✕ **Beira Mar.** One of several well-established and unpretentious restaurants behind the fish market, the Beira Mar has a comfortable, tiled interior. An impressive display of the day's catch shows you the best of the seafood, although as ever, you can end up paying top-dollar for dinner if you're not careful since it's all sold by weight. Make sure you know the price first, or stick to the menu—rice with clams or steaks cut from swordfish or tuna are always worth trying. ⊠ *Rua das Flores 6,* ☎ *21/483–0152. AE, DC, MC, V. Closed Tues.*

$$–$$$$ ✕ **O Pescador.** Fresh seafood fills the menu at this folksy restaurant, where a cluttered ceiling and maritime-related artifacts distract the eye. Sole is a specialty, and this is also a good place to try *bacalhau* (dried salt cod); it's often baked here, either with cream or with port wine and onions. ⊠ *Rua das Flores 10,* ☎ *21/483–2054. AE, DC, MC.*

$–$$$ ✕ **Dom Manolo.** In this Spanish-owned grill-restaurant, the waiters charge back and forth delivering excellent spit-roasted chicken to a largely local clientele. Accompany it with fries or salad, or both, and if you're still hungry, have a slab of the homemade crème caramel. The surroundings aren't sophisticated: there are paper tablecloths, holiday posters tacked to the walls, and billowing smoke as the cooks battle with the huge spit-roast machinery. But for inexpensive, down-to-earth food and company, this spot is hard to beat. ⊠ *Av. Marginal 13,* ☎ *21/483–1126. No credit cards.*

$–$$$ ✕ **Pizza Italia.** There's not much choice when it comes to tracking down a non-Portuguese restaurant in Cascais, so all the more praise to Pizza Italia. In its indoor dining rooms or on its sunny terrace you can choose from a range of authentic pizzas and pastas. ⊠ *Rua do Poço Novo 1,* ☎ *21/483–0151. MC, V. Closed Wed. No lunch.*

$$$–$$$$ ✕⌂ **Hotel Albatroz.** On a rocky outcrop above the crashing waves, this
★ gorgeous old house—once the summer residence of the dukes of Loulé—is the most luxurious of Cascais's hotels. Although expanded and modernized, its genteel character has been retained, particularly in the fabric-lined corridors and the cozy terrace bar. The traditionally decorated guest rooms combine elegance (old prints and floral drapes) with comfort (good beds and spacious bathrooms); it's worth paying extra for a sea view. The small, oval pool and the terrace overlook the ocean. A fine buffet breakfast is served in the Albatroz restaurant ($$$–$$$$), where fish dishes—grilled sole or baked cod stuffed with ham—are the specialty (reservations essential; jacket and tie). ⊠ *Rua Frederico Arouca 100, 2750,* ☎ *21/484–7380,* ℻ *21/484–4827. 37 rooms, 3 suites. Restaurant, bar, room service, saltwater pool, golf privileges, shops, baby-sitting. AE, DC, MC, V.*

$$$–$$$$ ⌂ **Estalagem Villa Cascais.** If Portugal's 18th-century writer Maria Amália de Carvalho could return today to her Cascais Bay harborfront

house, she would surely check in and open her laptop in the upmarket inn it has become. Each light-filled room is individually furnished—some with balconies or fireplaces—and all have sea views. In the bathroom, the hair dryer, music via a speaker, the phone, and the view of the greatly changed marina might surprise Doña Maria, but the huge tubs would not. The included buffet breakfast is served in a smaller room adjoining the cool, white restaurant, where meals are served either indoors or on a shaded, sea-view balcony (reservations advised). ⊠ *Rua Fernandes Tomas 1, 2750-342,* ☎ *21/486–3410,* FAX *21/484–4680. 10 rooms. Restaurant. AE, DC, MC, V.*

$$$ ⊡ **Hotel Baia.** This modern stone hotel fronted with white balconies overlooks fishing boats on the quayside and Cascais Bay. Your choice of rooms is straightforward: the 66 front rooms have balconies and sea views but are plain in the extreme; the rest face the town at the back but have been decorated with a bit more imagination. There's a private esplanade along the ground floor, with a lounge, restaurant, grill, café, and bar. Off-season discounts can cut room rates by as much as 40%. ⊠ *Av. Marginal, 2750-509,* ☎ *21/483–1033,* FAX *21/483–1095. 114 rooms. Restaurant, bar, café, grill, pool. AE, DC, MC, V.*

$–$$ ⊡ **Casa da Pérgola.** Set back from the road amid gardens, this intimate town house has been in the hands of the same family for more than a century. The decor throughout is refined and set solidly in the 19th century. A lovely painted-and-tiled facade sets a tone that's continued inside by the heavy drapes, impressive stairway, period furniture, and art; in the dining room, you eat breakfast surrounded by cabinets of old porcelain. You'll need to book well in advance to secure a room. ⊠ *Av. de Valbom 13, 2750-508,* ☎ *21/484–0040,* FAX *21/483–4791. 6 rooms. Dining room. No credit cards. Closed Nov.–Feb.*

Nightlife and the Arts

Cascais has plenty of bars and discos on and around the central pedestrian Rua Frederico Arouca and in Largo Luís de Camões. The trendy **Belbuerguer** (⊠ Travessa Visconde da Luz 20, ☎ 21/483–2312) serves burgers and fries to a rock-music accompaniment; it's busiest on Saturday night. **Chequers** (⊠ Largo Luís de Camões 7, ☎ 21/483–0926) booms out rock music into the square nightly in summer. You can hear fado, the mournful Portuguese folk music, at **Forte D. Rodrigo** (⊠ Rua de Birre 961, ☎ 21/487–1373). For drinks, try the English-style **John Bull** (⊠ Praça Costa Pinto 32, ☎ 21/483–3319) pub, whose customers spill out into the square on hot summer nights.

Outdoor Activities and Sports

FISHING
Contact the **Clube Naval de Cascais** (⊠ Esplanada Príncipe Luís Filipe, in front of Hotel Baia, ☎ 21/483–0125), which organizes deep-sea fishing outings.

GOLF
Quinta da Marinha (⊠ 4 km [2½ mi] west of Cascais, ☎ 21/468–9881) has an 18-hole course designed by Robert Trent Jones; there are also a pool and tennis courts within the resort complex.

HORSEBACK RIDING
A particularly good equestrian center at **Quinta da Marinha** (⊠ 4 km [2½ mi] west of Cascais, ☎ 21/486–9881 or 21/486–9084) offers year-round riding.

SURFING
You can rent surfing equipment from **Equinócio** (⊠ Varandas de Cascais 3, ☎ 21/483–5354).

Shopping

Cascais is the best shopping area on the Estoril Coast, with pedestrian streets lined with shops and small market stalls. For smart fashions, gifts, and handmade jewelry, browse around **Rua Frederico Arouca**. Near the church, in **Ceramicarte** (⊠ Largo da Assunção 3–4), Fatima and Luís Soares present their carefully executed, modern ceramic designs alongside more traditional jugs and plates, as well as a small selection of tapestries and artwork.

Markets are held north of town at Rua Mercado (⊠ Off Av. 25 de Abril) on Wednesday and Saturday; you'll find fruit, vegetables, cheese, bread, and flowers. On the first and third Sunday of each month, a large market is held at the **Praça de Touros** (bullring) on Avenida Pedro Álvares, west of the center.

Boca do Inferno

❸ *2 km (1¼ mi) west of Cascais.*

The most visited attraction in the area around Cascais is the forbiddingly named Mouth of Hell, one of several natural grottoes in the rugged local coastline. It's best to visit at high tide or in stormy weather, when the sea pounds the shoreline here, thrusting waves high onto the surrounding cliffs. You can walk along the fenced paths to the viewing platforms above the grotto and peer down into the abyss, and a path leads down to secluded spots on the rocks below, where fishermen cast their lines. Afterward, visit the daily roadside market of handicrafts, lace, and leather goods or one of the nearby cafés.

NEED A BREAK?   Walking along the coastal road west of Cascais, stop at the café-terrace **Esplanada Santa Marta** (⊠ Estrada da Boca do Inferno, ☏ 21/483–7779), which overlooks the tiny Santa Marta Beach and the adjacent lighthouse. This is a perfect spot for a cool drink on the way to or from the Boca do Inferno, a 20-minute walk beyond.

Guincho

❹ *9 km (5½ mi) north of Boca do Inferno.*

There's a superb wide beach at Guincho, where Atlantic waves pound onto the sand even on the calmest of days, providing perfect conditions for windsurfing (the annual world championships are often held here during the summer). The undertow here is notorious; even the best swimmers should take heed. Whether you surf or not, savor some fresh fish served at one of the restaurant terraces overlooking the beach. And if you don't want to drive—perhaps you would rather wash the meal down with wine and a glass of port?—it's a simple matter to come by bus, which leaves from outside Cascais's train station every two hours (7:45 AM–5:45 PM, journey time 25 minutes).

Dining and Lodging

$$–$$$ ✕🏠 **Estalagem do Forte Muchaxo.** The lovely location of this restaurant and inn, nestled in the rocks over Guincho beach, may draw you here from Cascais (10 km [6 mi] away). Although most of the comfortable rooms have splendid ocean views, those at the back overlook the nearby hills; the beach itself is just steps away. Despite the modern additions, the theme inside the main part of the building is thoroughly rustic, with stone floors, wood paneling, and maritime bric-a-brac hinting at the hotel's origins as a simple fishermen's café. Today, the inn contains one of the area's oldest and best-known restaurants ($$–$$$$), where fresh fish specialties (including *caldeirada,* Portuguese fish stew) are the order of the day. Meals are a little overpriced, and the service isn't always top-notch, but what you're ultimately paying for is the unrivaled view of the beach through picture windows. ⊠ *Praia do Guincho, 2750-642,* ☎ *21/487–0221,* 𝖥𝖠𝖷 *21/487–0444. 60 rooms. Restaurant, bar, pool. AE, DC, MC, V.*

SINTRA, SINTRA ENVIRONS, AND QUELUZ

Don't miss Sintra, long considered one of the most beautiful places in Portugal. The district's lush woods and valleys on the northern slopes of the Serra de Sintra (Sintra Mountains) have been inhabited since prehistoric times, although the Moors were the first to build a castle on their peaks. Later Sintra became the summer residence of Portuguese kings and aristocrats, and its late medieval palace is the greatest expression of royal wealth and power of the time. In the 18th and 19th centuries the area's charms were becoming widely known as English travelers, poets, and writers—including an enthusiastic Lord Byron—were drawn by the region's beauty. The poet Robert Southey described Sintra as "the most blessed spot on the whole inhabitable globe." Its historic importance has been recognized by UNESCO, which designated it as a World Heritage Site in 1995.

Visitors who lodge here tend to discover the town, then use it as a base for exploring the surrounding countryside. Consequently, the various local attractions listed in this section are arranged according to distance from Sintra, starting with the nearest attraction and ending at the coast. Driving is the easiest way to tour the area, but you could also take a guided tour (arranged through Sintra's tourist office) or see the sights by taxi. The nearest attractions are within walking distance or are accessible by bus or horse-and-carriage ride.

Sintra

★ ❺ *30 km (18 mi) northwest of Lisbon, 13 km (8 mi) north of Estoril.*

The palaces, gardens, wooded paths, and viewpoints of Sintra are enchanting, with horse-drawn carriages, country estates, and elegant old hotels enlivening its natural beauty. In front of Sintra Palace, tourists shop and sit at cafés while hawkers sell toys and souvenirs. But even at the height of summer, the region exudes its famous charm; tour buses are now largely banned from the main square; and with a little effort you can escape any crowds by taking one of several walks through the surrounding countryside. To explore Sintra, you might start at the tourist office (☞ Visitor Information *in* Lisbon's Environs A to Z, *below*) and—armed with local walking information—begin your discoveries.

★ The conical twin chimneys of the **Palácio Nacional de Sintra** (Sintra Palace), also called the Paço Real, are the town's most recognizable landmarks. There has probably been a palace here since Moorish times, although the current structure dates from the 14th century. The property was the summer residence of the House of Avis, Portugal's royal line, and it displays a fetching combination of Moorish, Gothic, and Manueline architectural styles. Some of its rooms are exceptional, and new bilingual descriptions in each of them let you enjoy the palace at your own pace. The **kitchen,** with its famous chimneys, is an intriguing stop, although despite its sheer size—imagine the life of a scullery maid here—it retains little of interest. Better is the **chapel,** decorated with some spectacular *mozarabic* (Moorish-influenced) *azulejos* (tiles) from the 15th and 16th centuries. The ceiling of the **Sala das Armas** is painted with the coats of arms of 72 noble families, and the grand **Sala dos Cisnes** has a remarkable ceiling of painted swans. One of the oldest rooms, the **Sala das Pegas,** figures in a well-known tale about Dom João I (1385–1433) and his dalliance with a lady-in-waiting. The king had the room painted with as many magpies as there were chattering court ladies, thus satirizing the gossips as loose-tongued birds. ⊠ *Largo Rainha D. Amelia,* ☎ *21/923–0085.* 🎫 *600$00, free Sun. 10–12:30.* 🕓 *Thurs.–Tues. 10–1 and 2–5; last admission 30 mins before closing. Closed Wed.*

NEED A BREAK? Well placed in Sintra's central square—with fine views of Sintra Palace—**Café Paris** (⊠ Largo Rainha D. Amelia, ☎ 21/923–2375) makes a pleasant, if pricey, stop for a drink or even a meal. Outside seating can be difficult to score; the lucky ones can soak up the bustling street scenes.

The tourist office's building also contains an art gallery, the **Galeria do Museu Municipal,** specializing in works associated with Sintra. ⊠ *Praça da República 23,* ☎ *21/924–4772.* 🎫 *Free.* 🕓 *Weekdays 9:30–noon and 2:30–7, weekends 2:30–7.*

The former fire station headquarters has been transformed into the **Museu do Brinquedo** (Toy Museum). Based on the collection of João Arbués Moreira, who began hoarding his toys when he was 14, the museum occupies more than four floors. Pick out your favorites from the thousands of toy planes, trains, and automobiles; dolls' furniture; rare lead soldiers; puppets; and a zillion-and-one other Christmas gifts and birthday presents—including some given to royal children. There's a café here, too. ⊠ *Rua Visconde de Monserrate,* ☎ *21/924–2171.* 🎫 *400$00.* 🕓 *Tues.–Sun. 10–6.*

If your stay is longer than a day or so, the **Museu Arqueológico de São Miguel di Odrinhas** is worth a visit. Its displays include locally found ancient and medieval objects. ⊠ *Av. Professor Dr. D. Fernando da Almeida,* ☎ *21/961–3574.* 🎫 *500$00.* 🕓 *Wed.–Sun. 10–1 and 2–6.*

Dining and Lodging

$–$$$$ ✕ **Tacho Real.** At the top of a steep flight of steps in the Old Town, this is where Sintra locals come for a celebratory night out. They can count on confident, traditional dishes cooked with panache, which means lamb, *leitão* (suckling pig), steaks, and game in season are all on the menu. ⊠ *Rua do Ferraria 4,* ☎ *21/923–5277. AE, MC, V. Closed Wed.*

$–$$$ ✕ **Alcobaça.** The friendly owner bustles around to make sure guests are well served in this restaurant up a side street in the town center. Try the excellent grilled chicken, arroz de marisco or tasty fresh clams *bulhão pato* (in garlic sauce)—served in simple surroundings that attract groups and Portuguese tourists in search of home cooking. ⊠ *Rua das Padarias 7–11,* ☎ *21/923–1651. MC, V.*

$ ✕ **Piriquita.** This classic old, tiled Sintra *pastelaria* (pastry shop) is *the* place for coffee and a pastry, particularly if you fancy trying one of the local queijadas. Sandwiches are available, too. It's a local joint and, at times, very crowded, so grab a table if you can, or stand and snack. ⊠ *Rua das Padarias 1,* ☎ *21/923–0626. No credit cards.*

$$$$ ✕🏨 **Hotel Palácio de Seteais.** This luxurious 18th-century palace sits
★ on pristine grounds 1 km (½ mi) or so from the center of Sintra. Built as a family home for the Dutch consul to Portugal, the palace is named "seven sighs" for the dismay people felt when the 1807–08 Treaty of Sintra yielded too much to their French wartime enemies. You'll enter under a superb arch that joins the palace's two wings: its public rooms are gloriously decorated with period furnishings, delicate frescoes, and

Arraiolos carpets; the guest rooms are individually styled, some with hand-painted wallpapers. If you're not planning an overnight stay, at least consider the splendid restaurant ($$$; reservations essential; jacket and tie), which serves a four-course set meal of impressive Continental dishes. In summer, coffee or afternoon tea on the terrace is a delight. ⊠ *Rua Barbosa do Bocage 8, 2710,* ☎ *21/923–3200,* ꜰꜱ *21/923–4277. 30 rooms, 1 suite. Restaurant, bar, pool, tennis court, horseback riding. AE, DC, MC, V.*

$$$–$$$$ ✕⊞ **Lawrence's Hotel.** Why did chefs from around Europe call, hoping to work at this 18th-century coaching inn when it reopened as a small luxury hotel in 1999 after a 50-year hiatus? Why did the U.S. Secretary of State soon arrive, as did the Netherlands' Queen Beatrix? You'll find clues in the harmonious convergence of four centuries: rooms are intimate but bathed in light from tall French windows; intriguing alcoves and handsome tiles team with the latest Internet hookups. Luxe touches like heated towel racks and crested linens abound, and personal service ranges from arranging jeep trips and golf packages to baby-sitting while you dine—very well. The menu at Lawrence's Restaurant ($$$–$$$$; reservations recommended) changes daily. The evening's specialties—served on Portugal's Vista Alegre porcelain under domed covers—might include fish soup *en croûte* (served in hollowed out bread) with coriander, roast duck, and a dessert flambéed at your table. Breakfast is included, whether you choose banana and bran or scrambled eggs, croissants, and a glass of Champagne. ⊠ *Rua Consiglieri Pedroso 38–40, 2710-550,* ☎ *21/910–5500,* ꜰꜱ *21/910–5505. portugalvirtual.pt/lawrences 11 rooms, 5 suites. Restaurant, bar, library. AE, DC, MC, V.*

$$$ ⊞ **Quinta da Capela.** This long, low 16th-century manor house, built by the dukes of Cadaval, presents superb, spacious rooms adorned with rugs and period furniture. The grounds also contain a garden, an old chapel, and a tree-shaded pool; the views stretch over to the Pena Palace (☞ *below*). Breakfast is served. The manor house is 3 km (2 mi) west of Sintra, off the road to Colares; a car is essential. ⊠ *Estrada de Monserrate, 2710,* ☎ *21/929–0170,* ꜰꜱ *21/929–3425. 8 rooms, 2 suites. Dining room, pool, sauna, exercise room. MC. Closed Nov.–Feb.*

$$$ ⊞ **Quinta das Sequóias.** On 40 acres of wooded grounds, just 1 km
★ (½ mi) beyond the Hotel Palácio de Seteais (☞ *above*), you'll find this lovely 19th-century manor house (look for the sign on the left side of the road), one of the only smoke-free properties in the area. It's an inspired conversion of an old property: one of the bathrooms has been cleverly built around monolithic boulders, and a tower contains a guest room as well as a flower-filled ground-floor sitting area; some rooms have views of the hills and coast. Antique touches proliferate: here an old parasol, there a period jewelry box. Buffet breakfasts (and light dinners if requested) are served in a large, galleried dining room that overlooks Pena Palace. The outdoor pool, Jacuzzi, and terrace form part of the landscaped gardens, and from the grounds you can walk to the gardens at Monserrate (☞ *below*). ⊠ *2 km [1 mi] from Sintra, past the Palácio de Seteais (Box 4), 2710-801,* ☎ ꜰꜱ *21/923–0342. 6 rooms. Bar, dining room, pool, hot tub, billiards. AE, DC, MC, V.*

$$$ ⊞ **Tivoli Sintra.** Right in the center of town and opposite the palace, the Tivoli makes the most of its location. In each room, balconies offer superb views of the local valley and distant ocean. The decor is a little dark, although renovations have brightened up the tiling in the bathrooms; furniture throughout is reproduction antique with a country feel. Do whatever it takes to score one of the four superior rooms, where enormous balconies provide even more tremendous views. Given the hotel's marvelous location, room rates are reasonable, especially with

15% winter reductions. ⊠ *Praça da República, 2710,* ☎ *21/923–3505,* FAX *21/923–1572. 75 rooms. Restaurant, bar. AE, DC, MC, V.*

$$
★ 🏠 **Casa Miradouro.** You can count yourself lucky if you've managed to book a room at this candy-striped 1890s house at the edge of Sintra (550 ft from the palace, downhill beyond the Tivoli Sintra). Its Swiss owner, the charming Mr. Kneubühl, has a keen eye for style and comfort and has done a superb job with all the decoration. Rooms have grand views, but equally attractive are the high-quality bathrooms, wrought-iron bedsteads, and polished tile floors. Breakfast is served in the downstairs dining room, which opens onto a summer terrace; although no other meals are served, you're only a (steep) five-minute walk from Sintra's restaurants. Rates drop by up to 25% off season. ⊠ *Rua Sotto Mayor 55, 2710,* ☎ *21/923–5900,* FAX *21/924–1836. 6 rooms. Breakfast room. No credit cards. Closed 6 wks mid-Jan.–Feb.*

Outdoor Activities and Sports

HORSEBACK RIDING

Sintra's pretty surroundings positively beg to be seen at a leisurely pace on horseback. Several local riding schools offer lessons; the local tourist office (☞ Visitor Information *in* Lisbon's Environs A to Z, *below*) can provide addresses and phone numbers.

Shopping

Sintra is a noted center for antiques, curios, arts, and crafts, although you'll need to choose carefully since the number of tourists keeps prices on the high side and also means a fair amount of poor-quality goods. Ceramics are plentiful, but too many are artless, mass-produced pieces; keep an eye out instead for special in-store displays and exhibitions of hand-painted ceramics, many of them reproductions of 15th-to 18th-century designs, signed by the artists.

For hand-embroidered linen tablecloths, bedspreads, towels, and sheets, visit **Violeta** (⊠ Rua das Padarias 19). Vintage port wines are on sale in **Camélia** (⊠ Praça da República 2), whose owners can recommend vintages; you can buy local cheese here, too. The small town of **Pêro Pinheiro** is known for its marble, with shops on both sides of the road selling stacks of cachepots, plaques, and other decorative garden objects. It's on route N9, 9 km (5½ mi) northeast of Sintra.

São Pedro de Sintra

6 *2 km (1¼ mi) southeast of Sintra.*

This little hillside village is most famous for its fair, the **Feira de São Pedro,** held every second and fourth Sunday of the month in the vast Praça Dom Fernando II (also called the Largo da Feira), where stalls are set up under the plane trees. Dating from the time of the Christian Reconquest, the fair is one of the best in the country, with livestock and agricultural displays, and local crafts, antiques, and food for sale. Even on nonfair days, it's worth coming to São Pedro to see the delightful village church in its own enclosed little square. There are also several good restaurants in São Pedro (☞ Dining, *below*), which makes it an attractive lunch stop.

The steep walk to São Pedro de Sintra along the main road from Sintra is not much fun, although you can cut out much of the distance by climbing up through the lush gardens of the **Parque Liberdade** (☉ June–Sept., daily 9–8; Oct.–May, daily 9–6), which starts just east of Sintra. Otherwise, local buses leave from outside the Sintra train station (weekdays every 30–40 minutes, reduced service on weekends), and you can catch one as it passes the tourist office; or take a taxi.

Dining

$$–$$$$ ✕ **Solar de São Pedro.** Right on the square, this distinctive restaurant has grandstand views of the bimonthly Sunday market—you'll have to book ahead for lunch if you want to eat then. There's a small menu of Portuguese specialties, but the São Pedro is best known for eclectic international food such as its fresh fish and grilled steaks. If it's full, or you don't fancy the menu, the market square has another three or four dining possibilities (mostly more moderately priced), so you won't go hungry. ✉ Praça Dom Fernando II 12, ☎ 21/923–1860. AE, DC, MC, V. Closed Wed.

$–$$$ ✕ **Cantinho de São Pedro.** Imaginative Portuguese cuisine with a French twist is served at this busy, rustic restaurant in a small courtyard of artisans' workshops, just off the main square. Locals consider the food well worth the wait for a table. Try the trout with almonds and cream or look for the fresh shellfish on the list of pratos do dia (dishes of the day). ✉ Praça Dom Fernando II 18, ☎ 21/923–0267. AE, DC, MC, V. Closed Mon.

Shopping

The **Lojas do Picadeiro** (✉ Praça Dom Fernando II) is a row of artisans' workshops that sell everything from wooden toys to rustic furniture and local art; a couple of taverns help restore flagging spirits.

Castelo dos Mouros

★ ❼ 3 km (2 mi) southwest of Sintra.

Only the battlemented ruins of the 8th-century Moorish Castle still stand today, but the extent of these gives a fine impression of the solid fortress that finally fell from Moorish hands when it was conquered by Dom Afonso Henriques in 1147. It's visible from various points in Sintra itself—the steps of Sintra Palace is a favored vantage point—but for a closer look follow the steep, partially cobbled road that leads up to the ruins, a walk that will take around 40 minutes. Buses now run this way, too, or rent one of the horse-drawn carriages outside Sintra Palace for a more romantic trip (☞ Guided Tours in Lisbon's Environs A to Z, below). Vast, panoramic views from the castle's serrated walls help explain why Moorish architects chose the site, and eagle-eyed visitors can also trace the remains of a mosque within the walls. ✉ Estrada da Pena, ☎ no phone. 🎟 Free. ☉ June–Sept., daily 10–7; Oct.–May, daily 10–5.

Palácio Nacional de Pena

★ ❽ 4 km (2½ mi) south of Sintra.

Of all the palaces in Sintra's environs, the most enjoyable is the drawbridged Pena Palace, a glorious conglomeration of turrets, ramparts, and domes washed in an array of pastel shades. It's a long but very pleasant walk up here from the center of Sintra (about 1½ hours), although there's bus service; you can also see the palace on one of the local tours or even come by horse and carriage. However, the walk from the Pena Palace back down to Sintra is delightful: you travel through shaded woods and have several opportunities to rest at viewpoints under the cork trees and take in the panoramic scenes.

Commissioned by Maria II's consort, Ferdinand of Saxe-Coburg, in 1840 and finished in 1885 when he was Fernando II, Pena Palace is a collection of clashing styles, from Arabian to Victorian. A splendid park surrounds the palace, filled with a lush variety of trees and flowers from every corner of the Portuguese empire. An electric bus takes you from the park gate up to the palace. Note an enormous statue on a nearby crag; it's Baron Eschwege (the building's German architect) cast as a medieval knight. The final kings of Portugal lived here, the last of whom—Dom Manuel II—went into exile in England in 1910 after a republican revolt. The pseudo-medieval structure, with its ramparts, towers, and great halls, is decorated in late Victorian and Edwardian furnishings—a rich, sometimes vulgar, and often bizarre collection of furniture, ornaments, and paintings that makes the guided tour very interesting. ⊠ *Estrada da Pena,* ☎ *21/923–0227.* 🖃 *600$00, free Sun. 10–2; electric bus ride 200$00.* ⊘ *Tues.–Sun. 10–12:30 and 2–4:30.*

At the **Cruz Alta,** a 16th-century stone cross, you are 1,782 ft above sea level, at the highest point of the Sintra Mountains. A direct path leads here from Pena Palace, starting beyond the statue of Baron Eschwege. It's an arduous climb, especially in the summer sun, but the views from this altitude are stupendous.

Monserrate

❾ *4 km (2½ mi) west of Sintra.*

The **gardens** here were laid out by Scottish gardeners in the mid-19th century at the behest of a wealthy Englishman, Sir Francis Cook. The grounds' centerpiece—the architecturally extravagant, Moorish-style, domed pavilion—is closed to visitors, but the gardens, with their streams, waterfalls, and Etruscan tombs, are worth a stop for their array of tree and plant species plus a vast collection of ferns. Labels, unfortunately, are few and far between. The gardens are a popular picnic spot; as you follow the paths that wind their way through the grounds, finding your own glade is easy. ⊠ *Estrada da Monserrate,* ☎ *21/923–1201.* 🖃 *200$00.* ⊘ *June–Sept., daily 9–7; Oct.–May, daily 10–5.*

En Route   Past Monserrate the road leads west for 3 km (2 mi) to the small village of **Colares,** associated with the locally produced red wine. The town, its winding streets alive with colorful flowers and trees, is also known for its parish church, which is adorned with ceramic tiles, and its main square, bordered by 18th-century houses. For terrific views of the sea and surrounding mountains, take the winding road that climbs up to the nearby village of **Penedo,** less than 2 km (1½ mi) away.

Cabo da Roca

★ **❿** *15 km (9 mi) west of Sintra, 20 km (12½ mi) northwest of Cascais.*

Between enchanting, culturally rich Sintra and the beach resort of Cascais you'll discover a totally different face of Lisbon's environs in this protected natural park. The windswept Cabo da Roca and its lighthouse mark continental Europe's westernmost point and are the main reason that most people make the journey. As with many such places, tourist stalls offer shell souvenirs and other gimmicks; an information desk and gift shop sells a certificate that verifies your visit. They do a brisk trade for these, but even without the certificate, the memory of this desolate granite cape will linger. The cliffs tumble to a frothing sea below, and on the cape a simple cross bears an inscription by Portuguese poet Luís de Camões. The cape can be reached from Cascais (30 minutes) or Sintra (40 minutes) by local bus, with regular departures from outside either town's train station.

OFF THE BEATEN PATH   **THE ATLANTIC COAST –** North of Cabo da Roca, the protected national parkland extends through the successive Atlantic-facing resort villages of **Praia Grande, Praia das Maças,** and **Azenhas do Mar.** The first two have good beaches, and all have public swimming pools and small restaurants. A fun way to reach Praia das Maças is on the 19th-century **tram** (the Elétrico de Sintra; ☎ 21/867–7681), which departs from Ribeira de Sintra, 4 km (2½ mi) north of town (hourly departures; 500$00; no service Monday). This passes through **Banzão** (just outside Colares) and offers particularly engaging views as it approaches the beach. The park's many contrasts are especially noteworthy as you ride or drive through the microclimate of **Serra de Sintra**.

Queluz

⓫ *15 km (9 mi) east of Sintra, 15 km (9 mi) northwest of Lisbon.*

Halfway between Lisbon and Sintra (just off route N249/IC19) is the town of Queluz, dominated entirely by its magnificent palace. The drive from Lisbon takes about 20 minutes, making this a good half-day option or a fine stop on the way to or from Sintra. It's also easy to take the train: get off at the Queluz-Belas stop, turn left outside the station, and follow the signs for the 1-km (½-mi) walk to the palace.

★ One of the most attractive of the royal residences near Lisbon, the **Palácio Nacional de Queluz** (Queluz National Palace) was inspired, in part, by the palace at Versailles. Intended as a royal summer residence, the salmon-pink rococo edifice was ordered by Dom Pedro III in 1747, and work began under the supervision of architect Mateus Vicente de Oliveira. Within five years it was fit to receive its first royal inhabitants, but it took another 40 years and the artistic endeavors of Frenchman Jean-Baptiste Robillon before Queluz acquired its famous romantic appearance and splendid gardens. Fronted by a huge cobbled square, the building is surrounded by Robillon's formal landscaping and waterways: the trees (brought from Amsterdam), statues (imported from London), ponds, canal, fountains, hedges—and the palace—all fit a carefully executed baroque plan that implies harmony and wholeness. After a 1934 fire, the palace was restored. It's used today for banquets, music festivals, official meetings attended by world leaders—and as accommodations for visiting heads of state.

You can tour the private apartments and elegant state rooms, including the frescoed Music Salon, the Hall of Ambassadors, and the mirrored Throne Room with its crystal chandeliers and gilt trim. Room furnishings and details—often of fine woods and precious metals from around the globe—are truly fit for a king. Walks in the formal gardens take you through orange groves and down avenues of oaks to azulejo-lined fountains and canals. ⊠ *Rte. IC19,* ☎ *21/435–0039.* 🎫 *Palace 600$00.* ⊙ *Wed.–Mon. 10–12:30 and 2–4:30.*

Dining and Lodging

$$$ ✕🏨 **Pousada de Dona Maria I.** This Queluz property is one of the jewels in the distinctive pousada network. The Royal Guard quarters beneath the clock tower opposite the palace have undergone stunning renovations: marble hallways lined with prints of old Portugal give way to high-ceilinged rooms furnished with exacting 18th-century reproductions. Decor and bathrooms are crisp and clean, and the building's original baroque theater has been retained as a meeting room. Only breakfast is served in the pousada itself, but across the road in the old palace kitchens, the **Restaurante de Cozinha Velha** ($$$–$$$$; reservations essential) takes full advantage of its heritage, with an imposing open fireplace and vast oak table. The cooking hits the mark, with Portuguese specialties occasionally tempered by a French touch. A spicy cataplana of salmon, monkfish, clams, and shrimp is just one superb main course. ⊠ *Rte. IC19, 2745-191,* ☎ *21/435–6158,* ℻ *21/435–6189. www.pousadas.pt 24 rooms, 2 suites. Restaurant, bar. AE, DC, MC, V.*

THE SETÚBAL PENINSULA

The Setúbal Peninsula, south of the Tagus River, is popular for its Costa da Caparica beaches, which provide the cleanest ocean swimming closest to Lisbon. Other attractions include the major port of Setúbal, some Roman ruins, and the scenic mountain range—the Serra da Arrábida—that separates the port from the peninsula's southernmost beaches and fishing villages.

If you're intent on eating seafood at Cacilhas, spending the day at a beach, or simply touring the town of Setúbal, traveling by public transportation from Lisbon is easiest. If you want to see most of the sights covered in this section, however—and particularly if you want to tour the southern coastal and mountainous region—you should rent a car. Apart from the ferry ride to Cacilhas, connections between the Setúbal Peninsula and Lisbon are via the capital's two bridges. Returning on the impressive Ponte 25 de Abril suspension bridge, you're guaranteed stupendous views of Lisbon. Avoid crossing during rush hour and on Friday and Sunday evenings, when the traffic can be horrendous. If you're heading directly for Setúbal, take the northern route across the Tagus River via the Vasco da Gama Bridge, from which a new highway cuts south. This less-direct route avoids the bottleneck over the Ponte 25 de Abril.

Cacilhas

⑫ *6 km (4 mi) south of Lisbon.*

Although a town in its own right, Cacilhas appears little more than a suburb of Lisbon, albeit one with the bonus of several reliable seafood restaurants along its main street, Rua do Ginjal. The town is immediately across the Tagus from the capital; at night, and especially on weekends, it's a popular destination for dining. Waiters armed with menus linger outside their doors, ready to pounce on passersby who can't decide where to eat; once inside, you're tempted with the best of the day's catch. The ferries run frequently from Terminal Fluvial, adjacent to Praça do Comércio, and from Cais do Sodré. One-way tickets cost 95$00, and the journey takes about 15 minutes.

The **Cristo Rei**—a huge, white statue of Christ, built in 1959—was modeled on the famous statue of Christ the Redeemer in Rio de Janeiro. The figure stands proudly above Cacilhas, its outstretched arms seemingly embracing the city of Lisbon across the water; indeed, it's something of a waterfront landmark and can be seen easily from almost any high point in Lisbon. Take the elevator to the platform beneath the statue's feet for remarkable panoramic views of the city, including the two bridges. If your schedule is tight, though, opt for the panorama from Lisbon's Torre Vasco da Gama (☞ Parque das Nações, *in* Chapter 1). Buses from Cacilhas dockside can take you directly to the Cristo Rei statue every 20–30 minutes, daily 8 AM–9 PM. Drivers can cross the Ponte 25 de Abril and follow the signs to the Cristo Rei. ☎ *No phone.* ☎ *250$00.* ☉ *Daily 9–7.*

Costa da Caparica

★ **⑬** *14 km (8½ mi) southwest of Lisbon; 8 km (5 mi) west of Cacilhas take the minor N377, a slower, more scenic route than the main road (IC20, off the A2/IP1).*

When Lisbon's inhabitants want to go to the beach, their preferred spot is the Costa da Caparica, a 20-km (12-mi) stretch of sand on the northwestern coast of the Setúbal Peninsula. The coastal strip centers on the lively resort of **Caparica** itself, at the northern end of the beach, less than an hour from the capital. Formerly a fishing village, it's now packed in summer with Portuguese tourists who come to enjoy the relatively unpolluted waters, eat grilled sardines, and stroll the seafront promenade. You may be able to avoid the crowds if you keep heading south toward the less accessible dunes and coves at the end of the peninsula. From June through September, a small narrow-gauge train departs from Caparica and travels along an 8-km (5-mi) coastal route, making stops along the way; a one-way ticket to the end of the line costs 500$00. Each beach is different: the areas nearest Caparica are family oriented, whereas the more southerly resorts tend to attract a younger crowd (there are some nudist beaches as well).

Palmela

⑭ *38 km (24 mi) southeast of Lisbon.*

The small town of Palmela lies in the center of a prosperous wine-growing area. Every September the community holds a good-natured **Festa das Vindimas** (Grape Harvest Festival) that draws the inhabitants of Palmela's whitewashed houses into the town's cobbled streets.

The village is dominated by the remains of a 12th-century castle that was captured from the Moors and enlarged by successive kings. In the 15th century the monastery and church of Sant'Iago were built within the castle walls. The buildings were damaged in the 1755 earthquake and lay abandoned for many years. After extensive restoration, a pousada was opened in the monastic buildings. From this height, on a clear day, you can see Lisbon.

Dining and Lodging

$$$ ×⌷ **Pousada de Palmela.** Set on a hill at the eastern end of the Arrábida range, this historic building was originally a medieval fortress and later a monastery. In 1979 it was converted into a luxury pousada, and the designers made inspired use of the flagstone corridors and old cloister (now a lounge). Most of the pleasant rooms have superb views of the valley and the sea; bathrooms are well equipped, and the beds comfortable. There's little trace of monastic asceticism: the monks' former refectory is now a dependable restaurant ($$–$$$) that serves traditional Portuguese food and a good range of wines. ⊠ *Follow signposts in and around town to pousada, 2950-997,* ☎ *21/235–1226,* 𝔽𝔸𝕏 *21/233–0440. www.pousadas.pt 28 rooms. Restaurant, bar. AE, DC, MC, V.*

Setúbal

⑮ *10 km (6 mi) south of Palmela, 50 km (31 mi) southeast of Lisbon.*

Sitting at the mouth of the Rio Sado, Setúbal is the country's third-largest port and one of its oldest cities. A significant industrial town in Roman times, it became one again during Portugal's Age of Discoveries and took off during the 19th century. Its center remains an attractive blend of medieval and modern, and the handsome Igreja de Jesus (☞ *below*) in itself makes the city worth a stop. Many travelers also use Setúbal as a spot to spend the night before driving on to the Algarve, since the Castelo de São Filipe has been converted into an exceptional pousada. Even if you decide to go on, you may want to dine here, or just pause to take in the views from the lofty castle.

Better still, spend half a day in the city, strolling attractive, cobbled pedestrian streets that open into pretty squares with cafés. Centrally located, the **tourist office** (☞ Visitor Information, *in* Lisbon's Environs A to Z, below) is built atop Roman ruins discovered during (and fortunately saved from) a construction project. Inside, you'll be standing above and peering down through the glass floor into a 5th-century fish-processing room. Near the port, an agreeable clutter of boats and warehouses is fronted by gardens, where you could stock up for a picnic at a huge, indoor fish-and-produce market (open Tuesday–Sunday 7–2).

★ The major sight in Setúbal is the 15th-century **Igreja de Jesus** (Church of Jesus), perhaps Portugal's earliest example of Manueline architecture, built with local marble and later tiled with simple but affecting 17th-century azulejos. The architect was Diogo de Boitaca, whose work here predates his contribution to Lisbon's Jerónimos Monastery. Six extraordinary twisted pillars support the vault; climb the narrow stairs to the balcony for a closer look. These details would soon become the very hallmark of Manueline style. Outside, you can still admire the original, although badly worn, main doorway and deplore the addition of a concrete expanse that makes the church square look like a roller-skating rink. ⊠ *Praça Miguel Bombarda,* ☎ *265/524772.* ⊠ *200$00 suggested donation.* ☉ *Tues.–Sun. 9:30–1 and 2–5:30.*

The original monastic buildings and Gothic cloister of the Church of Jesus now house the **Museu de Setúbal,** a museum that contains a fascinating collection of 15th- and 16th-century Portuguese paintings, several by the so-called Master of Setúbal. Other attractions include some lovely azulejos, local archaeological finds, and a coin collection. Renovations may close some sections. ⊠ *Rua Balneário Paula Borba,* ☎ *265/524772.* ⊠ *Free.* ☉ *Tues.–Sat. 9–noon and 2–5.*

Dining and Lodging

$$–$$$ ✕ **Rio Azul.** Locals frequent this seafood restaurant—hidden on a side street off Rua Luisa Todi, on the way to the castle, west of the harbor. It's a little tricky to find but is signposted from the main road. As you'd expect at a *marisqueira* (seafood restaurant), the dishes to go for are the fresh fish grilled to perfection and the arroz de marisco, a house specialty. ⊠ *Rua Placido Stichini 1,* ☎ *265/522828. AE, DC, MC, V. Closed Wed.*

$ ✕ **Alforge.** At this rather funky little bar-diner near the market (parallel to the main avenue), rough slabs of marble hang on the wall like old masters. At lunchtime, office workers hunker down to an excellent selection of daily grills—steaks to squid—accompanied by ceramic jugs of *vinho verde* (green wine). At night it's open until 2 AM for full meals or just drinks and sandwiches at the bar. ⊠ *Rua Regimento Infantaria 14,* ☎ *265/37675. No credit cards. Closed Sun.*

$$$ ✕🏠 **Pousada de São Filipe.** Atop a hill overlooking the town and the
★ Rio Sado, this 16th-century castle-cum-pousada is an exciting overnight stop. The approach to the main entrance from the parking lot is magnificent, up a tunneled flight of stairs and past an 18th-century chapel decorated with azulejos depicting the life of São Filipe. There are splendid views from the ramparts, and the traditionally decorated rooms are a delight, with carved headboards, tile floors, rugs, and white walls. The interior is also awash with azulejo tiling, especially in the welcoming bar; a canopied terrace in front of the reception area affords fine views of town, the bay, and the Tróia Peninsula. And the appealing restaurant ($$–$$$) has a kitchen strong on Portuguese cuisine, specializing in local cheeses and wines. ⊠ *Castelo de São Filipe, Estrada de São Filipe, 2900-300,* ☎ *265/523844,* ☏ *265/532538. 16 rooms. Restaurant, bar. AE, DC, MC, V.* 🐾

$–$$ 🏠 **Quinta do Patricio.** This manor house is close to the castle and provides a quaint alternative to the grand pousada. Furnishings throughout are homey, with open fireplaces and brightly colored rugs and paintings; from the large private garden you'll get some nice views of the town. There are also two separate apartments for rent on the grounds, one with a kitchen, the other romantically converted from a former windmill. Breakfast is served; other meals are on request, and reservations made well in advance are essential. ⊠ *Estrada de São Filipe, 2900,* ☎ FAX *265/33817. 3 rooms, 2 with bath; 2 apartments. Bar, pool. No credit cards.*

Peninsula de Tróia

⑯ *20 minutes from Setúbal by boat.*

Across the estuary from Setúbal is the Peninsula de Tróia, a long spit of land blessed with fine beaches and clean water, which area decision-makers are determined to retain. The peninsula has been much developed in recent years, and the large **Tróia Tourist Complex** here includes Robert Trent Jones Sr.'s **Tróia Golf Course** (one of Portugal's best), tennis courts, and other amenities. The area has managed to retain a little of its history, though: the peninsula is the site of the Roman town of Cetobriga, destroyed by a tidal wave in the 5th century. You can visit its scant ruins, opposite the marina. Car and passenger ferries to the peninsula run every 30–60 minutes (24 hours a day), from Setúbal's port.

Vila Nogueira de Azeitão

⑰ *14 km (9 mi) west of Setúbal.*

The region around the small town of Vila Nogueira de Azeitão, on the western side of the Serra da Arrábida (☞ *below*), retains a disproportionately large number of fine old manor houses and palaces. In earlier times, many of the country's foremost noblemen maintained country estates here, deep in the heart of a wealthy wine-making region. Wines made here by the José Maria da Fonseca Company are some of the most popular in the country (and one of Portugal's major exports); the best known is the dessert wine called Moscatel de Setúbal, available in any local bar or restaurant.

For a closer look at the wine business, seek out the headquarters of the **José Maria da Fonseca Company,** which stands on the main road through town. The intriguing tours allow you to see all stages of production, and take around 20–40 minutes depending on numbers in the group. ⊠ *Rua José Augusto Coelho 11,* ☎ *21/219–1500.* ☞ *Free.* ☉ *Daily tours throughout the year; call for times. Closed 2 wks at Christmas and New Year's.*

The town itself is little more than a straggle of buildings and shops along a dusty main road, although Vila Nogueira de Azeitão's agricultural traditions are trumpeted on the first Sunday of every month, when a **country market** is held in the center of town. Apart from the locally produced wine, you can buy queijo fresco—a good choice for a picnic lunch—as well as excellent fresh bread from one of the market's bakery stalls.

The grandest building in town is the 16th-century **Palácio de Tavora** (Tavora Palace), on the central Praça da República, once owned by the Duke of Aveiro. In the 18th century, the Marquês de Pombal accused the duke of collaborating in the assassination plot against the king, Dom José. Subsequently the duke was executed by the marquês, and the Tavora coat of arms was erased from the Sala das Armas in Sintra's National Palace. Unfortunately, the palace is not open for visits, but the badly worn Renaissance exterior is visible.

The 16th-century **Quinta das Torres** (☎ 21/208–0001), at Vila Fresca de Azeitão, 2 km (1¼ mi) east of Vila Nogueira de Azeitão, is now an inn with a restaurant. Set in beautiful gardens, the fine old building has been lovingly restored and has antique furniture and tapestries at every turn. The locally produced food served here is well prepared and moderately priced.

To view the best of the local estates, head to the **Quinta da Bacalhoa**, a late-16th-century L-shape mansion, whose pride and joy is its box-hedged garden, enlivened by striking azulejo-lined paths. You can't tour the villa, which is a private house, but the garden is open to the public and contains a pavilion with three pyramidal towers—the so-called Casa do Fresco—which houses the oldest azulejo panel in the country. Dating from 1565, it depicts the story of Susannah and the Elders. Scattered elsewhere are Moorish-influenced panels, fragrant groves of fruit trees, and enough restful spots to while away an afternoon. ⊠ *4 km (2½ mi) east of Vila Nogueira de Azeitão on N1,* ☎ *21/218–0011.* ☞ *250$00.* ☉ *Mon.–Sat. 1–5.*

Serra da Arrábida

⑱ *West of Setúbal, with access along the main N10 or minor N379; Portinho da Arrábida is 14 km (9 mi) southwest of Setúbal.*

Occupying the entire southern coast of the Setúbal Peninsula is the Parque Natural da Arrábida, dominated by the Serra da Arrábida, a 5,000-ft-high mountain range whose wild crags fall steeply to the sea. There's profuse plant life at these heights, particularly in the spring, when the rocks are carpeted with wildflowers. The park is distinguished by a rich geological heritage and numerous species of mammals, birds, butterflies, and other insects.

The main road through the park is the N10, which you can leave at Vila Nogueira de Azeitão to travel south toward the small fishing village of **Portinho da Arrábida,** at the foot of the mountain range. The village is a popular destination for Lisboetas, who appreciate the good local beaches. In summer, when the number of visitors makes parking nearly impossible, leave your car above the village and take the steep walk down to the water, where you'll find several modest seafood restaurants that overlook the port.

From Portinho da Arrábida, the lower, coastal road hugs the shore nearly all the way to Setúbal; the upper road leads to the ramshackle, white-walled **Convento de Arrábida,** an atmospheric 16th-century monastery built into the hills of the Serra da Arrábida. The views from here are glorious, but you'll have to contact the tourist office in Setúbal (☞ Visitor Information *in* Lisbon's Environs A to Z, *below*) in advance to arrange a visit to the monastery.

Sesimbra

⑲ *40 km (25 mi) south of Lisbon, 30 km (19 mi) southwest of Setúbal.*

Sesimbra, a lively fishing village surrounded by mountains and isolated bays and coves, owes its popularity to its proximity to the capital. And, despite high-rise apartments that now mar the approaches to the town, its few surviving narrow, central streets reflect its traditional past. Moreover, the long beach is lovely, if a little crowded in summer, and perfectly fine for swimming. The waterfront is guarded by a 17th-century fortress and overlooked by outdoor restaurants serving fresh-fish meals. A short walk along the coast to the west takes you to the main port, littered with nets, anchors, and coils of rope and packed with fishing boats—which unload their catches at entertaining auctions. More energetic visitors can make the 40-minute walk to the hilltop remains of a Moorish castle northwest of town. Several budget guest houses and seaview hotels cater mostly to Portuguese vacationers, but staying here overnight doesn't really add to the experience, especially since the Palmela and Setúbal pousadas are so close.

Dining

$–$$$ ✕ **Café Felipe.** Set in a line of sidewalk restaurants overlooking the waterfront, the Felipe is always busy with vacationers and locals digging into the terrific grilled fish—cooked outside on a charcoal grill—or arroz de marisco, the house specialty. There's no nicer spot for lunch, but you may have to wait in line for a table. It's worth it. ⊠ *Av. 25 de Abril,* ☏ *no phone. MC, V.*

Outdoor Activities and Sports

Sesimbra, a deep-sea fishing center, is renowned for the huge swordfish that are landed in the area. Ask around the port for local people who rent boats or consult the tourist office (☞ Visitor Information *in* Lisbon's Environs A to Z, *below*).

Cabo Espichel

⓴ *12 km (7 mi) west of Sesimbra.*

Espichel Cape, a salt-encrusted headland with a number of 18th-century pilgrimage houses and a forsaken church, is the southwestern point of the Setúbal Peninsula. It's a rugged and lonely place, where the cliffs rise hundreds of feet out of the stormy Atlantic. To the north, unsullied beaches extend as far as Caparica, with only local roads and footpaths connecting them. There are six buses a day here from Sesimbra.

LISBON'S ENVIRONS A TO Z

Arriving and Departing

Lisbon is the initial point of arrival for almost all the destinations covered here (☞ Lisbon A to Z *in* Chapter 1); from the city, it's easy to take public transportation or drive to all the surrounding towns. Driving south from Peniche-Óbidos, you can take the N8/IC1, rather than the main highway, if you prefer to see Sintra before Lisbon. If you're traveling north from the Algarve, then you reach the city of Setúbal and its peninsula before arriving in Lisbon.

Getting Around

By Boat

LisboFerries cross the river to Cacilhas (7 AM–9 PM) from Fluvial terminal, adjacent to Praça do Comércio. One-way tickets cost 95$00, and the journey takes about 15 minutes. For information on car ferries from Cais do Sodré, check with the Lisbon tourist office. From Setúbal there's 24-hour ferry service for cars (600$00) and foot passengers (140$00) across to the Tróia Peninsula; the journey takes about 20 minutes. Departures are every 30–60 minutes.

By Bus

Although the best way to reach Sintra and most of the towns on the Estoril Coast is by train from Lisbon, there are some useful bus connections between towns. Tickets are cheap (less than 600$00 for most journeys), and departures are generally every hour (less frequent on weekends); local tourist offices have current timetables.

At Cascais, the **bus terminal** (☎ 21/483–6357) outside the train station has regular summer service to Guincho (journey time 15 minutes) and Sintra (one hour). From the terminal outside the **Sintra** train station, there are half-hourly departures in summer to the resorts of Praia das Maças and Azenhas do Mar (30 minutes) in the west, and north to Mafra in Estremadura (one hour). There's also regular year-round service from Sintra to Cascais and Estoril (one hour). The most useful Sintra service, however, is the circular **Stagecoach** bus (daily, every hour 10–5; 500$00 ticket valid all day), which connects Sintra station, the town center, Castelo dos Mouros, and the Pena Palace. Timetables for all services in Sintra are available from the tourist office in the Sintra train station.

Buses to **Caparica** (45 minutes) depart from Praça de Espanha (Metro: Palhavã) in Lisbon, traveling over the Ponte 25 de Abril. Regular buses to Caparica also leave from the **quayside bus terminal** at **Cacilhas** (✉ Largo Aslfredo Diniz, ☎ no phone), the suburb immediately across the Tagus from Lisbon, which you can reach by ferry from the Fluvial terminal, adjacent to Praça do Comércio. Bus departures on both routes are as frequent as every 15 minutes in the summer, and services run from 7 AM until well after midnight, but can be very crowded. There's also a special beach bus (No. 75) that runs to Caparica every 15–30 minutes from the beginning of June to the beginning of September; pick it up in Lisbon at Campo Grande, Saldanha, or Rotunda metro stations, or outside the Amoreiras shopping center.

Express buses to **Setúbal** (45 minutes) leave every hour from Lisbon's Praça de Espanha (Metro: Palhavã); a local service also calls at Vila Nogueira de Azeitão (45 minutes) before traveling on to Setúbal (one hour). At **Setúbal bus station** (✉ Av. 5 de Outubro 44, ☎ 265/525051) you can connect with local services north to Palmela (20 minutes) and southwest to Sesimbra (30 minutes). The **Palmela** bus station is at **Largo do Chafariz D. Maria I** (☎ 21/235–0078). Six buses daily run a 30-minute trip from **Sesimbra** bus station (✉ Av. da Liberdade, ☎ 21/223–3071) to the southwestern Cabo Espichel.

By Car

Fast highways connect Lisbon with Estoril (A5/IC15) and Setúbal (A2/IP1), and the quality of other roads in the region is generally good. Take special care on hilly and coastal roads, though, and if possible, avoid driving out of Lisbon at the start of a weekend or public holiday or back in at the end. Both Tagus bridges—especially the Ponte 25 de Abril but also the dramatic Ponte Vasco da Gama—can be very slow. Parking can be problematic, too, especially in the summer along the Estoril Coast. When you do park, *never* leave anything visible in the car, and it's wise to clear out the trunk as well.

By Taxi

If you don't have your own car, it may pay—at least in time and convenience—to take a taxi. Cabs are relatively inexpensive, and you can usually agree on a fixed price that will include the round-trip to an attraction (the driver will wait for you to complete your tour). Tourist offices can give you an idea of what fares are reasonable for local trips.

By Train

Electric commuter trains travel the entire Estoril Coast, with departures every 15–30 minutes from the waterfront Cais do Sodré station in Lisbon, west of the Praça do Comércio. The scenic trip to Estoril, with splendid sea views, takes about 30 minutes, and four more stops along the seashore bring you to Cascais, at the end of the line. A one-way ticket to either costs 185$00; service operates daily 5:30 AM–2:30

AM. Trains from Lisbon's Rossío station, between Praça dos Restauradores and the Rossío, run every 15 minutes to Queluz (a 20-minute trip) and on to Sintra (40 minutes total). The service operates 6 AM–2:40 AM, and one-way tickets cost 155$00 to Queluz, 185$00 to Sintra. For current timetables for all train services in Lisbon's environs, call the **information line** (☎ 21/888–4025).

And thanks to a seven-year project completed in 1999, **Fertagus** (☎ ☎ 21/294–9700) trains from Lisbon's Sete Rios and Entre Campos stations now cross the Tagus River via the Ponte 25 de Abril. Passengers on the double-decker rail cars benefit from fine views, air-conditioning, and background music during the seven-minute crossing. Taxis at stations across the river can take you on to Cacilhas, Setúbal, and other towns on the Setúbal Peninsula. Trains run between 5:30 AM and 2 AM. From June through September a narrow-gauge railway runs for 8 km (5 mi) along the Costa da Caparica from the town of Caparica, on the Setúbal Peninsula. It makes 20 stops at beaches along the way, and a one-way ticket to the end of the line costs 500$00.

Contacts and Resources

Car Rental

There are better choices for car rentals in Lisbon (☞ Lisbon A to Z *in* Chapter 1), although the tourist offices in Cascais, Estoril, Sintra, and Setúbal can advise you of the local possibilities. Your options in the area include **Avis** (✉ Tamariz Esplanade, Estoril, ☎ 21/468–5728; ✉ Av. Luisa Todi 96, Setúbal, ☎ 265/526946), **Europcar** (✉ Av. Marginal, Centro Comércial Cisne, Bloco B, Lojas 4 and 5, Cascais, ☎ 21/486–4438), and **Hertz** (✉ Av. Luisa Todi 277, Setúbal, ☎ 265/533786).

Emergencies

General: ☎ 112. **Hospitals: Cascais Hospital** (✉ Corner of Av. Ultramar and Rua Padre J. M. Loureiro, ☎ 21/484–4071), **Setúbal Hospital** (✉ Rua Camilo Castelo Branco, ☎ 265/522133), **Sintra Health Center** (✉ Rua Visconde de Monserrate 2, ☎ 21/923–3400). **Pharmacies:** In all the towns, a notice on the door of every *farmácia* (drugstore) indicates the name and address of the nearest all-night pharmacy. **Police:** ☎ 21/483–1127 in Cascais; 21/468–1396 in Estoril; 265/522022 in Setúbal; 21/923–0761 in Sintra.

Guided Tours

Most travel agents and large hotels in Lisbon or its environs can reserve you a place on a guided tour. **Citirama** (✉ Av. Praia da Vitória 12-B, Lisbon, ☎ 21/355–8567) has half-day trips to Queluz, to Sintra, and to Estoril and a tour of the area's royal palaces (each 8,000$00); nine-hour tours of Mafra, Sintra, and Cascais (13,000$00, including lunch); and even an evening visit to Estoril's famous casino (13,000$00, including dinner). **Gray Line Tours** (✉ Av. Praia da Vitória 12-B, Lisbon, ☎ 21/352–2594) offers half-day trips into the Arrábida Mountain range and to local craft centers for around 9,000$00.

For guided tours of the Sintra area, ask at the tourist information center (☞ Visitor Information, *below*), which has current schedules and can sell tickets. Half-day tours typically encompass visits to all the principal sights and a wine tasting in Colares.

Sintratur (✉ Rua João de Deus 82, Sintra, ☎ 21/924–1238) runs old-fashioned horse-and-carriage rides in the Sintra area. A short tour of Sintra costs 8,000$00–9,000$00; longer trips cost between 11,000$00 and 15,000$00 and take in attractions as diverse as the Moorish Castle and Monserrate.

Telephones and Mail

For information, dial 118; operators speak English or will transfer you to one who does.

There are main post offices in **Cascais** (✉ Rua Manuel J. Avelar, ☎ 21/483–3175), **Sintra** (✉ Praça da República 26, ☎ 21/924–9825), and **Setúbal** (✉ Av. 22 de Dezembro, ☎ 265/522778).

Travel Agents

If you need a travel agent during your stay in the area, your best bet is to find one in Lisbon itself (☞ Lisbon A to Z *in* Chapter 1).

Visitor Information

ICEP, the Portuguese **national tourist office** with its main Lisbon office in the Palácio Foz (✉ Praça dos Restauradores, ☎ 21/346–3314 ✆), has information on the city's environs. Local tourist offices are usually open June–September, daily 9–1 and 2–6, sometimes later in the tourist-resort areas. Hours are greatly reduced after peak season, and most offices are closed Sunday.

Cabo da Roca (✉ Azóia, ☎ 21/928–0081), **Caparica** (✉ Praça da Liberdade, ☎ 21/290–0071), **Cascais** (✉ Av. Marginal, ☎ 21/486–8204), **Estoril** (✉ Arcadas do Parque, ☎ 21/466–3813), **Palmela** (✉ Castelo de Palmela, ☎ 21/233–2122), **Sesimbra** (✉ Largo da Marinha, off Av. dos Naufragios, ☎ 21/223–5743), **Setúbal** (✉ Travessa Frei Gaspar 10, ☎ 265/524284), **Sintra** (✉ Praça da República 23, ☎ 21/923–1157 or 21/924–1700; Sintra train station, ☎ 21/924–1623), **Queluz** (✉ Palácio Nacional de Queluz, ☎ 21/436–3415).

3 ESTREMADURA AND THE RIBATEJO

Populous Estremadura's rolling hills and glorious coastline contain some of the country's most famous towns and monuments. Bordering Estremadura on either side of the Rio Tejo is the Ribatejo—a famous bullfighting area and home to the shrine at Fátima—whose mainly flat lands fade into the vast plains of the southern Alentejo region.

By Dennis Jaffe

Updated by
Martha de la
Cal and Peter
Collis

ESTREMADURA OCCUPIES a narrow stretch of land along the coast, extending north from Lisbon to include the onetime royal residence of Leiria, 119 km (74 mi) from the capital city. Closely tied to the sea, which at no point in the province is more than a few miles away, the region is known for its fine beaches, coastal pine forests, and picturesque fishing villages. Some of these—such as Nazaré—have evolved, for better or worse, into popular resorts. Fruits and vegetables grow in fertile coastal valleys, and livestock contentedly graze in rich pastures, but Estremadura hasn't always been so peaceful. During the Wars of Reconquest, which raged from the 8th through the 13th centuries, it was the scene of a series of bloody encounters between Christians and Moors. In the aftermath of the wars, Portuguese sovereignty was secured with the defeat of the Spanish at Aljubarrota in 1385 and the turning back of Napoléon's forces in 1810 at Torres Vedras. The bloodshed left a positive legacy for today's traveler: Alcobaça and Batalha, masterpieces of religious architecture, were built to commemorate Portuguese victories.

The Ribatejo developed along both sides of the Rio Tejo (Tagus River), and it is this waterway, born in the mountains of Spain, that has shaped and sustained the province that carries its name. In the north, inhabitants tend groves of olive and fig trees, and the peaceful, sparsely populated landscape has changed little since the Romans settled.

Over the centuries Romans, Visigoths, Moors, and Christians built and rebuilt various castles and fortifications to protect the strategic Tagus. You'll see some fine examples along the river at Belver, Abrantes, and Almourol. Tomar, spanning the banks of the Nabão (a tributary of the Tagus) is dominated by the hilltop Convento de Cristo (Convent of Christ), an extraordinary example of medieval architecture, built in the 12th century by the Knights Templar. In the brush-covered hills at the western edge of the province lies Fátima, one of Christendom's most important pilgrimage sites. As it flows south approaching Lisbon, the Tagus expands, often overflowing its banks during the winter rains, and the landscape changes to one of rich meadows and pastures and broad, alluvial plains, where rice and other grains grow in abundance.

The Ribatejans are said to be more reserved than their fellow Portuguese—that is, until they step into the arena to test their mettle against a ton or so of charging bull. The Ribatejo is bullfighting country, the heartland of one of Portugal's richest and most colorful traditions. On the vast plains along the east bank of the Tagus, you'll encounter men on horseback carrying long wooden prods and often wearing the traditional waistcoats and stocking caps of their trade. These are *campinos,* the Portuguese "cowboys," who tend the herds of bulls and horses bred and trained for arenas throughout the country.

Pleasures and Pastimes

Beaches
Starting with Ericeira and extending north to São Pedro de Moel by Marinha Grande, there are a number of pleasant sandy beaches at convenient intervals along the coast. Some of the more popular beaches—where you'll find the customary range of facilities, hotels, and restaurants—are in Nazaré, Peniche, and Foz do Arelho.

Dining
In Estremadura restaurants, the emphasis is on fish, including the ubiquitous *bacalhau* (dried salt cod) and *caldeirada* (a hearty fish stew). The seaside resorts of Ericeira, Nazaré, and Peniche are famous

for fresh lobster. In Santarém and other spots along the River Tagus, an *açorda* (thick bread porridge) made with *savel*, a shadlike fish from the river, is popular, as are *enguias* (eels) prepared in a variety of ways. Pork is a key component in Ribatejo dishes, and roast lamb and kid are also widely enjoyed. Perhaps the result of a sweet-making tradition developed by nuns in the region's once-numerous convents, dessert menus abound with colorful-sounding—although often cloyingly sweet and eggy—dishes such as *queijinhos do céu* (little cheeses from heaven). The straw-color white wines from the Ribatejo district of Bucelas are among the country's finest.

Between mid-June and mid-September reservations are advised at upscale restaurants. However, most of the establishments we list are moderate or inexpensive, don't accept reservations, and have informal dining rooms where it's acceptable to share a table with other diners. Dress is casual at all but the most luxurious restaurants; any exceptions to the dress code or reservation policy are noted in the reviews. For price categories, *see* the chart under Dining *in* Smart Travel Tips A to Z.

Lodging

Estremadura is well equipped with quality lodgings, especially along the coast. In summer, you'll need reservations. Most establishments offer substantial off-season discounts. The Ribatejo has first-class hotels; the best accommodations in this region are the government-run inns called *pousadas*. The pousadas are small, some with as few as six rooms, so reserving well in advance is essential. There's also a number of high-quality, government-approved private guest houses. Look for signs reading TURISMO RURAL or TURISMO DE HABITAÇÃO. For information about pousadas contact **Enatur** (⊠ Av. Sta. Joana Princesa 10-A, Lisbon 1700, ☎ 21/844–2001, ℻ 21/844–2085).

For price categories, *see* the chart under Lodging *in* Smart Travel Tips A to Z.

Shopping

The regions around Alcobaça and Leiria are well known for their high-quality crystal and hand-blown glass. Traditional hand-painted ceramics are sold at shops and roadside stands throughout Estremadura. Caldas da Rainha, a large ceramics-manufacturing center, produces characteristic cabbage-leaf and vegetable-shape pieces. Traditional cable-stitch Portuguese fishermen's sweaters are for sale in towns all along the coast.

Water Sports

The clear waters and bizarre rock formations along Estremadura's coast make it a favorite with anglers, snorkelers, and scuba divers. A wet suit is recommended for diving and snorkeling, as the chilly waters don't invite you to linger long, even in summer. The area's most commonly caught fish are sea bass, bream, and red mullet.

Exploring Estremadura and the Ribatejo

The narrow province surrounding Lisbon and extending north along the coast for approximately 160 km (100 mi) is known as Estremadura, referring to the extreme southern border of the land the Portuguese reconquered from the Moors. This is primarily a rural region characterized by coastal fishing villages and small farming communities that mostly produce fruit and olives.

To the east of Estremadura, straddling both banks of the Tagus River, the Ribatejo is a placid, fertile region known for its vegetables and vineyards. As a consequence of its strategic location, the Ribatejo is home to a number of imposing castles.

Great Itineraries

Although you could cover these regions in a day or two, if you invest a few extra days, you'll be well rewarded. Three days will give you a feel for the region, five days will allow you to include a visit to the shrine at Fátima and the Convent of Christ at Tomar, and a full week will give you enough time to cover the major attractions as well as explore the countryside. With additional time you can easily extend your itinerary to include Évora and the Alentejo (☞ Chapter 4) or head north to Coimbra and the Beiras (☞ Chapter 6). Unless you have a great deal of time and patience, these regions are best explored by car. Trains don't serve many of the most interesting towns, and bus travel is usually slow.

Numbers in the text correspond to numbers in the margin and on the Estremadura and the Ribatejo map.

IF YOU HAVE 3 DAYS

Start with a visit to the imposing monastery and palace at **Mafra** ①, then head for the coast, with a stop at the popular seaside resort and fishing village of **Ericeira** ②. Continue north along the coast to **Peniche** ④, where an imposing fortress looms over the busy fishing harbor. Head inland to spend the night in the enchanting walled city of 🖼 **Óbidos** ⑥. The next morning continue north, stopping at ceramics shops in **Caldas da Rainha** ⑦. En route to 🖼 **Nazaré** ⑧, tour the church and cloister at **Alcobaça** ⑨, among Portugal's most impressive religious monuments. On your third day head inland to the magnificent monastery church in **Batalha** ⑩. The soaring multispired structure contains the tomb of Prince Henry the Navigator. Return to Lisbon along N1/IC2 with a stop in **Vila Franca de Xira** ⑫ (after joining the A1 toll road at Aveiras da Cima) to visit the museum devoted to bullfighting. If highway driving seems more appealing, take N356 east from Batalha and then A1 down to Vila Franca from the Fátima junction.

IF YOU HAVE 5 DAYS

Follow the above itinerary to **Batalha** ⑩, and then continue north to **Leiria** ⑪, whose principal attraction is its hilltop castle. Take N113 east to the A1 highway and drive down it to 🖼 **Fátima** ⑲, one of Christendom's most renowned pilgrimage destinations. The next morning, continue east on N113 to **Tomar** ⑳, an attractive town dominated by the hilltop Convent of Christ, which was once the headquarters of the Order of Knights Templar. After a few hours exploring Tomar and the convent, take N110 south and then join N358-2, a winding scenic road that follows the Rio Zêzere (Zêzere River) to its union with the Tagus. Just west of their confluence, on an island in the Tagus, is the **Castelo de Almourol** ㉒, one of Portugal's finest. From here, follow N118 southwest along the Tagus, stopping in **Alpiarça** ⑯ to visit the Casa dos Patudos, a large, turn-of-the-century country house containing the art collection of its former owner, and in **Almeirim** ⑭ stop to see the winery at the Quinta da Alorna. Spend the night in 🖼 **Santarém** ⑮, an important farming and livestock center with many fine historic sights. The next day return to Lisbon with a drive along the Tagus on N118 through the region of marshy plains known as the **Lezíria** ⑬.

IF YOU HAVE 7 DAYS

Leave Lisbon and head north to **Mafra** ①, then visit **Ericeira** ②. From here continue north along the coast, turning inland to **Torres Vedras** ③ to have a look at the castle and the fortifications erected by Wellington during the Peninsular War. Continue on to **Peniche** ④. If the weather is good, take the boat ride out to the **Ilhas Berlenga** ⑤. From Peniche

drive inland a few miles to 🏰 **Óbidos** ⑥. From Óbidos head north through **Caldas da Rainha** ⑦ and **Alcobaça** ⑨ to 🏰 **Nazaré** ⑧. The next morning visit 🏰 **Leiria** ⑪ and the glassworks at Marinha Grande. Stay in Leiria for two nights and use the town as a base to visit **Fátima** ⑲ and explore the Parque Natural das Serras de Aire e Candeeiros, where there are marvelous limestone grottoes at Mira de Aire, Alvados, and Santo António and hundreds of fossilized dinosaur footprints at Bairro. Leaving Leiria continue to **Tomar** ⑳. If you have time, stop in Ourem to visit its medieval castles before continuing to the lake at **Castelo de Bode** ㉑. To get a better feel for the countryside and visit a charming, out-of-the-way village, take N244-3 from 🏰 **Abrantes** ㉔ to **Sardoal** ㉕, an attractive backcountry hamlet. From Sardoal, N244-3 traces a broad loop through a heavily forested region before returning to the Tagus and joining the main highway N118 at the hilltop castle **Castelo de Belver** ㉖. Return on N118 to spend the night in Abrantes. In the morning visit the **Castelo de Almourol** ㉒ and continue to 🏰 **San-**

tarém ⑮ by way of **Alpiarça** ⑯ and **Almeirim** ⑭. The next morning return to Lisbon with a stop in **Vila Franca de Xira** ⑫.

When to Tour Estremadura and the Ribatejo

To avoid the busloads of tourists who inundate these places during July and August, visit the major monuments and attractions such as Óbidos and Mafra in the early morning. This also helps to beat the oppressive summer heat, particularly in the inland regions. The best time of year for touring is in early spring and from mid-September until late October. The climate during this period is pleasant, and attractions and restaurants aren't crowded. If throngs of people don't bother you, time your visit to Fátima to coincide with May 13, when between 500,000 and 1 million pilgrims overwhelm this otherwise sleepy country town. Less spectacular pilgrimages take place year-round.

ESTREMADURA

A tour through Estremadura includes visits to some of Portugal's most outstanding monuments and architectural treasures, including Mafra, Alcobaça, Óbidos, Tomar, and Batalha.

Mafra

❶ *28 km (17 mi) northwest of Lisbon.*

In 1711, after nearly three years of a childless union with his Hapsburg queen, Mariana, a despairing king João V vowed that should the queen bear him an heir, he would build a Franciscan monastery dedicated to St. Anthony. In December of that same year, a girl—later to become queen of Spain—was born; João's eventual heir, José I, was born three years later. True to his word, the king built the enormous

★ **Mosteiro Palácio Nacional de Mafra** (Monastery and Royal Palace), which looms above the small farming community of Mafra. The original project—entrusted to the Italian-trained German architect Friedrich Ludwig—was to be a modest facility that could house 13 friars. What finally emerged after 18 years of construction was an immense, rectangular complex that contained a monastery large enough for hundreds of monks, an imposing basilica, and a grandiose royal palace that has been compared to El Escorial outside Madrid, Spain. The numbers involved in the construction are mind-boggling: at times 50,000 workers toiled. There are 4,500 doors and windows, 300 cells, 880 halls and rooms, and 154 stairways. Perimeter walls that total some 19 km (12 mi) surround the park.

You'll be shown interesting details on the one-hour guided tour (offered in various languages), but the highlight is the magnificent baroque library: the barrel-vaulted, two-tiered hall contains some 40,000 volumes of mostly 16th-, 17th-, and 18th-century works and a number of ancient maps. The basilica, constructed entirely of limestone and containing 11 chapels, was patterned after St. Peter's in the Vatican. The balcony of the connecting corridor overlooks the high altar and was a favorite meeting place for Dom João and Mariana. This midway point between the "his" and "hers" royal bedrooms was considered neutral territory. When you're in the gilded throne room, notice the life-size renditions of the seven virtues, as well as the impressive figure of Hercules, by Domingos Sequeira. On display in the game room is an early version of a pinball machine. Note the hard-planked beds in the monastery infirmary; the monks used no mattresses.

You'll be fortunate if you arrive on a Sunday afternoon between 4 and 5, when the sonorous tones of the 92-bell carillon ring out across the countryside. ☎ 261/817550. ✉ 600$00, *including tour.* ◷ *Wed.–Mon. 10–1 and 2–5; tour times vary.*

🐾 A trek around the nearby royal game reserve, **Tapada Nacional de Mafra,** is a pleasantly verdant break from touring stone monuments. The huge, wall-enclosed area was once the private hunting ground of João V and is stocked with deer and other local fauna. You can opt for a guided tour by minitrain or on horseback, or go on your own by bicycle or on foot. All the visits begin weekdays at 10 AM and at 2 PM. The minitrain tour, however, leaves only when there are at least 20 passengers, and the horseback tours need to be booked a day in advance. On weekends, there are three visits daily, at 10 AM, 3 PM, and 4 PM, and the minitrain tour takes place with any number of passengers. ☎ 261/814240. ✉ 600$00 on foot, 1,250$00 by minitrain, 7,500$00 on horseback. ◷ *Daily 10–4.*

NEED A BREAK?   The **Pastelaria Fradinho** (☎ 261/815738), just across from the monastery, offers a welcome respite from the rigors of sightseeing. Light and cheerful, with tile decor, it specializes in little, homemade, friar-shape, egg-and-almond pastries called, predictably, *fradinhos* (little friars).

Ericeira

❷ *11 km (7 mi) northwest of Mafra.*

Ericeira, an old fishing town tucked into the rocky coast, is a popular seaside resort. The core of the town fans out from the sheer cliff, beneath which boats are hauled up onto a small, sheltered beach. In recent years, the growth of summer tourism has caused a proliferation of bars, pubs, discos, pizzerias, and the like in the increasingly gentrified but still attractive town center. But along the waterfront there are a number of traditional seafood restaurants that are popular with both locals and visitors. Either end of the town has good sand for sunbathing, but the south end is preferred by surfers.

Dining and Lodging

$ ✕🏨 **Hotel de Turismo.** Dramatically set at the edge of the breakers, this
★ sprawling, self-contained low-rise is a classic old Portuguese beach hotel. Public rooms are decorated with a delightful variety of colored tiles and accented with flowers and plants. Most of the spacious guest rooms have balconies with sea views. The large restaurant is lined with picture windows looking out on the water; you can opt to be served on the seaside terrace. The international menu emphasizes seafood, and the quality is good. ⊠ *Rua Porto Revez, 2655,* ☎ *261/860200,* ℻ *261/863146. 165 rooms. Restaurant, bar, 3 pools, beach, dance club. AE, DC, MC, V.*

$ 🏨 **Pedro O Pescador.** If you prefer your hotels on the small side, then you'll like this intimate, pastel blue, family-run place near the beach. Cheerful rooms have planked floors and are decorated with floral Alentejo furniture. The small, modern restaurant is frequented mostly by hotel guests but has a reputation for simple but excellent cooking. ⊠ *Rua Dr. Eduardo Burnay 22, 2655,* ☎ *261/869121,* ℻ *261/862321. 25 rooms. Restaurant, bar. AE, DC, MC, V.*

Torres Vedras

❸ *20 km (12 mi) northeast of Ericeira.*

Today a bustling commercial center crowned with the ruins of a medieval castle, Torres Vedras is best known for its extensive fortifications—a system of trenches and fortresses erected by Wellington in 1810 as part of a secret plan for the defense of Lisbon. It was here, at the

Lines of Torres Vedras, that the surprised French army under Napoléon's Marshal Masséna was routed. You can see reconstructed remnants of the fortifications on a hill above town and throughout the area.

Lodging

$$$ 🏨 **Golf Mar.** This hotel's idyllic location—on a rise overlooking a broad, sandy beach—is the main reason to stay here: the huge, concrete-block facade is hardly alluring, and the interior lacks inspiration. But if you're a golfer looking for a course, this is your only option in the region. The hotel is near the town of Lourinhã, 16 km (10 mi) northwest of Torres Vedras. ⊠ *Praia do Porto Novo, 2560,* ☎ *261/984157,* 🖷 *261/984621. 267 rooms, 9 suites. Restaurant, bar, indoor and outdoor pools, 9-hole golf course, 2 tennis courts, horseback riding, billiards, dance club. AE, DC, MC, V.*

$ 🏨 **Hotel Império.** A bright, cheerfully appointed modern hotel in the center of town, this is the place to stay if you're not interested in golf or a beachfront location. ⊠ *Praça 25 de Abril,* ☎ *261/314232,* 🖷 *261/321901. 47 rooms. Restaurant, bar, cafeteria. AE, MC, V.*

Outdoor Activities and Sports

GOLF

The one golf course in the region is at the beach at **Praia de Porto Nova** and is part of the Golf Mar hotel (☞ Dining and Lodging, *above*). The nine-hole course was designed by Frank Pennink. Reserve greens in advance, even if you're a hotel guest.

En Route For the most scenic drive to Peniche, return to the coast and follow N247 north for 43 km (27 mi) to Cabo Carvoeiro. About 3 km (2 mi) north of Torres Vedras is the archeological site Castro do Zambujal, the remains of an Iron Age settlement of people who worked the copper mines that once existed here. Farther on, the jagged coast is interrupted by fine beaches at Ribamar, Santa Cruz, and Areia Branca.

Peniche

❹ *32 km (20 mi) northwest of Torres Vedras.*

Situated in the lee of a rocky peninsula, Peniche is a major fishing-and-canning port that is also a popular summer resort known for its fine lace. The bustling harbor is watched over by a sprawling 16th-century **fortress.** (For a good view of the fortress and the harbor, drive out to Cabo Carvoeiro; the narrow road winds around the peninsula, along the rugged shore, and past the lighthouse and bizarre rock formations.) Until fairly recently the fortress was frequently used to incarcerate political prisoners. At one time its dungeons were full of French troops captured by the Duke of Wellington's forces. During the dictatorship that ended in 1974 it was a prison for opponents of the regime. With the restoration of a free democracy it became a museum. Visitors can tour the former cells as well as the small archeological exhibit. 🖼 *Free.* ☉ *Tues.–Sun. 10–noon and 2–5.*

The most interesting of the area's several churches is the 13th-century **Igreja de São Leonardo** (Church of St. Leonard) in nearby Atouguia da Baleia.

Dining and Lodging

$ ✕ **O Canhoto.** Unlike many of the expensive touristy restaurants along the harbor, O Canhoto puts less emphasis on the trappings and more on the food. This is a typical, no-frills Portuguese fish restaurant—set on a narrow side street—where you're almost always assured a good meal, especially if you ask for the *peixe do dia* (fish of the day). ⊠ *Rua Tenente Valadim 23,* ☎ *262/784512. MC, V.*

$ ✕⊡ **Hotel Praia Norte.** This well-equipped modern hotel set on a green lawn near the sea on the outskirts of Peniche was completely refurbished in 1999. The rooms aren't large, but they are light, pleasantly furnished, and well appointed. ⊠ *Av. Monsenhor Bastos, 2520,* ☎ *262/780500,* ℻ *262/780509. 92 rooms. Restaurant, bar, disco, 1 indoor pool, 1 outdoor pool, tennis court, dance club. AE, DC, MC, V.* ☜

$$ ⊡ **Hotel Atlântico Golfe.** Even if you're not a golfer, the views from your balcony (all rooms have them) over the links and the long, sandy beach will appeal. The hotel is located on a beach famed for the health-giving properties of its waters (attributed to the local rock). The rooms are spacious and well equipped. ⊠ *Praia da Consolacão, 2620,* ☎ *262/757700,* ℻ *262/750717. 90 rooms. Restaurant, bar, 1 indoor pool, 1 outdoor pool, sauna, 9-hole golf course, tennis court, exercise room, kennel. AE, DC, MC, V.*

Outdoor Activities and Sports
WATER SPORTS

A great alternative to a day at the beach for kids and adults is **Peniche Sportagua,** a large water-park complex with slides and separate adults' and children's swimming pools. The park also has a restaurant, snack bar, and disco. ⊠ *Av. Monsenhor M. Basto,* ☎ *262/789125.* ⊡ *Weekdays 1,300$00, 1,100$00 half day; weekends 1,500$00, $1,200 half day.* ⊙ *Mid-July–mid-Sept., daily 9–7.*

Ilhas Berlenga

⑤ *10 km (6 mi) northeast of Cabo Carvoeiro.*

The harbor at Peniche is the jumping-off point for excursions to the Berlenga Islands. The six small islands are a nature reserve and a favorite place for fishermen and divers. Berlenga, the largest of the group, is the site of the **Forte de São João Baptista,** a 17th-century fortress built to defend the area from pirates. There is a campground on the island, and a limited number of rooms are available. For information about accommodations, contact the Peniche tourist office (☞ Visitor Information *in* Estremadura and the Ribatejo A to Z, *below*).

The company Viamar operates regular summer boat services from Peniche to Berlenga. From May 15 to June 30 and again September 1 to September 15 there is one round-trip daily leaving at 10 AM and returning at 4:30 PM. July and August there are two round-trips daily at 9:30 AM and 11:30 AM, plus an evening boat that leaves at 5:30 PM and returns the following morning. There are also charter services. For information, ask at the Peniche tourist office.

Outdoor Activities and Sports
SCUBA DIVING

The clear (and somewhat chilly) waters and bizarre rock formations off the Berlenga Islands are popular with scuba divers and snorkelers. You can charter boats at the harbor in Peniche. Fishermen like these waters, too. The most commonly caught fish are sea bass, bream, and red mullet. A fishing license isn't required.

Óbidos

★ **⑥** *20 km (12 mi) east of Peniche.*

Once a strategic seaport but now left high and dry 10 km (6 mi) inland by the silting of its harbor, Óbidos is surrounded by fertile farmland. Cottages and cultivated fields abut the town walls where fishing boats and trading vessels once docked. As you approach Óbidos from the distance, you can see the bastions and crenellated walls standing as a hilltop sentinel guarding the now-peaceful valley of the Ria Arnoia. Enter the town through the massive, arched gates, and it may seem that you've been transported into medieval Portugal. The narrow Rua Direita, lined with boutiques and flower-bedecked white houses, runs the length of the town from the main gates to the foot of the castle: you may want to shop for ceramics and clothing on this street. The rest of the town is crisscrossed by a labyrinth of stone footpaths, tiny squares, and decaying stairways. Explore any route or all of them, for the town is small, and you can't really get lost. Each nook and cranny will offer its own reward.

Just be sure to include the **castelo** (castle) in your explorations. Extensively restored after suffering severe damage in the 1755 earthquake, the multitower complex—one of the finest medieval castles in Portugal—displays both Arabic and Manueline elements. Since 1952 parts of the castle have been a pousada.

Óbidos has a long association with prominent Portuguese women. So enchanted was the young Queen Isabel with Óbidos—which she visited with her husband, Dom Dinis, shortly after their marriage in 1282—that the king gave it to her as a gift, along with Abrantes and Porto de Móso; the town remained the property of the queens of Portugal until 1834. In the 14th century Inês de Castro sought refuge in this castle. Another queen associated with Óbidos was Leonor (the wife of João II), who came here in the 15th century to recuperate after the death of her young son; the town pillory bears Leonor's coat of arms.

The 17th-century artist Josefa de Óbidos came as a small child and lived here until her death in 1684. Some of her work may be seen in the *azulejo*-lined (tile-lined) **Igreja de Santa Maria** (St. Mary's Church), which dates from the 8th century.

Dining and Lodging

$$ ✕ **Alcaide.** From the upstairs dining room of this rustic tavern on the main street, you can enjoy a lovely view of the town. The Alcaide is often jammed with hungry sightseers, especially from May through October; this is not a quiet hideaway. The food, however, is always carefully prepared, and the service is attentive. Try the *coelho á Alcaide* (rabbit grilled and served with potatoes). ✉ *Rua Direita, between main gate and castle,* ☎ 262/959220. AE, DC, MC, V. Closed Mon.

$$ ✕ **A Ilustre Casa de Ramiro.** The decor here has Moorish motifs, but the food is authentically regional and probably the best around outside the Pousada do Castelo. You could do worse than try the *pato de arroz* (rice with duck). ✉ *Rua Porta do Vale (in an old building outside the walls),* ☎ 262/959194. AE, MC, V. Closed Wed.

$$$ ✕🏠 **Pousada do Castelo.** If you've ever fantasized about living in luxury within a medieval castle, this is a wonderful place to fulfill that wish. ★ This pousada occupies parts of the castle that Dom Dinis gave to his young bride, Isabel, in 1282. Except for the electric lights and the relatively modern plumbing, the style of the Middle Ages prevails throughout—from the guest rooms to the beautifully tiled lounge and dining room. Room 2, in one of the massive stone towers, is especially evocative of ancient times; other rooms are individually furnished with 16th- and 17th-century reproductions. In the restaurant, the food and service are worthy of royalty, and there's a curtained alcove where you can dine in privacy and still enjoy a splendid view of the castle walls and valley below. Try the *cabrito assado* (roast kid). ✉ *Paço Real, 2510,* ☎ 262/959105, FAX 262/959148. 6 rooms, 3 suites. Restaurant, bar. AE, DC, MC, V.

$ ✕🏠 **Albergaria Josefa d'Óbidos.** Built into the hillside at the town's main gate, this attractive, flower-bedecked country inn is the next best thing to the Pousada do Castelo. The rooms are outfitted with comfortable 18th-century reproductions, including massive wood furniture that enhances the old-inn feeling, even though the place was built in 1983. The Albergaría has several reproductions of Josefa d'Óbidos's works hanging in the bar. A large, rustic restaurant with an open brick grill serves a variety of regional specialties: try the *arroz de tamboril* (casserole with monkfish and rice) or one of the many varieties of bacalhau. The ambience of the otherwise-charming dining room is sometimes disturbed by the presence of large tour groups. ⊠ *Rua D. João de Ornelas, 2510,* ☎ *262/959228,* FAX *262/959533. 34 rooms, 2 suites. Restaurant, bar, dance club. AE, DC, MC, V.*

Caldas da Rainha

❼ *5 km (3 mi) north of Óbidos.*

Caldas da Rainha (Queen's Baths) is the hub of a large farming area best known for its sulfur baths. In 1484 Queen Leonor, en route to Batalha, noticed some people bathing in a malodorous pool. Having heard of the healing properties of the sulfurous water, the queen interrupted her journey to soak in the pool and became convinced of its beneficial effects. She decided to build a hospital on the site and reputedly was so enthusiastic that she sold her jewels to help finance the project. There's a bronze statue of Leonor in front of the hospital.

The expansive wooded park surrounding the spa contains the **Museu Malhoa,** a museum with works mostly by the local 19th- and 20th-century painter José Malhoa. ⊠ *Parque D. Carlos I,* ☎ *262/831984.* ⌨ *400$00, Sun. morning free.* ☉ *Tues.–Sun. 10–12:30 and 2–5.*

Also in the park is the **Museu de Cerâmica** (Ceramics Museum) in the house of the noted 19th-century ceramist, Rafael Bordalo Pinheiro. The collection contains ceramic works from all over the region, as well as works by Bordalo Pinheiro himself. ⊠ *Rua Dr. Elidio Amado,* ☎ *262/840280.* ⌨ *400$00, Sun. morning free.* ☉ *Tues.–Sun. 10–12:30 and 2–5.*

Dining and Lodging

$ ✕ **Adega Típica do Coto.** This popular local restaurant on the main street in Coto, 2 km (1¼ mi) north of Caldas, has a mainly Portuguese menu featuring many regional dishes. If it's in season, try the *javali* (wild boar). Another house specialty is the arroz de tamboril. The bread is baked fresh each day in a brick oven. ⊠ *Rua Principal, Coto,* ☎ *262/844898. AE, DC, MC, V.*

$ 🏨 **Hotel Cristal.** Most business travelers to the area choose this modern eight-story hotel, formerly the Malhoa, because it's conveniently located near the town center. The rooms are comfortable, but there aren't many details to indicate you're in Portugal. ⊠ *Rua António Sergio 31, 2500,* ☎ *262/840260,* FAX *262/842621. 111 rooms, 2 suites. Restaurant, bar, pool, sauna, dance club. AE, DC, MC, V.*

$ 🏨 **Quinta da Foz.** This large, two-story manor house dates from the
★ 16th century and is beautifully situated amid lawns and trees at the edge of the Óbidos Lagoon, some 15 minutes' walk from the beach. This is a quiet base from which to explore Caldas da Rainha, only 9 km (5½ mi) away, and other towns in the region. The bedrooms are large and comfortably furnished, with lots of flowers about. ⊠ *Largo do Areial, Foz do Arelho 2500,* ☎ *262/979369. 5 rooms, 2 apartments. Horseback riding. No credit cards.*

Outdoor Activities and Sports

WINDSURFING

The **Laguna de Óbidos** at Foz do Arelho is a lagoon that's popular with windsurfers. You can rent equipment at the beach: the cost for just the rig is about 1,500$00 per hour; rental and lessons cost about 3,000$00 per hour.

Shopping

Caldas da Rainha is famous for its cabbage-leaf and vegetable-shape ceramic pieces, and several of the town's factories and workshops can be visited if you reserve ahead of time. **Fábrica Rafael Bordalo Pinheiro,** named after the artist who made the Caldas da Rainha style famous, is certainly worth touring. To book a visit here, phone the factory showroom (✉ Rua Rafael Bordalo Pinheiro, ☎ 262/842353). Another leading factory worth visiting is **SECLA.** You can phone their showroom (✉ Rua S. Joáo de Deus, ☎ 262/824151) to book a tour.

Nazaré

❽ *24 km (15 mi) northwest of Caldas da Rainha. For the most interest-ing route, head west from Caldas along the lagoon to the beach town of Foz do Arelho, then take the coast road 26 km (16 mi) north.*

Not so long ago tourists could mingle on the beach with the black-stocking-capped fishermen and even help as the oxen hauled the boats in from the crashing surf. But Nazaré, one of the first quaint Portuguese fishing villages to feel the impact of tourism, is no longer a village and has long ceased to be quaint. The boats now motor comfortably into a safe, modern harbor, and the oxen have been put to pasture. The beach-front boulevard is lined with the usual assortment of restaurants, bars, and souvenir shops, and in summer the broad, sandy beach is covered with a multicolor quilt of tents and awnings.

To find what's left of the Nazaré once hailed by many as "the most picturesque fishing village in Portugal," come in the winter, and either climb the precipitous trail or take the funicular to the top of the 361-ft cliff called **Sitio.** Clustered at the cliff's edge overlooking the beach is a small community of fishermen who live in tiny cottages and seem unaffected by all that's happening below.

Dining and Lodging

$$$ ✕ **Arte Xavega.** On a hill overlooking the town, this is Nazaré's classi-est restaurant by far. Owner António Xavega's gardens and strategically placed house plants have contributed to the comfortable blend of ele-gance and intimacy. The international menu emphasizes local seafood specialties, including *arroz de marisco* (casserole of seafood and rice). ✉ *Ladeira Sitio-Meia Laranja, ☎ 262/562180. AE, DC, MC, V.*

$ ✕▥ **Ribamar.** This family-run restaurant-boardinghouse is on the main drag across from the beach; in summer it can be noisy, but the convenient location more than makes up for this. Bedrooms are small, but all are clean and well kept; ask for one that faces the sea. The restau-rant, decorated like a country tavern, has large windows overlooking the beach; seafood is the main attraction, particularly the caldeirada. ✉ *Rua Gomes Freire 9, 2450, ☎ 262/551158, ℻ 262/562224. 23 rooms. Restaurant, bar. AE, DC, MC, V.*

$ ▥ **Hotel Praia.** In spite of its popularity, Nazaré lacks a really first-rate hotel, but the 27-year-old, five-story Praia comes closest to filling the bill. The centrally located hotel is only about 50 yards from the sea, and the rooms, though not large, are well equipped and comfortably furnished. All have balconies, some with sea views. ✉ *Av. Vieira Guimaraes 39, 2450, ☎ 262/561423, ℻ 262/561436. 40 rooms. AE, DC, MC, V.*

Shopping

The many shops and stands along the beachfront promenade have a particularly good selection of traditional fishermen's sweaters. You'll also find a wide array of caps and plaid shirts (the best are made of wool rather than acrylic blends). It pays to shop around, as prices vary widely and bargaining is the order of the day.

Alcobaça

⑨ *10 km (6 mi) southeast of Nazaré, 20 km (12 mi) northeast of Caldas da Rainha.*

★ Alcobaça is the site of an impressive religious monument, the **Mosteiro de Alcobaça.** Like the monastery at Mafra, the church and monastery of St. Mary of Alcobaça were built as the result of a kingly vow, this time in gratitude for a battle won. In 1147, faced with stiff Muslim resistance during the battle for Santarém, Portugal's first king, Afonso Henriques, promised to build a monastery dedicated to St. Bernard and the Cistercian Order. The Portuguese were victorious, Santarém was captured from the Moors, and shortly thereafter a site was selected. Construction began in 1153 and was concluded in 1178. The church, the largest in Portugal, is awe-inspiring. The unadorned, 350-ft-long structure of massive granite blocks and cross-ribbed vaulting is a masterpiece of understatement: there's good use of clean, flowing lines, with none of the clutter found in the later rococo and Manueline architecture. At opposite ends of the transept, placed foot-to-foot some 30 paces apart, are the delicately carved tombs of King Pedro I and Inês de Castro. The story of Pedro and Inês, one of the most bizarre love stories in Portuguese history, was immortalized by Luís de Camões in the renowned epic poem *Os Lusiads.*

Pedro, son of King Afonso IV and heir to the throne, fell in love with the beautiful young Galician Inês de Castro, a lady-in-waiting to Pedro's Castilian wife, Constança. Fearful of the influence of Inês's family on his heir, the king banished her from the court. Upon the death of Constança, Pedro and Inês secretly married, and she lived in Coimbra, in a house later known as the Quinta das Lagrimas (the House of Tears); two sons were born of this union. King Afonso, ever wary of foreign influence on Pedro, had Inês murdered. Subsequently, Pedro took the throne and had Inês's murderers pursued: two of the three were captured and executed, their hearts wrenched from their bodies. Pedro publicly proclaimed that he had been married to Inês and arranged an elaborate and macabre funeral for his wife. Before the procession, Inês's fleshless body, in royal garb, was enthroned beside him, and the courtiers were forced to kiss her lifeless hand. She was then placed in the tomb in Alcobaça that Pedro had designed, which lay, according to his wishes, opposite his own—so that on Judgment Day the lovers would ascend to heaven facing each other.

The graceful twin-tiered **cloister** at Alcobaça was added in the 14th and 16th centuries. The Kings Hall, just to the left of the main entrance, is lined with a series of 18th-century azulejos illustrating the construction of the monastery. ⊠ *Praça 25 de Abril.* 🖾 *350$00.* ☉ *Daily 9–5.*

While in Alcobaça, you may want to visit the interesting **Museu Nacional do Vinho** (National Wine Museum) to see wine-making implements and presses. The museum is in an old winery, on N8 heading north at the edge of town. ⊠ *Rua de Leiria,* 🕿 *262/582222.* 🖾 *Free.* ☉ *Weekdays 9–noon and 2–5:30.*

Dining and Lodging

$ ✕ **Trindade.** This unpretentious restaurant is considered one of the town's best. The intimate dining room, lined with old photos of local scenes, reveals some of Alcobaça's history. Try the house specialty, açorda *de marisco* (with shellfish), and for dessert, the homemade pastry. ⊠ *Praça D. Afonso Henriques 22,* ☎ *262/582397. AE, MC, V. Closed Sat.*

$$ 🏨 **Santa Maria.** This pleasant hotel is in the gardens right in front of the monastery. The rooms are simply furnished and comfortable, and some have balconies. There's no restaurant, but there's an agreeable wood-paneled bar. ⊠ *Rua Dr. Francisco Zagalo,* ☎ *262/597395,* FAX *262/596715. 75 rooms. Bar. AE, DC, MC, V.*

$ 🏨 **Casa da Padeira.** Guests mingle freely with the hosts of this family-run inn, 5 km (3 mi) outside Alcobaça. The bedrooms are large, and each is furnished with period reproductions. The homemade, just-out-of-the-oven bread is the highlight of breakfast; dinner is available on request. ⊠ *Hwy. N8, São Vicente 2460 Alcobaça,* ☎ *262/505240,* FAX *262/505241. 8 rooms, 2 apartments. Dining room, bar, pool, miniature golf, billiards. AE, MC, V.*

Shopping

Alcobaça is well known for its fine lead crystal. **Casa Lisboa** (⊠ Praça 25 de Abril), across from the monastery, offers a good selection.

Batalha

★ ⑩ *18 km (11 mi) northeast of Alcobaça.*

Batalha, which means "battle" in Portuguese, is the site of the monastery church of **Santa Maria da Vitória** (St. Mary of Victory), built to commemorate a decisive Portuguese victory over the Spanish on August 14, 1385, in the battle of Aljubarrota. In this engagement the Portuguese king, João of Avis, who had been crowned only seven days earlier, took on and routed a superior Spanish force. In so doing he maintained independence for Portugal, which was to last until 1580, when the crown finally passed into Spanish hands. The heroic statue of the mounted figure in the forecourt is that of Nuno Álvares Pereira, who, along with John of Avis, led the Portuguese army at Aljubarrota.

The monastery, a masterly combination of Gothic and Manueline styles, was built between 1388 and 1533. Some 15 architects were involved in the project, but the principal architect was Afonso Domingues, whose portrait, carved in stone, graces the wall in the chapter house. In the great hall lie the remains of two unknown Portuguese soldiers who died in World War I: one in France, the other in Africa. Entombed in the center of the Founder's Chapel, beneath the star-shape, vaulted ceiling, is John of Avis, lying hand-in-hand with his English queen, Philippa of Lancaster. The tombs along the south and west walls are those of the couple's children, including Henry the Navigator. Perhaps the finest parts of the entire project are the Unfinished Chapels, seven chapels radiating off an octagonal rotunda, started by Dom Duarte in 1435 and left roofless owing to lack of funds. Note the intricately filigreed detail of the main doorway. 🎫 *400$00.* ☉ *Daily 9–5.*

There's a small **military museum** 5 km (3 mi) south of the monastery on N8. 🎫 *Free.* ☉ *Tues.–Sun. 10–noon and 2–5.*

Dining and Lodging

$$$ ✕🏨 **Pousada do Mestre Afonso Domingues.** This pousada, named for
★ the architect who designed the famous Batalha monastery, offers 20th-century comfort in a modern, two-story, white-stucco building, just steps from the historic monument. The good-size upstairs rooms have patterned wallpaper and are furnished in 17th- and 18th-century style; several look out on the monastery, as does the first-floor restaurant, with its polished *calçada* (pavement with small black stones on a white background) floor and wooden ceiling. The menu includes several types of bacalhau, and there's an extensive wine list. ⊠ *Largo Mestre*

Afonso Domingues 6, 2440, ☎ *244/765260,* FAX *244/765240. 19 rooms, 2 suites. Restaurant, bar. AE, DC, MC, V.*

$ 🏠 **Quinta do Fidalgo.** This historic two-story manor house close to the monastery has a homey ambience: you can gather and chat with other guests in the spacious living room or outside on the large terrace and in the pleasant garden. The rooms are comfortably and traditionally furnished. Reservations are advised in summer. ⊠ *Av. D. Nuno Álvares Pereira, 2440,* ☎ *244/765114,* FAX *244/767401. 5 rooms. Bar. No credit cards.*

Shopping

South of Batalha (on N8) there are a number of roadside shops with good selections of hand-painted ceramics featuring classic patterns.

OFF THE
BEATEN PATH

PARQUE NATURAL DAS SERRAS DE AIRE E CANDEEIROS – This sparsely populated region straddles the boundary between Estremadura and the Ribatejo and is roughly midway between Lisbon and Coimbra. Within its 75,000 acres of scrublands and moors, you'll find small settlements, little changed in hundreds of years, where farmers barely eke out a living. In this rocky landscape, stones are the main building material for houses, windmills, and the miles of walls used to mark boundary lines. In the village of Minde, you can see women weaving the rough patchwork rugs for which this region is known. The park is well suited for leisurely hiking or cycling. If you are driving, the N362, which runs for approximately 45 km (28 mi) from Batalha in the north to Santarém in the south, is a good route for exploring the area.

Leiria

🕚 *11 km (7 mi) north of Batalha.*

Leiria is a pleasant, modern, industrial town at the confluence of the Rios Liz and Lena (Liz and Lena rivers), overlooked by a wonderfully elegant medieval castle. The region is known for its handicrafts, particularly the fine hand-blown glassware from nearby Marinha. The **castle,** built in 1135 by Prince Afonso Henriques (later Portugal's first king), was an important link in the chain of defenses along the southern border of what was at the time the Kingdom of Portugal. When the Moors were driven from the region, the castle lost its strategic significance and lay dormant until the early 14th century, when it was restored and modified and became the favorite residence of Dom Dinis and his queen, Isabel of Aragon. With these modifications the castle became more of a palace than a fortress and remains one of the loveliest structures of its kind in Portugal. Within the perimeter walls you'll encounter the ruins of a Gothic church, the castle keep, and—built into the section of the fortifications overlooking the town—the royal palace. Lined by eight arches, the balcony of the palace affords a lovely view of the town. 🎫 *250$00.* ☉ *Daily 9–6:30.*

Dining and Lodging

$$ ✕ **O Casarão.** Five kilometers (3 miles) south of Leiria, in Azoia at the
★   Nazaré turnoff, O Casarão occupies a large rustic house surrounded by gardens. Chef José Rodrigues supervises the outstanding kitchen staff, while his wife, Clarissa, presides over the dining room. The service and presentation are flawless without being pretentious, and the extensive menu includes several ancient recipes from nearby monasteries. One of the best dishes is bacalhau *tibarna* (with olive oil, corn bread, and potatoes). Be sure to leave room for the *bolo pinão* (pine-nut cake). The comprehensive wine list displays the labels of 120 varieties. ⊠ *Cruzamento de Azoia,* ☎ *244/871080. AE, DC, MC, V. Closed Mon.*

$ ✕▥▤ **Eurosol.** A pair of modern, "medium-rise" hotels, the Eurosol and Eurosol Jardim, occupy a hilltop that's about a 15-minute walk from the town center. The lobbies and bedrooms are spacious and smartly furnished; and the eighth-floor restaurant is ringed with picture windows that give bird's-eye views of the town. ✉ *Rua Dom José Alves Correia da Silva, 2400,* ☎ *244/812201,* FAX *244/811205. 128 rooms, 7 suites. Restaurant, bar, pool, exercise room. AE, DC, MC, V.*

$ ▥▤ **Liz.** In the town center across from the park, this cozy old hotel has creaking floors and a lived-in feel. The large lounge, with its fireplace, can be particularly homey. Clean and comfortable bedrooms have plain furnishings. ✉ *Largo Alex, Herculano 10, 2400,* ☎ *244/814017,* FAX *244/815099. 41 rooms. Bar. AE, DC, MC, V.*

Shopping

Marinha Grande, just west of Leiria, is the center for the production of fine-quality lead crystal. You can visit several of the factories (opening times vary; call in advance). The most interesting are **Santos Barrosa** (✉ Zona da Estão–Cumeira, ☎ 244/569135), which charges a small admission fee, and **IVIMA** (✉ Av. 1 de Maio, ☎ 244/568621), where admission is free.

THE RIBATEJO

Featured in this region are such diverse sights as the bullfighting centers of Vila Franca de Xira and Santarém, the shrine at Fátima, and the fishing port of Nazaré.

Vila Franca de Xira

⑫ *30 km (18 mi) north of Lisbon via the A1 motorway.*

Vila Franca de Xira is an excellent place to see Portuguese bullfights, which are held from Easter through October. For more information call the tourist office (☞ Visitor Information *in* Estremadura and the Ribatejo A to Z, *below*). The bullring here, one of Portugal's finest, also contains a small museum with a collection of bullfighting memorabilia; it's open Tuesday–Sunday 10–12:30 and 2–6, and admission is free.

The Portuguese bullfight—known as the *tourada*—is quite different from any version of this ancient spectacle in Mexico or Spain. Here the bull's principal opponent is not a sword-carrying matador but a *cavaleiro*—a horseman elegantly attired as an 18th-century nobleman, with plumed hat and embroidered coat. Using exceptional equestrian skills, he provokes the bull and, just inches away from the animal's padded horns, manages to deftly place a colorfully festooned *bandarilha* (dart) in a designated part of the bull's back. With each pass of an ever shorter bandarilha, the danger to horse and rider increases—in spite of the bull's blunted horns. At the proper moment, when the bull is sufficiently fatigued, the final dart is placed, and with a flourish the cavaleiro exits the arena. (Following a decree by the Marquês de Pombal in the 18th century, bulls are not killed in Portuguese rings.)

The stage is now set for the *pega,* an audacious display of bravery with burlesque overtones. A group of eight men—called the *forcados*—dressed in bright-crimson vests and green stocking caps parades into the arena, and the leader, hands on hips, confronts the tired but still-enraged bull. When the bull charges, the leader meets him head on with a backwards leap and literally seizes the bull by the horns. While he tries to hang on to the furious bull's head, suspended between its horns, the other men rush in and, with one of them hanging on to its

BULLFIGHTING

ALTHOUGH THE TWO spectacles differ widely now, Portuguese and Spanish bullfights have a common origin. Both forms of the art of bullfighting were born in the Middle Ages in the struggle between Moors and Christians for the Iberian Peninsula; both were essentially arts of the nobility; and both were practiced by horsemen.

The horse was an important instrument of war in the Christian Reconquest, and the rider and his mount were both highly trained in the martial arts. As part of their training, Portuguese and Spanish knights would hone their equestrian skills and develop the dexterity of their horses in combat with the notoriously belligerent and agile Iberian fighting bulls. Long after these dangerous exercises lost their military utility, the noblemen continued to practice them for their own amusement. These displays of skill and courage, staged in castle courtyards and town squares, gradually evolved into the spectacle we know today.

During a bullfight a horse must make precisely timed movements in order to avoid being gored and to position its rider in the best location for placing his darts. This equestrian science developed out of fighting maneuvers, but over the years has been refined, most notably by the 18th-century Portuguese nobleman, Dom Pedro Alcántara e Meneses, fourth marquis of Marialva. The marquis, who held the rank of Master of the Horse to the Portuguese Court, established the rules that still govern the art of Portuguese equestrian bullfighting.

Bullfighting remained essentially the same in Portugal and Spain until the middle of the 18th century. Its subsequent development into two separate styles, the matador on foot becoming protagonist in Spain and the horseman continuing to play the leading role in Portugal, was due to the disapproval of Bourbon monarch Felipe V, who ascended to the Spanish throne in 1700. The king's French sensibilities were offended by the gore and violence of bullfighting and he soon prohibited the practice. Spain's noblemen were forced to comply. Bullfighting, however, had become too popular to disappear. The horsemen had always been assisted by a retinue of grooms and other helpers, and these lowly workers now took the art over for themselves.

In Spain, the evolution of bullfighting has produced the dramatic figure of the *matador,* a solitary protagonist who fights a deadly duel with his opponent from a proletarian position, on the ground. In Portugal, however, the aristocratic tradition of the horseman bullfighter has remained intact. The star of the show is the elegantly costumed *cavaleiro,* and the aim of the fight is not to kill the bull but to show off the courtly skills of the horse and its rider. Even today, horseback bullfighters tend to come from the wealthy and aristocratic segments of society, whereas the greatest matadors have typically come from more humble origins.

tail, try to force the animal to a standstill. At times this can be an amusing sight, but there's an ever-present element of danger (forcados have been killed during the pega). At the end of the spectacle, a few cows are led in to lure the bull from the ring. If he has shown exceptional bravery, the bull will be spared for stud purposes; otherwise, he will be slaughtered for the meat.

Had Hemingway and his buddies taken a wrong train and wound up in Vila Franca de Xira some 60 years ago, perhaps Pamplona would have remained an unsung, grimy industrial town, and the world would have flocked instead to the Ribatejo each year for one of Portugal's greatest parties. The first week of July sees the **Festa do Colete Encarnado** (Festival of the Red Waistcoat), during which the downtown streets are cordoned off, and the bulls are let loose as would-be bullfighters try their luck at dodging the charging beasts. At night the streets are alive with fado music and flamenco dancing. The running of the bulls also takes place during an autumn fair that's held in early October.

Not all the area sights are related to bullfighting. Young aviation enthusiasts will enjoy seeing the old planes at the **Museu do Ar** (Air Museum), in nearby Alverca. ✉ *At airport, 8 km (5 mi) south of Vila Franca de Xira,* ☎ *219/581294.* ✈ *300$00.* ☉ *Tues.–Sun. 10–8.*

Dining and Lodging

$$ ✕ **Redondel.** This restaurant inside the walls of the famous bullring
★ sees a lot of action and is considered Vila Franca's top eatery. There are high-vaulted brick ceilings, and in keeping with the theme, the dining room is adorned with bullfight posters and memorabilia. On the menu are regional dishes including açorda de saval. ✉ *Arcadas da Praça de Touros,* ☎ *263/272973. Reservations essential on bullfight and festival days. AE, DC, MC, V. Closed Mon.*

$ ✕▥ **Residencial Flora.** For simple but well-maintained budget accommodations, try this modern four-story hotel conveniently located in the center of town. It's even worth staying here for the restaurant. The small, homey N'O Cantinho do Ti Pedro (In Uncle Pedro's Place) is locally renowned for its excellent food at reasonable prices. It's best to book a table in advance if you're not staying here. ✉ *Rua Noel Perdigão 12, 2600,* ☎ *263/271272,* ℻ *263/276538. 19 rooms. Restaurant, bar. MC, V.*

$$$ ▥ **Quinta do Alto.** Once you drive through the massive iron gates of this hotel, you may have a hard time leaving. Situated on 50 choice acres of orchards, gardens, and vineyards in the hills high above the Tagus, just 30 minutes from the Lisbon airport, the Quinta do Alto—once the exclusive summer residence of a prominent Portuguese family—has been opened for paying guests. Instead of feeling like a lodger, you'll have the sense of visiting a wealthy friend or relative. Each of the 10 large bedrooms is comfortably furnished and has a luxurious bathroom; half the units have terraces with views of the countryside. Red brick adorns the vaulted ceilings, and the tile floors are enhanced with Arraiolos carpets. The price includes use of all the facilities and transportation to and from the airport. ✉ *Estrada de Monte Gordo, Vila Franca de Xira 2600,* ☎ *263/276850,* ℻ *263/276027. 10 rooms, 1 apartment. Bar, pool, sauna, tennis court, exercise room, squash. AE, DC, MC, V.*

$ ▥ **Lezíria Parque Hotel.** This four-story, modern hotel-and-apartment
★ complex offers the newest accommodations in Vila Franca de Xira. Conveniently situated off the main Lisbon–Oporto road, the hotel provides a comfortable base from which to explore the bull- and horse-breeding region across the Tagus River. The rooms are small and plainly furnished; there's a pleasant coffee shop on the ground floor. ✉ *Hwy. N1,*

Povos 2600, ☎ *263/276670,* FAX *263/276990. 71 rooms. Restaurant, bar, coffee shop. AE, DC, MC, V.*

Lezíria

⑬ *On the east bank of the Tagus River between Vila Franca de Xira and Santarém.*

The Lezíria refers to a region of marshy plains and rich pasturelands on the east bank of the Tagus. This area contains many stud farms, where the best bulls and horses in Portugal are bred. As you drive through the town of Benavente and the surrounding countryside, look for campinos in the fields working the bulls and horses.

Almeirim

⑭ *40 km (25 mi) northeast of Vila Franca de Xira, 4 km (2 mi) east of Santarém.*

Almeirim is a modest and not very interesting place now, although it was once at the center of an area that was a stomping ground for royalty and the Lisbon aristocracy. Nowadays it is visited mostly because it has a number of restaurants that serve a local delicacy called *sopa da pedra* (stone soup). It also has a working stud farm and a winery that can be visited at the **Quinta da Alorna.**

Santarém

⑮ *7 km (4 mi) northwest of Almeirim.*

Present-day Santarém, perched high above the Tagus, is an important farming and livestock center. Some historians believe that its beginnings date from as early as 1200 BC and the age of Ulysses. Its strategic location led several kings to choose it as their residence, and the Cortes (parliament) frequently met here. To get the feel of the town, walk up to the **Portas do Sol,** a lovely park within the ancient walls. From this vantage point you can look down on a sweeping bend in the river and beyond to the rich farmlands stretching into the neighboring Alentejo.

Thanks to its royal connections, Santarém is more richly endowed with treasures and monuments than other towns of its size. The Portuguese refer to it as their "Gothic capital." Of particular interest are the 17th-century Igreja Seminário (Seminary Church), built on the ruins of a royal palace, and the azulejo-bedecked Igreja da Marvila (Marvila Church).

Inside the **Museu Arqueológico** (Archaeological Museum), housed in the Romanesque church of São João de Alporão, you'll find interesting relics from the city's ancient past, including the finely sculpted tomb of Duarte de Meneses, which according to legend contains a single tooth, all that remained of the nobleman after his brutal murder by the Moors in Africa. The museum is on Rua Figueiredo Leal, directly across from the bell tower known as the Torre das Cabaças. ☎ *300$00.* ☉ *Tues.–Sun. 9–12:30 and 2–6:30.*

Also in Santarém is the **Igreja da Graça** (Graça Church), which contains the gravestone of Pedro Álvares Cabral, the discoverer of Brazil. There's also a tomb of the explorer in Belmonte, the town of his birth, but no one is really sure just what is in which tomb. Of note in this 14th-century Gothic church is the delicate rose window whose setting was carved from a single slab of stone. ⊠ *Largo Pedro Álvares Cabral.*

Dining and Lodging

$ ✕ **O Mal Cozinhado.** There's a strong flavor of the Ribatejo in this popular restaurant. The decor has the inevitable bullfight posters and a bull's head over the bar, but the husband-and-wife–run kitchen turns out some of the best regional fare in town. Try the pork dishes, especially the *lombinho com coentros* (tenderloin cooked with fresh coriander). ⊠ *Campo da Feira,* ☎ 243/323584. *AE, V.*

$ 🏨 **Alfageme.** This recently built, unpretentious establishment helps to fill out the otherwise sparse Santarém hotel scene. The rooms are comfortable but somewhat uninspired in their decor. ⊠ *Av. Bernardo Santareno 38, 2000,* ☎ *243/370870,* FAX *243/370850. 67 rooms. Restaurant, bar. MC, V.*

$ 🏨 **Quinta de Vale de Lobos.** This delightful two-story, 19th-century farmhouse—6 km (4 mi) from Santarém—sits among trees, ponds, and gardens. You can lounge in the large, comfortable living rooms and stroll in the adjacent woods; you also have access to a 600-acre hunting estate. The generously sized bedrooms and apartments are comfortably furnished. ⊠ *Hwy. N3, Azoia de Baixo 2000,* ☎ *243/429264,* FAX *243/429313. 4 rooms, 2 apartments. Pool. No credit cards.*

$ 🏨 **Vitória.** On a quiet street in a residential apartment building, Vitória provides a relaxing stopover. The owner of this eponymous family-run lodging, Senhora Vitória, will make you feel right at home. The old section is a bit drab, so try for a room in the newer wing. ⊠ *Rua Visconde 2, 2000,* ☎ *243/309130,* FAX *243/328202. 25 rooms. MC, V.*

Alpiarça

🔟 *10 km (6 mi) northeast of Santarém.*

Alpiarça is a pleasant little town where you'll have the chance to see how a wealthy country gentleman lived at the beginning of this century. The **Casa dos Patudos,** now a museum, was the estate of José Relvas, a diplomat and gentleman farmer. This unusual three-story manor house with its zebra-striped spire is surrounded by gardens and vineyards. An impressive assemblage of ceramics, paintings, and furnishings, including Portugal's foremost collection of Arraiolos carpets, is contained in the museum. ☎ *243/558321.* 🎟 *500$00.* ⊙ *Tues.–Sun. 10–noon and 2–5.*

Golegã

🔟 *25 km (16 mi) northeast of Santarém, 20 km (12 mi) northeast of Alpiarça.*

Golegã is one of Portugal's most notable horse-breeding centers. During the first two weeks of November, this is the site of the colorful **Feira Nacional do Cavalo** (National Horse Fair), the most important event of its kind in the country. It features riding displays, horse competitions, and stalls that sell handicrafts.

The **parish church** has a large Manueline portal, with interesting twisted columns and rope ornaments.

Torres Novas

🔟 *10 km (6 mi) northwest of Golegã.*

Torres Novas is best known for the crenellated, 14th-century hilltop **castle** that encloses a delightful garden. At the foot of the structure stands a caricature statue of Dom Sancho I—son and royal successor of Afonso Henriques—created by João Cutiliero, a prominent contemporary sculptor.

Dining and Lodging

$ ✕ **A Távola.** This simple, friendly, family-run neighborhood restaurant,
★   presided over by Sr. Joaquim and his wife, is good for such unsophisticated regional dishes as the *fritada de carnes* (assorted fried meats).
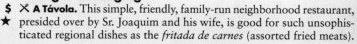

Since it's only about a 10-minute walk from the castle, A Távola makes a good dining spot after seeing the sights. ✉ *Av. Dr. Manuel de Figueiredo 12,* ☎ *249/823983. MC, V. Closed Sat. and 2 wks in Aug.*

$ ✕⊞ **Hotel dos Cavaleiros.** Facing the main square, this modern three-story hotel blends in well with the surrounding 18th-century buildings. Rooms are of a decent size and have plain, light-wood furnishings; ask for one on the third floor with a terrace. In spite of its sterile, coffee-shop appearance, the restaurant serves generous portions of well-prepared traditional dishes. Try the *espetada mista* (grilled pork, squid, and shrimp on a spit). ✉ *Praça 5 de Outubro, 2350,* ☎ *249/ 812420,* ✉ *249/812052. 57 rooms, 3 suites. Restaurant, bar. AE, DC, MC, V.*

Fátima

⓳ *20 km (12 mi) northwest of Torres Vedras, 16 km (10 mi) southeast of Batalha, 20 km (12 mi) southeast of Leiria.*

On the western flanks of the Serra de Aire lies Fátima, an important Roman Catholic pilgrimage site. (Ironically, this great Christian shrine is a village named after the daughter of Mohammed, the prophet of Islam!) If you visit this sleepy little Portuguese town in between pilgrimages, it will be difficult to imagine the thousands of faithful who come from all corners of the world to make this religious affirmation, cramming the roads, squares, parks, and virtually every square foot of space. Many of the pilgrims go the last miles on their knees.

When Pope John Paul II visited in 1991, it was estimated that more than 1 million people flocked to Fátima. Where there are so many people, there are bound to be opportunists, and Fátima is no exception—as shown by places like the "Virgin Mary Souvenir Shop" and the "Pope John Paul II Snack Bar."

It all began on May 13, 1917, when three young shepherds—Lucia dos Santos and her cousins Francisco and Jacinta—reported seeing the Virgin Mary in a field at Cova de Iria, near the village. The Virgin promised to return on the 13th of each month for the next five months, and amid much controversy and skepticism, each time accompanied by increasingly larger crowds, the three children reported successive apparitions. This was during a period of anticlerical sentiment in Portugal, and after the sixth reputed apparition, in October, the children were arrested and interrogated. But they insisted the Virgin had spoken to them, revealing three secrets. Two of these, revealed by Lucia in 1941, were interpreted to foretell the coming of World War II and the spread of communism and atheism. In a 1930 Pastoral Letter, the Bishop of Leiria declared the apparitions worthy of belief, thus approving the "Cult of Fátima." In May 2000, Francisco and Jacinta were beatified in a ceremony held at Fátima by Pope John Paul II. Lucia is still alive and is a Carmelite nun. The third secret, which was revealed after the beatification, foretold an attempt on the life of the Pope. On the 13th of each month, and especially in May and October, the faithful flock here to witness the passing of the statue of the Virgin through the throngs, to participate in candlelight processions, and to take part in solemn masses.

At the head of the huge esplanade is a large, neoclassical **basílica** (built in the late 1920s), flanked on either side by a semicircular peristyle. Other pilgrimage sites include the **Casa dos Pastorinhos**—the cottage in the nearby hamlet of Aljustrel, where the children were born—and the **Capela das Aparições** (Chapel of Apparitions), built on the spot where the appearances of the Virgin Mary are said to have taken place.

The **Museu de Cera** (Wax Museum), in the center of town, has tableaux representing the story. ☒ *700$00.* ☉ *May–Sept., daily 9:30–6:30; Oct.–Apr., daily 9:30–5:30.*

The largest caverns in Portugal are found in the honeycombed limestone **caves** in the hills to the south and west of Fátima. Within about a 25-km (15-mi) radius of Fátima, there are four sets of these grottoes—São Mamede (☎ 244/704302), Mira de Aire (☎ 244/440322), Alvados (☎ 244/440787), and Santo António (☎ 244/440787)—equipped with artificial lighting and elevators. Here you can see the subterranean world of limestone formations, underground rivers and lakes, and multicolor stalagmites and stalactites. The Fátima tourist office (☞ Visitor Information *in* Estremadura and the Ribatejo, *below*) can assist you with further details, including open hours, which vary by season. ☒ *650$00.*

Dining and Lodging

$$ ✕ **Tia Alice.** Considered the best restaurant in the area, Tia (Aunt) Alice
★ is concealed in an inconspicuous old house with French windows, across from the parish church near the sanctuary at Cova de Iria. A flight of wooden stairs inside leads to a small, intimate dining area with a wood-beam ceiling and stone walls. The *borrego assado* (roast lamb) is worth trying. ✉ *Rua do Adro,* ☎ *249/531737. AE, MC, V. Closed Mon. and July. No dinner Sun.*

$ ✕ **Retiro dos Caçadores.** A big brick fireplace, wood paneling, and stone walls set the mood in this cozy hunter's lodge, where the food is simple, but portions are hearty and the quality good. This is the best place in town for fresh game, especially coelho *com arroz* (with rice) and *perdiz* (partridge). ✉ *Lombo Egua,* ☎ *249/531323. MC, V. Closed Wed.*

$ 🛏 **Casa Beato Nuno.** This large pink-stucco inn, in a quiet setting just a few minutes' walk from the sanctuary, is run by the Carmelites but is open to visitors of all denominations. The austere rooms are clean and comfortable. ✉ *Av. Beato Nuno 51, 2496,* ☎ *249/533069,* 🖷 *249/ 532757. 136 rooms. Restaurant. MC, V.*

$ 🛏 **Hotel de Fátima.** Part of the Best Western chain, this modern four-story hotel is close to the sanctuary. With its spacious lobby, green-marble floors, and wood-paneled walls, it's generally considered Fátima's top hotel. ✉ *Rua João Paulo II, 2496,* ☎ *249/533351,* 🖷 *249/532691. 126 rooms, 7 suites. Restaurant, bar. AE, DC, MC, V.*

Tomar

⓴ *24 km (15 mi) east of Fátima, 20 km (12 mi) northeast of Torres Vedras.*

Tomar is an attractive town laid out on both sides of the Nabão River, with the new and old parts linked by a graceful, arched stone bridge. The river flows through a lovely park with weeping willows and an old wooden waterwheel.

In the Old Town, walk along the narrow, flower-lined streets, particularly Rua Dr. Joaquim Jacinto, where, in the heart of the old Jewish Quarter, you'll find the **Sinagoga de Tomar** (Tomar Synagogue), housed in a modest building. Built in the mid-15th century, this is the oldest Jewish house of worship in Portugal, though it is no longer used as such. Inside is a small museum with exhibits chronicling the Jewish presence in the country. The once-sizable Jewish population was considerably reduced in 1496 when Dom Manuel issued an edict ordering the Jews either to leave the country or convert to Christianity. Many, who became known as *marranos,* converted but secretly practiced their original religion. ✉ *Rua Dr. Joaquim Jacinto.* ☒ *Free (donations accepted).* ☉ *Daily 10–1 and 2–6.*

★ Atop a hill rising from the Old Town is the **Convento de Cristo** (Convent of Christ), a remarkable amalgamation of several centuries of architecture. You can drive to the top of the hill or hike for about 20 minutes along a path through the trees; at the top there are wonderful views from the castle walls. You enter through a formal garden lined with azulejo-covered benches. This was the Portuguese headquarters of the Order of Knights Templar, from 1160 until the order was forced to disband in 1314. Identified by their white tunics emblazoned with a crimson cross, the Templars were at the forefront of the Christian armies in the Crusades and during the years of struggle against the Moors. King Dinis in 1334 resurrected the order in Portugal under the banner of the Knights of Christ and reestablished Tomar as its headquarters. In the early 15th century, under the leadership of Prince Henry the Navigator (who for a time resided in the castle), the order flourished. The caravels of the era of discovery sailed under the order's crimson cross.

The oldest parts of this extraordinary architectural complex date from the 12th century: the towering castle keep, ringed by massive walls, and the **Charola**, sometimes called the Rotunda. Like many Templar churches, the fortresslike, 16-sided Charola, which originally stood on its own, is patterned after the Church of the Holy Sepulchre in Jerusalem and has an octagonal oratory at its core. (The paintings and wooden statues that decorate the interior of the Charola were added in the 16th century.) The medieval Templar nucleus of the Convento de Cristo acquired its Manueline church and cluster of magnificent cloisters during the next 500 years. To see what the Manueline style is all about, stroll through the church's nave with its many examples of the twisted ropes, seaweed, and nautical themes that typify the style, and be sure to look at the **chapter house window,** probably the most photographed one in Europe. Its lichen-encrusted sculpture evokes the feeling and spirit of the great age of discovery. ☎ 249/315089. 🖻 400$00. ☉ May–Sept., daily 9:15–6; Oct.–Apr., daily 9:15–12:30 and 2–5:15.

Tomar has several other buildings and sights worth visiting. On the way down the hill from the convent is the lovely little church of **Nossa Senhora da Conceição,** arguably Portugal's finest example of early Renaissance architecture, and across the river is the 13th-century church of **Santa Maria do Olival,** where the bones of several Templar knights are interred, including those of Gualdim Pais, founder of the order in Portugal. Popular belief—supported by some archaeological evidence—has it that the historic church was once connected with the Convent of Christ by a tunnel. In the gardens by the river there is an enormous working **waterwheel** of the sort once used in the region for irrigation. At Pegões, some 5 km (3 mi) northwest of town, is the 5-km-long (3-mi-long) **aqueduct** built in the 16th century to bring water to Tomar.

Dining and Lodging

$$ ✗ **A Bela Vista.** The date on the calçada reads "1922," which was when
★ the Sousa family opened this attractive little restaurant next to the old arched bridge. For summer dining there's a small, rustic terrace with views of the river and the Convent of Christ. Carrying on the family tradition, son Eugenio Sousa presides over the kitchen, which turns out great quantities of hearty regional fare. Try one of the house specialties, such as cabrito assado or *dobrada com feijão* (tripe with beans), and wash it down with a robust local red wine. ✉ *Marquês de Pombal 68,* ☎ *249/312870. No credit cards. Closed Tues.*

$$ ✗▥ **Hotel dos Templários.** A large, modern hotel set in a tranquil
★ park along the Nabão River, the Templários offers many units with views of the Convent of Christ. The big, airy dining room has picture

windows facing the park and serves interesting regional dishes. With its spacious grounds and reasonably priced luxuries, the hotel makes a good base from which to visit the area's many attractions. ✉ *Largo Candido dos Reis 1, 2300,* ☎ *249/321730,* 📠 *249/322191. 171 rooms, 5 suites. Restaurant, bar, indoor and outdoor pools, barbershop, beauty salon, tennis court, health club. AE, DC, MC, V.*

Castelo de Bode

㉑ *10 km (6 mi) southeast of Tomar.*

The dam on the Zêzere River at Castelo de Bode has created a huge artificial lake that fans out northward. This is one of Portugal's most popular water-sports areas. For information regarding boat excursions, which include lunch on board, inquire at the Hotel dos Templários in Tomar (☞ *above*) or at the dock by the Pousada de São Pedro (☞ *below*).

Dining and Lodging

$ ✕🏨 **Pousada de São Pedro.** Originally built in 1946 to house engi-
★ neers building the dam on the Zêzere River, this pousada sits on a wooded hill and overlooks the man-made lake. Its location—13 km (8 mi) from Tomar—makes it a good place from which to explore nearby villages. The restaurant, in a lovely setting, features high-quality regional fare. ✉ *Castelo de Bode 2300,* ☎ *249/381159,* 📠 *249/381176. 25 rooms. Restaurant. AE, DC, MC, V.*

Castelo de Almourol

★ ㉒ *16 km (10 mi) south of Tomar, 16 km (10 mi) east of Torres Novas. For the most scenic route from Castelo de Bode, take the N358-2 south along the Zêzere to where it joins the Tagus, then continue west 4 km (2 mi) on N3 to the castle turnoff.*

For a close look at Almourol Castle, a storybook edifice sitting on a craggy island downstream in the middle of the Tagus River, take the 1½-km-long (1-mi-long) dirt road leading down to the water. The riverbank in this area is practically deserted, making it a wonderful picnic spot. (In summer you can take a boat to the island.) The setting could hardly be more romantic: an ancient castle with crenellated walls and a lofty tower sits on a greenery-covered rock in the middle of a gently flowing river. The stuff of poetry and legends, Almourol was the setting for Francisco de Morais's epic *Palmeirim da Inglaterra* (*Palmeirim of England*).

NEED A BREAK? On N3 just west of the castle the good lunch stop **Restaurante Almourol** (✉ Cais de Tancos, Vila Nova da Barquinha, ☎ 249/710432) is in a lovely old house with gardens, orange trees, and a terrace overlooking the castle.

Constância

㉓ *4 km (2 mi) east of Almourol Castle.*

Peaceful little Constância is at the confluence of the Zêzere and the Tagus. It's best known as the town where Camões was exiled in 1548, the unfortunate result of his romantic involvement with Catarina de Ataíde, the "Natercia" of his poems and a lady-in-waiting to Queen Catarina. There's a bronze statue of the bard in a reflective pose at the riverbank. If you're unlucky and the wind is in the wrong direction, you may get an unpleasant whiff from the paper mill across the river. Fortunately, filtering has greatly reduced the possibility of this spoiling your visit.

Dining and Lodging

$ ✕🍴 **Quinta de Santa Barbara.** If you're looking for a place to immerse
★ yourself in the peace and quiet of the Portuguese countryside, look no
farther. The Quinta, a short drive from town, has several sprawling
buildings (a few of which date from the 16th century) and occupies
some 45 acres of farmland and pine forests overlooking the Tagus. This
country inn, opened in 1988, achieves a wonderful blend of old-world
charm and modern convenience. Each of the six spacious rooms in the
main house is individually furnished with 18th-century Portuguese reproductions and has a modern tiled bathroom. The small restaurant,
with a barrel-vault ceiling and stone walls, specializes in local dishes.
⊠ *2 km (1 mi) east of Constância on IP6; follow directions on sign at
traffic circle, 2250,* ☎ *249/739214,* FAX *249/739373. 6 rooms. Restaurant, bar, pool, tennis court, horseback riding. MC, V.*

Abrantes

㉔ *16 km (10 mi) east of Constância.*

Strategically situated on a hilltop overlooking the River Tagus, Abrantes
flourished and became one of the country's most populous and prosperous towns during the 16th century, when the river was navigable
all the way to the sea. With the coming of the railroad and the development of better roads, the town's commercial importance waned. The
main attraction here is the **castle** (built in the 16th century). Walk up
through the maze of narrow, flower-lined streets to the ruins of this
ancient fortress. Much of it is in disrepair, but with a bit of imagination you can conjure visions of what an impressive structure this must
have been. The attractive garden that has been planted between the
twin fortifications is a wonderful place to watch the sun set: the play
of light on the river and the lengthening shadows along the olive groves
provide an inspiring setting for an evening picnic.

Dining and Lodging

$ ✕ **O Fumeiro.** This pleasant and spacious restaurant is handily situ-
ated in the old part of town over a café. The food is simple but good,
consisting almost entirely of regional specialties. Try the *cabrito no forno*
(roast kid) if it's available. ⊠ *Rua do Pisco 9,* ☎ *241/363893. No credit
cards. Closed Mon.*

$ ✕🍴 **Hotel Turismo.** The hotel enjoys such a spectacular hilltop loca-
tion that it's a shame the hotel's architect couldn't come up with something more innovative than an exterior of pink stucco. Inside is a
different story: you'll find an inviting, clubby lounge with a fireplace
and comfy leather chairs. Guest rooms are small but comfortably furnished; many of the newer ones have terraces with wonderful vistas.
The dining room—lined with picture windows—also offers inspiring
views and is an excellent place to sample *palha de Abrantes* (straw of
Abrantes), a tasty local dessert consisting of a thick egg and almond
paste topped with yellow threadlike wisps made of eggs and sugar. ⊠
Largo de Santo António, 2200, ☎ *241/361271,* FAX *241/325218. 41
rooms. Restaurant, bar, pool, tennis court. AE, DC, MC, V.*

Sardoal

㉕ *12 km (7 mi) north of Abrantes on N244-3, 20 km (12 mi) northeast
of Constância on N358-2.*

Sardoal, an island of white houses with yellow trim and red-tile roofs
in a sea of wooded hills, is an enchanting place of narrow streets paved
with pebbles from nearby streams and flowers everywhere—hanging
from windows and balconies and lining the winding streets and alleys.

In such a spot you might expect art to flourish, and the 17th-century parish church *does* contain a collection of fine 16th-century paintings by the "Master of Sardoal," an unknown painter whose works have been found in other parts of the country and whose influence on other artists has been noted.

Castelo de Belver

㉖ *30 km (19 mi) southeast of Sardoal. Follow N244-3 through the pine-covered hills to Chão de Codes; take N244 south toward Gavião.*

A fairy-tale castle planted on top of a cone-shape hill (looking as if its top has been sliced off), the fortress of Belver was built in the last years of the 12th century by the Knights Hospitallers under the command of King Sancho I. The castle commands a superb view of the Tagus. In 1194 this region was threatened by the Moorish forces who controlled the lands south of the river, except for Évora. The expected attack never took place, and the present structure is little changed from its original design. The walls of the keep, which stands in the center of the courtyard, are some 12 ft thick, and on the ground floor is a great cistern of unknown depth. According to local lore, an orange dropped into the well will later appear bobbing down the river.

ESTREMADURA AND THE RIBATEJO A TO Z

Arriving and Departing

By Airplane
Estremadura and the Ribatejo are best served by Lisbon's international airport. For flight information, *see* Lisbon A to Z *in* Chapter 1.

By Car
Estremadura and the Ribatejo can be reached easily from Lisbon, since both provinces begin as extensions of the city's northern suburbs. There are two principal access roads from the capital: A1 (also called E80 and IP1), which is the Lisbon–Oporto toll road, provides the best inland access; A8 (also called IC1) is the fastest route to the coast. From Oporto there's easy access via the A1 tollway.

By Train
The region is served by the nightly Tren Hotel (Hotel Train), which departs from Lisbon's Santa Apolónia station at 10 PM and arrives in Madrid's Chamartin station at 8:40 the following morning. The *Sud Express,* linking Paris with Lisbon (Santa Apolónia station)—via the Spanish cities of Burgos and Salamanca—leaves Lisbon daily at 5:05 PM and arrives at Paris's Montparnasse station at 3 PM the following day. Passengers change onto a French TGV (high-speed train) at the Spain–France border to go on to Paris, and need special reservations for this leg of the journey. (Note that the *Sud Express* stops at Fátima, but be prepared for an additional bus or taxi ride. The actual town and shrine are some 25 km [16 mi] away from the station.)

Getting Around

By Bus
There are few, if any, places in this region that aren't served by at least one bus daily. Express coaches run by several regional bus lines travel regularly between Lisbon and the larger towns such as Santarém, Leiria, and Abrantes. If you have the time and patience, bus travel, which offers an opportunity to interact with locals, can be a rewarding and

inexpensive way to get around. At press time the Lisbon City Council was reorganizing the bus system; it's best to do your booking
through a travel agent (☞ *below*).

By Car

A car is by far the most efficient way to tour this region, where bus
service is often infrequent and train service virtually nonexistent. Driving will give you access to many out-of-the-way beaches and villages.
The roads are generally good, and traffic is light, except for weekend
congestion along the coast. There are no confusing big cities in which
to get lost, although parking can be a major problem in some of the
towns. However, drive with extreme caution. Affable as they are on
foot, the Portuguese are among Europe's most aggressive drivers.
There are major car-rental agencies in Leiria and Nazaré, as well as in
Lisbon.

By Train

Travel by train within central Portugal is not for people in a great hurry.
Service to many of the more remote destinations is infrequent—and in
some cases nonexistent. Even major tourist attractions such as Nazaré
and Mafra have no direct rail links. Nevertheless, trains will take you
to most of the strategic bases for touring the towns in this chapter.

The Lisbon–Oporto line (Santa Apolónia station) provides a reasonably frequent service to Vila Franca de Xira, Santarém, Torres Novas,
Tomar, and Fátima. Towns in the western part of the region, such as
Torres Vedras, Caldas da Rainha, Óbidos, and Leiria, are served on
another line from Lisbon's Rossío station.

Contacts and Resources

Emergencies

General: ☎ 112. **Hospitals: Caldas da Rainha Hospital Distrital** (⊠ Rua
Diário de Notícias, ☎ 262/830300), **Leiria Hospital Distrital** (⊠ Largo
D. Mel. Aguiar, ☎ 244/817000), **Tomar Hospital Distrital** (⊠ Av. Dr.
Candido Madureira, ☎ 249/321100). **Pharmacies:** All sizable towns
have at least one pharmacy open weekends, holidays, and after normal store hours. Local newspapers usually keep a schedule, and notices are posted on the door of every pharmacy.

Guided Tours

Few regularly scheduled sightseeing tours originate within the region,
but many of the major attractions are covered by a wide selection of
one-day tours from Lisbon. For information contact **Gray Line Tours**
(⊠ Av. Praia da Vitória 12-B, ☎ 213/522594) or **Citirama** (⊠ Av. Praia
da Vitória 12-B, ☎ 213/191090).

Boat trips on the São Cristovão, along the Zêzere River, depart in summer from the Estalagem Lago Azul (⊠ Hwy. N378, Ferreira do Zêzere,
Castanheira 2240, ☎ 249/361445), upstream from the Castelo de
Bode dam. The 4½-hour cruises cost 7,300$00 including lunch, but take
place only when there are enough passengers; this is most likely to happen on weekends and national holidays. For **reservations and information,** contact Hotel dos Templários in Tomar (⊠ Largo Candido
dos Reis 1, 2300, ☎ 249/310100).

Telephones

For information, dial 118; operators often speak English.

Travel Agencies

Many travel agencies in the region are small, with limited services and
no one who speaks English. However, **Meliá Europa** (⊠ Av. Cidade Mar-
ingá 25, ☎ 244/833850, ℻ 244/815346), in Leiria, has English-speak-

ing personnel and a full range of services (☞ *also* Travel Agencies *under* Lisbon A to Z *in* Chapter 1).

Visitor Information

ESTREMADURA

Alcobaça (✉ Praça 25 de Abril, ☎ 262/582377), **Batalha** (✉ Praça Mouzinho de Albuquerque, ☎ 244/765180), **Caldas da Rainha** (✉ Rua Eng. Duarte Pacheco, ☎ 262/831003), **Ericeira** (✉ Rua Eduardo Burnay 46, ☎ 261/863668), **Leiria** (✉ Jardim Lúis de Camões, ☎ 244/823773), **Lourinhã** (✉ Praia da Areia Branca, ☎ 261/422167), **Mafra** (✉ Av. 25 de Abril, ☎ 261/812023), **Nazaré** (✉ Av. República 17, ☎ 262/561194), **Óbidos** (✉ Rua Direita, ☎ 262/959231), **Peniche** (✉ Rua Alex. Herculano, ☎ 262/789571), **Torres Vedras** (✉ Rua 9 de Abril, ☎ 261/314094), and **Vila Franca de Xira** (✉ Rua Almirante Cándido dos Reis, 147, ☎ 263/276053).

THE RIBATEJO

Abrantes (✉ Largo da Feira, ☎ 241/362555), **Constância** (✉ Câmara Municipal, ☎ 249/739611), **Fátima** (✉ Av. José A. Correia da Silva, ☎ 249/531139), **Santarém** (✉ Rua Capelo e Ivens 63, ☎ 243/391512), **Tomar** (✉ Rua Serpa Pinto 1, ☎ 249/329000), and **Torres Novas** (✉ Largo do Paço, ☎ 249/812910).

4 ÉVORA AND THE ALENTEJO

Known as the granary of Portugal, the Alentejo is a thinly populated, largely agricultural region of grainfields and cork and olive trees. The landscape ranges from the breezy Atlantic beaches of the littoral to the fortress-crowned hills and rolling plains of the dry, inland areas. Ancient Évora, at the center of the region, is rich in history and architectural treasures.

By Dennis Jaffe

Updated by
Martha de la
Cal and Peter
Collis

THE ALENTEJO, which means "the land beyond the Rio Tejo (Tagus River)" in Portuguese, is a vast, sparsely populated area of heath and rolling hills punctuated with stands of cork and olive trees. It's the country's largest region, stretching from the rugged west coast beaches all the way east to Spain and from the Tagus in the north to the low mountains on the border of the Algarve, Portugal's southernmost region. Its central urban hub, Évora, is rich with traditional Portuguese architecture. Over the centuries the pastoral countryside has been the scene of innumerable battles: between Romans and Visigoths, Moors and Christians, Portuguese and Spaniards, Portuguese and French, and finally (in the 1830s) between rival Portuguese factions in a civil war. Few hilltops in the region are without at least a trace of a castle or fortress.

One of the Alentejo's major industries is cork, of which Portugal is the world's largest producer. This is not, however, an industry for people in a hurry. It takes two decades before the trees can be harvested, and they can be carefully stripped only once every nine years. The numbers painted on the trees indicate the year of the last harvest. Exhibits at several regional museums chronicle this delicate process and display associated tools and handicrafts.

The undulating fields of wheat and barley surrounding Beja and Évora, the rice paddies of Alcácer do Sal, and the vineyards of Borba and Reguengos de Monsaraz are representative of this region, Portugal's breadbasket. Traditions here are strong. Herdsmen tending sheep and goats wear the *pelico* (traditional sheepskin vest), and women in the fields wear broad-brim hats over kerchiefs and colorful, patterned dresses over trousers. Dwellings are dazzling white; more elegant houses have wrought-iron balconies and grillwork. The windows and doors of modest cottages and hilltop country *montes* (farmhouses) are trimmed with blue or yellow, and colorful flowers abound. The best time to visit the Alentejo is spring, when temperatures are pleasant and the fields are carpeted with wildflowers. Summer can be brutal, with the mercury frequently topping 100°F. As the Portuguese say, "In the Alentejo there is no shade but what comes from the sky."

Pleasures and Pastimes

Beaches
Some of Europe's finest and least crowded beaches are on the rugged stretch of Portugal's west coast that extends from the southern extreme of the Alentejo at Odeceixe north to the tip of the Tróia Peninsula. Some beaches—such as Praia do Carvalhal and Praia Grande at Almograve—don't have any facilities and are uncrowded even in July and August, when most of Europe's beaches are packed elbow to elbow. You can also find solitude by heading west on almost any of the unmarked tracks along the coast. The beaches at Vila Nova de Milfontes and at Porto Covo have restaurants and the usual beach facilities. Exercise great care when swimming on the west coast: the surf is often high, and strong undertows and riptides are common.

Castles
In much of the Alentejo, you can't drive far without seeing a castle or a fortress crowning one of the hills. Some, such as the castles at Estremoz and Alvito, have been restored and converted into luxurious *pousadas* (government-run inns). Others, including those at Castelo de Vide and Viana do Alentejo, are open for you to clamber about their battlements.

Dining

In the Alentejo, a region known as the country's granary, bread is a major part of most meals. It's the basis of a popular dish known as *açorda,* a thick, stick-to-the-ribs porridge to which various ingredients such as fish, meat, eggs, or shellfish are added. Açorda *de marisco*— bread with eggs, seasonings, and plenty of assorted shellfish—is one of the more popular varieties. Another version, açorda *Alentejana,* consists of a clear broth, olive oil, garlic, slices of bread, and poached eggs. Pork from the Alentejo is the best in the country and often is combined with clams, onions, and tomatoes in the classic dish *carne de porco Alentejana.* One of Portugal's most renowned sheep's milk cheeses— tangy, but mellow when properly ripened—is made in the Serpa region. Elvas, near the Spanish border, is known for its tasty sugar plums. Alentejo wines—especially those from around Borba and Reguengos de Monsaraz—are regular prizewinners at national tasting contests.

Between mid-June and mid-September reservations are advised at upscale restaurants. Many moderate or inexpensive establishments, however, don't accept reservations and have informal dining rooms where you share a table with other diners. Dress at all but the most luxurious restaurants is casual; any exceptions to the dress code or reservation policy are noted in the reviews. For price categories, *see* the chart under Dining *in* Smart Travel Tips A to Z.

Horseback Riding

The sparse population and minimal automobile traffic make this region a delight for equestrian outings. Whether for a few hours or a few days, you will get an authentic perspective of the Alentejo on horseback. Overnight tours are organized, with lodging at bed-and-breakfasts and meals both on the trail and at local restaurants. Trails provide a variety of backdrops—including castles, villages, and prehistoric sites.

Lodging

Much of the vast, primarily agricultural Alentejo is lacking in first-class hotels; the best accommodations in this region are the pousadas. Indeed, some of the finest in the country are in the Alentejo, including one in the old Lóios convent in Évora and another in the castle at Estremoz. Many of the pousadas are small, some with as few as six rooms, so reserving well in advance is essential. There are also a number of high-quality, government-approved private guest houses in the region. Look for signs that say TURISMO RURAL or TURISMO DE HABITAÇÃO. Several of these are included in our listings. For price categories, *see* the chart under Lodging *in* Smart Travel Tips A to Z.

Shopping

The brightly colored hand-painted plates, bowls, and figurines from the upper Alentejo are popular throughout Portugal. You'll find the best selection of this distinctive type of folk art in and around Estremoz, where the terra-cotta jugs and bowls are adorned with chips of marble from local quarries. Saturday morning the *rossío* (town square) is chock-full of vendors displaying their wares. Redondo and the village of São Pedro do Corval, near Reguengos de Monsaraz, are also good sources of this type of pottery, as is Évora. The village of Arraiolos, near Évora, is famous for its hand-embroidered wool rugs.

Swimming

In addition to swimming in the ocean at the many beaches along the west coast, many towns have modern municipal swimming pools—so even in the middle of the dry Alentejo, you'll never be very far from a refreshing dip. Water sports are also available, unlikely as it may seem, on some of the region's artificial reservoirs.

Exploring Évora and the Alentejo

The Alentejo, Portugal's largest region, contains a wide variety of attractions—from the rugged west coast beaches to the architectural treasures of Évora. The area is divided roughly into two parts: the more mountainous region north of Évora, and the flatter Lower Alentejo, in the southern part of the region.

Great Itineraries

You can make convenient loops starting and finishing in Lisbon, or you can extend your travels by continuing south to the Algarve from Beja or Santiago do Cacém. You should allow 10 days in order to get a feel for the region, exploring Évora and visiting some outlying attractions such as Monsaraz and Castelo de Vide. This will also allow time for a day or two of sunbathing on a west coast beach. If you skip the beach, you can cover the most interesting attractions at a comfortable pace in seven days. Three days will give you time to explore Évora and its surroundings along with one or two additional highlights.

Numbers in the text correspond to numbers in the margin and on the Évora, the Upper Alentejo, and the Lower Alentejo maps.

IF YOU HAVE 3 DAYS

Be sure to include ☷ **Évora** ①–⑳, one of Portugal's most beautiful cities, in your first day of exploring. The following morning visit the rug-producing town of **Arraiolos** ㉔ and then continue on to **Estremoz** ㉛ and its imposing fortress, which doubles as a pousada. Head east past **Borba** ㉚ and its marble quarries to **Vila Viçosa** ㉙, site of the Ducal Palace. Then continue south to the whitewashed village of ☷ **Terena** ㉘. In the morning visit the fortified hilltop town of **Monsaraz** ㉗ before returning to Lisbon.

IF YOU HAVE 7 DAYS

From Lisbon head for ☷ **Évora** ①–⑳. The next day explore the **Aqueduto da Agua da Prata** ㉑ and the prehistoric sites just outside town, which include the **Cromlech and the Menhir of Almendres** ㉒ and the **Dolmen of Zambujeiro** ㉓. On the way to ☷ **Estremoz** ㉛, stop at **Arraiolos** ㉔. From Estremoz head east to the fortified town of ☷ **Elvas** ㉝, stopping en route at **Borba** ㉚ and the Ducal Palace at **Vila Viçosa** ㉙. The following day continue to **Monsaraz** ㉗, with stops along the way at **Terena** ㉘ and the pottery shops in **São Pedro do Corval** ㉖. From Monsaraz head south to ☷ **Beja** ㉛, inspecting the Roman ruins at **São Cucufate** ㊹ en route. The next day head west to ☷ **Santiago do Cacém** ㊽ for more Roman ruins and a few hours at the beach. On your seventh day return to Lisbon, stopping along the way to see the castle at **Alcácer do Sal** ㊼.

IF YOU HAVE 10 DAYS

Spend two nights in ☷ **Évora** ①–⑳ to visit the town and its **Aqueduto da Agua da Prata** ㉑, the nearby prehistoric sites of **Cromlech and the Menhir of Almendres** ㉒ and the **Dolmen of Zambujeiro** ㉓, and neighboring **Arraiolos** ㉔. Then head for ☷ **Estremoz** ㉛, with a stop along the way to visit the castle and enjoy the spectacular view at **Évoramonte** ㉜. The next morning continue north to the **Coudelaria de Alter** ㊲ outside Alter do Chão. Then follow N245 north to ☷ **Castelo de Vide** ㊵, a friendly, whitewashed town known for its spa and healing waters. From here continue to ☷ **Marvão** ㊳ (spend two nights), a fortified town atop a sheer cliff. The most scenic approach from Castelo de Vide is via the serpentine back roads rather than the main highway. Using either Castelo de Vide or Marvão as a base, you can explore the **Parque Natural da Serra de São Mamede** ㊱. Rich in wildlife, the park is ideally suited for walking and enjoying the peaceful countryside. At

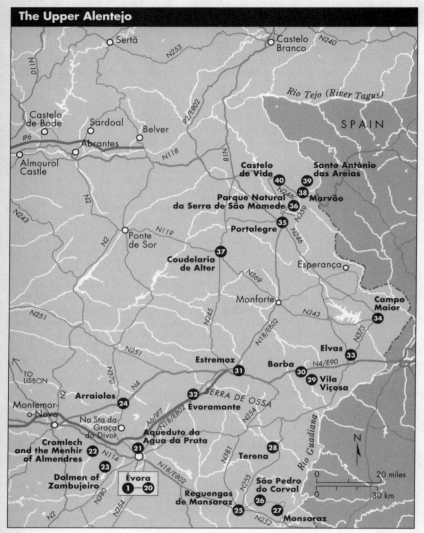

Santo António das Areias ㉟, just north of Marvão, are some two dozen prehistoric dolmens scattered among the chestnut groves. From Marvão take N359, which winds its way across the low mountains of the Serra de São Mamede to **Portalegre** ㉟. Spend a few hours here and continue to 🏨 **Elvas** ㉝, with its extensive fortifications and Manueline cathedral. Stop en route at **Campo Maior** ㉞, a pleasant town distinguished by its hilltop castle and tiny whitewashed houses with wrought-iron grillwork and balconies. The next morning visit **Borba** ㉚, known for its fine wines and marble quarries, then tour the Ducal Palace at **Vila Viçosa** ㉙. Continue south by way of **Terena** ㉘, **Reguengos de Monsaraz** ㉕, and **São Pedro do Corval** ㉖ to spend the night in 🏨 **Monsaraz** ㉗. The next day visit 🏨 **Beja** ㊹, a fortified town whose center still retains a Moorish character, stopping to see the Roman ruins at **São Cucufate** ㊹ en route. From Beja head west to 🏨 **Santiago do Cacém** ㊽ (spend two nights), where you can visit the Roman ruins and spend some time relaxing at the nearby beaches.

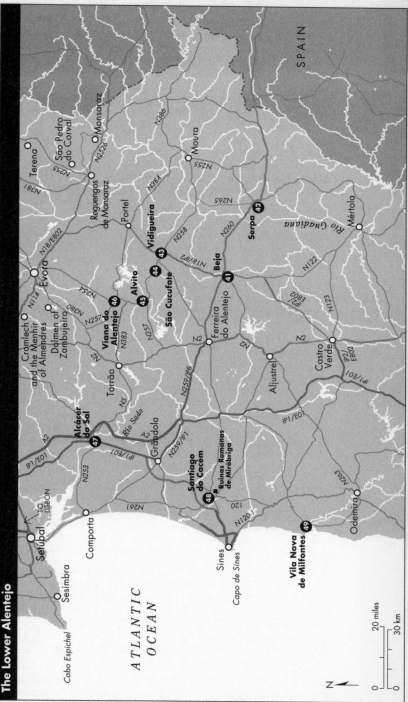

From Santiago do Cacém you can either head south to the Algarve or return to Lisbon. The most scenic route to Lisbon is the N261, which runs along the coast to the tip of the Tróia Peninsula; from there you can take the ferry across the Sado River estuary. You can also drive through the Sado River Nature Reserve by turning off at Comporta and following N253 to **Alcácer do Sal** ㊼. Visit the hilltop castle here and continue on to Lisbon via the A2 toll highway. Fifty kilometers (31 miles) south of Beja on the Guadiana River lies the pretty and historic little town of Mértola. The Phoenicians built a port here, later used by the Romans and the Moors. The entire town is considered a museum site, and dotted around it are a number of exhibits of great historical and artistic interest. The church, Igreja Matrix, on the slopes above the river, was once a mosque, and it retains many of its original Islamic features. After visiting the town you can return to Beja on N122 and spend the night there before heading west to the coast.

When to Tour Évora and the Alentejo

Spring comes early to this part of Portugal. Early April to mid-June is a wonderful time to tour, when the fields are full of colorful wildflowers. July and August are brutally hot, with temperatures in places such as Beja often reaching 100°F or more. Air-conditioned rental cars are rare, as are air-conditioned shops, restaurants, and hotels. By mid-September things cool off sufficiently to make touring this region a delight.

ÉVORA AND ENVIRONS

Dressed in traditional garb, shepherds and farmers with wizened faces that bear the markings of a lifetime in the baking Alentejo sun stand about Giraldo Square; a group of college girls dressed in jeans and T-shirts chat animatedly at a sidewalk café; a local businessman in coat and tie purposefully hurries by; and clusters of tourists, cameras in hand, capture the historic monuments on film—all this is part of a typical summer's day in Évora. The town is the flourishing capital of the central Alentejo and a university center. Sitting atop a small hill in the heart of a vast cork-, olive-, and grain-producing region, Évora—with its astonishing variety of inspiring architecture—stands out from provincial farm towns the world over: the entire inner city is a monument.

Although the region was inhabited some 4,000 years ago—as attested to by the dolmens and menhirs in the countryside—it was during the Roman epoch that the town called Liberalitas Julia in the province of Lusitania first achieved importance. A large part of present-day Évora is built on Roman foundations, of which the Temple of Diana, with its graceful Corinthian columns, is the most conspicuous reminder.

The Moors also made a great historical impact on the area. They arrived in 715 and remained more than 450 years. They were driven out in 1166, thanks in part to a clever ruse perpetrated by Geraldo Sem Pavor (Gerald the Fearless). Geraldo tricked Évora's Moorish ruler into leaving a strategic watchtower unguarded. With a small force, Geraldo took control of the tower. To regain control of it, most of the Moorish troops left their posts at the city's main entrance, allowing the bulk of Geraldo's forces to march in unopposed.

Toward the end of the 12th century, Évora's fortunes increased as the town became the favored location for the courts of the Burgundy and Avis dynasties; less than 164 km (102 mi) from Lisbon, it attracted many of the great minds and creative talents of Renaissance Portugal. Some of the more prominent residents at this time were Gil Vicente, the founder of Portuguese theater; the sculptor Nicolas Chanterene; and Gregorio Lopes, the painter known for his renderings of court life. Such a concentration of royal wealth and Renaissance creativity superimposed upon the existing Moorish town was instrumental in the development of the delicate Manueline-Mudéjar (elaborate, Moslem-influenced) architectural style. You can see fine examples of this in the graceful lines of the Palace of Dom Manuel and the turreted São Bras Chapel.

Évora is, above all, a town for walking. Wherever you glance as you stroll the maze of narrow streets and alleys of the old town, amid arches and whitewashed houses, you'll come face to face with reminders of the town's rich architectural and cultural heritage. The area surrounding Évora is a rich agricultural region with scattered small villages and some of Portugal's earliest inhabited sites.

Évora

★ *164 km (102 mi) southeast of Lisbon.*

★ ❶ The **Praça do Giraldo,** the bustling, arcade-lined square in the center of Old Town, is named after the city's liberator, Gerald the Fearless. During Caesar's time the square, marked by a large arch, was the Roman forum; in 1571 the arch was destroyed to make room for the fountain across from the entrance to the church. The graceful, flattened sphere made of white Estremoz marble was designed and executed by the Renaissance architect Afonso Álvares.

❷ Note the striking white Renaissance facade of the **Igreja de Santo Antão,** which stands at the top of the Praça do Giraldo. A medieval hermitage of the Knights Templar was razed in 1553 to make way for the present church, which has massive round pillars and soaring vaulted ceilings. The marble altar in bas-relief is a holdover from the primitive hermitage.

NEED A BREAK? The **Café Arcadia,** opposite the fountain on the Praça do Giraldo, is an Évora institution. The large hall, divided into snack bar and restaurant sections, is decorated with photos of the big bands that played here in the '40s. Tables set on the square are just the places from which to watch Évora on parade.

The narrow, cobblestone **Rua 5 de Outubro,** a pedestrian thoroughfare lined with shops and whitewashed houses with wrought-iron balconies, is one of the town's most attractive streets and connects the Praça do Giraldo and the cathedral. The massive, twin, asymmetric towers

★ ❸ and the battlement-ringed walls give the **Sé** (cathedral) a fortresslike appearance, a type of construction also seen in the Lisbon and Coimbra cathedrals. The Sé is a transitional Gothic-style building constructed in 1186 from huge granite blocks. It has been enhanced over the centuries with an octagonal, turreted dome above the transept; a blue-tile spire atop the north tower; a number of fine Manueline windows; and several Gothic rose windows. At the entrance, Gothic arches are supported by marble columns bearing delicately sculpted statues of the apostles. With the exception of a fine baroque chapel, the granite interior is somber. The cloister, a 14th-century Gothic addition with Mudéjar vestiges, is one of the finest of its genre in the country. Statues of the evangelists decorate the corners. Housed in the towers and chapter room is the **Museu de Arte Sacra da Sé** (Museum of Sacred Art). Of particular interest is a 13th-century ivory triptych, the *Virgin of Paradise,* whose body opens up to show exquisitely carved scenes of her life and whose head is a 16th-century wooden replacement, strangely out of proportion. The entrance fee to the museum also allows you to visit the cathedral's impressive cloisters. ▨ *Museum and cloisters 350$00.* ☉ *Tues. 2–5, Wed.–Sun. 9–noon and 2–5.*

Évora

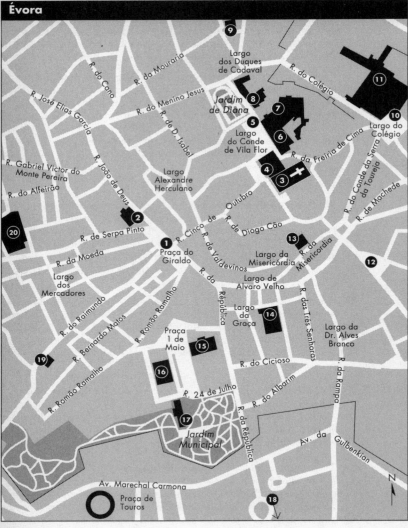

Largo dos Duques de Cadaval

R. do Colégio

Largo do Colégio

Jardim de Diana

Largo do Conde de Vila Flor

R. da Freiria de Cima

R. do Menino Jesus

R. de D. Isabel

R. da Mouraria

R. do Cano

R. José Elias Garcia

R. Gabriel Victor do Monte Pereira

R. do Alfeirão

R. João de Deus

Largo Alexandre Herculano

R. Cinco de Outubro

R. de Diogo Cão

R. de Serpa Pinto

R. da Moeda

Largo dos Mercadores

R. do Raimundo

R. Bernardo Matos

R. Romão Ramalho

R. Romão Ramalho

Praça do Giraldo

R. de Valdevinos

R. da República

Largo da Misericórdia

R. da Misericórdia

Largo de Alvaro Velho

Largo da Graça

R. das Três Senhoras

Largo da Dr. Alves Branco

R. do Conde da Serra da Tourega

R. de Machede

Praça 1 de Maio

R. do Cicioso

R. 24 de Julho

R. do Albarim

R. da República

R. da Rampa

Jardim Municipal

Av. da Gulbenkian

Av. Marechal Carmona

Praça de Touros

N

Biblioteca Pública 6

Ermida de São Bras 18

Igreja a Nossa Senhora da Graça 14

Igreja das Mercês 19

Igreja de Espirito Santo 10

Igreja de Misericórdia 13

Igreja de Santa Clara 20

Igreja de Santo Antão 2

Igreja de São Francisco 15

Igreja de São Mamede 9

Igreja dos Lóios 7

Largo da Porta de Moura 12

Mercado Municipal 16

Museu de Évora . . .4

Palácio de Dom Manuel 17

Palácio dos Duques de Cadaval 8

Praça do Giraldo 1

Sé 3

Templo Romano 5

Universidade de Évora 11

4 The **Museu de Évora** (Évora Museum) is in a stately, late-17th-century baroque building next to the Sé. The structure, once a palace that accommodated bishops, contains a rich collection of sculpture and paintings as well as interesting archaeological and architectural artifacts. The first-floor galleries, arranged around a pleasant garden, include several excellent carved pillars and a fine Manueline doorway. Among the early Portuguese paintings on display in the upstairs gallery are works attributed to the 16th-century Master of Sardoal. ✉ *Largo do Conde de Vila Flor,* ☎ 266/702604. 💰 250$00. ☉ *Tues. 2–5:30, Wed.–Sun. 9:30–12:30 and 2–5.*

★ **5** The well-preserved ruins of the **Templo Romano,** or Roman Temple, dominate a large plaza and are across from the Évora museum. The edifice, considered one of the finest of its kind on the Iberian Peninsula, makes use of the Corinthian style and was built during the 2nd or 3rd century AD. Although it has been referred to as the Temple of Diana, historians are uncertain as to which of the many Roman deities it was dedicated. The temple, largely destroyed during the invasions of the barbarian tribes in the early 5th century, was later used for various purposes, including that of municipal slaughterhouse in the 14th century. It was restored to its present state in 1871.

6 The **Biblioteca Pública** (Public Library) occupies the former town hall and contains an outstanding collection of rare books and manuscripts. These are not routinely on display, however. Bibliophiles need to obtain a reader's card to enter, a process that takes at least a day. ✉ *Largo do Conde de Vila Flor.* ☉ *Weekdays 9–12:30 and 2–5.*

7 The **Igreja dos Lóios** is adjacent to the former Convento dos Lóios, which is now the Pousada dos Lóios (☞ Dining and Lodging, *below*). To enter the church go down several steps and through a portal framed by a series of fan-shape arches in the flamboyant Gothic style. The sanctuary, dedicated to St. John the Evangelist, was founded in the 15th century by the Venetian-based Lóios Order. Its interior walls are covered with 18th-century *azulejo* (tile) panels created by Oliveira Bernardes, the foremost master of this unique Portuguese art form. The blue-and-white tiles depict scenes from the life of the church's founder, Rodrigo de Melo, who, along with members of his family, is buried here. The bas-relief marble tombstones at the foot of the high altar are the only ones of their kind in Portugal. Note the two metal hatches on either side of the main aisle: one covers an ancient cistern, which belonged to the Moorish castle that predated the church (an underground spring still supplies the cistern with potable water); and beneath the other hatch lie the neatly stacked bones of hundreds of monks. This bizarre ossuary was uncovered in 1958 during restoration work. Enhanced by the 16th-century Renaissance gallery, the cloister is now an integral part of the Pousada dos Lóios. ✉ *Largo Conde de Vila Flor,* ☎ 266/744307. 💰 500$00. ☉ *Tues.– Sun. 10–12:30 and 2–5.*

8 The **Palácio dos Duques de Cadaval** is readily identified by two massive stone towers that have pointed battlements. These towers, once part of a medieval castle that protected the town, were later incorporated into the Palace of the Dukes of Cadaval, a former residence of kings João I and João IV. A small gallery contains historic documents, paintings, and the unusual Flemish-style bronze tomb of Rui de Sousa, a signatory of the Treaty of Tordesillas. In 1494 the treaty divided the world into two spheres of influence: Spanish and Portuguese. Today, much of the palace is used by the city, but the ground-floor gallery is open to the public. ✉ *Largo Conde de Vila Flor.* 💰 300$00.

Opposite the Roman temple, the restful, tree-lined **Jardim de Diana** looks out over an aqueduct and the plains. From this park—in one sweeping glance that takes in the temple, the spires of the Gothic cathedral, the Lóios Church, and the 20th-century pousada housed in the convent—you can take in nearly 2,000 years of Portuguese history. A snack bar at the corner of the park is a great spot to sit and reflect on the architectural marvels before you.

⑨ The small **Igreja de São Mamede** (St. Mamede's Church) contains a vaulted ceiling decorated with baroque frescoes. Note the fine azulejos that cover the wall of the nave. On the east wall is a marble bust of the Renaissance humanist Andre de Resende, created by João Cuteliero, a well-known contemporary Portuguese sculptor. ⊠ *Rua da Mouraria.*

Facing the square known as the Largo do Colégio is the 16th-century **⑩ Igreja de Espirito Santo.** A squat structure with five arches in front, the church was originally a part of the ancient Évora University. The interior contains some fine azulejos and paintings, including artist Gregorio Lopes's painting of the *Last Supper.* As you explore the surrounding streets, you'll have a good view of the ancient town walls, and in some places, vestiges of the Roman foundations are visible.

From 1555 until its closure by the Marquis de Pombal in 1759, the **⑪ Universidade de Évora** was a Jesuit college; in 1979, after a lapse of more than 200 years, Évora University resumed classes. Although the enrollment is small, the college's presence has given new life and vigor to this ancient city. The large courtyard is flanked on all sides by a series of graceful buildings with double-tier, white-limestone, arched galleries in Italian Renaissance style. From the main entrance you'll see the imposing baroque facade of the gallery, known as the **Sala dos Actos** (Hall of Acts), which is crowned with allegorical figures and coats of arms carved in white marble quarried in the region. Lining the gallery's interior are azulejo works depicting historical, mythological, and biblical themes. ⊠ *Rua do Colégio.*

⑫ The **Largo da Porta de Moura**—perhaps Évora's most beautiful square— is characterized by paired stone towers that guard one of the principal entrances to the walled Old Town. Spires of the cathedral rise above the towers, and in the center of the square is an unusual Renaissance fountain. The large white-marble sphere, supported by a single column, bears a commemorative inscription in Latin dated 1556. Overlooking the fountain is the **Cordovil Mansion** (closed to the public), on whose terrace are several particularly attractive arches decorated in the Manueline-Mudéjar style. The square is in a lovely part of town with whitewashed houses and plenty of wrought-iron grillwork. ⊠ *Bounded by Ruas D. Augusto Eduardo Nunes, Enrique da Fonseca, Mendes Esteves, de Machede, and Miguel Bombarda.*

⑬ The interior of the 16th-century **Igreja de Misericórdia** (Mercy Church) is lined with large azulejo panels depicting scenes from the life of Christ; the unsigned 18th-century tiles are thought to be the work of António de Oliveira de Bernardes. ⊠ *Rua da Misericórdia.*

⑭ The **Igreja a Nossa Senhora da Graça** (Our Lady of Grace Church) is a splendid piece of classic Italian-style architecture. Note the impish figures perched above the portal: according to local legend, these four figures represent the first victims put to death in the Inquisition in Évora in 1543. The adjacent Largo de Alvaro Velho is an inviting square lined with metalsmith shops. ⊠ *Largo da Graça.*

⑮ After the cathedral, the **Igreja de São Francisco** is the grandest of Évora's churches. Its construction in the early 16th century, on the site of a former Gothic chapel, involved the greatest talents of the day, including Nicolas Chanterene, Oliver of Ghent, and the Arruda brothers, Francisco and Diogo. The magnificent architecture notwithstanding, the bizarre **Capela dos Ossos** (Chapel of the Bones) is the main attraction. The translation of the chilling inscription over the entrance reads: WE BONES WHO ARE HERE ARE WAITING FOR YOURS. The bones of some 5,000 skeletons dug up from cemeteries in the area line the ceilings and supporting columns. With a flair worthy of Charles Addams, a 16th-century Franciscan monk placed skulls jaw-to-cranium so they form arches across the ceiling; arm and leg bones are neatly stacked to shape the supporting columns. ⊠ *Praça 1 de Maio.* 🖾 *100$00.* ⊙ *Sun.–Fri. 9–12:30 and 2:30–5:30; closed during services.*

⑯ The **mercado municipal** (municipal market), facing the spacious Praça 1 de Maio, is housed in a large, sprawling building. Wander around the stalls that are crammed with fresh fruits, vegetables, fish, and meats to get an idea of what the Alentejo produces and consumes. Mornings, except for Sunday, the pavement in front of the market overflows with displays of colorful pottery. Across from the market, the extensive **Jardim Municipal** (Municipal Gardens) offer a pleasant respite from the rigors of sightseeing. They're landscaped with a variety of exotic plants and trees from all over the world.

⑰ At the entrance to the Municipal Gardens is the **Palácio de Dom Manuel.** Only a part of the former royal palace remains—restored after a fire in 1916. The existing wing displays a row of paired, gracefully curved Manueline windows, and on the south side of the building there's a notable arcade of redbrick sawtooth arches. Currently used as an art gallery, the palace has witnessed a number of historic events since its construction in the late 15th century. It was here, for instance, in 1497, that Vasco da Gama received his commission to command the fleet that would discover the sea route to India.

⑱ The **Ermida de São Bras** (St. Blaise Chapel), a curious structure built in the late 15th century, was the first important building in the Alentejo to join Gothic and Moorish elements to form the Gothic-Mudéjar style. The fortified church, a few hundred feet south of the city walls, is characterized by massive battlement-topped walls and a series of round towers crowned with steep spires. ⊠ *Rua da República.*

⑲ The **Igreja das Mercês** is a late-17th-century building with good examples of azulejos depicting scenes from the life of St. Augustine, the patron saint of the founding order of this church. There are also two unusual confessionals concealed behind tile panels. ⊠ *Rua do Raimundo,* ☎ *266/702604.* 🖾 *Free.* ⊙ *Tues.–Sun. 10–12:30 and 2–5.*

⑳ Behind the baroque facade of the **Igreja de Santa Clara** (Church of St. Claire) is an interior adorned with paintings, including a fine rendition on wood of the *Procession of Santa Clara* by the 16th-century Évora painter Francisco João.

Dining and Lodging

$$$ ✕ **Cozinha de Santo Humberto.** This is one of Évora's oldest traditional
★ restaurants and a good place to sample classic Alentejo cooking in what was once a wine cellar. Try the *sopa de peixe alentejana* (a mixed fish soup) or the *carne de porco com ameijoas* (small pieces of pork sautéed with clams). Game dishes such as grouse and partridge are particularly good in season (Santo Humberto, is, after all, the patron saint of hunters.) The list of Alentejo wines is excellent. ⊠ *Rua da Moeda 39,* ☎ *266/704251. AE, MC, V.*

$$$ ✕ **Fialho.** Amor and Gabriel Fialho are the third generation of Fial-
★   hos to operate this popular, traditional restaurant. The beamed ceil-
ing and painted plates on the walls lend a rustic ambience to what is
quite a sophisticated kitchen. You might start with a selection of ap-
petizers that includes an excellent *salada de polvo* (marinated octopus
salad) and as a main course try *coelho de convent a cartuxa* (roast rab-
bit with potatoes and carrots, according to a recipe from a nearby
monastery). A wide selection of Alentejo wines is offered. ⊠ *Travessa
das Mascarenhas 16,* ☎ *266/703079. AE, MC, V. Closed Mon.*

$ ✕ **Adega do Alentejano.** The atmosphere is pleasantly rustic in this
huge old Alentejo wine cellar, and the food is hearty and simple. Stick
to the very reasonable local wine from the barrel, and you'll be agree-
ably surprised by the bill. ⊠ *Rua Gabriel Vito do Monte Pereira 21-
A,* ☎ *266/744447. No credit cards.*

$$$ ✕🏨 **Pousada dos Lóios.** This luxurious pousada is in the historic 15th-
★   century monastery opposite the Roman Temple. Except for the small
size of the rooms, which were formerly the monks' cells, and the need
for anyone over 5′ 2″ to duck when entering, there's no trace of monastic austerity here. The opulent period furnishings compensate for the
cramped quarters, and the elegant public rooms deserve a visit even if
you don't plan to spend the night. Superbly prepared Alentejo specialties
are served in the restaurant, a marvel of Manueline details. ⊠ *Largo
Conde de Vila Flor, 7000,* ☎ *266/704051,* 𝖥𝖠𝖷 *266/707248. 31 rooms,
1 suite. Restaurant, bar, pool. AE, DC, MC, V.*

$ ✕🏨 **Évora Hotel.** On the route to Montemor-o-Novo, just outside
town, you'll find this pleasant, modern establishment. The public areas
are light and spacious, as is the dining room, which presents a delicious buffet of regional specialties. Rooms are generous in size, and
all have small balconies. ⊠ *Quinta do Cruzeiro (EN114), 7001,* ☎
266/734800, 𝖥𝖠𝖷 *266/707248. 114 rooms. Restaurant, bar, pool, sauna,
2 tennis courts, exercise room. AE, DC, MC, V.*

$$ 🏨 **Hotel da Cartuxa.** Building a two-story hotel—one with a truly rus-
tic feel *and* truly modern amenities—inside a 14th-century walled city
is no small feat. This establishment, however, proves that it can be done
successfully. The comfortable public areas are furnished with antiques.
Guest rooms are large and have tile baths; ask for a room at the back
for a view of the garden, pool, and Roman walls. ⊠ *Travessa da
Palmeira 4/6, 7000,* ☎ *266/739300,* 𝖥𝖠𝖷 *266/739305. 91 rooms. Restau-
rant, bar, pool, parking (fee). AE, DC, MC, V.*

$ 🏨 **Riviera.** This cozy, three-story old manor house is well situated be-
tween Giraldo Square and the Roman Temple. The small, cheerful entry
is decorated with colorful azulejos, and the guest rooms have floral wall-
paper. Furnishings are in the traditional, painted Alentejo style. ⊠ *Rua
5 de Outubro 49, 7000,* ☎ *266/703304,* 𝖥𝖠𝖷 *266/700467. 22 rooms.
Lounge. AE, DC, MC, V.*

$ 🏨 **Solar de Monfalim.** In a historic building that has a delightful arched
gallery, this comfortable, family-run guest house provides quiet, old-
fashioned hospitality in the heart of the Old Town. The rooms, although
small, are comfortably furnished, as is the TV lounge. ⊠ *Largo da Mis-
ericórdia 1, 7000,* ☎ *266/750000,* 𝖥𝖠𝖷 *266/742367. 26 rooms, 1 suite.
Bar. MC, V.*

Outdoor Activities and Sports

BALLOONING AND FOUR-WHEEL DRIVING

Hot-air balloon flights and four-wheel-drive excursions through the
Alentejo are offered by **Turibalão Lda.** (⊠ Largo Luis de Camões 14,
☎ 𝖥𝖠𝖷 266/706323).

Lucena Karting, a go-cart track on the outskirts of Évora (take N114 toward Montemor-o-Novo), provides an outlet for pent-up youthful energy. ✉ *Quinta Lucena (EN 114),* ☎ 266/896680, ℻ 266/893227. 🎫 *900$00 for 5-min spin around the track; 7,250$00 for 1 hr.* ☉ *Tues.– Sun. 10–7.*

Equeturi, a horse-riding center about 2 km (1 mi) from Évora on the road to Montemor-o-Novo, offers riding lessons and escorted rides in the countryside. Reservations are advised. ✉ *Quinta do Bacêlo, Santo Antonico,* ☎ 266/742884, ℻ 266/746606. 🐎

Aqueduto da Agua da Prata

㉑ *Extends 18 km (11 mi) north of Évora.*

The graceful arched Silver Water Aqueduct, which once carried water 18 km (11 mi) to Évora from the springs at Graça do Divor, is best seen along the road to Arraiolos. You can also see a section of it within Évora, along the Rua do Cano in the northwest corner of the city. Constructed in 1532 under the patronage of Dom João III, the aqueduct was designed by the famous architect Francisco de Arruda. Extensive parts of the system remain intact and can be seen from the road.

Cromlech and the Menhir of Almendres

㉒ *15 km (9 mi) west of Évora.*

A trip through the countryside surrounding Évora will take you to some of the earliest inhabited sites in Portugal. In Guadalupe, the site of a 17th-century chapel, near the grain-storage bins of the agricultural co-operative, is the Menhir of Almendres, an 8-ft-tall, Neolithic, stone obelisk. Several hundred yards away is the cromlech, 95 granite monoliths arranged in an oval in the middle of a large field.

Dolmen of Zambujeiro

㉓ *12 km (7 mi) southwest of Évora. From N380 (the Évora–Alcaçovas road) take the turnoff to Valverde.*

The 20-ft-high Dolmen of Zambujeiro is the largest of its kind on the Iberian Peninsula. This prehistoric monument is typical of those found throughout Neolithic Europe: several great stone slabs stand upright, supporting a flat stone that serves as a roof. These structures were designed as burial chambers.

Arraiolos

㉔ *22 km (14 mi) northwest of Évora.*

Arraiolos, dominated by the ruins of a once-mighty fortress, is a typical hilltop Alentejo village of whitewashed houses and narrow streets. What distinguishes it is its worldwide reputation as a carpet-producing center. In the 16th century, as Portuguese trade with the East grew, an interest developed in the intricate designs of the carpets from India and Persia, and these patterns served as models for the earliest hand-embroidered Arraiolos carpets. The colorful rugs are not mass-produced in factories but are handmade by locals in their homes and cottages. An authentic Arraiolos rug, made of locally produced wool, has some 44,000 ties per square meter. To discourage imitations, in 1992 the town council designed a blue seal of authenticity to be affixed to each carpet. There's a permanent exhibition of carpets in the **town hall.** 🎫 *Free.*

⊙ *Weekdays 9–12:30 and 2–5:30; weekend hrs vary; call the tourist office at Praça Lima Brito,* ☎ *266/499105, for information.*

Dining and Lodging

$$$ ✕⊞ **Pousada da Nossa Senhora da Assunção.** If you need to sleep on your decision about which carpet to buy, consider an overnight stay in this picturesque pousada. It's a little more than a kilometer outside of town in an old convent (Convento dos Lóios) that has been restored and tastefully padded with modern comforts. The restaurant decor is contemporary, but the menu favors traditional regional dishes. ⊠ *Val das Flores (take E-370 to Pavia),* ☎ *266/419340,* ℻ *266/419280. 30 rooms. Restaurant, bar, pool, tennis court. AE, DC, MC, V.*

Shopping

The main street of Arraiolos is lined with showrooms and workshops featuring the town's famous hand-embroidered wool rugs. Some of the best selections can be found at **Calantica** (⊠ Rua Alexandre Herculano 20, ☎ 266/499556) and **Condestavel** (⊠ Rua Bombeiros Voluntários 7, ☎ 266/499587), a large shop with branches in Évora and Lisbon.

THE UPPER ALENTEJO

The Upper Alentejo is a hilly, partly mountainous area that contains a number of interesting fortified towns. Some of Portugal's best wines are produced in the area between Borba and Reguengos de Monsaraz.

Reguengos de Monsaraz

㉕   *35 km (22 mi) southeast of Évora.*

Reguengos de Monsaraz, a sleepy little Alentejo town often simply called Reguengos, is arranged around a large square. Note the unusual pentagonal bell tower on the 19th-century Victorian church. The town, in the center of a large wine-producing region, is also known for its handwoven rugs.

São Pedro do Corval

㉖   *5 km (3 mi) northeast of Reguengos.*

The tiny hamlet of São Pedro do Corval, on the road to Monsaraz, is one of Portugal's major centers for inexpensive hand-painted pottery.

En Route   On the way to Monsaraz, just before the road begins to climb, you'll see an intriguing Moorish-style domed fountain across from the public laundry area, dated 1723 in Roman numerals. The road then snakes up the hill to a parking area outside the village walls; no cars except those of residents are permitted inside.

Monsaraz

★ **㉗**   *16 km (10 mi) east of Reguengos, 50 km (31 mi) southeast of Évora.*

The entire fortified hilltop town of Monsaraz is a living museum of narrow, stone-surfaced streets lined with ancient white houses. The town's 150 or so permanent residents (mostly older people) live mainly from tourism, and because they do so graciously and unobtrusively, Monsaraz has managed to retain its essential character.

Old women clad in black still sit in the doorways of their cottages and chat with neighbors, their ever-present knitting in hand. At the southern end of the walls stand the well-preserved towers of a formidable castle. The view from atop the pentagonal tower sweeps across the plain to the west and to the east over the Rio Guadiana (Guadiana River) to Spain. Within the castle perimeter is an unusual arena with makeshift slate benches at either end of an oval field. Bullfights are held here several times a year and always in the second week of September (during the festival of Senhora Jesus dos Passos, the village's patron saint).

The small **Monsaraz Museum,** next to the parish church, displays religious artifacts and the original town charter, signed by Dom Manuel in 1512. The former tribunal contains an interesting 15th-century fresco that depicts Christ presiding over figures of Truth and Deception. ⊠ 200$00. ☉ Daily 9–7.

The area around Monsaraz is dotted with megalithic monuments. The **Menhir of Outeiro,** 3 km (2 mi) north of town, is one of the tallest ever discovered.

Dining and Lodging

$$
★ ✕ **Casa do Forno.** The labor of love of two ambitious women (Gloria and Mariana), Casa do Forno is an upscale restaurant. At the entrance is a huge, rounded oven with an iron door, hence the name (*forno* is Portuguese for "oven"). Picture windows line the dining room and offer a spectacular view over the rolling plains. The Alentejan menu appropriately features roasts; one special dish worth trying is the *borrego Convento Orado* (roast lamb from an ancient recipe obtained at the nearby monastery). ⊠ *Travessa da Sanabrosa,* ☎ *266/557190. AE, MC, V. Closed Tues.*

$$ ✕ **Lumumba.** Set in one of the old village houses, this little restaurant has a devoted clientele on both sides of the border. The dining room is small, but there is an attractive terrace for outside dining with views over the valley to distant mountains. The menu is classic Alentejo, with good lamb and kid roasts and casseroles, but the grilled fish dishes are also excellent. Try the *chocos grelhados* (grilled squid) or *peixe espada grelhada* (charcoal-grilled blade fish). ⊠ *Rua Direita,* ☎ *266/557121. No credit cards. Closed Mon.*

$$$ ⊡ **Horta da Moura.** This self-contained miniresort is set on a working farm between the walled city and the Guadiana River. The main house, whose white-stucco facade has blue trim and an arched portico, is typical of Alentejo-style architecture. Inside, vaulted brick ceilings with wooden beams and traditional furnishings create a cozy atmosphere. The outlying buildings include stables, a riding school, a crafts room, a winery, and a recreation center with a large fireplace. The helpful staff eagerly arranges walking, horseback-riding, and cycling trips along the river, as well as four-wheel-drive and canoe excursions. Fishing trips can also be arranged. ⊠ *10 km (6 mi) east of Reguengos on E256 to Mourão, then 6 km (4 mi) on turnoff to Monsaraz, Reguengos de Monsaraz 7200,* ☎ *266/550100,* ᶠᴬˣ *266/550108. 6 rooms, 7 suites, 1 apartment. Pool, 2 tennis courts, horseback riding, fishing, bicycles, recreation room. AE, DC, MC, V.*

$ ⊡ **Estalagem Dom Nuno.** This small, rustic guest house—a true romantic hideaway—occupies an old, restored, white home on the main street of the walled town. Clean rooms with modern furnishings offer fantastic views over the valley—the sunsets alone are worth the price of a room. ⊠ *Rua do Castelo 6, 7200,* ☎ *266/557146,* ᶠᴬˣ *266/557400. 8 rooms. AE, DC, MC, V.*

Terena

㉘ *28 km (17 mi) north of Reguengos.*

A little jewel of a town, with a charter dating from 1262 and a castle on a hill, Terena is a place where tourists are still a pleasant curiosity. Drive—or better yet, stroll—along the narrow Rua Direita past the white houses, some with Gothic doorways, others with baroque or Renaissance ones. The small, well-preserved castle was one of several built in this area to defend the border with Spain, which lies across the Guadiana River, 11 km (7 mi) east.

Dining and Lodging

$ ✕⛩ **Casa de Terena.** A restored 18th-century house in an out-of-the-
★ way village has been turned into a charming inn. It has six comfortably furnished guest quarters, all with period reproductions. You eat your first meal of the day in what was once the stable but is now a delightful restaurant. ✉ *Rua Direita 45, 7250-065,* ☎ *268/459132,* FAX *268/459155. 5 rooms, 1 suite. Restaurant, bar. MC, V.*

Vila Viçosa

㉙ *18 km (11 mi) northeast of Terena.*

A quiet town with a moated castle, Vila Viçosa is in the heart of the fertile Borba plain. It has been closely linked with Portuguese royalty since the 15th century, but this association has not always been a happy one: in 1483 King João II, seeking to strengthen his grip on the throne, moved to eliminate the second Duke of Bragança, his brother-in-law and most formidable rival, who from Vila Viçosa controlled more than 50 cities, castles, and towns. After much intrigue and counterintrigue, the unfortunate Duke was beheaded in the main square of Évora.

Court life in Vila Viçosa flourished in the late-16th and early 17th centuries, when the huge palace constructed by the fourth Duke of Bragança (Jaime) was the scene of great royal feasts, theater performances, and bullfights. This all came to an abrupt end in 1640, when King João IV, the eighth Duke of Bragança and the first Portuguese to occupy the throne after 60 years of Spanish domination, elected to move his court to Lisbon. Thereafter, Vila Viçosa slipped into relative oblivion. In more recent times Portugal's second-to-last king, Carlos I, and the young Prince Luís Filipe spent their last night in the palace. The following day, February 1, 1908, in response to a royal decree that mandated exile for "political" crimes, they were assassinated by members of a secret political society while they were in an open carriage.

The **Paço Ducal** (Ducal Palace) and the adjacent *castelo* (castle) draw a great many visitors. Built of locally quarried marble, the main wing of the palace extends for some 360 ft and overlooks the expansive Palace Square and the bronze equestrian statue of Dom João IV. The interior of the palace was extensively restored in the 1950s and contains all you'd expect to find: azulejos, Arraiolos rugs, frescoed ceilings, priceless collections of silver and gold objects, Chinese vases, Gobelin tapestries, and a long dining hall adorned with antlers and other hunting trophies. The enormous kitchen is equipped with spits large enough to accommodate several oxen and enough gleaming copper to keep a small army of servants busy polishing. The apartments where the unfortunate Dom Carlos spent his last night have been maintained as they were. Carlos was quite an accomplished painter—some say a better painter than he was a king—and many of his works (along with private photos of Portugal's last royal family) line the walls of the apartments. The palace itself as well as its armory, its treasury, and the castle and hunting museum can each be visited in separate guided tours. ✉ *Terreiro do Paço,* ☎ *268/980659.* 🎫 *1,000$00 palace, 500$00 armory, 500$00 treasury, 500$00 castle.* ☉ *Apr.–Sept., Tues.–Sun. 9–1 and 3–5:30; Oct.–Mar., Tues.–Sun. 9–1 and 2:30–5.*

Following the tour of the Ducal Palace you can visit the nearby **Museu dos Coches** (Coach Museum), which features a collection of horse-drawn

AZULEJOS

T IS DIFFICULT TO FIND AN OLD building of any note in Portugal that isn't adorned somewhere or other with the predominantly blue-toned ceramic tiles called *azulejos*. The centuries-old marriage of glazed ornamental tiles to Portuguese architecture is one of those matches that seem to have been made in heaven.

After the Gothic period, large buildings made entirely of undressed brick or stone became a rarity in Portuguese architecture. Most buildings had extensive areas of flat plaster on their facades and interior walls that cried out for some form of decoration. The compulsion to decorate these empty architectural spaces produced the art of the fresco in Italy; in Portugal, it produced the art of the azulejo. The medium is very well suited to the deeply rooted Portuguese taste for intricate, ornate decoration. And, aesthetics aside, glazed tiling is ideally suited to the country's more practical needs. Durable, waterproof, and easily cleaned, the tile provides cool interiors during Portugal's hot summers and exterior protection from the damp onslaughts of Atlantic winters.

The term azulejo comes not from the word *azul* (blue in Portuguese), but from the Arabic word for tiles, *az-zulayj*. But despite the long presence of the Moors in Portugal, the Moorish influence on early Portuguese azulejos was actually introduced from Spain in the 15th century, well after the Christian reconquest. No examples of tile work from the time of the Moorish occupation have survived in Portugal.

The very earliest tiles found on Portuguese buildings were imported from Andalusia. They are usually geometric in design

and were most frequently used to form panels of repeated patterns. As Portugal's prosperity surged in the 16th century, the growing number of palaces, churches, and sumptuous town and country mansions created a demand for more tile ornamentation. Local production was small at first, and Holland and Italy were the main suppliers. The superb Dutch-made azulejos in the Paço Ducal in Vila Viçosa are famous examples from this period. The first Portuguese-made tiles had begun to appear in the last quarter of the 15th century, when a number of small factories were established, but three centuries were to pass before Portuguese tile making reached its peak.

The great figure in 18th-century Portuguese tile making is António de Oliveira Bernardes, who died in 1732. The school established by the master tile maker spawned the series of monumental panels depicting hunting scenes, landscapes, battles, and other historical motifs that grace many of the stately Portuguese homes and churches of the period. Some of the finest examples can be seen in the Alentejo—in buildings such as the old university in Évora and the parish church in Alcácer do Sal—as well as at the Castelo de São Felipe in Setúbal. In Lisbon's Museu do Azulejo (☞ Chapter 1) you can trace the development of tiles in Portugal from their beginnings to the present.

Portuguese tile making declined in quality in the 19th century, but a revival occurred in the 20th century, spearheaded by leading artists such as Almada Negreiros and Maria Keil. Today, some notable examples of the use of tile by contemporary artists can be seen in many of the capital's metro stations.

coaches and antique automobiles. (If you've already seen the coach museum in Lisbon, however, you can skip this one; it's interesting but isn't in the same league as the one in the capital city.) ✉ *Terreiro do Paço,* ☎ *268/980659.* 🎟 *150$00.* ⊙ *Apr.–Sept., Tues.–Sun. 9–1 and 3–5:30; Oct.–Mar., Tues.–Sun. 9–1 and 2:30–5.*

At the north end of the palace square is the **Porta do Nó** (Knot Gate) with its massive stone ropes—an intriguing example of the Manueline style.

Dining and Lodging

$$$ ✕🏨 **Pousada de D. João IV.** If you're hooked on the historical feel of Vila Viçosa, this state inn next door to the palace has all the atmosphere you'll need. It's in a restored 16th-century convent that's furnished with period reproductions. Its restaurant even serves you dishes based on old convent recipes. ✉ *Terreiro do Paço, 7160,* ☎ *268/980742,* FAX *268/ 980747. 33 rooms, 3 suites. Restaurant, bar, pool. AE, DC, MC, V.*

En Route   Driving between Vila Viçosa and Borba you'll see mountainous dirt-and-rock piles strewn about the countryside. These tailings are evidence of the many local quarries and are the residue of centuries of extracting the high-quality marble. Marble is generously used throughout the region, even in the most modest of buildings.

Borba

③⓪ *4 km (2½ mi) northwest of Vila Viçosa.*

Borba is one of the Alentejo's major wine producers, and the town's vintners have won many national prizes. The village has a pleasant conglomeration of modest whitewashed houses, noble mansions, and small churches—all beautifully decorated with marble.

Borba's most notable monument is the 18th-century **Fonte das Bicas**, a neoclassical white-marble fountain built to honor Queen Maria I, known as Maria the Pious, who reigned from 1777 to 1816.

Estremoz

③① *11 km (7 mi) west of Borba.*

Estremoz, which lies on the ancient road that connected Lisbon with Mérida, Spain, has been a site of strategic importance since Roman times, and the castle, which overlooks the town, was a crucial one of the Alentejo's many fortresses. Estremoz is most closely associated with Queen St. Isabel, although she spent only a short time here. Married to Dom Dinis—a Portuguese king—in 1282, she arrived in 1336 and after a brief stay became ill and died. The luxurious Pousada da Rainha Santa Isabel (☞ Dining and Lodging, *below*), which occupies the castle, was named for her. It was also in Estremoz in 1367 that the queen's grandson Pedro, the lover and secret husband of Inês de Castro, died. The Portuguese people loved Queen St. Isabel and over the ages have handed down many tales and legends of her humility and charity. A statue in the castle square commemorates her. From atop the castle tower you'll have a magnificent view over the Alentejo plains.

The **Museo Municipal** (Municipal Museum) is in a 16th-century almshouse across from the castle. Its displays chronicle the development of the region and range from Roman artifacts to contemporary pottery, including a collection of the brightly colored little figurines for which Estremoz is famous. ✉ *Largo D. Dinis,* ☎ *268/339200.* 🎟 *185$00.* ⊙ *Apr.–Sept., Tues.–Sun. 10–12:30 and 3–7; Oct.–Mar., Tues.–Sun. 10–12:30 and 3–5.*

The lower town, a maze of narrow streets and white houses, radiates out from the **Rossío,** a huge, unpaved square. Stands lining it sell the town's famous colorful pottery. In addition to the multicolored, hand-painted plates, pitchers, and dolls, note the earthenware jugs decorated with bits of local white marble.

NEED A
BREAK?

There are several refreshment stands and snack bars along the Rossío, but for more substantial fare try the **Café Alentejano.** From this popular 60-year-old café and its first-floor restaurant, you can watch the goings-on in the square.

The little farming museum, **Museu da Alfaia Agricola,** a short walk from the Rossío, has a collection of pre–machine age agricultural tools. ⊠ *Rua Serpa Pinto.* 🎫 *200$00.* ⊙ *Weekdays 9–12:30 and 2–5:30.*

Dining and Lodging

$ ✕ **Adega do Isaias.** Hidden away on a narrow side street a few min-
★ utes' walk from the square, this is the best place in town for hearty, no-nonsense roasts and grilled meats. The front part of the former wine cellar is a rough-looking bar; walk through to the dining area—a slop-ing, cement-floor cave that's lined with huge terra-cotta wine jugs. Dur-ing your meal you sit on benches at planked tables; expect the service to be casual, at best. But the food will be great, and the place—popu-lar with the locals—will probably be packed. ⊠ *Rua do Almeida 21,* ☎ *268/322318. No credit cards. Closed Sun.*

$$$ ✕🏠 **Pousada da Rainha Santa Isabel.** Occupying Estremoz's hilltop
★ castle and steeped in history, this pousada is one of the most luxuri-ous in the country. The sumptuous lobby and other public rooms dis-play literally tons of gleaming Estremoz marble and are decorated with 15th-century tapestries, Arraiolos rugs, and original paintings. The generous-size bedrooms are furnished with 17th- and 18th-century re-productions, and some of the rooms have elaborate four-poster beds. Just to sit in the baronial dining hall is a treat, and the food and ser-vice—in tune with the decor—are fit for a queen. The accent is on tra-ditional Alentejo dishes and old-fashioned recipes. Their *perdiz caçador* (partridge in red wine) is very good in the autumn. ⊠ *Largo D. Dinis,* *7100,* ☎ *268/332075,* 𝔽𝔸𝕏 *268/332079. 30 rooms, 3 suites. Restaurant,* *bar, pool. AE, DC, MC, V.*

$ 🏠 **Monte Dos Pensamentos.** This comfortable old manor house sur-
★ rounded by olive and orange trees is just 2 km (1¼ mi) from Estremoz. The living room and large bedrooms are cluttered with enough painted plates, dolls, and antiques to stock a good-size museum. The mood is casual and relaxed, and guests typically sit around the fire and share the cozy sitting room. ⊠ *Estrada Estação do Ameixial, 7100,* ☎ *268/* *333166,* 𝔽𝔸𝕏 *268/332409. 4 rooms. Bar, pool. No credit cards.*

Évoramonte

③② *17 km (10 mi) southwest of Estremoz, 42 km (26 mi) northeast of Évora.*

Évoramonte is a medieval town that sits along the western flank of the Serra da Ossa at an altitude of 1,550 ft. Drive up to the castle for a spectacular panoramic view that extends as far as the Serra da Estrela. The castle here, built in Italian Renaissance style, is distinguished by a massive round tower at each of its four corners. Also note the heavy Manueline ropes that run, like ribbons on a Christmas package, around the outside of the castle; they're joined together at the entrance with two tidy cement knots. (An interesting gastronomic aside: it was in Évo-ramonte that the famous *sopa Alentejana* is said to have originated. The convention held here in 1834 to end the civil war between the Liberals and the Miguelists took so long that by the end only stale bread was left to eat—and thus was born the popular Alentejo soup, made with stale bread, garlic, olive oil, coriander, and water.)

Elvas

③③ *40 km (25 mi) east of Estremoz, 15 km (9 mi) west of Spain.*

Another of the fortified Alentejo towns, Elvas—because of its proximity to the Spanish town of Badajoz—was from its founding an important bastion in warding off attacks from the east. The extensive fortifications, 17th-century Portugal's most formidable, are characterized by a series of walls, moats, and reinforced towers. The size of the complex can be best appreciated by driving around the periphery of the town.

Another distinguishing landmark, the 8-km (5-mi) **Aqueduto Amoreira** (Amoreira Aqueduct)—which took more than a century to build—is still in use today. It was started in 1498 under the direction of one of the era's great architects, Francisco de Arruda—who also designed the Aqueduto da Agua da Prata (☞ *above*)—but not until 1622 did the first drops of water flow into the town fountain.

The 16th-century **Igreja da Nossa Senhora da Assunção** (Church of Our Lady of the Assumption) at the head of the town square, the Praça da República, is worth a visit for its impressive triple-nave interior lined with 17th-century blue-and-yellow azulejos. The church was designed by Francisco de Arruda, architect of the Elvas aqueduct, but underwent subsequent modifications. It was a cathedral until the diocese was moved to Évora in the 18th century.

From the church, walk up the hill past a pillory and two stone towers (spanned by a graceful Moorish loggia) to the **castle.** At the battlements you'll have a sweeping view of the town and its fortifications. ⊠ *Praça da República.* 🎫 *Free.* ⊙ *Daily 9–12:30 and 2–5:30.*

Dining and Lodging

$$$ ✕🏨 **Pousada de Santa Luzia.** Opened in 1942, this was Portugal's first
★   pousada, and its convenient location—just 12 km (7 mi) from one of the major border crossings between Spain and Portugal—was no accident. The two-story, Moorish-style building has been remodeled several times, most recently in 1994. All bedrooms on the second floor are a good size and cheerfully decorated with hand-painted Alentejo furniture and bright floral fabrics. The modern tiled bathrooms are small but adequate. The large restaurant has arched windows overlooking an attractive garden and is a favorite with Elvas residents. One of the most popular dishes is *bacalhau dourado* (cod sautéed with eggs, potatoes, and onions). It's best to reserve a room in advance. ⊠ *Av. de Badajoz, 7350,* ☎ *268/637470,* 𝔽𝔸𝕏 *268/622127. 25 rooms. Restaurant, bar, pool, 2 tennis courts. AE, DC, MC, V.*

Campo Maior

③④ *19 km (12 mi) northeast of Elvas.*

Campo Maior, surrounded by rows of gentle hills covered with the Alentejo's ubiquitous cork and olive trees, is a quiet, sparsely populated corner of the country where little has changed over the years. You may notice the smell of roasting coffee lingering in the air: it isn't coming from a nearby café but from the several coffee-roasting plants in the area. Campo Maior is the center of Portugal's coffee industry.

Try to make it to this town during the first week of September, when nearly 100 streets and squares are covered with a rainbow-colored mantle of paper flowers and decorations. The decorations for each neighborhood are a closely held secret for months, as the women nimbly assemble the paper flowers and the men construct the wooden framing. When the festival opens, all is revealed in a blaze of color. Check with the local or regional tourist office for exact dates.

At the top of the hill is a castle that was reconstructed after a disastrous explosion in 1732. As you walk around the fortifications, you'll notice some tiny whitewashed dwellings with laundry fluttering about like flags in the breeze. The little buildings are the old army barracks, the only part of the military complex still occupied. Before leaving Campo Maior, stroll through the lower part of town, where the narrow streets are lined with many fine examples of wrought-iron grillwork and balconies, giving the town a Spanish appearance.

Portalegre

35 *47 km (29 mi) northwest of Campo Maior.*

Portalegre is the gateway to the Alentejo's most mountainous region, where the parched plains of the south give way to a greener, more inviting landscape. The town, which sits at the foot of the Serra de São Mamede, lacks the charm of the whitewashed hamlets in the south of the province but has long been noted worldwide for the quality of its tapestries. Handmade to order in a dilapidated former Jesuit monastery, the tapestries currently fetch prices of around $6,000 per square meter, and Portalegre is not a place for bargain hunters.

NEED A
BREAK?
In the municipal gardens in the town center, the **O Tarro** restaurant and snack bar has a pleasant terrace overlooking a pond and the sprawling gardens themselves.

To explore Portalegre, start at the park in the center of the lower town and walk uphill past a maze of shops and old houses to the twin-towered **cathedral.** The 18th-century facade of this, the town's most prominent landmark, is highlighted with marble columns and wrought-iron balconies. ☉ *Mon.–Sat. 8:30–noon and 3–6, Sun. 9–noon.*

The **Municipal Museum,** in a former seminary next to the cathedral, contains a wealth of religious art, including a gilded, 16th-century Spanish pietà. ☒ *Rua José Maria da Rosa,* ☎ *245/300120.* 🖾 *350$00.* ☉ *Wed.–Mon. 9:30–12:30 and 2–6.*

From the cathedral square, head east about 400 yards to the ruins of a once-formidable **castle,** whose tower walls afford a splendid view of the cathedral and its surroundings.

The **Museu José Regio** (José Regio Museum), just off Avenida Poeta José Regio, roughly midway between the cathedral and the castle, was named for a local poet who died in 1969. He bequeathed his varied collection of religious and folk art to the museum, which is in his former home. ☒ *Largo de Boa Vista,* ☎ *245/23625.* 🖾 *250$00.* ☉ *Tues.–Sun. 9:30–12:30 and 2–6.*

Dining and Lodging

$ ✗ **O Abrigo.** On a quiet street around the corner from the cathedral you'll find this small, husband-and-wife–run restaurant. You enter the cork-lined dining area through a snack bar. One of the best dishes on the menu is the *migas alentejanas* (a tasty fried-pork-and-bread-crumbs concoction), served on a terra-cotta platter. ☒ *Rua de Elvas 74,* ☎ *245/ 331658. MC, V. Closed Tues.*

$ **✕⟨⟩ Dom João III.** This modern multistory hotel is across from the city park. Although the lobby and hallways are somewhat institutional, the rooms are more pleasant; many have balconies overlooking the park. The large top-floor restaurant, a favorite with local businessmen, is ringed with picture windows looking over the town. The menu has international dishes as well as regional specialties. ⊠ *Av. da Liberdade, 7300,* ☎ *245/330192,* ℻ *245/330444. 58 rooms, 2 suites. Restaurant, bar, pool. AE, DC, MC, V.*

Parque Natural da Serra de São Mamede

㊱ *5 km (3 mi) northeast of Portalegre.*

Portalegre is the principal gateway to this recently established national park, which extends north to the fortified town of Marvão and to the spa of Castelo de Vide, and south to the little hamlet of Esperança on the Spanish border. Rural in character, the sparsely inhabited 80,000-acre park region is made up of small family plots, and sheepherding is the major occupation. The area is rich in wildlife, including many rare species of birds, as well as wild boars, deer, and wildcats. This is not a spectacularly scenic park like Yellowstone or Yosemite but rather a quiet place for hiking, riding, or simply communing with nature. For information about activities, contact the park office. ⊠ *Praceta Herois da India 8, Portalegre,* ☎ *245/203631,* ℻ *245/207501.*

Coudelaria de Alter

㊲ *22 km (14 mi) southwest of Portalegre.*

If you're interested in horses, you must visit the Coudelaria de Alter (Alter Stud Farm), which was founded by Dom João V in 1748 to furnish royalty with high-quality mounts. Dedicated to preserving and developing the extraordinarily beautiful Alter Real (Royal Alter) strain of the Lusitana breed, the farm has had a long, turbulent history. After years of foreign invasion and pillage, little remains of its original structures. Fortunately, the equine bloodline, one of Europe's noblest, has been preserved, and you can watch these superb horses being trained and exercised on the farm (phone ahead to make sure a visit is practical on the day you want to go). There are also three small but interesting museums here: one documents the history of the farm, one has a collection of horse-drawn carriages, and one has displays on the art of falconry. You can also watch falcons going through their daily training sessions. The town of Alter do Chão itself, with the battlements of a 14th-century castle overlooking a square, is also worth a stroll. ⊠ *The farm is on a dusty track 3 km (2 mi) northwest of Alter do Chão,* ☎ *245/610080.* ⊡ *Free.* ☉ *Farm daily 9:30–noon and 2–4:30.*

En Route For the most scenic approach to Marvão and the Serra de São Mamede from Portalegre, take N359 18 km (11 mi) to Marvão. The narrow but well-surfaced serpentine N359 rises to an elevation of 2,800 ft, past stands of birch and chestnut trees and small vegetable gardens bordered by ancient stone walls. At Portagem take note of the well-preserved Roman bridge.

Marvão

★ **㊳** *25 km (16 mi) northeast of Portalegre.*

The views of the mountains as you approach the fortress town of Marvão are spectacular, and the town's castle, atop a sheer rock cliff, commands a 360-degree panorama. Although you can drive through the constricted streets of this medieval mountaintop village, Marvão is best appreciated on foot. First head for the castle and climb to the tower. From here you can trace the course of the massive Vauban-style stone walls (characterized by concentric lines of trenches and walls, a hallmark of the 17th-century French military engineer Vauban), adorned at intervals with bartizans, to enjoy breathtaking vistas from different angles. Given its strategic position, it's no surprise that Marvão has been a fortified settlement since Roman times or earlier. The present castle was built under Dom Dinis in the late 13th century and modified some four centuries later, during the reign of Dom João IV.

At the foot of the path leading to the castle is the **Municipal Museum,** housed in the 13th-century Church of Saint Mary. The small gallery contains a diverse collection of religious artifacts, azulejos, costumes, ancient maps, and weapons. ✉ *220$00.* ☉ *Daily 9–12:30 and 2–5:30.*

The village, with some 300 mostly older inhabitants, is laid out in several long rows of tidy, white-stone dwellings terraced into the hill. The recently remodeled Pousada de Santa Maria (☞ Dining and Lodging, *below*) and the few guest houses and restaurants are well integrated into the village and do not detract from Marvão's pleasing traditional architecture.

Dining and Lodging

$$$$ ✕⌸ **Pousada de Santa Maria.** In 1976 several old houses within the
★   city walls were joined to create the Pousada de Santa Maria. The rooms are decorated with traditional Alentejo furnishings, and the restaurant serves some of the best regional dishes in the village. ✉ *Rua 24 de Janeiro 7, 7330,* ☎ *245/993201,* ℻ *245/993440. 29 rooms. Restaurant, bar. AE, DC, MC, V.*

$ ⌸ **Dom Dinis.** This comfortable country inn at the foot of the castle occupies a restored 200-year-old house with massive stone window and door frames. Bedrooms, which have fantastic cliffside views, are furnished with light pine furniture. ✉ *Rua Dr. Matos Magalhães, 7330,* ☎ ℻ *245/993236. 9 rooms. Restaurant, bar. AE, DC, MC, V.*

Santo António das Areias

❸❾ *5 km (3 mi) northeast of Marvão. Head north from Marvão on the small country road and follow signs.*

Scattered among the chestnut groves at Santo António das Areias are some two dozen prehistoric dolmens.

Castelo de Vide

❹⓪ *8 km (5 mi) west of Marvão. An intriguing backcountry lane connects Marvão with Castelo de Vide. About halfway down the hill from Marvão, turn to the right toward Escusa (watch for the sign) and continue through the chestnut- and acacia-covered hills to Castelo de Vide.*

A quiet, hilltop spa town, Castelo de Vide is graced with flowers that sprout from nearly every nook and cranny. When you encounter the local people, it will be clear that the beauty of Castelo de Vide has reached the hearts of its residents, who have kind and gentle natures. The large, baroque Praça Dom Pedro V is bordered by the Igreja de Santa Maria (St. Mary's Church) and the town hall. An alleyway to the right of the church leads to the village fountain, which taps one of the many springs in the area. (The waters are alleged to cure a wide variety of disorders ranging from diabetes to dermatitis.) The canopied, 16th-century marble fountain is the town symbol.

A cobblestone alley leads from the fountain up to the Juderia (Jewish Quarter). On the Rua da Juderia, a bare little room in a modest one-story cottage is all that remains of a **medieval synagogue** that was once the center of a thriving Jewish community. In the Middle Ages, as the town prospered, many Jews and Marranos (Jews forced to convert to Christianity) settled here. ⊠ *Free.* ◯ *June–Sept., daily 10–8; Oct.–May, daily 10–5:30.*

As you walk along, notice the many houses with Gothic doorways and their various designs. (The tourist brochures proclaim that Castelo de Vide has the largest number of Gothic doorways of any town in Portugal.) From the Juderia it's a short climb to the ruins of the **castle.** Go up into the tower and inside the well-preserved keep to the large Gothic hall, which has a picture window looking down on the town square and the church. ⊠ *Free.* ◯ *June–Sept., daily 10–8; Oct.–May, daily 10–5:30.*

Dining and Lodging

$$ ✕ **Sr. Marinos.** This comfortable, wood-paneled restaurant in the center of town has an unusually eclectic menu for this part of the country. It includes a number of French and Italian plates alongside some outstanding regional fare. The multilingual host will help out with translations. The wine list is as long as your arm. ⊠ *Praça Dom Pedro 6,* ☎ *245/901408. AE, MC, V. Closed Sun. and lunch Mon.*

$$ ✕🏨 **Hotel Garcia d'Horta.** Named after a notable 16th-century Jewish doctor and naturalist who lived in Castelo de Vide (his bust by modern sculptor João Cutileiro is in the garden), this attractive, tastefully appointed hotel offers some of the best accommodation value in the area. In addition, its restaurant, A Castanha ($$$$), is renowned for great Alentejan cooking and polished service. A stay here gets you a discount at the 18-hole Ammaia Golf Course, just a few miles away. ⊠ *Estrada de São Vicente 7320,* ☎ *245/901100,* 🆔 *245/901200. 52 rooms, 1 suite. Restaurant, bar, pool, golf privileges. AE, MC, V.*

$ ✕🏨 **Sol e Serra.** This three-story Mediterranean-style hotel at the edge of town is just a 10-minute walk from the castle. Large rooms have balconies looking over the park, and the bar with its spacious lounge, which overlooks the pool, is one of the town's most popular gathering places. The tastefully decorated restaurant with wooden beams is one of the few places in Portugal that offers a kosher menu. It also offers live music and folk-dancing displays every Friday June–September. ⊠ *Estrada de São Vincente, 7320,* ☎ *245/901301,* 🆔 *245/01337. 51 rooms. Restaurant, bar, pool. AE, DC, MC, V.*

Outdoor Activities and Sports

Five kilometers (3 miles) southeast of Castelo de Vide on N246-1 is the **Ammaia Golf Course** (⊠ Quinta do Prado, Marvão), an 18-hole facility with stunning views of the São Mamede mountain range. Greens fees range from 6,000$00 a day on weekdays to 8,000$00 a day on weekends.

THE LOWER ALENTEJO

Extending south of Évora and from the rugged west coast beaches east to the border with Spain, the Lower Alentejo is a vast, mostly flat region of wheat fields, cork oaks, and olive trees. It rains very little here, and the summer months are particularly hot.

Beja

41 *180 km (112 mi) southeast of Lisbon, 128 km (79 mi) south of Évora.*

Spread across a small knoll midway between Spain and the sea is Beja, the Lower Alentejo's principal agricultural center. In the town's streets and squares, shepherds wearing broad-brimmed hats and the traditional sheepskin vests mingle with townspeople. In the fields at the edge of town, gypsies still set up camp, with makeshift tents, horse carts, and open fires. These scenes from a rapidly disappearing way of life contrast sharply with the modernization taking place in the region.

Much of the old part of Beja still retains a significantly Arabic flavor, the legacy of more than 400 years of Moorish occupation. Students of the Portuguese language even claim that the local dialect has Arabic characteristics. Beja, founded by Julius Caesar and known as Pax Julia, was an important town in the Roman province of Lusitania during the first century. The name Pax Julia was chosen because it was here, after a long struggle, that peace was finally established between the Lusitanian chiefs and Julius Caesar. You can see Roman artifacts and other tokens of Beja's long history at the regional museum housed in the convent (☞ *below*) and at the excavations in nearby Pizões.

Facing a broad plaza in the center of the Old Town, the **Convento da Conceição** was founded in 1459 by the parents of King Manuel I. Favored by the royal family, this Franciscan convent thrived and became one of the richest of the period. The convent now houses the **Museu Regional Rainha Dona Leonor** (Queen Leonor Regional Museum), whose exhibits are of more interest to scholars of local history than to casual visitors; still, the building itself merits a visit. The church and cloisters display some fine azulejos from the 16th and 17th centuries, including panels depicting scenes from the life of St. John the Baptist, and a section of multicolored Moorish tiles. Upstairs, at the far end of the second-floor gallery, is the famous Mariana Window, named after a young Beja nun, Mariana Alcoforado. As the story goes, Mariana fell in love with a French count named Chamilly, who was in the Alentejo fighting the Spaniards. When he went back to France, the nun waited longingly and in vain at the window for him to return. The 1669 publication in France of five passionate love letters, known as the *Portuguese Letters*, written by Mariana to the count, documented the scandalous affair and brought a measure of lasting international literary fame to this provincial Alentejo town. ⊠ *Largo da Conceição.* 🎫 *100$00 (includes admission to Visigoth Museum; ☞ below).* ⊙ *Tues.–Sun. 9:30–12:30 and 2–5:15.*

The **Igreja de Santa Maria** (St. Mary's Church), across the square from the convent, was once a mosque, and can be easily recognized by its massive round pillars, Mudéjar arches, and its bell tower similar in design to that of the famed Giralda Tower in Seville.

NEED A BREAK?

The **Café Pastelaria Santa Maria,** opposite the church, has outside tables looking out on the convent square and is a pleasant spot for cake and coffee or a light lunch. A few steps away, in Rua dos Açoutados, the **Maltesinhas** tea house specializes in tea, scones, and cakes.

Castelo de Beja (Beja Castle) is an extensive system of fortifications, whose crenellated walls and towers chronicle the history of the town from its Roman occupation through its 19th-century battles with the French. ⊠ *Largo de Santo Amaro.* 🎫 *150$00.* ⊙ *June–Sept., Tues.–Sun. 10–1 and 2–6; Oct.–May, Tues.–Sun. 9–noon and 1–4.*

The **Museu Visigotico** (Visigoth Museum), next door to the castle in a 6th-century church, houses an impressive collection of tombstones, weapons, and pottery that documents the Visigoth presence in the region. ⊠ *Largo de Santo Amaro.* 🎫 *100$00; free with ticket to Convento da Conceição (☞ above).* ⊙ *Tues.–Sun. 10–12:30 and 2–5:30.*

Dining and Lodging

$ ✕ **A Esquina.** Good, plain local cooking is the attraction here, served with care in pleasant surroundings. There are few better places to try *lebre com feijão* (hare with beans). The wine list is short, but there's usually a good selection of Serpa cheeses. ⊠ *Rua Infante D. Henrique 26,* ☎ *284/389238. AE, V. Closed Sun.*

$ ✕ **Os Infantes.** You sit under vaulted ceilings while dining on traditional Alentejan fare in this agreeable restaurant: the food is basic, but skillfully prepared. The *ensopado de borrego* (lamb stew) and the migas alentejanos are recommended. ⊠ *Rua dos Infantes 14,* ☎ *284/322789. AE, MC, V.*

$$$ ✕🏨 **Pousada do Convento de São Francisco.** This pousada, set in spacious gardens, has been tastefully and comfortably converted from an old convent. The former chapel has been preserved and incorporated into the complex. The restaurant is excellent. Traditional Alentejo dishes make up most of the menu, but the *bacalhau com natas* (salt cod cooked with a cream sauce) is delicious. ⊠ *Largo Dom Nuno Álvares Pereira, 7800,* ☎ *284/328441,* FAX *284/329143. 34 rooms, 1 suite. Restaurant, bar, pool, 2 tennis courts, chapel. AE, DC, MC, V.*

$$ 🏨 **Monte Horta do Cano.** This converted farming estate is the place to stay if sybaritic rustic calm appeals. A kilometer and a half (1 mi) from Beja on the road to Fereira do Alentejo, it has six handsomely appointed rooms, each with private bathroom and air-conditioning. On tap for the energetic are tennis, swimming, and clay pigeon shooting. For those otherwise inclined there is an old wine cellar converted into a bar where fine Alentejo wines can be had with snacks of regional bread, cheeses, and cured sausage. ⊠ *Apartado 1118, 7800-249,* ☎ FAX *284/326156. 6 rooms. Bar, pool, tennis court. No credit cards.*

$ 🏨 **Cristina.** This comfortable *pensão* (pension) occupies a modern five-story building, conveniently located on one of the main shopping streets. Light and airy rooms are a bit sterile. ⊠ *Rua de Mértola 71, 7800,* ☎ *284/323035,* FAX *284/329874. 28 rooms, 3 suites. Bar. AE, DC, MC, V.*

Outdoor Activities and Sports

AIR EXCURSIONS

To enjoy a thrilling bird's-eye view of Beja, take a sightseeing flight in a small plane or in a microlight aircraft. For details and reservations, contact **Aerobeja** (⊠ Aeródromo Civil de Beja, ☎ 284/327003, FAX 284/328279). Flights take place only in June, July, and August.

Serpa

🔢 *29 km (18 mi) southeast of Beja.*

A sleepy agricultural town that seems to have missed the train of progress and development, Serpa is a place where men pass the time by gathering together in the compact Praça da República under the shadow of the ancient stone clock tower. Unemployment is high, and there's little else for many to do. In tiny cubbyholes along narrow, cobbled streets, carpenters, shoemakers, basket weavers, and other craftsmen work in much the same manner as their forefathers did generations earlier. Luckily for gourmets, craftsmen also continue to make one of Portugal's most renowned sheep's milk cheeses here in small factories around the town.

From the 13th-century castle walls, you can get a stunning view of the town. Note how an aqueduct forms an integral part of the walls. As for the huge ruined sections of wall tottering precariously above the entrance, they're the result of explosions ordered by the Duke of Ossuna during the 18th-century War of the Spanish Succession.

Within the castle walls there's a small **Municipal Museum** with archaeological and ethnographic exhibits. 💲 *Free.* ⊙ *Tues.–Sun. 9–12:30 and 2–5:30.*

Dining and Lodging

$$$ ✕▣ **Pousada de São Gens.** On a hill above the white houses and for-
★   tifications of Serpa, this modern, white-domed, Moorish-style pousada offers a relaxed and informal lodging option. The Arabic influence continues as you walk through the green-tile entrance to the lobby with its many arches and vaulted ceilings. Each of the rooms has a small terrace, and bright, cheery fabrics nicely offset the white walls and ceilings. The restaurant has a small, brick-floor dining room with an open fireplace, and in summer you may dine on the terrace looking over the pool and the plains. Tasty local specialties include *poejada de* bacalhau (fried with bread and seasoned with pennyroyal). ✉ *2 km (1 mi) south of Serpa (off E260 to Spain), 7830,* ☎ *284/544724,* ℻ *284/ 544337. 16 rooms, 2 suites. Restaurant, bar, pool. AE, DC, MC, V.*

Vidigueira

⑬   *32 km (20 mi) northwest of Serpa. For the most scenic route head north from Serpa on N265, a narrow road that parallels the Guadiana River as it runs through an isolated stretch of hills and cork trees. At the intersection with N258, follow signs to Vidigueira.*

Vidigueira, a quiet farm town in the middle of the Alentejo plain, is best known as the onetime home of Vasco da Gama, the Portuguese explorer whose voyage in 1497 opened the sea route to India. A statue of him stands in the main square. At the edge of town, in a setting of gardens and ponds, is a Carmelite chapel where the explorer's body lay from the time it was returned from India in 1539 until it was moved in 1898 to Lisbon's Jerónimos Monastery.

São Cucufate

⑭   *5 km (3 mi) west of Vidigueira.*

Standing in an olive orchard are the 2,000-year-old ruins of a Roman villa. The two-story building was part of an extensive Roman settlement. (Coins and other artifacts that have turned up indicate a 1st-century Roman presence here.) It's believed that the ground floor was used as a barn, with the living quarters above it. Remnants of the original heating and drainage systems are visible. The building was later adapted and used in the 13th century as a monastery. The frescoes in the little monastery chapel that still stands on the site were painted in the late 15th and early 16th centuries and have not been restored. 💲 *Free (donations accepted).* ⊙ *Chapel: Tues.–Sun. 9–12:30 and 2–5:30; other parts of site are always open.*

Alvito

⑮   *11 km (7 mi) west of the Ruins of São Cucufate.*

Alvito is a typical, sleepy Alentejo town that occupies a low hill above the Odivelas River. Noted for its fortresslike 13th-century parish church, the town also has a 16th-century castle recently converted into a pousada (☞ Dining and Lodging, *below*) and a number of modest houses with graceful Manueline doorways and windows.

Dining and Lodging

$$$ ✕▣ **Pousada do Castelo de Alvito.** This pousada is within the walls of the 15th-century fortress at the edge of the village. The essential architectural elements of a castle, including crenellated battlements and

massive round towers, have been retained, and there's a large garden and courtyard. The cozy restaurant serves a variety of Alentejo specialties, including an excellent bacalhau *caldeirada* (stew). ⊠ *Apartado 9, 7920,* ☎ *284/485343,* FAX *284/485383. 20 rooms. Restaurant, bar, pool, chapel. AE, DC, MC, V.*

Viana do Alentejo

46 *10 km (6 mi) north of Alvito.*

The attractive castle at Viana do Alentejo—with its rough stone walls, brick battlements, and round turrets—was constructed in 1313 to the very specific orders of Dom Dinis. He decreed that the pentagonal walls should be tall enough that a horseman with a lance measuring 9 *côvados* (an ancient unit of measure equal to 66 centimeters [26 inches]) couldn't injure anyone on the battlements. The fortified parish church within the walls of the castle—designed by the famous Diogo de Arruda—has a pleasing combination of battlements, spires, and ornate Manueline elements. Below the castle a delightful Renaissance fountain enhances the town square. Viana do Alentejo is also noted for a primitive-style pottery, sold in several small shops in town.

Dining

$ ✕ **S. Luís.** Set in the vaulted rooms of what was a medieval hospital adjoining the castle, this little family-run restaurant serves some of the best Alentejo food in the area (and is consequently packed on weekends, when the staff gets somewhat overstretched). The menu is short, simple, and composed entirely of local dishes. Try the *carne de porco assado com puré de patatas* (roast pork with mashed potatoes). ⊠ *Rua António Isidoro de Sousa 136,* ☎ *266/953116. No credit cards.*

Alcácer do Sal

47 *46 km (29 mi) northwest of Alvito, 60 km (37 mi) southwest of Évora. For the most scenic route from Alvito, take N383 west to Torrão, then follow N5 west, close to the Sado River through a sparsely populated region of pine and olive trees, to Alcácer do Sal.*

Because of its favored location and its salt, Alcácer do Sal was one of the first inhabited sites in Portugal; parts of the castle foundations are around 5,000 years old. The Greeks were here, and, of course, the Romans, who established the town of Salatia Urbs Imperatoria—a key intersection in their system of Lusitanian roads. During the Moorish occupation, under the name of Alcácer de Salaria, this became one of the most important Muslim strongholds in all of Iberia. In the 16th century Alcácer prospered as a major producer of salt, and a brisk trade was conducted with the northern European countries, which used it to preserve herring. The hilltop castle is the town's most prominent attraction. A series of red-tile-roof buildings descend from the castle in long, horizontal rows, reaching down the hill to the riverbank.

The marshlands and the estuary of the Sado River that extend to the west of Alcácer form the **Reserva Natural do Sado.** The riverbanks are lined with extensive salt pans and rice paddies, and the nature reserve gives shelter to wildlife such as dolphin, otter, white stork, and egret. From the beach town of Comporta, Route N261 runs south along the coast through a mostly deserted stretch of dunes and pine trees with some wonderful, undeveloped sandy beaches.

Dining and Lodging

$–$$ ✕ **O Brazão.** Don't be put off by the run-down exterior of this no-frills restaurant: it's the favorite eating place of local businesspeople. The open kitchen allows you to peek in and see for yourself what looks good. Sample the *ensopa da garoupa* (fish stew), a typical dish from this part of the country. ⊠ *Largo Prof. Francisco Gentil,* ☎ 265/ 622576. *No credit cards. Closed Sun.*

$$$ ✕⊞ **Pousada Dom Afonso II.** Housed in the ancient castle that overlooks the Sado River, this very attractive member of the Pousadas de Portugal chain has sweeping views over the rooftops of the town and the green plain across the river. The rooms are comfortably and tastefully appointed, and all are air-conditioned. ⊠ *Alcácer do Sal 7580,* ☎ 265/613070, FAX 265/613074. *33 rooms, 2 suites. Restaurant, bar, pool. AE, DC, MC, V.*

Santiago do Cacém

㊽ *40 km (25 mi) southwest of Alcácer do Sal, 64 km (40 mi) west of Beja.*

Santiago do Cacém, about 16 km (10 mi) inland at the junction of N120 and N261, is a quiet regional market town. The castle, built by the Knights of the Order of Santiago (St. James) on the site of Moorish ruins, dominates the town and affords sweeping views to the sea, marred only by the oil refineries at Sines. Inside the parish church, you can see a sculpture of St. James battling the Moors. The Old Town, a maze of narrow streets just below the castle, has a number of well-preserved 17th- and 18th-century manor houses.

The **Municipal Museum,** in a former prison at the center of town, offers several exhibits portraying various aspects of Alentejo life, including one that shows the stages of and implements used in cork production. ⊡ *Free.* ☉ *Tues.–Fri., 10–noon and 2–6, weekends 2–4.*

Just outside of town, off N121 to Ferreira do Alentejo, you can explore the excavations of the Roman city of **Miróbriga.** Originally this site was settled by the Celts in the 4th century BC; later, in the 1st century AD, it became a Roman town. The ruins, although not nearly as extensive or well preserved as those at Conimbriga near Coimbra, contain the interesting sanctuaries of Venus and Esculapius (god of medicine). The excavations—some of which were done in the 1980s by a team from the University of Missouri—are not currently being worked. ⊠ *Cumeadas.* ⊡ *300$00.* ☉ *Tues.–Wed. 9:30–12:30 and 2– 5:30; Thurs.–Sat. 9–12:30 and 2–5:30; Sun. 9–noon and 2–5.*

Dining and Lodging

$$ ✕ **O Retiro.** The joint efforts of an Austrian and his Portuguese wife have
★ turned this Alentejo cottage into a cozy international restaurant. Farm implements adorning the walls help set a down-home tone in this friendly but professional restaurant, which also serves good solid Portuguese fare. ⊠ *Rua Machado dos Santos 8,* ☎ 269/822659. *AE, MC, V. Closed Sun.*

$$ ✕⊞ **Pousada de Santiago.** Sitting atop a small rise at the end of town is
★ this rose-color, ivy-clad manor house surrounded by mature trees and gardens. One of the first pousadas created, the Santiago has had time to cultivate comfort. Over the years its guest and public rooms have been extensively remodeled so that you feel almost as if you're staying in a private house. Some rooms have views of the castle; all units are furnished with decorative Alentejan pieces. The intimate restaurant has a wood-beam ceiling and a tile fireplace, and you'll be served good-quality local favorites such as carne de porco Alentejana. In summer the terrace opens up for meals under the stars. ⊠ *Pousada de Santiago, 7540,* ☎ 269/822469, FAX 269/822459. *8 rooms. Restaurant, bar, pool. AE, DC, MC, V.*

$$ ✕⊞ **Quinta da Ortiga.** This lovely old country estate, just 5 km (3 mi)
★ from Santiago do Cacém (off IP8 to Sines), sits amid 10 acres of trees and farmland. Its interior decor—wood-panel ceilings and Arraiolos

carpets—can best be described as "luxury rustic." The ambience is reminiscent of a comfortable rural villa, and the intimate restaurant, which serves the cuisine of the region, is more like an old-style family dining room than a commercial establishment. Try this inn—managed by Enatur, the government organization that also handles the pousadas—for a quiet, comfortable base from which to enjoy the Alentejo's beaches. ⊠ *Apartado 67, 7540,* ☎ *269/822074,* FAX *269/822073. 14 rooms. Restaurant, bar, pool, horseback riding, chapel. AE, DC, MC, V. 1-wk stay with ½ board required July–Sept.*

Outdoor Activities and Sports

HORSEBACK RIDING

For instruction and for riding on the beach at nearby Sines, contact **Centro Equestre de Santo André** (⊠ Monte V. Cima, Santo André, ☎ 269/761235).

Vila Nova de Milfontes

⑲ *32 km (20 mi) southwest of Santiago do Cacém.*

Although the town itself is just another small resort without any special architectural merit, the location of Vila Nova de Milfontes at the broad mouth of the Mira River is delightful, and it has soft, sandy beaches on both sides of the river. Overlooking the sea is an ivy-covered fortress built on Moorish foundations in the late 16th century to protect Milfontes from the Algerian pirates who regularly terrorized the Portuguese coast. It was built on ancient foundations, for it was believed that the spirits there would ward off the pirates. In recent times, the converted edifice has been used as a guest house. It has now been restored and converted into a small inn.

Dining and Lodging

$$ ✕ **Restaurante O Pescador.** Appreciated for its good seafood specialties, this bustling, air-conditioned *marisqueira* (seafood restaurant) is owned by a husband and wife who started off as fish sellers in the nearby market. This is a popular choice with locals, by whom the restaurant is familiarly known as *"o Moura"* (Moura's place), after the owner's name. ⊠ *Largo da Praça 18,* ☎ *283/996338. AE, MC, V.*

$$ ✕▥ **Pousada Castelo de Milfontes.** This privately owned inn set in the town's restored castle is run along the lines of a guest house, albeit with some luxury touches. The door closes at midnight, and dinner is served at a set time with the guests seated around a common table. The rooms are comfortable, some have sea views, and all have private bathrooms. ⊠ *Vila Nova de Milfontes, 7645,* ☎ *283/998231,* FAX *283/997122. 7 rooms. Bar. No credit cards.*

$ ✕▥ **Duna Parque.** This pleasant apartment-hotel complex just outside town is a good option in the low season. From July through August the minimal rental period is three days, but at other times you can rent the apartments by the day. The one- to three-bedroom units with kitchenettes are in modern two-story blocks set in gardens that are a five-minute walk to the beach and a 10-minute walk to town. ⊠ *Eira da Pedra, 7645,* ☎ *283/996451. 45 units. Restaurant, bar, kitchenettes, pool, 2 tennis courts. AE, MC, V.*

ÉVORA AND THE ALENTEJO A TO Z

Arriving and Departing

By Airplane

You can fly into the airports at either Lisbon or Faro and then take ground transportation into the region. Évora is roughly 160 km (99 mi) from Lisbon and about 245 km (152 mi) from Faro. For flight information for Lisbon, *see* Chapter 1; for information about Faro's airport, *see* Chapter 5.

By Car

Three main roads connect the Alentejo with Spain: the N521 runs 105 km (65 mi) from Caceres, Spain, to the Portuguese border near Portalegre. On the border farther south, the A6 toll highway meets up with Spain's N.V highway from Madrid. To the south, the N433 runs from Seville, Spain, to Beja, 225 km (140 mi) away. The Alentejo can also be easily reached from the Algarve, its southern neighbor. The fastest and smoothest of the main routes are the IP1, which extends north from Albufeira, and the IP2, which branches east from it at Ourique.

Getting Around

By Bus

There are few, if any, places in this region that are not served by at least one bus daily. Express coaches run by several regional bus lines travel regularly between Lisbon and the larger towns such as Évora, Beja, and Estremoz. If you have the time and patience, bus travel, which offers an opportunity to come in close contact with locals, can be a rewarding and inexpensive way to get around. Since a number of different bus companies leave for the Alentejo from different terminals in Lisbon, it's best to have a travel agent do your booking.

By Car

A car is by far the most efficient way to tour the Alentejo, where distances are great and bus and train service infrequent. Driving will give you access to many out-of-the-way beaches and villages. The roads are generally good, and traffic is light. There are no confusing big cities in which to get lost, although parking can be a problem in some of the towns such as Évora. You'll encounter a good bit of construction on many of the Alentejo's main routes. There are two important new roads. The first is the toll highway A6, which branches off A2 running south from Lisbon and takes you as far as the Spanish border at Caia, where it links up with the N.V highway from Madrid. This road provides easy access to Évora and the Upper Alentejo. The other is A2 itself, which at press time had reached a point 16 km (10 mi) south of Grádola in the Alentejo, on its way south to the Algarve. This route also has a good nontoll alternative in the IP1/E01, a road that has seen great improvements in recent years. Farther inland and south of Évora, IP2/E802 is the best access for Beja and the southeastern Alentejo.

By Train

Travel by train in the vast Alentejo is not for people in a great hurry. Service to many of the more remote destinations is infrequent—and in some cases nonexistent. The towns of Alcácer do Sal, Évora, and Beja are connected with Lisbon by several trains daily. The trains leave from Barreiro station across the river, reached by a ferry boat connection from the river station in Praça do Comércio.

Contacts and Resources

Car Rental

Major car-rental agencies include **Hertz** (⊠ Dona Isabel 7/13, Évora, ☎ 266/701767) and **Europcar** (⊠ Rua Angola 3–5, Beja, ☎ 284/328128).

Emergencies

General: ☎ 112. **Hospitals:** The following cities have hospitals with emergency rooms, and their approaches are marked HOSPITAL; the emergency room is marked URGÊNCIAS. **Beja** (⊠ Hospital Distrital, Rua Dr. António F. C. Lima, ☎ 284/310200) and **Évora** (⊠ Hospital Distrital Espirito Santo, Largo Sr. da Pobreza, ☎ 266/740100). **Pharmacies:** All sizable towns have at least one pharmacy that's open weekends, holidays, and after normal store hours. Local newspapers usually keep a schedule, and notices are posted on the door of every pharmacy.

Guided Tours

Few regularly scheduled sightseeing tours originate within the region, but many of the major attractions are covered by a wide selection of one-day tours from Lisbon. For information in Lisbon, contact **Gray Line Tours** (⊠ Av. Praia da Vitória 12-B, ☎ 21/352–2594) or **Citirama** (⊠ Av. Praia da Vitória 12-B, ☎ 21/355–8567). Walking tours of Évora are available through **Mendes and Murteira** (⊠ Rua 31 de Janeiro 15-A, Évora, ☎ 266/703616), and the company can also organize bus tours of the district's prehistoric archaeological sites.

Telephones

For information, dial 118; operators often speak English.

Travel Agencies

Many travel agencies in the region are small, with limited services and no English-speaking personnel. In Évora, **Touralentejo** (⊠ Rua Miguel Bombarda 78, ☎ 266/702717, FAX 266/709231) has a full range of services and staff members who speak English.

Visitor Information

The main tourist office for the central part of the Alentejo is in Évora and is called the **Região de Turismo de Évora** (⊠ Rua de Aviz 90, ☎ 266/742534, FAX 266/705238). The main office for the Lower Alentejo is in Beja, and is called the **Região de Turismo da Planicie Dourada** (⊠ Praça da República 12, ☎ 284/310150, FAX 284/310151). The Upper Alentejo is represented by the **Região de Turismo de São Mamede,** in Portalegre (⊠ Estrada de Santana 25, ☎ 245/300770, FAX 245/204053). Most of the coastal part of the Alentejo is represented by the **Região de Turismo de Setúbal (Costa Azul)** (⊠ Travessa Frei Gaspar 10, ☎ 265/ 539120, FAX 265/539127) in Setúbal.

The most practical immediate sources of information for tourists are the local offices, called *postos de turismo*. In Central Alentejo: **Arraiolos** (⊠ Câmara Municipal, ☎ 266/499105), **Estremoz** (⊠ Rossio do Marquês de Pombal, ☎ 268/333541), **Évora** (⊠ Praça do Giraldo, ☎ 266/ 702671), **Vila Viçosa** (⊠ Câmara Municipal, ☎ 268/881101). In Lower Alentejo: **Alcácer do Sal** (⊠ Rua da República 66, ☎ 265/ 622565), **Beja** (⊠ Rua Capitão João Francisco de Sousa, ☎ 284/ 311913), **Mértola** (⊠ Largo Vasco da Gama 1, ☎ 286/612573), **Moura** (⊠ Largo de Santa Clara, ☎ 285/251375), **Santiago do Cacém** (⊠ Praça do Mercado Municipal, ☎ 269/826696), **Serpa** (⊠ Largo D. Jorge, ☎ 284/544727), **Sines** (⊠ Jardim das Descobertas, ☎ 269/634472). In Upper Alentejo: **Alter do Chão** (⊠ Palácio do Álamo, ☎ 245/ 610004), **Arronches** (⊠ Praça da República, ☎ 245/583210), **Campo Maior** (⊠ Rua Major Talaja, ☎ 268/688936), **Castelo de Vide** (⊠ Rua Bartolomeu Álvares da Santa 81, ☎ 245/901361), **Marvão** (⊠ Rua Dr. António Matos Magalhães, ☎ 245/933886), **Portalegre** (⊠ Palácio Póvoas-Rossio, ☎ 245/331359).

5   THE ALGARVE

Clean, sandy beaches and excellent sports facilities dot Portugal's southern coast, as do apartment complexes, hotels, discos, and bars, which sprout from every bay and cliff top. At the shore, interesting rock formations and grottoes make beaches more than sand and surf, whereas the inland countryside has a simple, rural atmosphere that seems a world away.

By Jules Brown

Updated by
Paul Murphy

Portugal's southernmost coastal region, the Algarve is the favorite destination of foreign visitors to the country. It's a well-known holiday center, with clean, sandy beaches and excellent sports facilities coupled with an equable climate and dining and lodging choices to suit all budgets. Many Europeans fly here directly and rarely stray more than a few miles from their resorts. Even for those visitors based in Lisbon, the Algarve is an easy 300-km (186-mi) drive south, and it provides an interesting contrast to the rest of the country.

Along with the region's popularity has come progress, and during the past two decades, the Algarve has been heavily developed, with parts of the once pristine, 240-km (149-mi) coastline now seriously overbuilt. In some areas the seashore is almost wall-to-wall with apartment complexes, hotels, discos, and bars.

Until the construction of the airport at Faro in the '60s, the Algarve was rarely visited by tourists, and for centuries before that it remained isolated from the rest of Europe. Phoenicians, Romans, and Visigoths established fishing and trading communities here, but it wasn't until the arrival of the Moors in the 8th century that the region became an important strategic settlement. It was the Moors who gave the province its name—El Gharb (the Land to the West)—and who established their capital at the inland town of Silves (then called Chelb). In those days it had direct access to the sea and at its peak was a grand city with a population of more than 30,000. Silves fell to the Christians in 1189, but the Moors weren't completely out of the region until the middle of the 13th century, leaving many tangible reminders of their 500-year rule: Arabic place-names; the white, cubelike houses in the coastal fishing villages; the popular fruits and sweets of the region; and the physical features of many of the people.

In the 15th century Prince Henry the Navigator established a town and a pioneering navigation school near Sagres, where principles were developed that would enable Portuguese mariners of the 16th century to explore much of the world. After this flurry of activity, though, the Algarve once again settled into obscurity.

The Algarve measures a mere 40 km (25 mi) north to south, bordered on the north by the Serra de Monchique (Monchique Mountains) and the Serra de Caldeirão (Caldeirão Mountains) and on the east by the Rio Guadiana (Guadiana River), a river that isolated the Algarve from contact with neighboring Spain. Over the centuries the region's geography has both enabled inhabitants to keep to themselves and provided many natural advantages. Its location in the south, protected by hills, makes the Algarve much warmer than any other place in the country. The vegetation is far more luxuriant; the land, originally irrigated by the Moors, supports a profusion of fruits, nuts, and vegetables; and the fishing industry has always flourished.

Despite heavy development in some places, the region still makes a fine coastal vacation spot. There are small fishing villages and secluded beaches, particularly in the west, that so far have escaped attention; an abundance of extraordinary rock formations and idyllic grottoes, also in the west; and to the east, a series of isolated sandbar islands and sweeping beaches that balance the crowded excesses of the middle. Even where development is at its heaviest, new construction takes the form of landscaped villa and apartment complexes made of local materials, which not only fit in well with the surroundings but also keep money circulating within the community. However, to see the Algarve at its best, it's often necessary to abandon the popular beaches for a drive inland. Here, rural Portugal still survives in hill villages, market towns, and agricultural landscapes, which, although only a few miles from the coast, seem a world away in attitude.

One word of warning: the Algarve is one of Europe's most popular sites for vacation and retirement homes. If you didn't know that before you arrived, you'll soon get the picture in towns such as Albufeira and Praia da Rocha, where an entire industry exists to persuade visitors to tour apartment developments and proposed sites in the hopes that they'll sign on the dotted line. You may be approached by agents offering all sorts of inducements (such as free gifts, meals, and drinks) to encourage you to visit time-share properties and villa complexes. Even if you do agree to go on a tour, *never* sign anything, regardless of the promises made.

Pleasures and Pastimes

Beaches
The glory of the Algarve is its beaches, which are generally clear and impressive—some of the finest in Europe. There are hundreds from which to choose on the long stretch of coast. Most beaches (especially those in the main resorts) have snack bars and showers, and many have watersports equipment for rent. Remember that although it's possible to wade out for a swim from most Algarve beaches, you should heed local warnings about currents and steeply sloping seabeds.

The best cove beaches are at Lagos. Interesting beaches with enormous rock formations include those at Albufeira and Praia da Rocha. If you require more breathing space, particularly if you're traveling with young children, try the strands near Olhão and Tavira; these and the beaches near Sagres are less populated than those at major resorts.

Bullfights
Unlike the Spanish, the Portuguese do not kill their bulls at the end of the fight, although they are slaughtered immediately afterwards, out of sight of the public. You can attend fights in the towns of Albufeira and Lagos; aficionados of the sport recommend attending the events held in August, which are fought by the country's top matadors (at other times, smaller bulls are used). Bullfights are held every Saturday at 5:30 PM April–June and September–October; in July and August they're held at 10 PM, when the day's heat has dissipated.

Dining
Algarvian cooking makes good use of local seafood. The most unusual of regional appetizers, *espadarte fumada* (smoked swordfish), is sliced thin, served with a salad, and best appreciated if accompanied by a dry white wine. Restaurants generally serve their own version of *sopa de peixe* (fish soup) as well as a variety of succulent shellfish: *perceves* (barnacles), *santola* (crab), and *gambas* (shrimp). Main courses often depend on what has been landed that day, but there's generally a choice of *robalo* (sea bass), *pargo* (bream), *atum* (tuna), and espadarte.

At simple beach cafés and harbor stalls the unmistakable smell of *sardinhas assadas* (charcoal-grilled sardines) permeates the air—they make a tempting lunch served with fresh bread and smooth red wine. Perhaps the most famous Algarvian dish is *cataplana*—a stew of clams, pork, onions, tomatoes, and wine, which takes its name from the lidded utensil used to steam the dish. You have to wait for cataplana to be specially prepared, but once you've tasted it, you won't mind waiting again and again.

In inland rural areas, game highlights most menus, with many meat dishes served *o forno* (oven roasted). Specialties include *cabrito* (kid), *leitão* (suckling pig), and *codorniz* (quail), as well as *ensopado de borrego* (lamb stew).

The Algarve is particularly known for its almonds, oranges, and figs. However, these rarely appear in restaurants, where the choice of dessert is often limited to flan, ice cream, and perhaps a fresh fruit salad. Typical Algarvian sweets include rich egg, sugar, and almond custards that reflect the Moorish influence, including *doces de amendoa* (marzipan cakes in the shapes of animals and flowers), *bolos de Dom Rodrigo* (almond sweets with egg-and-sugar filling), *bolo Algarvio* (cake made of sugar, almonds, eggs, and cinnamon), and *morgado de figos do Algarve* (fig-and-almond paste). You will find these on sale in *pastelarias* (cake shops) and in some cafés.

Unless otherwise noted, casual dress is acceptable throughout the Algarve. Reservations are not needed off-season, but in summer, you'll need them at most of the better restaurants. For price categories, *see* the chart under Dining *in* Smart Travel Tips A to Z.

Fishing

The best fishing waters are those off the shores of Sagres and Carrapateira (on the west coast), and local fishermen recommend October through January as the most fruitful—or, rather, fishful—months. You're likely to catch gray mullet, sea bass, moray eels, scabbard fish, and bluefish. Individuals and charter companies offer organized trips from various ports along the coast. Check the boards on quaysides for prices and departure times or consult local tourist offices.

Golf

The Algarve has some of Europe's best golf courses, designed by the likes of Henry Cotton, Frank Pennink, and William Cotton. It's a year-round game here, and all courses have a clubhouse with bar and restaurant, practice grounds, and equipment rentals. At the many hotels with golf facilities, greens fees are included in the room rate, or discounted. In the past few years, many Algarve courses have undergone renovations. The esteemed "Old Course" at Vilamoura—designed by Frank Pennink and one of the first to open in the Algarve about 30 years ago—is one such example. Restoration of the par 73, 6,500-yard course—which rises and falls through a pine forest with sea views along the way—was true to the original. Ask at local tourist offices for more information, including the brochure that gives details on all Algarve courses.

Lodging

The Algarve has some of Portugal's best hotels, whose leisure and sports facilities are second to none. There are busy beachside hotels in large resorts and secluded retreats in luxuriant country estates. Apartment and villa complexes with luxurious amenities are popular in the Algarve. Some properties—built on the most beautiful parts of the coast—are fancy, indeed. They may be a good distance from major towns, but most have bars, restaurants, shops, and other facilities.

Budget lodgings are also available. In most towns and resorts, you'll be approached by people offering very reasonably priced *quartos* (rooms) in private houses, which are almost always clean and cheerful, if small and with shared bathrooms. Don't expect to pay less than around 5,000$00 for a reasonable double room per night. Also don't agree to take a room without seeing it first, since it may be farther from the town center than you were led to believe. In summer, reservations at most places are essential, and rates often rise by as much as 50%

above off-peak prices. Since the weather from September through May is still good, you might want to consider an off-peak trip to take advantage of the lower prices. For price categories, *see* the chart under Lodging *in* Smart Travel Tips A to Z.

Nightlife

In the major resorts you'll find plenty of bars, discos, and clubs. If you prefer a quieter evening, the Algarve's open-air cafés are perfect for a drink and people-watching, and sometimes a traveling musician will stroll by. Many hotels also put on performances of fado and other traditional music. To gamble, head for one of the Algarve's three casinos—at Praia de Rocha, Vilamoura, and Monte Gordo—and remember to bring your passport as well as your wallet.

Shopping

All the main towns and villages have regular food markets, usually open daily from 8 until around 2. Among the best are those in Olhão, Tavira, Lagos, and Silves. Larger weekly and monthly markets, where a wider variety of produce and goods is sold, are held in Albufeira, on the first and third Tuesdays of the month; in Loulé, every Saturday; in Lagos, on the first Saturday of the month; in Portimão, on the first Monday; in Sagres, on the first Friday; in Silves, on the third Monday; and in Quarteira, largest of all, every Wednesday. Most major towns hold annual country fairs, where alongside the market stalls you'll find crafts and entertainment. Dates vary from year to year; check with tourist offices for details.

Probably the best town in which to shop is Portimão, where you can spend at least a half day browsing. In summer, the main resorts have a lot of casual roadside stalls (a good area is outside the lighthouse at Cabo São Vicente), at which you can buy items such as jewelry, handicrafts, art, and clothes. Look for reasonably priced hand-knit sweaters in stores throughout the Algarve, and even better bargains at roadside stalls. Handmade copper items and other metal crafts can be found in many towns, although the best places are probably Portimão, Lagos, and Loulé. Small woven sisal baskets make good souvenirs and are available nearly everywhere. You'll sometimes see women sitting in the doorways of their houses as they weave.

Water Sports

The coast is developing into a popular destination for mariners from all over the world, in particular those who come to escape the severe northern European winters. There are anchorage and harbor facilities at Faro, Lagos, Olhão, Portimão, Praia da Rocha, Sagres, and Vila Real. Snorkeling and scuba diving, possible at several places along the coast, are especially good in the western Algarve, where certified, experienced divers can explore the many caves and rock formations. Wind- and board surfing are popular at a number of spots as well. In fact, several of the more remote west coast beaches have recently begun to attract surfers from all parts of Europe. Windsurfing equipment is available throughout the Algarve; you can rent from stands on the beaches at Meia Praia (Lagos), Vale do Lobo, Albufeira, Armação de Pêra, Ferragudo, and Burgau, and at the Luz Bay Club. Waterskiing is less widely practiced, although it can be arranged.

Exploring the Algarve

The Algarve may be the simplest region in Portugal to explore, since the main roads—N125 and the IP1/E1—and the train line connect towns and villages along the entire coast. Towns are close together, and it's possible to see all of the Algarve in a week, albeit at a fairly brisk pace.

But even if you spend several days at one resort, you should make an effort to see both the eastern and western ends of the province and an inland town or two, for each has a very distinct character.

For touring purposes, the province can conveniently be divided into four sections, starting with Faro—the Algarve's capital—and the nearby beaches and inland towns. The second section encompasses the region east to the border town of Vila Real de Santo António, from which you may cross into Spain. The most built-up part of the coast, bursting with attractions, is found from Faro west to Portimão, while the fourth area covers Lagos, the principal town of the western Algarve, and extends west to Sagres and Cabo São Vicente.

Great Itineraries

Give yourself at least three days to take in the important sights. In five days you can see the sights, have a little time at the beach, linger over a delicious seafood lunch (or two) at a beachfront restaurant, and still have time to get away from the built-up coastal strip to some of the more remote inland villages. A seven-day stay will allow you to, perhaps, get in a game of golf or spend a few days simply relaxing on some of the many excellent beaches. After all, it was the discovery of these sandy stretches by sun-starved northern Europeans that transformed this sleepy province into one of Europe's most popular vacation spots.

Numbers in the text correspond to numbers in the margin and on the Algarve, Faro, and Lagos maps.

IF YOU HAVE 3 DAYS

Begin with a day exploring the provincial capital, **Faro** ①–⑨, and its surroundings. The following morning, head west to see the lighthouse at **Cabo São Vicente** ㊸ and the fortress and exhibition center at **Sagres** ㊷, where you can have lunch overlooking the cliffs. In the afternoon, head back to Faro, stopping along the way to visit **Lagos** ㉜–㊲ or **Portimão** ㉗. On day three, drive east to **Vila Real de Santo António** ⑰, at the border with Spain. En route you can explore **Olhão** ⑩, with its Moorish-style architecture, and **Tavira** ⑭, one of the Algarve's most attractive towns.

IF YOU HAVE 5 DAYS

After a day in and around **Faro** ①–⑨, drive west to visit **Portimão** ㉗ and the popular nearby beach resort of **Praia da Rocha** ㉙. Continue west to overnight in **Lagos** ㉜–㊲, an attractive and historic city whose origins go back to Carthaginian times. After seeing the sights in Lagos, head out to **Cabo São Vicente** ㊸ for some spectacular views from the lighthouse and then to **Sagres** ㊷. The next morning, follow N268 along the west coast to Aljezur, where you take N267 through a remote part of the Algarve to the delightful mountain town of **Monchique** ㉛. Enjoy lunch at one of the several terrace restaurants that afford sweeping views across the countryside to the sea. After lunch, head down the mountain on N266 to the coastal road N125 and swing east to **Olhão** ⑩ and **Tavira** ⑭. On your last day, visit the border town of **Vila Real de Santo António** ⑰.

IF YOU HAVE 7 DAYS

With a week, you can see the attractions of the five-day itinerary at a leisurely pace and still have a few days left to just bask on one of the Algarve's fine beaches. Simply pick a spot and spend an extra night nearby. If you like your beaches long and flat, then you will enjoy the sands of the Sotavento, the region extending east from Faro. The beaches off **Tavira** ⑭ and **Olhão** ⑩ are the best. The beaches of the Barlavento, west of Faro, often have dramatic cliffs and bizarre rock formations as a backdrop. Although recently subject to relentless high-

The Algarve

SPAIN

ATLANTIC OCEAN

Rio Chança
Rio Guadiana
R. de Foupana
R. de Odeleite
R. do Vascão
R. Mira

SERRA DE CALDEIRÃO
SERRA DE MONCHIQUE

to LISBON
Ourique
Odemira
Odeceixe
Aljezur
Carrapateira

Monchique **31**
Foia

São Bartolomeu de Messines **26**
Silves **25**
Dam
Lagoa **24**
Alvor **30**
Portimão **27**
Ferragudo **28**
Praia da Rocha **29**
Carvoeiro **23**
Cabo Carvoeiro
Praia da Galé
Armação de Pêra **22**
Albufeira **21**
Praia da Oura
Praia da Falesia **20**
Vilamoura
Vale do Lobo **18**
Praia de Faro
19
Loulé **13**
São Brás de Alportel **12**
Almansil
Estói **11**
Faro **1–9**
Olhão **10**
Ria Formosa
Ilha de Faro
Ilha da Culatra
Ilha da Armona
Armona
Ilha da Armona
Tavira **14**
Cacela Velha
Ilha de Tavira
Manta Rota
Praia da Manta Rota **15**
Monte Gordo **16**
Vila Real de Santo António **17**
Ayamonte
Golfo de Cádiz
Barranco Velho

Logos **32–37**
Praia da Luz **38**
Burgau **39**
Salema **40**
Praia da Salema
Vila do Bispo **41**
Sagres **42**
Ponta de Sagres
Cabo São Vicente
43

N265
N122
N2
N270
N124
N266
N125
N267
N268
N120
IP1/E1
E1

KEY
Rail Lines
Beach

N

10 miles
15 km

rise tourist development, the beaches of **Praia da Rocha** ㉙ are still magnificent. The beaches at **Lagos** ㉜–㊲ and nearby **Praia da Luz** ㊳ are also recommended.

When to Tour the Algarve

The Algarve's weather is welcoming year-round. Winters are mild, and spring is positively delightful. Summer is, of course, high season—with lodging at a premium, prices at their highest, and crowds at their thickest. But you'll also find warmer seas (compared to the Mediterranean, the Atlantic is always cool), piercing blue skies, and golden sands at the foot of glowing ocher-red cliffs.

If you can, avoid the high season, which runs from July through August. Although not quite as congested as many other European seaside resorts, the Algarve's beaches are best appreciated in late spring and early fall, when the water is quite pleasant for swimming and finding a secluded spot to lay out your beach blanket is much less challenging. From a scenic perspective, the Algarvian spring, with its rolling carpets of wildflowers, is hard to beat. If you seek solitude and are willing to endure swimming in an ocean that is definitely cold (a hotel pool would be a better bet!), a winter visit can be very pleasant. There are many bargains to be had, particularly with respect to accommodations and car rentals.

FARO AND ENVIRONS

Many people fly in to Faro and pass straight through on their way to beaches east and west, which is unfortunate. The city's attractive harbor and Old Town are both worthy of a night's stay or more, and its many facilities make it a fine base for touring the region. The towns that ring Faro contain their own sights worth seeing, from beaches and markets to churches and ruins.

Faro

❶ *300 km (186 mi) southeast of Lisbon.*

The provincial capital of the Algarve is a prosperous city of around 100,000 residents. Founded by the Moors, it was taken by Afonso III in 1249, at the end of the Arab domination. Much of its early architecture was lost in the late 16th century, when it was sacked by the English under the earl of Essex. It was further damaged by two 18th-century earthquakes, the latter of which, in 1755, also destroyed Lisbon. Remnants of the medieval walls and some historic buildings, however, can still be seen in the delightful **Cidade Velha** (Old Town). Here, quiet streets and squares, where balconies and tile work decorate even the most unappealing facade, are perfect for a stroll.

❷ You enter the Old Town through an 18th-century gate, the **Arco da Vila,** which stands in front of the central Jardim Manuel Bivar (Manuel Bivar Garden). Note the white-marble statue of St. Thomas Aquinas in a niche at the top and the storks that nest here permanently.

❸ The squat, mostly Renaissance-style **Sé** (cathedral) faces the Largo da Sé, a grand square bordered by orange trees and whitewashed palace buildings. The cathedral retains a Gothic tower but is mostly of interest for its stunning interior of decorated 17th- and 18th-century *azulejos* (tiles). Another highlight, on one side of the nave, is the red Chinoiserie organ, dating from 1751. Best of all, however, is the wonderful view from the top of the church tower, looking out over the Old Town rooftops and across the lagoon. ✉ *Largo da Sé.* 🎟 *250$00.* ⏲ *Mon.–Sat. 10–5 or 6; also open Sun. 8–1 for services.*

Arco da
Vila 2

Doca 6

Igreja de São
Francisco 5

Igreja do
Carmo 9

Museu
Maritimo 7

Museu
Municipal . . .4

Museu
Regional do
Algarve 8

Sé 3

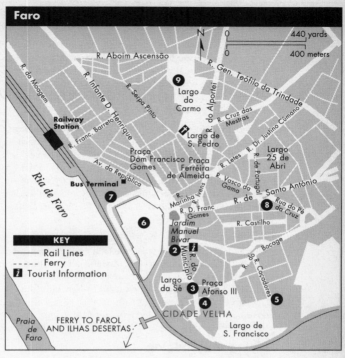

The 16th-century Convento de Nossa Senhora da Assunção (Convent of Our Lady of the Assumption) has been converted to house the

4 **Museu Municipal** (Municipal Museum). The conversion makes fine use of the convent's beautiful two-story cloister. The best displays are the archaeological collections, including fascinating Roman artifacts from local settlements predating Moorish Faro as well as Roman statues from the excavations at Milreu. ⊠ *Praça Afonso III 14,* ☎ *289/822402.* ⊠ *Free.* ☉ *Weekdays 10–6:30, Sat. 10–1.*

5 The plain facade of the **Igreja de São Francisco** (Church of St. Francis) gives no hint of the richness of its baroque interior. Inside are glorious 18th-century blue-and-white azulejos and a chapel adorned with gilt work. Ask for the key at the tourist office. ⊠ *Largo de São Francisco.* ⊠ *Free.*

6 The **doca** (dock)—flanked by Faro's main square, the Praça Dom Francisco Gomes, and the Manuel Bivar Gardens—is one of the prettiest places in town. You can sit at an outdoor café and watch the boats go about their business.

NEED A
BREAK?

The **Café Alianca** (⊠ Rua Francisco Gomes 7–11) is an old-style coffeehouse, between Rua Francisco Gomes and Rua Marinha. Inside you'll find a timeworn ambience and outside, sidewalk tables.

---

7 At the dockside **Museu Maritimo** (Maritime Museum), models of local fishing craft are displayed alongside full-size boats of war and exploration. ⊠ *Capitania do Porto de Faro,* ☎ *289/803601.* ⊠ *100$00.* ☉ *Weekdays 9:30–noon and 2:30–5.*

East of the harbor, in the pedestrian shopping streets around **Rua de Santo António,** you'll find much of what makes Faro tick as a tourist town: bars, restaurants, shops, and sidewalk hawkers touting souvenirs and snacks.

❽ Providing a bit of culture in an area otherwise dominated by stores and eateries, the **Museu Regional do Algarve** (Algarve Regional Museum) sheds light on local agricultural and fishing practices by way of various models and diagrams. Crafts and reconstructions of typical house interiors are displayed, too. ✉ *Rua do Pé da Cruz,* ☎ *289/27610.* 🎫 *300$00.* ⊘ *Weekdays 9–12:30 and 2–5.*

❾ Just northwest of the city center, the baroque **Igreja do Carmo** (Carmo Church), looking very out of place amid the modern buildings surrounding it, is flanked by twin bell towers. The real interest, however, is inside. A door to the right of the altar leads to the Capela dos Ossos (Chapel of the Bones), whose walls are covered in more than 1,000 skulls and bones of parishioners and monks—an eerie sight, to say the least. ✉ *Largo do Carmo.* 🎫 *100$00.* ⊘ *Weekdays 10–1 and 3–5, Sat. 10–1.*

Beach

Although thick with crowds in season and on weekends, the long, sandy beach on the Ilha de Faro (Faro Island), a sandbar 5 km (3 mi) southwest of Faro, is the closest beach to town. You can reach the beach, called the **Praia de Faro,** via a ferry to Farol on Ilha Culatra or to Ilha Deserta or by a 25-minute ride on Bus 16. ✉ *Bus stop opposite bus terminal; catch ferry at jetty below Old Town.* 🎫 *Ferry 300$00.* ⊘ *Buses leave hourly 8 AM–10 PM; July–Aug., 3 ferries daily.*

Dining and Lodging

$$ ✕ **Dois Irmãos.** In business since 1925, this large, pretty, centrally located restaurant (one of several good places on this street) specializes in cataplana, as evidenced by the utensils that hang from its wood-beam ceiling. Almost any of the other seafood dishes are worth trying, too. Just be sure to save room for the homemade flan. Choose your wine from one of the hundreds of bottles that line the upper walls. ✉ *Largo do Terreiro do Bispo 14–15,* ☎ *289/803912. AE, DC, MC, V.*

$$ ✕ **Mesa dos Mouros.** The Moors' Table occupies an ancient stone house right by the cathedral. You can either eat indoors or dine alfresco on a pretty little raised wooden terrace looking across the cobbled square, which is fringed with orange trees. Despite the antiquity of its surroundings, this is a very stylish modern restaurant serving good fish dishes and also Spanish *tapas* (snacks). ✉ *Largo da Sé,* ☎ *289/878873. MC, V.*

$ ✕ **Adega Nova.** This atmospheric *adega* (wine cellar) offers expertly prepared traditional Portuguese dishes in down-to-earth surroundings that foster the lively atmosphere. Drinks are served at the tile-covered bar, and you sit at long wooden tables and benches to eat. The restaurant is close to the train station in an otherwise dreary area. ✉ *Rua Francisco Barreto 24,* ☎ *289/813433. No credit cards.*

$$$–$$$$ ✕🏨 **Hotel La Reserve.** Tucked in the hills at Santa Bárbara de Nexe, a
★ few miles inland from Faro, this intimate hotel delivers luxury, seclusion, and comfort. The air-conditioned quarters (with a Moorish flavor) have private terraces or balconies, and lush plantings set off the low, white buildings. In a 6-acre park, the hotel has a rural atmosphere conducive to total relaxation, but you can work up an appetite at the tennis courts or pool and then satisfy it in the formal restaurant (reservations essential; closed Tuesday; no lunch). Elegant cuisine with a French accent is the fare, with game dishes as specialties, and there's a complimentary Continental breakfast. ✉ *Santa Bárbara de Nexe, 8000,* ☎ *289/999494; 289/999234 for restaurant,* ☎ 🖷 *289/999402. 12 studios, 8 duplexes. Restaurant, bar, pool, tennis courts. AE, DC, MC, V.*

$$$$ 🔲 **Hotel Eva.** From this well-appointed hotel on the main square, you
★ have magnificent views of the yacht-filled harbor, the sea, and Old Town.
There's a bar with occasional evening entertainment, as well as a
rooftop pool and top-floor restaurant. Guest rooms are modern and
comfortably furnished; ask for one overlooking the front. There's also
a courtesy bus to the town beach on nearby Faro Island. ✉ *Av. da
República 1, 8000,* ☎ *289/803354,* FAX *289/802304. 150 rooms.
Restaurant, bar, pool. AE, DC, MC, V.*

$ 🔲 **Residencial Algarve.** Just a few steps from the center of town, the
★ original building on this site was built in the 1880s for a wealthy maritime family. It was recently rebuilt to mirror the original style and features and is now possibly the nicest budget hotel in town. All rooms
have cable television and air-conditioning, breakfast is included, and
the brand new bathrooms are worthy of many a four-star hotel. ✉ *Rua
Infante Dom Henrique 52, 8000,* ☎ *289/895700,* FAX *289/895703. 14
rooms. Breakfast room. MC, V.*

Nightlife

Faro's central pedestrian streets are filled at night with throngs of café
goers, and **Rua do Prior,** in particular, is known for its wide selection
of stylish, late-closing bars. Friday night is the best time for bar-hop-
ping. **Kingburger** (✉ Rua do Prior 40) and **Diesel Bar** (✉ Travessa São
Pedro, off Rua do Prior) are current favorites. For a disco, visit trendy
24 Julho (✉ Rua do Prior 38), which stays open until 7 AM.

Olhão

🔟 *8 km (5 mi) east of Faro.*

During the Napoleonic Wars, the inhabitants of this small 18th-century
port town on the Ria Formosa (a *ria* is a briny river) defied the French
blockade on trade with Britain and profited greatly from smuggling. With
the proceeds, they built North African–style, cube-shape whitewashed
houses. In 1808, local fishermen reputedly sailed to Brazil to inform the
exiled Dom João VI that the French had departed from Portugal. Because of their loyalty and courage (they sailed without navigational aids),
the fishermen's home town was granted a town charter. Although modern construction has destroyed a great deal of its charm, Olhão's fishing port is still colorful, and its intricate Old Town quarter is appealing.
To get a bird's-eye view visit the parish church and climb its bell tower.

Beaches

Adding to the allure of the beaches here is the designation of this entire section of coastline, including islands and river inlets, as a nature
reserve because a great number of migratory birds flock to the area on
their way south for the winter. Of the nearby islands, **Armona** is the
best. About 15 minutes east of Olhão, it possesses some fine, isolated
stretches of sand, holiday villas, and café-bars. The sandy island of **Culatra,** 40 minutes east of Olhão, supports several ramshackle fishing
communities; at the southern village of **Farol** (meaning lighthouse), you'll
find agreeable beaches.

To get to the local beaches, take a **ferry.** If the kiosk is closed, you can
buy tickets on board. Schedules are available at the tourist office. ✉
Jetty east of town gardens. 🎫 *Round-trip: 160$00 Armona, 180$00
Culatra.* ⊙ *June–Sept., ferries run hourly; Oct.–May, 3 or 4 ferries daily.*

Shopping

One of the Algarve's best food **markets** (⊙ Mon.–Sat. 7–2) is held in
the riverfront buildings in the town gardens. Feast your eyes on the
shellfish for which Olhão is renowned; mussels, in particular, are a local
specialty.

Estói

⑪ *8 km (5 mi) northeast of Faro.*

This village has houses grouped on its slopes and is the site of the beautiful pink fairy-tale 18th-century **Palácio do Visconde de Estói** (Palace of the Counts of Estói). The palace itself is closed to the public and in the process of being converted into a luxury *pousada* (inn). You can, however, stroll around part of its formal gardens. ☎ *Free.* ⊙ *Mon.–Sat. 9–12:30 and 2–5:30.*

OFF THE
BEATEN PATH

MILREU – These Roman ruins, just ½ km (⅓ mi) northwest of Estói, were first excavated in 1876. The settlement was once known as Roman Ossonoba, and the remains—including a temple (later converted into a Christian basilica) and mosaic fragments adorning some of the 3rd-century baths—date from the 2nd through the 6th centuries. A few of the more portable pieces are on display in the gardens of Estói's Palace of the Counts and in Faro's Municipal Museum. ☎ *250$00.* ⊙ *June–Sept., Tues.–Sun. 9:30–12:30 and 2–6; Oct.–May, Tues.–Sun. 9:30–12:30 and 2–5.*

São Brás de Alportel

⑫ *7 km (4 mi) north of Milreu.*

The town of São Brás is a regional center for the processing of cork from the surrounding countryside.

Dining and Lodging

$$ ✕🖻 **Pousada de São Brás.** One of only two pousadas in the Algarve sits atop a hill where the air is pure and the views are splendid. It was built in the 1940s and has been lavishly refurbished for the 21st century; most of the original look was kept, though, and you'll find such touches as balconies embellished with heart cutouts. In public areas, bright yellow rattan furniture is covered with splashy green cloth, and lattice-work dividers provide a sense of privacy. Guest rooms are well appointed, as are their tile bathrooms. The restaurant serves traditional Portuguese cuisine, but is sadly lacking in atmosphere and quality. ⊠ *Estrada de Lisboa, 8150,* ☎ *289/842305,* FAX *289/841726. 31 rooms, 2 suites. Restaurant, bar, pool, tennis court. AE, DC, MC, V.* ☙

Loulé

⑬ *13 km (8 mi) west of São Brás de Alportel.*

This little market town, though undistinguished in many respects, is known for its crafts. The tiny, cobbled streets around the castle and the church—particularly Rua da Barbacà—are lined with whitewashed houses and workshops (closed Saturday afternoons and Sunday) where lace, leather, and copper goods are made. It's fascinating to wander this area, watch the craftspeople at work, and explore the nooks and crannies. Note the many houses with sculpted plasterwork on their white chimneys—a typical old Algarve sight. The rest of Loulé is overwhelmed by the main boulevard and modern buildings, but there's a pleasant municipal park at the top of town.

Once a Moorish stronghold, Loulé has preserved the ruins of its medieval **castelo** (castle), which houses the historical museum and archives as well as the tourist office. ⊠ *Largo Dom Pedro I.* ☎ *Free.* ⊙ *Daily 9–12:30 and 2:30–5.*

The restored 13th-century **Igreja Matriz** (Parish Church) is decorated with handsome tiles and wood carvings and has an unusual wrought-iron pulpit. ⊠ *Largo Pr. C. da Silva.* ⊙ *Mon.–Sat. 9–noon and 2–5:30.*

Lodging

$ 🏨 **Loulé Jardim Hotel.** Portuguese business types and locals are drawn to this hotel, which is far enough from the tourist bustle—off the main road on a small square—yet close enough to the shore. Rooms are modest and clean; prices leave you with extra money to buy some of those beautiful items crafted in town. ⊠ *Praça Manuel D'Arriaga, 8100,* ☎ *289/413094,* ℻ *289/463177. 52 rooms. AE, MC, V.*

THE EASTERN ALGARVE

The eastern portion of the province, known as the Sotavento, is a region of flat, sandy beaches. Although there has been some development along the coast, this is primarily a quiet, low-key area. Its principal towns, such as Tavira, are important fishing ports.

Tavira

★ ⑭   *30 km (19 mi) east of Loulé, 28 km (17 mi) east of Faro.*

At the mouth of the Rio Gilão (Gilão River), Tavira is considered by many to be one of the prettiest towns in the Algarve. With its castle ruins, riverfront gardens, old streets, and pastel-color houses strung along both sides of the quiet river, it's immediately endearing. Many of Tavira's white 18th-century houses retain their original doorways and coats-of-arms; others have peculiar four-sided roofs; and still others are completely covered in tiles. The town also has 37 churches, almost all dating from the 17th and 18th centuries.

Since Tavira is a tuna-fishing port, you'll find plenty of local color and fresh fish; tuna steaks, often grilled and served with onions, are on restaurant menus all over town at remarkably low prices. In the **harbor** area, you can sample no-frills dining at its best, alongside the fishermen, at any of the little café-restaurants across from the picturesque tangle of fishing boats and nets. The old covered **market,** once lined with an array of fresh fish, is being converted into a cultural and shopping center.

One of two river crossings, the low **bridge** adjacent to the arcaded Praça da República is of Roman origin, although it was rebuilt in the 17th century and again a few years ago after sustaining damage from floodwaters.

From the battlemented walls of the central **castelo,** you can look down over Tavira's many church spires and across the river delta to the sea. ⊠ *Stepped street off Rua da Liberdade.* 🎟 *Free.* ☉ *Weekdays 8–5:30, weekends 10–7.*

One of two major churches in Tavira, **Santa Maria do Castelo** (St. Mary of the Castle) was built on the site of a Moorish mosque in the 13th century. Although it was almost entirely destroyed by the 1755 earthquake, the church retains its original Gothic doorway.

The **Igreja da Misericórdia** (Misericórdia Church) is a beautiful Renaissance structure with a portal that dates from 1541. On Good Friday, a 10 PM candlelight procession begins at the church; it moves across the town's bridges, continues through the town, and returns to the church. From May through July, the church occasionally hosts musical performances during the Algarve International Classical Music Festival. ⊠ *West of Praça da República.* ☉ *Ask at the tourist office for opening times.*

Directly offshore and extending west for some 10 km (6 mi) is the **Ilha de Tavira,** a long offshore sandbar with several good beaches. The island is served by regular ferry service, and in summer a bus (marked QUA-

TRO ÁGUAS) shuttles from the center of town to the ferry's jetty. ⊠ *Jetty: 2 km (1¼ mi) east of Tavira.* 🕾 *150$00 round-trip.* ⊙ *May–June and Sept.–mid-Oct., ferries run hourly; July–Aug., ferries run every ½ hr.*

Dining and Lodging

$$ ✕ **Ponto de Encontro.** Cross the Roman bridge to this typical Portuguese restaurant beside a small square abloom with flowers and closed to traffic in summer. Dine inside amid tile walls and tables immaculately draped with linens. Or relax at outside tables to a view of the passing scene. Algarve-style swordfish grilled with garlic, tuna fried with onion, and other fresh fish dishes are specialties here. ⊠ *Praça Dr. António Padinha 39,* 🕾 *281/323730. AE, DC, MC, V.*

$$ ✕ **Restaurante Imperial.** Behind the riverside gardens, this restaurant is well known for its fish: clams, tuna, a tasty mixed fried-fish plate—you name it. In summer, there's seating on the sidewalk. Waiters are good at their job but a little aloof—after 40 years of service, the Imperial doesn't have to try hard to attract customers. Desserts are a tad disappointing here. ⊠ *Rua José Pires Padinha 22–24,* 🕾 *281/322306. MC, V. Closed Wed. Oct.–May.*

$$ ✕🏨 **Marés Residencial e Restaurante.** Only a stone's throw from the waterfront, this tiny hotel is above an excellent restaurant. Some of the rooms have balconies. Six rooms face the river; back rooms overlook a narrow street. The hotel has lovely wooden bannisters throughout, a sitting area, and a sauna that you can use for a small fee. ⊠ *Rua José Pieres Padinha 1134/140, 8800,* 🕾 *281/325815,* ℻ *281/325819. 15 rooms. Restaurant, sauna. AE, DC, MC, V.*

$ 🏨 **Residencial Princesa do Gilão.** Across the river from the main square, this small, gleaming white hotel stands on the quayside, offering fine views of both the river and the castle walls. All the rooms are modern and compact; request one that faces the front and has a balcony. Continental breakfast is available. ⊠ *Rua Borda de Água de Aguiar 10–12, 8800,* 🕾 *281/325171. 22 rooms. No credit cards.*

Manta Rota

⑮   *12 km (7½ mi) east of Tavira.*

There isn't much of a settlement here, but you will find a few bars, restaurants, and hotels; a campground; and some nice stretches of sand. A particularly nice strand is the offshore sandbar at the delightful, tiny, undeveloped village of **Cacela Velha.** Where the sandbars merge with the shore is the exceptional **Praia de Manta Rota.** Note that, from here to Faro, the underwater drop-offs are often steep and you can quickly find yourself in deep water.

Monte Gordo

⑯   *6 km (4 mi) east of Manta Rota.*

Pine woods and orchards break up the flat landscape around this large resort area, just 4 km (2½ mi) from the Spanish border. Relentlessly modern, Monte Gordo has plenty of hotels, restaurants, and nightspots but falls well short on charm and character. The long, 12-km (7-mi), flat **Praia de Monte Gordo** is a very popular beach. The seawater here has the highest average temperature in the country.

Dining and Lodging

$ ✕ **Mota.** This large, lively, unpretentious restaurant, which has been around for more than 30 years, is on the sands of the Praia de Monte Gordo near the Vasco da Gama Hotel. During the day you can drop in for a snack or salad if you don't want a full meal. You sit on the large covered terrace facing the ocean, and in the evening you're served seafood, grills, and regional dishes, while live music plays in the background. ⊠ *Praia de Monte Gordo, 8900,* ☎ *281/512340. No credit cards.*

$$ 🏨 **Alcázar.** Its unusual design makes this hotel one of the most striking in Monte Gordo. Outside, white balconies contrast with the red-brick facade; inside, sinuous arches and low, molded ceilings recall a cave's interior or that of an Arab tent. Guest rooms have their own terraces and window boxes. Alcazar has a pleasant atmosphere, a very accommodating staff, and a convenient location two blocks off the beach. ⊠ *Rua de Ceuta 9, 8900,* ☎ *281/510140,* FAX *281/510149. 95 rooms. Restaurant, bar, snack bar, pool, shops, dance club. AE, DC, MC, V.*

$$ 🏨 **Casablanca Hotel.** Not being on the main drag is a major advantage here, where the ambience is cozy with a strong Moorish feel. The solarium and the heated indoor pool help ward off a wintertime chill. ⊠ *Rua Sete, 8900,* ☎ *281/511444,* FAX *281/511999. 42 rooms. 1 indoor pool, 1 outdoor pool. AE, DC, MC, V.*

Nightlife

In addition to a wealth of nightclubs and discos, Monte Gordo has a **Casino** (⊠ Av. Infante, ☎ 281/512224) with blackjack and roulette, among other games, as well as a slot-machine room. From July through September, you can have dinner and see a cabaret show for 15,000$00; from October through June the cost is $10,000$00. You must be 18 or older to enter (bring your passport), and dressy-casual attire is best.

Vila Real de Santo António

🄗 *4 km (2½ mi) east of Monte Gordo, 47 km (29 mi) east of Faro.*

This town, on the Guadiana River, is the last stop before Spain. The original town was destroyed by a tidal wave in the 17th century and was not rebuilt until the late 18th century, when the Marquês de Pombal constructed a new, gridded town. Consequently, Vila Real, which took only five months to complete, is a showpiece of 18th-century town planning. Like most border towns, it's a lively place, with plenty of bars and restaurants and some traffic-free central streets that encourage evening strolling. For all that, however, there's very little to see.

You can take a **cruise** up the Guadiana River, which runs between Portugal and Spain. An all-day trip includes lunch, a stop for a dip in the river, and a final stop in the timeless village of Foz de Odeleite before returning by boat to Vila Real. The same tour company also offers half-day overland tours by jeep and full-day cruise–jeep tours that take you off the beaten path up to Foz de Odeleite. After lunch, you return by boat down the river to Vila Real. The company has shuttle service from all eastern and central Algarve hotels to the Vila Real de Santo António dock. *Riosul Viagens e Turismo Lda., Rua Tristão Vaz Teixeira 15 C, Monte Gordo,* ☎ *281/510201.* 🖃 *6,900$00 to 7,500$00, depending on pickup location.* ☉ *Trips May–Oct., Mon.–Sat.; Nov.–Apr., Thurs.–Sun.*

THE CENTRAL ALGARVE

The central Algarve, between Faro and Portimão, has the heaviest concentration of tourist resorts, some of which are household names in Europe. Nevertheless, in between built-up areas you can still discover quiet bays, amazing rock formations, and exclusive, secluded hotels and villas. With a car it's easy to travel the few miles inland that make all the difference: minor roads lead into the hills, to towns that have resisted the changes wrought upon the developed coast. Towns in this section are covered basically from east to west, with side trips north to these inland jewels.

Vale do Lobo

⓱ *10 km (6 mi) west of Faro.*

This luxury resort village—one of the Algarve's earliest—has superb facilities. Golf, tennis, and sailboarding are all popular.

Dining and Lodging

$$$$ ✕🏨 **Le Meridien Dona Filipa.** This luxurious hotel has a lavish, strik-
★ ing interior; superb service; and pleasant air-conditioned rooms with balconies (most of which overlook the sea). It's on extensive, beauti-fully landscaped grounds near the beach west of Faro. The hotel has its own tennis courts and is very close to the locally renowned Vale do Lobo Tennis Academy. A stay here also gets you a reduced fee at the San Lorenzo Golf Club, in Almansil, and discounts of 20% to 25% at other courses in the area, including the Vale do Lobo Golf Club. The hotel's chic restaurant offers an excellent international menu and an impressive wine list. ✉ *Vale do Lobo, Almansil 8135,* ☎ *289/357200,* FAX *289/394288. 147 rooms. Restaurant, bar, grill, pool, golf privileges, 3 tennis courts, shops, dance club. AE, DC, MC, V.* 🍽

Outdoor Activities and Sports

GOLF

The **Vale do Lobo Golf Club** (✉ Take N396 off N125 to Quarteira; con-tinue to Vale do Lobo and follow signs, ☎ 289/393939) has two 18-hole courses.

TENNIS

The **Vale do Lobo Tennis Academy** (✉ 8137 Vale do Lobo, ☎ 289/396991), one of Europe's best, has 14 all-weather courts, a bar, a pro shop, a pool, gym, steam room, and a restaurant.

Almansil

⓳ *2 km (1 mi) northeast of Vale do Lobe, 10 km (6 mi) northwest of Faro.*

Almansil straggles along the N125 due north of the major golf resorts of Quinta do Lago and Vale do Lobo. It provides services such as swim-ming pool supplies, lawn sprinklers, and so on to these communities. Of more interest to passing vacationers are the number of good restau-rants here. The best reason for visiting Almansil, however, is the chapel of **São Lourenço** (St. Lawrence), built in 1730. Notable are the chapel's blue-and-white, floor-to-ceiling azulejo panels and its intricate gilt work.

☾ **Atlantic Park** (✉ N125, Celões, ☎ 0800/204767) is an aquatic theme park filled with water-related rides. It's open daily 10–6. You pay 1,600$00 for a full day of splashing about, 1,200$00 if you arrive after 2 PM.

Dining and Lodging

$$ ✕ **Sr. Franco.** The finger-lickin' chicken that's grilled over charcoal pits in this large, spotless restaurant has won awards for owner Joaquim Guerréiro (he concocts a special seasoning of herbs and other natural ingredients found in the Algarve). For an even better dining experience order a side salad (with tomatoes, onions, and ample sprinkles of fresh oregano) and top everything off with a bottle of Portuguese *vinho verde,* a fruity, faintly sparkling wine. The food is well worth the 5-km (3-mi) trip southwest from Almansil. (✉ *Estrada de Quarteira, Escanx-inas,* ☎ 289/393756. AE, DC, MC, V.

$$$$ ✕🏨 **Hotel Quinta do Lago.** Set on 1,680 acres of pine woods and hills—surrounded by opulent private villas painted a dainty apricot, sparkling-blue beaches, and enough seclusion to appease the soul—this resort has pleased its visitors for many years. Golf is the main focus; a stay here gets you substantial discounts on fees at area courses. Numerous other sporting activities, from horseback riding to clay-pigeon shooting, can be arranged. The beach and sandbar are accessed via a wooden bridge. ✉ *Almancil, 8135,* ☎ *289/396666,* ℻ *289/394905. 132 rooms. 2 restaurants, 2 pools, 2 tennis courts. AE, DC, MC, V. www.quintadolagohotel.com*

Nightlife and the Arts

Some cottages next to the church of São Lourenço have been transformed into an **art gallery** (☎ 289/393281), which exhibits contemporary Portuguese works and holds occasional classical music concerts. Don't miss the delightful sculpture garden to the rear. In the Quinta do Lago resort area, you'll find **Allegro** (☎ 289/394627), a lounge where good taste blends with the sounds of a piano, and **T Clube** (☎ 289/ 396751), which appeals to a younger, disco crowd. It's closed September to April, except for New Year's Eve, Carnival, and Easter.

Outdoor Activities and Sports

GOLF

The Portuguese Open Championship has been held seven times at the **Quinta do Lago Golf Club** (☎ 289/390700), which features two 18-hole courses on the superb Quinta do Lago estate. The **San Lorenzo Golf Club** (✉ Hotel Le Meridien Dona Filipa, Vale do Lobo, ☎ 289/ 396522) has 18 of Europe's finest holes. If you're not a guest of the hotel, the greens fee is 24,500$00; hotel guests pay 5,000$00.

HORSEBACK RIDING

There are fully equipped riding centers at **Quinta dos Amigos** (✉ Escanxinas, ☎ 289/395269), where many locals keep their horses. Rates start at 3,500$00. At **Horses Paradise** (✉ Rua Cistoval Tires Norte, ☎ 289/394189) rates range from 3,500$00 to 7,000$00.

Vilamoura

㉚ *10 km (6 mi) northwest of Almansil.*

Once a prosperous Roman settlement, this highly developed upscale resort, built in the 1960s, possesses the Algarve's only marina. It also has several golf courses, a major tennis center, and other sports facilities, as well as luxury hotels and a casino.

The excavations of the Roman ruins at **Cêrro da Villa** (✉ Across from marina) have revealed an elaborate plumbing system as well as several mosaics.

Dining and Lodging

$$$$ ✕🏨 **Vilamoura Marinotel.** One of the Algarve's newest accommodations, the luxurious Marinotel overlooks Vilamoura's stupendous marina. Rooms have such thoughtful touches as VCRs, and the facilities are wide-ranging. Activities available at the marina include sailboat and motorboat excursions, deep sea fishing, and scuba diving. Many people think the Marinotel has the best places to eat in town: the grill overlooking the boats serves fish and has live music, whereas the restaurant that faces the hotel gardens specializes in Spanish and Portuguese food. ✉ *Vilamoura 8125,* ☎ *289/389988,* ℻ *289/389869. 387 rooms. Restaurant, 2 bars, grill, 2 pools, 2 tennis courts, boating, shops. AE, DC, MC, V.* 🐾

$$$ 🏨 **Hotel Dom Pedro Golf.** Part of a highly successful vacation complex, the Dom Pedro is close to the casino, not far from the splendid beach, and five minutes from the marina. Each bright room is attractively furnished and has a sea view; many rooms have balconies. ✉ *Vilamoura*

8125, ☏ 289/300700, 𝔽𝔸𝕏 289/300701. 261 rooms. Restaurant, bar, 3 pools, golf privileges, 3 tennis courts, shop. AE, DC, MC, V. ✎

Nightlife

A big part of Vilamoura's nightlife scene is its **Casino Vilamoura** (☏ 289/302999), open nightly 4 PM–3 AM. You'll find two restaurants, a new disco, and the usual selection of games, including slot machines. For 2,000$00 you can see the nightly show and have a complimentary drink. Dress is smart-casual, and you must be 18 to enter.

Outdoor Activities and Sports

GOLF

Vilamoura Golf Club has three courses with 18 holes, and a new course with nine holes: the "Old Course" at **Vilamoura** (☏ 289/310341), formerly known as Vilamoura I; the Vilamoura II, now known as **Laguna** (☏ 289/310349); **Pinhal** (☏ 289/310390), once called Vilamoura III; and the nine-hole **Millennium course** (☏ 289/310341). Greens fees and tee times vary with the seasons.

HORSEBACK RIDING

Horses are available for lessons and for trail rides at the **Centro Hipico de Vilamoura.** For more information ask at your hotel or fax the center (𝔽𝔸𝕏 289/302577).

SAILING

You can rent sailboats at the **Vilamoura Marina,** an enormous self-contained marina complex with apartments, shops, hotels, sporting and leisure facilities, and 1,000 berths. Just walk around the marina and enquire at any of the various kiosks that deal with water sports, fishing, and boat excursions.

If you'd like to relax and let someone else do the work, book a cruise on the **Condor de Vilamoura,** which sails toward Albufeira. ✉ Vilamoura Marina, ☏ 289/314070. 🎟 3,500$00 for 3 hrs; 7,000$00 for 7 hrs, including lunch. ☉ 2 cruises daily.

TENNIS

The **Vilamoura Tennis Center** (☏ 289/302369) has 12 courts and a pro shop, restaurant, and bar. Court fees start at 1,200$00.

Albufeira

★ ㉑   12 km (7½ mi) west of Vilamoura.

Brash Albufeira, a favorite with British holidaymakers, has mushroomed from an attractive fishing village into the Algarve's largest and busiest resort. The town beach attracts thousands of visitors daily, and the noisy center is dominated by cafés, bars, restaurants, discos, and souvenir shops. Albufeira ages a bit during the shoulder seasons when it draws older (often retired) visitors, mainly from northern Europe. (A few words of caution: streets leading into the older parts of town have steep inclines and may be difficult for some visitors to climb.)

Despite the crowds, Albufeira has much to commend it, and a lunchtime stop at one of the restaurants in the older part of town, overlooking the cliffs, is well worth your while. One of the last Algarve towns to hold out against the Christian army in the 13th century, Albufeira still has a distinctly Moorish flavor in parts, most apparent in the steep, narrow streets and whitewashed houses snuggled on the hill that marks the center of the Old Town.

🖐 **Zoo Marine,** 6 km (4 mi) northwest of Albufeira, is a popular marine park with low-key rides, swimming pools, performing parrots, and dolphin and sea lion shows. Hotel pickups are available. ⊠ *N125, Guia,* ☎ *289/560300.* 🎫 *2,450$00.* 🕙 *Mid-Mar.–late June and late Sept.– early Nov., daily 10–6; late June–late Sept., daily 10–8; early Nov.– mid-Mar., Tues.–Sun. 10–5.*

Beaches

On most summer days, the **town beach** (⊠ Reached by tunnel from Rua 5 de Outubro) is so crowded that it may be hard to enjoy its interesting rock formations, caves, and grottoes, not to mention sand and sea. If you want more space, you'll have to move farther afield. Possibilities include the beautiful beaches of **São Rafael** and **Praia da Galé,** 4 km (2½ mi) west on local roads, although there's been much recent development here, too. The coves and rocks are very attractive, but don't expect them to be deserted. **Praia da Falesia, Olhos d'Agua,** and **Praia da Oura** also fall within the ambit of Albufeira.

Dining and Lodging

$$$ ✕ **La Cigale.** This restaurant, 9 km (5 mi) east of Albufeira, is renowned among locals for its excellent French and Portuguese cooking. It's right on the beach, and the terrace is the most sought-after place to sit, although you'll have to reserve in advance. ⊠ *Olhas d'Agua,* ☎ *289/501637. DC, MC, V. Closed Dec.–Feb.*

$$–$$$ ✕ **A Ruina.** This big, multilevel, rustic restaurant on the beach is the
★ place to go for charcoal-grilled seafood, especially sardines or tuna steaks. Start with a shellfish salad and choose your main course from the display. You may sit outdoors on the beach or inside in one of two simple but attractively furnished dining rooms. There's a top-floor bar and a roof terrace, too. ⊠ *Cais Herculano, Praia dos Pescadores,* ☎ *289/ 512094. No credit cards.*

$$–$$$ ✕ **Cabaz da Praia.** You'll have spectacular views of the beach from
★ the cliffside terrace of this long-established restaurant. Its name means "beach basket," and it has been converted from an old fisherman's cottage. There's fine French-Portuguese cooking here—fish soup, grilled fish served imaginatively, and chicken with seafood. Try the soufflé, perhaps the restaurant's most popular dish. ⊠ *Praça Miguel Bombarda 7,* ☎ *289/512137. AE, MC, V. Closed Thurs. No lunch Sat.*

$$$ ✕🏨 **Hotel Montechoro.** This modern development in the village of Montechoro, 3½ km (2 mi) north of town, is ideal for those who like to be right on top of where all the action is. Guest rooms are furnished in an up-to-date style and either look out over the surrounding countryside or down onto "The Strip," the long street leading straight to Praia d'Oura that is lined with cheap bars, tacky shops, and boisterous nightlife options. Among the health and fitness facilities are pools, tennis and squash courts, and a sauna. There are four bars, the Montechoro Restaurant, and the rooftop Amendoeiras Grill—from which the views are stupendous. ⊠ *Av. Dr. Francisco Sá Carneiro, Montechoro 8200,* ☎ *289/589423,* 🖷 *289/589947. 362 rooms. Restaurant, 4 bars, grill, 2 pools, sauna, 8 tennis courts, exercise room, squash, shops, billiards. AE, DC, MC, V.*

$$$$ 🏨 **Sheraton Algarve Hotel.** This luxury hotel occupies a spectacular
★ cliff-top site 8 km (5 mi) east of town. It overlooks the sea and has direct access to a very fine beach via an exterior elevator. The architecture and decor blend traditional Moorish-style courtyards, fountains, and terraces with fine Portuguese tiles and furnishings. Up-to-the-minute facilities include a sauna, discounted rates on the Pine Cliffs nine-hole golf course, tennis courts, and an exercise room. An excellent buffet breakfast is included in the room rate. Service is superb. ⊠ *Praia da Falésia, 8200,* ☎ *289/500100,* 🖷 *289/501950. 215 rooms. 2 restaurants, bar, snack bar, 3 pools, sauna, golf privileges, 3 tennis courts, exercise room, beach. AE, DC, MC, V.* 🍴

$$$ ⊡ **Hotel Cerro Alagoa.** Popular with Europeans, who like to relax around the pleasant pool and garden, this modern hotel on the hill above town may be the most comfortable of Albufeira's central lodgings. Smart, well-equipped guest rooms have private balconies; be sure to ask for one with a sea view. It's a 10-minute walk to the center of town, which makes the hotel a good base for exploring. A courtesy bus runs you to nearby beaches. ⊠ *Via Rápida, 8200,* ☎ *289/588261,* 𝔽𝔸𝕏 *289/583199. 310 rooms. Restaurant, bar, indoor and outdoor pools, sauna, health club. AE, DC, MC, V.* ☜

Nightlife

Albufeira tries hard to maintain its reputation as the Algarve's number-one nightspot. Many bars and discos here have promotional nights that are enormously popular, with free or reduced-price drinks and free admission. The cacophonous bars lining the streets in the Old Town and on Montechoro's Avenida Sa Carneiro (better known as "The Strip") guarantee a good-time crowd. Of the discos, **Club 7½** (⊠ Rua São Gonçalo de Lagos) and **Silvia's** (⊠ Rua São Gonçalo de Lagos) hop nightly (bars until 3 AM, discos until 5 AM).

The trendiest nightspot in Albufeira is **Kiss** (⊠ Off Av. Sa Carneiro at the beach end), which often has celebrity guest DJs. It's crowded and not for the faint-hearted. For a less energetic evening, there's **Bizarro's** (⊠ Rua Latino Coelho), a laid-back, tastefully decorated bar on the cliffs by the Rocamar Hotel. The owner, the music (including a Brazilian guitarist once a week), and the atmosphere are all very mellow, and it's a perfect place to watch the sun go down.

Shopping

The **shopping center** (☎ 289/589905) on the bypass road above town has more than 60 shops and is open daily 10–10. For high-quality ceramics go to **Infante Dom Henrique House** (⊠ Rua Candido dos Reis 30).

Armação de Pêra

㉒   *14 km (9 mi) west of Albufeira.*

At this bustling resort, it's best to reserve your room near the sea, rather than behind the main road where apartment-hotels are crammed together and offer no views and little ambience. Year-round, local boats
☝ can take you on two-hour **cruises** to the caves and grottoes along the shore, past the Praia Nossa Senhora da Rocha (Beach of Our Lady of the Rocks) to the west—a beach named after the Romanesque chapel above it. To arrange tours, head to Praia Armação de Pêra beach—a wide sandy stretch with a pretty promenade—or Praia Nossa Senhora da Rocha beach and speak with the fishermen directly.

Dining and Lodging

$$$ ×⊡ **Hotel Garbe.** The bar, lounge, and restaurant—all with terraces that provide unhindered sea views—maximize the superb location of this squat, white complex. It sits atop a low cliff at the western end of the beach and is built on several levels, with steps to the beach below. Public rooms are bright and appealing; guest rooms have modern furnishings. ⊠ *Av. Marginal, 8365,* ☎ *282/315187,* 𝔽𝔸𝕏 *282/315087. 152 rooms. Restaurant, bar, coffee shop, pool. AE.* ☜

$$$$ ⊡ **Vila Vita Parc.** The pampering begins as soon as the wrought-iron gates open to welcome you. Decorated in gentle colors with dark-wood details, fireplaces, and tasteful Mediterranean-Moorish touches, this superb resort has the feel of an exclusive oasis. From its cliff-top setting, landscaped gardens wind down to two sequestered beaches. All rooms have either a sea or garden view or both. ⊠ *Armação de Pêra*

8365, ☎ 282/315310, ⓕ丸Ⅹ 282/315333. *182 rooms, 8 suites. 6 restaurants, 3 pools, 5 tennis courts, 9-hole golf course, putting green, beaches. AE, DC, MC, V.* ✎

$$$ 🏨 **Hotel Viking.** About 1 km (½ mi) west of town, the Viking stands near the coast, not far from a good, sandy beach. Its swimming pools (one for children) and bars are set between the main building and the cliff top. ✉ *Praia Nossa Senhora da Rocha, 8365,* ☎ *282/314876,* ⓕ丸Ⅹ *282/314852. 184 rooms. Restaurant, bar, 2 pools, boating, shops, dance club. AE, DC, MC, V.* ✎

Carvoeiro

㉓ *20 km (12 mi) west of Albufeira.*

Although the fishermen no longer work from the shores here, the village has maintained the character of a fisherman's settlement. It has a picturesque harbor with shell-shape beaches and interesting rock formations. Boats at the beach take groups on two-hour cruises to nearby caves.

Outdoor Activities and Sports

TENNIS

The **Carvoeiro Tennis Club** (✉ Mato Serão, ☎ 282/357847) has 12 courts as well as a fitness center, a swimming pool, and a restaurant.

Lagoa

㉔ *6 km (4 mi) north of Carvoeiro.*

This market town is primarily known for its wine, *vinho Lagoa;* the red is particularly good. The **winery,** open for tours, is on the main road just after the Carvoeiro junction, on the left.

☺ The best of the Algarve's several water parks is **Slide & Splash,** east of Lagoa. ✉ *Estombar,* ☎ *282/341685.* 🎫 *2,000$00 full day; 1,700$00 half day (after 1 PM).* ☉ *Sept.–June, daily 10–5:30; July–Aug., daily 10–7.*

Shopping

Along N125 in nearby **Porches,** you can stop at a variety of roadside shops that sell handmade pottery. **Olaria Pequena** (✉ N125, between Porches and Alcantarilha), which means "the small pottery," is owned and run by a friendly young Scot who has worked in the Algarve for many years and produces some beautiful handmade pieces.

Silves

★ ㉕ *7 km (4 mi) north of Lagoa, 11 km (7 mi) northeast of Carvoeiro.*

Once the Moorish capital of the Algarve, today Silves is one of the region's most intriguing inland towns. Rich and prosperous in medieval times, it remained in Arab hands until 1249, although not without attempts by Christian forces to take it. In 1189, following a siege led by Sancho I, the city was sacked by Crusaders, who subsequently put thousands of Moors to the sword. Silves finally lost its importance after its almost complete destruction by the 1755 earthquake. Today it's an enjoyable excursion from the coast; trains, buses, and a recently opened river service using traditional Portuguese gondola-like boats make the 20-km (12-mi) trip north from Portimão.

☺ The Moors built an early **fortress** here, which survived untouched until the Christian sieges. The remains you see today of this 12th-century sandstone fortress with its impressive parapets were restored in 1835 and still dominate the upper part of town. You can walk around the walls for expansive views over Silves and the surrounding hills, but the rest of the castle is a mere shell, its interior a modern garden watched over by a statue of Sancho I. The fortress is a great favorite with kids, who love to clamber about its massive walls and crenellated battlements. Keep an eye open, as some places have no guardrails. 🖼 *250$00. ☉ June–Sept., daily 9–8; Oct.–May, daily 9–5.*

The 12th- to 13th-century **Santa Maria da Sé** (Cathedral of St. Mary), built on the site of a Moorish mosque, saw service as the Cathedral of the Algarve until the 16th century. The 1755 earthquake and indifferent restoration have left it rather plain inside, but its exterior gargoyles and its tower are intriguing. 🖼 *Free; donations accepted. ☉ Mon.–Sat. 8:30–6:30, Sun. 8:30–1.*

Although the labels are in Portuguese, the items on display at Silves's **Museu Arqueologia** (Archaeological Museum) still give interesting insights into the area's history. A primary attraction is an Arab water cistern, preserved in situ, with a 30-ft-deep well. The museum is a few minutes' walk below the cathedral, off Rua da Sé. ⊠ *Rua das Portas de Loulé,* ☎ *282/444832.* 🖼 *300$00. ☉ Tues.–Sun. 10–6.*

NEED A   The **produce market,** liveliest in the morning, is at the foot of town, close
BREAK?   to the medieval bridge. If you arrive at lunchtime, you can have a deli-
           cious meal of spicy grilled chicken or fish from the outdoor barbecue at
           one of the simple restaurants facing the river that runs through town. The
           market is closed Sunday.

Dining

$$ × **Rui Marisqueira.** The food is the main event here, as the functional decor doesn't offer much in the way of atmosphere. The fish and shellfish are a remarkably good value, which is one reason the crowds from the coast come up into the hills to dine. Grilled sea bream and bass are usually offered, and there's locally caught game—wild boar, rabbit, and partridge—in season. ⊠ *Rua Comendador Vilarinho 27,* ☎ *282/442682. AE, MC, V. Closed Tues.*

$ × **Churrasqueira Valdemar.** At this inexpensive grill room on the riverfront behind the market, whole chickens are barbecued outside over charcoal. Eat under the stone arches and enjoy your *piri-piri* (spicy) chicken with salad, fries, and local wine. ⊠ *Facing the river, behind the market,* ☎ *no phone. No credit cards.*

São Bartolomeu de Messines

㉖ *20 km (12 mi) northeast of Silves.*

This attractive countryside village is a nice place for a coffee break. The **parish church** dates from the late 14th century and has interior columns of spiraling, ropelike stonework.

Portimão

㉗ *25 km (15½ mi) southwest of São Bartolomeu de Messines, 52 km (32 mi) northwest of Faro.*

Portimão is the most important fishing port in the Algarve. Even before the Romans arrived, there was a settlement here, at the mouth of the Rio Arade (Arade River). Devastated in the 1755 earthquake, the town was revived by the fish-canning industry in the 19th century. Although the colorful fishing boats now unload their catch at a modern terminal across the river, modern Portimão, sprawling with concrete high-rise buildings, remains a cheerful, busy place.

Rather than staying in Portimão, most visitors choose one of the excellent local beach resorts and visit Portimão as a day trip, especially to shop. If you prefer to stay in town, the local tourist office can help you find accommodations at one of the hotels or *pensões* (pensions), which are of reasonable quality.

NEED A BREAK?	Lunch outdoors at Portimão's **harborside** is a must. You sit at one of many inexpensive establishments, eating the excellent charcoal-grilled sardines (a local specialty), chewy fresh bread, and simple salads and drinking local red wine while around you the air is thick with barbecue smoke and the tang of the sea.

Dining

$$ ✕ **Kibom.** Set on a narrow pedestrian street in a typical Algarvian house, Kibom has represented the town in gourmet food competitions. The traditional Portuguese food here is highly recommended. Dishes include *arroz de marisco* (shellfish with rice), *feijoada de choco* (octopus with beans), and *cataplana de lagosta* (spiny lobster cataplana). ✉ *Rua Damião L Faria e Castro, off Rua Judice Biker,* ☎ *282/414623. AE, DC, MC, V. Closed Sun.*

$ ✕ **Flor da Sardinha.** This is one of several open-air eateries next to the bridge, by the fishing harbor. Fresh sardines are superbly grilled on stoves at the quayside and served to the crowds sitting in informal rows at plastic tables and chairs. A plateful of these delicious fish, with fries and a bottle of the local red wine, is one of Portugal's best treats—at giveaway prices. ✉ *Cais da Lota,* ☎ *282/424862. No credit cards.*

Shopping

Portimão's main shopping street is **Rua do Comércio.** Shops on **Rua de Santa Isabel** specialize in crafts, leather goods, ceramics, crystal, and fashions.

The enormous **Modelo Shopping Center** (✉ N124 at Av. Miguel Bombarda, toward Praia da Rocha), open daily 10–10, has a plethora of shops and restaurants under one roof. For handmade copper items and other metal crafts, visit **O Aquario II** (✉ Rua Vasco da Gama 41). **O Aquario III** (✉ Rua Direita, Loja 10) sells ceramics, porcelain, and crystal. There's a branch of the Parisian shoe store **Charles Jourdan** (✉ Rua de Santa Isabel 26). For leather goods, stop in at **Gaby's** (✉ Rua Direita 5 and Praça Visconde Bívar 15), which sells high-quality items. **Vista Alegre** porcelain can be found at O Aquario II and O Aquario III (☞ *above*).

Ferragudo

㉘ *5 km (3 mi) east of Portimão.*

Across the bridge from Portimão is the former fishing hamlet of Ferragudo. Despite its fine beach, Praia Grande, Ferragudo shows no sign of going down the mass-market tourist route of its neighbor across the river, Praia da Rocha. Right on the beach is the heavily restored 16th-century **Castelo de São João** (St. John's Castle), built to defend Portimão. Looking like a child's giant sand castle, it is now privately owned and there is no public access. Around Ferragudo's attractive **beach,** to the south, you can enjoy restaurants and bars and rent sailboards.

Dining

$$ ✕ **A Lanterna.** This well-run restaurant, on the main road just over the bridge from Portimão, serves exceptional, rich fish soup and smoked swordfish, both genuine Algarvian treats. Other seafood specialties are worthy, too. ✉ *Parchal,* ☎ *282/414429. MC, V. Closed Sun.*

Praia da Rocha

㉙ *3 km (2 mi) southeast of Portimão.*

Praia da Rocha was one of the first resorts in the Algarve to undergo a transformation for the mass market, and it's now dominated by high-rise apartments and hotels. Buses run throughout the day between the town and Portimão.

The 16th-century **Fortaleza de Santa Catarina** (Fortress of St. Catharine; ⊠ Av. Tomás Cabreira) was a defensive castle and provides wonderful views out to sea and across the River Arade to Ferragudo. Directly below, a new marina has just been completed. There's a long cement jetty that extends into the Atlantic. Praia da Rocha's excellent **beach** is made all the more interesting by a series of huge colored rocks worn into strange shapes by the wind and sea.

Dining and Lodging

$$ ✕ **Cabassa.** On a grassy terrace at the eastern end of town, the restaurant is far removed from the frenetic activity a few hundred yards away in the heart of the resort. It is known for its innovative Italian cooking, great-value Portuguese barbecue nights, and friendly young staff. ⊠ *Av. Tomás Cabreira,* ☎ *282/424307. MC, V. No lunch.*

$$ ✕ **Safari.** Set on a cliff above the beach, this lively restaurant has a distinctly African flavor. Seafood and delicious Angolan recipes are the best choices: try the chicken curry or one of the charcoal grills and enjoy your meal on the terrace. ⊠ *Rua António Feu,* ☎ *282/423540. AE, DC, MC, V.*

$$$–$$$$ 🏨 **Hotel Algarve-Casino.** The sea views from here are spectacular. Many of the public rooms are brightly decorated in Moorish style, and the spacious guest rooms have tile floors and balconies that face the water. The casino has a restaurant, shows, and, of course, gambling (slots open at 4 PM, the main floor at 7:30 PM; dress is casual). Among the numerous other facilities here are two saltwater pools, a beach bar, and a disco (open May–October) that's set into the rocks. *Av. Tomás Cabreira,* ☎ *282/415001,* 🅵🅰🆇 *282/415999. 209 rooms. 3 restaurants, bar, 2 pools, 2 tennis courts, health club, beach, boating, shops, casino, dance club. AE, DC, MC, V.* ☜

$$$ 🏨 **Bela Vista.** This small, tastefully decorated beachfront hotel was built
★ at the turn of the century as a private house in Moorish style. Magnificent azulejos, leaded stained-glass panels, a wonderful staircase, and a large open fireplace are just some of the remarkable features that make this inn so delightful—and so popular. Early reservations are essential during high season. ⊠ *Av. Tomás Cabreira,* ☎ *282/450480,* 🅵🅰🆇 *282/ 415369. 14 rooms. Bar. AE, DC, MC, V.*

Alvor

㉚ *5 km (3 mi) west of Praia da Rocha.*

Characterized by a maze of streets, lanes, and blind alleys that intersect one another, the handsome old port of Alvor is one of the Algarve's best examples of an Arab village. In summer, many vacationers are attracted to Alvor's huge **beach**; although it's not one of the region's best, it does usually have space to spare.

Dining and Lodging

$$$–$$$$ ✕🏨 **Le Meridien Penina.** This impressive golf hotel, on 360 well-main-
★ tained, secluded acres between Portimão and Lagos, has elegant public rooms and attentive service. It was one of the first luxury hotels in the Algarve, and recent renovations are keeping up the hotel's high standards. Most of the smartly furnished rooms have balconies;

those in back, with the best views, face the Serra de Monchique. A stay here gives you access to the superlative golf course, which was designed by Henry Cotton, with significantly reduced greens fees. A bus shuttles you (in five minutes) to and from the hotel beach, which has a restaurant (reservations essential) and water-sports facilities. A supervised children's village has its own pool and restaurant. There is a choice of five restaurants, including the Grill Room, which serves excellent Portuguese dishes, and the Sagres Restaurant, with its lively international theme evenings. ⊠ *Montes de Alvor, Penina 8502,* ☎ *282/420200,* FAX *282/415000. 196 rooms. 5 restaurants, 2 bars, grill, pool, sauna, 18-hole and two 9-hole golf courses, 6 tennis courts, horseback riding, beach, windsurfing, boating, shops, children's programs (summer), private airstrip. AE, DC, MC, V.* ☺

$$$ ✕▥ **Hotel Alvor Praia.** Rooms at this comfortable, split-level hotel
★ have views of the sea or the Serra de Monchique. The dining room has picture windows overlooking the coast, and there's a deck with a snack bar. Although it's an easy walk to the pleasant sands below, there's an elevator that can take you down. ⊠ *Praia dos Tres Irmãos, 8500,* ☎ *282/400900,* FAX *282/400999. 180 rooms, 18 suites. Restaurant, 3 bars, grill, snack bar, pool, sauna, golf privileges, 7 tennis courts, beach, shops. AE, DC, MC, V.* ☺

$$ ▥ **Aparthotel Torralta.** This large apartment complex near the beach is unappealing architecturally but has good-size rooms, fully equipped kitchens, a supermarket, and daily maid service—very good value all around, particularly out of season. Some of the leisure facilities are appealing to children, making this an excellent choice for families. ⊠ *Praia de Alvor, 8500,* ☎ *282/459211,* FAX *282/459171. 655 units. Restaurant, bar, grocery, pool, beauty salon, bowling, boating, billiards, dance club. AE, DC, MC, V.*

Monchique

③① *25 km (15½ mi) northeast of Alvor, 20 km (12½ mi) north of Portimão.*

This tiny market town is known for the lovely ride up to reach it. Although handicrafts, particularly carving and woodworking, are available, the quality is not top-notch.

OFF THE **FOIA –** A short drive west on N266–3 brings you to the highest point in
BEATEN PATH the Serra de Monchique. At 2,959 ft, the peak offers a café and panoramic views over the western Algarve.

Dining and Lodging

$ ✕ **Teresinha.** The interior decor of this modest restaurant is simple, but
★ real atmosphere can be found on the outdoor terrace, which overlooks a lovely valley and the coast. Located just west of Monchique, Teresinha offers good country cooking: a particularly tasty local ham as well as chicken specials done on the outdoor grill. ⊠ *Estrada da Foia,* ☎ *282/ 912392. MC, V.*

$-$$ ✕▥ **Estalagem Abrigo da Montanha.** This pleasant, rustic inn—in the heart of the Serra de Monchique—is noted for its magnolia trees, camellia-filled garden, and panoramic views. A leisurely lunch in the restaurant, where dependable regional dishes are prepared, makes for an enjoyable afternoon. If you want to stay longer to take in the scenery, be sure to reserve in advance for one of the welcoming rooms (all with views). ⊠ *Corto Pereiro, Estrada da Foia, 8550,* ☎ *282/912131,* FAX *282/913660. 15 rooms. Restaurant, bar, pool. AE, DC, MC, V.*

LAGOS AND THE WESTERN ALGARVE

From the bustling holiday town of Lagos, the rest of the western Algarve is easily accessible. This is the most unspoiled part of the region, with some genuinely isolated beaches and bays along an often wind-buffeted route that reaches to the southwest and the magnificent Cabo São Vicente.

Lagos

★ ㉜ *13 km (8 mi) west of Portimão, 70 km (43 mi) northwest of Faro.*

An attractive, busy fishing port with some beautiful cove beaches nearby, Lagos draws an international crowd. Here, you feel, is a town whose inhabitants follow a way of life that goes beyond catering to tourists, although there's no shortage of attractions for visitors. The main pedestrian streets leading off the central Praça Gil Eanes are lined with stores (Lagos has several good antiques shops), restaurants, cafés, and bars—all of which do a roaring business in summer.

The town has a venerable history, with sights to prove it. Lagos's deep-water harbor and wide bay have made it a natural choice for various groups of settlers, starting with the Carthaginians, who founded the town around 400 BC. Under the Moors, Lagos was a center for trade between Portugal and Africa. Even after the town fell to the Christians in 1241, trade continued and was greatly expanded under the rule of Prince Henry the Navigator, who used Lagos as his base. The town later became capital of the Algarve, a role it lost in 1756, after the great earthquake reduced much of it to rubble. Nonetheless, some interesting buildings remain, as does the circuit of defensive walls, built between the 14th and 16th centuries over older, Moorish bastions. Some of the best-preserved parts of the walls can be seen from near the expansive Praça da República, at the southwest end of Avenida dos Descobrimentos.

㉝ In the 15th century, the first African slave market in Europe was held under the arches of the old **Casa da Alfandega** (Customs House, ✉ Praça da República). The building now contains an art gallery with changing exhibits and is sometimes used as a space for small concerts and theater productions.

㉞ It was from the Manueline window of the **Governor's Palace** (✉ Praça da República) that the young king Dom Sebastião is said to have addressed his troops before setting off on his crusade of 1578. The crusade was a failure, and the king and his men died in Morocco at Alcácer-Quibir. (Dom Sebastião is further remembered by a much-maligned modernistic statue that stands in Praça Gil Eanes.)

★ ㉟ Lagos's most extraordinary building is the early 18th-century baroque **Igreja de Santo António** (Church of St. Anthony), off Rua General Alberto Silveira. The decoration inside is a riot of gilt extravagance made possible by the import of gold from Brazil. Dozens of cherubs and angels clamber over the walls, among fancifully carved woodwork and azulejos. ✉ *Rua Henriques Correira Silva,* ☎ *282/762301.* 🎟 *360$00.* ⊙ *Tues.–Sun. 9:30–12:30 and 2–5.*

㊱ The **Museu Municipal** (Municipal Museum) houses an amusing jumble of exhibits, including mosaics, archaeological and ethnological items, and a town charter from 1504—all arranged haphazardly. ✉ *Rua General Alberto Silveira,* ☎ *282/762301.* 🎟 *330$00.* ⊙ *Tues.–Sun. 9:30–12:30 and 2–5.*

㊲ The 17th-century fort **Ponta da Bandeira** defended the entrance to the harbor in bygone days. From inside the fort you can look out at sweep-

Casa da
Alfandega . **.33**

Governor's
Palace . . . . **.34**

Igreja de
Santo
António . . .**35**

Museu
Municipal . . **36**

Ponta da
Bandeira . . **.37**

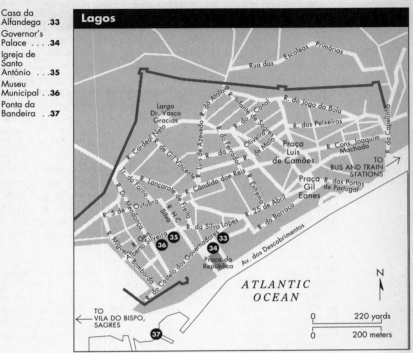

ing ocean views. ✉ *Av. dos Descobrimentos*, ☎ *282/761410.* 📷
320$00. ⊘ *Tues.–Sat. 10–1 and 2–6; Sun. 10–1.*

For an interesting perspective on the rock formations and grottoes of
the area's shoreline, take one of the short **cruises** offered by fishing boats
near the Ponta da Bandeira. Check for departure times at the boards
on the quayside.

Beaches

The largest beach near town and one of the best centers for water sports
is the 4-km (2½-mi) stretch of **Meia Praia,** to the northeast. You can
walk to the end of the beach closest to town in less than five minutes,
simply by crossing the footbridge. If you want to go farther along, however, you can take a bus from the riverfront Avenida dos Descobrimentos,
and in summer there's a ferry service a few hundred yards from Ponta
da Bandeira.

All the other good beaches are south of town and can be reached on
the main road (an extension of Avenida dos Descobrimentos). You can
drive to the prettiest one—**Praia de Dona Ana**—by following the signs
for the Hotel Golfinho (☞ Dining and Lodging, *below*) or take an enjoyable 30-minute walk along the cliff top. If you choose to hoof it,
pass the fort, turn left at the fire station, and follow the footpaths, which
go to the most southerly point, **Ponta da Piedade,** a spectacular, much-
photographed group of rock arches and grottoes visited by all the fishing boat cruises. To either side are several delightful cove beaches with
fascinating rock formations and beach cafés.

Dining and Lodging

$$$$ ✕ **No Patio.** This happy restaurant with an attractive inner patio is run
by a Danish couple, Bjarne and Gitte. The outstanding fare is best described as international with a Scandinavian accent. Specialties in-

clude Scandinavian-style herring, duck-liver mousse, and tenderloin of pork with a Madeira and mushroom sauce. ⊠ *Rua Lançarote de Freitas 46,* ☏ *282/763777. AE, MC, V. Closed Sun.–Mon.*

$$$ ✗ **Dom Sebastião.** Portuguese cooking, charcoal-grilled fish specials,
★   and unobtrusive service are the attractions at this cheerful restaurant on the main pedestrian street. You can dine inside at elegant candle-lighted tables set on a cobblestone floor or outside on the sidewalk terrace. While you ponder the menu, you'll be served an impressive array of appetizers (included in the cover charge). You may wish to start your meal with smoked swordfish, followed by grilled tuna or the cataplana—all extremely good. ⊠ *Rua 25 de Abril 20,* ☏ *282/762795. AE, DC, MC, V. Closed Sun. Oct.–May.*

$$ ✗ **O Galeão.** Tucked away on a backstreet, this restaurant is a popular local choice—so much so that you'll wait in line unless you've made a reservation. There's a bustling, informal atmosphere here, and the food is first-rate, particularly the steaks—for once, fish, although well cooked, isn't the main event. A reasonably priced wine list encourages you to sample regional choices; ask for advice if you're unsure. ⊠ *Rua da Laranjeira 1,* ☏ *282/763909. AE, DC, MC, V.*

$$ ✗ **Mirante.** Perched above the beautiful Praia de Dona Ana and just south of the town center, this restaurant shouts its fishermen's credentials loudly: a cork ceiling, ropes, and nets decorate the narrow interior. Mirante makes an excellent lunch stop or a place for an early dinner in summer, when the views over the sea are lovely. Try the splendid tuna steak stewed with onions and, for dessert, the filling homemade cream tart. The staff is very friendly and efficient. ⊠ *Praia de Dona Ana,* ☏ *282/762713. MC, V.*

$ ✗ **Piri-Piri.** This small, low-key restaurant, done in understated pastels, is on one of the main tourist streets and offers an inexpensive but extensive menu. The long list of Portuguese dishes includes a variety of market-fresh fish, but the house specialty is the tasty piri-piri chicken that gives the restaurant its name. ⊠ *Rua Afonso d'Almeida 10,* ☏ *282/763803. MC, V.*

$$$ 🛏 **Hotel de Lagos.** This state-of-the-art hotel is attractively laid out at
★   the eastern edge of the Old Town, within easy walking distance of the center. The rooms are strung across several levels, and the uniquely de-signed building includes gardens, lounges, and patios. Guest rooms are large and elegantly appointed, with attractive tiling everywhere—even on lamps and tabletops. A courtesy bus shuttles you to the Meia Praia beach, where the hotel has very good sports and beach facilities. You also get reduced greens fees at nearby golf courses. ⊠ *Rua Nova da Aldeia, 8600,* ☏ *282/769967,* ℻ *282/769920. 317 rooms. Restaurant, bar, 2 pools, golf privileges, 2 tennis courts, shops. AE, DC, MC, V.*

$$$ 🛏 **Hotel Golfinho.** On the cliffs above a pretty cove beach, this hotel maximizes its location with balconies, which give lovely views of the sea and inland reaches. The Golfinho is large and modern, but its rooms are done in traditional Portuguese style, with attractive wood and leather furniture. It's geared toward tour groups, and its amenities tend to be practical—there's a ground-floor coffee shop and terrace, where many guests congregate. The hotel is a little less than 1½ km (1 mi) from the town center, and a courtesy bus shuttles people back and forth all day. Cliff-top paths lead from here to beautiful cove beaches nearby. ⊠ *Praia de Dona Ana, 8600,* ☏ *282/769900,* ℻ *282/769999. 262 rooms. Restaurant, bar, coffee shop, pool, shops, dance club. AE, DC, MC, V.*

$ 🛏 **Pensão Mar Azul.** Its choice central location makes this simple, budget-priced pension a terrific value, although rooms that face the pedestrian thoroughfare can be noisy in high season. Rooms—some with a terrace—are clean and cheerful, with television (but no air-conditioning), and there's a comfortable community lounge. ⊠ *Rua 25 de Abril 13–1, 8600,* ☎ *282/769749 or 282/769143,* FAX *282/769960. 18 rooms. No credit cards.*

Nightlife

There's a whole cacophony of bars at the end of Rua 25 de Abril, playing music that's brutally loud at times. The most refined of these is **Bon Vivant** (⊠ Rua 25 de Abril), with a roof-top terrace way above the din. For late-night dancing and cuddling on couches with a fireplace nearby, try **Phoenix** (⊠ Rua 5 de Outubro 11), which plays disco and pop until 5 AM. An excellent bar is **Mullens** (⊠ Rua Cândido dos Reis 86), whose enthusiastic staff makes things swing until 2 AM; full meals are served, too. **Stevie Ray's Blues Jazz Bar** (⊠ Rua Senhora da Graça) is a very classy new place serving imported beers and French champagne.

Outdoor Activities and Sports

GOLF

The 18 holes of the **Palmares Golf Club** (⊠ Monte Palmares, Meia Praia, ☎ 282/762953) overlook Lagos Bay.

Praia da Luz

38 *6 km (4 mi) west of Lagos.*

Until a few years ago, there was an active fishing fleet at this lovely spot, and a favorite pastime was to watch the boats being hauled onto the broad sandy beach. The boats are gone now, but despite the wave of development that has hit the village, this is still an agreeable holiday destination. At the western edge of town is a delightful little church facing an 18th-century fortress, which once guarded against pirates and has now been converted to an attractive restaurant. Many of the accommodations available in Luz are in private villas and apartments; the tourist office in Lagos (☞ Visitor Information *in* The Algarve A to Z, *below*) may be able to advise about them.

Dining and Lodging

$$$ ✕ **Fortaleza.** Housed in a fortress whose foundations date from Moor-
★   ish times, this atmospheric restaurant does an admirable job of preparing international and local specialties. A classical guitarist plays on Tuesday evenings, while on Sunday there's a jazz barbecue during which you can enjoy Fortaleza's grounds and terrace, with its splendid sea views. ⊠ *Rua da Igreja 3,* ☎ *282/789926. MC, V.*

$$$ ✕🏨 **Ocean Club.** You may rent these well-appointed one-, two-, or three-bedroom self-service apartments (with daily maid service) for short or long stays, but you must reserve well in advance. The Ocean Club blends well with the old village surroundings, yet still provides a high level of comfort in its carefully decorated units. They're all near the beach, where the water-sports facilities are excellent. ⊠ *Rua Direita, 8600,* ☎ *282/ 789472,* FAX *282/789763. 210 apartments with kitchen. 2 restaurants, 3 pools, 3 tennis courts, playground. V.*

$$$ 🏨 **Bela Vista.** This smart hilltop hotel has a horseshoe configuration
★   that provides every room with a magnificent sea view. Each of the generous rooms and suites has an ample terrace and is outfitted with all the modern conveniences, including a coffeemaker. The hotel is family owned and attentively managed. With its excellent restaurant, two swimming pools, and close proximity (500 yards) to a fine beach, this is an ideal spot for an extended stay in the area. ⊠ *Praia da Luz, 8600,* ☎ *282/788655,* FAX *282/788656. 39 rooms, 6 suites. Restaurant, bar, 2 pools, sauna, tennis, health club. AE, DC, MC, V.* 🗣

Outdoor Activities and Sports

SCUBA DIVING

Lessons by certified instructors, wreck dives, and night dives are available at **Blue Ocean Divers** (⊠ Center Motel Ancora, Estrada de Porto de Mós, ☎ FAX 282/782718).

WINDSURFING

The broad bay provides an excellent venue for this exciting sport. Instruction and equipment rental are available directly on the beach.

Burgau

㊴ *4 km (2½ mi) west of Praia da Luz.*

This attractive fishing village has partly succumbed to the wave of tourism that has swept over the Algarve in recent years. Luckily, its fine beach remains unchanged, and the narrow, steep streets leading to it have held the masses back and helped to maintain the original character.

Salema

㊵ *5 km (3 mi) west of Burgau.*

Salema is blessed with a lovely, 1,970-ft-long beach at the foot of green hills. New development is fast changing the face of this pretty place, until recently a simple fishing village, but it's still very relaxed and low-key.

Outdoor Activities and Sports

GOLF

Sixteen kilometers (10 miles) west of Lagos you'll find the 18-hole course at **Parque da Floresta** (⊠ Budens, ☎ 282/690054).

Vila do Bispo

㊶ *6 km (4 mi) northwest of Salema.*

At the western terminus of the N125 highway, this small inland town is a quiet place. The interior of its **church**—right in the center of town—is covered with 18th-century azulejos.

Dining

$$ ✕ **Café Correia.** Favorites at this rustic family-run restaurant are the stuffed squid and the rabbit cooked with beer and an onion sauce. The wine list, presented in a well-worn ledger, contains 180 varieties, the oldest from the 1970s. ⊠ *34 José Cardoso,* ☎ *282/442455. No credit cards. Closed Sat.*

Sagres

㊷ *10 km (6 mi) southwest of Vila do Bispo, 3 km (2 mi) southeast of Cabo São Vicente.*

In the 19th century, this village, amid harsh, barren moorland, was rebuilt over earthquake ruins. Today there's little of note apart from a series of fine, sweeping beaches. The hostels that once were inside the Fortaleza de Sagres are gone, replaced with an exhibition center and spruced-up visitors' facilities.

★ ℭ Views from the **Fortaleza de Sagres** (Sagres Fortress), an enormous run of defensive walls high above the crashing waves, are spectacular. Its massive walls and battlements make it popular with young visitors. (It's about a 15-minute walk from the village to the tunnel-like entrance; three buses a day also run this way on weekdays.) The fortress was rebuilt in the 17th century, and although some historians have claimed that it was the site for Prince Henry's house and famous navigation school, it's more likely that Henry built his school at Cabo São Vicente. But this doesn't detract from the powerful atmosphere. Certainly the **Venta da Rosa** (Wind Compass, or compass rose) dates from Prince Henry's period. Only uncovered this century, this large circular construction made of stone and packed earth is set in the courtyard just inside the fortress. Of the same age is the restored and captivating **Graça Chapel.**

A stark, modern building within the fortress walls houses an **exhibition center** with revolving exhibits documenting the region's history, flora, fauna, and nautical themes. ☎ 600$00. ☉ *May–Sept., daily 10–8:30; Oct.–Apr., daily 10–6:30.*

Dining and Lodging

$$$ ✕☑ **Pousada do Infante.** Beautifully poised on the cliffs across the
★ bay from the fortress, this modern pousada (1960) is a delightful two-story country house. There are relatively few facilities here, but the inn does have one attraction that really matters—the glorious view of the sea and the craggy cliffs. The public rooms have Moorish embellishments—such as minarets and arches alongside the pool—and are very comfortable, particularly the terrace bar, a perfect place to watch the sun set. Guest rooms feel homey. The light, airy restaurant is a well-respected spot that serves locally caught fish. The service is accomplished, and the dessert selection noteworthy. After-dinner coffee is served on the terrace. ✉ *Sagres 8650,* ☎ *282/624222,* FAX *282/624225. 39 rooms. Restaurant, bar, pool, tennis court. AE, DC, MC, V. www.pousadas.pt*

$$–$$$ ✕☑ **Fortaleza do Beliche.** Two kilometers (1¼ miles) past Sagres on
★ the coastal road to Cabo São Vicente, the remnants of an isolated cliff-top fortress have been converted into the Fortaleza do Beliche, a restaurant and very small hotel that are an annex of the Pousada do Infante. The furnishings here are smart, and the rooms are comfortable. This is also an excellent spot for a meal, with good food served—perhaps amid the flicker of fire in the fireplace and the sparkle of the old chandeliers—in the dining room. ✉ *Sagres 8650,* ☎ *282/624124,* FAX *282/624225. 4 rooms. Restaurant, bar. MC, V. Closed Nov.–Mar.*

Nightlife

Since Sagres is a well-known haunt of young travelers, there are several music bars near the village square. **A Rosa dos Ventos,** in the square, and the **Last Chance Saloon,** on the road down to Praia da Mareta, open summertime, are both loud, lively, and open late.

Outdoor Activities and Sports

FISHING

Turinfo (✉ Praça da República, ☎ 282/620003) can organize fishing trips, jeep tours, and other tourist activities around the Sagres Peninsula.

Cabo São Vicente

★ ㊹ *6 km (4 mi) northwest of Sagres, 95 km (59 mi) west of Faro, 30 km (19 mi) southwest of Lagos.*

At the southwest tip of the European continent, where the land juts starkly into the rough waters of the Atlantic, is Cabo São Vicente, called *O Fim do Mundo* (The End of the World) by early Portuguese mariners. Legends attach themselves easily to this desolate place, which the Romans once considered sacred (they believed it was the place where the spirits of the light lived because with sunset the light disappeared). It takes its modern name from the martyr St. Vincent, whose relics were brought here in the 8th century; it is said that they were transported to Lisbon 400 years later in a boat piloted by ravens.

Most historians agree that it was here in the 15th century that Prince Henry built his house and the school of navigation where he trained his captains—including Vasco da Gama and Ferdinand Magellan—before they set out on their voyages of discovery. The ancient buildings were long ago destroyed by pirates and earthquakes.

The only remaining structure is a splendidly isolated **lighthouse,** the grounds of which are open to the public. The lighthouse keeper also occasionally opens the lighthouse to visitors, although this is at his discretion and there are no set opening times. The beacon is said to have the strongest reflectors in Europe—they cast a beam 96 km (60 mi) out to sea. The views from the lighthouse are remarkable. Turquoise water whips across the base of the rust-color cliffs below, the fortress at Sagres is visible to the east, and in the distance lies the immense Atlantic.

THE ALGARVE A TO Z

Arriving and Departing

By Airplane

International and domestic airlines use **Faro Airport** (☎ 289/800800; 289/800801 for flight information), which is 6 km (4 mi) west of town. The airport accommodates frequent flights from various European cities. TAP Air Portugal (☎ 808/205700) has regular daily service from Lisbon and Oporto. Flying time from Lisbon is 45 minutes; from Oporto, 90 minutes.

FROM THE AIRPORT

From mid-May to the end of October there is a free Aerobus service from Faro airport to Faro town center. It runs every day (except Tuesday) on the hour; just show your flight ticket when boarding. A taxi from the terminal building to the center of Faro costs around 1,400$00 (there's a small extra charge for baggage). Ask the airport tourist office for a list of prices for rides to other destinations throughout the region, but in any case always make sure that you agree on a price with the taxi driver before setting off. Buses 14 and 16 shuttle between Faro town and the airport hourly, 8 AM–9 PM (until 11 PM July–mid-September); buy tickets on board (140$00).

By Bus

Various companies run daily express buses between Lisbon and Lagos, Portimão, Faro, Tavira, and Vila Real de Santo António. Allow for 3½–4½ hours' travel time for all these destinations. Generally this is more comfortable than traveling by train, and some of the luxury coaches have a toilet, TV, and food service. Any travel agency in Lisbon can reserve a seat for you; in summer, book at least 24 hours in advance.

By Car

To reach the Algarve from Lisbon, cross the Ponte 25 de Abril and take the toll road to Setúbal. Beyond here, the main IP1 highway runs via Alcácer do Sal, Grândola, and Ourique, eventually joining N125, the main east–west thoroughfare near Guia, north of Albufeira. To reach Portimão, Lagos, and the western Algarve, turn right; go straight to reach Albufeira; and turn left for Faro and the eastern Algarve. The drive from Lisbon to Faro, Lagos, or Albufeira takes about three hours, longer in the summer, on weekends, and on holidays.

Visitors driving from Spain can now cross a suspension bridge over the Guadiana River, from Ayamonte to Vila Real de Santo António. There are no longer any border controls between Spain and Portugal.

By Train

There are regular daily departures to the Algarve from Lisbon's Barreiro station on the south banks of the Tagus. Purchase your ticket for a boat ride at Terminal Fluvial in front of the Praça do Comércio, which takes you across the river to the train station for all trains traveling in a southerly direction (☞ Lisbon A to Z *in* Chapter 1). The route runs through Setúbal to the rail junction of Tunes (3 hours from Barreiro) and continues on to Albufeira (another 10 minutes), Faro (another 40 minutes), and all stations east to Vila Real de Santo António (another 2 hours). For the western route to Silves (another 20 minutes) and Lagos (another hour), you must change trains at Tunes.

Getting Around

Public transportation in general is fairly good, if sometimes infrequent on Sundays and holidays. Regardless, this region is one of the few in Portugal where having a car isn't essential.

By Bus

The main form of public transportation in the Algarve is the bus, and every town and village has its own terminal. You may have to walk from the main road to the more isolated beaches, however. Tickets are relatively inexpensive, although a bus ride always costs more than the comparable train journey. Most ticket offices have someone who speaks at least a little English. The booklet *Guia Horário,* which costs 600$00 and is available at main terminals, lists every bus service, with timetables and information in English. Some local services are infrequent or don't run on Sunday.

The major terminals are at **Albufeira** (⊠ Av. da Liberdade, ☎ 289/589755), **Faro** (⊠ Av. da República, ☎ 289/899760), **Lagos** (⊠ Rossío de São João, ☎ 282/762944), **Portimão** (⊠ Av. Guanaré, ☎ 282/418120), and **Vila Real de Santo António** (⊠ Av. da República, ☎ 281/511807).

By Car

The east–west N125 extends 165 km (102 mi) from the Spanish border to Sagres, in the far west of the Algarve. It runs parallel to the coast but slightly inland, with clearly marked turnoffs to the beach towns. New, faster stretches of highway are under construction everywhere, and roadwork and diversions add to the traffic that's normally to be expected near the busy resorts. A new high-speed motorway, IP1, extends from the Spanish border to Alcantarilha, just west of Albufeira, and eventually it will run to Sagres. Beware that the standard of driving is very poor, and Portugal has some of the worst accident statistics in Europe. Especially on the N125, always drive defensively and be prepared for the antics of other drivers. In inland areas, minor country roads are not always well maintained; when driving at night in rural areas, look out for mopeds without lights. Signage in the area can be very confusing, but don't despair. Local officials have started replacing older tangles of signs with streamlined versions.

By Train

The railroad connects Lagos in the west with Vila Real de Santo António in the east—running close to N125. Several trains a day run the entire often-scenic route, which takes three to four hours; tickets are very reasonably priced, and the trip is pleasant. Some of the faster trains don't stop at every station, and some of the stations are several miles from the towns they serve, although there is usually a connecting bus. The main train stations generally have someone who speaks some English, but it's easiest to get information at the tourist offices. At the Faro and Lagos offices, timetables are posted. The major terminals are at **Faro** (⊠ Largo da Estação, ☎ 289/801726) and **Lagos** (⊠ Largo da Estação, ☎ 282/762987).

Contacts and Resources

Car Rental

Most of the major international firms have offices at Faro Airport, and many have branches elsewhere in the Algarve, too. Try **Auto Jardim** (⊠ Av. da Liberdade, Albufeira, ☎ 289/580500; ⊠ Faro Airport, ☎ 289/800881); **Avis** (⊠ Rua da Igreja Nova 13, Albufeira, ☎ 289/512678; ⊠ Faro Airport, ☎ 289/810120; ⊠ Largo das Portas de Portugal 11, Lagos, ☎ 282/763691; ⊠ Alto do Quintão, Praia da Rocha, ☎ 282/490250); **Budget** (⊠ Faro Airport, ☎ 289/818888); or **Hertz** (⊠ Faro Airport, ☎ 289/803956).

Emergencies

General: ☎ 112. **Hospitals:** Each region has a health center for primary medical (outpatient) treatment; local tourist offices can supply addresses and phone numbers. Hospitals include those at **Faro** (⊠ Rua Leão Penedo, ☎ 289/803411), **Lagos** (⊠ Rua do Castelo dos Governadores, ☎ 282/763034), and **Portimão** (⊠ Av. São João de Dios, ☎ 282/415115). **Pharmacies:** Each town has at least one pharmacy that stays open all night; consult the notice posted on every pharmacy's door for current schedules. **Police:** ⊠ Rua Serpa Pinto, Faro, ☎ 289/804924; ⊠ Rua General Alberto Silveira, Lagos, ☎ 282/762930.

Guided Tours

Many companies and individual fishermen along the coast hire out boats for excursions. These range from one-hour tours of local grottoes and rock formations to full-day excursions that usually involve a stop at a beach for a barbecue lunch. Main centers for coastal excursions are Albufeira, Vilamoura, Portimão, Tavira, Lagos, Sagres, Vila Real, and Armação de Pêra. Consult the tourist offices in these towns for details or simply wander down to the local harbor, where the prices and times of the next cruise will be posted.

Jeep "safaris" are a unique way to see fascinating inland villages on minor, rural roads. Lunch is usually included in the price. One safari operator is **Megatur** (⊠ Rua Conselheiro Bivar 80, Faro, ☎ 289/807648). Another is **Zebra Safari** (⊠ Apartado 836 Areias de S. João, Albufeira, ☎ 289/586860).

Telephones

For information, dial 118; operators often speak English.

Travel Agencies

There are travel agencies on practically every corner in every town in the Algarve. Most of these can book guided sightseeing tours. Some agencies are **Abreu** (⊠ Av. da República 124, Faro, ☎ 289/870900; ⊠ Rua Infante Dom Henrique 83, Portimão, ☎ 282/460560), one of the largest and oldest in the country, and **Space Travel** (⊠ Rua Conselheiro Bivar 36, Faro, ☎ 289/803915; ⊠ Rua Judice Biker 26A, Portimão, ☎ 282/416063).

Visitor Information

Albufeira (✉ Rua 5 de Outubro, ☎ 289/585279); **Armação de Pêra** (✉ Av. Marginal, ☎ 282/312145); **Carvoeiro** (✉ Praça do Carvoeiro, ☎ 282/357728); **Faro** (✉ Airport, ☎ 289/818582; ✉ Rua da Misericórdia 8–12, ☎ 289/803604); **Lagos** (✉ Sitio de São João, ☎ 282/763031); **Loulé** (✉ Edifício do Castelo, ☎ 289/463900); **Monchique** (✉ Largo dos Choroes, ☎ 282/911189); **Monte Gordo** (✉ Av. Marginal, ☎ 281/544495); **Olhão** (✉ Largo Sebastião Martins Mestre, 6A, ☎ 289/713936); **Portimão** (✉ Av. Zeca Afonso, ☎ 281/531800); **Praia da Rocha** (✉ Av. Tomás Cabreira, ☎ 282/419132); **Sagres** (✉ Rua Comandante Matoso, ☎ 282/624873); **Silves** (✉ Rua 25 de Abril, ☎ 282/442255); and **Tavira** (✉ Rua da Galeria 9, ☎ 281/322511).

6 COIMBRA AND THE BEIRAS

From the dune-lined beaches and wide, shallow lagoon of the Atlantic coast to the soaring mountains and fortified towns near the Spanish frontier, the face of the Beiras is constantly changing. Lacing the region together is the Rio Mondego, the region's lifeblood and the most Portuguese of all rivers.

By Dennis Jaffe

Updated by
Martha de la
Cal and Peter
Collis

T'S NOT FAR from one point in the Beiras to any other. In fact, you can drive from the Atlantic shore to the lonely fortified towns along the Spanish border—only 160 km (100 mi)—in the time it takes many residents of Los Angeles or London to commute to work. But within this small area you will encounter tremendous diversity.

To the east Portugal's highest mountains, the Serra da Estrela, rise to a height of nearly 6,600 ft and provide a playground of alpine meadows, wooded hills, and clear streams. High in the granite reaches of this range, a tiny trickle of an icy stream begins a tortuous journey to the sea. This is the Mondego River, praised in song and poetry as the most Portuguese of all rivers. The longest river entirely within Portugal and the lifeblood of the Beiras, it provides vital irrigation to fruit orchards and farms as it flows through the heart of the region. Coimbra, the country's first capital and home to one of Europe's earliest universities, rises above its banks. Closer to the sea, under the imposing walls of Montemor Castle, the river widens to nurture rice fields before finally merging with the Atlantic at the popular beach resort of Figueira da Foz.

Historically, this region has played an important role in Portugal's development. The Romans built roads, established settlements, and in 27 BC incorporated into their vast empire the remote province known as Lusitania, which encompassed most of what is now central Portugal, including the Beiras. They left many traces of their presence in the region, including the well-known and well-preserved ruins at Conímbriga, near Coimbra.

Next came the Moors, who swept through the territory in the early 8th century and played a leading role for several hundred years. Many of the region's elaborate castles and extensive fortifications show a strong Moorish influence. The fortified towns stretching along the Spanish frontier have been the scene of many fierce battles—from the seesaw struggle against the Moors (known as the Wars of Christian Reconquest) to battles with the Spanish, as the fledgling Portuguese nation fought the invaders from neighboring Castile.

The Beiras also played a part in Portugal's golden age of discovery. In 1500 Pedro Álvares Cabral, a nobleman from the town of Belmonte on the eastern flank of the Serra da Estrela, led the first expedition to come upon what is now Brazil. Much of the wealth garnered during this period, when tiny Portugal controlled so much of the world's trade, financed the great architectural and artistic achievements of the Portuguese Renaissance. Throughout the region there are fine examples of the Manueline style, the uniquely Portuguese art form that reflects the nation's nautical heritage. The cathedrals at Guarda and Viseu, the Monastery of Santa Cruz at Coimbra, and the Convent of Jesus in Aveiro are especially noteworthy.

During the 19th-century Peninsular War, between Napoléon's armies and Wellington's British and Portuguese forces, a decisive battle was fought in the tranquil forest of Buçaco. Later in the same century, this area witnessed a much more peaceful invasion, as people from all corners of Europe came to take the waters at such well-known spas as Luso, Curia, and Caramulo. Around the turn of the century, when the now tourist-packed Algarve was merely a remote backwater, Figueira da Foz was coming into its own as an international beach resort.

Pleasures and Pastimes

Beaches

There is a virtually continuous stretch of good sandy beach along the entire coastal strip known as the Beira Litoral—from Praia de Leirosa in the south to Praia de Espinho in the north. One word of caution: if your only exposure to Portuguese beaches has been the Algarve's southern coast, be careful here. West coast beaches tend to have heavy surf and strong undertows and riptides. If you see a red or yellow flag, do not go swimming. The water temperature on the west coast is usually a few degrees cooler than it is on the south coast.

You can take your choice of beaches. There are fully equipped resorts, such as Figueira da Foz and Buarcos, or if you prefer sand dunes and solitude, you can lay your mat down at any one of the beaches farther north. Just point your car down one of the unmarked roads between Praia de Mira and Costa Nova and head west. The beaches at Figueira da Foz, Tocha, Mira, and Furadouro (Ovar) are particularly well suited to children; they all have lifeguards and have met the European Union standards for safety and hygiene.

Dining

Along the coast, as would be expected, the accent is on fresh fish. At almost any of the ubiquitous beach bar–restaurants, you can't go wrong by ordering the grilled *peixe do dia* (fish of the day). In most cases it will have been caught only hours before and will be prepared outside on a charcoal grill. You'll usually be served the whole fish along with boiled potatoes and a simple salad. Wash it down with a chilled white Dão wine, and you have a tasty, healthy, and relatively inexpensive meal. In Figueira da Foz and also in the Aveiro region, *enguias* (eels), *lampreia* (lamprey), and *caldeirada,* a fish stew that is a distant cousin of the French bouillabaisse, are popular.

Moving inland, although fish is still readily available, the emphasis shifts to meat dishes. The Bairrada region, between Coimbra and Aveiro, and in particular the town of Mealhada are well known for *leitão assado* (roast suckling pig). In Coimbra the dish to try is *chanfana*; this is traditionally made with tender young kid braised in red wine and roasted in an earthenware casserole. In the mountains, fresh *truta* (trout) pan-fried with bacon and onions is often served, as is *javali* (wild boar). *Bacalhau* (salt cod) is found in one form or another on just about every menu in the region. Bacalhau *à brás* (fried in olive oil with eggs, onions, and potatoes) is one of many popular versions of this ubiquitous dish.

The Beiras contain two of Portugal's most notable wine districts: Bairrada and Dão. Particularly good years for these wines are 1983 and 1985; if you see a 1983 Porta dos Cavaleiros Reserva tinto (red) on a wine list, grab it. The full-bodied Dão will go wonderfully with your chanfana or leitão assado. This region is also justly famous for its contribution to the country's dessert menus, although many of these pastry delights, such as Coimbra's *arrufada* (a small cinnamon-flavored pastry), are rarely found far from home. The tangy sheep's cheese of the Serra da Estrela is popular throughout the country.

With the exception of some luxury hotel dining rooms, restaurants are casual in dress and atmosphere, although a bit less casual than in the southern parts of the country. The emphasis is generally more on the food than on the trappings. Except for pizza, ethnic food is virtually nonexistent. For price categories, *see* the chart under Dining *in* Smart Travel Tips A to Z.

Festivals

In the Beiras, people are respectful of their traditions and folklore, and just about every town and village celebrates some sort of festival or fair. Dates often vary from year to year. Check with local tourist offices for details.

Fishing

There is excellent trout fishing in the Rio Vouga (Vouga River) and in the rivers and lakes of the Serra da Estrela—particularly in the Rio Zêzere (Zêzere River), which cuts through one of Europe's deepest glacial valleys—and in the Comprida and Loriga lakes. The Beira Litoral is full of beaches and rocky outcroppings where you can try your luck with a variety of fish, including bass, bream, and sole. Check with the local tourist offices for information about obtaining permits. No permit is required for ocean fishing.

Lodging

Until recently, visitors to the Beiras in search of high-quality accommodations were almost solely dependent on the government-run chain of *pousadas* (inns) and a few venerable old luxury hotels, such as the Palace Hotel Buçaco. During the past few years, especially near the coast, a number of new hotels and inns have been built, and to keep up with the competition, many existing facilities have been refurbished. However, accommodations in the eastern portions of the Beiras are still limited. If you plan to travel during the busy summer months, study the maps and lodging recommendations and make advance reservations to avoid disappointment. There are seven pousadas within the Beiras; you can use them as bases to explore the entire region. (These pousadas are small; the one at Caramulo has just 12 rooms.) In addition, there are several government-approved private manor houses that take guests. Most establishments offer substantial off-season discounts. (High season varies by hotel but generally runs July 1–September 15.) For price categories, *see* the chart under Lodging *in* Smart Travel Tips A to Z.

National Parks

Outdoorsy types find much to enjoy in the region's national parks. The most popular is the rugged Parque Natural da Serra da Estrela. Portugal's largest national park, it's frequented by hikers, anglers, and those who just like to drink up its craggy alpine scenery. The newer, smaller, and less crowded Serra da Malcata was founded to help protect the Iberian lynx.

Shopping

The Beiras are rich in artisans' traditions, but surprisingly, even today much of what is made is only available within a limited geographic area. The region around Aveiro produces Portugal's finest china, including the well-known Vista Alegre brand. In the Serra da Estrela, the famous Serra cheese and *presunto* (cured ham) are available in most towns, along with hand-carved wooden kitchen implements and wicker baskets.

Exploring Coimbra and the Beiras

The Beiras region encompasses the provinces of the Beira Litoral (Coastal Beira), the Beira Baixa (Lower Beira), and the Beira Alta (Upper Beira), which together make up roughly one-quarter of continental Portugal's landmass. On the verge of being discovered, the Beiras contain some of the last remaining areas in Europe unscathed by mass tourism.

Portugal's first capital, the ancient university town of Coimbra, provides a good introduction to this part of the country. The western part of the region contains the seaside resort of Figueira da Foz and the canals and lagoons in and around Aveiro. Farther inland it includes Viseu, with its wonderful parks and historic old quarter. The mountain resort of Caramulo and the belle époque towns of Luso and Curia are some of the country's most popular spas. The eastern portion of the region includes Portugal's highest mountains—the Serra da Estrela—and extends to the chain of ancient fortified towns along the Spanish border.

Great Itineraries

If you have 10 days, you can explore the region's winding back roads and remote mountain hamlets at a comfortable pace and still have time to take in Coimbra and the beach resorts. A week is enough time to get the feel of Coimbra, visit a spa and the coast, and explore the Serra de Estrela. If you have just three days, you can visit Coimbra and the main towns and, if you keep moving, include a stretch of the coast and the mountains. In any case, traveling by car is the best way to explore this part of Portugal and to capture its essence.

Numbers in the text correspond to numbers in the margin and on the Beiras map and the Coimbra map.

IF YOU HAVE 3 DAYS

Start your first day in 🖫 **Coimbra** ①–㉔, with a stroll through the Old Town and the university. In the afternoon visit the Roman ruins at **Conímbriga** ㉕. The next day, follow the Mondego River to the beach resort of **Figueira da Foz** ㉗, head up the coast, and move inland to visit the china factory in **Vista Alegre** ㉙ and the Museum of the Sea at **Ílhavo** ㉚. Explore **Aveiro** ㉛, with its Old Town and famous Ria de Aveiro, and end the day by taking IP5 east to 🖫 **Viseu** ㉞. On your third morning, visit Viseu's cathedral and Grão Vasco Museum and then continue east on IP5 to **Guarda** ㊌, before returning to Coimbra through the **Parque Natural da Serra da Estrela.**

IF YOU HAVE 7 DAYS

With a week, you'll be able to slow down the pace a bit and also include a few more places. Start in 🖫 **Coimbra** ①–㉔ and **Conímbriga** ㉕, as above. The next day, explore the coast with visits to the beach resorts of 🖫 **Figueira da Foz** ㉗ and **Buarcos** ㉘, stopping on the way to visit the castle at **Montemor-o-Velho** ㉖. In the evening drive out to Cape Mondego to enjoy the view and the sunset. Continue along the dune-lined coast on the third day, and after stops in **Vista Alegre** ㉙ and **Ílhavo** ㉚, explore 🖫 **Aveiro**'s ㉛ Old Town. The following morning, take a boat trip through the narrow waterways and marshlands that make up the Ria de Aveiro and after lunch continue on to 🖫 **Viseu** ㉞ by way of **Ovar** ㉜ and the castle at **Santa Maria da Feira** ㉝. On your fifth day, continue east from Viseu and make a loop that includes visits to the fortified towns of **Celorico da Beira** ㊱, **Trancoso** ㊲, **Pinhel** ㊳, and **Almeida** ㊵—a pleasant drive through the sparsely settled countryside over little-traveled roads. Spend the night in the mountain bastion of 🖫 **Guarda** ㊌. The next morning, after visiting the cathedral and museum, drive through the mountainous **Parque Natural da Serra da Estrela,** exiting at Seia. Continue by way of **Penacova** ㊉ to the forest of 🖫 **Buçaco** ㊲, just north of Coimbra. Be sure to visit the opulent Palace Hotel and, if it's within your budget, spend the night; more modest accommodations are found in the nearby spa town of 🖫 **Luso** ㊳. On your last day, return to Coimbra.

IF YOU HAVE 10 DAYS

If you like castles and fortified towns, a little longer stay will allow you to view several interesting ones in the Beiras' eastern reaches.

After exploring **Coimbra** ①–㉔ and **Conímbriga** ㉕, head for the coast, with a stop at **Montemor-o-Velho** ㉖. Spend two nights at **Figueira da Foz** ㉗ so you can enjoy a day relaxing on the beach here or at **Buarcos** ㉘. In the evening take in the casino's show and the next morning follow the coast north to **Aveiro** ㉛, detouring inland to pause at **Vista Alegre** ㉙ and **Ílhavo** ㉚. On the fifth day, after touring the Ria de Aveiro and stopping in **Ovar** ㉜ and **Santa Maria da Feira** ㉝, take the scenic route (N227) to **Viseu** ㉞. From there, drive a circuitous route that takes in **Celorico da Beira** (51), **Trancoso** (52), **Pinhel** (53), and **Almeida** (55) and ends at **Guarda** (56) for the night. Alternatively, from Celorico da Beira take IP2 north to visit the prehistoric rock engravings in the archaeological park at Vila Nova de Foz Côa, skipping Pinhel on the way back down to Almeida. Continue south from Guarda to visit the historic town of **Belmonte** ㊼ and the unusual Roman building at Centum Celas. From Belmonte, trace an arc that includes the fortified mountain towns of **Sortelha** ㊻, **Sabugal** ㊺, and **Penamacor** ㊹, and overnight in the quiet provincial capital of **Castelo Branco** ㊶. In the morning, after seeing the gardens and exploring the town, head north through **Fundão** ㊸ to **Covilhã** ㊽, and spend a few hours exploring the **Parque Natural da Serra da Estrela.** Overnight at the pousada outside **Manteigas** or continue on for the 26 km (16 mi) to **Gouveia** ㊾. Leave the park via N17 southwest to **Penacova** ㊵, and from there drive to the forest of **Buçaco** ㊴. You can spend the night there (at the Palace Hotel) or in nearby **Luso** ㊳ before returning to Coimbra.

When to Tour Coimbra and the Beiras

The Beiras, and their interior regions in particular, are some of the few attractive places in Europe where you can enjoy a July or August vacation in relative solitude. Although the Beiras' coastal beaches are quite popular in summer, the crowds are nothing like those you'd encounter on the Algarve. The water along this stretch of coast is not as warm as it is farther south, and as a consequence the season is considerably shorter. Plan your beach time here between early June and mid-September.

With the exception of the eastern regions, the interior is not subject to the blazing heat of the Alentejo or the interior of the Algarve and so is well suited for summertime touring. Aside from occasional showers, the weather is comfortable between early April and mid-November. Winters, especially in the eastern mountain towns, are harsh.

COIMBRA AND ENVIRONS

Since its emergence as the Roman settlement of Aeminium, this city on the banks of the Mondego River has played an influential and often crucial role in the country's development. In Roman times, it was an important way station, the midway point on the road connecting Lisbon with Braga to the north, and a rival of the city of Conímbriga, across the river to the south. But by the beginning of the 5th century the Roman administration was falling apart, and Aeminium fell under the dominance of Alans, Swabians, and Visigoths in turn. Beset by constant tribal warfare, the riverside settlement had little chance to develop. But by the middle of the 7th century, under Visigoth rule, its importance was such that it had become the regional capital and center of the bishopric of Conímbriga. Upstart Aeminium had finally gained ascendancy over its rival Conímbriga to the south.

The Moorish occupation of Coimbra is believed to have occurred around the year AD 714, and it heralded a new era of economic de-

The Beiras

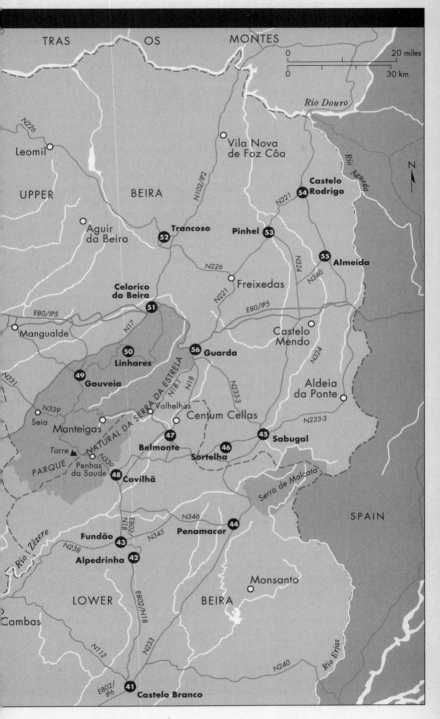

TRAS OS MONTES

20 miles

30 km

Rio Douro

Rio Águeda

N226

Leomil

UPPER BEIRA

Vila Nova
de Foz Côa

**Castelo
Rodrigo** 54

N221

N102/IP2

Aguir
da Beira

Trancoso 52

Pinhel 53

55 **Almeida**

N324

N340

N226

Freixedas

Celorico
da Beira

N221

E80/IP5

E80/IP5

51

Castelo
Mendo

Mangualde

N17

N324

50

56 Guarda

Linhares

49 **Gouveia**

Aldeia
da Ponte

N18

NT8-1

N233-3

N339

Valhelhas

Centum Cellas

N233-3

Seia

Manteigas

47

45 **Sabugal**

Torre

Belmonte

46

Penhas
da Saude

48 **Covilhã**

Sortelha

Serra de Malcata

PARQUE NATURAL DA SERRA DA ESTRELA

N339

SPAIN

Rio Zêzere

N346

44 **Penamacor**

E802/N18

N345

Fundão 43

N238

42

N18

Alpedrinha

Monsanto

E802/N18

LOWER BEIRA

Cambas

N112

N233

N240

Rio Erjas

E802/IP6

41 **Castelo Branco**

velopment for the city. For the next 300 years or so, Coimbra was a frontier post of Muslim culture. North of the city there are no traces of Moorish architecture, but Coimbra has retained tangible fragments of its Muslim past—remains of old Moorish walls, a small gate now part of the Machado de Castro Museum, the Arco de Almedina, once a gateway to the Moorish medina—and the surrounding country is full of place names that betray a Moorish origin.

After a number of bloody attempts, the reconquest of Coimbra by Christian forces was finally achieved in 1064 by Ferdinand, King of León, and Coimbra went on to become the capital of a vast territory extending north to the Rio Douro (Douro River) and encompassing much of what are now the Beiras. The city was the birthplace and burial place of Portugal's first king, Dom Afonso Henriques, and was the capital from which he launched the attacks against the Moors that were to end in the conquest of Lisbon and the birth of a nation. Coimbra remained the capital of the young Portuguese nation until late in the 13th century, when the court was transferred to Lisbon.

Several of Portugal's early kings were born in Coimbra, but the figure who has remained closest to the heart of the city was the Spanish-born wife of King Dinis, Isabel of Aragon. During her life, while her husband and son were away fighting wars, sometimes against each other, Isabel occupied herself with social works, battling prostitution and fostering education and welfare schemes for the young women of Coimbra. She helped found Coimbra's Poor Clairs Convent, and had her own tomb placed in it. Her jewels she bequeathed to the poor girls of Coimbra to provide them with wedding dowries. She died on a peacemaking mission to Estremoz in 1336. Her body was brought back to Coimbra, and almost immediately the late queen became the object of a local cult. Isabel was beatified in the 16th century, then canonized in 1625 by Pope Urban VIII after it was determined that her body had remained undecayed in its tomb in Coimbra.

Nowadays, Coimbra is best known for its university. Although it was first established in Lisbon by King Dinis I in 1290 and subsequently transferred back and forth between Coimbra and Lisbon, it was finally installed on its present site in 1537. Since then the university has played an important role in the life of both the city and the nation. During the 1960s, the university was a center of the unrest preceding the 1974 revolution. Many current political leaders were educated there, and Dr. António Salazar, the country's dictator from 1932 until 1968, taught economics at the university.

Essentially a college town, Coimbra is best visited when school is in session. The students proudly wear the traditional black capes and adorn their briefcases with colored ribbons denoting which faculty they attend (red for law and yellow for medicine, for example). Their presence adds much life to the city, and after final exams in May, students, with great exuberance, burn their colored ribbons in a ceremony called Queima das Fitas (Burning of the Ribbons).

To devotees of fado, that uniquely Portuguese art of musical expression, Coimbra has a very special significance. It is here on the banks of the Mondego that the second great style of fado was born. With the exception of a few bars where it's performed mostly for tourists, you won't find fado "shows" in Coimbra; here it's more a form of personal expression than entertainment. Wandering the narrow, steep passageways of the old university quarter, you're likely to hear plaintive sounds drifting through the night air. In contrast to the brasher Lisbon version, the Coimbra fado, performed only by men, is softer and gentler.

Musical accompaniment is played on the traditional heart-shape, 12-string guitar, and tradition dictates that you don't applaud. During the Queima das Fitas, the square in front of the old cathedral is full of people listening in silence to fado. During the student demonstrations of the 1960s, this music was used as a form of protest in much the same manner as the folk song was in the United States.

In a bucolic setting southwest of Coimbra, you'll find Conímbriga, one of the Iberian Peninsula's most important archaeological sites. It began as a small settlement in Celtic or possibly pre-Celtic times. In 27 BC, during his second Iberian visit, the emperor Augustus established a Roman province that came to be called Lusitania. It was in this period that, as the Portuguese historian Jorge Alarcão wrote, "Conimbriga was transformed by the Romans from a village where people just existed into a city worth visiting." It still is.

Coimbra

★ ❶ *165 km (102 mi) northeast of Lisbon.*

❷ The triangular plaza at the foot of the Ponte Santa Clara is the **Largo da Portagem.** The statue of Joaquim António de Aguiar, with pen in hand, represents the signing in 1833 of a decree banning religious orders throughout Portugal (the result of an anticlerical liberalism that had infused political thought throughout Europe at this time).

NEED A BREAK?
Why not succumb to the temptation of the pastry-filled windows of the cafés along the Rua Ferreira Borges? The **Café Nicola** (✉ Rua Ferreira Borges 35) is a good choice for sampling arrufada, Coimbra's most notable contribution to the great pastries of the world. This curved confection is said to represent the tortuous course of the Mondego River.

❸ On Rua Ferreira Borges, one of the city's principal shopping streets, the **Arco de Almedina** is a tall, graceful, arched opening in a massive stone wall. The 12th-century arch is one of the last vestiges of the medieval city walls, and above it are a Renaissance carving of the Virgin and Child and an early Portuguese coat of arms. The adjacent tower houses the city's historical archives and the *sino de correr* (warning bell), used from the Middle Ages until 1870 to signal the populace to return to the safety of the city walls. The tower is also used as an art gallery.

❹ **Rua Quebra Costas** is the main pedestrian link between the Baixa (Lower Town) and the Sé Velha. The street name translates to "backbreaker"; try carrying a heavy load of groceries up this steep incline, and you'll understand why it is an apt name.

★ ❺ The imposing **Sé Velha** (Old Cathedral) was designed and constructed in the 12th century. Made of massive granite blocks and crowned by a ring of battlements, the cathedral looks more like a fortress than a house of worship. (Engaged in an ongoing struggle with the Moors, the Portuguese, who were building and reconstructing castles for defense purposes throughout the country, often incorporated fortifications in their churches.) The harsh exterior is softened somewhat by graceful 16th-century Renaissance doorways. The somber interior has several interesting features, including a gilded wooden altarpiece, a late-15th-century example of the Flamboyant Gothic style, created by the Flemish masters Olivier of Ghent and Jean d'Ypres. The walls of the Chapel of the Holy Sacrament are lined with the touching, lifelike sculptures of Jean de Rouen, whose life-size Christ figure is flanked by finely detailed representations of the apostles and evangelists. The cloisters, built in the 13th century, are distinguished by a well-executed series of transitional

Arco de
Almedina . . .**3**
O Choupal . .**20**
Convento de
S.C.-a-Nova .**22**
Convento de
S.C.-a-Velha .**21**
Fonte dos
Judeus **16**
Jardim
Botânico **9**
Jardim de
Manga **15**
Justiça **19**
Largo da
Portagem . . .**2**
Museu
Machado . . .**6**
Palácio de Sobre
Ribas **11**
Parque de Santa
Cruz **8**
Pátio da
Inquisição . .**17**
Portugal dos
Pequenitos . .**23**
Praça do
Comércio . .**13**
Quinta das
Lágrimas . . .**24**
Rua da Sofia .**18**
Rua Quebra
Costas **4**
Santa Cruz .**14**
Sé Nova **7**
Sé Velha **5**
Torre de Anto .**12**
Universidade .**10**

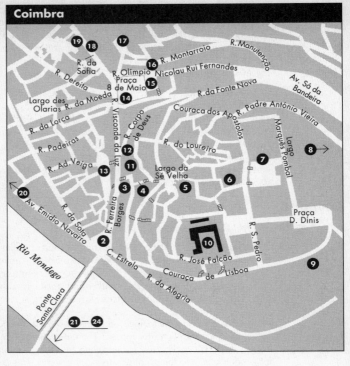

Coimbra

Gothic arches. ⊠ *Largo da Sé Velha,* ☎ *239/825273.* ▨ *Cathedral free; cloisters 100$00.* ⊙ *Daily 10–noon and 2–7:30.*

NEED A
BREAK? The cathedral square is ringed with cafés and restaurants. **Café Sé Velha** (⊠ Rua da Joaquim António Aguiar 136), decorated with *azulejos* (painted and glazed ceramic tiles) depicting local scenes, is one of the most inviting.

★ ❻ The **Museu Machado de Castro** (Machado de Castro Museum) contains one of Portugal's finest collections of sculpture, including works by Jean de Rouen and Master Pero, and an intriguing little statue of a mounted medieval knight. The Bishop's Chapel, adorned with 18th-century azulejos and silks, is a highlight of the upstairs galleries, which also contain a diverse selection of Portuguese paintings and furniture. The building, itself a work of art, was constructed in the 12th century to house the prelates of Coimbra; it was extensively modified 400 years later and was converted to a museum in 1912. If you're interested in Roman things, don't miss the well-preserved vaulted passageways in the basement built by the Romans as storerooms for the forum that was once here. Be sure to take in the view from the terrace of the Renaissance loggia. As you exit the museum, note the large 18th-century azulejo panel depicting Jerónimo translating the Bible. ⊠ *Largo Dr. José Rodrigues,* ☎ *239/823727.* ▨ *250$00, Sun. morning free.* ⊙ *Tues.–Sun. 9:30–12:30 and 2–5:30.*

❼ The 17th-century Jesuit **Sé Nova** (New Cathedral) was patterned after the baroque church of Il Gesù in Rome, as were many such churches of the day. ⊠ *Largo da Sé Nova.* ▨ *Free.* ⊙ *Daily 9–noon and 2–6:30.*

❽ **Parque de Santa Cruz** (Santa Cruz Park), east of the old city on Praça da República, offers a pleasant mixture of luxuriant vegetation, ornate fountains, and meandering walking paths.

⑨ Relief from Coimbra's oppressive summer heat can be found in the shade and greenery of the **Jardim Botânico** (Botanical Garden), not far from the university on Alameda Dr. Julio Henriques.

Built in 1634 as a triumphal arch, the **Porta Férrea** is adorned with the figures of the kings Dinis and João III. It marks the entrance to the principal university courtyard. ✉ *Praça Porta Férrea.* ☾ *Daily 9:30– 12:30 and 2–5.*

★ **⑩** The **Universidade Velha** (Old University) is steeped in tradition. Although there are modern dormitories and apartments available, many of the 20,000 students, some because of tradition and some for economic reasons, choose to live in one of approximately 30 old, ramshackle *repúblicas* (student republics) scattered around the university quarter. Groups of students live together (coed since the revolution) in these old houses, with the bare minimum in creature comforts, sharing costs and chores; the one indulgence they allow themselves is a cook. Traditionally to the left on the political spectrum, the repúblicas were a hotbed of anti-Salazar activity during the years of the dictatorship. The **República Bota-Abaixo** (✉ Rua São Salvador 6), near the Machado de Castro Museum, is a typical example of this Portuguese-style cooperative. The repúblicas are not really tourist attractions, nor are they open to the public, but if you can get an invitation, don't pass up the opportunity for a glimpse of Portuguese student life.

The statue in the center of the **university courtyard** is of Dom João III; it was during his reign that the university moved permanently to Coimbra. Walk to the far end of the courtyard for a view of the Mondego and across it to the Convento de Santa Clara-a-Nova. The double stairway rising from the courtyard leads to the graceful colonnade framing the **Via Latina** (Latin Way), the scene of colorful student processions at graduation time. Amid much pomp and ceremony, doctoral degrees are presented in the Ceremonial Hall's **Sala dos Capelos** (✉ 250$00, ☾ daily 10–noon and 2–5), which is capped by a fine paneled ceiling and lined with a series of portraits of the kings of Portugal.

The 18th-century **clock-and-bell tower,** rising above the courtyard, is one of Coimbra's most famous landmarks. The bell, which summons students to class and in centuries past signaled a dusk-to-dawn curfew, is derisively called the *cabra* (she-goat; an insulting term common in other parts of Europe, particularly the Mediterranean, and used here to express the students' dismay at being confined to quarters). In the southwestern corner of the courtyard is a building with four huge columns framing a set of massive wooden doors. It contains one of the world's most beautiful libraries, the **Biblioteca Joanina** (✉ 250$00, ☾ Mon.–Sat. 10–noon and 2–5). Constructed in the early 18th century, the library contains three dazzling book-lined halls and has one of the loveliest baroque interiors in the country. The large painting in the center is of Dom João V, the monarch responsible for the library's construction. Next door to the library is the **Capela de São Miguel,** with a fine 16th-century Manueline portal opening onto the courtyard. Begun in 1517, the chapel's glories are nevertheless from the 18th century. Its magnificent baroque organ, mannerist main altar, and rococo side altars are stunning.

⑪ The **Palácio de Sobre Ribas** (Palace above the Riverbanks) occupies a tower in the ancient walls in the lower part of the Old Town on Rua Sobre Ribas. Converted into a private residence in the 16th century, the exterior of the building is graced by several Manueline doorways and windows.

⓬ Now containing a regional handicrafts center, the converted **Torre de Anto** (Tower of Anto) was named for the nickname of Portuguese poet António Nobre, who lived in it during the 19th century. ⊠ *Rua Sobre Ribas.* ☉ *Handicrafts center weekdays 9–12:30 and 2–5:30.*

⓭ One of the Baixa's most attractive and active plazas, the **Praça do Comércio** is ringed with a variety of fashionable shops in 17th- and 18th-century town houses, while in its corners, street vendors sell everything from combs to carpets. In Roman times this was the site of the circus. The Rua Eduardo Coelho, which fans out from the square, is lined on both sides with shoe shops and was once known as the Street of the Shoemakers. Currently closed to the public, the Church of Sant'Iago, in the northeast corner, is a small, late-13th-century stone structure with finely carved Romanesque columns. At the opposite corner is the Church of São Bartolomeu. Dating from 957, it's one of the oldest churches in the city. Destroyed several times, it was rebuilt in its present form in 1756. The interior is of no special interest.

⓮ The **Igreja e Mosteiro de Santa Cruz** (Church and Monastery of Santa Cruz) is one of the country's richest in history and culture. The stark 12th-century stone facade is greatly enhanced by the Renaissance entrance, added as part of an extensive renovation in 1507. Unfortunately, much of the fine detail has been damaged by corrosion. Inside you will see the delicate features of the Renaissance altar carved in 1521 by Nicolas Chanterene. The high altar is flanked on either side by the intricately detailed tombs of the first two kings of Portugal, Dom Afonso Henriques and his son, Dom Sancho I. In the sacristy are several notable examples of 16th-century Portuguese painting. The lower portions of the interior walls are lined with azulejos depicting various religious motifs. From the sacristy, a door opens to the **Casa do Capítulo** (Silent Cloister); this double-tier Manueline cloister contains scenes from the Passion of Christ, attributed to Nicolas Chanterene. ⊠ *Praça 8 de Maio,* ☏ *239/822941.* ▨ *Church free; sacristy, chapter room, and cloister 200$00.* ☉ *Daily 9–noon and 2–5.*

NEED A BREAK?
Even if you aren't hungry or thirsty, take the time to stop at the **Café Santa Cruz** (⊠ Praça 8 de Maio), one of the most popular and unusual watering holes north of Lisbon. Until its conversion to more pedestrian uses in 1927, this was an auxiliary chapel for the monastery. Now its high-vaulted Manueline ceiling, stained-glass windows, and wood paneling provide a wonderful setting in which to indulge a favorite Portuguese pastime: sitting in a café with a strong, murky *bica* (Portugal's answer to espresso) and a brandy, reading the day's newspaper. It's closed Sunday.

⓯ A small park with an odd assortment of domed, rose-color turrets grouped around a fountain, the **Jardim de Manga** (Manga Garden) on Rua Olímpio Fernandes was designed by Jean de Rouen in the 16th century and once belonged to the cloisters of the Santa Cruz Monastery. The fountain symbolizes the fountain of life, and the eight pools radiating from it represent the rivers of paradise.

⓰ Across from the Manga Garden on Rua Olímpio Fernandes you'll find the impressive **Fonte dos Judeus** (Jewish Fountain). It dates from 1725 and marks one of the boundaries of the old Jewish quarter.

⓱ A small alley leads into the notorious **Pátio da Inquisição** (Courtyard of the Inquisition) on Rua Pedro da Rocha. This once-feared site is now home to the local Red Cross.

⑱ The broad, busy **Rua da Sofia** is one of the city's main thoroughfares. Developed in the 16th century, the road is famous for its many fine religious monuments, including the Carmo, Graça, São Pedro, and Santa Justa churches. To preserve the architectural integrity of the neighborhood, the entire street has been classified as a national monument.

⑲ The **Palácio da Justiça** (Hall of Justice) occupies a stately 16th-century building that was once the College of St. Thomas. To the left of the main entrance is a large azulejo panel depicting the goddess of justice watched over by a Knight Templar. The three panels in front read WORK, JUSTICE, and ORDER. Gracing the interior is a two-tier cloister, decorated with azulejo panels depicting historical themes associated with Coimbra. ⊠ *Rua da Sofia.* 🎟 *Free.* 🕑 *Weekdays 9–12:30 and 2–5:30.*

⑳ **O Choupal,** near the railroad bridge, is a pleasant wooded area along the river at the west end of the city. Originally a poplar grove planted as a buffer against floods, the park has a place in Coimbra's history as a setting for student serenades and poetic meditation. It's now used more by joggers than romantics.

On Rua de Baixo, across the river from the Largo da Portagem, is the
㉑ **Convento de Santa Clara-a-Velha** (Old Santa Clara Convent), a ruined Gothic church, presently being excavated from centuries-old flood deposits by restorers. Founded as a Poor Clairs convent in the early 14th century by Queen Isabel, widow of King Dinis and patron saint of Coimbra, the building was beset by periodic flooding and was finally abandoned in 1677. Both Queen Isabel and the tragic Inês de Castro were originally interred here.

㉒ High on the hill overlooking the Old Santa Clara Convent is the **Convento de Santa Clara-a-Nova** (New Santa Clara Convent), built in the 17th century to house the Poor Clair nuns who were forced out of their old convent by floods. The remains of Queen Isabel were also relocated here. Don't be put off by the barrackslike exterior of the huge building. The sumptuous baroque church and noble cloisters—the only parts of the convent open to visitors—shouldn't be missed. The remains of Queen Isabel lie in a magnificent silver shrine behind the main altar in the church, installed there by Coimbra townspeople in 1696. The queen's original tomb—she ordered it for herself in 1330— stands in the lower choir at the other end of the church. Carved out of a single block of stone, the splendid Gothic sarcophagus is decorated with sculpted polychrome figures of Franciscan friars and nuns. A sculpted effigy of the queen herself dressed in her Poor Clair habit lies on top. During the Peninsular War, the French general Massena used the convent as a hospital for 300 troops wounded during the battle of Buçaco. The carefully hidden convent treasures escaped the desecration inflicted on so many Portuguese monuments during this period. Don't leave Santa Clara without a relaxing stroll through the enormous cloisters. ⊠ *Rua Santa Isabel.* 🎟 *Church free; cloisters 100$00.* 🕑 *Daily 9–12:30 and 2:30–5:30.*

🦢 ㉓ At Coimbra's small, open-air theme park, **Portugal dos Pequenitos** (Portugal of the Little Ones), children will have great fun poking around the models of Portugal's most important buildings, built to the scale of a five-year-old child. Then they can compare them with what they have seen firsthand. ⊠ *Rossío de Santa Clara,* ☎ *239/853020.* 🎟 *400$00.* 🕑 *Sept.–Apr., daily 9–5:30, May–Oct., daily 9–7.*

㉔ Popular history has it that Dom Pedro and Inês de Castro lived with their children on this estate, which came to be known as **Quinta das Lágrimas** (House of Tears). It was here on a black January night in 1355 that Inês was killed by agents of Dom Pedro's father, Afonso IV. The

FADO

THE DRAMATIC IMAGE OF A black-shawled fado singer, head thrown back, eyes closed with emotion, has become an emblem of Portugal; the swelling, soulful song with the plaintive guitar accompaniment seems to embody Portugal's romantic essence. Fado's importance is such that when the great *fadista* Ámalia Rodrigues died in 1999, the government declared three days of national mourning and awarded her a state funeral. When the singing begins in a fado house, all talking ceases and a reverent silence descends on the tables.

But for all that, fado is not an extremely old tradition. The genre, probably an outgrowth of a popular sentimental ballad form called the *modinha,* seems to have emerged some time in the first half of the 19th century in the poor quarters of Lisbon. At first, fado was essentially a music of the streets, a bohemian art form born and practiced in the alleys and taverns of Lisbon's Mouraria and Alfama quarters. By the end of the century, though, fado had made its way into the drawing rooms of the upper classes. Portugal's last king, Dom Carlos I, was a fan of the form, and a skilled guitar player to boot.

Strictly an amateur activity in its early years, fado began to turn professional in the 1930s with the advent of radio, recording, and the cinema. The political censorship exercised at the time by Portugal's long-lasting Salazar dictatorship also contributed to the development of fado. Wary of the social comments *fadistas* might be tempted to make in their lyrics, the authorities leaned on them heavily. Fado became increasingly confined to fado houses, where the singers needed professional licenses and had their repertoires checked by the official censor.

Nowadays, although the tradition of fado sung in taverns and bars by amateurs (called *fado vadio* in Portuguese) is still strong, the place to hear fado—the Lisbon form of it, at least—is in a professional fado house. Called *casas de fado,* the houses are usually restaurants, too, and some of them mix the pure fado with folk dancing shows. The word "fado" means "fate" in Portuguese, and like the blues, fado songs are full of the fatalism of the poor and the deprived; laments of abandoned or rejected lovers; and tales of people oppressed by circumstances they cannot change.

There are two basic styles of fado: Coimbra and Lisbon. In both forms the singer is typically accompanied by three, or sometimes more, guitarists, at least one of whom plays the Portuguese guitar, a pear-shape twelve-string descendant of the English guitar introduced into Portugal by the British port wine community in Oporto in the 19th century. It is the Portuguese guitar that gives the musical accompaniment of fado its characteristically plaintive tone, as the player plays variations on the melody. The other instruments are usually classical Spanish guitars, which the Portuguese call *violas.*

Although the greatest names of Lisbon fado have been women, and the lyrics often deal with racy, down-to-earth themes, Coimbra fado is always sung by men, and the style is more lyrical than that of the capital. The themes tend to be more erudite, too—usually serenades to lovers or plaints about the trials of love. Coimbra fado is also a largely amateur expression, typically sung by university students.

18th-century manor house on the grounds—which has nothing to do with the Inês tragedy—has been turned into a hotel, but you can visit the gardens and the celebrated **Fonte dos Amores** (Fountain of Love), whose waters are said to be Dona Inês's tears. ⊠ *Rua António Augusto Gonçalves.* ☎ *150$00.* ⊙ *Daily 9–7.*

Dining and Lodging

$$$ ✕ **Dom Pedro.** The entrance, next to a car dealer, is hardly impressive,
★   but inside it's a different story. A tasteful blend of arches, tile, and wood creates just the right atmosphere in which to enjoy the excellent chanfana and *açorda de mariscos* (a sort of bread porridge mixed with eggs and mounds of fresh shellfish). There's an extensive list of Portuguese wines, and service is efficient without being stuffy. The restaurant is just a few steps along the riverfront from the tourist office. ⊠ *Av. Emidio Navarro 58,* ☎ *239/829108. AE, MC, V.*

$$$ ✕ **Trovador.** Seasoned travelers know well that the rule of thumb is to stay away from restaurants near such tourist sights as Coimbra's Sé. But Trovador—just a step away from the old cathedral—offers good service and regional food (although prices are on the high side by Coimbra standards) as well as a manor house decor. On Friday and Saturday you can listen to fado at dinner. ⊠ *Largo da Sé Velha 15–17,* ☎ *239/825475. MC, V.*

$ ✕ **Democrática.** The best that can be said about the decor is that it's functional, although wine barrels add a touch of rustic Portugal. The students and locals who frequent this popular old establishment are here for the food and the conviviality, however. The fare is simple and inexpensive. A tasty *caldo verde* (potato soup with shredded cabbage and sausage) and some fresh grilled fish make a typical meal. ⊠ *Travessa da Rua Nova 7,* ☎ *239/823784. MC, V. Closed Sun.*

$ ✕ **Zé Manel.** It's just a hole-in-the-wall in a back alley. The open kitchen is a jumble of pots and pans, walls are plastered with an odd assortment of yellowing paper announcements, and simple wooden tables and chairs constitute the decor, but the food is great and cheap. If you can get in (it's a favorite with students), don't pass this one up. For such a small place, there's an amazing choice of dishes, including a wonderful *sopa da pedra* (a rich vegetable soup served with hot stones in the pot to keep it warm). ⊠ *Beco do Forno 10/2,* ☎ *239/823790. Reservations not accepted. No credit cards. Closed 1st 2 wks in Aug.*

$$$ ✕🏠 **Quinta das Lágrimas.** This small hotel, open since 1996 on the
★   grounds of the estate where Inês de Castro was supposedly killed at the order of her husband's father, offers a nicely tuned blend of elegance, atmosphere, and modern comfort. The rooms are furnished simply but adequately. At the Arcadas da Capela restaurant, German-born chef Joachim Koerper makes a point of using home-grown herbs, fruits, and vegetables in the dishes, some of which have origins in the 18th century. ⊠ *Santa Clara 3040,* ☎ *239/802380,* 𝔽𝔸𝕏 *239/441695. 35 rooms, 4 suites. Restaurant, bar, pool, tennis court, golf. AE, DC, MC, V.*

$$ ✕🏠 **Astoria.** Occupying a prominent downtown location facing the Mondego, the domed, triangular Astoria (owned by the people who own the Buçaco Palace) has been a Coimbra landmark since its construction in 1927. In spite of a recent face-lift, the 1920s ambience has been largely maintained, although the aluminum windows around the balconies seem out of step. If you like your hotels with Old World charm and tradition and almost state-of-the-art comforts, then you will like this veteran. Ask for a room facing the river. The wood-paneled L'Amphitryon Restaurant is one of the city's finest in both ambience and quality, and Buçaco wines are served here. ⊠ *Av. Emidio Navarro 21, 3000,* ☎ *239/853020,* 𝔽𝔸𝕏 *239/822057. 64 rooms. Restaurant, bar. AE, DC, MC, V.*

$$ ✗⊞ Tivoli. This is currently a favorite with businesspeople. It's sleek, efficient, well located, and outfitted with all the latest gadgets. The only thing lacking is that certain sense of place that the other great hotels in the Tivoli chain have achieved: once in your comfortable room, you could be anywhere. The Porta Férrea restaurant serves excellent international and regional dishes in a subdued setting. ⊠ *Rua João Machado 4–5, 3000,* ☎ *239/826934,* FAX *239/826827. 90 rooms, 10 suites. Restaurant, bar, pool, health club. AE, DC, MC, V.*

$ ⊞ Dona Inês. This modern glass-and-marble hotel, conveniently located on the banks of the Mondego, is just a few minutes' walk from Coimbra's main commercial district. Although simply furnished, the rooms are light and airy. ⊠ *Rua Abel Dias Urbano 12, 3000,* ☎ *239/855800,* FAX *239/855805. 72 rooms, 12 suites. Restaurant, bar, tennis court. AE, DC, MC, V.*

$ ⊞ Larbelo. A quiet, family-run *residencial* (inn that was once a private residence) in an old, green-tile building, Larbelo has a good, central location facing the Largo da Portagem, adjacent to the tourist office. The 17 upstairs rooms have high, ornate ceilings; some rooms, particularly No. 209, have terrific views. Only breakfast is served here. ⊠ *Largo da Portagem 33, 3000,* ☎ *239/829092. 17 rooms, 9 with bath. Dining room. No credit cards.*

Outdoor Activities and Sports

HORSEBACK RIDING

Riding by the hour and excursions are available at the **Centro Hípico de Coimbra** (⊠ Mata do Choupal, ☎ 239/837695).

KAYAKING

April through October 15, the student-run **O Pioneiro do Mondego** (☎ 239/478385) conducts kayak trips on the Mondego River to Coimbra from Penacova, 25 km (16 mi) upstream. You're picked up at 10 AM in Coimbra and taken by minibus to the starting place in Penacova. The descent takes about three hours, but plan on a day for the whole outing. Call the English-speaking staff for information and reservations. Trips cost 3,000$00 per person, including kayak rental.

TENNIS

There are courts at the **Clube Tenis de Coimbra** (⊠ Av. Urbano Duarte, Quinta da Estrela, ☎ 239/403469). Nonmembers pay a 1,000$00 temporary membership fee plus a court fee of 500$00 per person per hour. Lessons with a pro are available. The club will lend rackets free of charge, but visitors must bring their own balls or buy from the club.

Shopping

The ceramics produced in and around Coimbra, mostly blue-and-white reproductions of delicate 17th- and 18th-century patterns, are among the loveliest in the country. You will come across numerous shops that sell these ceramics around the town. The Baixa district by the river is crowded with shops; Rua Ferreira Borges, Praça do Comércio, Rua Eduardo Coelho, Rua Fernão de Magalhães, and Rua Visconde da Luz create a cluster of major shopping streets.

Conímbriga

★ ㉕ *16 km (10 mi) southwest of Coimbra.*

You enter Conímbriga, an important archaeological site, via a brick reception pavilion with pools and gardens surrounding a museum. Exhibits chronicle the development of the site from its Iron Age origins, through its heyday as a prosperous Roman town, to its decline following the 5th-century barbarian conquests. The museum, which contains artifacts unearthed at the site, is best appreciated after visiting the excavations.

At the site's entrance is a portion of the original **Roman road** that connected Olissipo (as Lisbon was then known) and the northern town of Braga. If you look closely, you can make out ridges worn into the stone by cart wheels. The uncovered area represents just a small portion of the Roman city, but within this area are some wonderful mosaic floors. The 3rd-century **House of the Fountains** has a large, macabre mosaic depicting Perseus offering the head of Medusa to a monster from the deep, an example of the amazing Roman craftsmanship of the period.

Across the way is the **Casa do Cantaber** (House of Cantaber), named for a nobleman whose family was captured by invading barbarians in 465. A tour of the house reveals the comfortable lifestyle of Roman nobility at the time. Private baths included a *tepidarium* (hot pool) and *frigidarium* (cold pool). Remnants of the central heating system that was beneath the floor are also visible. Fresh water was carried 3 km (2 mi) by aqueduct from Alcabideque; parts of the original aqueduct can still be seen. There's daily bus service from Coimbra. (Buses leave from Rua João de Ruão 18—in the center of town close to the river—and drop you off right by the ruins entrance. The one-way fare is 270$00). ⊠ *Condeixa-a-Velha,* ☎ *239/941177.* ☞ *Ruins and museum 350$00.* ☉ *Ruins daily 9–6 (until 8 May–Sept.); museum Tues.–Sun. 10–8.*

Dining and Lodging

$ ✕⌂ **Pousada de Santa Cristina.** This pousada in the delightful town
★   of Condeixa-a-Nova makes an ideal base for visiting the Roman ruins at Conímbriga, 1 km (½ mi) to the south, and Coimbra, 15 km (9 mi) to the northeast. The pousada occupies a converted palace and contains spacious, comfortably furnished bedrooms and one of the area's best traditional restaurants. ⊠ *Rua Francisco Lemos (in the center of town), 3150,* ☎ *239/944025,* ℻ *239/943097. 45 rooms. Restaurant, bar, pool, tennis court. AE, DC, MC, V.*

THE WESTERN BEIRAS

The western Beiras encompass shore and mountain, fishing villages and country towns, wine country and serene forest. And within this varied landscape, you'll find an equally diverse selection of activities to pursue. Sights to see range from castles to cathedrals, monasteries to museums. For those more interested in R&R, you can lie in the sun by the Atlantic or sample the restorative powers of the air and water in any of a cluster of inland towns.

On the gentle-faced coast, long, sandy beaches and sunbaked dunes stretch from Figueira da Foz north toward the great lagoon at Aveiro, with its colorful kelp boats. A bit farther inland are the vineyards of the Dão region, the Serra do Caramulo range, the lush forests of Buçaco, and the sedate spa resorts of Curia and Luso.

Montemor-o-Velho

㉖   *20 km (12 mi) west of Coimbra, 16 km (10 mi) northwest of Conímbriga; the most scenic route, N341, runs from Coimbra along the south bank of the Mondego River.*

Occupying a strategic hilltop position overlooking the fertile Mondego basin between Coimbra and Figueira da Foz, Montemor-o-Velho figures prominently in the region's history and legends. One popular story tells how the castle's besieged defenders cut the throats of their own families to spare them a cruel death at the hands of the Moorish invaders; many died before the attackers were repulsed. The following day the escaping Moors were pursued and thoroughly defeated. Legend has it that all those slaughtered at Montemor were resurrected but forever carried a red mark on their necks as a reminder of the battle.

The **castle** walls and tower, which command the hill and fertile plains below, are largely intact, although little remains inside the impressive ramparts to suggest this was a noble family's home that once garrisoned 5,000 troops. Archaeological evidence indicates the hill has been fortified for more than 2,000 years. Although the castle played an important role in the long-standing conflict between the Christians and Moors, changing hands many times, the structure seen today is primarily of 14th-century origin. The two churches on the hill are also part of the castle complex; the Igreja de Santa Maria de Alcaçova dates from the 11th century and contains some well-preserved Manueline additions.

Here again are threads of the story of Inês de Castro, for in January 1355 Dom Afonso IV, meeting in the castle with his advisers, made the decision to murder her. In 1811 during the Napoleonic invasions, the castle was badly damaged. ▩ *Free.* ☉ *Tues.–Sun. 10–12:30 and 2–5.*

Figueira da Foz

㉗ *14 km (9 mi) west of Montemor-o-Velho.*

There are various theories as to the origin of the name Figueira da Foz. The consensus around the busy fishing harbor at this seaside resort favors the literal translation: "the fig tree at the mouth of the river." The belief is that when this was just a small settlement, oceangoing fishermen and traders from up the river would arrange to meet at the big fig tree to conduct their business. Although today there are no fig trees to be seen, the name has stuck.

Shortly before the turn of the century, with the improvement of road and rail access, Figueira, with its long, sandy beach and mild climate, developed into a popular resort. Today, although the beach is little changed, a broad four-lane divided boulevard runs along its length. The town side is lined with the usual mélange of apartments, hotels, and restaurants, but, fortunately, the beachfront has been spared from development.

One of the town's more curious sights is the 18th-century **Casa do Paço** (Palace House), the interior of which is decorated with about 7,000 Delft tiles. These Dutch tiles were salvaged from a shipwreck at the mouth of the harbor. ⊠ *Largo Prof. Vitor Guerra 4, around corner from main post office.* ▩ *Free.* ☉ *Weekdays 9:30–12:30 and 2–5.*

The triangular 17th-century **Fortaleza da Santa Catarina** (Santa Catarina Fortress), adjacent to the beachfront tennis courts, was occupied by the French during the early days of the Peninsular War.

NEED A
BREAK?

There are a number of brightly painted wooden-shack restaurants on the beach. These are wonderful places for fresh grilled fish or just a cold drink. **A Plataforma** is one of the best.

Palácio Sotto Mayor, a luxurious, elegantly furnished, French-style manor house, was constructed as part of the wave of development in the late 19th and early 20th centuries that made Figueira da Foz a world-class resort. Long in the hands of one of Portugal's leading families, the building now belongs to the owners of the casino, and local gossip has it that it was "donated" as payment for gambling debts. Its collection includes paintings and fine furnishings. ⊠ *Rua Joaquim Sotto Mayor,* ☎ *233/422121.* ☞ *200$00.* ☉ *Sept.–June, weekends 2–6; July–Aug., daily 2–6.*

Dining and Lodging

$$ ✕ **Quinta de Santa Catarina.** The fish dishes in this popular restaurant—set in a leafy garden on the outskirts of the town—are outstanding. The menu varies depending on the catch of the day, but ask if one of the *tambril* (monkfish) dishes is available. The house also does a really good *rojões á minhota* (Minho-style sautéed pork). ⊠ *Rua Joaquim Sotto Mayor.* ☎ *233/422178. AE, MC, V. Closed Mon.*

$ ✕ **O Peleiro.** In the quiet village of Paião, 10 km (6 mi) from Figueira,
★ is this popular restaurant that was once a tannery, and that's what the name means. Owner Henrique has achieved a tranquil ambience through the use of wood and tile. Heavy on regional specialties, the menu includes sopa da pedra—a must. Grilled pork or veal on a spit are also excellent, and there's a good wine selection. ⊠ *Largo Alvideiro, Paião,* ☎ *233/940159. MC, V. Closed 1st 2 wks May and Sept., and Sun.*

$$ ✕🏨 **Mercure.** Although this dowager of a hotel is beginning to show her age, she's still the top in-town choice. Formerly known as the Grande, the five-story, 1950s-vintage hotel is popular with tour groups and has a favored location overlooking the broad, sandy beach. Public and guest rooms are spacious and airy, and seafront rooms have small balconies. The large pool has a view of the beach. The restaurant—a big, rather sterile room—serves international dishes as well as regional specialties. ⊠ *Av. 25 de Abril, 3080,* ☎ *233/403900,* FAX *233/403901. 102 rooms. Restaurant, piano bar, pool. AE, DC, MC, V.*

$ 🏨 **Aparthotel Atlântico.** In this high-rise tower at the beach, the accommodations—apartments with kitchenettes—are small but adequate, with plain, functional furnishings. Some apartments have wonderful sea views. ⊠ *Av. 25 de Abril, 3080,* ☎ *233/433910,* FAX *233/433901. 70 apartments. Bar, kitchenettes, pool. AE, DC, MC, V.*

$ 🏨 **Ibis.** On a quiet street just a five-minute walk from the beach, this
★ small hotel has all the reasonably priced modern appointments Ibis fans expect, but unusually for the chain (which likes to construct new hotels), it's installed in a remodeled stone building built in 1914. ⊠ *Rua da Liberdade 32, 3080,* ☎ *233/426602,* FAX *233/420756. 50 rooms. Bar, breakfast room, pool. AE, DC, MC, V.*

$ 🏨 **Pensão Esplanada.** This turn-of-the-century corner house is across from the beach. The floors creak, and the rooms have seen better days. But this place is clean and well maintained, and the price is right. Ask for a room with a sea view. ⊠ *Rua Engenheiro Silva 86, 3080,* ☎ *233/422115,* FAX *233/429871. 19 rooms, 10 with bath. No credit cards.*

Nightlife

The **casino** is part of an entertainment complex that, although small by Las Vegas standards, is pretty big stuff for this part of the world. Built in 1886, the gambling room (minimum age 18; bring your passport), with its frescoed ceilings and chandeliers, provides a subdued atmosphere in which to try your luck at a variety of table games, including blackjack and American and Continental roulette. Banks of slot machines lie in wait in a separate room. Within the same building, there are also a large belle époque show room featuring a Vegas-type revue, two cinemas, and a piano bar. Although dress is casual, jeans and T-shirts are not permitted. ⊠ *Av. Bernado Lopes,* ☎ *233/ 408400.* ✑ *1,500$00 gambling room; 1,500$00 minimum cover for show.* ⊘ *Table games daily 5 PM–3 AM, slot machines 3 PM–3 AM; shows nightly at 11. Reservations for revue advised July–Sept.*

Outdoor Activities and Sports

BIKING

In summer, you can rent bikes and mopeds by the day and week at the **AFGA Travel Agency** (⊠ Av. Miguel Bombarda 79). **Gabriel Grácio** (⊠ Rua Dr. Calado 24) rents bicycles.

FISHING

There is good fishing for sea bream, bass, and mullet at Costa de Lavos and Gala beaches, just south of town.

TENNIS

There are good hard courts at the **Figueira da Foz Tennis Club** (⊠ Av. 25 de Abril, ☎ 233/422287). Court fees are 1,600$00 per hour per person, and lessons with a pro are available. Rackets can be rented.

WINDSURFING

Windsurfers can be rented at most of the popular beach resorts.

Buarcos

⊗ *2 km (1 mi) north of Figueira da Foz.*

This town, with its fine sandy beach, has retained some of the character of a Portuguese fishing village in spite of a heavy influx of tourists. Here colorfully painted boats are still pulled up onto the beach, and fishermen sit around mending nets.

OFF THE BEATEN PATH   **CAPE MONDEGO LIGHTHOUSE** – Take a trip out to the cape for a wonderful, uncluttered view of the coastline. The road traces a loop and returns to Buarcos.

Dining and Lodging

$$ ✕ **Teimoso.** Although the menu choices are varied, seafood is what put this seaside restaurant on the map. Locals and visitors alike gather in the dining room, which has large picture windows, to order the shellfish that comes fresh from the restaurant's huge saltwater tanks. ⊠ *Estrada do Cabo Mondego,* ☎ *233/432785. MC, V. Closed Wed.*

$ ✕🏨 **Clube Vale de Leão.** This self-contained cluster of Mediterranean-style, semidetached villas is unobtrusively nestled in the hills high above Buarcos. Rooms and apartments are small but comfortable, and the views over the bay are magnificent. The restaurant, a bit garish in decor, does a good job with both international and regional dishes. ⊠ *Vais-Buarcos, 3080,* ☎ *233/433057,* 🖷 *233/432571. 6 rooms, 17 studios, 1 apartment. Restaurant, piano bar, tea shop, pool, massage, sauna, 4 tennis courts, exercise room, squash. AE, DC, MC, V.*

Outdoor Activities and Sports

WATER SPORTS

Cape Mondego has good fishing for sea bream, bass, and mullet. Carp and barbel are caught in the Quiaios Lakes, northeast of town. The bay here is a popular windsurfing location, as are the Quiaios Lakes. Board surfers often find 10- to 12-ft waves at Quiaios Beach (just north of Cape Mondego).

En Route   The most scenic route north from Buarcos is a winding road that climbs through a wooded area to the little village of Boa Viagem (Good Journey). From here you can trace the course of the Mondego as it flows into the sea and then head north, following a narrow road that runs along the sand dunes to Aveiro, or turn inland to Vagos and pick up N109 to Vista Alegre.

Vista Alegre

㉙ *50 km (31 mi) northeast of Buarcos.*

Portugal's finest china is produced here by a business that was started in 1824 as a sort of commune. Housing was furnished for workers from all parts of the country, training was provided by French master craftsmen, and the clay came from the nearby town of Ovar. Today the settlement's large, tree-filled square is bordered by the factory, a china museum and gift shop, and a small 17th-century chapel with the delicately carved tomb of the chapel's founder.

Through its collection of hundreds of magnificent pieces, the **Museu Histórico da Vista Alegre** (Vista Alegre Historical Museum) traces development of chinaware. ⊠ *Fábrica Vista Alegre,* ☎ *234/320755.* ▭ *Free.* ☉ *Museum and gift shop Tues.–Fri. 9–12:30 and 2–5:30, weekends 2–5.*

Ílhavo

㉚ *2 km (1 mi) northeast of Vista Alegre.*

Said to have been founded by the Phoenicians, this small town is nowadays notable for the brightly tiled art nouveau houses that punctuate its otherwise unremarkable streets and the **Museu do Mar** (Museum of the Sea). Housed in a rather drab concrete building next to a fish-processing plant, the museum has an interesting collection documenting the region's close relationship with the sea and has some good early pieces of Vista Alegre china. ⊠ *Rua Vasco da Gama,* ☎ *234/ 321797.* ▭ *200$00.* ☉ *Wed.–Sat. 9–12:30 and 2–5:30, Sun. and Tues. 2–5:30.*

Aveiro

㉛ *4 km (2½ mi) north of Ílhavo, 56 km (35 mi) northeast of Buarcos.*

To refer to Aveiro as the Venice of Portugal, as is sometimes done, does not make for a good comparison. Yes, there are a few canals running through its center, and the swan-necked *moliceiros* (kelp boats) do remotely resemble Venetian gondolas, but that's the extent of the similarity. Aveiro's mood is not the drama and splendor of Venice but rather a quiet confidence and dignity.

Like Venice, though, Aveiro is first and foremost a water city. Its traditions are closely tied to the sea and to the **Ria de Aveiro,** the vast, shallow lagoon that fans out to the north and west of the city. This 45-km (28-mi) hydralike delta of the Vouga River was formed in 1575, when a violent storm caused shifting sand to block the river's flow into the ocean. The unique combination of fresh- and saltwater, narrow waterways, and tiny islands is bordered by salt marshes and lush pine forests, and the ocean side is lined with lovely sandy beaches. The tranquil Ria is the realm of the colorful moliceiros that glide gracefully along the shallow waterways, their owners harvesting seaweed.

Although you can drive through the Ria on back roads, the best way to see the area is by boat. From mid-June to mid-September, large excursion boats depart from the main canal just in front of the tourist office at 10 AM; they return at 5 PM. A stop is made along the way for lunch, which is not included in the 2,340$00 ticket. The boats can carry up to 80 passengers, but will leave with a minimum of 30. You can also take one- or two-hour trips on moliceiro boats (six passengers maximum) that leave four times a day from the same spot. The fare is 1,000$00 and 2,000$00, respectively.

With the loss of its seaport, Aveiro, once a major center for boats working the Newfoundland codfish banks, suffered a prolonged decline. It was only in 1808, when a breakwater was built of stones from the city's old fortifications, that a passage to the sea was reestablished and the town once again flourished. Deep-sea fishing was reinstituted, new industries were established, and the city took on the prosperous air it maintains today.

Aveiro is great for walking or cycling because it has no hills and its places of interest are so easily accessible. In many parts of the old town, the sidewalks and squares are paved with *calçada* (traditional Portuguese hand-laid pavement) in intricate nautical patterns.

Aveiro's most attractive buildings date from the latter half of the 15th century. In 1472 Princess Joana, daughter of King Afonso V, retired against her father's wishes to the **Convento de Jesus** (Convent of Jesus)—established by papal bull in 1461—where she spent the last 18 years of her life. This royal presence gave impetus to the city's economic and cultural development. After nearly four centuries of religious life, the convent was closed in 1874 upon the death of its last nun. It now contains the **Museu de Aveiro**, one of Portugal's most interesting museums, and doubly noteworthy in that the building itself is as remarkable as the collection. One of the highlights is the church, completed in the early 18th century. The interior is a masterpiece of baroque art, overwhelming in its richness. The elaborately gilded wood carvings and ornate ceiling by António Gomes and José Correia from Oporto are among the finest in Portugal. Scenes depicting the life of Joana, who was beatified in 1693, can be seen on blue-and-white azulejo panels, and Joana's tomb is in the lower choir. The multicolor inlaid-marble sarcophagus is supported at each corner by delicately carved angels. Other jewels are the 16th-century Renaissance cloisters, the splendid refectory lined with camellia motif tiles, and the chapel of São João Evangelista (St. John the Evangelist). The pieces on display, many brought from other convents, include sculpture, coaches and carriages, artifacts, and paintings—including a particularly fine 15th-century portrait of Joana by Nuno Gonçalves. ⊠ *Rua Santa Joana Princesa.* ▨ *250$00.* ☉ *Tues.–Sun. 10–5:30.*

The austere stone structure across from the Convent of Jesus, on Rua Santa Joana Princesa, is the Aveiro Cathedral, more commonly known as the **Igreja de São Domingos.** The interior of the church has no definitive architectural style but does contain some fine azulejos.

NEED A BREAK? — Looking onto the canal, just down the road from the tourism office, are several little coffee houses that specialize in regional *doces* (sweets). One of the best is **A Barrica** (⊠ Rua João Mendonça 26), which makes its own very good *ovos moles* (egg-yolk sweets) as well as biscuits and wafers of various sorts.

On the Praça da República, you'll find the graceful, three-story **Câmara Municipal** (Town Hall), which has a pointed bell tower. On the same plaza as the Town Hall, the 18th-century **Igreja da Misericórdia** (Mercy Church) has an imposing baroque portal; the walls of the otherwise sober interior are resplendent with blue-and-white azulejos.

The best place for viewing the brightly decorated fishing boats is along the **Canal de São Roque.** To the west of the canal are huge, glistening mounds of white salt, recovered by evaporation from the lagoon. At the northeast edge of the city, on Rua João de Moura, the **train station** displays some lovely azulejo panels depicting regional traditions and customs.

For restless youngsters, the large **city park** on Avenida Artur Ravara has a well-equipped playground and offers a welcome respite from the rigors of sightseeing with the family.

Dining and Lodging

$$ ✕ **A Barca.** This small, family-run restaurant draws a devoted clientele daily with its locally renowned fish dishes. It fills up very quickly, so go early or make a reservation. Although the style is homey, the cooking has won national gastronomical prizes. Try the *fritada de peixe* (fish fry) and the *amêijoas á bulhão pato* (clams in a garlic and coriander sauce). ✉ *Rua José Rabumba 5,* ☎ *234/426024. MC, V. Closed Sun.*

$$ ✕ **O Mercantel.** This restaurant is the brainchild of Senhor Costa da Lota, who, after 13 years of working at the nearby fish market, decided to try his hand at the other side of the business. He has done quite well. In 1990 O Mercantel took first prize in the national gastronomic fair in Santarem. Specialties include fresh fish, fish stew, and *arroz de marisco* (shellfish with rice). ✉ *Rua António dos Santos Le 16,* ☎ *234/428057. AE, DC, MC, V. Closed Mon.*

$$$ ✕🏨 **Pousada da Ria.** Built on the edge of the lagoon (about 30 minutes by car southwest of Aveiro), this light, airy, two-story inn is filled with and surrounded by plants and flowers. The entry is a tasteful blend of wood and tile, with a loft sitting area. Ten of the 19 cheerfully furnished rooms have large picture windows and look out over the water; you can stand on your balcony and watch the colorfully painted moliceiros glide by. Midway down the narrow, pine-covered peninsula that separates the lagoon from the sea, this pousada is in a great location for exploring. The restaurant has an open, spacious feeling and a lovely view. There's also a terrace for outside dining during the summer. The tasty *ensopada de cabrito* (kid stew) is recommended. ✉ *Murtosa 3870,* ☎ *234/860180,* 🖷 *234/838333. 18 rooms, 1 suite. Restaurant, bar, pool, tennis court. AE, DC, MC, V.*

$ ✕🏨 **Imperial.** If you like an efficient, modern hotel in the heart of a city, then the Imperial is for you. Rooms are comfortable but lack charm, although some on the upper floors have small balconies and nice views. The restaurant is luxurious without being ostentatious and is popular with the business community. Specialties include *enguias fritas* (fried eels) and *bacalhau com natas* (dried salt cod with cream). The breakfast buffet is the best in town. ✉ *Rua Dr. Nascimento Leitão, 3800,* ☎ *234/380150,* 🖷 *234/380151. 100 rooms, 8 suites. Restaurant, 2 bars. AE, DC, MC, V.*

$$ 🏨 **Hotel As Américas.** If you feel you need some modern comforts to go with the art nouveau feel of Aveiro, this is probably the hotel for you; it has both. A building from the 1920s has been converted into a bar, breakfast room, and games room. An attached modern building houses the well-equipped guest rooms. ✉ *Rua Engenheiro Von Hafe 20, 3800,* ☎ *234/384640,* 🖷 *234/384258. 70 rooms. Bar, breakfast room. AE, MC, V.* ✎

$ 🏨 **Arcada.** A comfortable, family-owned Portuguese classic more than 50 years old, this arched, four-story building with a red-tile roof is well kept, and its location at the foot of the bridge over the central canal couldn't be more convenient. Room size is adequate, and the furnishings vary from blond 1950s to traditional Portuguese. The lounge and bar are reminiscent of a gentleman's club slightly past its prime. ✉ *Rua*

Viana do Castelo 4, 3800, ☏ 234/404400, FAX 234/404401. 49 rooms, 1 suite. Bar, breakfast room. AE, DC, MC, V.

$ **Residencial do Alboi.** This small, modern hotel is on a quiet back street a few blocks from the main canal. It does not have a restaurant, but the bar is attractive, and the breakfasts are excellent. ✉ *Rua da Arrochela 6, 3800, ☏ 234/380390, FAX 234/380391. 22 rooms. Bar, breakfast room. AE, MC, V.*

Outdoor Activities and Sports

BIKING

Near the tourist office and at other spots in town are racks offering free bikes for touring the town and its surroundings. You insert a 200$00 coin to free the bike and you get it back when you return it. There are specially marked routes throughout town.

HORSEBACK RIDING

Escola Equestre de Aveiro (✉ Quinta do Chão d'Agra, Vilarinho, ☏ 234/912108), about 6 km (4 mi) north of Aveiro on N109, offers riding classes at all levels and trekking rides to explore the wetlands around Aveiro. Reservations are necessary for trekking. Prices range from 2,000$00 an hour for a group trek to 4,000$00 an hour for a single rider.

Shopping

The **Armazéms de Aveiro** (✉ Rua Conselheiro Luís de Magalhães 1) carries leading Portuguese brands of high-quality ceramics and chinaware, including Vista Alegre, Quinta Nova, and Artebus. They will also ship your purchases. The shopping mall **Forum Aveiro** (✉ Rua Batalhão Caçadores 10), beside the main canal in the center of town, has dozens of little shops and restaurants.

Ovar

㉜ *24 km (15 mi) north of Aveiro; head north on N109 from Aveiro to Estarreja, then turn west and follow N109-5 through quiet farmlands, and after crossing the bridge over the Ria, continue north on N327 to Ovar.*

At the northern end of the Ria, Ovar provides a convenient jumping-off point for visiting the string of beaches and sand dunes to the north. This small town, with its many tiled houses, is a veritable showcase of azulejos. The **Câmara Municipal** (Town Hall), built in the 1960s, is adorned with some unusually beautiful multicolor tile panels. The exterior of the late-17th-century **Igreja Matriz** (Parish Church) is completely covered with blue-and-white azulejos.

The small **Museu Regional de Ovar,** in an old house in the town center, exhibits many tiles and regional handicrafts. ✉ *Rua Heliodoro Slagado, ☏ 256/572822. 200$00. Daily 10–noon and 2–6.*

Santa Maria da Feira

㉝ *8 km (5 mi) northeast of Ovar.*

Your reward here is the lovely fairy-tale **Castelo de Santa Maria da Feira** (Castle of Santa Maria da Feira). The four square towers are crowned with a series of conical turrets in a display of Gothic architecture more common in Germany or Austria than in Portugal. Although the original walls date from the 11th century, the present structure is the result of modifications made 400 years later. From atop the tower you can make out the sprawling outlines of the Ria de Aveiro. ✉ *Largo do Castelo. 300$00. Tues.–Sun. 9–12:30 and 2–6.*

Viseu

⊛ *70 km (43 mi) southeast of Santa Maria da Feira, 60 km (37 mi) east of Aveiro; you can take the scenic but twisting and bone-jarring N227 across the Serra da Gralheira or the smoother, faster, but much less interesting IP1 and IP5.*

A thriving provincial capital in one of Portugal's prime wine-growing districts, the Dão region, Viseu has maintained the ambience of a country town in spite of its obvious prosperity. The newer part of town is comfortably laid out. Parks and wide boulevards radiate from a central traffic circle, but, unlike many Portuguese towns, through traffic does not have to go into its center.

A good place to start a visit is the tree-lined **Praça da República,** also known as the Rossío. This pleasant square is framed at one end by a massive **azulejo mural** depicting scenes of country life. The heroic figure in bronze, standing sword in hand, is Prince Henry the Navigator, the first duke of Viseu. The stately building across from the tile mural is the **Câmara Municipal.** Walk inside to admire the colorful Aveiro tiles and fine woodwork, and be sure to see the courtyard. Just to the south of the square, a graceful stairway leads to the 18th-century, baroque **Igreja dos Terceiros de São Francisco** (Church of the Brotherhood of St. Francis). Behind the church is a large, wooded park with paths and ponds, offering an ideal respite from the summer heat.

Almeida Moreira, the first director of the Grão Vasco Museum, bequeathed his home, a Moorish-style mansion on a hill, and a diverse collection of paintings, furniture, and ceramics to the city. Today it's the **A Casa-Museu de Almeida Moreira** (Almeida Moreira House and Museum). The house alone is worth the admission price. ⊠ *Rua Soar Cima,* ☎ *232/423769.* ⌨ *250$00.* ☉ *Tues.–Sun. 9:30–12:30 and 2–5:30.*

★ One of the most impressive squares in Portugal, the **Largo da Sé,** in the Old Town, is bounded by three imposing edifices—the cathedral, the palace housing the Grão Vasco Museum, and the Church of Mercy.

The **Sé,** a massive stone structure with twin bell towers, lends a solemn air to the large plaza that it faces. Construction on this cathedral was started in the 13th century and continued off and on until the 18th century, resulting in an interior marked by a mixture of Gothic and Manueline elements. Massive Gothic pillars support a network of twisted, knotted forms that reach across the high, vaulted roof; a dazzling, gilded, baroque high altar contrasts with the otherwise somber stone interior. The harsh lines of the upper level (added in the 18th century) appear awkward when compared with the graceful Italianate arches of the lower level, built in the 16th century in the style of the Italian Renaissance. The walls of the lower level are adorned with a series of excellent azulejo panels that depict various religious motifs. To the right of the Mannerist main portal is a double-tier cloister. A well-preserved, transitional, Gothic-style doorway connects the cloister with the cathedral. ⊠ *Largo da Sé.* ⌨ *Free.* ☉ *Daily 9:30–12:30 and 2–5:30.*

The second-floor galleries of the **Museu de Grão Vasco,** once the 16th-century Bishop's Palace, are devoted to the works of the great 16th-century Portuguese painter Vasco Fernandes (Grão Vasco) and his Flemish-influenced Viseu school, whose painters were appreciated for their naturalistic style and use of landscape. The museum is directly adjacent to the cathedral. ⊠ *Adro de Sé,* ☎ *232/422049.* ⌨ *300$00, free Sun. morning.* ☉ *Tues.–Sun. 9:30–12:30 and 2–5:30.*

The white, rococo **Igreja da Misericórdia** has soft, graceful lines that contrast sharply with the harsh, gray lines of the cathedral, which stands directly opposite. ⊠ *Largo da Sé.* 🎟 *Free.* ⊙ *Daily 9:30–12:30 and 2–5:30.*

★ The **Praça de Dom Duarte** is one of those rare places where just the right combination of rough stone pavement, splendid old houses, wrought-iron balconies, and views of an ancient cathedral (it's just below the Largo da Sé) come together to produce a magical effect. Try to be here at night, when the romance of the setting is further enhanced by the soft glow of the streetlights.

A statue of a warrior stands on a rock at the edge of town, on the road to Aveiro. It's a **monument to Viriáto,** the leader of the Lusitanian resistance to the Roman invasion in the 2nd century BC. Some historians believe this was the site of his encampment.

Dining and Lodging

$$ ✕ **O Cortiço.** In the heart of the old part of town, Viseu's most cele-
★ brated restaurant is known for the sometimes comical names of its dishes and more importantly for its intelligent use of old local recipes. Try the *coelho bêbedo* (drunk rabbit), which is rabbit stewed in red wine, or the bacalhau *podre* (rotten), which is actually a savory dish of cod braised in a tomato and wine sauce. ⊠ *Rua Augusto Hilario 47,* ☎ *232/423853. AE, DC, MC, V.*

$ ✕ **O Fontelo.** This storefront grill restaurant specializes in chicken that tastes as good as it looks in the window. ⊠ *Av. Afonso da Melo 45,* ☎ *232/424221. No credit cards. Closed Sat.*

$ ✕🏨 **Grão Vasco.** For many years the Grão Vasco has been Viseu's lead-
★ ing hotel. Its location in a wooded park just a few steps from the main square is ideal, offering the convenience of the city and the quiet of the countryside. Many of the rooms have balconies that look out on the oval pool. The restaurant serves a wide variety of principally Portuguese dishes. If it's in season, try the wild boar. ⊠ *Rua Gaspar Barreiros, 3500,* ☎ *232/423511,* 𝔽𝔸𝕏 *232/426444. 110 rooms. Restaurant, bar, pool. AE, DC, MC, V.*

$ ✕🏨 **Onix.** This cozy hotel on the outskirts of Viseu offers just the right
★ combination of tasteful decor and modern comfort. Ask for a room on the third floor with a balcony facing the Serra da Estrela. The restaurant offers good local cooking, and the service is efficient. ⊠ *Via Caçador (N16), 3500,* ☎ *232/479243,* 𝔽𝔸𝕏 *232/478744. 73 rooms. Restaurant, bar, pool. AE, DC, MC, V.*

$ 🏨 **Bela Vista.** This comfortable residencial on a quiet street about 1½ km (1 mi) from the center of town has rooms that are small but comfortable. ⊠ *Rua Alexandre Herculano 510, 3500,* ☎ *232/422026,* 𝔽𝔸𝕏 *232/428472. 44 rooms. No credit cards.*

$ 🏨 **Monte Belo.** This modern hotel, built in a quiet residential neighborhood just a few minutes' walk from the center of town, is a welcome addition to Viseu's rather sparse hotel scene. ⊠ *Urbanização Quinta do Bosque, 3500,* ☎ *232/415444,* 𝔽𝔸𝕏 *232/415400. 100 rooms, 16 suites. Restaurant, bar, pool, tennis court, health club. AE, DC, MC, V.*

Shopping

A walk along the Rua Direita, in Old Town, can be rewarding. The narrow street is lined with shops displaying locally made wood carvings, pottery, and wrought iron.

En Route Driving to Caramulo from Viseu takes you through the heart of the Dão region. Here you will see many vineyards, some carefully terraced. The wines pressed from these grapes are some of Portugal's finest.

Caramulo

⑤ *24 km (15 mi) southwest of Viseu.*

In the early part of this century, when tuberculosis was rife, people came here for the beneficial effects of the fresh mountain air. Although tuberculosis is no longer the problem it once was, Caramulo has not lost its appeal. People still come to enjoy the heather-clad wooded slopes and to walk through the lovely parks and gardens. Mineral water bottled at the nearby spring is popular throughout the country.

Ⓒ The unusual museum in the **Fundação Abel de Lacerda** (Abel de Lacerda Foundation) was founded and supported by a local doctor. Its varied collections, all from donations, include jewels, ceramics, and a fine assortment of paintings that represent such diverse artists as Salvador Dali, Pablo Picasso, and Grão Vasco. Next door is the **Museu do Automóvel**, whose collection of perfectly restored antique cars includes such rare items as a 1902 Darracq. Also on exhibit are vintage bicycles and motorcycles. ☎ *232/861270 (both museums).* 🎫 *1,000$00 (valid for both museums).* ⊙ *Daily 10–1 and 2–6.*

OFF THE
BEATEN PATH

CARAMULINHO – From the trailhead on N230-3, it's about a 30-minute climb to Caramulinho, at an elevation of 3,500 ft. Here at the tip of the Serra do Caramulo, you can look out across a vast panorama taking in the coastal plain to the west and the Serra da Estrela to the southeast.

Dining and Lodging

$ ✕🎏 **Pousada de São Jerónimo.** Reminiscent of an Alpine chalet, this
★ small pousada in the Serra do Caramulo has just 12 rooms. The reception area has lovely Arraiolos carpets hung on knotty-pine walls. Rooms are small but adequate, each with a modern marble bathroom and a small balcony with a table and chairs. Views are spectacular. The lounge, restaurant, and bar are divided by a see-through partition, and there's an inviting open fireplace. The cozy dining room's picture windows frame a mountain panorama that extends to the Serra da Estrela. The fare is country style, with chanfana *de borrego* (roast lamb, instead of kid, with red wine) one of the favorites. The pool, cabana bar, and a badminton court are in a private wooded park across from the main building. ✉ *1 km (½ mi) from Caramulo on N230, 3475,* ☎ *232/ 861291,* 📠 *232/861640. 12 rooms. Restaurant, bar, pool, badminton. AE, DC, MC, V.*

Águeda

⑥ *25 km (15½ mi) west of Caramulo, 18 km (11 mi) southeast of Aveiro.*

This industrial town is a center for the production of paper products and boasts an attractive parish church and several well-preserved manor houses. Although Águeda itself is not particularly appealing, the peaceful greenery of the surrounding countryside makes a visit to this area worthwhile.

Ⓒ Train buffs might like to take a 10-km (6-mi) side trip north to the **Museu Ferroviário** (Railway Museum) at Macinhata do Vouga, north of Águeda. The museum contains exhibits that include four steam locomotives dating from 1886. ✉ *At the train station,* ☎ *234/521123.* 🎫 *270$00.* ⊙ *Weekdays 9–1 and 2–5.*

Dining and Lodging

$ ✕🎏 **Estalagem da Pateira.** This modern, excellently equipped inn
★ complex is located on Portugal's biggest lake; 529 hectares of peaceful water, the private duck reserve of King Manuel I in the 16th cen-

tury (the name *pateira* comes from *pato*, Portuguese for duck). If you fancy the idea of being lulled to sleep by the croaking of frogs after a spectacular lake sunset, this is the place for you. The restaurant serves some excellent fare including a very good bacalhau com natas and fried eels. ⊠ *Fermentelos, 7 km west of Águeda, off Rte. 333, 3750,* ☎ *234/721219,* FAX *234/722181. 56 rooms, 1 suite. Restaurant, bar, café, pool, exercise room, boating. AE, DC, MC, V.*

Curia

③⑦ *16 km (10 mi) south of Águeda, 20 km (12 mi) north of Coimbra.*

This small but popular spa is in the heart of the Bairrada region, an area noted for its fine wines and roast suckling pig. The waters, with their high calcium and magnesium-sulfate content, are said to help in the treatment of kidney disorders. Curia offers a quiet retreat of shaded parks, a small lake, and grand belle époque hotels just a half hour's drive from the clamor of the summer beach scene. In fact, any of the three resorts in this area—Curia, Luso, and Buçaco—makes a good, quiet base for visiting the beaches and other area attractions. Coimbra, Aveiro, Figueira da Foz, the Serra do Caramulo, and Viseu are all within an hour's drive.

Dining and Lodging

$$ ✕ **Pedro dos Leitões.** Of the several restaurants specializing in suck-
★ ling pig, clustered on the N1 from Coimbra to Oporto, "Suckling Pig Pete" is the most popular. A meal here is one of those traditional things you do when you visit Portugal. You eat sardines by the old bridge in Portimão, and you have suckling pig at Pedro's in Mealhada. The size of the parking lot is a dead giveaway that this is no intimate little bistro. In the busy summer season, Pete's spitted pigs pop out of the huge ovens at an amazing rate. In spite of the volume, quality is maintained. ⊠ *N1, Mealhada,* ☎ *231/202062. MC, V. Closed Mon.*

$$ ✕⊞ **Curia Palace.** The approach down a long tree-lined drive past for-
★ mal gardens is like the beginning of an old movie. In fact, parts of the *Buster Keaton Story* were filmed here. Enter the spacious, polished, marble-floored reception area, and you're transported back to the Europe of the 1920s. The four-story hotel is the centerpiece of 15 acres of gardens, vineyards, a deer park, an aviary, orchards, and a duck pond—all of which supply produce for the hotel kitchen. A meticulously restored 18th-century water mill grinds wheat and corn for the bakery. There are also a winery, a distillery, and a chapel on the premises. The swimming pool is one of the largest in Portugal, and for car buffs there's a small collection of antique autos. Such facilities make this a wonderful place to stay with children. Bedrooms are large, with high ceilings and modern bathrooms, and the spacious corridors all have names (the Avenue of the Roses, for example). Room 255 is one of the larger rooms and has a fine view of the gardens. The dining room is light and airy—the enormous height of the ceiling broken somewhat by an encircling mezzanine—and the cuisine, prepared from garden-fresh ingredients, is excellent. ⊠ *Anadia 3780,* ☎ *231/512131,* FAX *231/515531. 114 rooms. Restaurant, bar, pool, miniature golf, 2 tennis courts, horseback riding, billiards, playground. AE, DC, MC, V. Closed Nov.–Mar.*

$$ ✕⊞ **Grande Hotel de Curia.** The task of taking a grand old 1890s spa
★ hotel and bringing it up to contemporary standards is not an easy one, but the Belver Hotel Group did just that. And it was not merely a cosmetic face-lift: new polished-marble floors, mahogany furniture and paneling, elegant bathroom fixtures, and fine carpets and draperies are some of the more visible changes. The hotel also has its own fully equipped, state-of-the-art health center, with a full-time medical staff.

Various exercise and diet programs are available. The restaurant, with wood-plank floors and soft draperies, exudes a subdued elegance. The menu is primarily international, with a few regional specialties. ⊠ *Anadia 3780,* ☎ *231/515720,* ℻ *231/515317. 78 rooms, 6 suites. Restaurant, bar, indoor and outdoor pools, hot tub, massage, sauna, Turkish bath, health club, library. AE, DC, MC, V.*

$ 🏠 **Quinta de São Lourenço.** This delightful 18th-century country manor house—surrounded by vineyards and pine groves—is in the tiny village of São Lourenço do Bairro. The house has six comfortable-size bedrooms with wooden floors, period furniture, and modern bathrooms. There's also a small apartment. Meals can be arranged upon request. ⊠ *3 km (2 mi) from Curia on N1 to Mugofores, São Lourenço do Bairro 3780,* ☎ *231/528168,* ℻ *231/528594. 6 rooms, 1 apartment. Bar, billiards, recreation room, library. No credit cards.*

Luso

38 *8 km (5 mi) southeast of Curia, 18 km (11 mi) northeast of Coimbra.*

This charming town, built around "the taking of the waters," is on the main Lisbon–Paris train line. It sits in a little valley at the foot of the Buçaco Forest and attracts visitors from all over the world. Like Curia, it has an attractive park with a lake, elegant hotels, and medicinal waters. The water emerges at a warm 27°C (81°F) from the Fonte de São João, a fountain in the center of town. Slightly radioactive and with a low-sodium and high-silica content, the water is said to be effective in the treatment of a wide range of kidney and rheumatic disorders.

Dining and Lodging

$ ✕ **O Cesteiro.** At the western edge of town just past the Luso bottling plant, this popular local restaurant serves simple fare that includes several types of cod, roast kid, and fresh fish. ⊠ *Rua Dr. Lucio Abranches,* ☎ *231/939360. MC, V.*

$$ ✕🏠 **Grande Hotel das Termas.** This hotel is a large, yellow-stucco complex in a park at the center of town. The buildings, constructed in 1945, are an architectural zero, but the interior is attractive. Rooms are large and airy, with modern, tiled bathrooms; some bedrooms have terraces that overlook the Olympic-size pool. The hotel is adjacent to the renowned Luso Spa, which offers a wide range of therapeutic programs. If you are looking for a hotel where you can settle in and really make use of the facilities, this place is ideal. The restaurant serves a good selection of international and regional foods in a pleasant environment with a view of the pool. ⊠ *Luso 3050,* ☎ *231/930450,* ℻ *231/930350. 173 rooms. Restaurant, bar, indoor and outdoor pools, sauna, miniature golf, dance club. AE, DC, MC, V.*

$ 🏠 **Pensão Alegre.** On a hill overlooking the park, this 19th-century
★ manor house has been receiving guests since 1931. The present owner, Manuel Alegre, took over the pension from his father. Filled with colorful tiles and rich wood, it exudes charm. If you're after Old World ambience and hospitality at bargain prices, look no farther. There are 20 rooms, all with high ceilings and plank floors. Ask for No. 103; it has a large terrace. Home-cooked meals are available on request. ⊠ *Rua Emidio Navarro 3050,* ☎ *231/930256,* ℻ *231/930556. 20 rooms. Dining room, pool. No credit cards.*

$ 🏠 **Vila Duparchy.** As you pass through the old gate and go up the long,
★ curved, tree-lined driveway, you'll soon realize this is no ordinary hotel. The two-story stucco house was built in the late 19th century. In 1988 Maria and Oscar Santos, the current resident owners, opened it as a guest house. Upstairs there are just six rooms; each has a fire-

place, a modern bath, and individually selected period furnishings. On the ground floor are three comfortable sitting rooms, which you share with the Santoses and other guests. The spacious grounds are full of trees and flowers, and there's a small swimming pool. Breakfast is included, and other meals, far superior to the local restaurant fare, are prepared on request. ⊠ *Just outside Luso on E234 to Mealhada, 3050,* ☎ *231/930790,* ℻ *231/930307. 6 rooms. Breakfast room, pool. AE, MC, V.*

Buçaco

● *3 km (2 mi) southeast of Luso, 16 km (10 mi) northeast of Coimbra.*

In the early 17th century, the head of the Order of Barefoot Carmelites, searching for a suitable location for a monastery, came upon an area of dense virgin forest. Having rejected an offer to settle in Sintra because there were too many distractions, he chose instead the tranquil forest of Buçaco. A site for the monastery was selected halfway up the hill on the greenest slope, and by 1630 the simple stone structure was occupied. To preserve their world of isolation and silence, the monks built a wall enclosing the forest. Their only link with the outside world was through one door facing toward Coimbra, which one of them watched over. The Coimbra Gate, still in use today, is the most decorative of the eight gates constructed since that time.

So concerned were the Carmelites for the well-being of their forest that they obtained a papal bull in 1643 calling for the excommunication of anyone caught cutting down even a single tree. They planted many trees, including a number of exotic varieties, and the forest flourished. Attracted by the calm and tranquility of the forest, individual monks would leave the monastery to be alone with God and nature. They built simple hermitages, where they would stay, without human companionship, for several months at a time. You can still see vestiges of these hermitages as you walk through the forest.

In 1810 this serenity was shattered by a fierce battle in which the Napoleonic armies under Massena were repulsed by Wellington's British and Portuguese troops. An obelisk marks the site of the Battle of Buçaco, a turning point in the French invasion of the Iberian Peninsula. In 1834, owing to the rise in anticlerical sentiment and the country's need for money to rebuild the economy after the war of succession between the two sons of King John VI, the government issued a decree ordering the confiscation of all monasteries and convents. The monastery was virtually abandoned. In the early years of this century, much of the original structure was torn down to construct—under the supervision of Italian architect Luigi Manini—what was to be a royal hunting lodge.

The small **Museu Militar de Buçaco** (Buçaco Military Museum) houses uniforms, weapons, and various memorabilia from the Battle of Buçaco. ▣ *200$00.* ☉ *Tues.–Sun. 9–5:30.*

★ The opulent, multiturreted, pseudo-Manueline extravaganza on the site of the monastery is the **Palace Hotel Buçaco** (☞ *also* Dining and Lodging, *below*). With the exception of one brief vacation and a dubious romantic fling involving the 20-year-old Manuel II, Portugal's last king, this "simple hunting lodge" was never used by the royal family. It became a prosperous hotel, and in the years between the two world wars it was one of Europe's most fashionable vacation addresses. Tales told in the local villages have it that during World War II, when neutral Portugal was a hotbed of espionage activity, Nazi agents ensconced in the tower rooms beamed radio signals to submarines off the coast.

Today the hotel is still going strong, somewhat of a dinosaur among the sleek new breed of glass-and-steel hostelries. Many come to Buçaco just to view this unusual structure, to stroll the shaded paths that wind through the forest, and to climb the hill past the Stations of the Cross to the Alta Cruz (High Cross), their efforts rewarded by the spectacular view extending all the way to the sea.

Dining and Lodging

$$$ ✕🖾 **Palace Hotel Buçaco.** Staying at the Palace, even if just for one night, ★ is an experience to be remembered. Yes, there's an elevator, but who can resist the temptation to walk up the grand, red-carpeted stairway, its walls lined with heroic azulejo panels, and past the suit of armor with electric lights for eyes—a refreshing bit of kitsch in the midst of so much splendor? A former royal hunting lodge set in a historic 250-acre forest, the hotel is a hodgepodge of architectural styles, ranging from Gothic to neo-Manueline to early Walt Disney. It's worth ordering a meal in the dining room just to sit at the finely laid table and take in the ornate, carved-wood ceiling, inlaid hardwood floors, and massive Manueline windows. In keeping with the decor, Chef Manuel Lorenço turns out some masterpieces of his own. The hotel also has its own winery: the fine Buçaco wines laid down in the cellars, which contain some 200,000 bottles, are only available here. ⊠ *Buçaco 3050,* ☎ *231/ 930101,* 🖷 *231/930509. 53 rooms, 6 suites. Restaurant, bar. AE, DC, MC, V.*

Penacova

⓴ *12 km (7½ mi) southeast of Buçaco, 12 km (7½ mi) northeast of Coimbra; from Buçaco, the most scenic route is N235, through wooded countryside along the foot of the Serra do Buçaco; from Coimbra, take N110 along the Mondego River.*

A delightful little town perched on a hill at the junction of three low mountain ranges, Penacova affords panoramic views wherever you look and wonderful opportunities for hiking. The attractive parish church in the town square was built in 1620.

OFF THE **MONASTERY IN LORVÃO –** In a delightful setting among the hills above BEATEN PATH the Mondego, this structure is patterned after the massive baroque edifice at Mafra. Archaeological evidence places the existence of a monastery here as far back as the 6th century, but the present church is principally an 18th-century construction. It has a fine carved choir and the intricate silver tombs of Teresa and Sancha, daughters of Dom Sancho I. A large part of the original monastery has been taken over by a psychiatric hospital, but you can visit the church, choir, and sacristy. There's also a small museum next door. ⊠ *Turnoff on N110, 2 km (1 mi) south of Penacova.* 🎫 *Free.* ☉ *Daily 10–5.*

Dining

$ ✕ **O Panorâmico.** This small family-run restaurant is an ideal spot to stop for lunch while driving through the lovely countryside. It's easy to see where the name came from: there's a wonderful panoramic view looking down on the Mondego as it snakes its way along to Coimbra. Maria da Graça, the proprietor, suggests the house specialty, *lampreia à mode de Penacova* (lamprey cooked with rice). ⊠ *Largo Alberto Leitão,* ☎ *239/477333. MC, V.*

Outdoor Activities and Sports

HIKING
Several paths lead over the hills to the monastery in Lorvão or through the vineyards and fields down to the Mondego.

KAYAKING

Between April 1 and October 15, there are kayak trips down the Mondego from Penacova to Coimbra. For more information contact the student-run **O Pioneiro do Mondego** (☎ 239/478385; ☞ *also* Outdoor Activities and Sports *in* Coimbra and Environs, *above*) or the local tourist office (☞ Visitor Information *in* Coimbra and the Beiras A to Z, *below*).

Shopping

This is the place to buy the intricately hand-carved willow toothpicks or cocktail spears that, in Europe, are found only in Portugal.

THE EASTERN BEIRAS

In the mountains and along the frontier with Spain, life is difficult. Winters are cold and harsh, and summers are broiling hot. The rugged mountains of the Serra da Estrela and the sparse vegetation of the stone-strewn high plateau present a sharp contrast to the sandy beaches, lush valleys, and densely forested mountains along the coast. As you drive east, the red-tile roofs and brightly trimmed white-stucco houses are replaced by stone-and-slate construction, reflecting the more somber environment.

This harsh, rocky country is a tough place to make a living, as crops do not flourish. Traditionally, many inhabitants supplemented their meager farming incomes by smuggling contraband across the Spanish border. Between 1950 and 1970, many of the villages lost their ablest workers to the factories of northern Europe; a half-million Portuguese went to France alone. As a consequence, many towns are populated primarily by senior citizens.

Still, it's worth visiting this region to stand atop a centuries-old castle wall and look out on the rugged beauty of the landscape. And in this part of the country, where tourists are still something of a curiosity, you'll find perhaps the warmest welcome.

Destinations are listed roughly from south to north, with some loops along the way. In between discussions of towns—some modern but many still dominated by what remains of their fortifications—is a visit to the Parque Natural da Serra da Estrela.

Castelo Branco

④   *150 km (93 mi) southeast of Coimbra.*

The provincial capital of Beira Baixa is a modern town of wide boulevards, parks, and gardens. Lying just off the main north–south IP2 highway, it's easily accessible from all parts of the country.

Of course there's an older section of town, where you'll find the **Praça Luís de Camões,** the town's best-preserved medieval square. The building with the arched stone stairway is the 16th-century **Town Hall.** At the top of the town's hill are the ruins of the 12th-century **Castelo Templario** (Templar's Castle). Not much remains of the series of walls and towers that once surrounded the town. Adjoining the castle is the flower-covered **Miradouro de São Gens** (St. Gens Terrace), which provides a fine view of the town and surrounding countryside.

A small regional museum, the **Museu Francisco Tavares Proença Junior** is housed in the old Episcopal Palace. In addition to the usual Roman artifacts and odd pieces of furniture, the collection contains some fine examples of the traditional *bordado* (embroidery) for which Castelo Branco is well known. Adjacent to the museum is a workshop where embroidered bedspreads in the traditional patterns are made and sold. ⊠ *Rua Bartolomeu da Costa,* ☎ *272/344277.* 🎫 *250$00, free Sun.* 🕐 *Daily 10–12:30 and 2–5:30.*

★ Take a stroll through the **Jardim do Antigo Paço Episcopal** (Garden of the Old Episcopal Palace). These 18th-century gardens are planted with rows of hedges cut in all sorts of bizarre shapes and contain a most unusual assemblage of sculpture. Bordering one of the park's five small lakes are a path and stairway lined on both sides with granite statues of the apostles, the evangelists, and the kings of Portugal. The long-standing Portuguese disdain for the Spanish is graphically demonstrated here; the kings who ruled when Portugal was under Spanish domination are carved to a noticeably smaller scale than the "true" Portuguese rulers. Unfortunately, many statues were damaged by Napoléon's troops when the city was ransacked in 1807. ⊠ *Rua Bartolomeu da Costa.* 🎫 *100$00.* 🕐 *May–Sept., daily 9–8; Oct.–Apr., daily 9–5.*

Dining and Lodging

$$ ★ ✕ **Praça Velha.** Set in a historic stone building on a lovely square (the plaque outside reads 1685), this is by far the best restaurant in town. Of the two dining rooms, the older section with the beamed ceiling and stone floors is preferred. One intriguing specialty is *bife na pedra* (steak served still cooking on a hot stone slab). ⊠ *Largo Luís de Camões 17,* ☎ *272/328640. AE, DC, MC, V.*

$$ 🏨 **Meliá Confort.** This modern hotel set atop a hill overlooking the town has all the conveniences you could wish for in additional to exceptionally good views. ⊠ *Rua da Piscina, 6000,* ☎ *272/329856,* 🏧 *272/329759. 97 rooms, 6 suites. Restaurant, bar, indoor pool, exercise room, 3 tennis courts, squash. AE, DC, MC, V.*

$ 🏨 **Rainha Dona Amelia.** The Dona Amelia is housed in a graceful, modern five-story building conveniently placed in the center of the town. The no-frills rooms are pleasant, functional, and airy. ⊠ *Rua de Santiago 15, 6000,* ☎ *272/326315,* 🏧 *272/326390. 64 rooms. Restaurant, bar. AE, MC, V.*

Shopping

Tradition in Castelo Branco dictates that a new bride make an embroidered bedspread for her wedding night. This custom is still followed, and these delicately patterned, hand-embroidered linen-and-silk spreads are among the finest examples of Portuguese handicrafts. There is a display-and-sales room next to the Museu Francisco Tavares Proença Junior (☞ *above*).

En Route As you travel north from Castelo Branco on N18, you cross broad plains dotted with olive trees. From here you can see the Serra da Estrela in the distance.

Alpedrinha

㊷ *30 km (19 mi) north of Castelo Branco.*

This village known for its fine fountains also has well-preserved remnants of the Roman road that connected this fertile agricultural region with the Spanish town of Merida.

Fundão

㊸ *5 km (3 mi) north of Alpedrinha, 36 km (22 mi) north of Castelo Branco, 16 km (10 mi) south of Covilhã.*

The pears and cherries grown in this region are the best in Portugal, and Fundão is the principal market town for the area's many orchards. It's also a convenient gateway to the fortified towns along the Spanish border. The 18th-century **parish church** is noted for its azulejos and decorative ceiling.

Dining and Lodging

$ ✕ **O Casarão.** This quiet neighborhood restaurant's three small dining areas have beamed ceilings and are divided by brick pillars. Owner José Pereira proudly proclaims that he serves the best food in Fundão, and in this restaurant-poor town he's probably right. Try the Oporto-style tripe. ⊠ *Rua José Germano da Cunha 2/4,* ☎ *275/752844. No credit cards. Closed Sat.*

$ ✕🏠 **Estalagem da Neve.** A small, cozy, Victorian-style inn on the road from Castelo Branco, it has small but comfortably furnished rooms. The restaurant, with its beamed ceiling and tiled walls, provides an inviting setting in which to enjoy a fine Portuguese meal. Try the trout or roast kid. ⊠ *Calçada de São Sebastião, 6230,* ☎ FAX *275/752215. 22 rooms, 6 with bath. Restaurant, bar, pool. MC, V.*

Penamacor

44 *28 km (17 mi) east of Fundão, 28 km (17 mi) southeast of Covilhã.*

Like many of the towns in this region, Penamacor is a mix of old and new. Dominated by the ruins of an ancient castle, it was a key link in the chain of strategically placed fortified towns. On its outskirts are newer stucco houses, many built by Portuguese emigrants with money earned working in France and Germany.

Up on the hill, the **castle** once guarded the northern approaches to the Tagus River. In the wake of the 11th- and 12th-century campaigns to reconquer this region from the Moors, Penamacor lay in ruins. In 1180 Dom Sancho I ordered the reconstruction of the fortifications. Although you can still find traces from that period, much of what you now see, including the solitary watchtower, dates from the early 16th century. The tower, which has no entrance, was used as an observation post and has a direct line of sight with the fortifications at Monsanto to the south and Sortelha to the north. If castle is closed, ask for key at tourist office.

The 16th-century **Igreja da Misericórdia** (Church of Mercy) is distinguished by a fine Manueline entrance. A rare octagonal **pillory** in front of the old town hall is also worth a look.

A small but interesting **regional museum** is housed in a building that was a political prison until the 1974 revolution. One of the original cells has been kept intact, and among the other exhibits is the only complete Roman crematorium on the Iberian Peninsula. ▨ *Free.* ☉ *Daily 10–noon and 2:30–5:30.*

Dining and Lodging

$ ✕🏠 **Vila Rica.** This 19th-century converted farmhouse is surrounded
★ by trees and gardens and is adjacent to a popular hunting area. Not coincidentally, the excellent restaurant serves many game dishes, including rabbit, quail, and wild boar. The 11 large bedrooms are simply but comfortably furnished. ⊠ *N233, 6090,* ☎ *277/394311,* FAX *277/394321. 11 rooms. Restaurant, bar, chapel. No credit cards.*

Sabugal

45 *20 km (12 mi) northeast of Penamacor, 36 km (22 mi) northeast of Covilhã; from Penamacor, follow N233 north across the high plateau.*

The main attraction here is the 13th-century **Castelo de Sabugal** (Sabugal Castle), which sits majestically atop a grassy knoll and is noted for its unusual pentagonal tower. Some historians maintain that the five sides represent the five shields of the Portuguese national coat of arms. Climb the stone stairs in the courtyard and walk around the battlements. The castle overlooks the Rio Côa (Côa River), an important tributary of the Douro. If castle is closed, ask for key at tourist office. *Free.* ☉ *Mon.–Sat. 10–5.*

OFF THE BEATEN PATH	**SERRA DA MALCATA NATURAL PARK –** One of Portugal's newest national parks, the Serra da Malcata is virtually unknown to foreigners. The 50,000-acre area along the Spanish border between Penamacor and Sabugal was created primarily to protect the natural habitat of the Iberian lynx, which was threatened with extinction. Although this isn't a place of rugged beauty and spectacular vistas, it's nevertheless an attractive, quiet region of heavily wooded, low mountains with few traces of human habitation. In addition to the lynxes, the park shelters wildcats, wild boars, wolves, and foxes.

Sortelha

★ ㊻ *10 km (6 mi) southwest of Sabugal, 26 km (16 mi) east of Covilhã.*

If you only have time to visit one fortified town, then this should be it. From the moment you walk through its massive ancient stone walls, you feel as if you're experiencing a time warp. Except for a few TV antennas, there's little to evoke the 20th century. The streets aren't littered with souvenir stands, nor is there a fast-food outlet in sight. Stone houses are built into the rocky terrain and arranged within the walls roughly in the shape of an amphitheater.

Perched above the village are the ruins of a small but imposing **castle.** The present configuration dates back mainly to a late-12th-century reconstruction, done on Moorish foundations; additional alterations were made in the 16th century. Note the Manueline coat of arms at the entrance. Wear sturdy shoes so that you can walk along the walls (you can circle the entire village this way). Children of all ages can let their fantasies run wild while taking in views of Spain to the east and the Serra da Estrela to the west. The three holes in the balcony projecting over the main entrance were used to pour boiling oil on intruders. Just to the right of the north gate are two linear indentations in the stone wall. One is exactly a meter (roughly a yard) long, and the shorter of the two is a *côvado* (66 centimeters [26 inches]). In the Middle Ages, traveling cloth merchants used these markings to ensure an honest measure.

Dining and Lodging

$ ✕ **Restaurante Dom Sancho.** This pleasant little restaurant in a restored
★ stone house in the main square began life as a bar that was the pet project of a local engineer. Since then it has become one of the more presentable restaurants in the vicinity. It specializes in game dishes like roast wild boar and venison. ⊠ *Largo do Corro,* ☎ *271/388267. No credit cards. Closed Tues.*

Although this medieval town has no hotels or pensions, several ancient stone houses have been converted into comfortable, although not luxurious, accommodations. They have running water and bathrooms and offer an unusual opportunity to actually live in a medieval Portuguese village. They fall at the low end of the $ category, and they do not accept credit cards. **Casa Arabe** (⊠ Rua da Mesquita, 6320, ☎ 271/ 381006) has one apartment that can accommodate up to four people. **Casas do Campanário** (⊠ Rua da Mesquita, 6320, ☎ 271/388198), next to the church, just inside the village walls, consists of two apartments, one with room for two persons and one that can take eight.

Belmonte

47 *14 km (9 mi) northwest of Sortelha, 20 km (12 mi) southwest of Guarda.*

As you approach Belmonte, three distinct objects that say a lot about the town catch your eye. The first two, the ancient castle and the church, represent its historic past, while the third structure, an ugly water tower, symbolizes the new industry of the town, now a major clothing-manufacturing center. Belmonte's importance can be traced back to Roman times, when it was an important outpost on the road between Merida, the Lusitanian capital, and Guarda. Elements of this road may still be seen.

Ask a Portuguese, or better yet any Brazilian, what Belmonte is best known for, and the answer will undoubtedly be Pedro Álvares Cabral. In 1500 this native son "discovered" Brazil and in doing so contributed to making Portugal one of the richest and most powerful nations of that era. The **monument to Cabral,** in the town center, is an important stop for Brazilians visiting Portugal.

Of the mighty complex of fortifications and dwellings that once made up the **castle,** only the tower and battlements remain intact. As you enter, note the scale-model replica of the caravel that carried Cabral to Brazil. On one of the side walls is a coat of arms with two goats, the emblem of the Cabral family (in Portuguese, *cabra* means "goat"). The graceful Manueline window incorporated into the heavy fortifications seems out of place. ⌂ *Free.* ☉ *Mon.–Sat. 10–12:30 and 2–5:30.*

Adjacent to the castle, a cluster of old houses makes up the **Juderia** (Jewish Quarter). Belmonte had (and, in fact, still has) one of the largest Jewish communities in Portugal. Many present-day residents are descendants of the Morranos, the Jews who were forced to convert to Christianity during the Inquisition. For centuries, many kept their faith in secret, pretending to be Christians while practicing their true religion behind closed doors. Such was their fear of repression, Belmonte's secret Jews did not emerge fully into the open until the end of the 1970s. The community remained without a synagogue until 1995.

The 12th-century stone **Igreja de São Tiago** (Church of St. James) contains fragments of original 12th-century frescoes and a fine pietà carved from a single block of granite. The tomb of Pedro Cabral is also in this church. Actually there are two Pedro Cabral tombs in Portugal, the result of a bizarre dispute with Santarém, where Cabral died. Both towns claim ownership of the explorer's mortal remains, and no one seems to know just who or what is in either tomb. If closed, ask at tourist office. ✉ *Adjacent to castle.* ⌂ *Free.* ☉ *Daily 10–6.*

OFF THE
BEATEN PATH

CENTUM CELLAS – A couple of miles outside Belmonte, on a dirt track leading off N18, is a strange archaeological find. This massive, three-story, solitary building constructed of granite blocks is thought to be of Roman origin, but experts are unable to explain what its function may have been. Some archaeologists believe it was part of a much larger complex. Excavations of the surrounding area are planned.

Dining and Lodging

$$$ ✕⌂ **Convento de Belmonte.** Just over a kilometer (½ mi) from Belmonte on the slopes of the Serra da Esperança, this attractive hotel complex was added to the national Pousadas de Portugal chain in 2000. The hotel is built around a restored Franciscan monastery founded in 1563 by a descendant of Pedro Álvares Cabral, the first European to reach Brazil. The blend of ancient and modern has been accomplished with considerable finesse. The rooms are well equipped, handsomely decorated, and have balconies with wide views over the surrounding hills. ✉ *Serra da Esperança, Apartado 35, 6250,* ☎ *275/910300,* FAX *275/910310. 23 rooms, 1 suite. Restaurant, bar, pool, 2 tennis courts. AE, DC, MC, V.* ⊗

$ ✕ⓕ **Belsol.** Pleasant and modest, the hotel is conveniently situated in a quiet spot off N18. Rooms are large, and a number have balconies with views of the Zêzere. Owner João Pinheiro is representative of a new breed of enterprising young Portuguese businesspeople looking to provide quality and service. The downstairs restaurant, although simple in decor, offers excellent food and is a favorite with local businesspeople. Try the fresh trout from the local rivers. ✉ *Quinta do Rio, 6250,* ☎ *275/912206,* FAX *275/912315. 55 rooms. Restaurant, bar, pool, playground. DC, MC, V.*

Covilhã

48 *16 km (10 mi) southwest of Belmonte, 48 km (30 mi) north of Castelo Branco.*

Although its origins go back to Roman times, there is little in present-day Covilhã of historic significance. Built into the foothills of the Serra da Estrela, the mostly modern town is closely linked to sheep raising. Its tangy *queijo da Serra*, a ewe's-milk cheese, is Portugal's most prized cheese, and the town is Portugal's most important wool-producing center. However, most visitors come to Covilhã because it is a convenient gateway to the Serra da Estrela.

Dining and Lodging

$ ✕ⓕ **Hotel Turismo.** This attractive, modern hotel at the eastern edge of town is the first new hotel to be built in Covilhã in several decades. The decor is simple but pleasant and functional. Among the local specialties served in the panoramic rooftop restaurant is fresh trout from nearby mountain streams. ✉ *Acesso a Variante, Quinta da Olivosa, 6200,* ☎ *275/324545,* FAX *275/324630. 60 rooms. Restaurant, bar, sauna, health club, squash, dance club. AE, DC, MC, V.*

$ ⓕ **Covilhã Parque Hotel.** Conveniently located near the town center, this large, modern hotel has the same ownership—and style—as the Hotel Turismo. It goes in for functional service rather than elaborate facilities. ✉ *Av. Frei Heitor Pinto, 6200,* ☎ FAX *275/327518. 134 rooms. Bar. AE, DC, MC, V.*

Parque Natural da Serra da Estrela

Until the end of the 19th century, this mountainous region was little known except by shepherds and local hunters. The first scientific expedition to the Serra was in 1881. Since that time it has developed into one of the country's most popular recreation areas. In summer the high, craggy peaks, alpine meadows, and rushing streams become the domain of hikers, climbers, and trout fishermen. The lower and middle elevations are heavily wooded with large stands of deciduous oak, sweet chestnut, and pine. Above the tree line, at about 4,900 ft, is a rocky, subalpine world of scrub vegetation, lakes, and boggy meadows that, in late spring, is transformed into a vivid, multicolored carpet of wildflowers. The Serra da Estrela Natural Park is home to many species of animals, the largest of which include wild boar, badger, and, in the more remote areas, the occasional wolf.

If you prefer to take in the scenery from the comfort of your car, the roads through the Serra da Estrela, although hair-raising at times, are well maintained and offer many inspiring vistas. The drive between Covilhã and Seia on N339, the highest road in the country, affords a breathtaking view of the Zêzere Valley. Along the way you will pass a small fountain marking the source of the Mondego River.

Dining and Lodging

$ ✕ **Cabana do Pastor.** A cozy mountain restaurant with a fireplace and
★   panoramic views, this is a good place to partake of the locally made cheese—queijo da Serra—and cured ham. It's also famed for its *cabrito no forno*, a succulent dish of roast kid. The restaurant is 12 km (7½ mi) southwest of Gouveia. ✉ *Behind souvenir shop on N339, Seia*, ☎ *238/311316. V.*

$$$ ✕🏨 **Pousada de São Lourenço.** At an elevation of 4,231 ft, this pou-
★   sada is in the heart of the Serra da Estrela, 13 km (8 mi) from Manteigas, a pleasant spa town at the foot of the Zêzere Valley. The remodeled granite mountain lodge is a favorite stopover for Portuguese and foreign visitors. Ample use of wood and brick in the rooms and a cozy fireplace in the lounge contribute to the high-country ambience. Ask for Room 207; it has a loft for sleeping and one of the best views. If you're just driving through, stop for lunch at the restaurant and try the unusual but delicious bacalhau *á lagareiro* (with corn bread, olive oil, and potatoes). ✉ *On E232 to Gouveia, Manteigas 6260*, ☎ *275/ 982450,* 📠 *275/982453. 21 rooms, 1 suite. Restaurant, bar. AE, DC, MC, V.*

$$ ✕🏨 **Hotel Serra da Estrela.** Originally built in the early part of this century as a tuberculosis sanitorium, this hotel 12 km (7½ mi) from Covilhã has been completely renovated. Rooms are large, and those in the front have good views of the valley. At an elevation of 3,936 ft, the hotel provides an excellent base for a few days in the mountains. The restaurant is bright and spacious, with lots of glass and wood. ✉ *Penhas da Saude (on the road to Torre), Covilhã 6203,* ☎ *275/310300,* 📠 *275/310309. 38 rooms. Restaurant, bar, snack bar, 3 tennis courts. AE, DC, MC, V.*

$$ ✕🏨 **Pousada de Santa Barbara.** In the pines high on the western
★   flank of the Serra da Estrela, 20 km (12 mi) southwest of Gouveia, this mountainside pousada offers a restful and cool respite from the summer heat. Many of the rooms have balconies supported by massive stone columns. The restaurant features a variety of tasty local dishes. ✉ *N17, Povoa das Quartas 3400,* ☎ *238/609551,* 📠 *238/609645. 16 rooms. Restaurant, bar, pool, tennis court. AE, DC, MC, V.*

$ 🏨 **Albergaria Senhora do Espinheiro.** This recently built mountain inn
★   is next to the Cabana do Pastor restaurant (☞ *above*), 12 km (7½ mi) from Gouveia. Both are the labors of love of António Mora, a big, gentle bear of a man who will enhance your stay or meal. The use of wood and tile throughout gives the inn a warm feeling. Rooms are small and furnished in pine; ask for one at the back, where the views are best. ✉ *N339, Seia 6270,* ☎ 📠 *238/312073. 23 rooms. Bar. AE, DC, MC, V.*

Outdoor Activities and Sports

CAMPING

There are several official campsites within the park, but you must bring your own camping gear.

HIKING

This is a hiker's paradise, amply supplied with well-marked trails. A comprehensive trail guide is available at tourist offices in the region (☞ Visitor Information *in* Coimbra and the Beiras A to Z, *below*), and, although it's in Portuguese, the maps, elevation charts, and pictures are useful.

SKIING

With the coming of winter and the first snows, the area becomes a winter playground, offering many Portuguese their only exposure to winter sports. Although there are five ski lifts at **Torre** (☎ 275/334933)—the highest point in continental Portugal, with an elevation of 6,539 ft— the conditions and facilities are not on a par with ski resorts in the rest of Europe. Still you will find a restaurant and sports-equipment shops, and you can rent gear. Lift tickets cost 2,500$00 a day during the week, and 3,000$00 a day on weekends.

Gouveia

49 *28 km (17 mi) northwest of Covilhã.*

Nestled into the western side of the Mondego Valley, this quiet town of parks and gardens is a popular base from which to explore the Serra da Estrela. The exterior of the baroque **parish church** is covered with blue-and-white tiles, and a series of well-executed azulejos depicting the Stations of the Cross lines the inside walls of the small, dimly lighted chapel across the street.

The **Museu Abel Manta,** in an 18th-century manor house, displays the paintings of this local 20th-century artist. 🎟 *Free.* ☉ *Tues.–Sun. 10– noon and 2–5.*

OFF THE BEATEN PATH

CANIL MONTES HERMÍNIOS – Gouveia is the principal center for the famous Serra da Estrela dogs, beautiful sheepdogs known for their loyalty and courage. In earlier days, when marauding wolf packs were an ever-present menace, the dogs wore metal collars with long spikes to protect their throats. To learn more about the dogs, you can visit the Montes Hermínios Kennels, one of the major breeding kennels in the Vale do Rossim. ⊠ *N232 between Gouveia and Manteigas, Solar do Cão da Serra, Estrada da Serra,* ☎ *238/492426.* ☉ *Visits by appointment.*

Dining and Lodging

$ ✕ **O Julio.** Thanks to the talents of chef and owner Julio, this simple, ★ unassuming restaurant was chosen to represent the Serra da Estrela region at the 1992 tourist fair in Lisbon. Try the *truta frita do Mondego* (fried trout from the Mondego River) or the *javali no forno* (roast wild boar). ⊠ *Travessa do Loureiro 1,* ☎ *238/498016. MC, V. Closed Tues.*

$ ✕🏨 **Hotel Gouveia.** This small, modern hotel on one of the main approaches to the Serra da Estrela offers comfortable rooms furnished in traditional style. Several have small balconies. The ground-floor O Foural restaurant is popular with local businesspeople; service is attentive, and the kitchen turns out delicious roast kid. If you like tennis, there are two courts you can use for free in the nearby city park. ⊠ *Av. 1 de Maio, 6290,* ☎ *238/494370,* 📠 *238/491010. 27 rooms, 4 suites. Restaurant, bar, pool. AE, DC, MC, V.*

Linhares

50 *16 km (10 mi) northeast of Gouveia.*

Atop a rocky outcrop on the northeastern shoulder of the Serra da Estrela at an elevation of 2,625 ft, this fortified hamlet is a good place for a lookout. This small, quiet village of stone houses, a church, and a few shops is encircled by walls, much of which remain intact, as do two square, crenellated towers from the time of King Dinis. There's a 16th-century pillory in front of the church.

Celorico da Beira

51 *14 km (9 mi) northeast of Linhares, 16 km (10 mi) northwest of Guarda.*

Celorico da Beira is a major producer of Serra cheese and the site of one of Europe's largest cheese markets, held every other Friday. The cheese is made from the best quality ewe's milk, using traditional methods. Production takes place between December and March.

Celorico also has the requisite **fortress,** and a large portion of the castle walls and an impressive tower are intact. ⌑ *Free.* ⊙ *Mon.–Sat. 10–12:30 and 2–5. Key to castle can be obtained at town hall.*

Dining and Lodging

$ ✕☷ **Mira Serra.** Owner Fernando Batista was the manager of a luxury hotel in the Algarve before striking out on his own with this modern four-story establishment. The rooms are comfortable and furnished in traditional style; some have small balconies. The restaurant prepares a delicious bacalhau à brás. ✉ *Just off IP5, 6360,* ☎ *271/742604,* 𝔽𝔸𝕏 *271/741382. 42 rooms. Restaurant, bar. AE, DC, MC, V.*

Trancoso

52 *18 km (11 mi) northeast of Celorico da Beira, 26 km (16 mi) northwest of Guarda.*

This town reached its pinnacle in 1282, when King Dinis chose it as the site for his marriage to Isabel of Aragon. Portions of the town's well-preserved castle walls and towers date from the 9th century. Above one of the gates, the **Porta do Carvalho,** you can make out the figure of a knight. This was a local lad who, during one of the many battles with the Spanish, left the safety of the castle walls to capture the Spanish flag. He was caught, but before being spirited away, he defiantly hurled the flag over the wall.

Pinhel

53 *38 km (24 mi) east of Trancoso; the best route is the scenic but tortuous N226 to Freixedas and N221 from there up to Pinhel.*

Sitting atop a hill in the Marofa range, this town was a key bastion during the wars of restoration. Pinhel's most striking remnants of the 17th century are two solitary towers that rise above town. On one of the towers, below the balcony facing the town, you can make out the graceful form of a Manueline window.

En Route Taking N221 north, you'll cross the Serra da Marofa and a desolate, rocky moonscape. Before some recent improvements, this stretch was known as the Accursed Road, because of its many bends.

Castelo Rodrigo

54 *12 km (7½ mi) northeast of Pinhel.*

This old fortified town is now mostly deserted, many of its former residents having emigrated to France and Germany. The ruins of the **fortress** afford a panoramic view of the surrounding countryside. In neighboring Figueira de Castelo Rodrigo, the 18th-century **parish church** contains several attractive gilded wooden altars.

Almeida

☁ ⑤⑤ *18 km (11 mi) southeast of Castelo Rodrigo.*

Enclosed within a star-shape perimeter of massive stone walls, moats, and earthen bulwarks lies the quiet little town of Almeida. Less than 10 km (6 mi) from the Spanish border, it has been the scene of much fighting over the centuries. This is a place for walking, clambering along the walls and bulwarks, and giving your imagination free rein—perhaps to conjure up ghosts of battles past.

Dining and Lodging

$$$ ✕▥ **Pousada Senhora das Neves.** Portuguese architect Cristiano Mor-
★ eira has mastered the difficult task of integrating this modern hotel into historic fortress walls. Public areas and guest rooms are spacious and light, and there are large terraces that look out across the high table-lands into Spain. You can sip your afternoon glass of chilled white port and imagine Wellington's troops facing Napoléon's armies on this very spot. The restaurant, divided into two inviting plank-floor din-ing rooms, serves a wide variety of regional dishes, including *sopa de peixe do Rio Côa* (a rich tomato-based soup made with fish from the nearby Côa River). The extensive wine list has more than 60 selections. ✉ *Rua das Muralhas, 6350,* ☎ *271/574283,* ℻ *271/574320. 20 rooms, 1 suite. Restaurant, bar. AE, DC, MC, V.*

$ ▥ **A Muralha.** This modern residencial, just outside the fortifications, is the creation of former schoolteacher Manuel Dias and his wife, Eliza. He has traded teaching English for running the 24-room resi-dencial, and Eliza oversees the small restaurant. The rooms are clean and simply furnished. Cork floors in the bedrooms and cork paneling in the hallways contribute to a homey atmosphere. The restaurant's specialties include cabrito no forno and an excellent oven-baked salt cod dish called *bacalhau á Muralha.* ✉ *Bairro de São Pedro, 6350,* ☎ *271/574357. 24 rooms. Restaurant, bar. MC, V.*

Guarda

⑤⑥ *38 km (24 mi) southwest of Almeida, 36 km (22 mi) northeast of Cov-ilhã, 60 km (37 mi) east of Viseu.*

At an elevation of about 3,300 ft, Guarda is Portugal's highest city and is aptly referred to by the four Fs: *forte, feia, fria, e farta* (strong, ugly, cold, and wealthy). A somber conglomeration of austere granite build-ings set in a harsh, uncompromising environment, Guarda is no charm-ing mountain hamlet. The winters are cold and gloomy, often cutting into the short springtime.

From pre-Roman times, Guarda has been a strategic bastion on the northeastern flank of the Serra da Estrela, protecting the approaches from Castile. The town is thought to have been a military base for Julius Caesar. Following the fall of the Roman Empire, the Visigoths and later the Moors gained control. Guarda was liberated in the late 12th cen-tury by Christian forces and, along with a number of towns in the re-gion, enlarged and fortified by Dom Sancho I.

The **castle tower,** on a small knoll above the cathedral, and a few seg-ments of wall are all that remain of Guarda's extensive fortifications. From atop the ruins there is an impressive view across the rock-strewn countryside toward the Castilian plains.

Construction on the fortresslike **cathedral** started in 1390 but wasn't completed until 1540. As a consequence, the imposing Gothic build-ing also shows Renaissance and Manueline influences. Although built on a smaller and less majestic scale, the cathedral shows similarities to the great monastery at Batalha. Inside, a magnificent four-tier relief contains more than 100 carved figures. The work is attributed to the 16th-century sculptor Jean de Rouen.

In the **Praça Luís de Camões,** a square lined with some fine 16th- and 18th-century houses, stands a statue of Dom Sancho I.

The **Museu da Guarda** (Guarda Museum), in a stately early 17th-century palace adjacent to the 18th-century Igreja da Misericórdia (Church of Mercy), is worth a visit. It documents the region's history with a collection of prehistoric and Roman objects, old paintings, documents, arms, and ecclesiastical art. ⊠ *Rua Alves Rocadas,* ☎ *271/213460.* 🎫 *250$00.* ☉ *Tues.–Sun. 10–12:30 and 2–5:30.*

Dining and Lodging

$ ✕ **Belo Horizonte.** Guarda is not noted for its good restaurants, but this modest establishment in the old quarter is one of the few exceptions. It features hearty regional fare and a different type of bacalhau daily. ⊠ *Largo de São Vicente 2,* ☎ *271/211454. AE, MC, V. Closed Sat.*

$ ✕🏨 **Hotel Turismo.** Since it opened in 1940 in a stately, country-style
★ manor house, the Turismo has been Guarda's leading hotel. The extensive use of wood and leather in the bar and lounges lends a comfortable, clubby atmosphere to the place. Bedrooms are adequate in size and furnished in traditional style. The restaurant serves the best food in town in a quiet, refined ambience. ⊠ *Praça do Município, 6300,* ☎ *271/223366,* ℻ *271/223399. 100 rooms, 2 suites. Restaurant, bar, pool. AE, DC, MC, V.*

$ 🏨 **Filipe.** This residencial offers plain but comfortable rooms and not a lot else. In an under-equipped town like Guarda it's a good choice if you don't plan to stay long and are looking for something inexpensive. ⊠ *Rua Vasco da Gama 9, 6300,* ☎ *271/223659,* ℻ *271/221402. 30 rooms. AE, DC, MC, V.*

COIMBRA AND THE BEIRAS A TO Z

Arriving and Departing

By Airplane

There are some international flights into Oporto (to the north); Lisbon, however, is the preferred choice for international air travelers. It's 160 km (99 mi) northeast from the Lisbon airport to Coimbra via the A1 highway.

By Bus

Rede Nacional de Expressos (☎ 21/354–5775 in Lisbon) provides comfortable bus service between Lisbon, Oporto, and Coimbra, and to other parts of the Beiras. International as well as regional services are available at the Rodoviário da Beira Litoral bus station in **Coimbra** (⊠ Av. Fernão de Magalhães, ☎ 239/855270), and at the Rodoviário da Beira Interior stations in **Castelo Branco** (⊠ Rodrigo Rebelo 3, ☎ 272/340120) and **Covilhã** (⊠ Central de Camionagem, ☎ 275/334914).

By Car

Although you can zip from Lisbon to Coimbra on the A1 toll highway in less than two hours or drive from Oporto to Coimbra in under an hour, smaller roads provide a much richer and more varied travel experience. The eastern part of the Beiras is readily accessible from Spain. It's 90 km (56 mi) on N620 from Salamanca and 320 km (199 mi) from Madrid to the border crossing at Vilar Formoso.

By Train

Coimbra, Luso, Guarda, Ovar, and Aveiro are on the main Lisbon–Oporto and Lisbon–Paris lines. Two trains arrive from and depart for Paris daily. There are also regular train services linking the principal cities in the Beiras with Madrid, Lisbon, and Oporto. In summer a daily car-train operates between Paris and Lisbon. There are three stations in Coimbra: Coimbra A (Estação Nova), along the Mondego River, a five-minute walk from the center of town (for domestic routes), Coimbra Parque (also for domestic routes), and Coimbra B (Estação Velha), 5 km (3 mi) west. International trains and trains from Lisbon and Oporto arrive at Coimbra B, where there's a free shuttle to Coimbra A. There are also bus links between stations. For information call ☎ 239/834998. Schedules for all trains are posted at all three stations.

Getting Around

By Bus

For those who choose not to drive, an extensive bus network provides the next best way of getting around. Vehicles of various vintages can take you to almost any destination, and unlike train stations, which are often some distance from the town center, bus depots are centrally located. Rural buses, often packed with people going to and from regional markets, provide a wonderful microcosm of Portuguese life. Regional and local bus schedules are posted at the terminals. Information may also be obtained at local tourist offices. Although this is a great way to travel and get close to the local people, it does require a great deal of time and patience.

By Car

The Beiras, with their many remote villages, are particularly suited to exploration by car. Distances between major points are short; there are no intimidating cities to negotiate; and except for the coastal strip in July and August, traffic is light. Roads in general are quite good and destinations well marked; however, parking is a problem in the larger towns.

Although it is possible to whiz through the region in a few hours on the Lisbon–Oporto highway or the IP5 that links Aveiro with Vilar Formoso at the Spanish frontier, resist the temptation. The heart and soul of the Beiras are to be found along the many miles of those squiggly little lines lacing the road map of Portugal.

By Train

Although the major destinations in this chapter are linked by rail, service to most towns, with the exception of Coimbra, is infrequent. The equipment on the Beira line, which connects Lisbon with Guarda and the Serra da Estrela, has been upgraded.

Using Coimbra as a hub, there are three main rail lines serving the Beiras. Line 110, the Beira Alta line, goes northeast to Luso, Viseu, Celorico da Beira, and Guarda. Line 100 extends south through the Ribatejo to intersect with Line 130, the Beira Baixa line, which runs from Lisbon northeast through Castelo Branco and Fundão to Covilhã, the gateway to the Serra da Estrela. Going north from Coimbra, Line 100 serves Curia, Aveiro, and Ovar and continues north to Oporto and Braga.

Contacts and Resources

Car Rental

If you don't get a car from one of the numerous agencies in Lisbon, try **Hertz,** which has offices in **Coimbra** (⊠ Rua Padre Estevão Cabral, Loja 6, ☎ 239/834750) and **Viseu** (⊠ Rua da Paz 21, ☎ 232/421846).

Avis also has offices in **Coimbra** (✉ Coimbra A railway station, ☎ 239/834786) and **Viseu** (✉ Hotel Grão Vasco, Rua Gaspar Barreiros, ☎ 232/435750) as well as in **Aveiro** (✉ Av. Dr. Lourenço Peixinho 181–B, ☎ 234/371041).

Emergencies

General: The national emergency number is 112. **Hospitals:** Hospitals with *urgências* (emergency rooms) are in **Castelo Branco** (✉ Hospital Amato Lusitano, Av. Pedro A. Cabral, ☎ 272/322133), **Coimbra** (✉ Hospital da Universidade de Coimbra, Praça Prof. Mota Pinto, ☎ 239/400400), **Figueira da Foz** (✉ Hospital Distrital da Figueira da Foz, Gala, ☎ 233/402000), and **Guarda** (✉ Hospital Sousa Martins, Av. Reinha Dona Amalia, ☎ 271/222133). **Pharmacies:** In all sizable towns, pharmacies operate on a rotating system for staying open after normal closing hours, including weekends and holidays. Consult a local newspaper or the notice posted on the door of every pharmacy.

Guided Tours

There are very few regularly scheduled guided tours originating in the Beiras. The **Departamento Cultural** (Cultural Department) in Coimbra's town hall organizes excellent one-day bus excursions to areas around Coimbra, but they take place once a month only. If you can catch one of these, the experience could be worthwhile. The tours usually include a rewarding introduction to regional home cooking. The Coimbra town hall tourist offices (☎ 239/832591 and 239/833202) can supply details. Other than that, the only regular tours of the Beiras originate either in Lisbon or in Oporto. For further information contact a travel agency.

Telephones and Mail

The central post office in Coimbra, **CTT Estação Central** (✉ Av. Fernão de Magalhães 223), is adjacent to the train station and is the center for *poste restante* (general delivery). Most other towns have just one central post office, where poste restante is received. For telephone directory assistance, dial 118; operators often speak English.

Travel Agency

In Coimbra, a useful agency is **Abreu** (✉ Rua da Sota 2, ☎ 239/855520).

Visitor Information

The regional tourist offices for Coimbra and the surrounding area are the **Região de Turismo do Centro** (✉ Largo da Portagem, Coimbra 3000, ☎ 239/833019) and its branch office in Figueira da Foz (✉ Praceta Dr. Marcos Viana, Av. 25 de Abril, 3080, ☎ 233/428895).

Within this region there are local tourist offices in **Arganil** (✉ Av. Forças Armadas, ☎ 235/204823), **Buarcos** (✉ Largo Tomas de Aquino, ☎ 233/433019), **Figueiró dos Vinhos** (✉ Av. Padre Diogo de Vasconcelos, ☎ 236/552178), **Lousã** (✉ Câmara Municipal, Rua D. João Santos, ☎ 239/990370), **Mira** (✉ Câmara Municipal, Praça da Republica, ☎ 231/480550), and **Penacova** (✉ Câmara Municipal, ☎ 239/470300).

For information about Aveiro and the Rota da Luz region, consult the **Região de Turismo da Rota da Luz** (✉ Rua João Mendonça 8, Aveiro 3800, ☎ 234/423680). The principal local tourist offices in this region are in **Águeda** (✉ Largo Dr. João Elísio Sucena, ☎ 234/601412), **Costa Nova** (✉ Av. José Estevão, ☎ 234/369560), **Ílhavo** (✉ Praça do Município, ☎ 234/325911), **Ovar** (✉ Edifício da Câmara, Rua Elias Garcia, ☎ 256/572215), and **Torreira** (✉ Av. Hintze Ribeiro, ☎ 234/838250).

The regional tourist office for the Dão-Lafões area is the **Região de Turismo de Dão-Lafões** (⊠ Av. Gulbenkian, Viseu 3500, ☎ 232/420950). Local tourist offices are in **Caramulo** (⊠ Estrada Principal do Caramulo, ☎ 232/861437), **Nelas** (⊠ Largo Prof. Veiga Simão, ☎ 232/944348), and **São Pedro do Sul** (⊠ Largo dos Correios, ☎ 232/711320).

The Serra da Estrela district is represented by the **Região de Turismo da Serra da Estrela** (⊠ Frei Heitor Pinto, Covilhã 6200, ☎ 275/319569). There are local tourist offices in **Belmonte** (⊠ Praça da Republica, ☎ 275/911488), **Castelo Branco** (⊠ Câmara Municipal, ☎ 272/330339), **Fundão** (⊠ Av. da Liberdade, ☎ 275/752770), **Gouveia** (⊠ Av. dos Bombeiros Voluntários, ☎ 238/492185), **Guarda** (⊠ Câmara Municipal, Largo do Município, ☎ 271/221817), **Manteigas** (⊠ Rua Dr. José Carvalho 2, ☎ 275/981129), **Oliveira do Hospital** (⊠ Casa da Cultura Cesár de Oliveira, Rua do Colégio, ☎ 238/609269), **Penamacor** (⊠ Av. 25 de Abril, ☎ 277/394316), and **Seia** (⊠ Praça do Mercado, ☎ 238/312272).

7 OPORTO AND THE NORTH

The vibrant, baroque-flavored city of Oporto is famous for the wine that bears its name, but the rest of the north is undiscovered country for most visitors. The Minho region combines beaches along its Atlantic coast with a lush inland area dotted with ancient towns. New roads have penetrated the northeastern Trás-os-Montes region, whose dramatic landscape is rich in wildlife and populated by castles, fortresses, and medieval villages.

By Jules Brown

Updated by
Martha de la
Cal and Peter
Collis

THE REMOTE CORNERS OF NORTHERN PORTUGAL seem far away in Oporto, a trading center since pre-Roman times and still a vibrant, cosmopolitan city. The Moors never had the same strong foothold here that they did farther south, and the city remained largely unaffected by the great earthquake of 1755; as a result, Oporto shows off a baroque finery lacking in Lisbon. Its grandiose granite buildings were financed by the trade that made the city wealthy: wine from the upper valley of the Rio Douro (Douro River, or River of Gold) was transported to Oporto, from where it was then exported. You can follow that trail today by boat or by the beautiful Douro rail line.

Although it's not immediately apparent, northern Portugal *is* a popular holiday destination—although most summer visitors are Portuguese returning to their hometowns from the south or from abroad. The north can be beautiful, as it is in the valley of the Douro River and the deep, rural heartland of the Minho, the coastal province north of Oporto; it can also be rugged, as in the Terra Fria (Cold Land), the remote uplands of the northern Trás-os-Montes (Beyond the Mountains). From here come the mysterious, prehistoric *porcas* (stone pigs), reminders of early tribes who scratched a living from the cold earth. Some towns, such as Chaves (Keys), bear curious names and complicated histories. Festivals such as the Holy Week parade at Braga (complete with a torchlight procession through dark old-town streets) evoke an earlier time.

The Minho, which takes its name from the river forming Portugal's northern border with Spain, is bounded by the Atlantic in the west and cut by the long, peaceful Rios Lima and Cávado (Lima and Cávado rivers). The Minho coast is advertised as the Costa Verde (Green Coast), a sweeping stretch of beaches and fishing villages named for its lush, green landscape. Some locations have been appropriated as resorts by the Portuguese, but there are still plenty of places where you can find solitary dunes or splash in the brisk Atlantic away from crowds. Inland you can lose yourself in villages with country markets and fairs that have hardly changed for hundreds of years. You'll also see that little of the green countryside is wasted. Vines are trained on poles and in trees high above cultivated fields, forming a natural canopy, for this is *vinho verde* country. This refreshing "green wine"—so called because it is drunk young—is a true taste of the north, one to which you'll quickly become accustomed as you sit, glass in hand, by a river or the coast and reflect upon the day's events.

To the northeast there's adventure at hand, in the winding mountain roads and remote towns and villages of the Trás-os-Montes region. After centuries of isolation, the area is being accessed by new roads, but there's still great excitement in getting off the beaten track and taking rattling bus rides into the far northeastern corners of the country. The imposing castle towers and fortress walls of this frontier region are a great attraction, but—unusual in such a small country—it's often the journey itself that's the greatest prize: traveling past voluminous manmade lakes, through forested valleys rich in wildlife, across bare crags and moorlands, and finally down to coarse, stone villages where TV aerials sit oddly in almost medieval surroundings.

Pleasures and Pastimes

Beaches

Swimming in the Atlantic can be very cold, even at the height of summer, and beaches along the Costa Verde are notoriously windswept. More pleasant is river swimming in the small towns along the Lima and Minho rivers, although you should take local advice about currents and pollution before plunging in. Ponte de Lima has a particularly nice wide, sandy beach. Espinho, south of Oporto, and the main resorts to the north (Póvoa de Varzim and Ofir) are the best places for water-sports enthusiasts. Equipment rental is usually available at the beaches, or you can inquire about renting gear at local tourist offices.

Castles

There are towers, castles, and forts galore to explore in this part of the country, some of them so complete they provide a virtual medieval playground. The best include those at Guimarães, Monção, Bragança, and Chaves. Don't miss the region's two vast ornamental staircases at the pilgrimage sights of Lamego and Bom Jesus do Monte.

Dining

The cooking in Oporto is rich and heavy. It's typified by the city's favorite dish, *tripas á moda do Porto* (Oporto tripe), a heavy concoction made with beans, chicken, sausage, vegetables, and spices. Elsewhere in Portugal residents of Oporto are known as *tripeiros* (tripe eaters)—a nickname earned when the city was under siege during the Napoleonic Wars, and tripe was the only meat available. However, tripe doesn't dominate the menu in Oporto, and dishes tend to resemble those served in the Minho region. *Caldo verde* (literally "green soup") is ubiquitous; it's made of potato and shredded kale (cabbage) in a broth and is usually served with a slice or two of *chouriço* sausage. Fresh fish is found all the way up the coast, and every town has a local recipe for *bacalhau* (dried cod); in the Minho it's often cooked with potatoes, onions, and eggs. *Lampreias* (lampreys)—eel-like fish—are found in Minho rivers from February through April and are a specialty of Viana do Castelo and Monção. Pork is the meat most often seen on menus, appearing in inventive stews and sausages. For adventurous palates a typically *Minhoto* dish is *papas de sarrabulho*, a hearty stew of shredded pork in a flour-thickened, cumin-scented, pig's-blood soup. Roast *cabrito* (kid) is very popular, too.

In the mountains wonderful *truta* (trout) is available at any town or village close to a river. Trás-os-Montes menus are enlivened by hearty meat stews, which usually include parts of the pig you may wish had been left out (an ear or a trotter, for example). Sausages are a better bet, particularly *alheira* (a legacy of the Sephardic Jews, who devised this mock sausage of chicken and spices to fool religious authorities) or chouriço, the spicy, smoked variety. The other smoked specialty of the region is *presunto de Chaves*, a delicious smoked ham from Chaves. Most dishes will be served with *batatas* (potatoes) or *arroz* (rice), both fine examples of staples being raised to an art form. Spuds here, whether roasted, boiled, or fried, have an irresistibly nutty and sweet flavor. Rice is lightly sautéed with chopped garlic in olive oil before adding water, resulting in a side dish that could easily be devoured as a main course.

The wine available throughout the north is of very high quality. The Minho region's vinho verde is a light, young, slightly sparkling red or white wine. The taste is refreshing, both fruity and acid. Both reds and whites are served chilled (most people prefer the white), and vinho verde goes exceptionally well with fish and shellfish. Vinho verde made from the *Alvarinho* grape in the region of Monção is prized throughout the country. Port enjoys the most renown of the local wines (ask for *vinho do Porto*), but the Douro region, where port comes from, also produces some of Portugal's finest table wines. Other good regions for wine include the area around Chaves, particularly at Valpaços, which produces some excellent, full-bodied, and almost creamy reds.

On the whole, restaurants in Oporto and the north offer extremely good value, although the smaller ones often do not accept credit cards. Dress throughout the region is informal, and reservations are usually unnecessary. For price categories, *see* the chart under Dining *in* Smart Travel Tips A to Z.

Fishing

Inland, especially in the northeast, fishing is a traditional leisure activity. The best freshwater fishing is in the Lima and Minho rivers, where trout can be caught. Local tourist offices can assist with fishing licenses.

Lodging

Most of the lodgings in the Minho and Trás-os-Montes are very reasonably priced compared to their counterparts elsewhere in the country—perhaps a reflection of the previous lack of attention paid by tourists to these regions. The government-run group of *pousadas* (inns) offers a variety of settings in the north, from a 12th-century monastery in Guimarães to more rustic, hunting-lodge digs high on a hill in Bragança. In Oporto, however, matters are much the same as in Lisbon, and, if at all possible, you should reserve a room well in advance to avoid disappointment. The north also hosts some of the country's most famous festivals and markets, at which times available lodging quickly dries up; book well in advance if your visit coincides with a festival (☞ Festivals and Seasonal Events *in* Smart Travel Tips A to Z).

The Turismo no Espaço Rural (Manor House Tourism) network allows you to spend time at a variety of historic manor houses, country farms, and little village cottages scattered throughout the Minho. Most of these converted 17th- and 18th-century buildings are found in the lovely rural areas around Ponte de Lima, where the manor house organization **Turihab**—Associação de Turismo de Habitação (✉ Praça da República, ☎ 258/741672 ℻ 258/741444, 🐢)—has its headquarters and a central reservations office (☎ 258/741672, 🐢). For price categories, *see* the chart under Lodging *in* Smart Travel Tips A to Z.

Shopping

The north is an excellent region in which to shop for souvenirs, with a wide range of folk art and crafts available in many towns and villages. Oporto, of course, has the best selection of shops, but don't miss the smaller towns of the Minho, which often specialize in particular handicrafts; Vila do Conde, for example, is known for its lace. The region's weekly and monthly markets are also famous throughout Portugal for having the best local crafts at very reasonable prices.

Exploring Oporto and the North

The north of Portugal can be divided into three basic regions—Oporto and its immediate environs (the nearby coastal resorts and the Douro Valley), the evergreen Minho and Costa Verde to the north, and the somewhat remote and untamed Trás-os-Montes area to the east, a region still slightly short on tourist amenities yet long on spectacular scenery and superb country cooking.

Great Itineraries

Oporto is just 3½ hours north of Lisbon by highway or express train, so even a short trip to Portugal can include a night or two here. From Oporto, it's only another two hours through the Minho and along the Costa Verde coastline up to the Spanish border, or another three–four hours east to the less visited Trás-os-Montes and the eastern border with Spain. Traveling by car allows you the freedom to stop and start as inspiration strikes, although trains also have a compelling charm.

It takes only a day or two to experience the more urban pleasures of Oporto and its wine lodges and the nearby coastal resorts. Several more days would permit a visit to the history-rich towns of Braga or Guimarães or a trip through the lovely scenery of the Douro Valley. A full week would allow you to cover all of this and the peaceful inland towns and villages along the rivers Lima and Minho, or you could set off for the remote northeastern Trás-os-Montes and its fascinating towns of Bragança and Chaves. Two weeks would give you the opportunity to do the complete circuit and return sated on the riches of the north.

Numbers in the text correspond to numbers in the margin and on the North: Douro, Minho, and Trás-os-Montes map and the Oporto map.

IF YOU HAVE 3 DAYS

Devote the morning of your first day to ▣ **Oporto** ①–⑬, followed by an afternoon tour of the port-wine lodges in Vila Nova de Gaia, across the Douro River. Before turning in, spend some time enjoying the lively riverside cafés and restaurants. In the morning, drive north through the sandy coastal towns of **Vila do Conde** ⑭, **Póvoa de Varzim** ⑮, and **Ofir and Esposende** ⑯. After the bracing air, shopping to the sound of the waves, and a seafood lunch, head inland to the ancient Visigothic city of ▣ **Braga** ㉒, sometimes referred to as the religious capital of the country, with its profusion of churches and its sumptuous Easter celebrations. Overnight there or in the delightfully medieval ▣ **Guimarães** ㉔, which you should explore on day three. Worth a side trip from either town is the nearby, fascinating hilltop **Citânia de Briteiros** ㉓, site of an ancient Iron Age settlement.

Alternatively, you could spend your second two days savoring the pastoral pleasures of the Douro Valley. Follow the winding N108 road east from Oporto along the north bank of the river. Don't miss the view at Entre-os-Rios, where the Douro and Tâmega rivers converge. Head back up toward **Penafiel** ⑱, admiring the sculptural beauty of the terraced hillside vineyards; this region is known for its vinho verde and Romanesque churches, a legacy of the wine-making Benedictine monks. Stop here for some religion and a respite from the road and then move on to ▣ **Amarante** ⑲, one of the north's most picturesque towns, its halves joined by a narrow 18th-century bridge. It's worth overnighting here. On day three, wind your way southeast along N101, passing through Mesão Frio, to the Douro, where you can follow the river east to **Pêso da Régua** ⑳, heart of the port-wine country, and tour a wine cellar or two. Across the river and a bit farther south is **Lamego** ㉑; don't miss the town's most famous monument, the impressively baroque 18th-century pilgrimage shrine of Nossa Senhora dos Remédios. From either of these towns, it's not far to **Vila Real** ㉝, gateway to the remote and beautiful region of Trás-os-Montes. You could spend the night here and head east the next day, or return to Oporto.

IF YOU HAVE 5 DAYS

Spend a day and night in ▣ **Oporto** ①–⑬, then head inland and north. Take two days to explore ▣ **Braga** ㉒, **Citânia de Briteiros** ㉓, and ▣ **Guimarães** ㉔. On day four go west to **Barcelos** ㉕, folk-art center of the country; try to arrive on a Thursday, when the large weekly market is filled with purveyors of everything from live pigs to hand-painted pottery. Continue north to graceful ▣ **Viana do Castelo** ㉖, along the banks of the Lima River. Wander its narrow stone streets (with a stop at the municipal museum—a must for lovers of ceramics) and stay the night in the luxurious art deco pousada on a hill overlooking town or drive up along the Costa Verde to **Caminha** ㉗ or one of the other partially walled castle towns along the Spanish border: ▣ **Vila Nova de Cerveira** ㉘, **Valença do Minho** ㉙, and **Monção** ㉚.

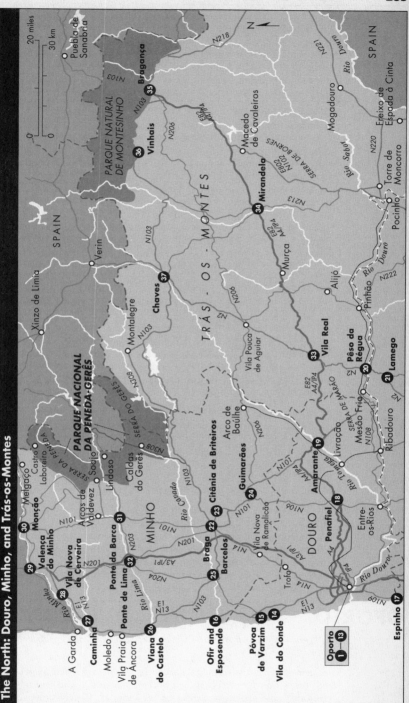

The North: Douro, Minho, and Trás-os-Montes

On day five, head to quaint Arcos de Valdevez and rent a rowboat for a couple of leisurely hours on the river, then continue on to two nearby towns with beautiful bridges, **Ponte da Barca** ㉛, with its 15th-century arched passageway, and **Ponte de Lima** ㉜, graced with a long, low Roman footbridge. If you're in Ponte de Lima on the second Monday of the month, you'll be able to visit the oldest market in the country. From here, set your sails back to Oporto or Lisbon, or on to Trás-os-Montes.

IF YOU HAVE 7 DAYS

Oporto ①–⑬ is the ideal first day and night for your explorations. On day two, head inland for **Penafiel** ⑱ (stop to admire the architecture of its granite mansions and to sample the local vinho verde) and ⌸ **Amarante** ⑲, where you can have dinner in the romantic, old part of town and spend the night. Next day, onward to ⌸ **Vila Real** ㉝, the capital and first sizable town in the Trás-os-Montes region. Rosé-wine lovers might want to visit the nearby Solar de Mateus, a baroque mansion open to the public; the building's facade adorns the widely exported Mateus wine label. On day four, head northeast to Murça and admire the town's Iron Age granite porca, the largest of what are believed to be many ancient fertility symbols dotting the region. Farther north is the attractive town of **Mirandela** ㉞; visit the 17th-century Palácio dos Tavoras, today used as the town hall. Stay on the IP4 and head into the Serra de Nogueira toward the northeastern corner of the country. Eventually you'll see the great castle at ⌸ **Bragança** ㉟ rising in the distance; plan on spending two nights here. On day five, visit the sights of the city, which dates from about 600 BC. Next day, head west along the N103, one of the most spectacular drives in the country. You'll pass through **Vinhais** ㊱ on the way to **Chaves** ㊲, originally settled as a Roman military base and still popular today for its thermal springs. From Chaves, you could head back toward Vila Real and on to a final night in Oporto.

Another alternative would be to stay on the N103 and continue west until reaching the lake and hydroelectric dam system along the Cávado River. The winding road allows for marvelous views and has several access points into the **Parque Nacional da Peneda-Gerês** where you could quite understandably choose to stay overnight (the São Bento Pousada overlooks the Caniçada dam) for a bit of hiking in the woods, or you could continue down the road to ⌸ **Braga** ㉒, spend the night, and then return to Oporto.

When to Tour Oporto and the North

It's best to visit the north in summer, when Oporto and the Costa Verde have a generally warm climate, but be prepared for drizzling rain at any time. Coastal temperatures in the north are a few degrees cooler than in the south. Inland, and especially in the northeastern mountains, it can be very hot in summer and cold, hard going in winter.

OPORTO ①

★ *321 km (199 mi) north of Lisbon, 255 km (158 mi) southwest of Bragança.*

Industrious Oporto—Portugal's second city, with a population of a half million—considers itself the capital of the north and, more contentiously, the economic center of the country. Locals support this claim by quoting a typically down-to-earth maxim: "Coimbra sings, Braga prays, Lisbon shows off, and Oporto works." Certainly wherever you look, there's evidence of a city in robust financial health. Massive new business developments on the outskirts give way to a fashionable commercial area in the heart of town; shops and restaurants bustle with big-spending locals; and the city's buildings, churches, and monuments—both old and new—impress with their solid construction. There's poverty here, of course, primarily down by the river in the ragged older areas, parts of which are positively medieval. But in the shopping centers, the stately stock exchange building, and the affluent port-wine industry, Oporto oozes confidence.

This emphasis on worth rather than beauty has created a solid city rather than a graceful one. The public buildings tend to be sober. Gray and ocher tones often dominate facades. But the city abounds in fine buildings and interesting perspectives. It's quite impressive at first sight if you approach from the south, and its glorious location on a steep hillside above the Douro River affords exhilarating views.

The river has influenced the city's development since pre-Roman times, when the town of Cale on the left bank prospered sufficiently to support a trading port, called Portus, on the site of today's city. Under the Romans this twin town of Portus-Cale became a thriving commercial center, and it continued to be successful despite the later ravages of Moorish occupation and Christian reconquest. Given the outward-looking nature of its inhabitants, it's fitting that Henry the Navigator—the great explorer king—was born here at the end of the 14th century.

The importance of the river trade to the city is reflected in its current name, whose use began in early medieval times. Porto, as the city is called in Portuguese, means simply "port," and over the centuries the city has traded widely in fish, salt, and wine. As the result of an agreement with England in 1703, the region's most notable product—wine, made from the grapes of the Douro's vineyards—found a new market and was shipped out of the city in ever-increasing quantities. The port-wine trade is still big business, based just over the river from the city, in the suburb of Vila Nova de Gaia (site of the Roman town of Cale).

Exploring Oporto

❶ You'll do best to tour Oporto on foot, taking buses or taxis to the few outlying attractions. The **Avenida dos Aliados** is an imposing, sloping boulevard that lies at the commercial heart of the city and points toward the river. Providing some welcome open space in Oporto's busy center, it is planted with bright flower beds and lined with grand buildings, including the broad **Câmara Municipal** (Town Hall), which stands at the top of the avenue. A tall bell tower sprouts from the roof of this palacelike, early 20th-century building, inside of which an impressive Portuguese wall tapestry is displayed. At the other end of the avenue, **Praça da Liberdade** is the hub from which Oporto radiates. Two statues adorn the square: a cast of Dom Pedro IV sitting on a horse and an unusual, modern statue of the great 19th-century Portuguese poet and novelist Almeida Garrett. The odd, oval-shape **Igreja dos Clérigos** (Clergy Church) is visible from Praça da Liberdade if you peer down Rua dos Clérigos.

| NEED A BREAK? | Oporto's old-style coffeehouses once rivaled Lisbon's in opulence and literary legend. Most, such as the famed **Café Imperial,** in Praça da Liberdade, have adapted to modern fast-food styles. Happily, two notable ones have survived and are perfect places to sit and sip a *cimbalino* (espresso) and imbibe Oporto's past as you watch the city go about its business. The splendidly ornate **Majestic Café** (✉ Rua de Santa Catarina 112) is on a busy pedestrian shopping street, a short walk from Avenida dos Aliados. Just around the corner is the attractively restored **Confeitaria do Bolhão** (✉ Rua Formosa 339), another evocative reminder of Oporto's past. |

Oporto (Porto)

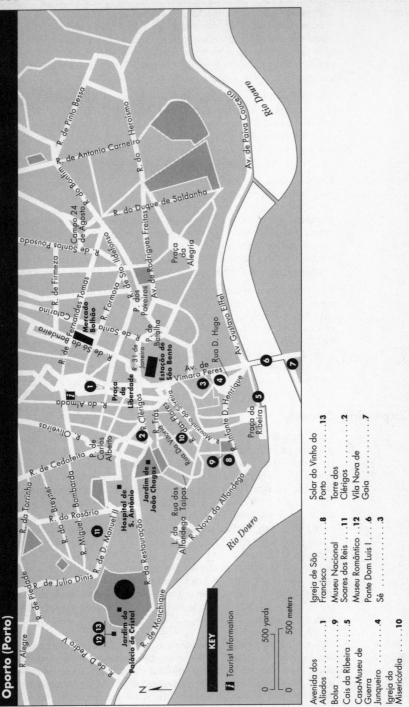

KEY

i Tourist Information

0   500 yards

0   500 meters

Avenida dos
Aliados **1**

Bolsa **9**

Cais da Ribeira . . .**5**

Casa-Museu de
Guerra
Junqueiro **4**

Igreja da
Misericórdia **10**

Igreja de São
Francisco **8**

Museu Nacional
Soares dos Reis . . .**11**

Museu Romântico . .**12**

Ponte Dom Luis I . . .**6**

Sé **3**

Solar do Vinho do
Porto **13**

Torre dos
Clérigos **2**

Vila Nova de
Gaia **7**

★ ⊙ ❷ The **Torre dos Clérigos,** the Tower of Clergy Church, is an immediately recognizable finger on the Oporto skyline. Designed by Italian architect Nicolau Nasoni and begun in 1754, it consists of six stories that leap to a height of 249 ft, making it one of the tallest towers in the country. There are 225 steep stone steps to the belfry, and the very considerable effort required to climb them is rewarded by stunning views of Old Town, the river, and beyond to the mouth of the Douro. The church itself, also built by Nasoni, predates the tower and is an elaborate example of Italianate baroque architecture. ⊠ *Rua dos Clérigos,* ☎ *22/200–1729.* ☜ *Tower 200$00; church free.* ⊙ *Tower daily 10–noon and 2–5; church Mon.–Tues. and Thurs.–Sat. 10–noon and 2–5, Sun. 10–1.*

Use the pedestrian underpass from the Praça da Liberdade to cross to the **Estação de São Bento,** Oporto's central railroad station; the main hall is decorated with enormous *azulejos* (tiles) depicting the history of Portuguese transportation. From the steps of the train station, you can look across to the city's cathedral.

❸ Originally constructed in the 12th century by the parents of Afonso Henriques (the first king of Portugal), Oporto's granite **Sé** (Cathedral) has been rebuilt twice: first in the late 13th century and again in the 18th century, when the architect of the Torre dos Clérigos, Nasoni, was among those commissioned to work on its expansion. Despite these renovations, it remains a severe, fortresslike structure, perched on a sweeping terrace over Old Town, which is a few minutes' walk to the south. It's an uncompromising testament to the city's medieval wealth and power. Sheer size apart, the cathedral's interior is unusually disappointing, and only when you enter the two-story 14th-century **cloisters** (☜ 250$00) does the building come to life. Decorated with gleaming azulejos, a staircase added by Nasoni leads to the second level and into a magnificent, richly furnished chapter house, from which there are fine views through narrow windows. Nasoni also designed the **Paço dos Arcebispos** (Archbishops' Palace), behind the cathedral, although since it was converted to offices, visitors can see no farther than the impressive 197-ft-long facade. ⊠ *Terreiro da Sé,* ☎ *22/205–3644.* ☜ *Free.* ⊙ *Mon.–Sat. 9–12:30 and 2:30–6, Sun. and holidays 2:30–6.*

❹ **Casa-Museu de Guerra Junqueiro** (Guerra Junqueiro House and Museum), another 18th-century building attributed to Oporto's favorite architect, Nasoni, lies on Rua de Dom Hugo, a narrow street that curves around the eastern side of the cathedral. This white mansion was home to the poet Guerra Junqueiro (1850–1923). However, the short tour of the elegant interior and enviable collection of furniture, sculpture, paintings, and silver is less than enlightening if you don't speak Portuguese. ⊠ *Rua de Dom Hugo 32,* ☎ *22/205–3644.* ☜ *150$00, free weekends.* ⊙ *Tues.–Sat. 10–12:30 and 2–5:30, Sun. 2–5.*

Rua de Dom Hugo leads you by way of steep steps that cut through surviving sections of the medieval city walls into a web of tangled alleys, leaning buildings, and down-at-the-heel street markets. This decaying neighborhood has missed out on the city's economic progress, however colorful the timeworn buildings with their long rows of balconies may appear. The stepped alleys all eventually emerge at the river-
★ ❺ front quayside of the Ribeira District. Along the **Cais da Ribeira** (Ribeira Pier) there are a small daily market and a string of excellent fish restaurants and *tascas* (taverns) built into the street-level arcade of the old buildings (☞ Dining, *below*). In the Praça da Ribeira, people sit and chat around an odd, modern, cubelike sculpture; farther on, steps lead up to a raised walkway, backed by tall houses, that runs above the river. The pier also provides the easiest access to the lower level of the middle bridge across the Douro.

⑥ The two-tier **Ponte Dom Luís I** (Dom Luís I Bridge) was built in 1886 and leads directly to the suburb of Vila Nova de Gaia. Its real glory, however, is not its practical calling but the nearly magical view it affords of downtown Oporto. A jumble of red-tile roofs on pastel-color buildings mixes with gray-and-white Gothic and baroque church towers, and all is reflected in the majestic Douro; if the sun is shining just right, everything appears to be washed in gold.

★ **⑦** **Vila Nova de Gaia,** across the Douro River from central Oporto, has been the headquarters of the port-wine trade since the late 17th century, when import bans on French wine led British merchants to look for alternative sources. By the 18th century, the British had established companies and a regulatory association at Oporto to control the quality of the wine they were importing from Portugal. The wine was transported from vineyards on the upper Douro to port-wine "lodges" (warehouses) at Vila Nova de Gaia, where it was allowed to mature before being exported. Very little has changed in the relationship between Oporto and the Douro since those days, as wine is still transported to the city, matured in the warehouses, and bottled. However, instead of traveling down the river on traditional *barcos rabelos* (flat-bottomed boats), the wine is now carried by truck. A couple of the boats are moored at the quayside on the Vila Nova de Gaia side.

There are more than 25 companies with *adegas* (port-wine lodges) in Vila Nova de Gaia (many still foreign-owned), from such well-known names as Sandeman, Croft, and Cockburn to lesser-known Portuguese firms, such as Ramos Pinto and Borges. All are signposted within a few minutes' walk of each other, and their names are displayed in huge white letters across their roofs. Each company offers free guided tours of its facility and the fascinating process of port-wine making and bottling—tours that always end with a tasting of one or two wines and an opportunity to buy bottles from the company store. Children are usually welcome and are often fascinated by the huge warehouses and all sorts of interesting machinery. The major lodges are open weekdays 9–12:30 and 2–7, Saturday 9–12:30, from June though September; the rest of the year, tours end at 5 and are conducted only on weekdays. Tours begin regularly, usually when enough visitors are assembled. The tourist office at Vila Nova de Gaia (☞ Visitor Information *in* Oporto and the North A to Z, *below*) offers a small map of the main lodges and can advise you on hours of the smaller operations.

Vila Nova de Gaia isn't solely devoted to the port-wine trade. Combine a tour of the wine lodges with a visit to the **Casa-Museu de Teixeira Lopes,** the home of the sculptor António Teixeira Lopes (1866–1942), who was born here. It contains some excellent sculpture as well as a varied collection of paintings by Teixeira Lopes's contemporaries. The collection of books, coins, and ceramics is also interesting. ⊠ *Rua Teixeira Lopes 32,* ☎ *22/370–2095.* ☞ *Free.* ⊙ *Oct.–May, Tues.–Sat. 9:30–12:30 and 2–5:30; June–Sept., Tues.–Sat. 9:30–12:30 and 2–5:30, Sun. 1–7.*

From Vila Nova de Gaia you can cross back to the city, using the narrow footway on the upper level of the Dom Luís I Bridge, which puts you on Avenida de Vimara Peres, close to the cathedral. But at 200 ft above the river and with traffic thundering past, this is not a crossing for the faint of heart or for those who have tasted of the port "not wisely but too well." To continue the city tour, retrace your path to the Cais da Ribeira.

Away from the water, Rua do Infante Dom Henrique, which used to be known as Rua dos Ingleses (English Street), contains shipping offices and warehouses. Where it meets Rua de São João stands the granite **Feitoria Inglêsa** (Factory House of the British Association), built at the end of the 18th century as the headquarters of the Port Wine Shippers' Association. (It's not open to the public.)

A statue of Prince Henry stands in the nearby Praça do Infante Dom Henrique, which also holds a remarkable church. The late-14th-century **Igreja de São Francisco** (Church of St. Francis) may be an undistinguished Gothic building on the outside, but it has an astounding interior. The profusion of gilded carving was added in the mid-18th century and swarms over every inch of the building—up the pillars, over the altar, and across the ceiling. An adjacent museum houses valuable furnishings from the Franciscan monastery that once stood here. ⊠ *Rua do Infante Dom Henrique,* ☏ 22/200–6493. 🎫 *500$00.* ⊘ *Sept.–June, Tues.–Sat. 9–noon and 2–5; July–Aug., daily 9–5.*

The **Bolsa,** Oporto's 19th-century, neoclassical stock exchange, is behind the Igreja de São Francisco and takes up much of the site of the old Franciscan monastery. Guided tours (the only way to see the interior) stroll around the huge, showy edifice, much of it in questionable taste. The Arab-style ballroom, in particular, has critics as numerous as the glowing adjectives with which the guides describe it. ⊠ *Rua Ferreira Borges,* ☏ 22/339–9000. 🎫 *Guided tours 800$00.* ⊘ *Apr.–Oct., daily 9–7; Nov.–Mar., 9–12:30 and 2–5:30.*

North of the stock exchange, at Largo de São Domingos, Rua das Flores—a street known for its silversmiths and striking wrought-iron balconies—leads toward São Bento station. Although it dates from the 16th century, the **Igreja da Misericórdia** (Mercy Church) was largely remodeled two centuries later by Nicolau Nasoni. Call at the adjacent offices, and you will be shown the *Fons Vitae* (Fountain of Life), considered one of the country's finest paintings. It's an anonymous Renaissance work of brilliant colors, showing the founder of the church, Dom Manuel I, his queen, and their eight children kneeling before a crucified Christ. ⊠ *Rua das Flores,* ☏ 22/200–8371. 🎫 *Church free, Fons Vitae 300$00.* ⊘ *Weekdays 9–12:30 and 2–5:30.*

Rua das Taipas will lead you to the Jardim João Chagas (João Chagas Gardens), where the Palácio da Justiça (Palace of Justice) towers on your left. Facing the corner of the gardens is the 18th-century Hospital de Santo António. A former royal palace west of the hospital is now the **Museu Nacional Soares dos Reis,** a museum named for the 19th-century Portuguese sculptor whose works are contained within. The large art collection includes several Portuguese primitive works of the 16th century as well as superb collections of silver, ceramics, glassware, and costumes. ⊠ *Rua de Dom Manuel II,* ☏ 22/339–3770. 🎫 *350$00, free Sun.* ⊘ *Tues. 2–6, Wed.–Sun. 10–12:30 and 2–6.*

Follow Rua de Dom Manuel II to the Jardim do Palácio de Cristal (Crystal Palace Gardens), named for a 19th-century palace that once stood here—it was replaced in the 1950s by an enormous domed pavilion used for sports and exhibitions. On the far side of the Crystal Palace Gardens is the **Museu Romântico** (Romantic Museum), featuring period furniture in a charming 19th-century country house called the Quinta da Macierinha. ⊠ *Rua de Entre Quintas 220,* ☏ 22/609–1131 or 22/606–6207 for guided tours. 🎫 *150$00, free weekends.* ⊘ *Tues.–Sat. 10–12:30 and 2–5:30, Sun. 2–6.*

The ground floor of the Quinta da Macierinha is of special interest, for here the **Solar do Vinho do Porto** (Port Wine Institute) offers relaxed tastings of Oporto's famous wine in much the same fashion as its counterpart in Lisbon. However, Oporto's Solar has a much friendlier reputation, and in addition, the wine has only had to travel across the river before being served. Tasting prices vary but start at 100$00 per glass. ⊠ *Rua de Entre Quintas 220,* ☎ *22/609–4749.* ⊘ *Mon.–Sat. 2–midnight.*

This is a fine place to end your tour of the city, and when it's time to return downtown, either catch Bus 78 (which runs along Rua de Dom Manuel II, past the Soares dos Reis Museum, to Praça da Liberdade) or jump into a taxi.

OFF THE
BEATEN PATH

MUSEU DE ARTE CONTEMPORÂNEA - FUNDAÇÃO DE SERRALVES – The Serralves Foundation Museum of Contemporary Art is in western Oporto, beyond the range of any walking tour. The museum, which occupies the Serralves Mansion, set in spacious and pleasant gardens, displays the work of contemporary Portuguese painters, sculptors, and designers. Exhibitions change constantly, and the museum sometimes closes for two weeks at a time for rehanging. Check with the tourist office for the latest information. You can take either a taxi or Bus 3, 19, 21, 35, or 78. The journey takes about 30 minutes from the town center. ⊠ *Rua de Serralves 977,* ☎ *22/618–0057.* ⊠ *800$00.* ⊘ *Tues.–Sun. 10–7.*

Dining

$$$ ✕ **O Escondidinho.** High-quality food from the Douro region and a range of French-influenced dishes are served in this restaurant on a central shopping street. The surroundings are engaging, and a tiled entrance announces a country-house decor. Steak is prepared no less than six ways (try the woodsy-smoky version with truffles), and the sole is always deliciously fresh. The *pudim flan* (egg custard) is outstanding. ⊠ *Rua dos Passos Manuel 144,* ☎ *22/200–1079. Reservations essential. AE, DC, MC, V. Closed Sun.*

$$$
★ ✕ **Portucale.** At the top of the modern building that houses the hotel Albergaria Miradouro, the Portucale is known equally for the excellence of its food and the citywide views from its windows. Dishes are rich, making imaginative use of local ingredients such as tripe and game, and mountain-style roast cabrito is sometimes served. After dinner, sip some port from the impressive selection. ⊠ *Rua da Alegria 598,* ☎ *22/537–0717. Reservations essential. AE, DC, MC, V.*

$$ ✕ **Bule.** This is an especially good choice for a summer lunch if the weather is good. In addition to offering some of the best cooking in town, it has a pretty little outside terrace for umbrella-shaded dining. The inside dining room is spacious and comfortable, the service impeccable. The *pato assado* (roast duck), a succulent house specialty, is definitely worth considering, as is the *bacalhau à lagareiro* (salt cod baked with onions and garlic in olive oil). ⊠ *Rua de Timor 128,* ☎ *22/618–8777. AE, DC, MC, V. Closed Sun. and 1st 2 wks Aug.*

$$ ✕ **Bull and Bear.** If you are hooked on the basic flavors of northern Portuguese cooking but could do with a lighter touch to go with them, this comfortable, modern restaurant, set in the Oporto stock exchange building, has the answer. Chef and owner Miguel Castro Silva adds French and Italian touches to traditional Portuguese recipes and comes up with unusual and very successful combinations like *ameijoas com feijão manteiga* (clams with butter beans) and *linguado com molho de amêndoa* (sole with almond sauce). ⊠ *Av. da Boavista 3431,* ☎ *22/610–7669. AE, DC, MC, V. Closed Sun. No lunch Sat.*

$$ ✕ **Casa Aleixo.** Surprisingly, given the high quality of its food and service, this restaurant remains almost unknown to out-of-towners. The locals know better, and it's a popular place with city gourmets. The decor and furnishings are comfortable, if unremarkable; the service excellent. The *cabrito assado no forno* (roast kid) is one of the best you'll find in the north, but it's served only on Friday at dinner. The *polvo*

com arroz de polvo (octopus with rice) is a mouth-watering treatment of a traditional Oporto dish. The wine list is exceptionally good and varied. ⊠ *Rua da Estação 216,* ☎ *22/537–0462. AE, MC, V. Closed Sun. and 2 wks in Aug.*

$$ ✕ **Casa Filha da Mãe Preta.** One of the best known of Oporto's riverside restaurants, this place is in the row of old buildings that line the Cais da Ribeira. The pleasant first-floor dining room is decorated with azulejos and has arched windows that look across the river to the port-wine lodges of Vila Nova de Gaia. You'll need to reserve (or get there early or late) to get a window table. Stick with such simple fish specialties as *lulas grelhadas* (grilled squid) or *pez espada* (grilled blade fish). Most of the grilled dishes come with an ample serving of rice; unless you're going to share the dish with someone else, ask for a *meio dose* (half serving). ⊠ *Cais da Ribeira 39–40,* ☎ *22/208–6066. AE, DC, MC, V. Closed Sun.*

$$ ✕ **O Macedo.** This agreeable, friendly little restaurant is housed in an attractively restored old building looking over the Douro estuary a 10-minute drive from the center of town. The menu has a tempting selection of meat and fish dishes that provides a change from the more traditional Oporto fare found in many restaurants. Try the *goraz assado no forno* (oven-baked sea bream), for instance, or the *bife de fillet mignon com natas à Macedo* (house-style filet mignon with cream sauce). The wine list is exceptionally good. ⊠ *Rua do Passeio Alegre 552,* ☎ *22/617–0166. AE, MC, V. Closed Sun. and 2 wks in Aug.*

$$ ✕ **O Tripeiro.** This is just the place to try Oporto-style tripe, which is nearly always on the menu in one form or another. In case you don't appreciate Oporto's favorite food, the spacious restaurant is also good for most meat dishes, and there are several bacalhau specialties, too. Along with the typically Portuguese food comes typically Portuguese decor: wooden ceiling beams, whitewashed walls, and potted plants throughout. ⊠ *Rua de Passos Manuel 195,* ☎ *22/200–5886. AE, DC, MC, V. Closed Sun.*

$ ✕ **Casa Nanda.** This restaurant is the epitome of what the Portuguese call a tasca, a small, homely, tavern-cum-restaurant offering plain home cooking without frills. The difference here is that the cook and co-owner Fernanda Maria learned her skills from a legendary figure in the history of Oporto restaurants, a tasca keeper of great fame who was popularly known as "Mamuda" because of her impressive bosom. The experience shows. This is a great place to try a *cozido à Portuguesa* (a monumental dish of boiled meats and vegetables), but phone first to see if it is available that day. ⊠ *Rua Alegria 394,* ☎ *22/537–0575. No credit cards. Closed Sun. and 2 wks in July.*

$ ✕ **O Castiço da Sé.** Above a bar on a steep Old Town street close to the cathedral, this tiny upstairs dining room does a roaring lunchtime trade. Make a stab at the indecipherable handwritten menu, and you'll be rewarded with huge portions of grilled and stewed meat and fish, which come with salad and vegetables. The clientele is mostly local businesspeople, who know a bargain when they see one. The stone walls, beams, and lanterns provide atmosphere, while the fine food is dispensed with little ceremony. Be prepared to wait in line at lunchtime. ⊠ *Rua da Bainharia 18,* ☎ *no phone. No credit cards.*

$ ✕ **Chez Lapin.** Another favorite place on the Cais da Ribeira, this restaurant occupies two floors of an old building overlooking the river and has an attractive outside terrace. The air-conditioned dining rooms are small, and the folksy decor stops just short of being overpowering, but the food is excellent. The menu is made up of traditional but sometimes uncommon Oporto dishes like *bacalhau e polvo assado no forno* (salt cod and octopus baked in the oven) and *caldeirada de peixe* (fish stew), all served in generous portions. The restaurant also owns five traditional rabelo riverboats it rents out for river trips from the quay in front of the restaurant. ⊠ *Rua Canastreiros 48,* ☎ *22/200–6418. Reservations essential. AE, DC, MC, V.*

$ ✕ **Majestic Café.** One of Oporto's grand old coffeehouses, the turn-
★ of-the-century-style Majestic doubles as a reasonably priced grill-restaurant. Sit amid the sculpted wood, carved nymphs, and mirrors and choose from a fair list of steaks, burgers, and omelets, or just take coffee and cake or a drink. There's a delightful enclosed patio that's the perfect place to dine on a summer's eve; if you come on Friday or Saturday night, your meal will be accompanied by live piano music. There's also an art gallery downstairs. ⊠ *Rua de Santa Catarina 112,* ☎ *22/200–3887. AE, MC, V. Closed Sun.*

$ ✕ **Pedro dos Frangos.** In an area full of budget restaurants, the popular Pedro dos Frangos stands out for the quality of its barbecued chicken, which grills temptingly in the window. If you're in a hurry, sit at the bar, although it's more comfortable upstairs in the plain dining room, where ordering a *meia frango* gets you a sublime half chicken and fries. Order a side of the delicious *esparregado* (greens, usually spinach or turnip tops, sautéed with olive oil and garlic, then pureed), and you'll have plenty of energy to go out and see the rest of the city. ⊠ *Rua do Bonjardim 219–223,* ☎ *22/200–8522. No credit cards. Closed Tues.*

$ ✕ **Traçadinho.** A long bar invites you to take an aperitif before descending to the vaulted dining room in this popular traditional restaurant. The *bacalhau à Traçadinho* (baked salt cod with onions and tomatoes) is legendary, as is the cozido à Portuguesa. ⊠ *Rua da Madeira 186,* ☎ *22/200–5624. No credit cards. Closed Sun.*

Lodging

$$$$ 🏨 **Infante de Sagres.** Oporto's first luxury hotel built after World
★ War II is named after the city's most famous son, Prince Henry the Navigator, and does indeed provide formal, princely service. Visiting royalty have been happy to stay here, and you'll be pleased by its very central location, close to Avenida dos Aliados. Public areas are very impressively decked out, in a style closer to the 1890s than the 1990s, with a lot of intricately carved wood. Guest rooms have a more 20th-century character; all are supremely comfortable and have marble bathrooms. ⊠ *Praça D. Filipa de Lencastre 62, 4000,* ☎ *22/200–8101,* FAX *22/205–4937. 83 rooms. Restaurant, bar. AE, DC, MC, V.*

$$$$ 🏨 **Ipanema Park.** This elegant tower of a hotel is a 15-minute taxi ride west from the center of town, so it's not the most convenient sightseeing base. What it does have is an uncluttered position with views overlooking the Douro estuary and the Atlantic, plus a formidable array of facilities. The rooms are equipped with every modern convenience, and although the decor doesn't tell you you're in Portugal, the views do. ⊠ *Rua de Serralves 124, 4150-702,* ☎ *22/610–4174,* FAX *22/610–2809. 281 rooms. Restaurant, bar, 1 outdoor pool and 1 indoor pool, 2 tennis courts, hot tub, sauna, health club. AE, DC, MC, V.* ☜).

$$$ 🏨 **Boa-Vista.** This little hotel overlooks the Douro estuary and the sea a 10- to 15-minute taxi ride or 20-minute bus ride west from the center of town. It's not ideal for touring the city, but its considerable charm compensates for the off-center location. The handsome mid-19th-century building was converted into a hotel 50 years ago, and subsequent renovations haven't detracted from its elegant appearance. The guest rooms are small, but are attractively appointed and well equipped with modern conveniences. Ask for one with a sea view. ⊠ *Esplanada do Castelo 58, 4150-196,* ☎ *22/618–0083,* FAX *22/617–3818. 69 rooms. Restaurant, bar, cafeteria. AE, MC, V.*

$$$ 🏨 **Dom Henrique.** The Dom Henrique attracts business travelers who want a central base; its elegant rooms and amenities are spread through-

out the 22 floors of an octagonal downtown tower. Spacious guest quarters are well appointed; many have superb city views—as do the main restaurant and bar. Although perhaps not the place for a leisurely vacation, the hotel is ideal if you need more than just the basic comforts. ⊠ *Rua Guedes de Azevedo 179, 4000-009,* ☎ *22/200–5755,* FAX *22/ 201–9451. 112 rooms. Restaurant, bar, grill. AE, DC, MC, V.*

$$$ 🏨 **Mercure Batalha.** This attractive modern hotel has a very convenient central location a block or two away from Avenida dos Aliados. The rooms are elegantly appointed and have the customary four-star comforts like minibar, satellite TV, and air-conditioning. You can get sweeping views over the city from a wide terrace at the top of the building. ⊠ *Praça da Batalha 116, 4050-453,* ☎ *22/200–0571,* FAX *22/205–4756. 149 rooms. Restaurant, bar, games room. AE, DC, MC, V.*

$$$ 🏨 **Tivoli Porto Atlântico.** This small hotel lies west of the city center,
★ off Avenida da Boavista, in a residential suburb near the Serralves Foundation Museum of Contemporary Art. The comfortable interior is unobtrusively modern. Guest rooms share a terrace and have every little amenity, right down to a shoe-shine kit; bathrooms are marble-clad and luxurious. A fine buffet breakfast is the only meal served, but there's an excellent French-style restaurant, the Foco, associated with and adjacent to the hotel. ⊠ *Rua Afonso Lopes Vieira 66, 4100-020,* ☎ *22/ 609–4941,* FAX *22/606–7452. 58 rooms. Restaurant, bar, indoor and outdoor pools. AE, DC, MC, V.*

$$$ 🏨 **Tuela Torre.** This modern apartment hotel is a good alternative if you feel like doing your own cooking. Each two-bed apartment has a fully equipped kitchen plus amenities such as TV, direct-dial phone, and air-conditioning. If you tire of the kitchen stove, the Torre has another hotel a block away with a good restaurant. The hotel is in the western part of the city, a 10-minute taxi ride from the center. Bus connections are frequent. ⊠ *Rua Goncalo Sampaio 282, 4150-483,* ☎ *22/ 607–1800,* FAX *22/610–1810. 148 apartments. AE, DC, MC, V.*

$$ 🏨 **Grande Hotel do Porto.** Once Oporto's finest hotel, the Grande of-
★ fers a touch of old-fashioned style at reasonable prices. It's on the city's best shopping street, and most visitors are immediately impressed with its turn-of-the-century public rooms and restaurant and its efficient staff. Guest rooms are furnished with such modern touches as air-conditioning and satellite TV, but the hotel's genteel ambience has been preserved. ⊠ *Rua de Santa Catarina 197, 4000,* ☎ *22/200–8176,* FAX *22/205–1061. 100 rooms. Restaurant, bar. AE, DC, MC, V.*

$$ 🏨 **Nave.** This moderately priced modern hotel is functional rather than charming, but it is conveniently located a 10-minute walk from the center, and the rooms are comfortable and well equipped. ⊠ *Av. Fernão de Magalhães 247, 4300,* ☎ *22/589–9030,* FAX *22/589–9039. 81 rooms. Restaurant, bar, cafeteria. AE, DC, MC, V.*

$ 🏨 **Pensão dos Aliados.** The well-equipped, comfortable rooms in this excellent *pensão* (pension) are usually in great demand, partly because the location is bang in the center of town. The delightfully ornate turn-of-the-century building that houses the place is a listed city landmark. ⊠ *Rua Elisio de Melo 27, 4000,* ☎ *22/200–4853,* FAX *22/200–2710. 45 rooms. Bar, cafeteria. AE, MC, V.*

$ 🏨 **Pensão Estoril.** The Estoril offers functional but comfortable rooms with cable TV and phones at very reasonable rates. It's in a quiet location near the city center and has a terrace, a bar, and metered parking in a nearby square. Ask for a room with a balcony overlooking the back garden area. ⊠ *Rua de Cedofeita 193, 4000,* ☎ *22/200–2751,* FAX *22/208–2468. 18 rooms. Bar. No credit cards.*

$ 🏨 **Pensão Pão de Açúcar.** Centrally located just off the Avenida dos Aliados, this pensão offers a lot for its relatively modest rates. You can choose between a simple room—small, but equipped with TV and minibar—a suite, or a top-floor room opening onto a terrace with tables and chairs. The room decor is art nouveau. ⊠ *Rua do Almada 262, 4050,* ☎ *22/ 200–2425,* ℻ *22/205–0239. 44 rooms, 6 suites. Bar. AE, MC, V.*

$ 📺 **Pensão Peninsular.** Centrally located between the São Bento station and Praça da Liberdade, this small, popular hotel has a grand tiled entrance hall, spic-and-span rooms with TVs, and a modern—if slightly cheerless—bar. ⊠ *Rua Sá da Bandeira 21, 4000,* ☎ *22/200–3012,* ℻ *22/208–4984. 57 rooms. Bar. AE, MC, V.*

Nightlife and the Arts

For concerts and recitals consult the tourist office (☞ Visitor Information *in* Oporto and the North A to Z, *below*), whose staff will advise you on events. Noted as a center for modern art, Oporto enjoys regular exhibitions at the Serralves Foundation Museum of Contemporary Art, as well as at a variety of galleries, some of which are on the main street, Avenida da Boavista. Films in Oporto are shown in their original language; check local newspapers for current listings.

Bars
The nicest places for an evening drink are the old-style cafés; try the **Majestic** (⊠ Rua de Santa Catarina 112, ☎ 22/200–3887; ☞ *also* Dining, *above*), open Monday–Saturday until around 10 PM. For a glass of port, the best place is the newly remodeled **Solar do Vinho do Porto** (⊠ Rua de Entre Quintas 220, ☎ 22/609–4749), which is open until midnight every day except Sunday. **Anikibóbó** (⊠ Rua da Fonte Taurina 36, ☎ 22/332–4619), down on the Ribeira waterfront, is where Oporto's intellectual and artistic crowd hang out until the early hours (it's open from 10 PM to about 4 AM every day). The odd name was the title of a film made by Portugal's famed film director Manuel de Oliveira. The decor is old stone, set off by modern paintings, and a little garden out back is great on warm nights.

Casinos
For a more sophisticated—or just riskier—evening's entertainment, there are two casinos within reach of Oporto (☞ Espinho *and* Póvoa de Varzim *in* Oporto's Environs: The Coast and the Douro, *below*). Both are open daily throughout the year 3 PM–3 AM and feature dining, dancing, and cabaret in addition to the gaming tables. You must be 18 to enter (bring your passport), and smart-casual dress is recommended.

Dancing and Music
Oporto has a number of fashionable discos west of the city center in the new commercial developments along the Douro estuary; these clubs usually open around 11 PM and close at 4 AM. In the Centro Comercial Brasília, try the **Brasília Clube** (☎ 22/609–3256). A very funky, very hip crowd shows up late at **Indústria** (⊠ Av. do Brasil 843, ☎ 22/ 617–6806), in the Centro Comercial da Foz. Music from the 1960s and '70s is the draw at **Twins** (⊠ Rua do Passeio Alegre 994, ☎ 22/ 618–5740).The **Mal Cozinhado** (⊠ Rua do Outeirinho 13, ☎ 22/208– 1319) is a lively restaurant with traditional folk music and dancing, including the plaintive sounds of fado, Monday–Saturday.

Outdoor Activities and Sports
Golf
There are two golf clubs at resorts south of Oporto (☞ Espinho *in* Oporto's Environs: The Coast and the Douro, *below*).

Soccer
The main sporting obsession in Oporto is soccer, and the city has one of the country's best teams, **FC Porto,** which rivals Lisbon's Benfica for

domestic fame and fortune. Matches are played September through May at the **Antas Stadium** (⊠ Av. de Fernão de Magalhães, ☎ 22/557–0400) in the east of the city; Buses 6, 78, and 88 run past it. Other good regional teams are **Guimarães** and **Boavista,** both small soccer clubs that have enjoyed considerable success in recent years.

Shopping

The best areas to shop are the downtown streets off the central Praça da Liberdade—particularly on Rua 31 de Janeiro, Rua dos Clérigos, Rua de Santa Catarina, Rua Sá da Bandeira, and Rua das Flores. You'll see port on sale throughout the city. But first taste the wine at either the Solar do Vinho do Porto or the lodges at Vila Nova de Gaia (☞ Exploring Oporto, *above*). You may want to buy a bottle of the more unusual white port, drunk as an aperitif, as it's not commonly sold in North America or Britain.

Crafts

Traditionally, Rua das Flores has been the street for silversmiths. **Pedro A. Baptista** (⊠ Rua das Flores 23) deals in antique and modern silver. Gold-plated filigree is also a regional specialty, and examples are numerous along the same street and along Rua de Santa Catarina. Rua 31 de Janeiro and nearby streets are the center of the shoe trade, and many shops create made-to-measure shoes upon request.

For a general handicrafts emporium, try **Artesanato dos Clérigos** (⊠ Rua da Assunção 33, next to Clérigos Tower). The **Artesanato Centro Regional de Artes Tradicionais** (Center for Traditional Arts; ⊠ Rua da Reboleira 37), in the Ribeira District, sells an excellent selection of regional arts and crafts.

Market

For a good general market, visit the **Mercado Bolhão,** held Monday–Saturday at Rua Formosa and Rua Sá da Bandeira (then stop at the Confeitaria do Bolhão, a delicious-smelling pastry and candy shop at Rua Formosa 339, for your choice of exquisite cakes).

Shopping Malls

New shopping centers are a feature of Oporto's burgeoning commercial life. One of the best is **Via Catarina Shopping** (⊠ Rua Santa Catarina). Unlike most, this mall is centrally located in an old restored building. The top floor is occupied by little restaurants, all with old Oporto decor. The **Centro Comercial de Brasília** (⊠ Av. da Boavista), in the city's northwest, is another popular mall, and so is the **Shopping Center Cidade do Porto** (⊠ Rua do Bom Sucesso).

OPORTO'S ENVIRONS: THE COAST AND THE DOURO

Both north and south of Oporto are relaxing resort towns much favored by locals. To the north there are beaches in nearby Foz do Douro and Matosinhos, but they're unattractive places, much influenced by the industrial port of Leixoes. Espinho, south of Oporto, and the main resorts to the north (Vila do Conde, Póvoa de Varzim, Ofir, and Esposende) are the best places for water-sports enthusiasts, with equipment rental establishments often right on the beaches.

Inland, the beautiful Douro Valley awaits, with its carefully terraced vineyards dotted with farmhouses stepping down to the river's edge. Drives along the river lead to romantic ancient towns where you may want to stop for a while, rent a rowboat, and do some paddling. If all

that rowing works up a powerful thirst, this is the heart of prizewin-
ning wine country, and every town has charming bars where you can
pull up a chair, order a bottle and a plate of *petiscos* (mixed appetizers), and watch small-town life go by.

Vila do Conde

★ ⑭   *27 km (17 mi) north of Oporto.*

Vila do Conde has a long sweep of fine sand, a fishing port, and a strug-
gling but interesting shipbuilding industry that has been making wooden
boats since the 15th century. The yards are probably Europe's oldest,
and the traditional boat-making skills used in them have changed surprisingly little over the centuries. It was here that the replica of Bartolomeu Dias's caravel was made in 1987 to commemorate his historic
voyage around the Cape of Good Hope 500 years earlier. Urban and
industrial sprawl mars the outer parts of town, but the historic center
has winding streets and centuries-old buildings. Try to time your visit
to coincide with the Festas de São João, held June 23–24 every year.
As in Oporto, locals gather for feasting and boisterous street celebrations; many end up on the beach, building bonfires and waiting for
the first sunbeams of St. John's Day (☞ *also* Festivals and Seasonal
Events *in* Smart Travel Tips A to Z).

The town is further distinguished by the huge **Convento de Santa Clara**
(Convent of St. Claire), overwhelming the north bank of the Rio Ave
(Ave River), on which the town is situated. The convent was founded
in the 14th century by Dom Afonso Sanches and his wife, Dona Teresa
Martins, and it retains its original cloister and the beautiful tombs of
its founders. The convent is open Monday–Saturday 9–noon and 2–
5. The 16th-century **Igreja Matriz** (Parish Church), in the center of town
near the market, is worth seeing for its superb Gothic portal.

Shopping

Vila do Conde has been known for its lace since the 17th century, and
it remains the center of a flourishing lace industry today. If you're looking for souvenirs, the tourist office will direct you to a lace-making school,
Escola de Rendas, that welcomes visitors. There you can see how the
famed *rendas de bilros* (bone lace) is made. Local artisans also produce excellent sweaters, which are on sale in shops and at stands along
the road in town. An international handicrafts exhibition takes place
here every year, usually at the end of July.

Póvoa de Varzim

⑮   *4 km (2½ mi) north of Vila do Conde, 31 km (20 mi) north of Oporto.*

Póvoa de Varzim has a long beach, but the town has little of Vila do Conde's
charm (except for the many shops and roadside stalls that sell similarly
beautiful and reasonably priced hand-knit sweaters). It is, instead, a major
resort, with high-rise hotels used mostly by vacationing Portuguese. The
waterfront casino, which is open daily 3 PM–3 AM, attracts much attention. Entertainment includes nightly floor shows; you must be 18 to enter
(take along your passport), and smart-casual dress is your best bet.

Ofir and Esposende

⑯   *17 km (11 mi) north of Póvoa de Varzim, 46 km (29 mi) north of Oporto.*

Ofir, on the south bank of the River Cávado estuary, has a lovely beach
with sweeping white sands, dunes, pinewoods, and water sports—a combination that has made it a popular resort in recent years. On the opposite bank of the river, Esposende, which also has a beach, retains

elements of the small fishing village it once was. Mid-August sees the Festas do São Bartolomeu do Mar (Festival of St. Bartholomew of the Sea; ☞ *also* Festivals and Seasonal Events *in* Smart Travel Tips A to Z). You'll have to drive here to appreciate these twin towns: the train line runs inland at this point, passing through Barcelos.

Espinho

17 *18 km (11 mi) south of Oporto.*

South of Oporto, frequent trains and Route N109 run past a string of quiet family beaches to Espinho. Built on a grid pattern, this has become an increasingly fashionable resort over the years, with a full range of leisure facilities and good shopping. A casino, open daily throughout the year 3 PM–3 AM, has dining, dancing, and cabaret in addition to gaming tables; foreign visitors must present their passports (18 is the minimum age), and although there's no formal dress code, smart and casual is most appropriate. The long, sandy beach is very popular in summer, but you can find some space by walking through the pinewoods to less developed areas to the south.

Outdoor Activities and Sports

The 18-hole **Oporto Golf Club** (✉ Espinho-Paramos, ☎ 22/734–2008), founded in 1890 by members of the Port Wine Shippers' Association, is just 2 km (1¼ mi) south of Espinho. Greens fees are 8,000$00 for 18 holes on weekdays, 10,000$00 weekends (but nonmembers can play only until 10 AM). The club hires out carts and other equipment. The **Clube de Golfe de Miramar** (✉ Praia de Miramar, ☎ 22/762–2067) has nine holes and is 5 km north of Espinho. Greens fees are 7,500$00 for 18 holes. On weekends it's 9,000$00.

OFF THE
BEATEN PATH

THE DOURO TRAIN LINE – Even if you're driving, it's worth considering at least a day trip using the Douro train line. The main route runs 40 km (25 mi) inland from Oporto, past Penafiel, then swings south to join the Douro River and follow the north bank of the river to Pêso da Régua, a 2½-hour journey. From here the train continues east to the end of the line at Pocinho, providing a glorious 70-km (43-mi) ride that hugs the river all the way. Between Penafiel and the Douro, at Livração, the Tâmega line branches off the main line and runs northeast up the Tâmega River tributary to Amarante. This 25-minute ride is well worth taking. The little single-carriage diesel train ambles along the meandering Tâmega Valley high above the river, and the views at every twist and turn are enchanting. The economic viability of both routes has been under review for a number of years. Cuts have been made in the service, but at press time the lines were still operating and widely used by locals. From the end of May to the middle of October, the Oporto-based company **Ferreira & Rayford Turismo** (✉ Rua de S. Francisco 4, ☎ 233/393950) organizes train excursions on the Régua–Ferradosa stretch of the Douro line in a train pulled by a 1924 Henschel & Sohn steam locomotive. The same company offers a number of boat cruises up the Douro River.

Penafiel

18 *40 km (25 mi) east of Oporto.*

The valleys surrounding Penafiel are terraced with vineyards, whose grapes are used to make the slightly sparkling vinho verde. Other than some fading mansions, there's little in the town itself to see, but do stop for a glass of the always-refreshing local wine.

Amarante

★ **⑲** *33 km (20 mi) east of Penafiel, 60 km (37 mi) northeast of Oporto.*

Small, agreeable Amarante is charming, if ever a town deserved the adjective, and it's the one place in Oporto's environs that really demands an overnight stop. Straddling the Tâmega River, its halves are joined by a narrow 18th-century bridge that stretches above the river's tree-shaded banks. Although the river is polluted (which precludes swimming), it's beautiful to look at. Rowboats and pedal boats are for hire at several points along the riverside paths.

NEED A
BREAK?

Along Rua 31 de Janeiro, the narrow main road leading to the bridge, several small cafés and restaurants have terraces that overlook the river. Enjoy a drink, a snack, or a meal as you soak up the views. On the other side of the river, the big, modern **São Gonçalo Café** in the square beside the church has outside tables in summer, ideal for a restful break. It also has lunch and dinner service.

On the north side of the Tâmega River is the imposing 16th-century **Convento de São Gonçalo** (Convent of St. Gonçalo). The effigy of the saint, in a room on the left of the altar, is reputed to guarantee marriage to anyone who touches it. Not surprisingly, his features have almost been worn away over the years, as desperate suitors try one last time for success. ⊠ *Praça da República.* ⊠ *Free.* ☉ *Daily 8–6.*

Adjacent to Amarante's church are the cloisters and associated buildings of the convent, now housing the tourist office and the **Museu Municipal Amadeo de Souza-Cardoso.** The museum displays an excellent collection of modern Portuguese art, the nucleus of which is an important group of works by Cubist painter Souza-Cardoso, who was born in the area. In 1906 Souza-Cardoso moved to Paris and shared a studio with Modigliani. He returned to Portugal in 1914 and died four years later, at the early age of 31. The museum also hosts temporary exhibitions and has a number of interesting archaeological pieces. Curiously, the museum's star exhibits are the *diabos* (devils), a pair of 19th-century carved wooden figures connected with ancient fertility rites. They were venerated on St. Bartholomew's day, every August 24, when the devil was thought to run loose. The originals were destroyed by the French in the Peninsular War. In 1870, the Archbishop of Braga ordered the present two burned because of their pagan function. The São Gonçalo friars didn't feel free to go that far, but they did emasculate the male diabo, in which state he survives today. ⊠ *Alameda Teixeira de Pascoães,* ☎ *255/420236.* ⊠ *200$00.* ☉ *Tues.–Sun. 10–12:30 and 2–5:30.*

Dining and Lodging

$$ ✕ **Restaurante Amaranto.** This spacious, comfortably appointed modern restaurant sits atop a hotel near the center of town. There's nothing especially charming about the location, but the menu has excellent regional fare (if it's available, try the *ensopado de borrego* [lamb stew]), and there are panoramic views over much of the town from the window tables. ⊠ *Edifício Amaranto, Rua Acácio Lino,* ☎ *255/422006. AE, DC, MC, V.*

$ ✕ **A Quelha.** The restaurants along Rua 31 de Janeiro may have river views, but they don't necessarily serve the best food. This friendly, ham-and-garlic-bedecked little place—behind a service station off a square at the end of the main street—has no views, but the regional fare served on its wooden tables is fantastic. The menu changes daily. Come early, because it gets packed. ⊠ *Largo do Arquinho,* ☎ *no phone. No credit cards.*

$ ✕☲ **Pousada de São Gonçalo.** The small, modern São Gonçalo pousada is 20 km (12 mi) east of Amarante on the road to Vila Real. In the Serra do Marão at an altitude of nearly 3,000 ft, it offers wonderful views. The rugged terrain outside is matched by rustic decor within, including lovely wood furniture, a large fireplace, and tile floors. Having worked up an appetite in the hills, you can count on the restaurant to satisfy you with good, hearty regional fare. *Costaletas de porco com feijão branco de tomatada* (pork chops served with white beans cooked with tomatoes), a bottle of red wine from the pousada's carefully chosen list, and creamy cinnamon-scented *arroz doce* (rice pudding) will make you feel that all's right with the world, or at least with the north of Portugal. ✉ *Curva do Lancete, Ansiães 4600,* ☎ *255/461113,* ℻ *255/461353. 15 rooms. Restaurant, bar. AE, DC, MC, V.*

$ ☲ **Albergaria Dona Margarita.** This friendly and recently refurbished hotel (known for years as Hotel Silva) backs onto the river. Some of the rooms have French windows that open onto a long balcony with splendid views of the river and adjacent gardens; there's also a pretty terrace for calm contemplation of the river. The rooms are simply furnished but comfortable. Breakfast is the only meal served: in summer you can have it on the terrace. ✉ *Rua Cândido dos Reis 53, 4600,* ☎ *255/432110,* ℻ *255/437977. 22 rooms. Breakfast room. No credit cards.*

$ ☲ **Hotel Navarras.** The Navarras is part of a modern shopping complex in the center of Amarante, a five-minute walk from the river. Decor throughout is smart and up-to-date, although unexceptional, and service is competent. The hotel has a covered pool. ✉ *Rua António Carneiro, 4600,* ☎ *255/431036,* ℻ *255/432991. 61 rooms. Restaurant, bar, pool, shops. AE, MC, V.*

Outdoor Activities and Sports

GOLF

Golfe de Amarante (☎ 255/446060), at Quinta da Devesa, 5 km (3 mi) southwest of Amarante, is an 18-hole golf course with superb mountain views. The facilities include bar, restaurant, golf shop, and a driving range. Greens fees are 4,000$00 for nine holes, 5,500$00 for 18 on weekdays. Weekends, it's 6,000$00 and 8,000$00 respectively.

WATER SPORTS

There are great swimming pool facilities perched over the river 5 km (3 mi) outside Amarante at the **Parque Aquático** (Aquatic Park). ✉ *Fregin,* ☎ *255/446310.* ▭ *1,500$00.* ☉ *Daily 9–7.*

Shopping

The riverside beyond the municipal museum is the site of the local **market,** held every Wednesday and Saturday, which are perhaps the best days to be in Amarante. Until lunchtime this entire area is alive with activity, and the usually peaceful town is disturbed by manic traffic racing along the main street and over the bridge.

Pêso da Régua

❷⓿ *35 km (22 mi) southeast of Amarante, 108 km (67 mi) east of Oporto.*

This small river port is in the heart of port-wine country, and through it passes all the wine from the vineyards of the Upper Douro Valley on its way to Oporto. Local wine lodges offer tours of their cellars, which make a nice contrast to the large-scale operations in Vila Nova de Gaia.

Lamego

㉑ *13 km (8 mi) south of Pêso da Régua, 121 km (75 mi) southeast of Oporto.*

A prosperous wine-producing town, Lamego is rich in baroque churches and mansions, although none is so impressive as the town's most famous monument—the 18th-century pilgrimage church and shrine of **Nossa Senhora dos Remédios** (Our Lady of Cures). It stands on a hill to the west of the town center, and a marvelous granite staircase leads up the hillside to the church. The steps and terraces are decorated with azulejos, small chapels, and statues; at the top, rest under the chestnut trees and enjoy the view over the town to the distant mountains. During the Festas de Nossa Senhora dos Remédios, the annual pilgrimage to the shrine, many penitents climb the steps on their knees, just as they do at the shrine of Bom Jesus, near Braga. The main procession is September 8, but the festivities start at the end of August and include concerts, dancing, parades, a fair, and torchlight processions.

THE MINHO AND THE COSTA VERDE

The coastline of Minho Province, north of Oporto, is known as the Costa Verde, a largely unspoiled stretch of small towns and sandy beaches that runs all the way to the border with Spain. Most coastal towns are easily accessible by train from Oporto, and regular buses connect with the most interesting inland destinations. By car, a leisurely tour of the major points of interest could occupy three or four days.

The weather in this region of Portugal is more inclement than elsewhere, a fact hinted at in its name: the Costa Verde is green because it sees a disproportionate amount of rain. It's a land of emerald valleys, endless pine-scented forests, and secluded beaches that are beautiful but not for fainthearted swimmers. Summers can be cool, and swimming in the Atlantic is bracing at best. "These are real beaches for real people," is the reply when visitors complain about the water temperature.

Days spent at the coast can be alternated with trips inland to medieval towns along the lush Lima River or through the historic border settlements along the Minho River. Everywhere are remains of ancient civilizations; you'll come across dolmens, Iron Age dwellings, and Celtic and Roman towns. Old traditions are carefully incorporated into modern-day hustle and bustle. Up here, you'll see more than the occasional oxcart loaded with some sort of crop, being led by a long-skirted, wooden-shoed woman on both highway and country lane.

Braga

㉒ *53 km (33 mi) northeast of Oporto.*

Braga is one of the outstanding surprises of northern Portugal. Its attractive city center has many fine buildings whose baroque facades face small squares and pedestrian streets. A city of ancient origin, Braga prospered under the 6th-century Visigoths, when it became an important bishopric, marking the start of the religious authority it maintains today. Braga's later archbishops often wielded greater power than the Portuguese kings themselves. During the city's golden age, in the 16th century, Braga was beautified with churches, palaces, and fountains, many of which were subsequently altered in the 18th century.

The city feels like the religious capital it is. Shops that sell religious items—from candles to hand-carved angels—line the pedestrian streets around the cathedral. The Semana Santa (Holy Week) festivities here—including eerie torchlight processions of hooded participants—are some of Portugal's most impressive. Braga also has a conservative reputation; the military coup that brought Salazar to power began here. However, the city seems increasingly dynamic, both in its local economy and artistic life, and its population of 65,000 is growing fast. The preserved city center is now surrounded by noisy streets and apartment blocks, and traffic congestion is assuming legendary proportions.

The center of Old Town is marked by the huge **Sé** (Cathedral), originally Romanesque in character but now an impressive blend of styles. The delicate Renaissance stone tracery on the roof is particularly eye-catching. Enter from the main Rua do Souto through the 18th-century cloister; the cathedral interior is on your left, and there are various interesting chapels. Steps by the entrance to the cathedral lead to the **Museu de Arte Sacra** (Museum of Religious Art), which has a fascinating collection of religious art and artifacts, including a 14th-century crystal cross set in bronze. From the magnificent *coro alto* (upper choir), which you cross as part of the treasury tour, there are views of the great baroque double organ. Across the cloister, you'll see the **Capela dos Reis** (Kings' Chapel), a 14th-century chapel containing the tombs of Afonso Henriques's parents, Henry of Burgundy and his wife, Teresa. ☎ 253/263317. 🖃 *Cathedral free; 300$00 treasury tour and museum entry.* ⊙ *Daily 8:30–12:30 and 2:30–6:30.*

Across narrow Rua do Souto from the Sé is Largo do Paço, a park flanked by the well-proportioned **Paço dos Arcebispos** (Archbishops' Palace), which overlooks an attractive, castellated fountain. Parts of the building date from the 14th century. Today it's occupied by faculties from the city's university and functions as the public library, one of the most impressive in the country, with more than 300,000 volumes.

The pedestrian Rua Diogo de Sousa leads down from the cathedral and Archbishops' Palace to one of the city's former gateways, the 18th-century **Arco do Porta Nova.** Past the Arco do Porta Nova and to the right is the **Palácio dos Biscainhos** (Biscainhos Palace), a baroque mansion typical of many in the city. The elegant rooms are furnished in 18th-century style and display silver and porcelain collections. Interestingly, the ground floor of the palace is stone flagged, which allowed carriages to run through the interior to the stables beyond. At the back of the palace is a formal garden with decorative tiles. ⊠ *Rua dos Biscainhos,* ☎ *253/204650.* 🖃 *300$00.* ⊙ *Tues.–Sun. 10–noon and 2–5:30.*

Past the garden gateway of the Biscainhos Palace, you'll find the **Zona Arqueológica** (Archaeological Zone), which contains the excavations of an old Roman city known as Bracara Augusta. (The site isn't usually open to the public.) To the east, the Roman city stretched as far as the large Largo de São Tiago.

NEED A BREAK?	There are two inexpensive cafés in the arcade at Praça da República, either of which makes a pleasant stop. **Café Astoria** is the most elegant, with mahogany-paneled walls, mirrors, marble tables, and a molded ceiling. **Café Viana** has been in business since 1871 and serves a wider variety of snacks. It's also a good place for breakfast and offers views of the fountain and gardens.

The city center is found at the **Praça da República,** the square at the head of Braga's elongated central gardens. The west side of the square is arcaded, and behind it stands the dominating 14th-century tower, the **Torre de Menagem,** which is being restored.

There are several interesting historical sights a short distance from the city. The **Capela de São Frutuoso de Montélios,** about 3½ km (2 mi) north of town on the N205-4, is one of Portugal's oldest buildings. The original chapel is believed to have been built in the 7th century in the form of a Greek cross. The chapel was partially destroyed by the Moors, and rebuilt in the 11th century. Only one brick vault and the cupola remain, but it is one of the few examples left of pre-Romanesque architecture in Portugal. Some 4 km (2½ mi) northwest of Braga on the N205-4 stand the impressive and romantic ruins of the **Mosteiro de Tibães,** built as a Benedictine monastery in the 11th century and rebuilt at the end of the 19th century. There are four cloisters to be seen, with some fine examples of azulejos. On a hilltop 5 km (3 mi) west of Braga on the N309 is the **Santuário Nossa Senhora do Sameiro,** after Fátima the most important Marian shrine in Portugal, visited annually by hundreds of thousands of pilgrims. The church itself is of little architectural interest. All can be visited by bus from Braga's city center; inquire at the tourist office (☞ Visitor Information, *in* Oporto and the North A to Z, *below*) for timetables.

Dining and Lodging

$$ ✕ **Restaurante Inácio.** Just outside the 18th-century town gate, this well-known restaurant serves solid regional fare. Bacalhau is a good bet, as is the roast kid. The house wine is on the raw side, but the wine list is decent so you have plenty of other options. Service in the stone-clad interior is brisk and efficient. ⊠ *Campo das Hortas 4,* ☎ *253/513235. Reservations essential. AE, DC, MC, V. Closed Mon.*

$$ ✕ **Sameiro.** This long-established restaurant is situated at the top of the Sameiro Sanctuary hill, and it is worth the climb. The dining room is spacious and pleasantly furnished, and the views are superb. The menu is traditional northern Portuguese. No concessions are made to foreign influences; simply very good old-fashioned fare. Try the *arroz de vitela com pastelinhos de marisco* (a veal and rice concoction with little seafood pastries), or one of the various bacalhau dishes that are always on the menu. ⊠ *Sameiro,* ☎ *253/675114. No credit cards. Closed Mon.*

$ ✕ **Alexandre.** This family-run restaurant, known for years as O Cantinho, changed its name in a recent move to a more convenient site. But the same owners still preside over a kitchen that turns out good regional fare and serves it up in a friendly, no-frills fashion to a doting clientele drawn from all walks of life. The cabrito is legendary with regulars. The wine list is adequate, but confined to local varieties. ⊠ *Campo das Hortas 10,* ☎ *253/614003. MC, V. Closed Mon.*

$$ ✕🏠 **Hotel de Turismo.** This smart, modern hotel is on a main road just a few minutes away from the center of town. The rooms are well equipped and have balconies, although the views are mostly of traffic. The restaurant is good, however, and there is a rooftop pool. ⊠ *Praceta João XXI, Av. da Liberdade, 4700,* ☎ *253/612200,* ₣ₐₓ *253/ 612211. 134 rooms. Restaurant, bar, pool. AE, DC, MC, V.*

$$ ✕🏠 **Hotel do Elevador.** Many seasoned travelers to the north have made
★ this hotel on a wooded hilltop 3 km (2 mi) outside Braga their top choice. The hotel is named after the 19th-century water-operated funicular that hoists the foot-weary up to the top of the hill. Recent remodeling has preserved most of the hotel's charm. The restaurant, Panorâmico do Elevador, scores highly for its food and for its gorgeous panoramic views. ⊠ *Parque do Bom Jesus do Monte, 4700,* ☎ *253/603400,* ₣ₐₓ *253/ 676679. 23 rooms. Restaurant, bar. AE, DC, MC, V.*

$ 🏠 **Albergaria Senhora a Branca.** This modern inn is in the center of town and offers very good value. The rooms are on the small side, but they are attractively furnished and all have TV, air-conditioning, radio, and phone. ✉ *Largo da Senhora a Branca 58, 4710,* ☎ *253/269938,* ℻ *253/269937. 18 rooms, 2 suites. Bar. AE, DC, MC, V.*

$ ⌨ **Dona Sofia.** Close to the Sé, this small, pleasant, well-appointed hotel may well be the best bargain in town. The only meal served is breakfast, but otherwise there's nothing lacking in terms of basic comforts, and the staff is friendly. ✉ *Largo São João de Souto 131, 4700,* ☎ *253/263160,* ℻ *253/611245. 34 rooms. Breakfast room. MC, V.*

Nightlife

Braga has an active nightlife. Its café-bars in the arcaded Praça da República—such as **Café Viana,** which is open 8 AM to midnight, and **Café Astoria,** open 8 AM to 11 PM—are good places for a drink and are lively at any time of the day or night. In the square **Campo da Vinha** in the center of town the nightlife goes on until 2 AM in no fewer than 10 discos. **Salsa** (✉ Rua de Diu) has a Latin American bent and sometimes has live bands from Brazil.

Outdoor Activities and Sports

You can rent a pedal boat (600$00 an hour) for a trip along the Cávado River near Braga. Contact the **Clube Nautico de Prado** (☎ 253/923840) in the nearby hamlet of Prado.

Bom Jesus do Monte

★ ♻ *5 km (3 mi) east of Braga.*

Many people visit Braga specifically to see the pilgrimage center of Bom Jesus do Monte, a 1,312-ft-high, densely wooded hill east of the city. Here, a stone staircase, started in 1723, climbs up to an 18th-century sanctuary-church, whose terrace commands wonderful views. But it's the stairway itself—a marvel of baroque art—that's the most extraordinary attraction. Many pilgrims climb up on their knees. Fountains placed at various resting places represent the five senses and the virtues, and small chapels display a series of tableaux, with life-size figures illustrating the Stations of the Cross. If you don't want to climb up the staircase (which would be a pity), you can drive up the winding road or pay 50$00 and take the funicular. There are restaurants, refreshment stands, and even a couple of hotels beside the sanctuary at the top. On weekends the area is popular with local families, who come here to picnic. Buses run every half hour from the center of Braga.

Citânia de Briteiros

❷❸ *7 km (4 mi) southeast of Braga, 15 km (9 mi) northwest of Guimarães. From Guimarães, go north toward Braga on N101 and after 8 km (5 mi), turn right at Caldas das Taipas (Caldelas on some maps).*

Citânia de Briteiros, the fascinating remains of a Celtic *citânia* (hill settlement), dates from around 300 BC and was probably not abandoned until AD 300, making it one of the last Celtic strongholds against the Romans in Portugal. The walls and foundations of 150 huts and a meeting house have been excavated (two of the huts have been reconstructed to show their original size), and paths are clearly marked between them. Parts of a channeled water system also survive. The site was excavated in the late 19th century by Dr. Martins Sarmento, who gave his name to the museum in Guimarães (☞ *below*), where most of the finds from Briteiros were transferred. If you intend to visit the site, don't miss the museum. ⌧ *Free.* ♾ *Daily 9–6.*

Guimarães

★ ㉔ *22 km (14 mi) southeast of Braga, 51 km (32 mi) northeast of Oporto.*

Afonso Henriques was born in 1110 in Guimarães, and Portuguese schoolchildren are taught that *"aqui nasceu Portugal"* ("Portugal was born here") with him. Within 20 years he was being referred to as king of *Portucale* (the united Portuguese lands between the Minho and Douro rivers) and had made Guimarães the seat of his power. From this first "Portuguese" capital, Afonso Henriques drove south, taking Lisbon back from the Moors in 1147. Today Guimarães is a town proud of its past, and this is evident in a series of delightful medieval buildings and streets. In the narrow, cobbled thoroughfares of the Old Town, small bars open onto the sidewalk; balconied, pastel-color houses overhang little squares; and flowers brighten windowsills. Festivals in July and August bring celebration to Guimarães's streets (☞ Festivals and Seasonal Events *in* Smart Travel Tips A to Z).

The best place to start exploring is at the **Castelo** (Castle) at the top of the town. It was built (or at least reconstructed from earlier remains) by Henry of Burgundy; his son, Afonso Henriques, was born within its great battlements and flanking towers. Standing high on a solid rock base above the town, the castle has been superbly preserved. A path leads down from the castle walls to the tiny Romanesque **Igreja de São Miguel de Castelo** (☉ church has irregular hours), the plain chapel where it's believed that Afonso Henriques was baptized. ⊠ *Rua D. Teresa de Noronha.* ☒ *Free.* ☉ *Tues.–Sun. 9:30–12:30 and 2–5.*

The **Paço dos Duques** (Palace of the Dukes), below the castle, is a much-maligned, renovated 15th-century palace belonging to the dukes of Bragança. Critics claim that the restoration during the Salazar regime, which turned the building into an official state residence, damaged it irrevocably. Certainly the palace's brick chimneys and turrets bear little relation to the original structure, which was an atmospheric ruin for many years. You can judge for yourself on a guided tour of the interior, where you'll find much of interest—from tapestries and furniture to porcelain and paintings. You can book guided tours at the main desk. ☏ *253/412273.* ☒ *400$00 June–Sept. (tour included); 250$00 Oct.–May (tour included).* ☉ *Daily 10–12:30 and 2–5.*

Walk down Rua de Santa Maria into the peaceful Old Town, and the centuries roll away with every step. You'll see granite archways, wooden balconies, iron grillwork, and paving stones. In Largo da Oliveira, a delightful square enclosed by buildings, stands the Romanesque **Colegiada de Nossa Senhora da Oliveira** (Church of Our Lady of the Olive Branch). It was founded in the 10th century to commemorate one of Guimarães's most enduring legends. Wamba, elected king of the Visigoths in the 7th century, refused the honor and thrust his olive-branch stick into the earth, declaring that only if his stick were to blossom would he accept the crown—whereupon the stick promptly sprouted foliage. In the square in front of the church, an odd 14th-century Gothic canopy sheltering a cross marks the alleged spot.

The convent buildings surrounding the Colegiada de Nossa Senhora da Oliveira house the **Museu Alberto Sampaio,** a beautifully displayed collection of religious art. The cloister itself holds medieval statuary, sarcophagi, and various coats of arms, but the interior rooms provide the highlight: a 14th-century silver triptych of the Nativity, full of animation and power. This is said to have been captured from the King of Castile at the crucial Battle of Aljubarrota and presented to the victorious Dom João I, whose tunic, worn at the battle, is preserved in a glass case nearby. ⊠ *Largo da Oliveira,* ☎ *253/412465.* 🎫 *250$00.* ⊙ *Tues.–Sun. 10–12:30 and 2–5.*

Close to the Alberto Sampaio Museum, the **Museu de Arte Primitiva e Moderna** (Museum of Primitive and Modern Art) houses Portugal's most important collection of naïve art. The works are from several different countries and are attractively displayed. ⊠ *Largo da Oliveira,* ☎ *253/414186.* 🎫 *Free.* ⊙ *Weekdays 9–12:30 and 2–5:30.*

<table>
<tr><td>NEED A
BREAK?</td><td>An inexpensive café in Largo da Oliveira, A Medieval has seats outside in the square. Relax over coffee and a cake every day but Sunday.</td></tr>
</table>

The Old Town streets peter out at the Almeida da Liberdade, a swath of gardens at the southern end of Guimarães, whose benches and cafés are often full. Here the **Igreja de São Francisco** (Church of St. Francis) has a chancel decorated with 18th-century azulejos depicting the life of the saint. The church also has a fine Renaissance cloister. ⊠ *Largo de São Francisco,* ☎ *253/412228.* ⊙ *Daily 9–noon and 3–6.*

★ At the top of the Largo do Toural is the excellent **Museu Martins Sarmento.** Like the ☞ **Museu Alberto Sampaio,** it's contained within the cloister and buildings of a church, the **Igreja de São Domingos.** The museum has rich finds from the Celtic settlement of Citânia de Briteiros (☞ *above*), as well as Lusitanian and Roman stone sarcophagi, a strange miniature bronze chariot, various weapons, and elaborate ornaments. Two finds stand out: the decorative, carved stone slabs known as the *pedras formosas* (beautiful stones)—one of which was found at a funerary monument at Briteiros—and the huge, prehistoric, granite *Colossus of Pedralva,* a figure of brutal power thought to have been used in ancient fertility rites. ⊠ *Rua de Paio Galvão,* ☎ *253/415969.* 🎫 *300$00.* ⊙ *Tues.–Sun. 9:30–noon and 2–5.*

Dining and Lodging

$$$ ✕🏨 **Pousada de Santa Marinha.** Overlooking the town from the
★ Penha National Park to the northwest, this pousada occupies a beautifully converted 12th-century monastery that was founded by the wife of Dom Afonso Henriques to honor the patron saint of pregnant women. The history contained within the building is almost tangible: some of the attractive guest rooms used to be monks' cells, and antiques from Lisbon's Ajuda Palace brighten the public rooms, which are already knockouts with extraordinarily lovely azulejo panels gracing the walls. The great stone dining room (serving regional and Continental dishes) was once the monastery kitchen. *Rojões á Minhota* (pieces of browned pork, reddened with paprika and then simmered until meltingly tender and served with mixed pickled vegetables) is delicious here, especially when you sop up the sauce with chunks of *broa* (a dense, chewy corn bread). A fitting dessert is *toucinho do céu,* which translates as "bacon from heaven" but is actually an exceedingly rich egg-and-almond pudding cake. ⊠ *Estrada de Penha, 4800,* ☎ *253/514453,* 🗚 *253/514459. 49 rooms, 2 suites. Restaurant, bar. AE, DC, MC, V.*

$ ✕🏨 **Pousada da Nossa Senhora da Oliveira.** An elegant mansion, this pousada was fashioned when various adjacent 16th- and 17th-century town houses in the center of Guimarães were remodeled. Antique reproductions throughout provide Old World atmosphere, and the service, too, is straight from the old school—courteous and efficient. Guest rooms are elegantly cheerful, if not particularly large, but there's compensation at hand in the superb restaurant (reservations essential), whose windows overlook the lovely Largo da Oliveira. A large fireplace catches the eye, and the menu features a wide range of regional Minho dishes; try *coelho á fundador* (a fragrant fricassee of rabbit scented with fennel and red wine). A local favorite for dessert is the *bolo de amêndoa* (a dense almond cake made with flour and mashed potatoes). Even if you don't stay here, this would make a fine place for lunch while sightseeing. The one drawback to staying here is that the noise from traffic on the surrounding streets can be a problem for light sleepers. ⊠ *Rua de Santa Maria, 4800,* ☎ *253/514157,* ℻ *253/514204. 16 rooms. Restaurant, bar. AE, DC, MC, V.*

Shopping

Guimarães is a center for the local linen industry. The fabric is hand-spun and hand-woven, then embroidered, all to impressive effect; it is available in local shops. Here the weekly market is on Friday.

Barcelos

㉕ *12 km (7 mi) west of Braga, 60 km (37 mi) northeast of Oporto.*

Easily reachable by car or train and attractively situated on the banks of the Cávado River, Barcelos is the center of a flourishing handicrafts industry, particularly ceramics and wooden toys and models. It pays to come here if you plan to carry home a host of souvenirs. Unquestionably, the best time to visit is during the famous weekly market.

★ ㋛ The **Feira de Barcelos** (Barcelos Market), held every Thursday in the central Campo da República, is one of the largest in the country. It starts very early in the morning. Stalls appear overnight, and on market day the square resembles a small city, with rows of covered booths selling almost anything you can think of. This is a great place to buy traditional Barcelos ceramics (brown pottery with yellow-and-white decoration) as well as more workaday earthenware, baskets, rugs, glazed figurines (including the famous Barcelos cock), decorative copper lanterns, and wooden toys. Plus there are mounds of vegetables, fruits, cheese, fresh bread and cakes, clothes, shoes, leather, and kitchen equipment. At times—when the early mist rises off the ground, the cries of the vendors ring the air, and the smell of roasting chestnuts wafts across the square—it seems almost medieval. Parking is available, although you may have to maneuver around a pig or cow for a spot.

NEED A
BREAK?

There are several attractive cafés in the center of town. From the market in the Campo da República, head for the **Avenida da Liberdade** and to the front of the tourist office building on the **Largo Dr. José Novais** for clean, well-lighted places to sit, have a cup of coffee and some pastry, and think about heading back to the market to get an extra suitcase for all the great stuff you just bought.

From the Campo da República, Rua Dom António Barroso leads down through the Old Town toward the river. On the left, the former medieval town tower now houses the tourist office and the **Centro de Artesanato** (Artisans' Center), which brings together some of the best local handicrafts. Ceramic dishes and bowls, often signed by the artist, are a good buy. Figurines, too, are popular, although none approach the individuality of those made by the late Rosa Ramalho and Mistério, local potters whose work first made famous the ceramics of Barcelos. ⊠ *Torre de Menagem, Largo de Porta Nova,* ☎ *253/811882.* ☉ *Mon.–Sat. 9–noon and 1:30–5:30.*

The Cávado, crossed by a medieval bridge, is shaded by overhanging trees and bordered by municipal gardens. High above the river stands the ruin of the medieval Paço dos Condes (Palace of the Counts), whose grounds constitute the **Museu Arqueológico** (Archaeological Museum). Among the empty sarcophagi and stone crosses is the 14th-century crucifix known as the Cruzeiro do Senhor do Galo (Cross of the Rooster Man). According to local legend, after sentencing an innocent man to death, a judge prepared to dine on a roast fowl. When the condemned man said, "I'll be hanged if that cock doesn't crow," the rooster flew from the table and the man's life was spared. The Barcelos cock is on sale in pottery form throughout the town; indeed, it's become almost a national symbol. ⊠ *Paço dos Condes.* 🎫 *Free.* ☉ *Oct.–Apr., daily 9–5:30; May–Sept., daily 9–7.*

Ceramic buffs can indulge in their passion for pottery in the **Museu de Olaria** (Pottery Museum), a five-minute walk from the town's medieval bridge. The collection of more than 6,000 pieces—including selections from current and now-extinct Portuguese workshops, private donations, and excavation finds from both Portugal and all over the world—resides in a spacious and well-lighted ocher-color building. ⊠ *Rua Cónego Joaquim Gaiolas,* ☎ *253/824741.* 🎫 *260$00.* ☉ *Tues.– Sun. 10–12:30 and 2–6.*

Dining and Lodging

$ ✕ **Restaurante Bagoeira.** The little Pensão Bagoeira has been closed for major remodeling, but its restaurant continues to operate, to the relief of the town's Thursday market vendors for whom it has become a traditional venue. Dishes are prepared in full view of hungry customers on a huge old range that splutters and hisses. The decor is rustic, with a wood ceiling, black metal chandeliers, and vases of fresh flowers. *Grelhados* (grilled meats and fish) are the specialty. The place fills up early Thursdays. ⊠ *Av. Dr. Sidonio Pais 495,* ☎ *253/811236. AE, DC, MC, V.*

$ 🏠 **Quinta de Santa Combra.** Just 5 km (3 mi) from Barcelos on the road to Famalicão, this fine 18th-century manor house offers bed and breakfast in a rustic decor of wooden beams and granite. ⊠ *Lugar de Crujães,* ☎ 🗚 *253/832101. 6 rooms. Breakfast room, pool. AE.*

Viana do Castelo

★ ㉖ *45 km (28 mi) northwest of Barcelos, 71 km (44 mi) north of Oporto.*

An enjoyable resort at the mouth of the Lima River, Viana do Castelo has been a prosperous trading center since it received its town charter in 1258. Although you shouldn't miss the excellent local beach, Praia do Cabedelo (reached by ferry from the riverside at the end of the main street), there's plenty in town to occupy an inveterate stroller. Ask the folks at the tourist office for their English-language brochure, which includes a walking tour of the town.

Many of Viana's finest buildings date from the 16th and 17th centuries, the period of its greatest prosperity, and the town's best face is presented in the old streets and squares that radiate from the charming Praça da República. The most striking building here is the **Misericórdia,** a 16th-century almshouse, whose two upper stories are supported, unusually, by tall caryatids (carved, draped female figures). The stone fountain, also Renaissance in style, harmonizes perfectly with the surrounding buildings, which include the restored town hall and its lofty arcades.

NEED A BREAK? **Natário,** a small café right off the main drag, is a perfect place to soak up the Minho atmosphere. The proprietor makes his own pastries, cakes, and croquettes. It has been rumored that the Brazilian writer Jorge Amado comes here for coffee when he's in town. ⊠ *Rua Manuel Espregueira 37,* ☎ *no phone.* ☉ *Daily 8 AM–10 PM.*

A 10-minute walk west across the town's main avenue, the Avenida dos Combatentes da Grande Guerra, takes you to the **Museu Municipal** (Municipal Museum), housed in one of Viana's most impressive mansions. The early 18th-century interior has been carefully preserved, and the collection of 17th-century ceramics and ornate period furniture shows how wealthy many of Viana's merchants were. ⊠ *Largo de São Domingos,* ☎ *258/820678.* ▣ *250$00.* ⊙ *Tues.–Sun. 10–noon and 2–5.*

A little ways beyond the municipal museum are the great ramparts of the **Castelo de São Tiago da Barra,** the 16th-century fortification that added the words "do Castelo" to the town's name and protected Viana against attack from pirates eager to share in its wealth. Outside the walls, Viana holds a large market every Friday.

An *elevador* (funicular railway) behind the train station climbs to the modern basilica of **Santa Luzia,** a white, domed building overlooking the town from its wooded heights. The views from the steps are magnificent, and a staircase to the side allows access to the very top of the dome for some extraordinary coastal vistas. Be warned that this steep climb, up a very narrow staircase to a little platform, is for the agile only. ⊠ *Estrada de Santa Luzia.* ▣ *Funicular 75$00, dome 50$00.* ⊙ *Basilica 10–noon and 2–6; funicular operates 10–7, every 30 mins.*

Dining and Lodging

$$ ✕ **Taverna do Valentim.** This locally renowned seafood restaurant
★   near the fishing docks was once a fishermen's tasca and has retained the feel of its rustic beginnings. It serves nothing but fish dishes and is usually packed (reservations are recommended). Try the caldeirada de peixe, a spicy stew containing several varieties of fish. If you're lucky you'll be entertained on the piano by the owner. ⊠ *Rua Monsignor Daniel Machado 180,* ☎ *258/827505. MC, V. Closed Sun.*

$$ ✕ **Os Tres Potes.** The cellarlike dining room, converted from a 16th-century bakery, gets very busy in summer as people crowd in to eat to the accompaniment of the weekend folksinging and dancing sessions. Sitting at tables under stone arches or on the open-air terrace, you can choose from a fine range of regional dishes: start with a bowl of caldo verde or the *aperitivos regionais* (a selection of ham, spicy sausage, cheese, and olives); move on to the house-style baked bacalhau and potatoes or try the exceedingly tender *polvo grelhado* (grilled octopus). There's a good wine list, too. For dessert, have the house specialty: hazelnut cake. ⊠ *Beco dos Fornos 7, off Praça da República,* ☎ *258/829928. Reservations essential. MC, V.*

$$$ ✕▦ **Pousada Santa Luzia do Monte.** Majestically situated on a wooded,
★   rocky outcrop behind the basilica, this country mansion overlooks the town and coast. The pousada has been restored to its original sumptuous 1920s style. The grand public rooms are a delight—especially in winter, when the fireplaces add crackling, romantic warmth to the sometimes chilly lounges—as are the private gardens and terrace. There's an outdoor pool, too. Guest rooms are spacious and have glamorous marble bathrooms; some have a beautiful view of the sea. The restaurant serves regional and Continental cuisine in an enchanting setting, with sweeping views of both the countryside and the Atlantic. Archaeology buffs will be pleased to note that in front of the hotel are the recently excavated remains of an Iron Age settlement. ⊠ *Monte de Santa Luzia, 4900,* ☎ *258/828889 or 258/828890,* ℻ *258/828892. 48 rooms. Restaurant, bar, pool, tennis court. AE, DC, MC, V.*

Nightlife

The center of Viana do Castelo is lively in the summer, and several bars and cafés cater to the mostly Portuguese tourists. **Ministerio** (⊠ Rua do Tourinho 41) is a lively, popular bar with loud music. On the town beach, Praia da Cabedelo, the **Cybar** disco is popular. People, mostly young, also flock to **Foz Caffe,** another Praia da Cabedelo night spot.

Shopping

Viana is regarded as the folk capital of the region and specializes in producing traditional embroidered costumes, which are worn at the most important festivals. These make colorful souvenirs, although the town also sells less elaborate crafts, including ceramics, lace, and jewelry. The large Friday market is a good place to shop, and the tourist office also has a nice selection of items.

En Route Leaving Viana, both the train and the N13 continue north, following the coast and passing a succession of small villages with delightful beaches. There are good stretches of sand at the resorts of **Vila Praia de Âncora** and **Moledo,** and if you keep your eyes open, you'll find some side roads that lead to fairly isolated beaches.

Caminha

㉗ *25 km (16 mi) north of Viana do Castelo, 97 km (60 mi) north of Oporto.*

At Caminha you reach the Minho River, which forms the border with Spain. The fortified town hall on the main square once was part of Caminha's defenses; its loggia, supported by graceful pillars, is very pleasing to the eye. There's a 16th-century clock tower in the square, too; the nearby parish church resembles a Gothic fortress and was built a century earlier, when Caminha was an important port. The rich interior of the church and the surviving mansions in the surrounding streets are reminders of the town's former wealth, but by the 17th-century Caminha had lost much of its business to Viana do Castelo.

Vila Nova de Cerveira

㉘ *12 km (7 mi) northeast of Caminha.*

With granite hills on one side and the Minho River on the other, Vila Nova de Cerveira is another border town with history dating from the 13th century, when it was fortified to ward off any marauding Spaniards. Nowadays, the Spanish who do come ashore on the ferry that connects Vila Nova to the Spanish town of Goian come in cars (not on horseback) for day trips and good shopping. The most visited building in town is a medieval castle that has been converted into the luxurious, government-run Pousada de Dom Dinis (☞ Dining and Lodging, *below*).

Dining and Lodging

$ ✕🏨 **Pousada de Dom Dinis.** Open since 1982, this pousada was built inside the town's 14th-century fortified castle walls, which face the Minho River. Ancient, mottled buildings within the ramparts now house the guest rooms, which have been enhanced by lovely reproductions of traditional Minho furniture. Some rooms have private patios. The modern restaurant features local Minho dishes, including the popular river fish. In season, lamprey is a particular favorite. Enjoy *robalo grelhado com molho manteiga* (grilled bass with butter sauce). For dessert, try the pears poached in red wine. ✉ *Praça da Liberdade, 4920,* ☎ *251/708120,* ℻ *251/708129. 29 rooms. Restaurant, bar. AE, DC, MC, V.*

Valença do Minho

㉙ *15 km (9 mi) northeast of Caminha, 123 km (76 mi) northeast of Oporto.*

Valença do Minho is the major border crossing point in this area, with road-and-rail service to Spain. Valença's Old Town is enclosed by per-

fectly preserved walls, which face the similarly defended Spanish town
of Tuy. Strolling along the river and ramparts is very pleasant—even
more so in the evening, when the day-trippers from Spain have retreated
to their own side of the river. As at Vila Nova de Cerveira, Valença's
fortifications contain a pousada, from which there are fine river views.

Monção

③⓪ *18 km (11 mi) northeast of Valença do Minho, 144 km (89 mi) northeast of Oporto.*

The riverside town of Monção is another fortified border settlement
with a long history of skirmishes with the Spanish. In town there are
the remains of a 14th-century castle that withstood a desperate siege
in 1368. When the Portuguese supplies ran low, a local woman baked
some cakes with the last of the flour and sent them to the Spaniards
with the message that there was plenty more where that came from.
The bluff worked, the Spanish retreated, and the little cakes are still
on sale in town. A spa to the east of Monção attracts some tourists,
but the town is generally peaceful. If you stop, try a glass of the local
vinho verde, a noteworthy wine available in several bars.

En Route South of Monção the N101 traverses glorious rural countryside before descending to the valley of the Rio Vez (Vez River), a tributary of
the Lima. **Arcos de Valdevez,** 35 km (22 mi) south of Monção, makes
a nice stop. It's a typically serene little river town, where you can rent
rowboats for a closer look at the surroundings. Five kilometers (3 miles)
farther south you arrive at the Lima itself, one of the most beautiful
rivers in the country. It was known to the Romans as the River of Oblivion, because its blissful beauty was said to make travelers forget their
home. Ask at the tourist office (☞ Visitor Information, *in* Oporto and
the North A to Z, *below*) about walks along the ancient Roman roads.

Ponte da Barca

③① *5 km (2 mi) south of Arcos de Valdevez on N101, 39 km (24 mi) south
of Monção.*

At the old town of Ponte da Barca, the *ponte* in question is a beautiful, 10-arched bridge, built in the 15th century. At the junction of four
main roads, the small town has been an important market center for
centuries, and the Tuesday market held on the riverside here is well
worth catching. On other days you can spend time quite happily walking along the riverbank.

Ponte de Lima

★ ③② *18 km (11 mi) west of Ponte da Barca on N203, 57 km (35 mi) southwest of Monção.*

Ponte de Lima is as delightful a town as you're likely to come across
in the region. The graceful bridge here is of Roman origin, long and
low and open only to foot traffic; drivers cross a concrete bridge at
the edge of town. The square tower near the old bridge still stands guard
over the town, while beyond, in the narrow streets, there are several
fine 16th-century mansions and a busy market. Walking around town,
you'll return again and again to the river, which is the real highlight
of a visit. A wide beach usually displays lines of drying laundry, and
a riverside avenue lined with plane trees leads down to the Renaissance
Igreja de Santo António dos Capuchos. The twice-monthly Monday
market, held on the riverbank, is the oldest in Portugal, dating from
1125. On market days and during the mid-September **Feiras Novas** (New

Fairs; ☞ Festivals and Seasonal Events *in* Smart Travel Tips A to Z) you'll see the town at its effervescent best.

NEED A
BREAK?

The main square by the old bridge in Ponte de Lima has a central fountain and benches and is ringed by little cafés—the perfect places to stop for a leisurely drink.

Dining and Lodging

$$ ✕ **Restaurante Encanada.** Close to the market, the Encanada is adjacent to the tree-lined avenue along the riverfront. A terrace provides river views. The menu is limited, but you can count on good local cooking, with dishes that depend on what's available at the market. Try one of the Minho dishes such as rojões á Minhota accompanied by a vinho verde. ⊠ *Mercado Municipal,* ☎ *258/941189. AE, MC, V. Closed Thurs.*

$ ✕🏠 **Turismo no Espaço Rural** (Rural Tourism). The Ponte de Lima re-
★   gion is well known for its Manor House Tourism program; the organizing body, Turihab, has its central reservations office in Ponte de Lima. Bookings are for a minimum stay of three nights at each house. The cost includes bed and breakfast, although some manor houses will also arrange other meals on request. There are 26 properties in the area, mostly concentrated on the north bank of the Lima River, no more than several miles from town. Facilities are usually minimal; houses may have a communal lounge or bar, a pool or access to local swimming facilities, fishing, and gardens. Most manor houses do not take credit cards. Ask about the early 18th-century **Paço de Calheiros,** which has lovely gardens; the 17th-century **Casa de Pomarchão** (closed Dec.–Jan.); the **Moinho de Estorãos,** a converted water mill by an old Roman bridge (🕒 May–Sept.); and the 18th-century manor house **Casa do Outeiro.** ⊠ *Praça da República, 4990,* ☎ *258/741672 or 258/742827,* 📠 *258/ 741444.*

Parque Nacional da Peneda-Gerês

★   *Lindoso, in the park's center section, is 30 km (19 mi) east of Ponte da Barca.*

The 172,900-acre Peneda-Gerês National Park, bordered to the north by the frontier with Spain, was created in 1970 to preserve the diverse flora and fauna that exist in the region. Even a short trip to the main towns and villages contained within the park shows you wild stretches of land framed by mountains, woods, and lakes. Access is free, and general information is available at tourist offices in Braga and Viana do Castelo. There's also an information center at Caldas do Gerês where you can get a walking map and more specific hints.

Accommodations are concentrated mostly in the attractive spa town of **Caldas do Gerês,** in the southern section around the Serra do Gerês (Gerês Mountains). It's a two-hour drive from Braga; turn off the N103 just after Cerdeirinhas, along the N304; there's bus service, too, from Braga to Cerdeirinhas and Caldas do Gerês. The central region of the park is accessible from Ponte da Barca, from which N203 leads to **Lindoso,** or from Arcos de Valdevez, from which the minor N202 leads to the little village of **Soajo.** Both towns offer basic accommodations and superb hiking. To see the northern part of the park, encompassing the Serra da Peneda (Peneda Mountains), it's best to come from Melgaço, a small town on the Minho River, 25 km (15½ mi) east of Monção. From Melgaço, it's 27 km (17 mi) on the N202 to the village of **Castro Laboreiro,** at the northernmost point of the park. There's just one small hotel—and lots of fine long-distance hiking.

TRÁS-OS-MONTES

The remote and beautiful region of Trás-os-Montes, in Portugal's extreme northeast, attracts very few foreign visitors. The name means "Beyond the Mountains," and though new roads have made it easier to reach in recent years, exploring the region still requires a certain sense of adventure. Great distances separate the fascinating towns, and twisting roads can test your patience. Medieval villages exist in a landscape that alternates between splendor and harshness, and the population, thinned by emigration, retains rural customs that have all but disappeared elsewhere. Many still believe in the evil eye, witches, wolfmen, golden-haired spirits living down wells, and even the cult of the dead.

Having a car is the easiest way to tour the region, but making the trip by car would mean missing out on some of the finest train journeys in the country. The trip from Oporto to Mirandela provides an excellent opportunity to see the changing landscape, and you can take a bus on to Bragança. But it is slow going. Both trains and buses stop at every village, and the journey could take more than nine hours.

Vila Real

㉝ *116 km (72 mi) northeast of Oporto. By train from Oporto, change at Pêso da Régua (☞ above) to the Corgo line.*

The capital of Trás-os-Montes has the only significant industry in the northeast and has modern suburbs and a traffic-choked center to match. Still, Vila Real is superbly situated between two mountain ranges, and much of the city retains a small town air. Although there's no great wealth of sights, it's worth stopping here to stroll down the central avenue, which ends at a rocky promontory over the gushing River Corgo. A path around the church at the head of the promontory provides views of stepped terraces and green slopes. At the southern end of the avenue, a few narrow streets are filled with 17th- and 18th-century houses, their entrances decorated with coats of arms.

The finest baroque work in Vila Real is the **Capela dos Clérigos** (Chapel of the Clergy), also called the Capela Nova (New Chapel), a curious fan-shape building set between two heavy columns. ⊠ *Between Rua 31 de Janeiro and Rua Direita.* 🎟 *Free.* ⊗ *Daily 10–noon and 2–6.*

★ An exceptional baroque mansion built in the mid-18th century, the **Solar de Mateus** is 4 km (2½ mi) east of Vila Real. Its U-shape facade—with high, decorated finials at each corner—is recognized worldwide as the building pictured on the Mateus Rosé wine label. The building is believed to have been designed by Nasoni (architect of Oporto's Clérigos Tower), and typically, the huge portal is approached by a double staircase. Set back to one side is the chapel, with an even more extravagant facade. The elegant interior is open to the public, as are the formal gardens, which are enhanced by a "tunnel" of cypress trees that shade the path. ⊠ *N322 (road to Sabrosa), Mateus,* ☎ *259/323121.* 🎟 *1,000$00 for full guided tour; 600$00 gardens only.* ⊗ *Guided tours Dec.–Feb., daily 10–1 and 2–5; Mar.–May and Oct.–Nov., daily 9–1 and 2–6; June–Sept., daily 9–7.*

The **Sogrape** winery, in front of the Mateus mansion, offers tours of its premises. At the end of the tour, you'll have an opportunity to taste the wine and perhaps purchase a bottle. ⊠ *N322 (road to Sabrosa),* ☎ *259/323074.* 🎟 *Free.* ⊗ *Weekdays 10–noon and 2–5.*

Dining and Lodging

$ ✕ **O Aldeão.** A popular local restaurant, the Aldeão piles its plates high with Portuguese specialties, which include a full range of grilled meats. The steak comes garnished with a bit of everything and satisfies even the largest of appetites. A regional favorite, *feijoada branca á transmontana* (a hearty white-bean-and-smoked-sausage stew), is prepared to perfection here. Service is friendly, the surroundings straightforward, and the prices unbeatable for this quality and quantity of food. ⊠ *Rua Dom Pedro de Castro 70,* ☎ *259/324794. MC, V.*

$$$ ✕⊞ **Pousada do Barão de Forrester.** This pousada is named for Baron Forrester, a 19th-century Scotsman whose family members were successful port vintners and whose remarkable and beautiful map of the Douro River helped open the river to navigation. A nice alternative if you don't feel like staying in Vila Real, it's in Alijó, some 30 km (18 mi) southeast. Time fades away as you sit reading by the fire in the lounge, glass of port at your side. The restaurant has two terraces for sunlit lunches and star-filled suppers. Try the river mackerel in marinade, the bacalhau *meia desfeita* (cut into fine strips and served raw in an olive-oil marinade), or the alheira. ⊠ *Rua José Rufino, Alijó 5070,* ☎ *259/959215,* ℻ *259/959304. 20 rooms. Restaurant, bar, pool, tennis court, fishing. AE, MC, V.*

$ ⊞ **Miracorgo.** This hotel is a rather unattractive modern block in the center of town, but its exterior can be forgiven once you've secured a room that faces the valley, with views of the dramatic stepped terraces of the Corgo below. The handsome reception area, bright guest rooms, and good service make the hotel even more of a draw. ⊠ *Av. 1 de Maio 76–78, 5000,* ☎ *259/325001. 166 rooms. Bar, indoor pool, health club, shops. AE, DC, MC, V.*

Shopping

Vila Real is the place to purchase some world-famous, slightly sparkling rosé wine direct from the source: the winery close to the Solar de Mateus. The Sogrape (☞ *above*) winery, just before the mansion, offers tours of its premises and has bottles (or cases) for sale.

En Route The main road northeast of Vila Real (the N15) has recently been straightened for much of its length. You'll drive through exceptionally fine, high countryside; rolling, arable land continues as far as **Murça,** 40 km (25 mi) away. Here you'll see the most famous of the ancient zoomorphic images, and the largest of the Iron Age porcas, which are found all over the region. This particular granite boar stands on a plinth in the town's central square and is presumed to be a fertility symbol.

Mirandela

❹ *72 km (45 mi) from Vila Real. Train service, via Tua from Pêso da Régua, runs through pastures and barley fields, following the course of the Tua River, a tributary of the Douro.*

Mirandela, an attractive town midway between Vila Real and Bragança, has a medieval castle and a Roman bridge with 20 arches of uneven sizes. The grandest monument, however, is the 17th-century **Palácio dos Tavoras** (Tavora Palace), right in the center of town. Its great facade has elaborate pediments and baroque ornaments. Once the residence of the prominent Tavora family, it's now used as the town hall.

Bragança

🟤 *60 km (37 mi) northeast of Mirandela, 255 km (158 mi) northeast of Oporto.*

This ancient town in the very northeastern corner of Portugal has been inhabited since Celtic times (from about 600 BC). The town lent its name to the noble family of Bragança (or Braganza), whose most famous member, Catherine, married Charles II of England; the New York City borough of Queens is named for her. Descendants of the family ruled Portugal until 1910; their tombs are contained within the church of São Vicente de Fora in Lisbon (☞ Chapter 1). Unfortunately, since improved roads have encouraged development, the approaches to Bragança have been spoiled by many ugly new buildings.

★ ☙ Above the modern town rises the magnificent 15th-century **castelo** (castle), found within the ring of battlemented walls that surround the **cidadela** (citadel), the best-preserved medieval village in the country and one of the most thrilling sights in Trás-os-Montes. This fortified town developed as the medieval community drew close to its castle for protection. Within the walls you'll find the **Domus Municipalis** (City Hall), a rare Romanesque civic building dating from the 12th century. It's always open, but you may need to get a key from one of the local cottages for the **Igreja de Santa Maria** (Church of St. Mary), a building with Romanesque origins that has a superb 18th-century painted ceiling. Another prehistoric granite boar stands below the castle keep, this one with a tall medieval stone pillory sprouting from its back. The keep itself, the **Torre de Menagem,** (🕐 Fri.–Wed. 9–noon and 2–5) now contains a military museum (🎫 250$00) that's well worth visiting. ☎ 273/322378. 🕐 *Castle and walls always open.*

As you leave the castle walls on your way back down to town along this route, you'll pass the Renaissance **Igreja de São Bento,** with a fine Mudejar (Moorish-style) vaulted ceiling and a gilded retable. The church may or may not be open.

The exhibits at the **Museu do Abade de Baçal,** housed in Bragança's former bishop's palace, were collected by a local priest with eclectic tastes. The Abade de Baçal, who died in 1947, acquired prehistoric pigs, ancient tombstones, furniture, local costumes, fine silver, coins, and paintings—anything that caught his eye. ⊠ *Rua do Consilheiro Abílio Beca 27,* ☎ *273/331595.* 🎫 *400$00.* 🕐 *Tues.–Sun. 10–5.*

Once you've seen the castle and nearby buildings, you've seen almost everything Bragança has to offer. The central cathedral is unusually small and disappointing, but the modern town center is attractive in its way, with a wide central avenue and several cafés that open onto the sidewalk in summer. You'll easily exhaust all the local sights in under a day, but it's worth staying overnight for the views of the castle from the pousada on the outskirts of town.

Dining and Lodging

$$–$$$ ✕ **La Em Casa.** This low-key but attractive town center restaurant sits between the castle and the cathedral. It serves regional Portuguese food with—unusual this far inland—a decent menu of fish and shellfish. These are expensive, though. You can get a more moderately priced meal by choosing from the extensive selection of meat dishes, and there's a reasonable tourist menu, too. If you're lucky, you might catch one of the occasional evening fado performances. ⊠ *Rua Marquês de Pombal,* ☎ *273/322111. Reservations essential. AE, DC, MC, V. Closed Mon.*

$ ✕⊞ **Pousada de São Bartolomeu.** Bragança's pousada is on a hill just
★   to the west of the town center and offers terrific views of the citadel.
It's a modern building, although very comfortable; its bar-lounge has
an open fireplace and wooden furnishings. Guest rooms are rustically
decorated and have balconies. It doesn't really matter that the pousada
is a few miles from all the in-town restaurants, since the on-site formal dining room, which serves good stews and game dishes, is the best
in Bragança. ✉ *Estrada do Turismo, 5300,* ☎ *273/331493,* ☒ *273/
323453. 28 rooms. Restaurant, bar, tennis court. AE, DC, MC, V.*

Shopping

Bragança has locally made ceramics, and there's also a good crafts shop
within the walls of the citadel. Baskets, copper objects, pottery, woven
fabrics, and leather goods are all well made.

OFF THE   **SOUTH OF BRAGANÇA –** Trás-os-Montes is remote to begin with, and the
BEATEN PATH   minor roads south of Bragança are even more isolated; a number of attractive small towns are the reward of a wandering drive through the
area. The IP4 leads southeast through high, cultivated country to **Mirando do Douro,** a winding 84-km (52-mi) journey to the Spanish border that takes the better part of two hours. A small town with a
Renaissance cathedral and cobbled streets, Miranda do Douro has an
excellent pousada, where you can stop before crossing into Spain;
Zamora is due east. Back in Portugal the N221 shadows the frontier for
the 50-km (31-mi) drive southwest to **Mogadouro,** formerly a border
stronghold and now a market town with a 13th-century tower. Continue
south for 46 km (29 mi), and you'll reach the oddly named **Freixo de
Espada á Cinta** (Ash Tree of the Girded Sword), which retains a tall defensive tower and a fine parish church. Or turn off the N221 14 km (9
mi) before Freixo and take the N220 to **Torre de Moncorvo,** which surrounds an enormous church with a high, solid tower. Just to the north
you can pick up the main N102, which eventually joins the IP4, running
between Vila Real and Bragança.

Vinhais

③⑥   *31 km (19 mi) west of Bragança.*

Vinhais provides a welcome break from the beautiful although rather
desolate scenery along the N103—bleak uplands with the mountains
of Spain to the north and the distant mass of the Serra da Estrela (Estrela Mountains) to the south. Most probably a pre-Roman *castro* (settlement), the present town was founded in the 13th century by King
Sancho II. Its most notable sight is the structure housing the former
Convento de São Francisco (Convent of St. Francis), whose great
baroque facade incorporates two churches. The church has a beautiful painted ceiling.

En Route   Shortly before reaching Chaves, you'll see the ruins of the 13th-cen-
tury **Castelo do Monforte** (Monforte Castle), built upon the site of an
earlier Roman fort, a remote outpost of the great empire.

Chaves

★ ③⑦   *55 km (34 mi) west of Vinhais, 96 km (60 mi) west of Bragança.*

Chaves was known to the Romans as Aquae Flaviae (Flavian's Waters), in honor of the emperor Flavian. They established a military base
here and popularized the town's thermal springs, which are still in use
today. The impressive 16-arch Roman bridge across the Tâmega River,
at the southern end of town, dates from the 1st century AD and dis-

plays two original Roman milestones. Today Chaves is characterized most by a series of fortifications built during the late Middle Ages, when the city was prone to attack from all quarters. The town lies only 12 km (7½ mi) from the Spanish border. Its name means "keys"—whoever controlled Chaves held the keys to the north of the country.

Of the town's three surviving defensive structures, the most obvious landmark is the great, blunt fortress overlooking the river, the 14th-century **Torre de Menagem** (Castle Keep). As at Bragança, this now houses a military museum, and its grounds offer grand views of the town. The tower is surrounded by narrow, winding streets filled with elegant houses, most of which have lovely carved wood balconies on their top floors. ⊠ *Largo da Câmara Municipal de Chaves,* ☎ *276/340500.* 🖅 *200$00.* ☉ *Daily 9–noon and 2–5.*

In Praça de Camões, the main square below the Torre de Menagem, the late-17th-century **Igreja da Misericórdia** (Church of Mercy) is lined with huge panels of blue-and-white azulejos that depict scenes from the New Testament. The **Museu da Região Flaviense,** adjacent to the church, is thoroughly recommended for its indiscriminate hodgepodge of local archaeological finds and relics that tell the town's history; it's open Tuesday–Friday 9:30–12:30 and 2–5, weekends 2–4:30.

The spa buildings are contained within the **Parque Termal** (Thermal Park), below the tower and close to the river. Local legend has it that the hot water here was cast up from the entrails of the underworld, which is exactly what a mouthful tastes like. ⊠ *Largo das Termas,* ☎ *276/332445.* 🖅 *Free.* ☉ *Apr.–Oct., daily 9–5.*

Dining and Lodging

$ ✗ **O Pote.** A little way out of town on the Bragança road, this family-run restaurant has no pretensions. It serves tasty Portuguese food to an enthusiastic local clientele. Ask about the daily specials. You can't go wrong if you choose the *posta á mirandesa* (grilled steak seasoned with olive oil and garlic). To reach the restaurant, cross the bridge from the town center and drive for 1 km (⅔ mi). The restaurant is on the right, and parking is available. ⊠ *Estrada da Fronteira,* ☎ *276/321226. No credit cards. Closed Mon.*

$$$ ✗🏨 **Forte de São Francisco.** This remarkable hotel has been created out of the ruins of a 16th-century Franciscan monastery listed as a national monument. Inside, it's a sober but attractive blend of ancient stone and modern simplicity. Outside, massive walls surround extensive gardens and courtyards. The Franciscan monks would no doubt have frowned on the modern comforts of the elegant and well-equipped guest rooms and the sumptuous food served in the restaurant, although they might have winked at the pleasures of the hotel's fabulously well-stocked wine cellar installed in their old water cistern. ⊠ *Rua do Tabolado 35, 5400,* ☎ *276/333700,* 🖷 *276/333701. 58 rooms. Restaurant, bar, cafeteria, pool, tennis court. AE, DC, MC, V.*

$ ✗🏨 **Trajano.** The basement restaurant of the Hotel Trajano is a good place to try the presunto and chouriço for which the town is famous. *Truta á transmontana* (river trout wrapped in paper-thin slices of smoky presunto) is another good choice, served with boiled potatoes and salad. There's a reasonably priced selection of local wines to accompany your meal, which is served promptly on elegantly rustic monogrammed plates. Such touches, and the very attentive service, more than make up for the rather subdued basement surroundings. The good service continues upstairs, where the hotel's pleasant guest rooms are cheerily decorated in Portuguese country style. ⊠ *Travessa Cândido dos Reis, 5400,* ☎ *276/332415,* 🖷 *276/327002. 39 rooms. Restaurant, bar. AE, MC, V.*

$ 🏨 **Hotel Aquae Flaviae.** Although it bears the ancient Roman name for Chaves, this is a gleaming modern hotel, adjacent to the Parque Termal and a cannon shot away from the town's fortified tower. The rooms are spacious and attractively decorated. The facade has an art-deco touch—it looks more like an enormous movie house than a hotel—and the interior impresses with its smooth lines and polished surfaces. ⊠ *Praça do Brasil, 5400,* ☎ *276/309000,* 𝔽𝔸𝕏 *276/309010. 170 rooms. Restaurant, bar, piano bar, pool, shops. AE, DC, MC, V.*

En Route If you continue west along the N103 for 35 km (22 mi) you'll come to an enormous system of lakes and hydroelectric dams along the Cávado. At this point you can make a short side trip to see the ruined castle at **Montalegre,** which is visible from miles around. Take a right turn onto the N308 and drive for 12 km (7½ mi). The views are worth the detour. Back on the N103, you'll follow along the edge of the great lake system, skirting drowned valleys in an endless series of long loops. Allow plenty of time, because you're sure to want to stop often to take in the incredible views. To the north is the Parque Nacional da Peneda-Gerês (☞ *above*); there are occasional access points along the road. Finally, after passing the village of Cerdeirinhas, the road runs for 30 km (19 mi) through rocky heights and down tree-clad slopes to reach Braga, where you are firmly in the center of the Minho province again.

OPORTO AND THE NORTH A TO Z

Arriving and Departing

By Airplane

Oporto's **Sá Carneiro Airport** (☎ 22/943–2400) is 13 km (8 mi) north of the city and is the gateway to all of northern Portugal. There's direct service from European and South American cities but not from the United States. TAP runs regular flights from Lisbon. The airport has car-rental agencies and money-exchange facilities. In addition, there are regional airports handling light plane flights in **Bragança** (☎ 273/381175) and **Vila Real** (☎ 259/336620). For the service between these two cities and Lisbon, contact the airline Omni at either of the two regional airports or at **Lisbon airport** (☎ 21/445–8600).

BETWEEN THE AIRPORT AND CENTER CITY

Buses 56 and 87 run from the airport to downtown Oporto and cost 165$00. It takes up to an hour, depending on the traffic, to reach the stop at Cordoaria, the area behind the Clérigos Tower. Taxis are available, too, outside the terminal; the fare will run 3,000$00–3,500$00 including the 300$00 baggage charge if you have any.

By Train

Most trains into Oporto (including those from Lisbon) arrive at **Estação de Campanhã** (⊠ Campanhã, ☎ 22/535–4141), just east of the city center. From here, you can take a five-minute connecting train ride to the central **Estação de São Bento** (⊠ Praça Almeida Garrett, ☎ 22/536–4141); connecting trains run regularly. When leaving Oporto, be sure to budget in plenty of time from São Bento Station to make your connection. For the express service to and from Lisbon, you may want to reserve your seat at least a day in advance.

Trains from Guimarães and from the coast immediately north of the city use the **Estação da Trindade** (⊠ Rua Alferes Malheiro, ☎ 22/200–4833). The station is a few minutes' walk from downtown Oporto, behind the town hall at the top of Avenida dos Aliados.

From Spain, the Vigo–Porto train uses the Tuy/Valença border crossing and runs south down the Costa Verde to Oporto via Viana do Castelo. These trains usually stop at the Campanhã and São Bento stations, but some only stop at Campanhã, and you'll have to change for São Bento.

Getting Around

By Boat

Cruises on the Douro River are offered by various companies based in Oporto. These range from short trips taking in Oporto's bridges and the local fishing villages to one- and two-day cruises that include meals and accommodations. Expect to pay around 2,000$00 for one- to two-hour cruises, most of which depart several times daily from the Cais da Ribeira, at the foot of Oporto's Old Town. The longer cruises, some in traditional rabelo riverboats, usually involve taking a train from the Estação de São Bento that connects with a boat farther up the Douro. The cost for these can run from 8,000$00 for a day trip with lunch to 32,500$00 for a two-day trip with meals and overnight hotel stay included. These longer, up-river cruises usually leave once or twice a week from May to October. Contact the tourist office in Oporto for details and schedules (☞ Visitor Information, *below*).

One of the oldest companies is **Endouro** (⊠ Rua da Reboleira 49, Oporto, ☎ 22/332–4236). **Turisdouro** (⊠ Rua Machado dos Santos 824, Vila Nova de Gaia, ☎ 22/3708429) specializes in rides on sailboats traditionally used to transport port wine downriver. Ferreira & Rayford (⊠ Rua de S. Francisco 4, Oporto, ☎ 22/339–3950 specializes in longer cruises from the up-river town of Régua. More information can be obtained from the tourist office (☞ Visitor Information, *below*) in Oporto.

By Bus and Tram

Oporto has a very good public transportation system, consisting of buses and trams. The tourist office provides a city map with all the main routes and numbers. Main stops are at Praça da Liberdade, Praça de Dom João I, and Cordoaria, behind the Clérigos Tower. Bus 78 runs from Praça da Liberdade, past the Soares dos Reis Museum and the Palácio de Cristal gardens, along the main Avenida da Boavista, to the Museum of Contemporary Art. Trams 1 and 18 make a pleasant run along the river to the beach at Foz.

All bus rides within the inner metropolitan zone—this includes most places you'll want to see—cost 180$00 if you buy your ticket on the bus and 90$00 if you buy it at an STCP kiosk. The price for an outer zone ticket is 125$00 bought at the kiosk, 180$00 on board. Punch the ticket in a machine when you board the bus. A 10-ride ticket can be bought for 800$00. All tickets are available at the STCP kiosks at the main bus stops. The tourist office on Rua Clube dos Fenianos issues its own Passe Turístico; it costs 800$00 for one day of unlimited rides, 1,100$00 for two days, and includes discounts for certain museum visits.

Outside the city system there's a confusion of bus companies in the north, with several providing service between the same destinations. Generally, however, companies use one central station in each town. Major terminals are found at Oporto, Braga, Guimarães, Vila Real, and Chaves. The best source of information about departures is the local tourist office, since bus station personnel invariably speak no English. However, most bus stations do offer timetables for main routes, which you should be able to decipher with the aid of a dictionary.

The main company operating in Trás-os-Montes is **Cabanelas** (☎ 22/200–5637), whose terminal in Oporto is at Rua da Ateneu Comercial.

Bus trips in this region are slow and, on some of the minor routes, uncomfortable. One useful tip is to take the bus rather than the train between the neighboring towns of Guimarães and Braga. It's only 22 km (14 mi) on the road, but the circuitous train ride involves two changes.

By Car

Outside Oporto a car is the most convenient way to get around, but be prepared for lengthy journeys, particularly in the northeast, where roads can be tortuous. Many roads have been improved in recent years—the fast IP4 highway between Oporto and Bragança has been completed, and there are quick routes from Oporto to towns both north and south, as well as to Braga in the northeast. However, given the nature of Portuguese terrain, some journeys will never be anything but slow. Examples are the routes Bragança–Chaves–Braga (N103), Vila Real–Chaves (N2), and Bragança–Mirando do Douro (N218). It's best simply to accept the roads' limitations, slow down, and appreciate the scenery.

Off the beaten track, particularly in the northeast, always check with local tourist offices to make sure that the routes you wish to follow are navigable. Road work and winter landslides can cause detours and delays. In isolated regions, take special care at night, because many roads are unlighted and unpaved.

On Foot

You'll be able to walk around most of central Oporto, although be prepared for the hills, which can prove tiring in the summer heat. The city is very congested, so leave your car at your hotel while sightseeing in the city. Central parking is difficult to find, and much of the downtown area (in particular, the riverside and the winding streets of the Old Town below the cathedral) is not accessible to cars.

By Taxi

In Oporto there is a taxi stand in Praça da Liberdade, or you can phone for a cab (☎ 22/507–3900). Make sure that the driver switches on the meter. If you have phoned for the cab, the cabbie will have already done so from wherever he picked up the call. If not, the starting charge is 260$00 and then 65$00 per kilometer or fraction. If you have suitcases you pay 300$00 extra, but not per bag. It's customary, but not obligatory, to give your driver a small tip (up to 10% of the fare). Note that taxis add a surcharge for crossing the Ponte Dom Luís I to Vila Nova de Gaia, the suburb known for its port wine.

By Train

All the region's train routes originate in Oporto; from here some of the finest lines in the country stretch out into the river valleys and mountain ranges of the northeast. Even if you've rented a car, try to take a day trip on at least one of the beautiful lines that traverse the region.

The **Douro Line** runs from Oporto's São Bento Station east to Pocinho via Livração, Pêso da Régua, and Tua (a four-hour journey). Three narrow-gauge lines branch off from it: the **Tâmega Line,** linking Livração with beautiful Amarante (25 minutes); the **Corgo Line** from Pêso da Régua to Vila Real (one hour); and the **Tua Line** from Tua to Mirandela (two hours). The trains on these lines generally have just one class of car, and the trains usually stop at every station. Journeys are slow but rewarding. Recently there have been service cuts on the minor lines, and some route sections have been closed altogether. The lines mentioned above should still be operational, but for reservations and current schedules contact **Estação São Bento** (☎ 22/536–4141) or the tourist office in Oporto (☞ Visitor Information, *below*).

Trains on the main route north along the Costa Verde depart approximately hourly from both São Bento and Campanhã stations and run through Barcelos and Viana do Castelo, as far as Valença do Minho. Branch lines connect with Braga and Guimarães.

Contacts and Resources

Car Rental

All the major companies are represented at Oporto's Sá Carneiro Airport, and some have offices at the larger hotels. Other addresses include **Avis** (⊠ Rua Guedes de Azevedo 125, Oporto, ☎ 22/205–5947; ⊠ Braga train station, Largo da Estação, ☎ 253/427205; ⊠ Rua do Gontim 35, Viana do Castelo, ☎ 258/8180540), **Europcar** (⊠ Rua de Santa Catarina 1158, Oporto, ☎ 22/205–7737; ⊠ Campanhã Station, Oporto, ☎ 22/518–0723), and **Hertz** (⊠ Rua de Santa Catarina 899, Oporto, ☎ 22/339–5300; ⊠ Rua Gabrial P. Castro 28, Braga, ☎ 253/616744; ⊠ Av. Conde da Carreira, Viana do Castelo, ☎ 258/822250).

Emergencies

General: The general emergency number is 112. **Hospitals: Hospital de Santa Maria** (⊠ Rua de Camões 906, Oporto, ☎ 22/550–4844); **Hospital Geral de Santo António** (⊠ Largo Professor Abel Salazar, Oporto, ☎ 22/207–7500); **Hospital de São João** (⊠ Alameda Professor Hernâni Monteiro, Oporto, ☎ 22/252–7151). **Pharmacies:** Pharmacies take turns staying open late. Schedules and addresses are posted on the door of each establishment, and listings of late-night services are carried in the local press.

Guided Tours

BICYCLE

For something different, consider seeing the region on two wheels. **ExperiencePlus!** (⊠ 1925 Wallenberg Dr., Fort Collins, CO 80526, ☎ 303/484–8489 or 800/685–4565) offers 11-day biking tours through the valleys and vineyards of the Minho wine country.

BUS

In Oporto, consult a tourist office or travel agency (☞ Visitor Information, *below*) for the latest information on bus tours of the city. Usually these last a half day and take in all the principal sights, including a visit to the port-wine lodges (where the vintage is stored) at Vila Nova de Gaia. Short river cruises from Oporto are also a pleasant way to orient yourself (☞ By Boat *in* Getting Around, *above*).

For tours farther afield, **Citirama** (⊠ No office in Oporto; bookings are made through travel agencies or Lisbon office, ☎ 21/319–1090) and **SGV Viagens e Turismo** (⊠ Rua Damião de Góis 425, ☎ 22/557–4000) operate half- and full-day coach tours throughout the region to destinations as diverse as the Douro Valley, the Costa Verde, and Parque Nacional da Peneda-Gerês. Consider, too, the longer cruises operated by Endouro (☞ By Boat *in* Getting Around, *above*), which cover the towns of the Douro Valley.

Telephones and Mail

The **main post office** in Oporto is in Praça General Humberto Delgado (☎ 22/208–0251). It is open weekdays 8 AM–10 PM, Saturday 8–8. General-delivery mail (mark it POSTE RESTANTE) is received here, and telephones are available for local, regional, or international calls. The cashier will indicate which phone to use, and you pay afterward. (Note that most of the public pay phones can be used for all types of calls. The newest of the coin-operated phones take all the coins from 10$00 to 200$00; the oldest, of which there are fewer and fewer, accept coins from 10$00 to 50$00 only. You can buy cards for card-operated phones with 50 or 120 minute units in most tobacconists, news stands, and phone company outlets. For general information, dial 118; operators often speak English.

Travel Agencies

In Oporto, you'll find several travel agencies around the central Avenida dos Aliados. Reliable ones include **Abreu** (✉ Av. dos Aliados 207, ☎ 22/204–3500) and **Top Tours,** agents for American Express (✉ Rua Alferes Malheiro 96, Oporto, ☎ 22/207–4020).

Visitor Information

OPORTO AND ENVIRONS

There are three **tourist offices** in Oporto: one just east of Avenida dos Aliados (✉ Praça Dom João I 43, ☎ 22/205–7514), one to the west of the town hall, at the top of Avenida dos Aliados (✉ Rua Clube dos Fenianos 25, ☎ 22/339–3470), and one south of Praça da Liberdade on the way down to Cais da Ribeira (✉ Rua Infante Dom Enrique, 63, ☎ 22/200–9770). There's also a tourist office at the **airport** (☎ 22/941–2534) and at **Vila Nova de Gaia** (✉ Rua General Torres 1141, 4400, ☎ 22/379–0994).

There are tourist offices in the following Oporto environs towns: **Amarante** (✉ Rua Cândido dos Reis, 4600, ☎ 255/432980), **Espinho** (✉ Corner of Ruas 6 and 23, 4500, ☎ 227/340911), **Esposende** (✉ Rua 1 de Dezembro, 4740, ☎ 253/961354), **Lamego** (✉ Av. Visconde Guedes Teixeira, 5100, ☎ 254/612005), **Póvoa de Varzim** (✉ Praça Marquês de Pombal, 4490, ☎ 252/298120), and **Vila do Conde** (✉ Rua 25 de Abril, 4480, ☎ 252/642700).

THE MINHO AND THE COSTA VERDE

Arcos de Valdevez (✉ Av. da Marginal, 4970, ☎ 258/516001), **Barcelos** (✉ Torre de Menagem, Largo da Porta Nova, 4750, ☎ 253/811882), **Braga** (✉ Av. da Liberdade 1, 4700, ☎ 253/262550), **Caminha** (✉ Rua Ricardo Joaquim Sousa, 4910, ☎ 258/921952), **Gerês** (✉ Caldas de Gerês, 5300, ☎ 253/391133), **Guimarães** (✉ Alameda S. Dâmaso 83, 4800, ☎ 253/412450), **Monção** (✉ Largo do Loreto, 4950, ☎ 251/652757), **Ponte da Barca** (✉ Largo da Misericórdia, 4980, ☎ 258/452899), **Ponte de Lima** (✉ Praça da República, 4990, ☎ 258/942335), **Valença do Minho** (✉ Av. de Espanha, 4930, ☎ 251/823374), **Viana do Castelo** (✉ Praça da Erva, 4900, ☎ 258/822620), **Vila Nova de Cerveira** (✉ Rua Dr. A. Duro, 4920, ☎ 251/795787), and **Vila Praia de Âncora** (✉ Av. Dr. Ramos Pereira, 4915, ☎ 258/911384).

TRÁS-OS-MONTES

Bragança (✉ Av. Cidade de Zamora, 5300, ☎ 273/381273), **Chaves** (✉ Terreiro de Cavalaria, 5400, ☎ 276/340661), and **Vila Real** (✉ Av. Carvalho Araújo 94, 5000, ☎ 259/322819).

8 MADEIRA

The scent of flowers and the sound of
waterfalls fill Madeira's sea-washed air.
Birds of paradise grow wild; pink and
purple fuchsia weave lacy patterns up pastel
walls; and jacaranda trees create purple
canopies over roads and avenues. The
natural beauty of this island is like no other,
from the cliffs that plummet seaward to
mountain summits cloaked in silent fog. The
magic has captivated travelers for five
centuries and promises to continue in
today's fast-changing world.

By Deborah
Luhrman

Updated by
Alys Bohn

MADEIRA IS A MOUNTAINOUS, subtropical island carpeted with flowers and punctuated with waterfalls cascading down improbably steep, green canyons. Warmed by Atlantic currents in winter and cooled by trade winds in summer, the island is 900 km (558 mi) southwest of Lisbon–at roughly the same latitude as Casablanca.

In the middle of the island is a backbone of high, rocky peaks and the crater of a now-extinct volcano. Steep ravines fan out from the center like spokes of a wheel. Although Madeira is only 57 km (35 mi) long and 22 km (14 mi) wide, distances seem much greater, as the roads climb and descend precipitously from one ravine to the next. In the same island group are tiny Porto Santo, about 50 km (31 mi) northeast, which has a sandy beach popular with locals and its 5,000 inhabitants; the Ilhas Desertas, a chain of waterless, unpopulated islands 20 km (12 mi) southeast of Madeira; and the also-uninhabited Ilhas Selvagens, much farther south, near Spain's Canary Islands.

Madeira was discovered and claimed for Portugal in 1419–20 by explorer João Gonçalves Zarco, whose statue stands at the main intersection in Funchal, the capital. Because the uninhabited island was then covered with a nearly impenetrable forest, Zarco named it Madeira, which means "wood" in Portuguese. In the 15th and 16th centuries the colony grew rich from sugar plantations. Later, Madeira's wine industry sustained the island's growth, and more recently, tourism has become big business.

Funchal exudes a British air, dating back to the mid-16th-century marriage of the Portuguese princess, Catherine of Bragança, to England's King Charles II, which marked the end of Spain's domination of Portugal. The marriage contract gave the English the right to live on Madeira, plus valuable trade concessions. Charles in turn gave Madeirans an exclusive franchise to sell wine to England and its colonies. The island's wine boom lured many British families to Funchal, and vacationers followed to enjoy the mild winters.

Today the British still flock to Madeira—many via good-value hotel packages. It's also a popular destination for Germans and Scandinavians, who enjoy downtime in Funchal and hiking the island's famous network of *levadas,* inland irrigation canals converted into superb walking trails. A reserved crowd enjoys Madeira's magnificent blend of sun and seascapes, good food and lodging, tranquil gardens, and afternoon teatime. And although travelers whose priority is cosmopolitan action until dawn will be unfulfilled by Madeira, others—of almost any age, nationality, and fitness level—are likely to be caught in its magic spell.

Historically Madeira has been a winter resort, but—like much else on the island—that is changing. Christmas week, when every tree in Funchal is decorated with lights and the main boulevard becomes an open-air folk museum, is still the most popular time to visit, along with New Year's Eve, when cruise ships from everywhere pull into the harbor for an incomparable fireworks display from the hills surrounding Funchal. Festivals—celebrating flowers in April, the island's patron saint in August, and wine in September—are popular, too.

But now, despite nostalgia for Madeira's past, the island is entering a period of major growth, with the Aeroporto da Madeira as the catalyst. Thanks to a European Union–led infusion of some $500 million, it became fully intercontinental in September 2000. In anticipation of the new arrivals, hotel beds increased by 2,000 in 2000–to 25,000 and counting. (Fortunately, height and architectural restrictions are in place, along with popular interest in observing them.) At least one property on Funchal's oceanfront "hotel row" has reclaimed land from the sea and then, under a complex arrangement, rented it from the government. A 5-km (3-mi) promenade, including a pedestrian tunnel, now extends from a new swimming complex to downtown. And a new, Austrian-engineered cable car connects "Old Town" Madeira with the island's world-famous "toboggan" rides from the heights at Monte.

But although the island is small, don't assume that development will overwhelm it. Rather, it's the island's amazingly rugged interior that overwhelms all who experience it. Multiple microclimates; exotic topography and vegetation; a new UNESCO World Heritage Nature Site, Laurissilva Forest; and designated nature reserves create an amazing ecodestination—much of it laced with irrigation canals that double as world-renowned walking trails. With this awesome heritage, Madeira has the power to keep its core a sanctuary for centuries to come.

Pleasures and Pastimes

Dining

Numerous restaurants on Madeira specialize in island cuisine, and most typical meals revolve around a deep-sea fish known as *espada* (often called "scabbard fish" because of its long, swordlike shape). This soft, white fish is served everywhere and prepared dozens of ways, from poached à la Provençal to fried with bananas. You can see freshly caught espada, which are really quite ugly (although very delicious), at the Mercado dos Lavradores (Workers' Market) in Funchal or in iced displays at many restaurants. In all the world, espada are fished commercially only in the deep, offshore waters of Madeira and Japan. The fishermen set out in the early evening in small boats, lower lines baited with specially prepared squid to the depths of the ocean, and laboriously pull up the catch. The fishermen take Sunday off, however, so don't look for fresh espada on Monday. Seafood fans should also try the Portuguese version of bouillabaisse, *caldeirada de peixes variados,* a slowly simmered combination of fish, shellfish, potatoes, tomatoes, onions, and olive oil. The other popular fish plate is *bife de atum,* a hearty tuna steak. Those with more adventurous tastes should search out *polvo com vinagre*—a tangy octopus salad.

A favorite meal of tourists and locals alike is *espetada,* a beef shish kebab seasoned with bay leaves and butter. Traditionally it was a party dish prepared in the country over open fires, and the meat was skewered on bay twigs. Nowadays, the delicacy is served on iron skewers hung vertically from special stands placed in the center of each table so the kebabs are shared by all diners. Another specialty is *carne de vinhos e alhos* (pork marinated in wine, oil, garlic, and spices, then gently boiled and quickly browned over a high flame). Also worth trying are *milho frito* (fried cubes of savory corn pudding), a side dish native to Madeira, and *bolo de caco,* a round, flat bread made with sweet potatoes traditionally cooked on a hot stone.

Typical desserts are bananas (small, sweet, silvery ones, which are not exported), mango, *paw paw* (papaya), *anonas* (custard apples), and *maracujá* (passion fruit). Don't leave without trying the *bolo de mel,* a spicy honey cake made with molasses and traditionally served with a glass of Madeira, the unique wine that has become synonymous with the island. Most restaurants serve Madeira (indeed, many offer diners a complimentary glass). Look also for *vinho da casa,* a local table wine. It's much cheaper than imported ones and generally of high quality.

Coral, a light lager, is the local *cerveja* (beer). For a tasty nonalcoholic drink, try *brisa maracujá,* a sparkling passion-fruit soda.

For price categories, *see* the chart under Dining *in* Smart Travel Tips A to Z.

Fishing

Madeira and Porto Santo are meccas for those hoping to reel in huge blue marlin, yellowfin tuna, albacore, swordfish, and dorado. The European marlin weight record—1,212 pounds—was set here. In fact, the list of gilled gentry inhabiting the surrounding waters also includes bigeye tuna, barracuda, dolphinfish, wahoo, and shark.

Folkloric Traditions

Although many islanders prefer more sophisticated leisure pastimes, Madeira proudly makes the most of its folkloric traditions for tourists and at holiday time. No matter when you visit, there's a good chance you'll see folk dances performed at a restaurant or hotel. Costumed dancers whirl to the music of a small guitarlike instrument called a *machête.* Musicians also shake a colorful pole decorated with tiny folkdancer dolls that jangle like a tambourine.

Hiking

The island is covered with fabulous footpaths that run among the mountain peaks and alongside the levadas. These canals crisscross the island and often flow through tunnels, bringing valuable water from the mountains to the tiny terraced farms. You can follow the thin cement or dirt paths that run alongside the levadas for hundreds of miles. The footpaths were made so the *levadeiro,* the person tending the levadas, could clear anything that blocked the flow of water. Although most were built much more recently, some date from as far back as the 15th century.

The island has many microclimates and a varied topography. You'll encounter powerful jagged mountains, desertlike valleys, waterfalls, dense forest, and luxuriant hillsides. Every view seems better than the last. One of the most breathtaking is from Madeira's highest peak, 6,106-ft Pico Ruivo. On a clear day you can nearly see from one end of the island to the other. The tourist office has several publications listing hikes of varying length and difficulty.

Lodging

Accommodations in Funchal range from majestic old hotels to small, quiet *pensãos* (pensions). If you venture out to explore the island, you may want to stay in a *pousada* (which means resting place, not to be confused with mainland Portugal's government-owned *pousadas*). You'll find these two small, quiet inns in the heart of Madeira's mountains. At the Pousada do Pico do Arieiro at 6,107 ft, you'll feel as if you're above the clouds because sometimes you actually are. Several low-key inns and bed-and-breakfasts are also scattered around the island.

Some of the larger Madeiran hotels cater to package-tour operators, who offer better prices and reserve huge blocks of rooms during peak holiday-travel periods. This may be one place where do-it-yourself travelers are better off going through an agency. For price categories, *see* the chart under Lodging *in* Smart Travel Tips A to Z.

Wine Tasting

Madeira's wines have been enjoyed for more than 500 years. They graced the tables of Napoléon, Russian czars, and even George Washington. In fact, the glasses raised to toast the signing of America's Declaration of Independence were filled with this island's delicious elixir. And Shakespeare wrote of Falstaff's willingness to trade his soul for "a cup of Madeira and a cold capon." The fortified wine is served as an aperitif or with dessert, depending on its sweetness. Unlike other wines, Madeira is heated to produce its distinctive mellow flavor—a process that supposedly developed after thirsty sailors sampled the Madeira that had been shipped through equatorial heat and discovered its improved taste. The four varieties of Madeira are, from driest to sweetest, *Sercial, Verdelho, Boal,* and *Malmsey.*

The many famous brands of Madeira include Blandy's, Leacock's, and Cossart Gordon, to name a few. Although all are now produced by the Madeira Wine Company, each brand is blended to maintain the individual characteristics unique to each. To learn the history of these wines, see how they're made, and sample a few, you can visit the São Francisco Wine Lodge in Funchal or the Henriques & Henriques Vinhos (Winery) in Câmara de Lobos.

Exploring Madeira

Geographically, Madeira has five regions: Funchal, the capital; its environs; the eastern side of Madeira; the central peaks, gorges, and plateaus of the interior; and the powerful cliffs of the rocky northwest coast. Additionally, there are the neighboring islands of Porto Santo and Ilhas Desertas, although if time is limited, Madeira's pleasures are more than enough.

Great Itineraries

To tour Madeira, begin in Funchal. It's small, and its charm is contagious. Although it can be thronged with tour groups–especially when a large cruise ship arrives for a day, it's not hard to avoid them. Nearly 80% of visitors never leave Funchal—understandably, given its laid-back pleasures, but a great mistake in view of what lies inland.

To fully appreciate the island, get out—by rental car, taxi, even tour bus if that's the only option—and explore Madeira's greatest asset: nature. The rocky mountains and green hillsides, moors and narrow valleys could hold their own with New Zealand or Scotland, which are frequently invoked as comparisons. Hike or amble along a levada in the central part of the island. Spend a night or two inland or on the north coast. Consider giving this floating garden at least a few days to work its magic and invade your psyche with its lushness and raw drama. The biggest mistake of all would be to wait until the last day to explore the interior. If you're taking a scheduled tour, begin with half-day trips to orient yourself; full-day tours can involve many hours of sitting in a minivan or bus negotiating narrow roads and switchbacks, leaving you frustrated that, just when you'd like to stop for a picnic or even 10 minutes to admire the view, you can't.

Three days are the minimum for exploring Funchal and its environs, along with some of the interior or the western coast; five days allows for a less hurried and more complete exploration of the island including the northeast; a full week lets you circumnavigate the "big" island and perhaps spend a day on nearby Porto Santo. Allow plenty of time when driving around the island. Destinations often appear close on the map but take a long time to reach, due to winding mountain roads and slow-moving trucks.

Numbers in the text correspond to numbers in the margin and on the Madeira and Funchal maps.

IF YOU HAVE 3 DAYS

For many visitors, a three-day jaunt to Madeira is the perfect way to end (or begin) a visit to mainland Portugal. Devote your first day to the flower-bedecked capital city of ⚐ **Funchal** ①–⑬. Start day two early, heading for the hills just outside the city. In the morning, visit the nearby **Jardim Botânico,** planted on the grounds of an aristocratic plantation. Also in the vicinity is the mountain village of **Monte** ⑭, home of the unusual snowless sled ride. Next, go west from Funchal toward **Pico dos Barcelos,** whose view of the city can easily use up a roll of film. Then move on to the coast and a late lunch in or near the charming fishing village of **Câmara de Lobos** ⑰. Continue to **Cabo Girão** ⑱, with its spectacular views across the island. The terrain changes to forests as you continue along the coast to **Ribeira Brava** ⑲, another lovely seaside village. Turn inland through a rugged canyon and into a vivid green forest, all the while being sprayed by waterfalls cascading down the canyon walls. You'll soon come to the magical, mystical, cloud-shrouded peaks of the ⚐ **Serra de Agua** ⑳. Plan well ahead to stay overnight here at the charming pousada. On your last day, wake up very early and walk in the mountains. Keep an eye on the time, though, as it can be a three- to four-hour drive back to Funchal, where you can spend another night or catch a flight to Lisbon or home.

IF YOU HAVE 5 DAYS

Spend your first day and night getting into the island rhythm by exploring ⚐ **Funchal** ①–⑬. During the morning of your second day, explore its environs and visit the **Jardim Botânico** and **Quinta do Palheiro** (Blandy Gardens) with its amazing array of flowers. Next, head toward the village of **Monte** ⑭ for a quick look around. Afterward, using a good road map, follow the road to Poiso. Here, turn left and follow the signs to ⚐ **Pico do Arieiro** ㉖. You'll be driving above the tree line into what looks like a moonscape leading to the island's third-highest mountain. Plan well ahead to overnight in the memorable pousada here, and the next day, head out for an exhilarating hike. If you're up to the challenge, try to reach Pico Ruivo. The next morning, backtrack to Poiso and head north to **Ribeiro Frio** ㉗. You could walk a levada or stop at Victor's Bar, near the village's trout hatchery. Notice the dramatic change in landscape from brown-and-gold tones to rich greens and blues as you drive north. Next head for **Santana** ㉘ to see the thatched-roof houses for which the village is famous, then west along the coast road toward ⚐ **São Vicente** ㉒. Be sure to have film on hand, as the views are staggering. You can either overnight in São Vicente or push on to ⚐ **Porto Moniz** ㉓, farther along the same incredible coastal road. Watch for the many roadside waterfalls, some of which may cascade right over your car.

In Porto Moniz pick up picnic fare, then travel the coast toward Santa and turn inland toward **Rabaçal** ㉔, full of waterfalls and quiet pools. Follow the road to **Paúl da Serra** ㉕, the closest thing to flatland on the island, where you'll see sheep grazing across the moors. Next, follow the signs to the pretty, flower-filled town of Canhas and on to the coastal road back into Funchal. Spend your fourth night and the next day enjoying the capital; then bid the island a fond *até a prossima* (until next time) and head for the 21st-century airport.

IF YOU HAVE 7 DAYS

If you're lucky enough to have a week's time, you might combine the suggested five-day itinerary described above with one of two options: **Porto Santo,** the tiny, fast-developing resort island 50 km (31 mi) northeast of Madeira still provides sun-lovers with a 10-km (6-mi) stretch of golden sand and some scenic walks or drives. The don't-miss sight is the **Casa de Cristóvão Colombo** (Columbus Museum and Home), actually the house of the first governor, who also happened to be the ex-

Madeira

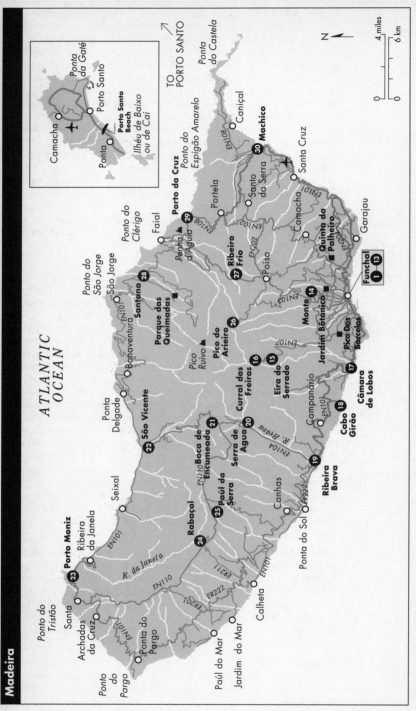

ATLANTIC OCEAN

TO PORTO SANTO

N

4 miles
6 km

Ponta da Gaté
Ponta Santo
Porto Santo
Camacha
Porto Santo Beach
Ilhéu de Baixo ou de Cai

Ponta do Castela
Canigal
Machico ③⓪
Santa Cruz
Ponto do Espigão Amarelo
Ponto da Cruz
Porto da Cruz ②⑨
Portela
Santo da Serra
Camacha
Quinta da Palheiro
Garajau
Faial
Ponto do Clérigo
Penha d'Águia
Ribeiro Frio ②⑦
Poiso
Funchal ① ⑬
Monte ⑭
Ponto do São Jorge
São Jorge
Santana ②⑧
Parque das Queimadas
Pico do Arieiro ②⑥
Jardim Bôtanico
Pico Dos Barcelos
Bonaventura
Pico Ruivo
Curral das Freiras ①⑥ ①⑤ Eira do Serrado
⑰
Câmara de Lobos
São Vicente
Ponta Delgada
②②
②①
Boca de Encumeada
②⓪ Serra de Agua
Campanário
Cabo Girão ①⑧
Seixal
Paúl da Serra
⑲
Ribeira Brava
Porto Moniz ②③
Ribeira da Janela
②⑤ Rabaçal
②④
Canhas
Ponta do Sol
Ponto do Tristão
Santa
Archadas da Cruz
Ponta do Pargo
R. da Janela
Calheta
Paúl do Mar
Jardim do Mar

plorer's father-in-law. Alternatively, **Funchal's** appeal makes it worth at least two more days.

When to Tour Madeira

The island's lower elevations are blessed by constant soft, warm breezes, and lush, subtropical vegetation that perfumes the air year-round. Every day seems like spring. The Christmas and New Year's period is the busiest; book far in advance. Summer can also be crowded, especially during August, when the Portuguese take vacations.

FUNCHAL

When colonists arrived in Madeira in July 1419, the valley they settled was a mass of bright yellow fennel, or *funchal* in Portuguese. Today the bucolic fields are gone, and the community that replaced them is the self-governing island's bustling business and political center.

Exploring Funchal

To get to know Funchal best, spend time at the waterfront, market, and city squares—daily haunts of the islanders. At press time, the **Teleférico da Madeira,** an Austrian-engineered cable car, was about to begin running 42 cars from the Fortaleza de São Tiago and the Mercado dos Lavradores up to Monte. The nine-minute ride promises to be a good way to savor gorgeous views over the city.

A Good Walk

A good place to start is at **Parque Santa Catarina** ①, which overlooks the harbor and Avenida Arriaga, Funchal's main street. In spring, the jacaranda trees that line both sides are vivid purple. (You can walk here from any of the big seafront hotels first—either on the promenade edging the ocean or along the Avenida do Infante slightly inland.) From Avenida Sá Carneiro, descend to the **Porto do Funchal** ②, take in the fresh sea air, and enjoy watching any ships that may be arriving. Across Avenida do Mar from the yacht harbor is the **Palácio de São Lourenço** ③. One block east of the palace is **parlamento** (parliament), housed in the restored 16th-century **Antiga Alfândega** ④.

Continue west along the waterfront to the **Fortaleza de São Tiago** ⑤, which houses a small museum of contemporary art. Head back the way you came, but at the traffic circle head up Rua Profetas to the **Mercado dos Lavradores** ⑥, where pyramids of tropical fruits, as well as flowers and fish, are sold. If you're interested in learning more about the flowers in the market or seeing exotic plants from four continents, resolve to visit (probably on another day) the **Jardim Botânico** (Botanical Garden), just outside town.

Return to Rua Dr. Fernão Ornelas, the main commercial street of Funchal. It changes into Rua do Aljube and then to Avenida Arriaga at the 15th-century **Sé** ⑦. From the square in front of the cathedral, go north on Rua João Tavira and turn right at Rua do Bispo to the **Museu de Arte Sacra** ⑧, in the old bishop's house. When strolling on Avenida Arriaga, stop at the **Adegas de São Francisco du Vinho** ⑨, if not for a tour at least to try some Madeira. Now, choose from two alternatives.

The first: head uphill and north three blocks on Rua São Francisco and Calçada Santa Clara for the **Museu Municipal** ⑩. Afterward, climb Calçada Santa Clara to **Museu da Quinta das Cruzes** ⑪, housed in a gracious mansion built, it's said, on the spot where Madeira's discoverer João Zarco once lived. The big pink building near the top of Calçada Santa Clara is **Convento de Santa Clara** ⑫, where he is buried. Near the convent, you can't miss the old walls of the **Fortaleza do Pico** ⑬,

Adegas de
São Francisco
du Vinho 9

Antigua
Alfândega . . .4

Convento de
Santa
Clara 12

Fortaleza de
São Tiago . . .5

Fortaleza
do Pico 13

Mercado dos
Lavradores . .6

Museu da
Quinta das
Cruzes . . .11

Museu de
Arte Sacra . . .8

Museu
Municipal . .10

Palácio
de São
Lourenço 3

Parque
Santa
Catarina 1

Porto do
Funchal 2

Sé 7

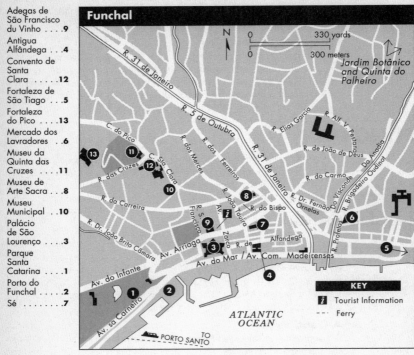

which dominates the upper part of the city. From here, you may want to end your day with a trip outside the city to **Quinta do Palheiro,** also known as the Blandy Gardens, where the heady scent of the blooms will relax you for the rest of your evening in Funchal.

As an alternative, retrace your steps to the colorful cacophony of the Mercado dos Lavradores, where Fridays are best (but Tuesdays through Saturdays are also fine) for examining the fish selections. Continue east along Rua de Santa Maria, parallel to the sea. With the arrival of the Teleférico da Madeira, Funchal's Old Town is fast changing. Hammers and paint brushes are out in force as shops and restaurants spruce up their businesses. Meander along, poking around the shops, to Fortaleza de São Tiago on Rua do Porto de São Tiago. Its walls and battlements date back to at least the early 17th century, and the Museum of Contemporary Art housed in its former governors' quarters could have an exhibition of interest. Artillery originally bristled from the fort's three levels, with staircases connecting them and continuing down to sea level.

Sights to See

★ ❾ **Adegas de São Francisco du Vinho** (St. Francis Wine Lodge). Here you can see how wine barrels are made, visit cellars where the wine is stored, and hear tales about Madeira wine. (The wineries, however, are outside town and are closed to visitors.) One legend has it that when the Duke of Clarence was sentenced to death in 1478 for plotting against his brother, King Edward IV, he was given his choice of execution methods. He decided to be drowned in a "vat of Malmsey," a barrel of the drink! There's plenty of time for tasting at the end of the visit. ⊠ *Av. Arriaga 28,* ☎ *291/223065.* ☞ *500$00.* ۞ *Tours weekdays at 10:30 and 3:30, Sat. at 11; wine shop weekdays 9–7.*

❹ **Antiga Alfândega** (Old Customs House). This stately building houses Madeira's parliament. Its original 16th-century Manueline style was amended with baroque renovations following the devastating 18th-century earthquake that almost leveled faraway Lisbon. From this building deputies govern the island, which is part of Portugal but enjoys greater autonomy than mainland provinces. ⊠ *Av. do Mar and Av. das Comunidades Madeirenses.*

⑫ Convento de Santa Clara (Santa Clara Convent). Inside, the painted wood walls and ceiling are lined with ceramic tiles, giving the sanctuary an Arabic look. ⊠ *Calçada de Santa Clara,* ☎ *291/742602.* ⊙ *Daily 10–noon and 3–5.*

❺ Fortaleza de São Tiago. The construction of this fortress was started by 1614, if not earlier, when French corsairs had begun to threaten Funchal Bay's coveted deep-water harbor. Thanks to continuous use—by British troops when their nation was allied with Portugal against Napoléon, and during the visit of the Portuguese king Dom Carlos in 1901—much of the fort has been preserved. A former governor's house inside it is now the **Museu de Arte Contemporânea,** housing small, changing exhibitions emphasizing works from the 1960s and later, most by local artists. ⊠ *Rua do Portão de São Tiago,* ☎ *291/226456.* ⊙ *Open Mon.–Sat. 10–12:30 and 2:30–5:45.*

⑬ Fortaleza do Pico. The Fort of the Peak was built in the late 1500s to protect the settlement against pirate attacks. One of the worst raids on Funchal was in the 16th century by the pirating nobleman Bertrand de Montluc, who sacked the churches and stole barrels of Madeira. He resold the wine to his noble friends and unwittingly helped spread the reputation of the island's drink. Today the fort is home to Pico Radio, a local radio station. ⊠ *Calçada do Pico.* ⊙ *Daily 9–6.*

OFF THE
BEATEN PATH

QUINTA DO PALHEIRO – Also known as Blandy Gardens, this 30-acre estate is owned by the Blandy wine family. Garden enthusiasts come for the camellia trees that bloom between December and April and for the formal gardens with flowering perennials. You can stroll the grounds, but you can't tour the family's house. The gardens are 5 km (3 mi) northeast of Funchal. Head out of town on N101, the road to the airport. At the fork make a left onto N102 and follow the signs toward Camacha. Also, Bus 36 departs weekday mornings at 9:45 from the intersection of Avenida do Mar and Avenida das Comunidades Madeirenses (next to the marina, in front of the Palácio de São Lourenço). It returns at 1 PM. 🎟 *1,000$00.* ⊙ *Weekdays 9:30–12:30.*

★ ❻ Mercado dos Lavradores (Workers' Market). Riotous displays of orchids, bird-of-paradise flowers, anthuriums, and other, less exotic blooms are sold in the center patio of this market by women who sometimes dress in Madeira's native costume—a full, homespun skirt with yellow, red, and black vertical stripes and an embroidered white blouse. Downstairs, the lower-level seafood market displays the day's catch. Note the rows of fierce-looking espada. Their huge, bulging eyes are caused by the fatal change in pressure between their deep-water habitat and sea level. ⊠ *Rua Brigadeiro Oudinot.* ⊙ *Weekdays 7 AM–8 PM.*

OFF THE
BEATEN PATH

JARDIM BOTÂNICO (Botanical Garden) – Garden aficionados won't want to miss this collection of well-labeled subtropical plants—including anthuriums, bird-of-paradise plants, and a large cactus collection—from four continents, displayed on the grounds of an old plantation. Savor wonderful views of Funchal, and catch the petrified trunk of a heather tree that's 10 million years old. There's also a simple natural-history museum, and an adjoining orchid garden with year-round flowers. You can reach the gardens, 3 km (2 mi) northeast of Funchal, via Bus 30, which stops across the street from the market in front of Madeira's Electric Company. To hike up, turn uphill on Rua da Rochina from Avenida Arriaga to Caminho do Meio and follow it for at least 45 minutes. ⊠ *Caminho do Meio,* ☎ *291/200200.* ⊡ *300$00.* ⊙ *Daily 10–6.*

⓫ **Museu da Quinta das Cruzes.** The building is impressive, and so is the collection of antique furniture inside. Of special interest are the palanquins—lounge chairs once used to carry the grand ladies of colonial Madeira around town. Outside the Quinta is a botanical garden filled with stone columns and tombstones. ⊠ *Calçada do Pico 1,* ☎ *291/741388.* ⊡ *350$00.* ⊙ *Tues.–Sat. 10–12:30 and 2–6.*

❽ **Museu de Arte Sacra** (Museum of Sacred Art). Here you'll find Flemish paintings, polychrome wood statues, and other treasures gathered from the island's churches. Most of the paintings were commissioned by the first merchants of Madeira, many of whom came from Brugge, Belgium. For example, the *Adoration of the Magi* was painted in 1518 for a rich merchant from Machico and paid for not in gold, but in sugar. You can tell how important sugar was to the island by examining the coat of arms of Funchal, which depicts five loaves of sugar in the shape of a cross. ⊠ *Rua do Bispo 21,* ☎ *291/228900.* ⊡ *450$00.* ⊙ *Tues.–Sat. 10–12:30 and 2:30–5:30, Sun. 10–1.*

NEED A BREAK?   A good place to stop for a light lunch or afternoon tea is **O Patio** (⊠ Rua da Carreira 43, ☎ 291/227376), which entirely lives up to its name—it's a tiled open-air patio. At the same address, **Livraria Inglesa,** Funchal's only English-language bookstore, sells magazines, novels, and books about Portugal.

❿ **Museu Municipal** (City Museum). Animals found on Madeira and in its seas—including a ferocious-looking collection of stuffed sharks—are on display here. Attached is a small aquarium, where you can watch the graceful movements of an octopus and view a family of sea turtles. ⊠ *Rua Mouraria 31,* ☎ *291/229761.* ⊡ *200$00.* ⊙ *Tues.–Fri. 10–6, weekends noon–6.*

❸ **Palácio de São Lourenço** (St. Lawrence Palace). Built in the 17th century as Madeira's first fortress, this palace is still used as a military headquarters. You can walk the grounds, but on occasions when the building is open to visitors, it's by prior appointment (ask at the tourist office). ⊠ *Av. Zarco and Av. Arriaga.*

❶ **Parque Santa Catarina.** At the top of this park, where flowers bloom year-round, is a pink mansion called **Quinta Vigia,** the residence of the president of Madeira. In the center of the park rests the tiny **Capela de Santa Catarina** (St. Catherine's Chapel), built by Zarco in 1425 and one of the oldest buildings on the island. ⊠ *Between Av. do Infante and Av. Sá Carneiro, overlooking the harbor.*

❷ **Porto do Funchal.** This is where growing numbers of cruise ships moor for one- or two-day visits to the island, and where big container ships—mostly from northern Europe—unload. Walk east on Avenida Comunidades Madeirenses (known as Avenida do Mar), the seafront boulevard, and enjoy the view.

NEED A BREAK?   A classic spot to sit back and smell the jacaranda is the **Casa Minas Gerais** (⊠ Av. do Infante 2, at Rua João Brito Câmara, ☎ 291/223381). Pick out your pastry from the central bar, and a waiter will bring it to your table with a pot of tea or coffee.

❼ Sé (Cathedral). Renowned for its ceiling with intricate geometric designs of inlaid ivory, this cathedral (currently undergoing restoration) reveals an Arabic influence throughout. Don't miss the carved choir stalls in the side entrance and in the chancel (they depict the prophets and the apostles), or the tilework at the side entrance and in the belfry. ⊠ *Av. Arriaga,* ☎ *no phone.* ⊙ *Daily 9–11 and 4–6.*

Dining

$$$$ ✕ **Les Faunes.** Named for the series of Picasso lithographs that adorns
★ the walls, Les Faunes is the crown jewel of Reid's Palace hotel (☞ Lodging, *below*). The interior is done in a sophisticated blue-gray, with tables on two tiers guaranteeing stunning views of Funchal at night. A pianist plays romantic music during your meal. The nouvelle menu changes daily, but expect to find such dishes as artichoke custard with sweet red-pepper sauce, carpaccio of sea bass with caviar, duck breast baked with peaches, and hot passion-fruit soufflé. ⊠ *Reid's Palace, Estrada Monumental 139,* ☎ *291/763001. Reservations essential. Jacket and tie. AE, DC, MC, V. No lunch.*

$$$ ✕ **Casa Dos Reis.** A favorite with regular visitors to Madeira, the Casa dos Reis serves high-quality international food in a dining room reminiscent of Grandma's house. Lobster crepes, sole in lemon-mustard sauce, and medallions of veal sautéed in Armagnac are all among the accomplished chef's repertoire. For dessert, try the pears poached in wine. ⊠ *Rua Penha de França 6,* ☎ *291/225182. AE, DC, MC, V.*

$$$ ✕ **Casa Madeirense.** Wedged into a restored house next to Reid's Palace (☞ Lodging, *below*), this restaurant has been lavishly decorated with tile, hand-painted murals, and a bar that resembles one of the thatch-roof houses of Santana. The menu leans heavily toward fresh seafood and regional dishes (including espada), which the chef likes to dress up with tropical fruits and flambé presentations. ⊠ *Estrada Monumental 153,* ☎ *291/766700. AE, DC, MC, V. Closed Mon.*

$$–$$$ ✕ **Casa Velha.** This restored 19th-century house has been converted into an inviting eatery that appeals to eye and stomach. Ceiling fans, exuberant floral displays, tiled walls, white-lace curtains, and green tablecloths hint at the care paid to the menu offerings. Start with salmon fillets with shrimp or seafood cream soup, then seafood fricassee or *frango assado* (grilled chicken). Dessert might be a pear poached in red wine or mango au gratin. The coffee is good and strong. ⊠ *Rua Imperatriz Dona Amelia 69,* ☎ *291/225749. AE, MC, V.*

$$–$$$ ✕ **O Celeiro.** The farmhouse decor here provides a dignified atmosphere
★ for the traditional Portuguese home cooking. A favorite for business lunches, the dining room fills up at night with a mix of tourists and locals celebrating special occasions. Among the most popular items are the Algarve-style *cataplanas,* seafood stews served in special copper-lidded pots. *Pudim,* a flanlike pudding, makes a soothing dessert. ⊠ *Rua dos Aranhas 22,* ☎ *291/230622. MC, V.*

$$–$$$ ✕ **Golden Gate.** Just steps from the tourist office in the heart of Funchal, this restaurant-café makes a perfect lunch stop. Sit in the modern airy interior or capture one of the tables that flank the sidewalk, and enjoy light local dishes. You can end your meal with such delicious desserts as *sorvete de banana e maracujá* (sorbet with bananas and passion fruit). ⊠ *Av. Arriaga 29,* ☎ *291/234383. AE, DC, MC, V.*

$$–$$$ ✕ **Quinta Palmeira.** This lovely private estate, built in 1735, has been converted into a restaurant and funky bar. You can dine in the airy, pastel dining room or out on the large terrace, where island specialties and international dishes are served with creative flair. Try espada *com bananas e molho de maracujá* (with a rich banana and passion-fruit sauce) or *filete de carneiro com molho de menta* (grilled lamb fillet with a fresh mint sauce). For dessert, try the *cassata de abacate* (homemade avocado ice cream). ⊠ *Av. do Infante 5,* ☎ *291/221814. AE, DC, MC, V.*

$$ ✕ **Carochinha.** Amber Victorian lamps, candlelight, and lace tablecloths make the atmosphere romantic at this English-style restaurant beside the municipal gardens. Lunch fare is typically salad or traditional British roast beef and Yorkshire pudding. Evening diners usually go for specialties with French accents, such as duck in orange sauce and coq au vin. Afternoon tea is served weekdays 3:30–5:30, with scones and jam. ⊠ *Rua São Francisco 2A,* ☎ *291/223695. AE, DC, MC, V. Closed Sun.*

$$ ✕ **A Seta.** It's not fancy, and the parking area is crammed with tour
★ buses, but this restaurant on a hill above Funchal serves some of the island's best espetada. You'll share long narrow tables with other diners, while waiters dodge in and out among folk dancers and fado singers. The meat is cooked over a charcoal fire; then the skewers are suspended from wrought-iron hooks at each table. It's touristy, but the food is good and the entertainment has a certain charm. ⊠ *Estrada do Livramento 80,* ☎ *291/743643. AE, DC, MC, V. Closed Wed.*

$ ✕ **Combatentes.** The inexpensive daily lunch specials in this large, plain dining room behind the municipal gardens are popular with Funchal's businesspeople. Big portions of simple Madeiran cooking, such as espada, tuna, and grilled pork chops, are served with milho frito. If you want something lighter, try the *sopa de tomate e cebola com ovo* (tomato and onion soup, garnished with a poached egg). ⊠ *Rua Ivens 1,* ☎ *291/221388. Reservations not accepted. MC, V.*

$ ✕ **Pizzaria Xaramba.** When young Madeirans want a break from seafood, they often head for this packed place tucked behind the church in the old section of town. Individual-size pizzas are prepared behind a long bar as hungry customers watch. The ovens stay hot until 3 AM, and the tiny restaurant fills up late at night, so come early or be prepared to wait for a table. ⊠ *Rua Portão São Tiago 11,* ☎ *291/ 229785. Reservations not accepted. No credit cards. No lunch.*

Lodging

$$$$ 🏨 **Cliff Bay Resort.** Down the coast from Reid's Palace hotel (☞ *below*) on the outskirts of town, this elegant resort sits on a spectacular promontory, overlooking the Atlantic and the Bay of Funchal. Cheerful rooms have sweeping views of bay, ocean, or inviting gardens. Marble bathrooms come with twin sinks. ⊠ *Estrada Monumental 147, 9000-100,* ☎ *291/707–0707,* 𝖥𝖠𝖷 *291/762525. 201 rooms. 4 restaurants, 3 bars, pool, saltwater pool, massage, sauna, golf privileges, health club. AE, DC, MC, V.*

$$$$ 🏨 **Reid's Palace.** This is a marvelously old-fashioned and decadently
★ luxurious hotel where the corridors smell of furniture wax and a bellhop plays a chime to announce dinner—at which black-tie (or, at least, a dark suit and tie) are de rigueur. Since 1891, a mix of royalty and film stars, tycoons and statesmen (including Winston Churchill, whose restored suite you can stay in) have frequented Reid's. In fact, it's considered one of the most gracious hotels in the world. A 15-minute walk or free shuttle from the center of town and commanding a rocky point, it is surrounded by 10 acres of gardens, full of hibiscus, salvia, and jasmine. The large rooms are extremely comfortable, with pastel bedspreads, fresh linen sheets daily, and wide balconies with sea views. Baths include big showerheads, towel warmers, and Molton Brown toiletries. ⊠ *Estrada Monumental 139, 9000-098,* ☎ *291/717171,* 𝖥𝖠𝖷 *291/700– 7177. 130 rooms, 32 suites. 5 restaurants, 3 bars, 3 saltwater pools, sauna, spa, golf privileges, 2 tennis courts, exercise room, waterskiing, billiards. AE, MC, V.* 🐢

$$$-$$$$ ⊞ **Crowne Plaza Resort Madeira.** The rectangular design of this ocean-front newcomer is far from unique, but all of the light, cheerful rooms and suites have unobstructed ocean views and perks to assure easy vacation living. Baths come with magnifying mirrors, closets with skirt hangers, and suites have hydromassage tubs. Panoramic elevators take guests down to the water-sports facilities at sea level, which includes sailing, pedal boats, and a PADI dive center. ⊠ *Estrada Monumental 176–177, 9000-100,* ☎ *291/717700,* FAX *291/717701. 276 rooms, 24 suites. 4 restaurants, pub, 4 pools, 2 tennis courts, squash, boating, business services. AE, MC, V.* ⊛

$$$-$$$$ ⊞ **Savoy Hotel.** With its library, tea lounge, manager's cocktail parties, outdoor and heated indoor pools, concerts, fresh flowers, and its location an easy 10-minute walk from downtown, the Savoy can be used as either a self-contained resort (you can choose a half-board option) or a hospitable base for island discovery. Rooms and suites come with foothill or ocean views. Attached to the hotel by lovely gardens, the Royal Savoy Resort will open in late 2001 with a mix of timeshare and hotel accommodations. The two properties will share pool, spa, and other facilities. ⊠ *Rua Imperatriz D. Amelia 108/112, 9000-542,* ☎ *291/222031 or 291/222039,* FAX *291/223103. 325 rooms, 12 suites. 4 restaurants, café, 4 pools, spa, driving range, putting green, 2 tennis courts, business services, meeting rooms. AE, MC, V.* ⊛

$$$ ⊞ **Eden Mar.** This seven-story inn is one of Funchal's several hotels offering good-value packages. It's a favorite with families, who settle in for long stays and appreciate the kitchenettes in each unit. The lobby is white marble, but the rest of the hotel has a homey floral-print decor and cheerful tiled bathrooms. All rooms have sea views. ⊠ *Rua do Gorgulho 2, 9004-537,* ☎ *291/762221,* FAX *291/761966. 70 suites, 37 studios. Restaurant, bar, coffee shop, kitchenettes, indoor pool, saltwater pool, sauna, exercise room, squash. AE, MC, V.*

$$$ ⊞ **Pestana Carlton Madeira.** Many guests at this 18-story beachfront high-rise, 10 minutes on foot from central Funchal, have come every season since the hotel opened in 1971. They're no doubt attracted by the friendly service and the range of sports facilities. The Carlton has a bustling lobby furnished in a passé '70s-modern style and large bedrooms with terraces overlooking ocean or mountains. Ask for one of the large tiled terraces on the first four floors. All rooms have coordinated drapes and bedspreads in airy pastel colors and baths with Portuguese tile. ⊠ *Largo António Nobre 9000,* ☎ *291/239500,* FAX *291/227284. 377 rooms. 4 restaurants, 3 bars, 2 saltwater pools, miniature golf, tennis court, windsurfing, dive shop, dance club. AE, DC, MC, V.*

$$$ ⊞ **Quinta Bela Vista.** Formerly the mansion of Dr. Roberto Monteiro,
★ this elegant hotel in the hills above Funchal provides a hospitality that makes you feel you're visiting a well-to-do family friend. The original house contains a sophisticated restaurant and four guest rooms. Other rooms are in two buildings, constructed in the same gracious colonial style as the main house. Guest quarters have French doors that open onto the gardens and are classically decorated with mahogany furniture, four-poster beds, and beautifully framed pastoral prints. ⊠ *Caminho do Avista Navios 4, 9000-129,* ☎ *291/764144,* FAX *291/765090. 72 rooms. Restaurant, bar, pool, hot tub, sauna, tennis court, exercise room. AE, DC, MC, V.*

$$-$$$ ⊞ **Ocean Park Resort Hotel.** At the end of Funchal's seafront promenade, this sleek newcomer is about a 25-minute walk from town. One of the 10 floors is nonsmoking, and four rooms are for travelers with disabilities. All the well-equipped rooms have sea-view balconies (some also overlooking each other); suites come with Jacuzzi tubs. The re-

sort has free transport to Funchal's center. The heated indoor pool is excellent. ✉ *Estrada Monumental, 9000-100,* ☎ *291/702000,* FAX *291/702020. 260 rooms, 57 suites. 3 restaurants, 3 bars, tea shop, 2 pools, spa, squash, dance club. AE, MC, V.* ⌕

$$–$$$ 🏨 **Pestana Carlton Park Hotel.** Part of the Casino da Madeira complex designed by Oscar Niemeyer, the architect of Brasilia (capital of Brazil), this drab concrete hotel sits next to what looks like a nuclear reactor but is actually the casino. Inside, though, it's pleasant: public rooms, bright with lots of glass and mirrors, are flooded with light from floor-to-ceiling windows that overlook gardens and the sea. Guest rooms are bright and airy, and the restaurant is popular for its buffet dinner and folklore performances. ✉ *Quinta da Vigia 67 9000-513,* ☎ *291/233111,* FAX *291/232076. 400 rooms. 2 restaurants, 2 bars, coffee shop, saltwater pool, hot tub, sauna, tennis court, health club, casino, convention center. AE, DC, MC, V.*

$$ 🏨 **Quinta da Penha França.** In an unbeatable area—just above Funchal Harbor—this place pleases those who prefer their resorts casual rather than glitzy. The homey, four-story white Portuguese manor house with green shutters is surrounded by gardens and a sunny pool. Every room is slightly different, and the furnishings border on the antique. A seaside wing, about a five-minute walk from the main house, opened in 1995. Although the wing is newer, with large terraces overlooking the sea, rooms here are much less charming. ✉ *Rua da Penha França 2, 9000-022,* ☎ *291/229087,* FAX *291/229261. 73 rooms. 2 restaurants, bar, 2 saltwater pools, billiards. AE, MC, V.*

$ 🏨 **Estrelicia.** Named for Madeira's exotic bird-of-paradise flower, this Best Western accommodation is the topmost of three high-rise towers built uphill from the hotel strip. Perhaps because of its somewhat inconvenient location, the hotel is an especially good value. Large, carpeted guest rooms have gold bedspreads and brown leather chairs. ✉ *Caminho Velho da Ajuda, 9000,* ☎ *291/765131,* FAX *291/761044. 145 rooms. Restaurant, 2 bars, saltwater pool, tennis court, dance club. AE, MC, V.*

$ 🏨 **Hotel Madeira.** This hotel on a quiet street in central Funchal has a marble lobby and tiny rooftop pool. Rooms are basic but carpeted, and the beds are comfortable. Each room has a balcony, some overlooking the municipal gardens. ✉ *Rua Ivens 21, 9000-046,* ☎ *291/230071,* FAX *291/229071. 53 rooms. Restaurant, bar, pool. AE, MC, V.*

Nightlife and the Arts

Much of Funchal's evening entertainment is sedate and centers around the big hotels, which offer Las Vegas–style floor shows and bands for cheek-to-cheek dancing.

Nightlife

BARS

A fairly recent addition to the nighttime scene is **Formula One** (✉ Rua do Favila 5, just north of Carlton Hotel, ☎ 291/775755), a combination pub and disco where you can have an intimate chat in a cozy alcove or dance the night away under flashing strobe lights. For an unusual evening's entertainment, try the Japanese-style **Karaokki Bar** (✉ Hotel do Mar, Estrada Monumental, ☎ 291/761001), where would-be singing stars from the audience have a chance to show their stuff. If you're looking to meet someone or simply to have a quiet chat against a backdrop of live jazz, an "in" spot is the terrace-bar **Salsa Latina** (✉ Rua Imperatriz D. Amélia 101, ☎ 291/225182).

CABARET

Young entertainers perform nightly dinner shows at the ⊞ **Pestana Carlton Madeira** (⊠ Largo António Nobre, ☎ 291/231031) and the ⊞ **Pestana Carlton Park** (⊠ Quinta da Vigia 67, ☎ 291/233111).

CASINO

Gamblers will want to try their luck in the **Casino da Madeira** (⊠ Av. do Infante, ☎ 291/209100), which is open Sunday–Thursday 8 PM–3 AM, Friday–Saturday 8–4. Its unusual building was designed by architect Oscar Niemeyer. The entrance fee is 500$00, and you must be at least 18 years old; dress is smart casual (no sports shoes allowed).

DISCOS

Most joints usually jump until 4 AM. Funchal's elegant younger set gravitates to **Copacabana** (⊠ Av. do Infante, ☎ 291/231121), a postmodern disco beneath the casino, or **Vespas** (⊠ Av. Sá Carneiro 60, ☎ 291/234800), a warehouse-style disco next to the docks. The over-30 crowd prefers **O Farol** (⊠ Largo António Nobre, ☎ 291/231031) at the Madeira Carlton Hotel, where hits from the '70s and '80s are mixed in with contemporary disco tunes. Another hot spot is **Formula One** (☞ Bars, *above*).

FADO

A steady stream of tourists fills the tables of the Funchal fado club **Marcelino Pão y Vinho** (⊠ Travessa da Torre 22-A, ☎ 291/230834). In the center of the Old Town, the club attracts aficionados as well as the just plain curious, who come to hear Portugal's soulful national music played each night from 9:30 until about 2 AM. Also in the neighborhood is **Arsenios** (⊠ Rua de Santa Maria 169, ☎ 291/224007), which is open for lunch and dinner, with both fado and Brazilian music.

The Arts

THEATER

The **Teatro Municipal Baltazar Diaz** (⊠ Av. Arriaga, ☎ 291/220416), in Funchal, offers occasional concerts and plays. The local newspaper carries listings, but the easiest way to find out the schedule is to check posters outside the theater. You can buy tickets at the box office.

Outdoor Activities and Sports

Fishing

Fishing excursions can be arranged at the Funchal Harbor through **Turipesca** (☎ 291/231063).

Golf

Golf enthusiasts have managed to carve two courses from Madeira's hillsides. The oldest club is the 27-hole, Robert Trent Jones, Jr.–designed **Campo de Golfe da Madeira** (⊠ Hwy. N102, ☎ 291/552345 or 291/552356), near the airport in Santo da Serra. Greens fees are 5,000$00–8,000$00. And even golfers who came unprepared to play can enjoy their game at 18-hole **Palheiro Golf** (⊠ São Gonçalo, ☎ 291/792116), designed by Cabel Robinson and set in a pine forest at the edge of Blandy Gardens. It's operated by a consortium of five-star hotels. Greens fees are 11,000$00, with right- and left-handed clubs for rent and fine views of town from the clubhouse restaurant.

Scuba Diving

Madeira is too far north for colorful tropical fish, but divers enjoy the clear, still seas of summer and report lots of interesting marine life and coral formations. The diving center at the ⊞ **Madeira Carlton Hotel** (⊠ Largo António Nobre, ☎ 291/934611) rents scuba gear; prices start at 3,000$00. The **Crowne Plaza Resort Madeira** (☞ Lodging, *above*) has a PADI dive center.

Swimming

Slightly west of Funchal are public swimming pools and sea access at the **Lido Swimming Complex** (⊠ Rua Gorgulho, 🖃 230$00; ☉ summer, daily 8:30–7, winter, daily 9–6) and at **Quinta Magnolia**'s complex (⊠ Rua Dr. Pita, ☎ 291/764598; 🖃 135$00; ☉ daily 8–5:30), which has beautiful views of the city. At press time a new complex at **Poças do Governador,** with two large saltwater pools curving into the coastal rocks, was scheduled to open in June 2001. Cool sea temperatures move many swimmers into the better-heated hotel pools. Admission to the attractive indoor pool at the **Ocean Park Resort Hotel** (☞ Lodging, *above*) costs 5,000$00, 3,000$00 of which can be a credit toward snack bar or restaurant food and drink.

Shopping

In addition to wine, island merchants specialize in embroidered table linens, needlepoint, basketry, and tropical flowers. Two of the oldest shops on the island are the **Casa Regional** (⊠ Av. Zarco 15, ☎ 291/224943), across from the post office, and **Casa do Turista** (⊠ José S. Ribeiro 2, ☎ 291/24907), near the Funchal marina.

Basketry

The wickerwork industry of Madeira is centered in the village of Camacha, about 10 km (6 mi) northeast of Funchal, where there's a large cooperative shop on the main square that sells every imaginable type of basket as well as some wicker furniture. Most of the work is done at home, and on many rural roads it's common to see men carrying large bundles of willow branches to be used for basketry. Although you'll find baskets and other wicker items all over Funchal, **Sousa & Gonçalves** (⊠ Rua do Castanheiro, ☎ 291/223626) is one of the largest manufacturers and exporters.

Clothing

Red Globe (⊠ Av. Arriaga 43, ☎ 291/229551) sells sportswear as well as dressy women's clothes at moderate prices. **Roddier** (⊠ Rua das Pretas 23, ☎ 291/228601), the upmarket French chain, has one of its boutiques near the post office. If you've forgotten your designer jeans or need a casual-chic outfit, this window-walled shop could have it.

Embroidery

Thousands of local women spend their days stitching intricate floral patterns on organdy, Irish linen, cambric, and French silks. Their handiwork decorates tablecloths, place mats, and napkins, all of which are expensive (and almost all need ironing). When buying embroidery, make sure it has a lead seal attached, certifying it was made on the island and not imported. One of the most popular shops is **Patricio & Gouveia** (⊠ Rua do Visconde de Anadia 33, ☎ 291/220801), where you can visit the upstairs factory and see the white-uniformed employees stencil patterns and check production; the actual embroidery is done by an army of women in their homes. Some of the most beautiful work can be found at the **Casa do Turista** (⊠ José S. Ribeiro 2, ☎ 291/224907), near the Funchal marina. Another shop with exquisitely finished work is **Bordados de Madeira** (⊠ Rua Visconde de Anadia 44, ☎ 291/223241).

Flowers

Tropical flowers, such as orchids and birds-of-paradise, are available boxed from any florist for shipping home. (It's legal to bring flowers into the United States from Madeira as long as they're inspected at the U.S. airport upon arrival.) Flower stands in the market and behind the church in Funchal also sell bouquets wrapped to withstand an airplane ride home. The **Quinta Boa Visita** (✉ Rua L. F. Albuquerque, ☎ 291/220468) grows orchids and will pack them for shipping.

Needlepoint

Needlepoint and tapestry making were introduced to Madeira in the early part of this century by a German family. You can visit their factory, **Kiekeben Tapestries** (✉ Rua da Carreira 194, ☎ 291/222073), and buy pieces at their shop, **Bazar Maria Kiekeben** (✉ Av. do Infante 2, ☎ 291/227857), which also has a branch in Tampa, Florida.

SIDE TRIPS FROM FUNCHAL

Monte

★ ☺ ⑭ *6 km (4 mi) northeast of Funchal. Take Bus 20 or 21, a taxi, or the new teleférico from downtown.*

If you drive from Funchal, turn up Rua 31 de Janeiro to reach the village of Monte, home of one of Madeira's oddest attractions: the snowless sled ride. Although the toboggans may seem a bit touristy, you really should check them out. Sled drivers, lined up on the street by the church, wear white, with goatskin boots soled with rubber tires. The sleds look like big wicker baskets on wooden runners and have cushioned passenger seats. Two drivers run alongside the sled, controlling it with ropes as it careens over the slippery cobblestones for the 20-minute ride back to Funchal. The runners are greased with lard, but if the basket starts going too fast, drivers jump on the back to slow it down. The sleds were first created to carry only supplies from Monte to Funchal; later, passenger sleighs hauled as many as 10 people at a time and required six drivers. Now you can catch the cable car up, and regard the sled as pure fun.

Before taking your sled ride, stop at the white-stucco church **Nossa Senhora do Monte** (Our Lady of the Mountain). The tiny statue above the altar was found by a shepherdess in the nearby town of Terreira da Luta in the 15th century and has become the patron saint of Madeira. The small church also contains the tomb of Emperor Charles I of Austria, the last Hapsburg monarch, who died here from tuberculosis in 1922 after being sent to the beneficial climate of Madeira.

NEED A BREAK? If you need refreshment before sledding back to Funchal, stop at the **Bar Rosemarie,** just up the hill to the right of the church. While sipping your beer, notice the old photos of sleds and drivers. Not much has changed over the years.

Eira do Serrado

⑮ *16 km (10 mi) northwest of Funchal. Head west out of Funchal on Rua Dr. João Brito Câmara, which turns into the new highway, and go to the miradouro (lookout) at Pico dos Barcelos.*

The *miradouro* (viewpoint) at Eira do Serrado looks over the Grande Curral—the crater of a long-extinct volcano in the center of the island, sometimes referred to as the belly button of Madeira. From here, Pico Ruivo and the craggy summits of central Madeira look like a granite city shimmering in the sunlight or shrouded in mist. Island legend says the peaks are the castle fortress of a virgin princess, who can be seen sleeping peacefully in the *rocha da cara* (rock face). It's said that she wanted to live in the sky like the clouds and the moon, and was so unhappy at being earthbound that her father—the volcano god—caused an earthquake that pushed the rocky cliffs high into the sky so she could live near the heavens.

Curral das Freiras

⓰ *From Pico dos Barcelos, continue on N107 and follow signs to the village of Curral das Freiras, which is 6 km (4 mi) north of Eira do Serrado.*

If you drive from Eira do Serrado, you'll pass through a series of switchbacks and two tunnels that lead down to the village of Curral das Freiras (Nuns' Shelter). The sisters of the Convent of Santa Clara took refuge here from bands of lonely, marauding pirates. Nearly the geographic center of Madeira, the valley sits in the middle of a circle of extinct volcanoes that long ago pushed the island up from the bottom of the sea.

WESTERN MADEIRA

The western part of Madeira includes the greenest and lushest part of the island: in some places you can see a dozen waterfalls spilling into a cool pine forest. On the dramatic north coast, a narrow highway clings to the cliff face and passes under and through several more waterfalls. You can't avoid getting your car wet.

Câmara de Lobos

⓱ *20 km (12 mi) west of Funchal on coastal route N101.*

From Funchal, you'll pass many banana plantations en route to Câmara de Lobos—a fishing village made famous by Winston Churchill, who came here (in a borrowed Rolls-Royce equipped with a bar) to paint the multicolored boats and the fishermen's tiny homes during a stay at Reid's Hotel in 1950. A plaque marks the spot where he set up his easel. Although the coast here is inevitably changing as commutes to jobs in Funchal grow more popular, the boats are still here, pulled up onto the rocky beach during the day. You can also still glimpse women doing the wash in public fountains and bare-bellied children running riot in the narrow streets. A crumbling promenade, which protrudes from the main plaza, offers views west to Cabo Girão.

If you're interested in sampling some Madeira wine, visit the **Henriques & Henriques Vinhos** (winery), in the center of town. You'll be made to feel right at home during a tour of a state-of-the-art facility that combines high technology with down-home hospitality. And yes, the bottles are for sale. ⊠ *Sitio de Belém,* ☎ *291/941551.* 🎫 *Free.* ☉ *Weekdays 9–1 and 2–5:30.*

Dining and Lodging

$$ ✕ **Santo António.** To try some of Madeira's most authentic and delicious espetada, seek out this unassuming restaurant in the hills 5 km (3 mi) above Câmara de Lobos in the hamlet of Estreito near the Funchal–Ribeira Brava Highway. The big dining room is plain, with a linoleum floor and paper tablecloths, but daylight floods through the windows, and espetadas are grilled over an open hearth. For dessert, try the mango fruit shake with a dash of Cointreau. ⊠ *Estreito,* ☎ *291/945439. MC, V.*

$ ✕ **Coral Bar.** This welcoming restaurant sits just behind the cathedral up the hill from the port. Choose between the pleasant tables on the plaza and the simple rooftop terrace overlooking Madeira's most famous fishing village and beyond to Cabo Girão. The day's catch is unloaded about a block away and served in big earthenware bowls. Try the delicious *peixe mista* (a combination of grilled fish, squid, and prawns) or the espada with fried bananas. ✉ *Largo República 2,* ☎ *291/942469. AE, DC, MC, V.*

$$$–$$$$ ✕🍴 **Estalagem Quinta do Estreito.** Just above Câmara de Lobos, this new inn is charmingly integrated into a former wine estate house and ideally situated for access to the Levada do Norte, one of Madeira's most popular walking trails. Guests enjoy views across fields and down to the sea. The inn's 48-room wing still smells like the polished new oak lavishly used in the floors and marble bathrooms. Simple, balconied rooms feature extra luxuries like heated towel racks and a welcoming bottle of wine and Madeira cake. Stairs lead up to a tower library that invites lazy lingering. The Bacchus Restaurant, serving nouvelle Madeira cuisine, may be reason enough for a visit. You can get here from Funchal via taxi or Bus 3 or 137. ✉ *Rua Jose Joaquim da Costa, Estreito de Câmara de Lobos, 9325-034,* ☎ *291/910530,* FAX *291/910549. 48 rooms. Restaurant, 3 bars, pool, sauna, library. MC, V.* ✆

Cabo Girão

⑱ *16 km (10 mi) west of Câmara de Lobos, 32 km (20 mi) west of Funchal.*

At 1,900 ft, Cabo Girão is on one of the highest sea cliffs in the world. From here you can see ribbons of terraces carved out of even the steepest slopes and farmers daringly cultivating grapes or garden vegetables. Neither machines nor animals are used on Madeiran farms because the plots are so small and difficult to reach. Not long ago, farmers blew into conch shells as a means of communication with neighbors across the deep ravines.

Ribeira Brava

⑲ *14 km (9 mi) west of Cabo Girão, 46 km (29 mi) west of Funchal.*

This pleasant village, with a pebbly beach and bustling seafront fruit market, was founded in 1440 at the mouth of the Ribeira Brava (meaning "wide river"); hence the name. It is one of the sunniest spots on the island. Visit the ruins of the 17th-century **Forte de São Bento,** built to protect the townspeople from pirates. The fort now houses the local tourist office.

En Route From Ribeira Brava, turn right on N104, where the road snakes through a sheer-sided canyon. In every direction you can see high waterfalls tumbling down canyon walls and into a pine forest.

Serra de Agua

⑳ *7 km (4 mi) north of Ribeira Brava.*

This is an ideal starting spot for a good hike in Madeira's interior. In fact, whether you hike or not, you may want to spend the night here at the stone pousada, surrounded by moss-green rocks, ferns, and more waterfalls.

Dining and Lodging

$$ ✕🍴 **Pousada dos Vinháticos.** This tiny stone lodge perched on the edge of a pine forest provides accommodations for nature lovers, most of whom swear this is the most beautiful part of Madeira. Do bring a good novel—or companion—in case of fog, which can weave an otherworldly spell of its own. Guest rooms are invitingly cheerful in shades of blue, green, and orange; ask for the log cabin accommodations. Madeira specialties, such as espetada and carne de vinhos e alhos are featured in the restaurant. ✉ *Hwy. N104 between Brava and Encumeada*

Pass, 9350, ☎ *291/952344 or 291/765658,* FAX *291/952140. 21 rooms. Restaurant. AE, MC, V.* 🐾

Boca de Encumeada

㉑ *6 km (4 mi) north of Serra de Agua, 41 km (25 mi) northeast of Funchal.*

The road from Funchal climbs northeast until it reaches Boca de Encumeada (Mouth of the Heights), where there are good views of both the north and south coasts of Madeira. Many hiking trails begin here.

São Vicente

㉒ *15 km (9 mi) northwest of Encumeada, 56 km (35 mi) northwest of Funchal.*

At the town of São Vicente, the road joins the one-lane north-coast highway that's chiseled out of the cliff face and is said to be one of the most expensive road projects, per mile, ever undertaken. In the early 19th century, workers in baskets were suspended by rope so they could carve out ledges and tunnels along the planned route. Proceed with caution and make sure to sound your horn when going around blind curves. Large tour buses constantly use this narrow road; if you happen to meet one, you may be forced to back up to a turnout.

Dining and Lodging

$–$$ ✕📷 **Estalagem do Mar.** All the rooms in this basic inn have ocean views. Bedrooms are sea-green and white with floral curtains and bedspreads. The sparkling white-tile bathrooms are a comfortable place to freshen up after a day of exploring the area. ⊠ *Fajã da Areia, 9240,* ☎ *291/840010,* FAX *291/840019. 83 rooms. Restaurant, indoor and outdoor pools. MC, V.*

En Route   As you wind west along the coast, there are a number of waterfalls ahead: at one point the road passes behind a falls, and there's another delightful fall cascading right onto the road, so you have to drive through it. Stop at one of the viewpoints and notice the windbreaks, made of thick mats of purple heather, which protect the terraced vineyards. You'll pass through Seixal, the site of many respected vineyards.

Porto Moniz

㉓ *16 km (10 mi) west of São Vicente.*

Porto Moniz, with its natural pools formed by ancient lava, is the destination of nearly all visitors taking full-day trips in Madeira. But unless they stay to enjoy a hotel's facilities, there's not much to do here except splash around the pools (no changing facilities), eat, and sunbathe: it's getting here that's fun. This northernmost village on the island was a 19th-century whaling station. Lovely old houses and twisting cobblestone streets make it absolutely picturesque, and its serenity makes it a good place to spend the night.

Dining and Lodging

$ ✕📷 **Residencial Orca.** The tidy, simple rooms here are as pleasant as can be for a low-budget hotel. However, if you want to make your stay here unforgettable, be sure to specify a seaside room. Large, tiled terraces overlook the lava-walled pool and past that, the blue-green sea. The Orca Restaurant, with equally good views, serves espada prepared in every way imaginable. Try it fried with orange, banana, kiwi, or passion fruit. ⊠ *By rocks at end of road,* ☎ *291/853359. 16 rooms. Restaurant, saltwater pool. AE, MC, V.*

En Route As you drive along the winding uphill road to the viewpoint at **Santa,** be sure to look back and see the patterns made by the scrub windbreaks in the village of Porto Moniz. At the fork, turn left on N204, a road that crosses through Madeira's wildest area, providing a unique perspective of both sides of the island.

Rabaçal

㉔ *22 km (14 mi) from Porto Moniz.*

If you have time, take the hair-raising lane to Rabaçal, a remote trailhead from which a network of trails fans out in all directions. Madeirans love to come here to picnic alongside the cascades. Be sure to bring all food with you. Rabaçal is also a good spot to begin a walk along a levada; this irrigation system was built more than 250 years ago without cement and still serves as a water source for much of the island.

Paúl da Serra

㉕ *5 km (3 mi) southeast of Rabaçal.*

Past Rabaçal, the road heads into a moorland called Paúl da Serra (Desert Plain), where sheep and cattle graze and seagulls spiral above the marshes. This is the closest thing to flatland in Madeira, and it looks strangely out of place. The landscape is scrubby and evocative of the high-altitude plateaus of Norway or Scotland.

En Route From Paúl da Serra, you can turn right on N209 and follow signs south to the village of **Canhas.** The twisting road passes more terraced farms and houses with flowering gardens and in 20 km (12 mi) joins the southern coastal road N101, which returns you to Funchal. Or you can take the route to Encumeada and rejoin the main road.

CENTRAL PEAKS AND THE VILLAGE OF SANTANA

The barren high peaks of central Madeira offer spectacular views and ample opportunity for hiking. This part of the island includes the much-photographed village of Santana, with its thatch-roof A-frame houses.

Pico do Arieiro

★ **㉖** *7 km (4½ mi) northwest of Poiso, 30 km (19 mi) northeast of Funchal. Head out of Funchal on Rua 31 da Janeiro, which turns into N103 as it passes the village of Monte. At the pass of Poiso (10 km [6 mi] north of Monte), turn left and follow signs to Pico do Arieiro.*

Pico do Arieiro, at 5,963 ft, is Madeira's second highest mountain. On your way here, you'll travel over a barren plain above the tree line: watch for errant sheep and goats wandering across the pavement on their way to graze stubbly gorse and bilberry. Stop in the parking lot of the pousada and make the short climb to the lookout, where you can scan the rocky central peaks. There are views of the clouds (below unless you're in them), and to the southeast is the Curral das Freiras crater. Look in the other direction and try to spot the huge **Penha d'Aguia** (Eagle Rock), which stretches up like a monolith on the north coast. The trail from the lookout that crosses the narrow ridge leads to **Pico Ruivo** (6,104 ft), the highest point on the island. Winter days can be chilly at these heights, so there's usually an inviting fire blazing in the pousada's bar.

Dining and Lodging

$$ ★ ✕⊡ **Pousada do Pico do Arieiro.** Designed for visitors who would rather hike, work on their novel, or play chess than sunbathe, this inn is high above the tree line. The exterior of the white-stucco building is bleak, but inside you'll find cozy, balconied rooms with chintz curtains and bedspreads. On clear days, the dining room and breakfast terrace have spectacular views of the mountains. Try the traditional island cooking, including delicious soups, good for warming when you come in from the bracing mountain air. A specialty is smoked ham with spinach. ⊠ *Mailing address: Box 478, Funchal 9006,* ☎ *291/230110 or 291/ 702030,* ℻ *291/228611. 25 rooms. Restaurant. AE, MC, V.* ✆

Ribeiro Frio

★ ㉗   *11 km (7 mi) north of Poiso.*

The landscape grows more lush on the northern side of the island, and the road is full of waterfalls. At the village of Ribeiro Frio, there's a trout hatchery, the starting point for an interesting 40-minute levada walk to the lookout of Balcões (meaning "balcony") and the longer hike along a levada to Portela. This is one of the easiest and prettiest walks on the island, ideal for those who are not even slightly passionate hikers. At Balcões jagged peaks tower behind you, and there are views of a sleepy valley dotted with minuscule houses.

Dining

$$ ✕ **Victor's Bar.** After your hike, stop at this marvelous family-owned mountain restaurant for afternoon tea and the best bolo de mel on the island. More substantial meals, including trout prepared many ways, are served here, too. Inside the rustic wood-and-glass building are a couple of welcoming fireplaces. Ask the owners, Victor Reinecke and his wife Nanda, about their highly personalized jeep safaris into Madeira's most remote and beautiful corners. ⊠ *N103,* ☎ *291/ 575898. AE, DC, MC, V.*

En Route   Continue north from Ribeiro Frio on N101 and follow signs to **Faial,** with the road descending in a series of steep curves into a deep ravine. The tiny A-frame huts that dot the terraces along the steep sides are barns for cows, which are prohibited from grazing. There's no horizontal pastureland, and they could easily fall off a ledge.

Santana

★ ㉘   *18 km (11 mi) northwest of Ribeiro Frio, 39 km (24 mi) north of Funchal.*

Santana is a village famous for its A-frame, thatch-roof cottages (*palheiros*) painted in bright colors. Most of these are upscale versions of traditional Madeiran homes. Sadly, this style has been replaced elsewhere on the island by nondescript concrete-block houses.

OFF THE   **PARQUE DAS QUEIMADAS –** From Santana, you can follow a road that
BEATEN PATH   leads southwest to this spot, where you can stop to picnic or pick up a
               hiking trail that goes to Pico Ruivo.

Dining and Lodging

$$–$$$ ✕⊡ **Quinta do Furão.** Set amid a newly planted vineyard high on the cliffs with sweeping views of the sea, this 43-room hotel and restaurant is a premier draw on the north coast. Funchal residents are even helicoptered here for Sunday lunches. Food is a cut above the typical island fare, featuring such dishes as steak in pastry with Roquefort sauce, and prawns on a spit with avocado sauce. Local north-coast wines are

served. ✉ *Achado do Gramacho, 9230,* ☎ *291/570100,* ℻ *291/ 572131. 43 rooms. Restaurant. AE, DC, MC, V.*

Porto da Cruz

㉙ *20 km (12 mi) southeast of Santana.*

The road from Santana to Porto da Cruz skirts the back of the landmark **Penha de Aguia,** whose sheer cliffs tower over the village. Positioned in a fertile valley filled with tiny farms and gardens, the town is as pretty as any on Madeira. It's also where you can find the island's last working sugar mill, used during March and April to make *aguardente.* This fire water, a sugarcane brandy, can be tasted at the small no-name bar opposite the church.

En Route   Start your climb again on N101 and continue to **Portela,** where the view looks south over the gentler valley of Machico. From here it's an easy drive through pine woods and sugarcane fields and into the town of Machico.

Machico

㉚ *15 km (9 mi) southeast of Porto da Cruz, 26 km (16 mi) northeast of Funchal.*

Local folklore says the bay of Machico was discovered in 1346 by two English lovers, Robert Machin and Anne d'Arfet, who set sail from Bristol to escape Anne's disapproving parents. The couple's ship was thrown off course by a storm and wrecked in this bay. Anne died a few days after becoming ill, and Robert then died of a broken heart. But their crew, according to legend, escaped on a raft, and news of the island made its way back to Portugal. (Legend also has it that Shakespeare heard the story before he wrote *The Tempest.*) When the explorer Zarco arrived in 1420, he found a wooden cross with the lovers' story and the church—the island's first—where they were buried. He named the place in memory of Machin. You can visit the replacement church and wander through the old quarter. Among the handful of atmospheric café-restaurants is the Mercado de Velho, a café with an outdoor terrace housed in a former market.

OFF THE BEATEN PATH

CANIÇAL – Multicolored boats bob in water that has been witness to this village's long history as a whaling station, which it remained until the not-so-distant year of 1981. The Whaling Museum still tells the story. In 1985, 5 acres of the sea surrounding the town were designated a national park for marine life. On the way to Caniçal, 10 km (6 mi) northeast of Machico, stop for a coffee at Bar Crespo.

PORTO SANTO

Beachcombers have long loved Porto Santo, some 50 km (31 mi) northeast of Madeira. This tiny island is very dry, and its golden beach runs along the entire south coast. But it is currently undergoing real development, and the increase in the number of beds here is bound to change the island's "getting away from it all" attraction.

Exploring Porto Santo

If you decide to make the trip, the 2½-hour ferry ride from Funchal ends in Vila Baleira. You'll find cobblestone streets, whitewashed buildings, and a park containing an idealized statue of Christopher Columbus. Before gaining fame and his place in history, he married

Isabela Moniz, daughter of Bartolomeu Perestrelo, the first governor of the island, in 1479. She died not long after, at the time of the birth of their son.

The **Casa de Cristóvão Colombo** (Columbus Museum and Home) is in the old governor's house. Inside, lithographs illustrate the life of Columbus, and there are copies of 15 portraits of the discoverer, which prove nobody really knows what he looked like. Ask to see the restored kitchen and bedroom in the upper part of the house. ⊠ *Travessa de Sacristia,* ☎ *291/938405.* 🎟 *Free.* ⊙ *Weekdays 9:30–5:30, Sat. 9:30–noon.*

One of your first stops on the island should be at the scenic **Portela** viewpoint, which overlooks the harbor, the town, and the long ribbon of beach. Move on to **Serra de Foca,** where a track passes old salt flats before winding down to a rocky beach popular with divers. As you continue around the island, you may have to dodge goats grazing along the edges of the road.

Pico do Castelo is a favorite picnic spot, named for the castle that once stood here to protect the town from pirates. Only four cannons remain. The young pine trees planted on the slopes will never grow taller than 9 ft so the view won't be obstructed. From here it's an easy walk to **Pico do Facho** (1,552 ft), the highest point on the island.

Fonte da Areia (Spring in the Sand) flows out of a sandstone cliff. Women came here to do their washing before water began to be piped into town. As you head to the southern tip of the island, you'll pass several windmills in disrepair that were once used for grinding wheat.

Pico das Flores—another lookout—at the end of a bumpy ride offers fine views of Madeira and the rocky, uninhabited islet called Ilhéu de Baixo. Back on the road that runs along the beach, encroaching development becomes apparent: you'll see a handful of high-rise apartment blocks—if not more by the time you arrive.

Dining and Lodging

$$ ✕ **Gazela.** Not far from the Campo de Cima Airport, this large, modern dinner house is where islanders go for Sunday lunch or to celebrate special occasions. The menu is basic Madeiran—espada, espetada, and a seafood soup. ⊠ *Campo de Cima,* ☎ *291/984425. MC, V.*

$ ✕ **Arsénios.** Red-and-white-check tablecloths are your clue that this is the place for pizza, spaghetti, and lasagna. Portuguese specialties are also served in the rustic, comfortable dining room. ⊠ *Av. Dr. Manuel Pestana Jr.,* ☎ *291/984348. AE, DC, MC, V.*

$ ✕ **Baiana.** A covered patio serves as a combination sidewalk café and town meeting place, as just about everybody wanders by in the morning for coffee. Baiana also serves sandwiches, *feijoada* (bean stew), and carne de vinhos e alhos. ⊠ *Rua Dr. Nuno S. Teixeira,* ☎ *291/984649. AE, MC, V.*

$ ✕ **Pôr do Sol.** This fish restaurant sits at the far end of the beach, near Ponta da Calheta. Just 24 tables fill the simple dining room slung with fishing nets—or dine on the sun terrace. There's a free shuttle to and from town. ⊠ *Ponta da Calheta,* ☎ *291/984380. Reservations not accepted. AE, DC, MC, V.*

$ ✕ **Teodorico.** In this farmhouse restaurant, authentic espetada is *the* dish, best accompanied by carafes of local dry red wine and *pão de caco,* the local bread. Choose outdoor tables made from tree stumps or a tiny tiled dining room with a wood-burning oven. ⊠ *Sera de Fora,* ☎ *291/982257. No credit cards. No lunch.*

$$–$$$ 🏨 **Hotel Porto Santo.** On the beach about a 15-minute walk from town,
★   this hotel is a beachcomber's dream—at least until more development

comes. There's a country-club atmosphere, with numerous sports activities, a library-lounge, and rooms overlooking the countryside instead of the beach. They're heavily booked throughout August, but during spring and fall you may have the place to yourself. ⊠ *Campo de Baixo, Porto Santo 9400, ☎ 291/982381, FAX 291/982611. 94 rooms. Restaurant, 2 bars, saltwater pool, miniature golf, tennis court, Ping-Pong, bicycles. AE, DC, MC, V.*

$$ 🏨 **Torre Praia Suite Hotel.** Right on the beach, a five-minute walk from the center of town, this simple two-story hotel was built around an old watch tower that now houses the restaurant. All rooms come with kitchenettes, and the hotel has all the amenities you need for a relaxing holiday in the sun. ⊠ *Rua Goulart Medeires, 9400, ☎ 291/985292, FAX 291/982487. 67 suites. Restaurant, bar, coffee shop, pool, sauna, health club.*

$ 🏨 **Praia Dourada.** This comfortable white-stucco hotel in the middle of the village is a five-minute walk from the beach and is popular with budget-minded German and Portuguese travelers. The corridors are dark, but the carpeted rooms are bright, and there's a small pool with a sundeck. ⊠ *Rua D. Estevão D'Alencastre, 9400, ☎ 291/982315, FAX 291/982487. 180 rooms. Saltwater pool. AE, DC, MC, V.*

Outdoor Activities and Sports

Camping
On Madeira there are really no organized campgrounds, but on Porto Santo **Parque Porto** is a stretch of beach just waiting—thus far—for you to unroll your sleeping bag and pitch a tent. Contact the Porto Santo Tourist Office (☎ 291/983111).

Scuba Diving
For underwater excursions and boat trips in Porto Santo contact **The Dive Center** (⊠ Rua J. G. Zarco 5, ☎ 291/982162).

MADEIRA A TO Z

Arriving and Departing

By Airplane
Funchal's new airport opens the island to nonstop flights from North America for the first time, but at press time they had not been scheduled. Numerous flights link Funchal with Lisbon, London, and other European capitals. Planes arrive at the **Aeroporto da Madeira** (☎ 291/524941 or 291/524972), east of Funchal in Santa Cruz and about 35 minutes away by car. The island is served by **TAP Air Portugal** (⊠ Av. Comunidades Madeirenses 8–10, Funchal, ☎ 291/239290; ⊠ Aeroporto da Madeira, ☎ 291/524362), which has frequent flights daily from Lisbon (1¾ hrs) and London (4 hrs). **British Airways** (⊠ Rua São Francisco 8, Funchal, ☎ 291/524864 or 291/524362) has nonstops between London and Funchal several times a week. A Canadian charter operator, **Lawson Tours** (⊠ 2 Carlton St., Suite 620, Toronto, Ontario M5B 1J2, ☎ 416/977–3000; 800/268–9126 in Canada; FAX 416/977–7782) offers summer flights between Toronto and Funchal.

The 15-minute interisland flight to Porto Santo from Madeira provides spectacular low-altitude views of Machico and São Lourenço Peninsula. **TAP Air Portugal** (☞ *above*) runs a shuttle between the islands four times daily, six times during the summer months. One-way fares start at 6.800$00. Reservations should be made in advance, especially for July and August.

By Boat

The *Lobo Marinho* ferry sails from Madeira to Porto Santo every day except Tuesday. Boats leave Funchal Harbor at 8 AM and return at 6 PM. The sometimes choppy one-way passage takes 2½ hours. Tickets cost 9,250$00 round-trip, and you can buy them on board or through the Porto Santo Line Office (⊠ Rua da Praia 4, ☎ 291/226511), which is open weekdays 9–12:30 and 2:30–6. For sailings on summer weekends, buy tickets in advance.

Getting Around

By Bus

Madeira has two extensive bus systems frequently used by visitors and islanders. Yellow buses serve Funchal and its surrounding neighborhoods: Buses 1 and 3 run west from the city and make stops along Estrada Monumental, where most of the hotels are; beige-and-red buses fan out to other points on the island. Both systems leave from an outdoor terminal at the end of Avenida do Mar, near Funchal's Old Town. Generally several buses a day travel to each village on the island, but schedules change constantly, so inquire at your hotel or the tourist office for departure times.

By Car

The best way to explore Madeira is by car. Although it's a small island, the terrain is steep, so driving can be tortuously slow. For example, the twisting, turning drive from Funchal to Porto Moniz on the western end is only 156 km (97 mi) round-trip, but takes all day. Also, be aware that there are few road signs (get a good map).

Porto Santo roads are easy to handle by car, but most visitors cover the 6-mi-long island on foot or by taxi. It's fairly easy to hail cabs as they cruise around, and you can also phone for one (☎ 291/982334).

Contacts and Resources

Car Rental

Although rates are often cheaper when booked from home, most major car-rental companies have offices at the airport and in Funchal, including **Avis** (⊠ Largo António Nobre 164, ☎ 291/763495 or 291/764546), **Atlas** (⊠ Rua da Alegria 23, ☎ 291/223100), **Budget** (⊠ Hotel Duas Torres, Estrada Monumental, ☎ 291/765619), **Europcar** (⊠ Aeroporto da Madeira, ☎ 291/524633), and **Hertz** (⊠ Assomada-Caniço, ☎ 291/935360). On Porto Santo call **Moinho** (⊠ Hotel Praia Dourada, Rua Estevão D'Alencastre, ☎ 291/982403 or 291/982780).

Emergencies

General: ☎ 112. In Funchal call the **police** (☎ 291/222022), **fire department** (☎ 291/222122). **Hospitals: Clínica de Santa Luzia** (⊠ Rua da Torrinha 5, Funchal, ☎ 291/233434) offers 24-hour emergency service by a specialized team. **Clínica de Santa Catarina** (⊠ Rua 5 de Outubro 115, Funchal, ☎ 291/741127) also has 24-hour medical service. **Pharmacies** are open at night and on Sunday according to a rotating schedule. Dial 166 for information.

Guided Tours

BOAT

Boat excursions near Funchal's coast take place year-round. Choose from a 2½-hour charter to Cabo Girão and back, costing 3,250$00 per person, or a full day (7½-hour) sail to the Ilhas Desertas, including lunch on board and plenty of time for swimming and tanning, for 7,500$00 per person. (Certain areas are banned to boats, and scuba is banned everywhere, as this is a nature reserve and refuge for endangered monk seals.) Tickets are available in advance; ask at the tourist office for schedules or contact **Costa do Sol, Lda.** (⊠ Marina do Funchal, Funchal, ☎ 291/238538 or 291/224390).

HIKING

Viva Travel (⊠ Rua Serpa Pinto 32A, Funchal, ☎ 291/203900, 291/231064, or 291/231065) offers a different hiking tour through the mountains every day. Levels of difficulty vary, and each excursion includes something extra, such as a peek at local weavers or a wine tasting in a hidden cave. Additional companies organizing walking tours are **Turismo Verde e Ecologico da Madeira (TURIVEMA)** (☎ 291/766109), **Montanhismo Animação e Práticas de Aventura (MAPA)** (☎ 291/757063), and **Terras de Aventura & Turismo** (☎ 291/776818).

ISLAND

Travel agencies specializing in island tours abound in Funchal. Visits usually include multilingual motor-coach tours to Cabo Girão, the inland peaks, Porto Moniz, and the village of Santana, as well as meals. Some of the best operators are **Blandy's** (⊠ Av. Zarco 2, Funchal 9006, ☎ 291/200600 or 291/222318) and **Orion** (⊠ Rua de João Gago, 2-A, Funchal, ☎ 291/228822).

WINE TASTING

Blandy's (☞ Island, *above*) runs full-day excursions for wine lovers on Friday, visiting vineyards on the north side of the island, as well as the village of Santana.

Telephones

The general information number on Madeira is **118.** For operator-assisted calls dial 098.

Visitor Information

In **Funchal,** Madeira's busy tourist office (⊠ Av. Arriaga 18, ☎ 291/229057 or 291/225658) is open weekdays 9–8 and weekends 9–6. It dispenses maps, brochures, and up-to-date information on the constantly changing bus schedules. There are also tourist offices in **Machico** (⊠ Forte do Amparo, Praça José António Almada, ☎ 291/962289) and **Ribeira Brava** (⊠ Forts de São Bento, Vila de Ribeira Brava, ☎ 291/951675), both open weekdays 9–12:30 and 2–5 and weekends and holidays 10–12:30. On the island of Porto Santo, a tiny **tourist office** (⊠ Av. Henrique Vieira de Castro, Vila Baleira, ☎ 291/982361) with a helpful staff attends to visitors weekdays 9–5:30 and weekends and holidays 10–12:30.

9 BACKGROUND AND ESSENTIALS

Portraits of Portugal

Smart Travel Tips A to Z

WHERE EUROPE AND THE ATLANTIC MEET

West across the Iberian Peninsula from Spain's arid plains and burning sun, Portugal's landscape unfolds in astonishing variety to reveal a mountainous, green interior and a sweeping coastline. Portugal provides many things you might expect if you're familiar with Spain, including fine food and wine, spectacularly sited castles, medieval hilltop villages, and excellent beaches. But the similarities are far outweighed by the country's delightful distinctions. Portugal seems to revel in its often contrary identity. Despite its proximity, the language is a world apart from Spanish; and although, like Spain, Portugal has a Mediterranean air, it firmly faces the Atlantic. Even the people seem undecided as to their origins, looking markedly Celtic in the north and rather Moorish in the south. But most important, in Portugal you can still travel into the heart of the provinces and be among few, if any, other visitors.

High economic growth and heavy foreign investment have benefited large sectors of the population. Many people are employed in the tourism industry, which now accounts for about 10% of the country's gross national product. Accordingly, the resort areas and cities are now anything but undiscovered: the Algarve coast, for example, is one of Europe's most visited regions. Lisbon, too, has rapidly acquired the trappings of a forward-looking commercial capital. Many of its turn-of-the-century buildings are being replaced by skyscrapers, and renovation and modernization have touched every part of the capital. Much of the architecture and culture that once made Portugal unique now stand side by side with contemporary styles and lifestyles. Away from Lisbon and the busy Algarve, however, there are still country villages, isolated beaches, crumbling historic towns, and hidden valleys that have barely changed over the past few hundred years.

The Ancients, the Romans, and the Moors

Blessed with a salubrious climate and abundant game and fish, this part of the Iberian Peninsula once supported a flourishing prehistoric population. Many traces of ancient culture remain: the sculpted-stone boar fertility symbols in Trás-os-Montes; the huge Colossus of Pedralva, a mysterious seated granite figure on display in the Museu Martins Sarmento in Guimarães; the fascinating megalithic structures throughout the Alentejo; and the Paleolithic rock engravings in northern Portugal. The later arrival of Celtic peoples in northern Portugal (700 BC–600 BC) is recorded in a series of *citânias* (fortified hill settlements) throughout the Minho; the most impressive example is at Briteiros, between Braga and Guimarães. Phoenicians traded at the site of present-day Lisbon, and the Carthaginians and Greeks set up trading posts on Portugal's southern shore. But it wasn't until the Roman annexation of the peninsula after the Second Punic War (218 BC–202 BC) that the region came under any kind of unified control.

There was resistance to the Roman advance, particularly in central Portugal, where the heroic chieftain Viriatus of the Lusitani tribe held the legions at bay for several decades, until his defeat in 139 BC. Much from the Roman period survives in modern Portugal. Roads, aqueducts, and bridges (such as those at Chaves and Ponte de Lima) were built, and cities founded. The most substantial remains are near Coimbra, where there are well-preserved ruins of a Roman town called Conímbriga, and at Santiago do Cacém, where remnants of another

Portrait

Roman town, Miróbriga, have been excavated. Évora has one of the best preserved Roman temples on the Iberian Peninsula. A less obvious Roman relic is the system of vast agricultural *latifundia* (estates) established in the Alentejo. Here the Romans introduced the crops that are now mainstays of the Portuguese economy: wheat, barley, olives, and grapes.

The Moorish invasion of the Iberian Peninsula in 711 had a lasting effect on the country, particularly in the south, where place-names and people's features still reflect those times. The Moors established a capital at Silves in the Algarve (derived from the Moorish, *al-Gharb,* meaning "west of the land beyond"), planted great orchards on irrigated land, and spread a Moorish Arab culture of great significance, although they allowed freedom of worship.

Arab rule stood firm until the 12th century, when Christian forces under Dom Afonso Henriques moved south from their stronghold at Guimarães in the Minho to take Moorish towns and castles at Leiria, Santarém, and Sintra. The ramparts and battlements of these fortresses are visible today, a reminder of both the Moorish genius for siting defenses and of the Christian effort in overcoming them. The most significant victory was at Lisbon in 1147, with the storming of the Moorish fortress on the site of the present-day Castelo de São Jorge. A Burgundian by descent, Afonso Henriques was by then being called the first king of all Portugal, and he ordered the building of Lisbon's proud *Sé* (Cathedral) to celebrate the victory. Many other churches in Portugal mark the path of the reconquest (as the Moors were pushed south), particularly the numerous Romanesque chapels that cover the landscape between the Rios Minho and Douro (Minho and Douro rivers).

Southern Alentejo and the Algarve remained in Arab hands until the mid-13th century, by which time the fledgling kingdom of Portugal extended to its current borders. The country reached its final shape in 1260, when Afonso III—who retook Faro and the western Algarve from the Moors—moved the capital from Coimbra to Lisbon.

An Empire on the Atlantic

The early kings of Portugal, from the dynastic House of Burgundy, quickly established their independent country. Although the nation was recognized by the neighboring Castilian rulers, fortresses were built along the Spanish frontier as a precaution. Those at Beja and Estremoz are evocative examples. A Cortes (Parliament) was assembled, and a university founded, initially in Lisbon in 1290 but transferred to Coimbra in 1308. (The grand university buildings that you see in Coimbra today date from the 16th century, when the scholastic foundation was declared permanent; it remained the only university in Portugal until this century.)

The House of Burgundy was succeeded by the House of Aviz, whose first king, Dom João I, roundly defeated the Castilian army at the Battle of Aljubarrota (1385) to end any lingering Castilian thoughts of dominion over Portugal. This significant victory secured Portugal's independence for nearly two centuries and allowed the country's kings to turn their attention to the maritime ventures that were to guarantee them fabulous colonial wealth. João I marked the victory by building the extraordinary abbey of Santa Maria da Vitória at Batalha in Estremadura, not far from the battlefield. Triumphant in tone, the abbey celebrates not only the Portuguese release from Castilian interference, but also an important historic link with England. The Treaty of Windsor, signed a year after the battle, confirmed the Anglo-Portuguese alliance, and in 1387 João I married Philippa of Lancaster, daughter of John of Gaunt. Philippa and João are buried side by side in the abbey's chapel, as are their children, one of whom was Prince Henry the Navigator, the man who did the most to influence Portugal's rapid 15th-century expansion.

Based at Sagres, on the western tip of the Algarve, Prince Henry surrounded himself with sailors, mapmakers, and astrologers. These men were the first to establish the principles of navigation on the high seas. The caravel, a ship capable of navigating in a cross-wind, was developed, and famous maritime discoveries were soon under way: Madeira and the Azores were discovered in 1419 and 1427, respectively, and by 1460 (when Henry died) the west coast of Africa was known to Portuguese seamen. There were no limits to the inquisitiveness or to the bravery of the sailors. Bartolomeu Dias rounded the southern tip of Africa in 1487, naming it the Cape of Good Hope; just 10 years later, Vasco da Gama reached India; and in 1500 Pedro Álvares Cabral sailed to Brazil. By the mid-16th century, the Portuguese empire had spread over four continents, with trading posts in the Far East and a monopoly in force throughout the Indian Ocean.

The wealth gained from this aggressive expansion knew no bounds. Portugal was at the height of its influence, with Lisbon the richest city in Europe, and under Dom Manuel I (1495–1521) the Crown intervened to take a fifth of the maritime trading profits. Manuel began to adorn Portugal with buildings and monuments worthy of an imperial power, and the late-Gothic architecture that evolved has since come to be called the Manueline style. If there's any doubt about the brimming confidence of that era, one look at the Manueline buildings will dispel it immediately. The interior decoration of the Igreja de Jesus (Church of Jesus), begun in 1494 in Setúbal, near Lisbon, is considered the earliest example of the Manueline style. It was soon overshadowed by exuberant works in the capital itself, at Belém's Mosteiro dos Jerónimos (Jerónimos Monastery) and Torre de Belém (Belém Tower). The abbey of Batalha was transformed by its Manueline renovations, in particular the portal of the Capelas Imperfeitas (Unfinished Chapels), which is among the most impressive of all Manueline works. A tour of any of these buildings is a requisite to understanding the untrammeled power and influence of 16th-century Portugal as well as the country's strong national identity. The pride in these buildings, which goes beyond mere architectural prowess, is most evident in Tomar's Convento de Cristo, whose supreme Manueline ornamentation stands as the most eloquent reminder of the Portuguese age of *os descobrimentos* (the discoveries).

The buildings have survived, but the glories of the Portuguese empire were relatively short-lived. Arts and literature flourished for a while with the emergence of the 16th-century dramatist Gil Vicente and the publication in 1572 of the great poet Luís de Camões's epic *Lusiads,* which told of the proud era of discovery. But the disastrous crusade in Morocco by the young Dom Sebastião in 1578, during which the king perished alongside most of the country's nobility, allowed Phillip II of Spain to renew a claim on Portugal. Camões died in the same year Portugal fell to Spain, and it's said his last words were, "I am dying at the same time as my country."

Portugal's Dark Ages

Spanish rule lasted 60 years (1580–1640), during which time many of Portugal's overseas possessions were lost. In 1640 the Portuguese took back their throne when a nobleman from the powerful Portuguese House of Bragança was installed as Dom João IV: the Bragança dynasty would last until the first years of the 20th century. Fueled by the gold and diamonds extracted from Brazil, the Bragança rulers spent extravagantly on the massive monastery at Mafra (which employed 50,000 workmen), the university library at Coimbra, and the decoration of the Capela de São João Baptista (Chapel of St. John the Baptist) in Lisbon. While such irrationally grand projects progressed, the country's domestic economy weakened and its society remained feudal.

It took the appalling devastation of the 1755 earthquake, which destroyed Lisbon, to breathe new life into commerce and industry. The king's chief minister at the time, the Marquês de

Portrait

Pombal, ordered that the capital's dead be buried and the living fed. He then created a new, planned Lisbon that employed the most advanced architectural and social ideas of the age and resulted in an elegant but restrained style of building known as Pombaline. To walk through downtown Lisbon today is to walk through shades of the 18th century, starting in the colonnaded riverside square, the Praça do Comércio, and through the gridded Baixa (Lower) District, expressly designed by Pombal to house the commercial concerns he was keen to promote. Lisbon's glory is its 18th-century buildings and its sense of measured space. Such town planning is repeated elsewhere in Portugal, most notably in the gridded streets of Vila Real de Santo António, the Algarve's easternmost town.

These developments proved to be mere diversions from the economic, social, and moral poverty of the Portuguese crown. Napoléon's invasions during the Peninsular War left the country devastated, and the monarchy was finally overthrown in 1910. A republic was proclaimed, but the rot of instability had set in, and during the next 16 years 44 governments attempted to rescue Portugal from its malaise. A coup d'état followed in 1926, and from 1928 onward the country was governed by the right-wing dictatorship of António Salazar, who—first as minister of finance, then as prime minister—was strongly influenced by the contemporary Italian and Spanish fascist movements led by Mussolini and Franco, respectively. The dictatorship lasted until 1974.

Contemporary Politics, Culture, and Economy

In the 20th century, industrialization bypassed Portugal; the economy remained agricultural, the political system was unreformed, and the lot of the people didn't improve. The country preserved its age-old traditions and customs within an almost feudal social structure, causing it to fall behind developing nations. Portugal was ready for change. In 1968 its government appointed Dr. Marcelo Caetano

to replace then-dictator António de Oliveira Salazar, who had just suffered a severe stroke. Long-brewing discontent among young career army officers in the African colonies of Angola and Mozambique led to the revolution that occurred six years later, on April 25, 1974, in which Caetano was ousted in a virtually bloodless coup (six people were killed). Huge demonstrations in support of the left-wing, officer-led Movimento das Forças Armadas (Armed Forces Movement) left no doubt that Portugal had entered a new era. The remaining colonies were granted independence. Initially it was a relatively peaceful operation in Mozambique and Guinea-Bissau, but in Angola and East Timor (now part of Indonesia) it was fraught with conflict. Land on the huge estates of the Alentejo was redistributed, and in the name of democracy, free elections produced a popular Socialist government.

Today Portugal is a stable country, its people keen to share in the prosperity offered by the developments within the European Union (EU), of which it held the presidency in 1992. In 1994 Lisbon was selected as European City of Culture, and the capital saw massive redevelopment prior to its hosting of the 1998 World Expo. You may find the stability surprising, given the relatively short time since the revolution, and indeed it speaks well for the inherent qualities of the Portuguese. Moreover, since 1975 more than 700,000 refugees from former Portuguese colonies in Africa and Asia have been absorbed into the country—a remarkable integration in that short period, given that the refugees now represent more than 7% of the total population.

The refugees have inspired welcome change in Portugal; in Lisbon, for example, African music and dance is popular, and dozens of places serve authentic Brazilian, Mozambican, Angolan, and Goan food. And in the final chapter of Portugal's colonial adventures, because the country agreed to take in as many citizens of Macau as wished to leave before the handover of that territory to China in 1999, more Chinese and Macanese restaurants have opened. There's a buoyancy in other cultural matters, too, with Lisbon, Oporto, Coimbra, and other major towns offering the best in contemporary Portuguese art, music, and dance. The painter Maria-Helena Vieira da Silva is the most famous name Portugal has produced this century, although others have also been influential, including pioneer modernist Almada Negreiros and Amadeo de Souza-Cardoso (who has a separate gallery for his works in Amarante). Contemporary writers whose works are translated into English include José Cardoso Pires, António Lobo Antunes, and José Saramago (winner of the 1998 Nobel Prize for literature). Architects strive to re-create that imperial Portuguese sense of confidence in their buildings—Lisbon's vast, colorful Amoreiras shopping and residential complex, the Centro Cultural in Belém, and the Expo Urbe development are as bold as such projects come.

Political stability and artistic confidence couldn't have been maintained without improvements in the economy, and there have been great strides forward since 1974. Membership in the EU has undoubtedly helped, with grants and subsidies paying for the modernization of agriculture; massive aid and loans from the United States have also played a part. One effect of this regeneration is that Portugal has become more expensive over the last few years, although you're unlikely to find costs prohibitive. The government, of course, faces its own problems, not least a marked disparity in economic development between the north and south of the country. In addition, there are relatively high illiteracy and infant mortality rates; inflation causes concern; and agriculture is stubbornly inefficient, despite modernization.

The challenges to the government and people of Portugal in the new millennium are clear, and there are few countries in Europe better equipped to deal with them—a young democracy often has an uncommon will to succeed. But there's a challenge to visitors, too. Take time to get off the beaten track, and you'll be rewarded—more than anywhere else in western Europe—with glimpses of a traditional life and culture that have been shaped by the memories of empire and tempered by the experience of revolution.

THE PLEASURES OF PORTUGUESE WINE

With the exception of those classic kings of wines, port and Madeira, the wines that Portugal produces are mainly honest and straightforward. This is a country where you can enjoy an endless procession of delicious experiments for little more than the cost of a good beer. You can also buy wines of some age at a very moderate cost.

Portuguese wine-making stretches back beyond the Romans to the Phoenicians; it flourished under the teetotaling Muslims, and went through a checkered time after the Moors were expelled. A firm link with Britain enabled the wine trade to remain prosperous, especially where port was concerned. Trade between the two countries predates the 1386 Treaty of Windsor possibly by two centuries. After a long period of spasmodic development, with some regions flourishing and others, such as the Algarve, almost ceasing production, the situation was taken in hand by the Marquês de Pombal. In 1756 he demarcated the regions, geographically delineating growing areas and controlling their output and marketing; the port-making region was the first to be demarcated.

Demarcation, and the attendant quality control, took off in the first years of this century. Today there are 10 regions officially demarcated—the Algarve, Moscatel de Setúbal, Bucelas, Carcavelos, Colares, Bairrada, Dão, Douro, Vinho Verde, and the island of Madeira. Several areas that are still undemarcated also produce excellent wines. The official body that regulates wine production is the Instituto do Vinho do Porto, based in Lisbon. It controls all the facets of viniculture and of marketing, runs competitions, promotes cooperatives, and empowers growers to use a *selo de origem* (seal of approval). Rather like the French *appellation d'origine contrôlée*, the seal acts as a guarantee of a wine's pedigree.

The Algarve and the Alentejo

In the Algarve wine is produced on a narrow strip of land that stretches between the mountains and the sea. Algarve wine is largely red and is usually no better than an undistinguished table wine. Among the better makes are Lagoa and Tavira.

Alentejo vineyards are almost all in the top part of the province, around Évora and over toward the Spanish border. The wines they produce are now among the best in Portugal— Redondo, Borba (with its lovely dark color and slightly metallic flavor), Reguengos, and Vidigueira. The reds are rich in color, the whites pale and fruity.

Moscatel de Setúbal

Wines produced on the Setúbal Peninsula are well known abroad, mainly through the 150-year efforts of the House of Fonseca, based in Azeitão. The Moscatel that Fonseca—together with the small vine growers who make up the local cooperative a few miles east of Azeitão in Palmela—produces is best known as a fortified dessert wine, aged and with a mouthwatering taste of honey. If you find some that is, say, 25 years old, you'll see that it has developed a licorice color; enjoy its sweet scent and taste. Fonseca and the cooperative produce many other wines besides the Moscatel—fine reds (notably one called Periquita, or "little parrot"); rosés, of which Lancers and Faisca are often exported; and a few regular whites.

Bucelas

The Bucelas region is about 30 km (19 mi) north of the Lisbon, in the valley of the Rio Trancão (Trancão River). Although wine from here has a considerable history and was very popular with the British soldiers under Wellington in the Peninsular War, this is quite a small demarcated region, and all the wine it produces appears under the Caves Velhas label. Bucelas wine is usually straw colored, with a distinctively full nose and a fruity taste that can sometimes verge on the citrusy. It goes extremely well with veal, poultry, and fish.

Carcavelos

Carcavelos consists of just one small vineyard, the Quinta do Barão, set between Lisbon and Estoril along a stretch of coast. This isn't an easy wine to find—the yearly output is small—but if you like wines with a history, it's worth looking for. Carcavelos is another fortified dessert wine, topaz colored, with a nutty aroma and a slightly almond taste, mostly drunk as an aperitif.

Colares

The Colares region is at the westernmost tip of Portugal, beyond Sintra. It's a fairly hostile place for vine growing, with sandy soil and exposure to the Atlantic winds. But it has a long and distinguished history of wine production, and it yields some very individual vintages. The red improves with age (it can be a little astringent when young) and has a full ruby color, an aromatic nose, and an aftertaste likened to black currants. One label to seek out is Colares Chita. The Colares whites are straw colored, slightly nutty in taste, and—like the reds—improve with age. They should be drunk well chilled.

Bairrada and Dão

Not far south of Oporto is the coastal region of Bairrada. Although it was not that long ago—1979—that Bairrada was demarcated, the quality of its output suggests that it probably should have received that status long before. This is a region made up mainly of small holdings, gathered into six cooperatives. Taken all together, they turn out a fairly large quantity of wine. The reds are of an intense color, with a delicious nose and a fruity, rich, and lasting taste. They mellow with age and go very well with stronger dishes such as game, roasts, and pungent cheeses. There aren't too many whites in this region, and most of them are slightly sparkling (*espumantes*). The whites mirror the reds in their slightly darkish straw color, with a heavy, rather spicy nose. They go well with fish, pasta, and pâtés. One of the biggest names in the region is Aliança, although several others such as São Domingos and Frei João are worth tracking down. The hotel at Buçaco has its own wines in an extensive cellar.

The Dão region is just south of the Douro, in the mountainous heart of the north, and is crossed by the valleys of the Dão, Mondego, and Alva rivers. The climate is capricious—cold, wet winters, scorchingly hot summers. Unlike the sandy or clay soils to the south, the terrain is made up of granite and schist, a rock that shatters easily. Much of the wine here is red and is matured in oak casks for at least 18 months before being bottled. When mature, Dão wines have a dark reddish-brown color—almost the hue of garnets—a "complex" nose, and a lasting velvety taste. They're best drunk at room temperature after being allowed to breathe well, and they go with roast lamb and pork. Look for São Domingos, Terras Altas, and Porta dos Cavaleiros, or any of the labels where "Dão" precedes the name of the supplier—Dão Aliança, Dão Caves Velhas, Dão Serra, or Dão Fundação. Dão whites are less common. They spend shorter times (10 months or so) maturing in casks and have the color of light straw, a full nose, and a dry, earthy flavor. The white Grão Vasco or the Meia Encosta is worth trying.

Douro and Port

The secret of port is found first of all in the nature of the arid, volcanic soil and the hothouse temperature of the Douro Valley. Some 800 years ago, when the father of Afonso Henriques took possession of his new domain between Douro and Minho, he planted a stock brought from Burgundy. "Eating lava and drinking sunshine," the Burgundy vines stretched, little by little, to the river's edge. They fought a bitter fight, strangling in ravines, wandering in fits and starts, to force their roots through schistose soil. Nothing but the vine could survive in this torrid pass. With tireless obstinacy, the men of the Douro broke up slate, built terraces with stone retaining walls, struggled against drought and phylloxera, and made the lost valley the most prosperous in Portugal.

The region comes alive during the grape gathering, which lasts for several weeks. (In lower-level vineyards, the gathering is often finished long before the higher plantations are ripe.) From dawn until dusk women fill the baskets that the men carry on their backs, supporting as much as 150 pounds with the aid of a leather band looped over their foreheads. They descend in long files toward the *lagares* at the foot of the slopes and pile the fruit in these enormous vessels, ready for treading. More than 40 varieties of grape go into making port, creating a wide diversity of taste. The harvesters gather about the vats before the must has begun to ferment; the atmosphere is steamy, the feverish excitement of new wine induces singing and dancing. In the spring the young wine goes down by road to the lodges in Vila Nova de Gaia. Since the building of a dam across the river the transporting of wine in traditional *rabelos,* boats that look somewhat like ancient Phoenician craft, has ceased.

Port, born as it is of a soil rich in lava, is divided into two great families—vintage and blended. When a year is outstanding—as in 1945, '47, '48, '55, '58, '63, '70, '75, '77, '80, '83, '85, and '94—the wine is unblended and, after reinforcement and bottling, left to mature. These are the vintage wines, which will take upwards of 20 years to mature; the old bottles, dusty with cobwebs, are brought up from the cellar for wed-

Portrait

dings and christenings and must be decanted before drinking. Most port, however, is a carefully studied blend of new wine with old vintages. For a long time, when England was the biggest market for port, the first choice was given to full-bodied tawnies; these were served at the end of dinner, with cheese or an apple and walnuts. However, there's a lot to be said for the white ports, either sweet, as an after-dinner drink, or dry, as an aperitif with ice and a twist of lemon.

In Oporto you can visit a lodge to learn more about port, taste it, and maybe buy a bottle. Seeing these huge old cellars and finding out about the long, fascinating history of port is a memorable experience. Language won't be a problem, as there has been an alliance for more than 200 years between the English and Portuguese in the port trade, and many of the families are bilingual.

Not all the wine produced in the Douro region is port. The reds here are of a deep ruby color, extremely fruity, and with a rounded taste. They go well with richer foods, a variety of meats, casseroles, and stews—anything that tends to be well flavored with herbs. The whites are dry, by and large, and have a pleasant pale-yellow color with a full nose. They go well with salads, hors d'oeuvres, and chicken dishes. Look for Mesão Frio, San Marco, Quinta da Cotto, and Santa Marta.

Vinho Verde
Portugal's largest demarcated region is divided into six subregions: Monção, Lima, Amarante, Basto, Braga, and Penafiel. Inland from the coast and threaded by a sequence of westward-flowing rivers, the region has a fairly mild climate and the country's highest rainfall. The vineyards here are often terraced, climbing hillsides away from the rivers like agricultural fortifications. In places they march alongside and arch over roads, the vines held up on colonnaded rows of pillars. The grapes hang so high they ripen in direct sunlight without any rising heat from the ground.

The name vinho verde, which translates as "green wine," refers not to the wine's color but to the fact that it's not aged. If you enjoy wine purely as a refreshing, mildly intoxicating beverage—a kind of celestial 7-Up—vinho verde is *the* drink—gently sparkling (what the experts call *pétillant*), with a delicate fruity flavor, it embodies the coolness and fragrance of summer gardens. Vinho verde goes well with any kind of seafood. The reds are important to the region, but will mostly be found on their home ground; they don't travel much. They're also refreshingly thirst quenching, sharp rather than heavy, with a vermilion-to-purple color. They go ideally with any meat dish. Look for Alvarinho and Quinta de São Claudio.

Madeira
Like port, Madeira—the wine and its preparation—is a way of life, and a way of life in which Portuguese and British families are bound together. When Charles II married Catherine of Bragança in 1662 he, perhaps foolishly, declined to accept the island, which was offered as part of her dowry. Madeiran soil is volcanic, and its beaches, such as they are, are black. The temperate climate here, which can be humid in summer, provides exactly the conditions in which vines can thrive—although they seldom grow below 300 feet above sea level; that warmer zone is taken up by bananas and sugarcane.

Madeira is a fortified wine, and most often blended. Boal and Malmsey or Malvasia styles are sweet and heavy, and make excellent dessert wines; Verdelho, not so sweet, is a nice alternative to sherry; and Sercial, dry and light, makes an excellent aperitif. All are attractive—particularly when they're really aged—occasional wines. The labels to look for—and they date back in some cases for a couple of centuries—include Blandy, Cossart Gordon, Rutherford and Miles, Leacock, and Miles and Luís Gomes. A visit to a wine lodge in Funchal is an educational and delectable way to spend a couple of hours.

Portuguese Wine Terms

Adamado	Medium sweet
Adega	Wine vault
Adega cooperativa	Wine cooperative
Aguardente	Brandy
Branco	White
Bruto	Extra dry (for sparkling wines)
Caves	Wine cellars
Colheita	Grape harvest (thus a vintage, e.g., Colh. 1980)
Doce	Sweet
Espumante	Sparkling wine
Garrafeira or *reserva*	Fine, mature wine, or a special vintage
Generoso	A sweet dessert wine, highly alcoholic
Meio seco	Medium dry
Região demarcada	Demarcated region
Rosado	Rosé
Seco	Dry
Tinto	Red
Velho	Old
Vinho da mesa	Table wine
Vinho da casa	House wine
Vinho do porto	Port

Portrait

SMART TRAVEL TIPS A TO Z

Basic Information on Traveling in Portugal, Savvy Tips to Make Your Trip a Breeze, and Companies and Organizations to Contact

AIR TRAVEL

BOOKING

When you book **look for nonstop flights** and **remember that "direct" flights stop at least once.** Try to avoid connecting flights, which require a change of plane.

Price is just one factor to consider when booking a flight: frequency of service and even a carrier's safety record are often just as important. Major airlines offer the greatest number of departures. Smaller airlines—including regional and no-frills airlines—usually have a limited number of flights daily. On the other hand, so-called low-cost airlines usually are cheaper, and their fares impose fewer restrictions, such as advance-purchase requirements. Safety-wise, low-cost carriers as a group have a good history—about equal to that of major carriers.

International flights on a country's flag carrier are almost always nonstop; U.S. airlines often fly direct.

Ask your airline if it offers electronic ticketing, which eliminates all paperwork. There's no ticket to pick up or misplace. You go directly to the gate and give the agent your confirmation number. There's no worry about waiting in line at the airport while precious minutes tick by.

CARRIERS

When flying internationally, you must usually choose between a domestic carrier, the national flag carrier of the country you're visiting, and a foreign carrier from a third country. You may, for example, choose to fly TAP Air Portugal to Portugal. National flag carriers have the greatest number of nonstops. Domestic carriers may have better connections to your home town and serve a greater number of gateway cities. Third-party carriers may have a price advantage.

➤ TO AND FROM PORTUGAL: **British Airways** (☎ 800/247–9297). **Continental** (☎ 800/231–0856). **TAP Air Portugal** (☎ 888/221–7370). **TWA** (☎ 800/892–4141).

➤ FROM THE U.K.: **British Airways** (☎ 020/8897–4000; 0345/222–111 outside London). **TAP Air Portugal** (☎ 020/7630–9223).

➤ AROUND PORTUGAL: Domestic air travel options are limited in mainland Portugal. **TAP Air Portugal** (☎ 888/221–7370 in the U.S.; 808/205700 in Portugal) and **Portugália** (☎ 21/8425559 in Portugal) fly between Lisbon, Oporto, and Faro. **Omni** (☎ 21/445–8600 in Portugal) has regular flights to Vila Real and Bragança. **Aerocondor** (☎ 21/846–4964 in Portugal) operates a charter service to regional destinations and to Spain and France. **Tap Air Portugal** and **Sata** (☎ 21/843–7700 in Portugal) have regular flights to the Azores, and **Sata** provides interisland flights on the archipelago.

CHECK-IN & BOARDING

Assuming that not everyone with a ticket will show up, airlines routinely overbook planes. When everyone does, airlines ask for volunteers to give up their seats. In return, these volunteers usually get a certificate for a free flight and are rebooked on the next flight out. If there are not enough volunteers, the airline must choose who will be denied boarding. The first to get bumped are passengers who checked in late and those flying on discounted tickets, so **get to the gate and check in as early as possible,** especially during peak periods.

Always **bring a government-issued photo I.D. to the airport.** You may be asked to show it before you are allowed to check in.

CUTTING COSTS

The least expensive airfares to Portugal must usually be purchased in advance and are nonrefundable. It's smart to **call a number of airlines, and when you are quoted a good price, book it on the spot**—the same fare may not be available the next day. Always **check different routings** and look into using different airports. Travel agents, especially low-fare specialists (☞ Discounts & Deals, *below*), are helpful.

Consolidators are another good source. They buy tickets for scheduled international flights at reduced rates from the airlines, then sell them at prices that beat the best fare available directly from the airlines, usually without restrictions. Sometimes you can even get your money back if you need to return the ticket. Carefully read the fine print detailing penalties for changes and cancellations, and **confirm your consolidator reservation with the airline.**

➤ CONSOLIDATORS: **Cheap Tickets** (☎ 800/377–1000). **Discount Airline Ticket Service** (☎ 800/576–1600). **Unitravel** (☎ 800/325–2222). **Up & Away Travel** (☎ 212/889–2345). **World Travel Network** (☎ 800/409–6753).

ENJOYING THE FLIGHT

Smoking is forbidden on all regular TAP Air Portugal, Portugália, and Omni flights. For more legroom, **request an emergency-aisle seat.** Don't sit in the row in front of the emergency aisle or in front of a bulkhead, where seats may not recline. If you have dietary concerns, **ask for special meals when booking.** These can be vegetarian, low-cholesterol, or kosher, for example. On long flights, try to maintain a normal routine, to help fight jet lag. At night, **get some sleep.** By day, **eat light meals, drink water** (not alcohol), and **move around the cabin** to stretch your legs.

FLYING TIMES

Flying time to Lisbon is 6½ hours from New York, 9 hours from Chicago, and 15 hours from Los Angeles. The flight from London to Lisbon is about 2½ hours.

HOW TO COMPLAIN

If your baggage goes astray or your flight goes awry, complain right away. Most carriers require that you **file a claim immediately.**

➤ AIRLINE COMPLAINTS: U.S. Department of Transportation **Aviation Consumer Protection Division** (✉ C-75, Room 4107, Washington, DC 20590, ☎ 202/366–2220, airconsumer@ost.dot.gov, www.dot.gov/airconsumer). **Federal Aviation Administration Consumer Hotline** (☎ 800/322–7873).

RECONFIRMING

Although the trend on international flights is to drop reconfirmation requirements, many airlines still ask you to reconfirm each leg of your international itinerary. Failure to do so may result in your reservation being canceled.

AIRPORTS

The major gateway to Portugal is Lisbon's Portela Airport, approximately 8 km (5 mi) north of the center of the city.

BIKE TRAVEL

Portugal is one of Europe's more mountainous countries. Although country roads can sometimes be crowded with speeding trucks, bicycle trips can take you along some unforgettably scenic routes, and there are great mountain bike opportunities in the country's rugged hills.

➤ LOCAL RESOURCES: **Federação Portuguesa de Cicloturismo** (✉ Av. Miguel Bombarda 147, Segungo - D, Lisbon 1050-164, ☎ 21/315–6086).

BIKES IN FLIGHT

Most airlines accommodate bikes as luggage, provided they are dismantled and boxed. For bike boxes, often free at bike shops, you'll pay about $5 from airlines (at least $100 for bike bags). International travelers can sometimes substitute a bike for a piece of checked luggage at no charge; otherwise, the cost is about $100. Domestic and Canadian airlines charge $25–$50.

BUS TRAVEL

The Eurolines/National Express consortium runs regular bus service from the United Kingdom (out of London's Victoria Coach Station) to Lisbon, Oporto, Coimbra, Fátima, Faro, Lagos, and other destinations. The company also has service from Paris, its other major hub. In Lisbon Intercentro Eurolines handles inquiries about Eurolines transportation. There are many companies that offer service between Spain and Portugal and to Portugal from other parts of Europe, so it's best to make arrangements with a travel agent.

Bus service within Portugal is fairly comprehensive, and in some places, such as the Algarve, buses are the main form of public transportation. Buses also give you a chance to come in contact with locals, and some luxury coaches even have TVs and food service—a comfortable way to travel. That said, you should note that bus travel can be slow; it can also be difficult to arrange on your own. For schedules within Portugal it's best to inquire at tourist information offices, since routes and companies change frequently, and bus company personnel rarely speak English. If you buy from a specific bus company's ticket office, give yourself plenty of time to purchase before you depart. Most travel agents can sell you a bus ticket in advance; it's always wise to reserve a ticket at least a day ahead, particularly in summer for destinations in the Algarve.

➤ FROM THE U.K.: Contact **Intercentro Eurolines** (✉ Rua Actor Taborda 55, Lisbon, ☎ 21/357–1745), **National Express/Eurolines** (☎ 0990/808080; 0990/143219 for information; 01582/488970 for ticket cancellation; **Campus Travel** (✉ 52 Grosvenor Gardens, London SW1W 0AU, ☎ 020/7730–8235), or any National Express–appointed agent.

BUSINESS HOURS

BANKS

Banks are open weekdays 8:30–3. Money exchange booths at airports and train stations are usually open all day (24 hours at Portela Airport in Lisbon).

MUSEUMS & SIGHTS

Most museums and palaces open at 10, close for lunch from 12:30 to 2, and then reopen until 5. They're usually closed on Mondays and holidays, but a few close on Tuesdays or Wednesdays and holidays. A few major museums stay open at midday.

PHARMACIES

Pharmacies are usually open weekdays 9 to 1 and 3 to 7, Saturdays 9 to 1. When they are closed, pharmacies display a card on their doors indicating where the nearest all-night, late-night, or Sunday-opening, pharmacy can be found.

SHOPS

One of the most inconvenient things about shopping in Portugal is the midday closing of most shops for approximately two hours. Although *hipermercados* (giant supermarkets), *supermercados* (regular supermarkets), and shopping centers have mushroomed in recent years and are typically open seven days a week 10 AM–midnight, most shops are open weekdays 9–1 and 3–7, Saturday 9–1. In December, Saturday hours are the same as weekdays. Shops are closed on Sunday.

CAMERAS & PHOTOGRAPHY

EQUIPMENT PRECAUTIONS

Always **keep your film and videotapes out of the sun.** Carry an extra supply of batteries, and **be prepared to turn on your camera or camcorder** to prove to security personnel that the device is real. Always **ask for hand inspection of film,** which may become clouded after successive exposure to airport X-ray machines, and **keep videotapes away from metal detectors.**

➤ PHOTO HELP: Kodak Information Center (☎ 800/242–2424). *Kodak Guide to Shooting Great Travel Pictures,* available in bookstores or from Fodor's Travel Publications (☎ 800/533–6478; $18 plus $5.50 shipping).

CAR RENTAL

Rates in Lisbon begin at around $45 a day and $160 a week for an economy car with unlimited mileage. This does not include VAT tax on car rentals, which is 17%.

➤ MAJOR AGENCIES: **Alamo** (☎ 800/ 522–9696; 020/8759–6200 in the U.K.). **Avis** (☎ 800/331–1084; 800/ 331–1084 in Canada; 02/9353–9000 in Australia; 09/525–1982 in New Zealand). **Budget** (☎ 800/527–0700; 0870/607–5000 in the U.K., through affiliate Europcar). **Dollar** (☎ 800/ 800–6000; 0124/622–0111 in the U.K., through affiliate Sixt Kenning; 02/9223–1444 in Australia). **Hertz** (☎ 800/654–3001; 800/263–0600 in Canada; 020/8897–2072 in the U.K.; 02/9669–2444 in Australia; 09/256– 8690 in New Zealand) **National Car Rental** (☎ 800/227–7368; 020/8680– 4800 in the U.K., where it is known as National Europe).

CUTTING COSTS

To get the best deal, **book through a travel agent who is willing to shop around.** You should also **look into fly/drive packages.** In recent years, for example, TAP Air Portugal has had an arrangement with Avis, where round-trip airfare to Lisbon also included a free rental car for three to five days.

Also **ask your travel agent about a company's customer-service record.** How has the company responded to late plane arrivals and vehicle mishaps? Are there often lines at the rental counter? If you're traveling during a holiday period, does a confirmed reservation guarantee you a car?

Do **look into wholesalers,** companies that do not own fleets but rent in bulk from those that do and often offer better rates than traditional car-rental operations. Payment must be made before you leave home.

➤ WHOLESALERS: **Auto Europe** (☎ 207/842–2000 or 800/223–5555, FAX 800/235–6321, www.autoeurope. com). **Europe by Car** (☎ 212/581– 3040 or 800/223–1516, FAX 212/246– 1458, www.europebycar.com). **DER Travel Services** (⌧ 9501 W. Devon Ave., Rosemont, IL 60018, ☎ 800/ 782–2424, FAX 800/282–7474 for information; 800/860–9944 for brochures, www.dertravel.com). **Kemwel Holiday Autos** (☎ 800/ 678–0678, FAX 914/825–3160, www. kemwel.com).

INSURANCE

When driving a rented car you are generally responsible for any damage to or loss of the vehicle. Before you rent see what coverage your personal auto-insurance policy and credit cards already provide.

REQUIREMENTS & RESTRICTIONS

In Portugal your own driver's license is acceptable. An International Driver's Permit is a good idea; it's available from the American or Canadian automobile association, and, in the United Kingdom, from the Automobile Association or Royal Automobile Club.

SURCHARGES

Before you pick up a car in one city and leave it in another, **ask about drop-off charges or one-way service fees,** which can be substantial. Note, too, that some rental agencies charge extra if you return the car before the time specified in your contract. To avoid a hefty refueling fee, **fill the tank just before you turn in the car.**

CAR TRAVEL

AUTO CLUBS

➤ IN AUSTRALIA: **Australian Automobile Association** (☎ 06/247–7311).

➤ IN CANADA: **Canadian Automobile Association** (CAA, ☎ 613/247– 0117).

➤ IN NEW ZEALAND: **New Zealand Automobile Association** (☎ 09/377– 4660).

➤ IN PORTUGAL: **Automóvel Clube de Portugal** (⌧ Rua Rosa Araújo 24/26, 1200 Lisbon, ☎ 21/318–0100 general information; 21/942–9103 for breakdowns south of Pombal; 22/ 834–0001 for breakdowns north of Pombal).

➤ IN THE U.K.: **Automobile Association** (AA, ☎ 0990/500–600), **Royal Automobile Club** (RAC, ☎ 0990/ 722–722 for membership; 0345/121– 345 for insurance).

➤ IN THE U.S.: **American Automobile Association** (☎ 800/564–6222).

EMERGENCY SERVICES

All large garages in and around towns have breakdown services, and you'll see orange emergency (SOS) phones along turnpikes and highways. The national automobile organization, Automóvel Clube de Portugal (☞ Auto Clubs, *above*), provides reciprocal membership with AAA and other European automobile associations.

GASOLINE

Gas stations are plentiful throughout Portugal. Prices are controlled by the government and are the same everywhere. At press time gasoline cost 186$00 a liter (approximately ¼ gallon) for 98 octane *sem chumbo* (unleaded), 178$00 for 95 octane unleaded, and 125$00 for diesel. Credit cards are frequently accepted at gas stations.

ROAD CONDITIONS

Major work is being done on Portugal's highway system; commercially operated *autoestradas* (toll roads with four or more lanes identified with an "A" and a number) link the principal cities up the coast from Lisbon as far as Valença, on the northern border with Spain, circumventing congested urban centers. Another autoestrada is gradually pushing south from the capital toward the Algarve, and a toll road now links Lisbon with Portugal's eastern border with Spain and the highway to Madrid. Many main national highways (labeled with "N" and a number) have been upgraded to toll-free, two-lane roads identified with "IP" (Itinerario Principal) and a number. Highways of mainly regional importance are being upgraded to IC (Itinerario Complementar). Roads labeled with "E" and a number are routes that connect with the Spanish network. Because road construction is still underway, you may find that one road can have several designations— A, N, IP, E, etc.—on maps and road signs.

Tolls seem steep in Portugal, but time saved by traveling the autoestradas usually makes them worthwhile. Minor roads are often poor and winding with unpredictable surfaces. The local driving may be faster and less forgiving than you're used to, and other visitors in rental cars on unfamiliar Algarve roads can cause problems: drive carefully.

In the north the IP5 shortens the drive from Aveiro to the border with Spain, near Guarda. Take extra care on this route, however. It's popular with trucks (you may find yourself stuck behind a convoy), *and* it has many curves and hills. The IP4 connects Oporto through Vila Real to once-remote Bragança. You can pick up the IP2 just southwest of Bragança and continue (with some interruptions owing to ongoing construction) to Ourique in the Alentejo, where it connects to the IP1 straight down to Albufeira on the southern coast. This same IP1 is now an autoestrada from Albufeira east across the Algarve to the Spanish border near Ayamonte.

Heading out of Lisbon, there's good, fast access to Setúbal and to Évora and other Alentejo towns, although rush-hour traffic on the 25 de Abril Bridge across the Tagus River can be frustrating. An alternative is to take the 17-km-long (11-mi-long) Vasco da Gama Bridge (Europe's second-longest water crossing after the Chunnel) across the Tagus estuary to Montijo and then link up with southbound and eastbound roads. Signposting on these fast roads is not always adequate, so keep your eyes peeled for exits and turnoffs.

ROAD MAPS

Contact the national automobile association, Automóvel Clube de Portugal (☞ Auto Clubs, *above*) for a first-rate road map of Portugal.

RULES OF THE ROAD

Driving is on the right. At the junction of two roads of equal size, traffic coming from the right has priority. Vehicles already in a traffic circle have priority over those entering it from any point. The use of seat belts is obligatory. Horns should not be used in built-up areas, and a reflective red warning triangle, for use in a breakdown, must be carried. The speed limit on turnpikes is 120 kph (74 mph); on other roads it's 90 kph (56 mph), and in built-up areas, 50 kph–60 kph (30 mph–36 mph).

Billboards warning you not to drink and drive dot the countryside, and punishable alcohol levels are low. Portuguese drivers are notoriously rash, and the country has one of the highest traffic fatality rates in Europe—**drive defensively.**

CHILDREN IN PORTUGAL

When traveling in Portugal you'll see children of all ages accompanying their parents everywhere, including bars and restaurants. Shopkeepers will smile and offer your child a *bombom* (candy), and even the coldest waiters tend to be friendlier when you have a child with you. Kitchens are usually willing to fix something special for children, but you won't find children's menus anywhere. On the road, even the smallest *tasca* (town restaurant-bar) can make a *sandes de queijo* (cheese sandwich), and roast chicken (*frango assado*) is on most menus. Museum admissions, buses, and metro rides are generally free for children under 5 and half-price for children under 12.

Be sure to plan ahead and **involve your youngsters** as you outline your trip. When packing, include things to keep them busy en route. On sightseeing days try to schedule activities of special interest to your children. If you are renting a car, don't forget to **arrange for a car seat** when you reserve.

FLYING

If your children are two or older, **ask about children's airfares.** As a general rule, infants under two not occupying a seat fly at greatly reduced fares or even for free. When booking, **confirm carry-on allowances** if you're traveling with infants. In general, for babies charged 10% of the adult fare you are allowed one carry-on bag and a collapsible stroller; if the flight is full, the stroller may have to be checked or you may be limited to less.

Experts agree that it's a good idea to use safety seats aloft for children weighing less than 40 pounds. Airlines set their own policies: U.S. carriers usually require that the child be ticketed, even if he or she is young enough to ride free, since the seats must be strapped into regular seats.

Do **check your airline's policy about using safety seats during takeoff and landing.** And since safety seats are not allowed just everywhere in the plane, get your seat assignments early.

When reserving, **request children's meals or a freestanding bassinet** if you need them. But note that bulkhead seats, where you must sit to use the bassinet, may lack an overhead bin or storage space on the floor.

LODGING

Most hotels in Portugal allow children under a certain age to stay in their parents' room at no extra charge, but others charge for them as extra adults; be sure to **find out the cutoff age for children's discounts.**

SIGHTS & ATTRACTIONS

Places that are especially appealing to children are indicated by a rubber duckie icon in the margin.

CONSUMER PROTECTION

Whenever shopping or buying travel services in Portugal, **pay with a major credit card** so you can cancel payment or get reimbursed if there's a problem. If you're doing business with a particular company for the first time, **contact your local Better Business Bureau and the attorney general's offices** in your own state and the company's home state, as well. Have any complaints been filed? Finally, if you're buying a package or tour, always **consider travel insurance** that includes default coverage (☞ Insurance, *below*).

➤ BBBs: **Council of Better Business Bureaus** (✉ 4200 Wilson Blvd., Suite 800, Arlington, VA 22203, ☎ 703/276–0100, FAX 703/525–8277 www.bbb.org).

CUSTOMS & DUTIES

When shopping, **keep receipts** for all purchases. Upon reentering the country, **be ready to show customs officials what you've bought.** If you feel a duty is incorrect or object to the way your clearance was handled, note the inspector's badge number and ask to see a supervisor. If the problem isn't resolved, write to the appropriate authorities, beginning with the port director at your point of entry.

IN AUSTRALIA

Australian residents who are 18 or older may bring home $A400 worth of souvenirs and gifts (including jewelry), 250 cigarettes or 250 grams of tobacco, and 1,125 ml of alcohol (including wine, beer, and spirits). Residents under 18 may bring back $A200 worth of goods. Prohibited items include meat products. Seeds, plants, and fruits need to be declared upon arrival.

➤ INFORMATION: **Australian Customs Service** (Regional Director, ⊠ Box 8, Sydney, NSW 2001, Australia, ☎ 02/9213–2000, FAX 02/9213–4000, www.customs.gov.au).

IN CANADA

Canadian residents who have been out of Canada for at least 7 days may bring home C$500 worth of goods duty-free. If you've been away less than 7 days but more than 48 hours, the duty-free allowance drops to C$200; if your trip lasts 24–48 hours, the allowance is C$50. You may not pool allowances with family members. Goods claimed under the C$500 exemption may follow you by mail; those claimed under the lesser exemptions must accompany you. Alcohol and tobacco products may be included in the 7-day and 48-hour exemptions but not in the 24-hour exemption. If you meet the age requirements of the province or territory through which you reenter Canada, you may bring in, duty-free, 1.14 liters (40 imperial ounces) of wine or liquor *or* 24 12-ounce cans or bottles of beer or ale. If you are 16 or older you may bring in, duty-free, 200 cigarettes and 50 cigars. Check ahead of time with Revenue Canada or the Department of Agriculture for policies regarding meat products, seeds, plants, and fruits.

You may send an unlimited number of gifts worth up to C$60 each duty-free to Canada. Label the package UNSOLICITED GIFT—VALUE UNDER $60. Alcohol and tobacco are excluded.

➤ INFORMATION: **Revenue Canada** (⊠ 2265 St. Laurent Blvd. S, Ottawa, Ontario K1G 4K3, Canada, ☎ 613/993–0534; 800/461–9999 in Canada, FAX 613/991–4126, www.ccra-adrc.gc.ca).

IN NEW ZEALAND

Homeward-bound residents 17 or older may bring back $700 worth of souvenirs and gifts. Your duty-free allowance also includes 4.5 liters of wine or beer; one 1,125-ml bottle of spirits; and either 200 cigarettes, 250 grams of tobacco, 50 cigars, or a combination of the three up to 250 grams. Prohibited items include meat products, seeds, plants, and fruits.

➤ INFORMATION: **New Zealand Customs** (Custom House, ⊠ 50 Anzac Ave., Box 29, Auckland, New Zealand, ☎ 09/300–5399, FAX 09/359–6730), www.customs.govt.nz.

IN PORTUGAL

Visitors age 15 and over are permitted to bring in 200 cigarettes, or 100 cigarillos, or 50 cigars, or 250 grams of loose tobacco. Those 17 years of age and older may bring in one liter of liquor over 22 proof and two liters of wine. Perfume is limited to 50 grams, eau de cologne to ¼ liter. It's a good idea to carry along sales receipts for expensive personal belongings to avoid paying export duties when you leave.

➤ INFORMATION: **Direção Geral das Alfândegas** (⊠ Rua da Alfândega 5, Lisbon, ☎ 21/881–3818).

IN THE U.K.

If you are a U.K. resident and your journey was wholly within the European Union (EU), you won't have to pass through customs when you return to the United Kingdom. If you plan to bring back large quantities of alcohol or tobacco, check EU limits beforehand.

➤ INFORMATION: **HM Customs and Excise** (⊠ Dorset House, Stamford St., Bromley, Kent BR1 1XX, U.K., ☎ 020/7202–4227, www.hmce.gov.uk).

IN THE U.S.

U.S. residents who have been out of the country for at least 48 hours (and who have not used the $400 allowance or any part of it in the past 30 days) may bring home $400 worth of foreign goods duty-free.

U.S. residents 21 and older may bring back 1 liter of alcohol duty-free. In addition, regardless of your age, you are allowed 200 cigarettes and 100 non-Cuban cigars. Antiques, which the U.S. Customs Service defines as objects more than 100 years old, enter duty-free, as do original works of art done entirely by hand, including paintings, drawings, and sculptures.

You may also mail or ship packages home duty-free: up to $200 worth of goods for personal use, with a limit of one parcel per addressee per day (except alcohol or tobacco products or perfume worth more than $5); label the package PERSONAL USE and attach a list of its contents and their retail value. Do not label the package UNSOLICITED GIFT or your duty-free exemption will drop to $100. Mailed items do not affect your duty-free allowance on your return.

➤ INFORMATION: **U.S. Customs Service** (✉ 1300 Pennsylvania Ave. NW, Washington, DC 20229, www.customs.gov; inquiries ☎ 202/354–1000; complaints c/o ✉ 1300 Pennsylvania Ave. NW, Room 5.4D, Washington, DC 20229; registration of equipment c/o ✉ Resource Management, ☎ 202/354–1000).

DINING

The explosion of fast-food restaurants in recent years hasn't dented the Portuguese affection for old-fashioned, white-tablecloth dining—even though the tablecloth may now be made of paper at economy spots. Hamburger places do a roaring lunchtime trade in towns all over the country, but so do the traditional little restaurants that offer office workers home cooking at a modest price. These simple places tend to cluster in commercial sections of towns. Don't expect much in the line of decor, and if you have trouble squeezing in, remember the rule of thumb: if it's packed it's probably good.

Portugal has its share of plush luxury restaurants, but while they can be good, they seldom measure up to their counterparts in other European countries. The best food by far tends to be found in the moderately priced and less expensive spots. Restaurants featuring charcoal-grilled meats and

fish, called *churasqueiras,* are also popular (and often economical) options, and the Brazilian *rodízio*-type restaurant, where you are regaled with an endless offering of spit-roasted meats, is entrenched in Lisbon, Oporto, and the Algarve. Shellfish restaurants called *marisqueiras* are especially numerous up and down the Portuguese coast, but while the lobsters and mollusks and their like are generally fresh and good, they tend to be pricey. Restaurant prices fall appreciably when you leave the Lisbon, Oporto, and Algarve areas, and portion sizes tend to increase the farther north you go.

As in many European countries, Portuguese restaurants serve an *ementa* (or *prato*) *do dia,* or set menu. This can be a real bargain—usually 80% of the cost of three courses ordered separately.

The restaurants we list in this book, each indicated by a knife-and-fork icon, ✕, are the cream of the crop in each price category. Establishments marked with ✕🏨 stand out equally for their restaurants and their rooms. Dollar-sign ratings are based on the following categories in Portuguese escudos:

CATEGORY	COST*
$$$$	over 6,500$00
$$$	4,000$00–6,500$00
$$	2,500$00–4,000$00
$	under 2,500$00

per person for a three-course meal, including tax and service, but not drinks

MEALTIMES

Breakfast is the lightest meal; lunch, the main meal of the day, is served between noon and 2:30, although nowadays, office workers in cities often grab a quick sandwich in a bar instead of stopping for a big lunch. About 5 there's an afternoon break for coffee or tea and a pastry, and dinner is eaten around 8. Unless otherwise noted, the restaurants listed in this guide are open daily for lunch and dinner.

RESERVATIONS & DRESS

Reservations are always a good idea: we mention them only when they're essential or not accepted. Book as far ahead as you can, and reconfirm as soon as you arrive. We mention dress only when men are required to wear a jacket or a jacket and tie.

DISABILITIES & ACCESSIBILITY

Portugal is not one of the easiest countries for travelers with disabilities, although efforts are slowly being made to accommodate those voyagers for whom the word "travel" all too often means travail. Many of the smaller towns and out-of-the-way hilltop castles have difficult terrain. Things are beginning to change, however, and buildings constructed here within the last five years should be accessible, as are some of the larger museums and other tourist sites. It's best to check either with the tourist office or directly with the hotel, or with your travel agent before booking a reservation or heading off to a museum or other attraction.

MAKING RESERVATIONS

When discussing accessibility with an operator or reservations agent, **ask hard questions.** Are there any stairs, inside *or* out? Are there grab bars next to the toilet *and* in the shower/tub? How wide is the doorway to the room? To the bathroom? For the most extensive facilities meeting the latest legal specifications, **opt for newer accommodations.**

➤ COMPLAINTS: **Disability Rights Section** (✉ U.S. Department of Justice, Civil Rights Division, Box 66738, Washington, DC 20035-6738, ☎ 202/514–0301 or 800/514–0301; 202/514–0383 TTY; 800/514–0383 TTY, 🖷 202/307–1198, www.usdoj. gov/crt/ada/adahom1.htm) for general complaints. **Aviation Consumer Protection Division** (☞ Air Travel, *above*) for airline-related problems. **Civil Rights Office** (✉ U.S. Department of Transportation, Departmental Office of Civil Rights, S-30, 400 7th St. SW, Room 10215, Washington, DC 20590, ☎ 202/366–4648, 🖷 202/366–9371) for problems with surface transportation.

TRAVEL AGENCIES

In the United States, the Americans with Disabilities Act requires that travel firms serve the needs of all travelers. Some agencies specialize in working with people with disabilities.

➤ TRAVELERS WITH MOBILITY PROBLEMS: **Access Adventures** (✉ 206 Chestnut Ridge Rd., Scottsville, NY 14624, ☎ 716/889–9096, dltravel@ prodigy.net), run by a former physical-rehabilitation counselor. **CareVacations** (✉ 5-5110 50th Ave., Leduc, Alberta T9E 6V4, Canada, ☎ 780/986–6404 or 877/478–7827, 🖷 780/986–8332, www.carevacations.com), for group tours and cruise vacations. **Flying Wheels Travel** (✉ 143 W. Bridge St., Box 382, Owatonna, MN 55060, ☎ 507/451–5005 or 800/535–6790, 🖷 507/451–1685, thq@ll.net, www.flyingwheels.com).

DISCOUNTS & DEALS

If you're undeterred by potentially wet weather, consider traveling November to March, when many hotels discount their rates by up to 20%. In Lisbon and Oporto, check with the tourist office about discount cards offering discounted travel on public transport, reduced or free entrance to certain museums, and discounts in some shops and restaurants.

Be a smart shopper and **compare all your options** before making decisions. A plane ticket bought with a promotional coupon from travel clubs, coupon books, and direct-mail offers may not be cheaper than the least expensive fare from a discount ticket agency. And always keep in mind that what you get is just as important as what you save.

DISCOUNT RESERVATIONS

To save money, **look into discount reservations services** with toll-free numbers, which use their buying power to get a better price on hotels, airline tickets, even car rentals. When booking a room, always **call the hotel's local toll-free number** (if one is available) rather than the central reservations number—you'll often get a better price. Always ask about special packages or corporate rates.

When shopping for the best deal on hotels and car rentals, **look for guaranteed exchange rates,** which protect you against a falling dollar. With your rate locked in, you won't pay more, even if the price goes up in the local currency.

➤ AIRLINE TICKETS: ☎ 800/FLY–ASAP.

➤ HOTEL ROOMS: **Steigenberger Reservation Service** (☎ 800/223–5652, www.srs-worldhotels.com). **Travel Interlink** (☎ 800/888–5898, www.travelinterlink.com).

PACKAGE DEALS

Don't confuse packages and guided tours. When you buy a package, you travel on your own, just as though you had planned the trip yourself. Fly/drive packages, which combine airfare and car rental, are often a good deal. If you **buy a rail/drive pass,** you may save on train tickets and car rentals. All Eurail- and Europass holders get a discount on Eurostar fares through the Channel Tunnel.

ELECTRICITY

To use your U.S.-purchased electric-powered equipment, **bring a converter and adapter.** The electrical current in Portugal is 220 volts, 50 cycles alternating current (AC); wall outlets take plugs with two round prongs.

If your appliances are dual-voltage, you'll need only an adapter. Don't use 110-volt outlets marked FOR SHAVERS ONLY for high-wattage appliances such as blow-dryers. Most laptops operate equally well on 110 and 220 volts and so require only an adapter.

EMBASSIES AND CONSULATES

➤ AUSTRALIA: **Australian consular section** (✉ Av. da Liberdade 110, 2°, Lisbon, ☎ 21/340–4666).

➤ CANADA: **Canadian embassy** (✉ Av. da Liberdade 144–156, 4°, Lisbon, ☎ 21/316–4600).

➤ NEW ZEALAND: **New Zealand consular representative** (✉ Av. António Augusto de Aguiar 122, 9°, Lisbon, ☎ 21/350–9690).

➤ UNITED KINGDOM: **U.K embassy** (✉ Rua de São Bernardo 33, Lisbon, ☎ 21/396–1191).

➤ UNITED STATES: **U.S. embassy** (✉ Av. das Forças Armadas, Lisbon, ☎ 21/727–3300).

EMERGENCIES

The national number for emergencies is 112, which is the universal EU emergency number.

GAY & LESBIAN TRAVEL

The Portuguese are generally very liberal in their attitudes, and gay and lesbian travelers should have no particular difficulties. Even in small towns the rules are those of discretion and good taste that apply to heterosexual couples, too.

➤ GAY- & LESBIAN-FRIENDLY TRAVEL AGENCIES IN PORTUGAL: **Ilga Portugal** (✉ Rua de São Lazaro 88, Lisbon, ☎ 21/887–3918). **Opusgay** (✉ Rua da Ilha Terceira 34, 2°, Lisbon, ☎ 21/315–1396).

➤ GAY- & LESBIAN-FRIENDLY TRAVEL AGENCIES IN THE U.S.: **Different Roads Travel** (✉ 8383 Wilshire Blvd., Suite 902, Beverly Hills, CA 90211, ☎ 323/651–5557 or 800/429–8747, FAX 323/651–3678, leigh@west.tzell.com). **Kennedy Travel** (✉ 314 Jericho Turnpike, Floral Park, NY 11001, ☎ 516/352–4888 or 800/237–7433, FAX 516/354–8849, kennedytravel1@yahoo.com, www.kennedytravel.com). **Now Voyager** (✉ 4406 18th St., San Francisco, CA 94114, ☎ 415/626–1169 or 800/255–6951, FAX 415/626–8626, www.nowvoyager.com). **Skylink Travel and Tour** (✉ 1006 Mendocino Ave., Santa Rosa, CA 95401, ☎ 707/546–9888 or 800/225–5759, FAX 707/546–9891, skylinktvl@aol.com, www.skylinktravel.com), serving lesbian travelers.

HEALTH

Sunburn and sunstroke are common problems in summer in mainland Portugal and virtually year-round in Madeira. On a hot, sunny day, even people not normally bothered by a strong sun should cover up. Carry sunscreen for nose, ears, and other sensitive areas; be sure to drink enough liquids; and above all, limit your sun exposure for the first few days until you become accustomed to the heat. No special shots are required before visiting Portugal (except for yellow-fever shots if you want to visit Madeira and have come from an infected area).

HOLIDAYS

New Year's Day (January 1); Mardi Gras, in Lisbon and many other towns (February 27, 2001; February 12, 2002); Good Friday (April 13, 2001; March 29, 2002); Liberty Day (April 25); Labor Day (May 1); Portugal's and Camões Day (June 10); St. Anthony's Day, Lisbon (June 13); Assumption (August 15); Republic Day (October 5); All Saints' Day (November 1); Independence Day (December 1); Feast of the Immaculate Conception (December 8); Christmas Eve and Christmas Day (December 24 and 25).

If a national holiday falls on a Tuesday or Thursday, many businesses also close on the Monday or Friday in between, for a long weekend called a *ponte* (bridge).

INSURANCE

The most useful travel-insurance plan is a comprehensive policy that includes coverage for trip cancellation and interruption, default, trip delay, and medical expenses (with a waiver for preexisting conditions).

Without insurance you will lose all or most of your money if you cancel your trip, regardless of the reason. Default insurance covers you if your tour operator, airline, or cruise line goes out of business. Trip-delay covers expenses that arise because of bad weather or mechanical delays. Study the fine print when comparing policies.

If you're traveling internationally, a key component of travel insurance is coverage for medical bills incurred if you get sick on the road. Such expenses are not generally covered by Medicare or private policies. U.K. residents can buy a travel-insurance policy valid for most vacations taken during the year in which it's purchased (but check preexisting-condition coverage). British and Australian citizens need extra medical coverage when traveling overseas.

Always **buy travel policies directly from the insurance company**; if you buy them from a cruise line, airline, or tour operator that goes out of business you probably will not be covered for the agency or operator's default, a major risk. Before making any purchase, **review your existing health and home-owner's policies** to find what they cover away from home.

➤ TRAVEL INSURERS: In the U.S.: **Access America** (✉ 6600 W. Broad St., Richmond, VA 23230, ☎ 804/285–3300 or 800/284–8300, FAX 804/673–1586, www.previewtravel.com), **Travel Guard International** (✉ 1145 Clark St., Stevens Point, WI 54481, ☎ 715/345–0505 or 800/826–1300, FAX 800/955–8785, www.noelgroup.com).

➤ INSURANCE INFORMATION: In the U.K.: **Association of British Insurers** (✉ 51–55 Gresham St., London EC2V 7HQ, U.K., ☎ 020/7600–3333, FAX 020/7696–8999, info@abi.org.uk, www.abi.org.uk). In Canada: **Voyager Insurance** (✉ 44 Peel Center Dr., Brampton, Ontario L6T 4M8, Canada, ☎ 905/791–8700, 800/668–4342 in Canada). In Australia: **Insurance Council of Australia** (☎ 03/9614–1077, FAX 03/9614–7924). In New Zealand: **Insurance Council of New Zealand** (✉ Box 474, Wellington, New Zealand, ☎ 04/472–5230, FAX 04/473–3011, www.icnz.org.nz).

LANGUAGE

Despite its Slavic-sounding inflections and nasal intonations, Portuguese is essentially a romance language, of Latin origin, and is the seventh most widely spoken language in the world. Portuguese is difficult to pronounce and understand (most people speak quickly and elliptically); if, however, you have a fair knowledge of a Latin language, you may be able to read a little Portuguese. Just be aware that, with some cognates, appearances can be deceptive—it's best to double-check terms in a pocket Portuguese–English dictionary. Any attempt you make to speak Portuguese will be warmly appreciated. In large cities and major resorts many people speak English and, occasionally, French.

LODGING

Portugal offers accommodations to suit every taste and budget, from palaces to pensions, from old-fashioned mansions to ultramodern hotels. Many visitors design their itineraries around *pousadas* (☞ *below*). Luxurious resorts provide self-contained surroundings that can tempt guests not to leave. There are new high-rise hotels in cities, *residências* (in what were once private homes—the term *residencial* is also often used), and apartment-style accommodations (with suites or one-bedroom units and kitchenettes) in the smallest of towns.

The lodgings we list are the cream of the crop in each price category. We always list the facilities that are available—but we don't specify whether they cost extra: when pricing accommodations, always ask what's included and what costs extra. Assume that no meals are included in the price unless we specify otherwise. Dollar-sign ratings are based on the following categories in Portuguese escudos.

CATEGORY	COST*
$$$$	over 40,000$00
$$$	20,000$00–40,000$00
$$	15,000$00–20,000$00
$	under 15,000$00

All prices are for a standard double room, including tax, in high season (off-season rates may be lower).

APARTMENT & VILLA RENTALS

If you want a home base that's roomy enough for a family and comes with cooking facilities, **consider a furnished rental.** These can save you money, especially if you're traveling with a group. Home-exchange directories sometimes list rentals as well as exchanges.

➤ INTERNATIONAL AGENTS: At Home Abroad (✉ 405 E. 56th St., Suite 6H, New York, NY 10022, ☎ 212/421–9165, FAX 212/752–1591, athomabrod@aol.com, www.athomeabroadinc.com). Hideaways International (✉ 767 Islington St., Portsmouth, NH 03801, ☎ 603/430–4433 or 800/843–4433, FAX 603/430–4444 info@hideaways.com, www.hideaways.com; membership $99). Hometours International (✉ Box 11503, Knoxville, TN 37939, ☎ 865/690–8484 or 800/367–4668, hometours@aol.com, http://thor.he.net/~hometour/).

Interhome (✉ 1990 N.E. 163rd St., Suite 110, N. Miami Beach, FL 33162, ☎ 305/940–2299 or 800/882–6864, FAX 305/940–2911, interhomeu@aol.com, www.interhome.com). Vacation Home Rentals Worldwide (✉ 235 Kensington Ave., Norwood, NJ 07648, ☎ 201/767–9393 or 800/633–3284, FAX 201/767–5510, vhrww@juno.com, www.vhrww.com). Villas and Apartments Abroad (✉ 1270 Avenue of the Americas, 15th floor, New York, NY 10020, ☎ 212/897–5045 or 800/433–3020, FAX 212/897–5039, vaa@altour.com, www.vaanyc.com).

CAMPING

There are more than 100 good campgrounds in Portugal. One of the largest and best equipped is **Lisboa Camping**, set in the Monsanto woods off the Estoril autoestrada not far from the city center. It has tennis, a swimming pool, a bank, a restaurant, cafés, fully furnished four- to six-bed cabins, a chapel, a library, a game room, and a minimarket. Another very pleasant site is five minutes from Guincho Beach, Cascais; it's operated by Orbitur (☞ Information, *below*), which also has several other well-equipped camps, some with four-person chalets to rent.

➤ INFORMATION: For a list of campgrounds, contact tourist offices; the **Federação Portuguesa de Campismo e Caravanismo** (Portuguese Camping and Caravanning Federation, ✉ Av. Coronel Galhado 24, Lisbon 1000, ☎ 21/812–6900); or **Orbitur** (✉ Rua Diogo Couto 1–8F, Lisbon 1100, ☎ 21/811–7000).

COUNTRY HOUSES

Manors, farm estates, and country houses have been modified to receive small numbers of guests, in a fairly new venture called Turismo de Habitação (Country House Tourism), mostly operating in the north of the country. These guest houses, which offer an alternative kind of comfort, are in bucolic settings removed from the cities, near parks or monuments, and in historic villages. Breakfast is always included in the price.

➤ INFORMATION: **ANTER** (✉ Rua 24 de Julho 1, Évora, 7000, ☎ 266/

749420) for homes in central Portugal and the south; **Direção-Geral do Turismo, Divisão do Turismo no Espaço Rural** (⌧ Av. António Augusto de Aguiar 86, Lisbon 1099, ☎ 21/286–7958); and **Turihab** (⌧ Praça da República, Ponte de Lima 4990, ☎ 258/741672 or 258/742827) for accommodations in more rural areas in the north of the country.

HOME EXCHANGES

If you would like to exchange your home for someone else's, **join a home-exchange organization,** which will send you its updated listings of available exchanges for a year and will include your own listing in at least one of them. It's up to you to make specific arrangements.

➤ EXCHANGE CLUBS: **HomeLink International** (⌧ Box 650, Key West, FL 33041, ☎ 305/294–7766 or 800/638–3841, FAX 305/294–1448, usa@homelink.org, www.homelink.org; $98 per year). **Intervac U.S.** (⌧ Box 590504, San Francisco, CA 94159, ☎ 800/756–4663, FAX 415/435–7440, intervacus@aol.com, www.intervacus.com; $93 per year includes two catalogues).

HOSTELS

No matter what your age, you can **save on lodging costs by staying at hostels.** In some 5,000 locations in more than 70 countries around the world, Hostelling International (HI), the umbrella group for a number of national youth-hostel associations, offers single-sex, dorm-style beds and, at many hostels, rooms for couples and family accommodations. Membership in any HI national hostel association, open to travelers of all ages, allows you to stay in HI-affiliated hostels at member rates; one-year membership is about $25 for adults (C$26.75 in Canada, £9.30 in the U.K., $30 in Australia, and $30 in New Zealand); hostels run about $10–$25 per night. Members have priority if the hostel is full; they're also eligible for discounts around the world, even on rail and bus travel in some countries.

➤ ORGANIZATIONS: **Hostelling International—American Youth Hostels** (⌧ 733 15th St. NW, Suite 840, Washington, DC 20005, ☎ 202/783–6161, FAX 202/783–6171, hiayhserv@hiayh. org, www.hiayh.org). **Hostelling International—Canada** (⌧ 400–205 Catherine St., Ottawa, Ontario K2P 1C3, Canada, ☎ 613/237–7884, FAX 613/237–7868, info@hostellingintl.ca, www.hostellingintl.ca). **Youth Hostel Association of England and Wales** (⌧ Trevelyan House, 8 St. Stephen's Hill, St. Albans, Hertfordshire AL1 2DY, U.K., ☎ 0870/870–8808, FAX 01727/844126, customerservices@yha.org.uk, www.yha.org.uk). **Australian Youth Hostel Association** (⌧ 10 Mallett St., Camperdown, NSW 2050, Australia, ☎ 02/9565–1699, FAX 02/9565–1325, www.yha.com.au). **Youth Hostels Association of New Zealand** (⌧ Box 436, Christchurch, New Zealand, ☎ 03/379–9970, FAX 03/365–4476, info@yha.org.nz, www.yha.org.nz).

HOTELS

Good accommodation can sometimes be sparse in the more remote inland areas but, in general, Portugal is well equipped with excellent and reasonably priced hotels. All tourist accommodation is officially graded with a star or a category rating according to the degree of comfort and number of facilities offered. This rating can occasionally be misleading because quality is difficult to grade, but in general the system works. Hotels are rated from one to five stars in ascending order of comfort and price. Pensions come in first, second, and third categories, first being the most luxurious. The state-owned *pousadas* (inns) are a category of their own, but they fall into the four- or five-star hotel range. Almost all hotel rooms have basic amenities like private bathrooms and telephone, but from two stars up you can expect increasing levels of comfort and service including air-conditioning, cable or satellite TV, and often a minibar and room service.

High season means not only the summer months, but also the Christmas and New Year's holiday period on Madeira, Easter week throughout the country, and anytime a town is holding a festival. However, in the off-season (generally November through March), many hotels' rates are as much as 20% lower. In Portugal, a Continental breakfast is often included in the price of the room.

All hotels listed have private bath unless otherwise noted.

➤ INFORMATION: Contact the **Portuguese National Tourist Office** (✉ 590 5th Ave., New York, NY 10036, ☎ 212/354–4403 or 212/354–4404, FAX 212/764–6137) for their basic hotel directory, in addition to the list of Hotels de Charme, a newly associated group of small hotels and pousadas throughout the country.

➤ TOLL-FREE NUMBERS: **Best Western** (☎ 800/528–1234, www.bestwestern.com). **Choice** (☎ 800/221–2222, www.hotelchoice.com). **Comfort** (☎ 800/228–5150, www.comfortinn.com). **Four Seasons** (☎ 800/332–3442, www.fourseasons.com). **Hilton** (☎ 800/445–8667, www.hilton.com). **Holiday Inn** (☎ 800/465–4329, www.basshotels.com). **Le Meridien** (☎ 800/543–4300, www.forte-hotels.com). **Quality Inn** (☎ 800/228–5151, www.qualityinn.com). **Sheraton** (☎ 800/325–3535, www.starwood.com). **Westin Hotels & Resorts** (☎ 800/228–3000, www.westin.com).

POUSADAS

The term *pousada* is derived from the Portuguese verb *pousar* (to rest). Portugal has an easily accessible network of more than 40 of these state-run hotels, which are in wonderfully restored castles, palaces, monasteries, convents, and other charming historic buildings. Each pousada is set in a particularly scenic and tranquil part of the country and is tastefully furnished with traditional regional crafts, antiques, and artwork. All have restaurants that present regional specialties; you may stop for a meal or a drink at a pousada without spending the night. Rates are reasonable, considering that most pousadas are four- or five-star hotels and a stay in one can be the highlight of a visit. However, they're extremely popular with foreigners and Portuguese alike, so make reservations in advance, especially in summer, since some have 10 or fewer rooms.

➤ INFORMATION: **Enatur** (✉ Av. Sta. Joana a Princesa 10-A, Lisbon 1700, ☎ 21/844–2001, FAX 21/844–2085,

guest@pousadas.pt); in the United States, **Marketing Ahead** (✉ 433 5th Ave., New York, NY 10016, ☎ 212/686–9213 or 800/223–1356, FAX 212/686–0271); in the United Kingdom, **Keytel International** (✉ 402 Edgeware Rd., London W2 1ED, ☎ 020/7402–8182).

SPAS

Portugal has been favored with a profusion of thermal springs, whose waters reputedly can cure whatever ails you. In the smaller spas, hotels are rather simple; in the more famous ones, they're first-class. Most are open from May through October.

➤ INFORMATION: Contact the Portuguese tourism office nearest you, **Marketing Ahead** (☞ *above*), or the **Associação Nacional dos Industriais de Aguas Minero-Medicinais de Mesa** (✉ Av. Miguel Bombarda 110–2, Lisbon 1050, ☎ 21/794–0574).

MAIL & SHIPPING

POSTAL RATES

Airmail letters to the United States and Canada cost 145$00 for up to 15 grams. Letters to the United Kingdom and other countries in the EU cost 90$00 for up to 20 grams. Letters within Portugal are 65$00. Postcards are charged at the same rate as letters. Stamps (*selos*) can be bought at post office counters or from machines scattered about Lisbon or in main post offices.

RECEIVING MAIL

If you are on the move it is best to have your mail sent to American Express (☎ 800/543–4080); call for lists of offices in Portugal. An alternative is to have mail held at a Portuguese post office; have it addressed to *poste restante* or *lista de correios* (general delivery) in a town you'll be visiting. Postal addresses should include the name of the province and district—for example, Figueira da Foz (Coimbra).

MONEY MATTERS

As Portugal moves to catch up with the rest of Europe, prices keep climbing. Lisbon is still not as expensive as most other international capitals, but it's not the extraordinary bargain it used to be. The coastal resort areas from Cascais and Estoril down to the Algarve can also be expensive, but lower-price hotels and restaurants catering mainly to the package-tour trade are certainly popular. If you head off the beaten track you'll find substantially cheaper food and lodging.

Transportation is still cheap in Portugal when compared with the rest of Europe. Gas prices are controlled by the government, and train and bus travel are inexpensive. Highway tolls are steep but may be worth the cost if you want to bypass the small towns and villages. Flights within the country on the state-owned TAP Air Portugal are costly.

Here are some sample prices. Coffee in a bar: 80$00 (standing), 150$00 (seated). Draft beer in a bar: 100$00 (standing), 175$00 (seated). Bottle of beer: 150$00. Small glass of wine in a bar: 80$00. Glass of port: 175$00–2,000$00, depending on brand and vintage. Bottle of ordinary table wine (*vinho da casa*): 900$00; half bottle, 450$00. Coca-Cola: 200$00. Ham-and-cheese sandwich: 300$00. One-kilometer taxi ride: 450$00 (but the meter keeps ticking in traffic jams). Local bus ride: 165$00 if purchased from driver. Subway ride: 100$00. Ferry ride in Lisbon: 110$00–300$00 one-way depending on destination. Opera or theater seat: about 4,000$00–6,000$00, depending on location. Nightclub cover charge: 3,000$00–5,000$00. Fado performance: 2,500$00 cover charge or 5,000$00–6,000$00 for dinner. Movie ticket: 800$00 (most cinemas offer cheaper tickets on Monday). Foreign newspaper: 260$00–450$00.

Prices throughout this guide are given for adults. Substantially reduced fees are almost always available for children, students, and senior citizens. For information on taxes, *see* Taxes, *below*.

ATMS

ATMs are ubiquitous in Portugal; you'll find them in practically every street in every town. The Portuguese use them for banking, and for paying bills and taxes, and the system, called the MB or Multibanco system, is state-of-the-art and reliable. The cards most frequently accepted are Visa, MasterCard, American Express, Eurocheque, Eurocard, and Electron. You need a four-digit pin to use ATMs in Portugal.

➤ ATM LOCATIONS: Call **Cirrus** (☎ 800/424–7787) for locations in the U.S. and Canada or check out the Web site (www.mastercard.com) for locations worldwide. You can also call **Plus** (☎ 800/843–7587) for locations in North America or use the ATM locator at the Web site (www.visa.com). Your local bank can also help you find locations.

CREDIT CARDS

Should you use a credit card or a debit card when traveling? Both have benefits. A credit card allows you to delay payment and gives you certain rights as a consumer (☞ Consumer Protection, *above*). A debit card, also known as a check card, deducts funds directly from your checking account and helps you stay within your budget. When you want to rent a car, though, you may still need an old-fashioned credit card. Although you can always *pay* for your car with a debit card, some agencies will not allow you to *reserve* a car with a debit card.

Otherwise, the two types of plastic are virtually the same. Both will get you cash advances at ATMs worldwide if your card is properly programmed with your personal identification number (PIN). (For use in Portugal, your PIN must be four digits long.) Both offer excellent, wholesale exchange rates. And both protect you against unauthorized use if the card is lost or stolen. Your liability is limited to $50, as long as you report the card missing.

Throughout this guide, the following abbreviations are used: **AE**, American Express; **DC**, Diner's Club; **MC**, MasterCard; and **V**, Visa.

➤ REPORTING LOST CARDS: **American Express** ☎ (21/392–5727); call collect to report loss or theft. **MasterCard** ☎ (800/811272). **Visa** ☎ (800/811107).

CURRENCY

Portugal's currency unit is the escudo, which is divided into 100 centavos. The number of escudos is written to the left of the $ sign and the centavos to the right; thus, 2 escudos and 50 centavos is written 2$50. Coins are issued for 200$00, 100$00, 50$00, 20$00, 10$00, 5$00, and 1$00. Bills in circulation are for 10,000$00, 5,000$00, 2,000$00, 1,000$00, and 500$00. Units of 1,000$00 are often referred to as contos. At press time, the exchange rate was about 224$00 to the U.S. dollar, 151$00 to the Canadian dollar, 327$00 to the pound sterling, 128$00 to the Australian dollar, and 96$00 to the New Zealand dollar.

CURRENCY EXCHANGE

For the most favorable rates, **change money through banks.** Although ATM transaction fees may be higher abroad than at home, ATM rates are excellent because they are based on wholesale rates offered only by major banks. You won't do as well at exchange booths in airports or rail and bus stations, in hotels, in restaurants, or in stores. To avoid lines at airport exchange booths, **get a bit of local currency before you leave home.**

➤ EXCHANGE SERVICES: **International Currency Express** (☎ 888/278–6628 for orders, www.foreignmoney.com). **Thomas Cook Currency Services** (☎ 800/287–7362 for telephone orders and retail locations, www.us.thomascook.com).

TRAVELER'S CHECKS

Do you need traveler's checks? It depends on where you're headed. If you're going to rural areas and small towns, go with cash; traveler's checks are best used in cities. Lost or stolen checks can usually be replaced within 24 hours. To ensure a speedy refund, buy your own traveler's checks—don't let someone else pay for them: irregularities like this can cause delays. The person who bought the checks should make the call to request a refund.

OUTDOORS & SPORTS

➤ FISHING: Contact the tourist office for a booklet on fishing throughout the country. For fishing in the Lisbon area, try the **Clube dos Amadores de Pesca de Lisboa** (⊠ Travessa do Adro 12–1, Lisbon 1100, ☎ 21/356–1375) and the **Clube dos Amadores de Pesca da Costa do Sol** (⊠ Rua dos Fontainhos 16, Cascais 2750, ☎ 21/284–1691).

➤ GOLF: Contact the tourism office for detailed descriptions of courses and a list of greens fees or the **Federação Portuguesa de Golf** (Portuguese Golf Federation, ⊠ 9 Rua Almeida Brandão 39, Lisbon 1200, ☎ 21/867–4658).

➤ HORSEBACK RIDING: Contact the **Federação Equestre Portuguesa** (Portuguese Equestrian Federation; ⊠ Av. Manuel Maia 24, Lisbon 1000, ☎ 21/847–4582) or the **Centro Equestre de Loures** (Equestrian Center of Loures; ⊠ Quinta da Maneta, Loures, ☎ 21/983–5945).

➤ TENNIS: Tennis pros offer classes almost all year long in the resorts; contact the tourism office for a list of courts in the resort areas. For further information, contact the **Federação Portuguesa de Tenis** (Portuguese Tennis Federation; ⊠ Box 210, Linda-a-Velha 2795, ☎ 21/419–5244 or 21/419–8472).

➤ WATER SPORTS: Contact the **Federação Portuguesa de Vela** (Portuguese Sailing Federation; ⊠ Doca de Belém, Lisbon 1300, ☎ 21/364–7324 or 21/364–1152), the **Associação Naval de Lisboa** (Lisbon Naval Association; ⊠ Doca de Belém, Lisbon 1300 ☎ 21/363–5861); or **Federação Portuguesa de Atividades Subaquáticas** (Portuguese Underwater Sports Federation; ⊠ Rua Francisco Maria Cardoso 39, Lisbon 1200, ☎ 21/846–0174); **Federação Portuguesa de Canoagem** (Portuguese Canoeing Federation, ⊠ Rua António Pinto Machado 60, 4100 Porto, ☎ 22/609–8020). For surfing, head to Carcavelhos, along the coast toward Cascais; rent a board there at **Windsurf de Carcavelhos** (⊠ Rua Principale, Loja 1, ☎ 21/456–5731) and continue on to the awesome beach at Guincho, where shooting a curl is popular even in the mild winters. Water-skiers should contact the **Clube Naval de Cascais** (Cascais Naval Club;

✉ Esplanada Principe D. Luis Filipe, Cascais 2750, ☎ 21/483–0125).

PACKING

The Portuguese, like the Spanish, tend to dress up more than do Americans or the British, but attitudes to clothes have become more relaxed in recent years. Nowadays, the young tend to be more informal in their attire than their parents, and country folk more formal than big city dwellers. Jeans, however, are generally paired with a collared shirt and, if necessary, a sweater or jacket. Dressier outfits are needed for more expensive restaurants, nightclubs, and fado houses, though, and people still frown on shorts in churches. Away from the beaches, bathing suits on the street or in restaurants and shops are not considered good taste. Sightseeing calls for casual, comfortable clothing (well-broken-in low-heel shoes, for example). Summer can be brutally hot; spring and fall, mild to chilly; and winter, cold and rainy. Sunscreen and sunglasses are a good idea any time of the year, since the sun in Portugal is very bright.

In your carry-on luggage, **pack an extra pair of eyeglasses or contact lenses** and **enough of any medication you take** to last the entire trip. You may also ask your doctor to write a spare prescription using the drug's generic name, since brand names may vary from country to country. In luggage to be checked, **never pack prescription drugs or valuables.** To avoid customs delays, carry medications in their original packaging. And don't forget to carry with you the addresses of offices that handle refunds of lost traveler's checks.

CHECKING LUGGAGE

How many carry-on bags you can bring with you is up to the airline. Most allow two, but not always, so make sure that everything you carry aboard will fit under your seat or in the overhead bin, and get to the gate early. Note that if you have a seat at the back of the plane, you'll probably board first, while the overhead bins are still empty.

If you are flying internationally, note that baggage allowances may be determined not by piece but by weight—generally 88 pounds (40 kilograms) in first class, 66 pounds (30 kilograms) in business class, and 44 pounds (20 kilograms) in economy.

Airline liability for baggage is limited to $1,250 per person on flights within the United States. On international flights it amounts to $9.07 per pound or $20 per kilogram for checked baggage (roughly $640 per 70-pound bag) and $400 per passenger for unchecked baggage. You can buy additional coverage at check-in for about $10 per $1,000 of coverage, but it excludes a rather extensive list of items, shown on your airline ticket.

Before departure, **itemize your bags' contents** and their worth, and label the bags with your name, address, and phone number. (If you use your home address, cover it so potential thieves can't see it readily.) Inside each bag, **pack a copy of your itinerary.** At check-in, **make sure that each bag is correctly tagged** with the destination airport's three-letter code. If your bags arrive damaged or fail to arrive at all, file a written report with the airline before leaving the airport.

PASSPORTS & VISAS

When traveling internationally, **carry your passport** even if you don't need one (it's always the best form of I.D.) and **make two photocopies of the data page** (one for someone at home and another for you, carried separately from your passport). If you lose your passport, promptly call the nearest embassy or consulate and the local police.

ENTERING PORTUGAL

Citizens of Australia, Canada, New Zealand, the United Kingdom, and the United States need only a valid passport to enter Portugal for stays of up to 60 days. Visas are required for longer stays and, in some instances, for visits to other countries in addition to Portugal.

PASSPORT OFFICES

The best time to apply for a passport or to renew is in fall and winter. Before any trip, check your passport's expiration date, and, if necessary, renew it as soon as possible.

➤ AUSTRALIAN CITIZENS: **Australian Passport Office** (☎ 131–232, www.dfat.gov.au/passports).

➤ CANADIAN CITIZENS: **Passport Office** (☎ 819/994–3500; 800/567–6868 in Canada, www.dfait-maeci.gc.ca/passport).

➤ NEW ZEALAND CITIZENS: **New Zealand Passport Office** (☎ 04/494–0700, www.passports.govt.nz).

➤ U.K. CITIZENS: **London Passport Office** (☎ 0870/521–0410, www.ukpa.gov.uk) for fees and documentation requirements and to request an emergency passport.

➤ U.S. CITIZENS: **National Passport Information Center** (☎ 900/225–5674; calls are 35¢ per minute for automated service, $1.05 per minute for operator service; www.travel.state.gov/npicinfo.html).

REST ROOMS

In Portugal, all public facilities like restaurants, cinemas, theaters, libraries, service stations, and railway stations are required to have public toilets, though train stations are likely to have pay toilets. Rest rooms can range from marble-clad opulence to little better than primitive, but in most cases they are reasonably clean. You are likely to find lamentably few public toilets anywhere that are adapted for travelers with disabilities. Women's rest rooms are often looked after by an attendant who customarily receives a tip of 50 to 100 escudos.

SENIOR-CITIZEN TRAVEL

In Portugal, senior citizens usually qualify for museum admission discounts—sometimes of as much as 50% off the cost of an adult ticket. To qualify for age-related discounts, **mention your senior-citizen status up front** when booking hotel reservations (not when checking out) and before you're seated in restaurants (not when paying the bill). When renting a car, ask about promotional car-rental discounts, which can be cheaper than senior-citizen rates.

➤ EDUCATIONAL PROGRAMS: **Elderhostel** (✉ 75 Federal St., 3rd floor, Boston, MA 02110, ☎ 877/426–

8056, FAX 877/426–2166, www.elderhostel.org). **Interhostel** (✉ University of New Hampshire, 6 Garrison Ave., Durham, NH 03824, ☎ 603/862–1147 or 800/733–9753, FAX 603/862–1113, learn.dce@unh.edu, www.learn.unh.edu).

STUDENTS IN PORTUGAL

➤ I.D.s & SERVICES: **Council Travel** (CIEE; ✉ 205 E. 42nd St., 14th floor, New York, NY 10017, ☎ 212/822–2700 or 888/268–6245, FAX 212/822–2699, info@councilexchanges.org, www.councilexchanges.org) for mail orders only, in the U.S. **Travel Cuts** (✉ 187 College St., Toronto, Ontario M5T 1P7, Canada, ☎ 416/979–2406 or 800/667–2887 in Canada, www.travelcuts.com).

➤ STUDENT TOURS: **Contiki Holidays** (✉ 300 Plaza Alicante, Suite 900, Garden Grove, CA 92840, ☎ 714/740–0808 or 800/266–8454, FAX 714/740–2034).

TAXES

VALUE-ADDED TAX

Value-added tax (IVA in Portuguese) is 12% for hotels. By law prices must be posted at the reception desk and should indicate whether tax is included. Restaurants are also required to charge 12% IVA. Menus generally state at the bottom whether tax is included (*IVA incluido*) or not (*mas 12% IVA*). When in doubt about whether tax is included in a price, ask: *Está incluido o IVA* (ee-vah)?

A number of shops, particularly large stores and shops in holiday resorts, offer a refund of the 17% IVA sales tax on large purchases (the purchase must be a single item worth more than 11,700$00, about $85). Be sure to ask for your tax-free check; you show your passport, fill out a form, and the store mails you the refund at home.

Global Refund is a V.A.T. refund service that makes getting your money back hassle-free. The service is available Europe-wide at 130,000 affiliated stores. In participating stores, **ask for the Global Refund form** (called a Shopping Cheque). Have it stamped like any customs form by customs officials when you leave the

European Union. Then take the form to one of the more than 700 Global Refund counters—conveniently located at every major airport and border crossing—and your money will be refunded on the spot in the form of cash, check, or a refund to your credit-card account (minus a small percentage for processing).

➤ V.A.T. REFUNDS: **Global Refund** (✉ 707 Summer St., Stamford, CT 06901, ☎ 800/566–9828, FAX 203/674–8709, taxfree@us.globalrefund.com, www.globalrefund.com).

TELEPHONES

During the last two years or so Portugal has been updating its phone system, causing phone numbers to change throughout the country. All numbers now have nine digits, the first two being the area code when in or around Lisbon and Oporto, the first three when it's anywhere else in the country. All fixed phone area codes now begin with 2. Mobile phone numbers also have nine digits and begin with 9. If you dial an old number, you will usually hear a recording stating the new number.

AREA & COUNTRY CODES

The country code for Portugal is 351. When dialing a Portuguese number from abroad, dial the nine-digit number after the country code.

DIRECTORY & OPERATOR ASSISTANCE

For general information, dial 118 (operators often speak English). The international information and assistance numbers are 171 for operator-assisted calls; 172 for collect calls; and 177 for information (the operators speak English).

INTERNATIONAL CALLS

Calling abroad can be awkward from public pay phones because of the noise and is expensive from hotels, which often add a considerable surcharge. The best way to make an international call is to go to the local telephone office and have someone place it for you. Every town has an office, and big cities have several. When the call is connected, you will be sent to a quiet cubicle and charged according to the meter. If the price is 500$00 or more, you may pay with Visa or MasterCard. In Lisbon the main telephone office is in the Praça dos Restauradores, right off the Rossío.

To make an international call yourself, dial 00 followed directly by the country code (1 for the United States, 44 for the United Kingdom, 61 for Australia, and 64 for New Zealand) and the area code and number. The Portuguese telephone directory contains a list of all of the principal world country codes and the codes for principal cities.

LONG-DISTANCE CALLS

To make calls to other areas within Portugal, precede the provincial code with 0 (most phone booths have a chart inside listing the various province codes). The 0 is unnecessary when dialing from outside Portugal.

LONG-DISTANCE SERVICES

AT&T, MCI, and Sprint access codes make calling long distance relatively convenient, but you may find the local access number blocked in many hotel rooms. First ask the hotel operator to connect you. If the hotel operator balks, ask for an international operator, or dial the international operator yourself. One way to improve your odds of getting connected to your long-distance carrier is to travel with more than one company's calling card (a hotel may block Sprint, for example, but not MCI). If all else fails, call from a pay phone.

➤ ACCESS CODES: **AT&T Direct** (☎ 800/800128 in Portugal; 800/ 222–0300 for other areas). **MCI WorldPhone** (☎ 800/800123 in Portugal; 800/444–4141 for other areas). **Sprint International Access** (☎ 800/800187 in Portugal; 800/ 877–4646 for other areas).

PUBLIC PHONES

One way to make a local call is to go into a café or bar and ask the bartender if you may use the phone. Bar phones are metered, and the bartender will charge you after you've finished. (Expect to pay a higher rate than the one you would pay in a public phone booth.)

The easiest way to call from a public booth is to use a Portugal Telecom calling card, which can be purchased at post offices, newspaper shops, and tobacconists for either 850$00 or 1,800$00. The phones that accept them have digital readouts, so you can see your time ticking away, and they are uncomplicated to use—the booths have instructions in several languages, including English. With coin-operated phones you insert coins and wait for a dial tone. The minimum cost for a local call is 20$00, 50$00 to call another area, for which you must dial the area code. On the old pay phones, you line up the coins in a groove on top of the dial, and they drop down as needed.

TIME

Portugal sets its clocks according to Greenwich Mean Time, five hours ahead of the U.S. East Coast. Portuguese summer time (GMT plus one hour) requires an additional adjustment from late March to late October.

TIPPING

Service is included in café, restaurant, and hotel bills, but waiters and other service people are poorly paid, and you can be sure your contribution will be appreciated. However, if you received bad service, never feel obligated (or intimidated) to leave a tip. An acceptable tip is 10%–15% of the total bill, and if you have a sandwich or *petiscos* (appetizers) at a bar, leave less, just enough to round out the bill to the nearest 100 escudos. Cocktail waiters get 50$00–75$00 a drink, depending on the bar.

Taxi drivers get about 10% of the meter, but more for long rides or extra help with luggage, and there is an official surcharge for airport runs and baggage. Hotel porters are tipped 100$00 a bag; 100$00 also goes for room service or a doorman who calls you a taxi. If you stay in a hotel for more than two nights, tip the maid about 100$00 per night. The concierge should be tipped for any additional help he or she gives you. Tour guides should be tipped about 200$00–500$00; ushers in theaters or bullfights, 100$00; barbers, at least 100$00; hairdressers, at least 200$00

for a wash and set. Washroom attendants are tipped 100$00.

TOURS & PACKAGES

Because everything is prearranged on a prepackaged tour or independent vacation, you'll spend less time planning—and often get it all at a good price.

BOOKING WITH AN AGENT

Travel agents are excellent resources. But it's a good idea to collect brochures from several agencies as some agents' suggestions may be influenced by relationships with tour and package firms that reward them for volume sales. If you have a special interest, **find an agent with expertise in that area**; ASTA (☞ Travel Agencies, *below*) has a database of specialists worldwide.

Make sure your travel agent knows the accommodations and other services of the place they're recommending. Ask about the hotel's location, room size, beds, and whether it has a pool, room service, or programs for children, if you care about these. Has your agent been there in person or sent others whom you can contact?

Do some homework on your own, too: local tourism boards can provide information about lesser-known and small-niche operators, some of which may sell only direct.

BUYER BEWARE

Each year consumers are stranded or lose their money when tour operators—even large ones with excellent reputations—go out of business. So **check out the operator.** Ask several travel agents about its reputation, and try to **book with a company that has a consumer-protection program.** (Look for information in the company's brochure.) In the United States, members of the National Tour Association and the United States Tour Operators Association are required to set aside funds to cover your payments and travel arrangements in the event that the company defaults. It's also a good idea to choose a company that participates in the American Society of Travel Agents' Tour Operator Program (TOP); ASTA will act as mediator in any disputes between you and your tour operator.

Remember that the more your package or tour includes the better you can predict the ultimate cost of your vacation. Make sure you know exactly what is covered, and **beware of hidden costs.** Are taxes, tips, and transfers included? Entertainment and excursions? These can add up.

➤ TOUR-OPERATOR RECOMMENDATIONS: **American Society of Travel Agents** (☞ Travel Agencies, *below*). **National Tour Association** (NTA; ✉ 546 E. Main St., Lexington, KY 40508, ☎ 859/226–4444 or 800/ 682–8886, www.ntaonline.com). **United States Tour Operators Association** (USTOA; ✉ 342 Madison Ave., Suite 1522, New York, NY 10173, ☎ 212/599–6599 or 800/468–7862, ℻ 212/599–6744, ustoa@aol.com, www.ustoa.com).

TRAIN TRAVEL

Train services in Portugal range in quality from luxurious to the "interesting experience, but I'll go by car next time" variety. The network covers most of the country, though it is thin in the Alentejo region. The cities of Lisbon, Coimbra, Aveiro, and Oporto are linked by the fast and extremely comfortable Alfa and Alfa Pendular (tilt train) services, and these are as good as anything you'll find in Europe. Most other major towns and cities are connected by InterCidade trains, which are reliable, though slower and less luxurious than the Alfa trains. The regional services that connect smaller towns and villages tend to be infrequent and slow, with stops at every station along the line.

The standards of comfort vary from Alfa train luxury, with air-conditioning, food service, and airline-type seats, to the often spartan conditions on regional lines. Most InterCidade trains have bar and restaurant facilities, but the food is famously unappealing. A first-class ticket will cost you 40% more than a second-class one and will buy you more leg and elbow room, but not a great deal more on the Alfa and InterCidade trains. The extra cost is definitely worth it on most regional services,

however. Smoking is restricted to special carriages on all Portuguese trains.

CUTTING COSTS

To save money, **look into rail passes.** But be aware that if you don't plan to cover many miles you may come out ahead by buying individual tickets.

Portugal is one of 17 countries in which you can **use Eurailpasses,** which provide unlimited first-class rail travel, in all of the participating countries, for the duration of the pass. If you plan to rack up the miles, get a standard pass. These are available for 15 days ($610), 21 days ($790), one month ($980), two months ($1,386), and three months ($1,714).

In addition to standard Eurailpasses, **ask about special rail-pass plans.** Among these are the Eurail Youthpass (in second class for those under age 26; $427–$1,198), the Eurail Saverpass (which gives a discount for two or more people traveling together), a Eurail Flexipass (which allows 10 or 15 travel days within a two-month period; $720 and $948, respectively), the Euraildrive Pass and the Europass Drive (which combines travel by train and rental car). It's best to **purchase your pass before you leave** for Europe.

Many travelers assume that rail passes guarantee them seats on the trains they wish to ride. Not so. You need to **book seats ahead even if you are using a rail pass;** seat reservations are required on some European trains, particularly high-speed trains, and are a good idea on trains that may be crowded—particularly in summer on popular routes. You will also need a reservation if you purchase sleeping accommodations.

➤ INFORMATION AND PASSES: **Rail Europe** (✉ 226–230 Westchester Ave., White Plains, NY 10604, ☎ 800/438–7245, ℻ 800/432–1329; ✉ 2087 Dundas St. E, Suite 105, Mississauga, Ontario L4X 1M2, ☎ 905/602–4195. **DER Travel Services** (✉ 9501 W. Devon Ave., Rosemont, IL 60018, ☎ 847/692–4141; 800/ 782–2424 for reservations, ℻ 888/ 712–5727). **CIT Tours Corp** (✉ 15

W. 44th St, 10th floor, New York, NY 10036, ☎ 800/248–7245 for rail; 800/248–8687 for tours and hotels).

➤ PUBLICATION: **Guide to European Passes** (✉ Back Door, Box 2009, Edmonds, WA 98020, ☎ 425/771–8304, FAX 425/771–0833; free) by Rick Steves leads you through the maze of different passes. You can order passes from the same source.

RESERVATIONS

Advance booking is not required on Portuguese trains but is definitely recommended in the case of popular services like the Alfa trains. Reservations are also advisable for other trains if you want to avoid long queues in front of the ticket window on the day the train leaves. You can avoid a trip out to the station to make the reservation by asking a travel agent to take care of it for you.

TRANSPORTATION AROUND
PORTUGAL

Car travel is by far the best way to see the country, although it isn't the cheapest: car-rental and fuel prices are high. Rail travel is economical, but many parts of inland and southern Portugal are simply not accessible by train alone. One option is to combine the advantages of the two forms of travel by using the fast Lisbon to Oporto train service to take you to places like Coimbra and Aveiro, and then use these cities as bases for rental car excursions. An extensive bus network provides what is probably the best all-around means of travel in Portugal in terms of access, comfort, and cost. Competition has produced increasingly good services and kept fares down to extremely reasonable levels. Book through a travel agency. Domestic air travel is very rarely a reasonable option. The regular flights between Lisbon and Oporto save you minimal time over the three-hour fast train service available between the two cities. The Lisbon to Faro flights operated by TAP Air Portugal and Portugália have something to offer if time is a factor since there is no fast train service to the Algarve.

TRAVEL AGENCIES

A good travel agent puts your needs first. Look for an agency that has been in business at least five years, emphasizes customer service, and has someone on staff who specializes in your destination. In addition, **make sure the agency belongs to a professional trade organization.** The American Society of Travel Agents (ASTA), with 27,000 agents in some 170 countries, is the largest and most influential in the field. Operating under the motto "Integrity in Travel," it maintains and enforces a strict code of ethics and will step in to help mediate any agent-client disputes if necessary. ASTA also maintains a Web site that includes a directory of agents. (If a travel agency is also acting as your tour operator, *see* Buyer Beware *in* Tours & Packages, *above.*)

➤ LOCAL AGENT REFERRALS: **American Society of Travel Agents** (ASTA; ☎ 800/965–2782 24-hr hot line, FAX 703/684–8319, www.astanet.com). **Association of British Travel Agents** (✉ 68–71 Newman St., London W1P 4AH, U.K., ☎ 020/7637–2444, FAX 020/7637–0713, information@abta.co.uk, www.abtanet.com). **Association of Canadian Travel Agents** (✉ 1729 Bank St., Suite 201, Ottawa, Ontario K1V 7Z5, Canada, ☎ 613/237–3657, FAX 613/521–0805, acta.ntl@sympatico.ca). **Australian Federation of Travel Agents** (✉ Level 3, 309 Pitt St., Sydney 2000, Australia, ☎ 02/9264–3299, FAX 02/9264–1085, www.afta.com.au). **Travel Agents' Association of New Zealand** (✉ Box 1888, Wellington 10033, New Zealand, ☎ 04/499–0104, FAX 04/499–0827, taanz@tiasnet.co.nz).

VISITOR INFORMATION

➤ PORTUGUESE NATIONAL TOURIST OFFICE: In the U.S.: ✉ 590 5th Ave., 4th floor, New York, NY 10036, ☎ 212/354–4403, FAX 212/764–6137. In Canada: ✉ 60 Bloor St. W, Suite 1005, Toronto, Ontario M4W 3BS, ☎ 416/921–7376, FAX 416/921–1353. In the U.K.: ✉ ✉ 22–25A Sackville St., London W1X 1DE, ☎ 020/7494–1441.

➤ U.S. GOVERNMENT ADVISORIES: **U.S. Department of State** (✉ Overseas Citizens Services Office, Room 4811 N.S., 2201 C St. NW, Washington, DC 20520, ☎ 202/647–5225 for interactive hot line, 301/946–4400 for computer bulletin board, FAX 202/647–3000 for interactive hot line); enclose a self-addressed, stamped, business-size envelope.

WEB SITES

Do check out the World Wide Web when you're planning. You'll find everything from current weather forecasts to virtual tours of famous cities. Fodor's Web site, www.fodors.com, is a great place to start your on-line travels. When you see a 🖥 in this book, go to www.fodors.com/urls for an up-to-date link to that destination's site.

TAP Air Portugal's site, at **www.TAP-AirPortugal.pt/,** has flight schedules and booking information. At **www.portugal.org/,** the Welcome to Portugal Web site is slow to load but is rich in information about the country's various regions. For full information about each of Portugal's state-owned inns in the Enatur chain, visit **www.pousadas.com.**

WHEN TO GO

The tourist season begins in spring and lasts through the autumn. In midsummer it is never unbearably hot (except in parts of the Algarve and on the mainland plains), and it is especially pleasant along the coast, where a cool breeze springs up in the evening. Winter is mild and frequently rainy, except in Madeira, where winter has long been popular; off-season travelers throughout the country have the advantage of reduced hotel rates. In the Algarve, springtime begins in February with a marvelous range of wildflowers. Late September and early October herald Indian summer, which ensures warm sunshine through November.

CLIMATE

The following are average daily maximum and minimum temperatures for major cities in Portugal.

➤ FORECASTS: **Weather Channel Connection** (☎ 900/932–8437), 95¢ per minute from a Touch-Tone phone.

FARO

Jan.	59F	15C	May	72F	22C	Sept.	79F	26C
	48	9		57	14		66	19
Feb.	61F	16C	June	77F	25C	Oct.	72F	22C
	50	10		64	18		61	16
Mar.	64F	18C	July	82F	28C	Nov.	66F	19C
	52	11		68	20		55	13
Apr.	68F	20C	Aug.	82F	28C	Dec.	61F	16C
	55	13		68	20		60	10

LISBON

Jan.	57F	14C	May	71F	21C	Sept.	79F	26C
	46	8		55	13		62	17
Feb.	59F	15C	June	77F	25C	Oct.	72F	22C
	47	8		60	15		58	14
Mar.	63F	17C	July	81F	27C	Nov.	63F	17C
	50	10		63	17		52	11
Apr.	67F	20C	Aug.	82F	28C	Dec.	58F	15C
	53	12		63	17		47	9

PORTO

Jan.	55F	13C	May	68F	20C	Sept.	75F	24C
	41	5		52	11		57	14
Feb.	57F	14C	June	73F	23C	Oct.	70F	21C
	41	5		55	13		52	11
Mar.	61F	16C	July	77F	25C	Nov.	63F	17C
	46	8		59	15		46	8
Apr.	64F	18C	Aug.	77F	25C	Dec.	57F	14C
	48	9		59	15		41	5

FESTIVALS AND SEASONAL EVENTS

Religious festivals, called *festas* and *romarias*, are held throughout the year. Some of the leading annual festivals, fairs, and folk pilgrimages are listed below. Verify the dates with the people at the Portuguese tourism office, who can also send you a complete list of events.

➤ FEB.–MAR.: Festivities of Carnival (Mardi Gras), the final festivals before Lent, are held throughout the country, with processions of masked participants, parades of decorated vehicles, and displays of exuberant flowers.

➤ MAR.–APR.: The large, colorful Feira do Março, held in Aveiro, has been celebrated for more than 500 years. It features folk music and dancing on weekends. Holy Week festivities are held in Braga, Ovar, Póvoa de Varzim, and other cities and major towns, with the most important events taking place on Monday, Thursday, and Good Friday. On the second Sunday after Easter, Loulé hosts the Romaria da Senhora da Piedade (Festival of Our Lady of Mercy), a pilgrimage and procession to the local shrine of Monte da Piedade. The Flower Festival, in the last week of April, brightens downtown Funchal with a carpet of flowers, a parade, and a lot of music.

➤ EARLY–MID-MAY: Legend has it that, in the early 16th century, a peasant who insisted on working on the Day of the Holy Cross saw a perfumed, luminous cross appear on the ground where he was digging. Ever since, Barcelos has held the colorful Festas das Cruzes (Festival of the Crosses), which includes a large fair, concerts, an affecting procession, and a spectacular fireworks display on the River Cavado. Celebrations enlivened by performances of traditional song and dance take place on May 1 in Loulé. During the May pilgrimage to Fátima thousands converge on the town from all over the world to commemorate the first apparition of the Virgin to the shepherd children on May 13, 1917. In Coimbra, the Queima das Fitas (Burning of the Ribbons) celebrated by the university students is quite a party.

➤ MAY–JULY: The Algarve International Classical Music Festival, a series of concerts that features leading Portuguese and foreign artists, is held in Faro, Tavira, Albufeira, Portimão, and Lagos.

➤ JUNE: Monção celebrates the Festa do Corpo de Deus (Festival of Corpus Christi), which includes a symbolic battle between good and evil. Amarante hosts the Festa de São Gonçalo (Festival of St. Gonçalo), when the saint is commemorated by the baking of phallus-shape cakes, which are then exchanged between unmarried men and women. Other celebrations include a fair, folk dancing, and traditional singing. The Feira Nacional (National Fair) in Santarém is the most important such event in Portugal, with bullfighting, folk songs and dancing, and fair amusements. Each June 29 São Pedro de Sintra hosts the large Festa de São Pedro (St. Peter's Day) with riotous hullabaloo. Santos Popularos in Lisbon honors Santo António, the city's patron saint, on June 13, as well as Saint John on June 23 and 24. The festivities for St. John are especially colorful in Oporto, where the whole city erupts with bonfires and barbecues and every corner has its own *cascatas* (arrangements with religious motifs). Locals roam the streets, hitting passersby on the head with, among other things, leeks and plastic hammers.

➤ JUNE–SEPT.: For four weeks every summer the Noites de Queluz (Queluz Nights) festival is staged in the gardens of the Palácio Nacional. Complete with costumed cast and orchestra, this event mimics the concerts, fireworks displays, and other activities held in the gardens to amuse Queen Maria I, who lived in the palace throughout her long reign (1777–1816) and whose eccentric behavior earned her the name "Mad" Queen Maria. The Sintra Festival runs from June through September every year and features piano recitals, operas, and ballet in the town's palaces, churches, and parks. Performances in the gardens of the Palácio de Seteais are especially popular.

➤ JULY: Silves hosts a **beer festival,** where you can sample all the different kinds of Portuguese beer, watch folk dances, and listen to music. This month also sees the annual **Cascais Jazz Festival** in Cascais. The **Festa do Colete Encarnado** (Festival of the Red Waistcoat) in Vila Franca de Xira honors the *campinos* (cowboys) who guard the brave bulls in the pastures of the Ribatejo. Downtown streets are cordoned off, and bulls are let loose as would-be bullfighters try their luck at dodging the charging beasts. Held in even-numbered years, Coimbra's **Festas da Rainha Santa** (Festival of the Queen Saint) is marked by colorful processions and fireworks along the River Mondego. In Guimarães the **Festas de São Torcato** (Festival of Saint Torcato) consists of a fair and a procession to the nearby village of São Torcato. The **Feira de Santiago** (Santiago Fair) in Setúbal includes various folkloric events, rides, food stalls, and other entertainment. Faro's **Festa e Feira da Senhora do Carmo** (Festival and Fair of Our Lady of Carmen) consists of a religious procession and an agricultural fair.

➤ JULY–AUG.: The **Estoril Music Festival** features leading Portuguese and foreign artists in Estoril, Cascais, and other towns of the Estoril Coast.

➤ AUG.: The first Sunday of the month sees Guimarães's **Festas Gualterianas** (Festival of St. Walter), a boisterous evening that dates from the 15th century. Mirandela's **Festa de Nossa Senhora do Amparo** (Festival of Our Lady of Aid), also on the first Sunday, includes dancing, games, and fireworks. On the second Sunday, auto drivers celebrating the **Festa de São Cristovão** (Festival of St. Christopher) converge on the church in Penha, near Guimarães, to commemorate their patron saint. Gouveia's **Festa do Senhor do Calvario** (Festival of Our Lord of Calvary) features a colorful procession, a handicrafts fair, games, and a sheepdog competition. The **Festa de Nossa Senhora do Monte** (Festival of Our Lady of the Mountain) attracts pilgrims from all corners of the island. Ofir and Es-

posende celebrate the **Festas do São Bartolomeu do Mar** (Festival of St. Bartholomew of the Sea), when rowdy revelries can be enjoyed at the water's edge. Machico celebrates the **Santissimo Sacramento** (Sacred Sacrament) festival with a sunset bonfire of pine-tree logs, branches, and cones in the center of town under a specially constructed ceremonial arch. The spectacular **Romaria de Nossa Senhora da Agonia** (Procession and Fair of Our Lady of Sorrows) is held in Viana do Castelo on the weekend closest to August 20. The three-day festival features a procession in which a statue of the Lady is carried over carpets of flowers to a chapel, a parade of fishermen who head down to the sea to be blessed by a bishop, a parade of local beauties in colorful hand-embroidered costumes, and a huge fireworks display.

➤ AUG.–SEPT.: Viseu's **Feira de São Mateus** (St. Matthew's Fair), an important agricultural event with folk dancing and singing, has been held since the Middle Ages. During the **Festas de Nossa Senhora dos Remédios** (Festival of Our Lady of Remedies), the annual pilgrimage to the shrine, many penitents climb the steps on their knees. The main procession is September 8, but the festivities start at the end of August and include concerts, dancing, parades, a fair, and torchlit processions. The *moliceiros* (kelp boats) are given a fresh coat of paint and can be seen racing against each other during the **Festa da Ria** (Ria Festival) held throughout August and September in the Ria de Aveiro.

➤ SEPT.: The **Romaria de São Gens** (Festive Pilgrimage of St. Gens) brings ceramic vendors from all over the country to Freixo de Cima, west of Amarante. The **Festas de Nossa Senhora de** (Our Lady of Nazaré Festival) includes bullfights, folk dancing and singing, and processions of Nazaré fishermen carrying the Lady's image on their shoulders. The **Festa das Vindimas** (Grape Harvest Festival) in Palmela has a symbolic treading of the grapes and a blessing of the harvest, accompanied by a parade of harvesters, wine tastings, the election of the Queen of the Wine, and fireworks. In Ponte de Lima the

Feiras Novas (New Fairs)—an enjoyable festival, which, despite its name, isn't really all that new (it has been held since the 12th century)—includes a fair, a procession, fireworks, and music. During the **Festas de Nossa Sehnora de Boa Viagem** (Our Lady of Good Voyage Festival) in the ancient town of Moita (near Setúbal), the focus is on the blessing of the fishing boats. In the annual **Folk Music and Dance Festival,** singing and dancing in all the Algarve's larger towns culminate at Praia da Rocha with performances by groups from all over the country. A **Wine Harvest Festival,** which involves plenty of singing, dancing, and wine tasting, is celebrated in both Funchal and nearby Estreito da Câmara de Lobos.

➤ OCT.: Faro's **Feira de Santa Iria** (Fair of St. Iria) is another happy excuse to hold traditional celebrations for several days. The **October pilgrimage to Fátima** brings thousands to Fátima to honor the last apparition of the Virgin on October 12, 1917. **Feira de Outubro** (October Fair) in Vila Franca de Xira, a short distance from Lisbon, has farming and agricultural activities, handicraft displays, bullfights, and a running of the bulls in the streets.

➤ LATE-OCT.–EARLY NOV.: The Algarve's **Feira de Outubro** (October Fair) gathers together crafts, goods, and produce from villages throughout the Serra de Monchique. The **National Gastronomy Festival** in Santerém consists of traditional regional dishes, cooking contests, and lectures. At Chaves's **Feira dos Santos** (Saints' Fair) you can buy anything from livestock and farm equipment to wool capes, regional black pottery, rugs, baskets, and gold jewelry. **St. Martin's Fair and the National Horse Show** in Golegã combine parades of saddle horses and bullfight horses with riding competitions, handicrafts exhibitions, and wine tasting.

➤ DEC.: **St. Sylvester's Festival,** on New Year's Eve, transforms Funchal into a vast fairground, with bands of strolling dancers and singers, thousands of lights, and breathtaking fireworks.

➤ MID-JAN.–EARLY FEB.: Among the notable festas during this period are those in honor of **São Gonçalo and São Cristovão** in Vila Nova de Gaia, **São Gonçalinho** in Aveiro, **Nossa Senhora de Candeias** in Mourão, and **São Sebastião** in Santa Maria da Feira in Aveiro.

NORWAY
Bergen

ICELAND
Reykjavik

SCOTLAND
Edinburgh

North
Sea

Skag

DENMARK

NORTHERN
IRELAND

Belfast

IRELAND   Irish
Dublin   Sea   UNITED
                      KINGDOM
             WALES
                                              Hambur

Cardiff   ENGLAND   NETHERLANDS
                                    Amsterdam
London   The Hague
                        Rotterdam
                                              GER
ATLANTIC   Brussels   Bonn
OCEAN   English Channel
                        BELGIUM
                                   Frankfurt
             Paris
                      LUXEMBOURG

                      FRANCE   Zürich   Mu
                                    Bern
                                    SWITZERLAND
                        Lyon   LIECHTENS
                                    Milan   Ve

                                    Monte
                              Nice Carlo
PORTUGAL   ANDORRA Marseille MONACO
             Madrid   Florence

Lisbon   Barcelona Corsica
             SPAIN

Seville   Granada   Sardinia
                        Balearic
                        Islands   Tyrrhe
Gibraltar   Mediterranean Sea

MOROCCO   ALGERIA
                     0   400 miles
                                        TUNISIA
                     0   600 km

Oslo

SWEDEN

Stockholm

Göteborg

Copenhagen

Kattegat

FINLAND

Gulf of Bothnia

Helsinki

Gulf of Finland

Tallinn

ESTONIA

Riga

LATVIA

LITHUANIA

Kaunas

RUSSIA

Vilnius

Kaliningrad

P O L A N D

Warsaw

Kraków

Baltic Sea

Berlin

N Y

Prague

CZECH
REPUBLIC

Vienna

Salzburg

AUSTRIA

Bratislava

SLOVAKIA

Budapest

HUNGARY

SLOVENIA

bljana

Zagreb

CROATIA

BOSNIA AND
HERZEGOVINA

Sarajevo

Belgrade

SERBIA

YUGOSLAVIA

MONTENEGRO

Podgorica

KOSOVO

Priština

Novi Sad

Tiranë

ALBANIA

Skopje

MACEDONIA

Sofia

BULGARIA

Bucharest

ROMANIA

Chişinău

MOLDOVA

UKRAINE

Kiev

Minsk

BELARUS

RUSSIA

Moscow

St. Petersburg

Black Sea

Istanbul

Ankara

T U R K E Y

Rome

Adriatic Sea

I T A L Y

Naples

MALTA

Sea

Sicily

Ionian Sea

GREECE

Aegean Sea

Athens

Crete

CYPRUS

Mediterranean Sea

Portugal

0   50 miles
0   50 km

N

ATLANTIC
OCEAN

SPAIN

Minho
Valença
Viana
do Castelo
Lima
Serra do Gerês N103
Barcelos
Braga
Chaves
Bragança
Póvoa de Varzim
Guimarães
Tâmega
Vila do Conde
Amarante
A4/IP4
Mirandela
N102/IP2
Oporto
Penafiel
Vila Real
Mogadouro
Espinho
Douro
Lamego
Duoro
Oliveira
dos Azeméis
Moimenta
da Beira
Albergaria-a-Velha
S. Pedro
do Sul
Sabot
Aveiro
Vouga
Viseu
Pinhel
IP5
Mealhada
Sta. Comba
Dão
Mira
Cantanhede
Mondego
Guarda
Coimbra
Serra da Estrêla
Covilhã
Figueira
da Foz
Arganil
Fundão
Zêzere
Penamacor
Pombal
Serra da
Gardunha
N233
Leiria
Proença-
a-Nova
Castelo
Branco
Nazaré
Batalha
Ourém
IP2
Alcobaça
Fátima
Tomar
Nisa
Caldas
da Rainha
Sta.
do Aire
IP6
Abrantes
NII8
Óbidos
Torres
Novas
Tagus
Aveiras de Cima
Portalegre
Torres Vedras
Santarém
Ponte
de Sor
Mafra
Tejo
Vila Franca
de Xira
IP2
Sintra
Lisbon
Sorraia
Avis
Badajoz
Cascais
Estoril
N10
Arraiolos
Estremoz
A6
Elvas
Seixal
Montemor-
o-Novo
A6/IP1
Vila
Viçosa
Guadiana
Setúbal
Sado
Sra. de Ossa
Cabo
Espichel
Alcácer
do Sal
Évora
Reguengos
TO THE
AZORES
N2
Sines
Ferreira do
Alentejo
Moura
Cabo de
Sines
Santiago
do Cacém
IP1/E1
Beja
Vilaverde de Ficalho
TO MADEIRA
ISLAND
Castro
Verde
Serpa
Odemira
Ourique
N122
N120
Mira
Mértola
Chança
Guadiana
Almodôvar
Monchique
ALGARVE
Vila do Bispo
Portimão
EN125
S. Brás de Alportel
Cabo de
S. Vicente
Lagos
IP1
Vila Real de
S. António
Sagres
Albufeira
Tavira
Faro
Olhão

PORTUGUESE VOCABULARY

If you have reading knowledge of Spanish and/or French, you will find Portuguese easy to read. Portuguese pronunciation, however, can be somewhat tricky. Despite obvious similarities in Spanish and Portuguese spelling and syntax, the Portuguese sounds are a far cry—almost literally so—from their ostensible Spanish equivalents. Some of the main peculiarities of Portuguese phonetics are the following.

Nasalized vowels: If you have some idea of French pronunciation, these shouldn't give you too much trouble. The closest approach is that of the French *accent du Midi*, as spoken by people in Marseille and Provence, or perhaps an American Midwest twang will help. Try pronouncing *an, am, en, em, in, om, un,* etc., with a sustained *ng* sound (e.g., *bom = bong,* etc.).

Another aspect of Portuguese phonetics is the vowels and diphthongs written with the tilde: *ã, ão, ães*. The Portuguese word for wool, *lã*, sounds roughly like the French word *lin*, with the *-in* resembling the *an* in the English word "any," but nasalized. The suffix "-tion" on such English words as "information" becomes in Portuguese spelling *-ção*, pronounced *-sa-on*, with the *-on* nasalized: *Informação*, for example. These words form their plurals by changing the suffix to *-çoes*, which sounds like "*-son-ech*" (the *ch* here resembling a cross between the English *sh* and the German *ch*: hence *informações*).

The cedilla occurring under the "c" serves exactly the same purpose as in French: It transforms the "c" into a *ss* sound in front of the three so-called "hard" vowels ("a," "o," and "u"): e.g., *graça, Açores, açúcar*. The letter "c" occurring without a cedilla in front of these three vowels automatically has the sound of "k": *pico, mercado, curto*. The letter "c" followed by "e" or "i" is always *ss*, and hence needs no cedilla: *nacional, Graciosa, Terceira*.

The letter "j" sounds like the "s" in the English word "pleasure." So does "g" except when the latter is followed by one of the "hard" vowels: hence, *generoso, gigantesco, Jerónimo, azulejos, Jorge*, etc.

The spelling *nh* is rendered like the *ny* in "canyon": e.g., *senhora*.

The spelling *lh* is somewhere in between the *l* and the *y* sounds in "million": e.g., *Batalha*.

In the matter of syllabic stress, Portuguese obeys the two basic Spanish principles: (1) in words ending in a vowel, or in "n" or "s," the tonic accent falls on the next-to-the-last syllable: *fado, mercado, azulejos*; (2) in words ending in consonants other than "n" or "s," the stress falls on the last syllable: *favor, nacional*. Words in which the syllabic stress does not conform to the two above rules must be written with an acute accent to indicate the proper pronunciation: *sábado, república, politécnico*.

Numbers

1	um, uma
2	dois, duas
3	três
4	quatro
5	cinco
6	seis
7	sete
8	oito
9	nove
10	dez
11	onze
12	doze
13	treze
14	catorze
15	quinze
16	dezaseis
17	dezasete
18	dezoito
19	dezanove
20	vinte
21	vinte e um
22	vinte e dois
30	trinta
40	quarenta
50	cinquenta
60	sessenta
70	setenta
80	oitenta
90	noventa
100	cem
110	cento e dez
200	duzentos
1,000	mil
1,500	mil e quinhentos

Days of the Week

Monday	Segunda-feira
Tuesday	Terça-feira
Wednesday	Quarta-feira
Thursday	Quinta-feira
Friday	Sexta-feira
Saturday	Sábado
Sunday	Domingo

Months

January	Janeiro
February	Fevereiro
March	Março
April	Abril
May	Maio
June	Junho
July	Julho
August	Agosto

September	Setembro
October	Outubro
November	Novembro
December	Dezembro

Useful Phrases

Do you speak English?	Fala Inglês?
Yes	Sim
No	Não
Please	Por favor
Thank you	Obrigado/a
Thank you very much	Muito obrigado/a
Excuse me, sorry	Desculpe, Com licença
I'm sorry	Desculpe-me
Good morning or good day	Bom dia
Good afternoon	Boa tarde
Good evening or good night	Boa noite
Goodbye	Adeus
How are you?	Como está?
How do you say in Portuguese?	Como se diz em Português?
Tourist Office	Turismo
Fine	Optimo
Very good	Muito bem (muito bom)
It's all right	Está bem
Good luck	Felicidades (boa sorte)
Hello	Olá
Come back soon	Até breve
Where is the hotel?	Onde é o hotel?
How much does this cost?	Quanto custa?
How do you feel?	Como se sente?
How goes it?	Que tal?
Pleased to meet you	Muito prazer em o (a) conhecer
The pleasure is mine	O prazer é meu
I have the pleasure of introducing Mr., Miss, Mrs., or Ms. . . .	Tenho o prazer de lhe apresentar o senhor, a senhora . . .
I like it very much	Gosto muito
I don't like it	Não gosto
Don't mention it	De nada
Pardon me	Perdão
Are you ready?	Está pronto?
I am ready	Estou pronto
Welcome	Seja benvindo
What time is it?	Que horas são?
I am glad to see you	Muito prazer em o (a) ver
I don't understand	Não entendo
Please speak slowly	Fale lentamente por favor
I understand (or It is clear)	Compreendo (or) Está claro
Whenever you please	Quando quizer
Please wait	Faça favor de esperar
Toilet	Casa de banho
I will be a little late	Chegarei um pouco atrasado
I don't know	Não sei
Is this seat free?	Está vago este lugar?

Vocabulary

Would you please direct me to . . . ?	Por favor indique-me . . . ?
Where is the station, museum . . . ?	Onde fica a estação, museu . . . ?
I am American, British	Eu sou Americano, Inglês
It's very kind of you	É muito amavel
Please sit down	Por favor sente-se

Sundries

cigar, cigarette	charuto, cigarro
matches	fosforos
dictionary	dicionário
key	chave
razor blades	laminas de barbear
shaving cream	creme de barbear
soap	sobonete
map	mapa
tampons	tampões
sanitary pads	pensos higiénicos
newspaper	jornal
magazine	revista
telephone	telefone
envelopes	envelopes
writing paper	papel de carta
airmail writing paper	papel de carta de avião
postcard	postal
stamps	selos

Merchants

bakery	padaria
bookshop	livraria
butcher's	talho
delicatessen	charutaria
dry cleaner's	limpeza a seco
grocery	mercearia
hairdresser, barber	cabeleireiro, barbeiro
laundry	lavandaria
shoemaker	sapateiro
supermarket	supermercado

Emergencies/Medical

ill, sick	doente
I am ill	Estou doente
I have a fever	Tenho febre
My wife/husband/ child is ill	Minha mulher/marido/criança está doente
doctor	doutor/médico
nurse	enfermeira/o
prescription	receita
pharmacist/chemist	farmacia
Please fetch/call a doctor	Por favor, chame o doutor/medico
accident	acidente
road accident	acidente na estrada
Where is the nearest hospital?	Onde é o hospital mais proximo?
Where is the American/ British Hospital?	Onde é o hospital Americano/ Britanico?
dentist	dentista

X-ray	Raios-X
aspirin	aspirina
painkiller	analgésico
bandage	ligadura
ointment for bites/stings	pomada para picadas
cough mixture	xarope para a tosse
laxative	laxativo
thermometer	termómetro

On the Move

plane	avião
train	comboio
boat	barco
taxi	taxi
car	carro/automovel
bus	autocarro
seat	assento/lugar
reservation	reserva
smoking/no-smoking compartment	compartimento para fumadores/não fumadores
rail station	estação caminho de ferro
subway station	estação do Metropolitano
airport	aeroporto
harbor	estação mártima
town terminal	estação/terminal
shuttle bus/train	autocarro/comboio com ligação constante
sleeper	cama
couchette	beliche
porter	bagageiro
baggage/luggage	bagagem
baggage trolley	carrinho de bagagem
single ticket	bilhete de ida
return ticket	bilhete de ida e volta
first class	primeira classe
second class	segunda classe
When does the train leave?	A que horas sai o comboio?
What time does the train arrive at . . . ?	A que horas chega o comboio a . . . ?

INDEX

Icons and Symbols

★   Our special recommen-
    dations
✕   Restaurant
🏠   Lodging establishment
✕🏠 Lodging establishment
    whose restaurant war-
    rants a special trip
🐥   Good for kids (rubber
    duck)
☞   Sends you to another
    section of the guide for
    more information
⊠   Address
☏   Telephone number
🕐   Opening and closing
    times
🎟   Admission prices
✇   Sends you to
    www.fodors.com/urls
    for up-to-date links to
    the property's Web site

Numbers in white and black
circles ③ ❸ that appear on
the maps, in the margins, and
within the tours correspond
to one another.

A

A Casa-Museu de Almeida
Moreira, 239
Abrantes, 122, 142
Adegas de São Francisco du
Vinho, 311, 312
Águeda, 241–242
Airports, 343
Albufeira, 196–198, 365
Alcácer do Sal, 149, 152,
174–175
Alcântara (Lisbon), 53–54
Alcobaça, 121, 122, 130–
131
Alentejo. ☞ Évora and the
Alentejo
Alfama district (Lisbon), 39–
43
Algarve, 180–213, 367
Almansil, 194–195
Almeida, 218, 219, 255
Almeirim, 121, 123, 136
Alpedrinha, 247
Alpiarça, 121, 123, 137
Alvito, 173–174
Alvor, 202–203
Amarante, 264, 266, 280–
281, 365
American Express, 356
Amoreiras, 48, 49
Antiga Alfândega, 311,
312–313
Apartment and villa rentals,
353

Aquarium, 53
Aqueduct (Tomar), 140
Aqueduto das Aguas Livres,
48, 49
Aqueduto da Agua da Prata,
149, 159
Aqueduto Amoreira, 166
Archaeological sites
Algarve, 187, 190, 195, 200,
204, 208–209
Coimbra and the Beiras, 227,
230–231, 232, 245, 246,
248, 250, 254, 255
Évora and the Alentejo, 155,
159, 167, 169–170, 171,
173, 175
Oporto and the North, 283,
284, 285, 288–289, 292,
296, 298
Arco da Vila, 186
Arco de Almedina
(Coimbra), 223
Arco do Porta Nova (Braga),
283
Arcos de Valdevez, 292
Armação de Pêra, 198–199
Armona, 189
Arraiolos, 149, 159–160
Art galleries, 47, 49–50, 77,
103, 195, 204
Atlantic Coast, 107–108
Atlantic Park, 194
ATMs, 356
Auto racing, 98
Aveiro, 218, 219, 235–238,
365, 367
Avenida da Liberdade
(Lisbon), 48, 49
Avenida dos Aliados
(Oporto), 267
Azenhas do Mar, 107–108
Azulejos, 42, 163

B

Bairro Alto (Lisbon), 45–47
Baixa district (Lisbon), 43–
44
Ballooning, 158
Banking hours, 344
Barcelos, 264, 288–289,
365
Basilica da Estrêla, 47
Batalha, 121, 131–132
Beaches
Algarve, 181, 188, 189, 192,
197, 201, 202, 205, 208
Coimbra and the Beiras, 216,
234
Estremadura and the Ribatejo,
119
Évora and the Alentejo, 147
Lisbon's environs, 98, 101,
107, 109–110, 112
Oporto and the North, 261–
262

Beiras. ☞ Coimbra and the
Beiras
Beja, 149, 150, 170–172
Belém (Lisbon), 53–58
Belmonte, 219, 250–251
Biblioteca Joanina, 225
Biblioteca Pública, 155
Bicycling, 234, 238, 343
tours, 302
Boat travel, 114, 144, 300,
330–331. ☞ Also Ferries
Boating, 78
Boca de Encumeada, 324
Boca do Inferno, 93, 101
Bolsa, 271
Bom Jesus do Monte, 285
Borba, 149, 150, 164
Bowling, 78
Braga, 264, 266, 282–285,
365
Bragança, 266, 296–297
Buarcos, 218, 219, 234–235
Buçaco, 218, 219, 244–245
Bullfighting, 49, 79, 133–
135, 161, 181
Burgau, 208
Bus travel, 344, 363
Algarve, 210, 211
Coimbra and the Beiras, 256,
257
Estremadura and the Ribatejo,
143–144
Évora and the Alentejo, 177
Lisbon, 83, 84, 86
Lisbon's environs, 114–115
Madeira, 330
Oporto and the North, 300–
301
Business hours, 344

C

Cable car, 311
Cabo da Roca, 93, 94, 107–
108
Cabo Espichel, 94, 114
Cabo Girão, 309, 323
Cabo São Vicente, 184, 209–
210
Cacela Velha, 192
Cacilhas, 93, 94, 109
Cais da Ribeira (Oporto),
269
Caldas da Rainha, 121, 122,
128–129
Câmara de Lobos, 309, 322–
323
Câmara Municipal (Aveiro),
236
Câmara Municipal (Oporto),
267
Câmara Municipal (Ovar),
238
Câmara Municipal (Viseu),
239
Cameras and photography,
344

Caminha, *264, 291*
Camping, *252, 329, 353*
Campo Maior, *150, 166–167*
Campo Pequeno (bullring), *49, 79*
Canal de São Roque, *236–237*
Canhas, *325*
Caniçal, *327*
Canil Montes Hermínios, *253*
Cape Mondego Lighthouse, *234*
Capela das Aparições, *138*
Capela de Santa Catarina, *314*
Capela de São Frutuoso de Montélios, *284*
Capela de São João Baptista, *46*
Capela dos Clérigos, *294*
Capela dos Ossos, *157*
Capela dos Reis, *283*
Car rentals, *344–345, 363.* ☞ *Also under specific cities and areas*
Car travel, *345–346, 363*
Algarve, *210–211*
Coimbra and the Beiras, *256, 257*
Estremadura and the Ribatejo, *143, 144*
Évora and the Alentejo, *177*
Lisbon, *83, 84*
Lisbon's environs, *115*
Madeira, *330*
Oporto and the North, *301*
Caramulinho, *241*
Caramulo, *241*
Carvoeiro, *199*
Casa da Alfandega, *204*
Casa de Cristóvão Colombo, *309, 328*
Casa do Cantaber, *231*
Casa do Paço, *232*
Casa dos Bicos, *39, 41*
Casa dos Pastorinhos, *138*
Casa dos Patudos, *137*
Casa-Museu de Guerra Junqueiro, *269*
Casa-Museu de Teixeira Lopes, *270*
Cascais, *93, 94, 98–101, 366*
Casinos, *96, 193, 196, 233–234, 276, 279, 319*
Castelo (Bragança), *296*
Castelo (Guimarães), *286*
Castelo (Loulé), *190*
Castelo (Óbidos), *127*
Castelo (Tavira), *191*
Castelo Branco, *219, 246–247*
Castelo de Almourol, *121, 122, 141*
Castelo de Beja, *171*
Castelo de Belver, *122, 143*
Castelo de Bode, *122, 141*
Castelo de Sabugal, *248–249*
Castelo de Santa Maria da Feira, *238*

Castelo de São João, *201*
Castelo de São Jorge, *38, 39, 41*
Castelo de São Tiago da Barra, *290*
Castelo de Vide, *149, 169–170*
Castelo dos Mouros, *93, 106*
Castelo Rodrigo, *254*
Castelo Templario, *246*
Castles
Algarve, *190, 191, 201*
Coimbra and the Beiras, *231–232, 238, 246, 248–249, 250*
Estremadura and the Ribatejo, *127, 132, 137, 141, 142, 143, 160–161*
Évora and the Alentejo, *147, 162, 166, 167, 168–169, 170, 171, 172–173, 174, 175*
Lisbon, *41*
Lisbon's environs, *106*
Oporto and the North, *262, 286, 290, 297*
Caverns, *139*
Celorico da Beira, *218, 219, 254*
Centro Cultural de Belém, *54, 77*
Centro de Arte Moderna, *38, 48, 49–50*
Centro de Artesanato, *288*
Centum Cellas, *250*
Cêrro da Vila, *195*
Chaves, *266, 297–299, 367*
Chiado (Lisbon), *45–47, 80*
Children, attractions for
Algarve, *187, 194, 196–197, 198, 199–200, 205, 208–209*
Coimbra and the Beiras, *227, 235, 237, 241, 249, 250, 255*
Estremadura and the Ribatejo, *124, 135, 139*
Lisbon, *41–42, 50, 58*
Madeira, *321*
Oporto and the North, *269, 285, 286, 288, 296*
Children, traveling with, *347*
Churches, convents, and monasteries
Algarve, *186–187, 188, 190, 191, 194, 200, 204, 208*
Coimbra and the Beiras, *223–224, 226, 227, 236, 238, 239–240, 244, 245, 248, 250, 253, 254, 255–256*
Estremadura and the Ribatejo, *123–124, 125, 127, 130, 131, 136, 137, 138, 140*
Évora and the Alentejo, *153, 155, 156, 157, 166, 167, 171*
Lisbon, *41, 42, 46, 47, 55*
Lisbon's environs, *98, 111, 113*

Madeira, *313, 314, 315, 321*
Oporto and the North, *267, 269, 271, 278, 280, 282, 283, 285, 286, 287, 290, 294, 296, 297, 298*
Cidade Velha (Faro), *186*
Cidadela, *296*
Citânia de Briteiros, *264, 285*
Climate, *364*
Coimbra and the Beiras, *215–259, 365, 366*
Colares, *107*
Colegiada de Nossa Senhora da Oliveira, *286*
Concerts, *77–78*
Conímbriga, *218, 219, 230–231*
Constância, *141–142*
Consulates, *351*
Consumer protection, *347*
Convento da Conceição, *171*
Convento de Arrábida, *113*
Convento de Cristo, *140*
Convento de Jesus (Aveiro), *236*
Convento de Santa Clara (Funchal), *311, 313*
Convento de Santa Clara (Vila do Conde), *278*
Convento de Santa Clara-a-Nova, *227*
Convento de Santa Clara-a-Velha, *227*
Convento de São Francisco (Vinhais), *297*
Convento de São Gonçalo, *280*
Convento do Carmo, *38, 45, 46*
Convents. ☞ Churches, convents, and monasteries
Cordovil Mansion, *156*
Costa da Caparica, *93, 94, 109–110*
Costa Verde, *282–293, 303*
Coudelaria de Alter, *149, 168*
Country house rentals, *353–354*
Country market (Vila Nogueira de Azeitão), *112*
Covilhã, *219, 251*
Credit cards, *356*
Cristo Rei, *109*
Cromlech and the Menhir of Almedres, *149, 159*
Cruises, *193, 198, 205*
Cruz Alta, *107*
Culatra, *189*
Curia, *242–243*
Curral das Freiras, *322*
Currency, *87, 357*
Customs and duties, *347–349*

D
Diner's Club, *356*
Disabilities and accessibility, *350*

Discounts, *350–351*
Doca (Faro), *187*
Dolmen of Zambujeiro, *149, 159*
Domus Municipalis
(Bragança), *296*
Douro, *277–282*
Douro train line, *279, 301*
Duties, *347–349*

E

Eastern Beiras, *246–256*
Eira do Serrado, *321–322*
Electricity, *351*
Elevador da Glória, *38, 45, 46*
Elevador de Santa Justa, *38, 44*
Elevators, *44, 46, 86, 290*
Elvas, *149, 150, 166*
Embassies, *351*
Emergencies, *346, 351*
Algarve, 212
Coimbra and the Beiras, 258
Estremadura and the Ribatejo, 144
Évora and the Alentejo, 177–178
Lisbon, 87–88
Lisbon's environs, 116
Madeira, 330
Oporto and the North, 302
Ericeira, *121, 124*
Ermida de São Bras, *157*
Espinho, *279*
Esposende, *264, 278–279, 366*
Estação se São Bento, *269*
Estói, *190*
Estoril, *93, 94, 96–98, 366*
Estoril coast, *95–102*
Estremadura and the Ribatejo, *119–145*
Estremoz, *149, 164–165*
Évora and the Alentejo, *147–178*
Évoramonte, *149, 165–166*

F

Fado music, *75–76, 228, 319*
Faial, *326*
Faro, *184, 186–191, 364, 365, 366, 367*
Fátima, *121, 122, 138–139, 365, 367*
Feira de Barcelos, *288*
Feira de São Pedro, *105*
Feira Nacional do Cavalo, *137*
Feiras Novas, *292–293*
Feitoria Inglêsa, *271*
Ferragudo, *201*
Ferries, *86, 189*
Festa das Vindimas, *110*
Festa do Colete Encarnado, *135*
Festivals and seasonal events, *365–366.* ☞ *Also under specific cities and areas*

Figueira da Foz, *218, 219, 232–234*
Film, *78*
Fishing, *357*
Algarve, 182, 209
Coimbra and the Beiras, 217, 234
Lisbon's environs, 100, 114
Madeira, 307, 319
Oporto and the North, 263
Foia, *203*
Fonte da Areia, *328*
Fonte das Bicas, *164*
Fonte dos Judeus, *226*
Fortaleza da Santa Catarina (Figueira da Foz), *232*
Fortaleza da Santa Catarina (Praia da Rocha), *202*
Fortaleza de Sagres, *208–209*
Fortaleza de São Tiago, *311, 313*
Fortaleza do Pico, *311–312, 313*
Forte de São Bento, *323*
Forts
Algarve, 199–200, 202, 204–205, 208–209
Coimbra and the Beiras, 232, 254
Estremadura and the Ribatejo, 125
Madeira, 313, 323
Oporto and the North, 296, 298
Four-wheel driving, *158*
Funchal, *309, 311–321, 367*
Fundação Abel de Lacerd, *241*
Fundão, *219, 247–248*
Funicular-railway system, *86, 290*

G

Galeria do Museu Municipal, *103*
Gardens
Coimbra and the Beiras, 225, 226, 247
Évora, 156, 157
Lisbon, 41, 47, 54–55
Lisbon's environs, 107, 113
Madeira, 313–314
Gay and lesbian travelers, *76, 351*
Go-carts, *159*
Golegã, *137, 367*
Golf, *357*
Algarve, 182, 194, 195, 196, 207, 208
Estremadura, 125
Évora and the Alentejo, 170
Lisbon, 78
Lisbon's environs, 92, 98, 100, 112
Madeira, 319
Oporto and the North, 276, 279, 281
Gouveia, *219, 253, 366*

Governor's Palace, *204*
Guarda, *218, 219, 255–256*
Guimarães, *264, 286–288, 366*
Guincho, *93, 94, 101–102*

H

Health concerns, *351*
Henriques, Dom Afonso, *41, 56*
Henriques & Henriques Vinhos, *322*
Hiking, *245, 252, 307, 326*
tours, 331
Holidays, *352*
Home exchanges, *354*
Horseback riding, *357*
Algarve, 195, 196
Coimbra and the Beiras, 230, 238
Évora and the Alentejo, 148, 159, 176
Lisbon's environs, 100, 105
Hospitals. ☞ Emergencies *under specific cities and areas*
Hostels, *354*
House of the Fountains, *231*

I

Icons and symbols, *376.* ☞ *Also* Web sites
Igreja a Nossa Senhora da Graça, *156*
Igreja da Graça, *136*
Igreja da Misericórdia (Aveiro), *236*
Igreja da Misericórdia (Chaves), *298*
Igreja da Misericórdia (Oporto), *271*
Igreja da Misericórdia (Penamacor), *248*
Igreja da Misericórdia (Tavira), *191*
Igreja da Misericórdia (Viseu), *239–240*
Igreja da Nossa Senhora da Assunção (Elvas), *166*
Igreja das Mercês, *157*
Igreja de Espirito Santo, *156*
Igreja de Jesus, *111*
Igreja de Misericórdia (Évora), *156*
Igreja de Nossa Senhora da Assunção (Cascais), *98*
Igreja de Santa Clara, *157*
Igreja de Santa Luzia, *41*
Igreja de Santa Maria (Beja), *171*
Igreja de Santa Maria (Bragança), *296*
Igreja de Santa Maria (Óbidos), *127*
Igreja de Santo Antão, *153*
Igreja de Santo António, *204*
Igreja de São Bento, *296*
Igreja de São Domingos (Aveiro), *236*

Igreja de São Domingos
(Guimarães), *287*
Igreja de São Francisco
(Évora), *156–157*
Igreja de São Francisco
(Faro), *187*
Igreja de São Francisco
(Guimarães), *287*
Igreja de São Francisco
(Oporto), *271*
Igreja de São Leonardo, *125*
Igreja de São Mamede, *156*
Igreja de São Miguel de
Castelo, *286*
Igreja de São Roque, *38, 45,*
46
Igreja de São Tiago, *250*
Igreja do Carmo, *188*
Igreja dos Clérigos, *267*
Igreja dos Lóios, *155*
Igreja dos Terceiros de São
Francisco, *239*
Igreja e Mosteiro de Santa
Cruz, *226*
Igreja Matriz (Loulé), *190*
Igreja Matriz (Oporto), *278*
Igreja Matriz (Ovar), *238*
Ilha de Tavira, *191–192*
Ilhas Berlenga, *121, 126*
Ílhavo, *218, 219, 235*
Instituto do Vinho do Porto,
38, 45, 46–47
Insurance, *352*
for car rentals, 345
Island tours, *331*

J

Jardim Botânico (Coimbra),
225
Jardim Botânico (Funchal),
311, 313–314
Jardim Botânico (Lisbon),
46, 47
Jardim Botânico (Madeira),
309
Jardim Botânico da Ajuda,
54–55
Jardim da Estrêla, *38, 46, 47*
Jardim de Diana, *156*
Jardim de Manga, *226*
Jardim do Antigo Paço
Episcopal, *247*
Jardim Municipal (Évora),
157
Jardim Zoológico, *38, 48, 50*
José Maria da Fonseca
Company, *112*
Juderia (Belmonte), *250*

K

Kayaking, *230, 246*

L

Lagoa, *199*
Lagos, *184, 186, 204–207,*
365
Lamego, *264, 282*
Language, *352*

Largo da Porta de Moura
(Évora), *156*
Largo da Portagem
(Coimbra), *223*
Largo da Sé (Viseu), *239–240*
Largo das Portas do Sol
(Lisbon), *39, 42*
Leiria, *121, 122, 132–133*
Lezíria, *121, 136*
Lighthouses, *210, 234*
Linhares, *253*
Lisbon, *34–89*
Lisbon's environs, *91–117*
Loulé, *190–191, 365*
Lower Alentejo, *170–176*
Luggage, *358*
Luso, *218, 219, 243–244*

M

Machico, *327, 366*
Madeira, *305–331*
Mãe d'Agua, *49*
Mafra, *121, 123–124*
Mail, *355. ☞ Also under*
specific cities and areas
Manta Rota, *192*
Manteigas, *219*
Marvão, *149, 168–169*
MasterCard, *356*
Meia Praia, *205*
Menhir of Outeiro, *161*
Mercado dos Lavradores,
311, 313
Mercado municipal (Évora),
157
Metro (Lisbon), *86*
Military museum (Batalha),
131
Milreu, *190*
Minho, *282–293, 303*
Miradouro de São Gens, *246*
Miradouro Santa Luzia
(Lisbon), *39, 41*
Mirandela, *266, 295, 366*
Miróbriga, *175*
Misericórdia (Viana do
Castelo), *289*
Modern City (Lisbon), *47–*
52
Moledo, *291*
Monasteries. ☞ Churches,
convents, and
monasteries
Monastery in Lorvão, *245*
Monção, *264, 292, 365*
Monchique, *184, 203*
Money, *355–357*
Monsaraz, *149, 150, 160–*
161
Monsaraz Museum, *161*
Monserrate, *107*
Montalegre, *299*
Monte, *309, 321*
Monte Gordo, *192–193*
Montemor-o-Velho, *218,*
219, 231–232
Montes Herminios Kennels,
253
Monument to Cabral, *250*

Monument to Viriáto, *240*
Monumento dos
Descobrimentos, *38, 55*
Mosteiro de Alcobaça, *130*
Mosteiro de São Vicente, *39,*
41
Mosteiro de Tibães, *284*
Mosteiro dos Jerónimos, *38,*
55
Mosteiro Palácio Nacional de
Mafra, *123*
Municipal Museum
(Marvão), *169*
Municipal Museum
(Portalegre), *167*
Municipal Museum (Santiago
do Cacém), *175*
Municipal Museum (Serpa),
173
Murça, *295*
Museo Municipal (Estremoz),
164
Museu Abel Manta, *253*
Museu Alberto Sampaio,
286–287
Museu Arqueologia (Silves),
200
Museu Arqueológico
(Barcelos), *288–289*
Museu Arqueologico
(Santarém), *136*
Museu Arqueológico de São
Miguel di Odrinhas, *103*
Museu Arqueológico do
Carmo, *46*
Museu Calouste Gulbenkian,
38, 48, 50
Museu Conde de Castro
Guimarães, *99*
Museu da Alfaia Agricola,
165
Museu da Guarda, *256*
Museu da Marinha, *38, 55*
Museu da Marioneta, *39,*
41–42
Museu da Quinta das Cruzes,
311, 314
Museu da Região Flaviense,
298
Museu das Artes Decorativas,
38, 39, 42
Museu de Arte Antiga, *38,*
53–54, 57
Museu de Arte
Contemporânea (Funchal),
313
Museu de Arte
Contemporânea—Fundação
de Serralves, *272*
Museu de Arte Popular, *38,*
57
Museu de Arte Primitiva e
Moderna, *287*
Museu de Arte Sacra
(Braga), *283*
Museu de Arte Sacra
(Funchal), *311, 314*
Museu de Arte Sacra
(Lisbon), *46*

Museu de Arte Sacra da Sé, 153
Museu de Aveiro, 236
Museu de Cera, 139
Museu de Cerâmica, 128
Museu de Évora, 155
Museu de Grão Vasco, 239
Museu de História Natural, 46, 47
Museu de Olaria, 289
Museu de Setúbal, 111
Museu do Abade de Baçal, 296
Museu do Ar, 135
Museu do Automóvel, 241
Museu do Azulejo, 42–43
Museu do Brinquedo, 103
Museu do Chiado, 45, 47
Museu do Mar (Cascais), 98–99
Museu do Mar (Ílhavo), 235
Museu dos Coches (Vila Viçosa), 162, 164
Museu Exilio, 96
Museu Ferroviário, 241
Museu Francisco Tavares Proença Junior, 246–247
Museu Histórico da Vista Alegre, 235
Museu José Regio, 167
Museu Machado de Castro, 224
Museu Malhoa, 128
Museu Maritimo, 187
Museu Martins Sarmento, 287
Museu Militar (Lisbon), 39, 42
Museu Militar de Buçaco, 244
Museu Municipal (Faro), 187
Museu Municipal (Funchal), 311, 314
Museu Municipal (Lagos), 204
Museu Municipal (Viana do Castelo), 290
Museu Municipal Amadeo de Sousa-Cardosa, 280
Museu Nacional de Coches (Lisbon), 38, 57
Museu Nacional do Vinho, 130
Museu Nacional Soares dos Reis, 271
Museu Regional de Ovar, 238
Museu Regional do Algarve, 188
Museu Regional Rainha Dona Leonor, 171
Museu Romântico, 271
Museu Visigotico, 171
Museums
Algarve, 187, 188, 200, 204
Coimbra and the Beiras, 224, 235, 236, 238, 239, 241, 244, 253, 256

Estremadura and the Ribatejo, 128, 130, 135, 136, 137, 139
Évora and the Alentejo, 153, 155, 161, 162, 164, 165, 167, 169, 171, 173, 175
hours, 344
Lisbon, 41, 42–43, 46, 47, 50, 55, 57
Lisbon's environs, 96, 98–99, 103, 111
Madeira, 313, 314, 327, 328
Oporto and the North, 269, 271, 272, 280, 283, 286–287, 288–289, 290, 296, 298

N

National parks, 168, 217, 249, 266, 293
Nature reserves, 107, 113, 124, 174, 293
Nazaré, 121, 122, 129–130, 366
Nightlife and the arts. ☞ Under specific cities and areas
The North. ☞ Oporto and the North
Nossa Senhora da Conceição, 140
Nossa Senhora do Monte, 321
Nossa Senhora dos Remédios, 282

O

O Choupal, 227
Óbidos, 121, 122, 126–128
Oceanário de Lisboa, 38, 52, 53
Ofir, 264, 278–279, 366
Olhão, 184, 189
Olhos d'Agua, 197
Oporto and the North, 261–303, 365
Outdoor activities and sports, 357–358. ☞ Also specific sports; under specific cities and areas; Water sports
Ovar, 218, 219, 238, 365

P

Packing, 358
Paço dos Arcebispos (Braga), 283
Paço dos Arcebispos (Oporto), 269
Paço dos Duques, 286
Paço Ducal, 162
Palace Hotel Buçaco, 244–245
Palaces
Algarve, 190, 204
Coimbra and the Beiras, 225, 227, 232, 244
Estremadura, 123–124
Évora and the Alentejo, 155, 157, 162

Lisbon, 50–51, 57–58
Lisbon's environs, 102–103, 106–107, 108, 112
Madeira, 314
Oporto and the North, 283, 286, 295
Palácio da Ajuda, 57–58
Palácio da Justiça (Coimbra), 227
Palácio de Dom Manuel, 157
Pálacio de São Lourenço, 311, 314
Palácio de Sobre Ribas, 225
Palácio de Tavora (Vila Nogueira de Azeitão), 112
Palácio do Visconde de Estói, 190
Palácio dos Biscainhos, 283
Palácio dos Duques de Cadaval, 155
Palácio dos Marqueses da Fronteira, 38, 48, 50–51
Palácio dos Tavoras (Mirandela), 295
Palácio Foz, 51
Palácio Nacional de Pena, 93, 106–107
Palácio Nacional de Queluz, 108
Palácio Nacional de Sintra, 102–103
Palácio Sotto Mayor, 232–233
Palmela, 93, 94, 110, 366
Parks
Coimbra and the Beiras, 224, 237, 251–253
Estremadura and the Ribatejo, 132
Évora and the Alentejo, 168
Lisbon, 51, 52–53
Lisbon's environs, 99, 105, 113
Madeira, 314, 326
Oporto and the North, 298
Parque das Nações, 52–53
Parque de Queimadas, 326
Parque de Santa Cruz, 224
Parque do Marechal Carmona, 99
Parque Eduardo VII, 38, 48, 51
Parque Liberdade, 105
Parque Nacional da Peneda-Gerés, 266, 293
Parque Natural da Serra da Estrela, 218, 219, 251–253
Parque Natural da Serra de São Mamede, 149–150, 168
Parque Natural das Serras de Aire e Candeeiros, 132
Parque Santa Catarina, 311, 314
Parque Termal, 298
Passports and visas, 358–359
Patio da Inquisição, 226

Paúl da Serra, *309, 325*
Pedal boats, *285*
Penacova, *218, 219, 245*
Penafiel, *264, 266, 279*
Penamacor, *219, 248*
Penedo, *107*
Penha D'Aguia, *325, 327*
Peniche, *121, 125–126*
Peninsula de Tróia, *112*
Peso da Régua, *264, 281*
Pharmacies, *344.* ☞ *Also*
    Emergencies *under*
    specific cities and areas
Photography, *344*
Pico das Flores, *328*
Pico do Arieiro, *309, 325–*
    326
Pico do Castelo, *328*
Pico do Facho, *328*
Pico dos Barcelos, *309*
Pico Ruivo, *325*
Pillory, *248*
Pinhel, *218, 219, 254*
Planetário Calouste
    Gulbenkian, *58*
Ponta da Bandeira, *204–205*
Ponta da Piedade, *205*
Ponte da Barca, *266, 292*
Ponte de Lima, *266, 292–*
    293, 366–367
Ponte Dom Luis I, *270*
Ponte 25 de Abril, *58*
Porta do Carvalho, *254*
Porta do Nó, *164*
Porta Férrea, *225*
Portalegre, *150, 167–168*
Portas do Sol, *136*
Portela, *327, 328*
Portimão, *184, 200–201,*
    365
Portinho da Arrábida, *113*
Porto da Cruz, *327*
Porto do Funchal, *311, 314*
Porto Moniz, *309, 324–325*
Porto Santo, *309, 327–329*
Portugal dos Pequenitos, *227*
Port-wine lodges, *46–47,*
    270, 312
Pousadas, *355*
Póvoa de Varzim, *264, 278,*
    365
Praça da Liberdade (Oporto),
    267
Praça da República (Braga),
    283
Praça da República (Viseu),
    239
Praça de Dom Duarte (Viseu),
    240
Praça do Comércio
    (Coimbra), *226*
Praça do Comércio (Lisbon),
    38, 43, 44
Praça do Giraldo (Évora),
    153
Praça dos Restauradores
    (Lisbon), *38, 48, 51*
Praça Luis de Camões
    (Castelo Branca), *246*

Praça Luis de Camões
    (Guarda), *256*
Praça Marquês de Pombal
    (Lisbon), *48, 51*
Praia da Falesia, *197*
Praia da Galé, *197*
Praia da Luz, *186, 207–208*
Praia da Oura, *197*
Praia da Rocha, *184, 186,*
    202, 367
Praia das Maças, *107–108*
Praia de Dona Ana, *205*
Praia de Faro, *188*
Praia de Manta Rota, *192*
Praia de Monte Gordo, *192*
Praia de Porto Nova, *125*
Praia Grande, *107–108*
Price categories
dining, 349
lodging, 353

Q

Queluz, *93, 108*
Quinta da Alorna, *136*
Quinta da Bacalhoa, *113*
Quinta das Lágrimas, *227,*
    229
Quinta do Palheiro, *309,*
    312, 313
Quinta Vigia, *314*

R

Rabaçal, *309, 325*
Regional Museum
    (Penamacor), *248*
Reguengos de Monsaraz,
    150, 160
Reserva Natural do Sado, *174*
Rest rooms, *359*
Ria de Aveiro, *235*
The Ribatejo. ☞ Estremadura
    and the Ribatejo
Ribeira Brava, *309, 323*
Ribeiro Frio, *309, 326*
Rossío (Estremoz), *165*
Rossío (Lisbon), *37, 43, 44*
Rua de Santo António (Faro),
    187–188
Rua da Sofia (Coimbra), *227*
Rua das Portas de Santo
    Antão (Lisbon), *48, 51–52*
Rua 5 de Outubro (Évora),
    153
Rua Garrett (Lisbon), *45, 47*
Rua Quebra Costas
    (Coimbra), *223*
Ruins, *190, 195, 284*

S

Sabugal, *219, 248–249*
Sagres, *184, 208–209*
Sailing, *92, 196*
Salema, *208*
Santa, *325*
Santa Engraça, *41*
Santa Luzia, *290*
Santa Maria da Feira, *218,*
    219, 238, 367

Santa Maria da Sé, *200*
Santa Maria da Vitória, *131*
Santa Maria do Castelo, *191*
Santa Maria do Olival, *140*
Santana, *309, 326–327*
Santarém, *121, 122–123,*
    136–137, 365, 367
Santiago do Cacém, *149,*
    150, 175–176
Santo António das Areias,
    150, 169
Santuário Nossa Senhora do
    Sameiro, *284*
São Bartolomeu de Messines,
    200
São Brás de Alportel, *190*
São Cucufate, *149, 150, 173*
São Lourenço, *194*
São Pedro de Sintra, *93,*
    105–106, 365
São Pedro do Corval, *149,*
    150, 160
São Rafael, *197*
São Vicente, *309, 324*
Sardoal, *122, 142–143*
Scuba diving, *126, 208,*
    319–320, 329
Sé (Braga), *283*
Sé (Évora), *153*
Sé (Faro), *186*
Sé (Funchal), *311, 315*
Sé (Lisbon), *38, 39, 42*
Sé (Oporto), *269*
Sé (Viseu), *239*
Sé Nova (Coimbra), *224*
Sé Velha (Coimbra), *223–*
    224
Senior citizens, *359*
Serpa, *172–173*
Serra da Arrábida, *93, 94,*
    113
Serra da Malcata Natural
    Park, *249*
Serra de Agua, *309, 323–*
    324
Serra de Foca, *328*
Sesimbra, *93, 94, 113–114*
Setúbal, *93, 94, 110–112,*
    366
Setúbal Peninsula, *109–114*
Shipping and mail, *355*
Shopping. ☞ *Under specific*
    cities and areas
Shopping hours, *344*
Silves, *199–200, 366*
Sinagoga de Tomar, *139*
Sintra, Sintra environs, and
    Queluz, *93, 94, 102–108*
Sitio, *129*
Skiing, *253*
Sled ride, *321*
Slide & Splash, *199*
Soccer, *79–80, 276–277*
Sogrape Winery, *294*
Solar de Mateus, *294*
Solar do Vinho do Porto,
    271–272
Sortelha, *219, 249*
South of Bragança, *297*

Spas, *169, 242, 293, 355*
Sports. ☞ Outdoor
    activities and sports;
    Water sports
Student travel, *359*
Surfing, *100*
Swimming, *79, 148, 320*
Symbols and icons, *376.*
    ☞ *Also* Web sites
Synagogues, *139, 170*

T

Tapada Nacional de Mafra,
    124
Tavira, *184, 191–192, 365*
Taxes, *359–360*
Taxis
    Lisbon, *84, 86*
    Lisbon's environs, *115*
    Oporto and the North, *301*
Telephones, *360–361.* ☞
    *Also under specific cities
    and areas*
Templo Romana, *155*
Tennis, *357*
    Algarve, *194, 196, 199*
    Coimbra and the Beiras, *230,
    234*
    Lisbon, *79*
    Lisbon's environs, *98*
Teatro Nacional, *44*
Terena, *149, 150, 161–162*
Theater, *44, 78, 319*
Time, *361*
Timing the visit, *364.* ☞
    *Also under specific cities
    and areas*
Tipping, *361*
Tomar, *121, 122, 139–141*
Torre de Anto, *226*
Torre de Belém, *38, 58*
Torre de Menagem
    (Bragança), *296*
Torre de Menagem (Chaves),
    298
Torre dos Clérigos, *269*
Torre Vasco da Gama, *52, 53*
Torres Novas, *137–138*
Torres Vedras, *121, 124–125*

Tours, guided. ☞ *Under
    specific cities and areas*
Tours and packages, *361–362*
Town Hall (Castelo Branco),
    246
Train travel, *362–363*
    Algarve, *211–212*
    Coimbra and the Beiras, *257*
    Estremadura and the Ribatejo,
    143, 144
    Évora and the Alentejo, *177*
    Lisbon, *84–85*
    Lisbon's environs, *115–116*
    Oporto and the North, *279,
    299–300, 301–302*
Trams, *87, 300–301*
Trancoso, *218, 219, 254*
Transportation, *363*
Trás-os-Montes, *294–299,
    303*
Travel agencies, *363.* ☞
    *Also under specific cities
    and areas*
Traveler's checks, *357*
Tróia Tourist Complex, *112*

U

Universidade de Évora, *156*
Universidade Velha, *225*
Upper Alentejo, *160–170*

V

Vale do Lobo, *194*
Valença do Minho, *264,
    291–292*
Viana do Alentejo, *174*
Viana do Castelo, *264, 289–
    291, 366*
Vidigueira, *173*
Vila do Bispo, *208*
Vila do Conde, *264, 278*
Vila Franca de Xira, *121, 123,
    133, 135–136, 366, 367*
Vila Nogueira de Azeitão,
    94, 112–113
Vila Nova de Cerveira, *264,
    291*
Vila Nova de Gaia, *270–
    271, 367*

Vila Nova de Milfontes, *176*
Vila Praia de Âncora, *291*
Vila Real, *264, 266, 294–
    295*
Vila Real de Santo António,
    184, 193
Vila Viçosa, *149, 150, 162,
    164*
Vilamoura, *195–196*
Villa rentals, *353*
Vinhais, *266, 297*
Visa (credit card), *356*
Visas and passports, *358–
    359*
Viseu, *218, 219, 239–240,
    366*
Visitor information, *363–
    364.* ☞ *Also under
    specific cities and areas*
Vista Alegre, *218, 219, 235*

W

Walking, *301*
Water parks, *194, 199*
Water sports, *357–358*
    Algarve, *183*
    Coimbra and the Beiras, *234*
    Estremadura and the Ribatejo,
    120
    Oporto and the North, *281*
Waterwheel, *140*
Web sites, *364*
Western Beiras, *231–246*
Western Madeira, *322–325*
Whaling Museum, *327*
Windsurfing, *128–129, 208,
    234*
Wine, *46–47, 82, 110, 112,
    130, 136, 164, 199, 239,
    270–271, 279, 294, 307–
    308, 312, 322, 337–341*
Wine tours, *112, 322, 331*

Z

Zona Arqueológica (Braga),
    283
Zoo Marine, *196–197*
Zoos, *38, 48, 50, 196–197*

FODOR'S PORTUGAL

EDITOR: Sharron S. Wood

Editorial Contributors: Stephanie Adler, Alys Bohn, Jules Brown, Peter Collis, Martha de la Cal, Dennis Jaffe, Laura M. Kidder, Deborah Luhrman, Paul Murphy, Mark Sullivan

Editorial Production: Ira-Neil Dittersdorf

Maps: David Lindroth, *cartographer*; Rebecca Baer and Bob Blake, *map editors*

Design: Fabrizio La Rocca, *creative director*; Guido Caroti, *art director*; Jolie Novak, *senior picture editor*; Melanie Marin, *photo editor*

Cover Design: Pentagram

Production/Manufacturing: Angela L. McLean

COPYRIGHT

Fifth Edition

ISBN 0-679-00676-1

ISSN 0071-6510

SPECIAL SALES

Fodor's Travel Publications are available at special discounts for bulk purchases for sales promotions or premiums. Special editions, including personalized covers, excerpts of existing guides, and corporate imprints, can be created in large quantities for special needs. For more information, contact your local bookseller or write to Special Markets, Fodor's Travel Publications, 280 Park Avenue, New York, NY 10017. Inquiries from Canada should be directed to your local Canadian bookseller or sent to Random House of Canada, Ltd., Marketing Department, 2775 Matheson Boulevard East, Mississauga, Ontario L4W 4P7. Inquiries from the United Kingdom should be sent to Fodor's Travel Publications, 20 Vauxhall Bridge Road, London SW1V 2SA, England.

PRINTED IN THE UNITED STATES OF AMERICA

10 9 8 7 6 5 4 3 2 1

IMPORTANT TIP

Although all prices, opening times, and other details in this book are based on information supplied to us at press time, changes occur all the time in the travel world, and Fodor's cannot accept responsibility for facts that become outdated or for inadvertent errors or omissions. So **always confirm information when it matters,** especially if you're making a detour to visit a specific place.

PHOTOGRAPHY

Bob Krist, *cover (Albufiera in the Algarve)*

Corbis: *2 top right, 2 bottom right, 3 top left, 3 bottom left, 28D, 30M, 30O.* Tony Aruzza, *13D.* Jonathan Blair, *22C.* Hans George Roth, *22B.*

DIAF: *Guittot, 11D.* Rosine Mazin, *7E.* Giovanni Simeone, *9I, 9K, 10B, 14A, 15E, 17D.* Jean-Daniel Sudres, *1, 18B.* Yvan Travert, *8H, 13E, 20A.*

Blaine Harrington III, *10A, 12A, 30K.*

Houserstock: Jan Butchofsky-Houser, *6B, 15D, 17C.* Dave G. Houser, *6A, 6C, 11F, 12B, 12C, 19D, 28A.*

The Image Bank: Grant V. Faint, *7F, 28F.* Guido A. Rossi, *15C.*

Instituto Português de Museus: António Chaves, *19E, 19F, 28E.*

Junta de Turismo da Costa do Estoril, *10C, 25, 28C.*

Len Kaufman, *4–5, 13F, 21C.*

Liaison Agency: Giulio Andreini, *23D.* Sigrid Estrada, *16B.* Alain Evrard, *28I.* Patrick Frilet, *16A.*

Jorge Miranda, *28G.*

Portuguese National Tourist Office: *3 top right.* Nuno Calvet, *2 bottom center, 28H.* Eça, *11E.* José Manuel, *23E.* João Paulo, *2 top left, 2 bottom left, 17C, 26.*

Pousadas de Portugal, *30J, 30N.*

Quinta das Seqúoias, *30P.*

Região de Turismo do Algarve, *3 bottom right, 17E.*

Região de Turismo do Centro, *24.*

Região de Turismo do Évora, *14B.*

Região de Turismo do Oeste, *27.*

Restaurante Tavares, *30L.*

Stone: Robert Frerck, *8G, 18A, 21D.* Erica Lansner, *32.* Kevin Schafer, *7D.* Walter Schmid, *22A, 23F.* Jamey Stillings, *14 center.*

Nik Wheeler, *9J, 21B, 28B.*

ABOUT OUR WRITERS

Every vacation is important. So here at Fodor's, we've pulled out all the stops in preparing *Fodor's Portugal*. To help you zero in on what to see in Portugal, we've gathered some wonderful color photos of the key sights in every region. To show you how to put it all together, we've created great itineraries. And to direct you to the places that are truly worth your time and money, we've rallied the team of endearingly picky know-it-alls we're pleased to call our writers. Having seen all corners of the regions they cover for us, they're real experts. If you knew them, you'd poll them for tips yourself.

During numerous visits to Portugal, **Alys Bohn** has focused on Lisbon and fallen in love with Madeira. Her eclectic career has included editing books and scholarly papers, working as a travel consultant, co-authoring a travel romance novel, and contributing to newspapers, books, and magazines. Now based in the Hudson River valley, she is senior editor for *Recommend Magazine* and a freelance travel writer.

Jules Brown, who wrote the Great Itineraries, has a soft spot for Portugal, which he first visited in 1985. A decade ago, he researched and wrote the chapters on Lisbon, Lisbon's Environs, Oporto and the North, and the Algarve for the original edition of this guide, though in recent years his travels have taken him further afield. As a freelance writer based in Yorkshire, England, he has written guidebooks to Scandinavia, Barcelona, Sicily, Hong Kong, Washington, D.C., and Great Britain, and he's a regular contributor to the travel pages of the United Kingdom's *Daily Mail*. Between them, **Martha de la Cal** and **Peter Collis,** freelance writers based in Lisbon, covered the north and central regions of Portugal—a lot of ground, indeed. Martha is a correspondent for *Time* magazine. Peter has had many gigs as a writer and journalist and currently spends much of his time writing, translating, and editing texts for Portuguese cultural foundations and travel publications. Both writers have lived the best part of the past 40 years on the Iberian Peninsula.

Paul Murphy has been travel writing for 11 years, during which time he has authored 35 guidebooks and contributed to as many again. He specializes in the Mediterranean (and near neighbors) and is especially fond of the Algarve, covering it regularly over the last 7 years. He also writes for British magazines.

Don't Forget to Write

We love feedback—positive and negative—and follow up on all suggestions. So contact the Portugal editor at editors@fodors.com or c/o Fodor's, 280 Park Avenue, New York, New York 10017. Have a wonderful trip!

Karen Cure
Editorial Director